The New Can[illegible]

Prepared by
The Cartographic Department
of the Clarendon Press

Advisory Editor
Quentin Stanford

Oxford University Press
70 Wynford Drive
Don Mills, Ont.
M3C 1J9

23456789 - 5432109

Printed in Canada by
The Bryant Press Limited

ISBN 0-19-540263-4

Metric Commission Canada
has granted use of the
National Symbol
for Metric Conversion

Contents

COUNTRIES OF THE WORLD
Population and Other Selected Statistics — Inside front cover

CANADA
Statistics on Population, Production, & Trade — iii

Title	Representative fraction (R/f) (approx.)	Page
Canada–Population	1:24 000 000	1
Canada–Physiographic Regions	1:24 000 000	2
Canada–Geology	1:24 000 000	3
Inset: Pleistocene Glaciation		
Canada–Soils	1:24 000 000	4
Canada–Climate	1:44 000 000	5
Canada–Agriculture & Forestry	1:24 000 000	6
Canada–Water Resources & Electrical Power	1:24 000 000	7
Canada–Natural Resources & Native Peoples	1:19 000 000	8-9
Canada–Manufacturing	1:19 000 000	10-11
Insets: Southwest Ontario, St. Lawrence Valley	1:2 000 000	
Canada *	1:19 000 000	12-13
Québec, Newfoundland *	1:8 000 000	14-15
Atlantic Provinces *	1:5 000 000	16-17
Ontario *	1:8 000 000	18-19
Central Canada	1:1 150 000	20-1
Lake Ontario & Upper St. Lawrence	1:1 150 000	22-3
Western Provinces *	1:5 000 000	24-5
Prairie Provinces	1:5 000 000	26–7
British Columbia *	1:5 000 000	28-9
Inset: Southwestern British Columbia	1:2 500 000	
The Territories *	1:8 000 000	30-1
Toronto, Montreal, Ottawa	1:400 000	32
Winnipeg, Detroit, Washington, Boston	1:400 000	33
Chicago, Pittsburgh	1:400 000	34
New York	1:400 000	35
San Francisco, Vancouver, Seattle	1:400 000	36
Los Angeles	1:400 000	37
North & South America–Physical	1:44 000 000	38-9
Insets: Build, Minerals	1:160 000 000	
North & South America–Vegetation	1:44 000 000	40-1
Insets: Annual Rainfall, Land Use	1:160 000 000	
North & South America–Population & Communications	1:44 000 000	42-3
Inset: Political	1:108 000 000	
U.S.A. & Central America	1:19 000 000	44-5
Inset: Panama Canal	1:1 500 000	
Eastern United States	1:8 000 000	46-7
Western United States	1:8 000 000	48-9
Northeastern United States	1:2 000 000	50-1
Mexico & Cuba	1:6 250 000	52-3
South America	1:25 000 000	54-5
Central South America	1:7 750 000	56
Atlantic Ocean	1:63 000 000	57

*These maps include panels with area, communications, population, and production statistics for each province and the Territories.

Title	Representative fraction (R/f) (approx.)	Page
Europe–Physical	1:19 000 000	58
Inset: Climate Graphs		
Europe–Climate	1:19 000 000	59
Inset: Climate Graphs		
Europe–Population & Communications	1:19 000 000	60
British Isles	1:4 750 000	61
Insets: Power, Population		
British Isles	1:2 200 000	62-3
Inset: Channel Islands		
Europe	1:12 600 000	64-5
Inset: Ruhr	1:1 000 000	
Western Europe	1:6 250 000	66-7
Inset: Corsica & Sardinia		
Eastern Europe	1:6 250 000	68-9
Scandinavia	1:6 250 000	70-1
Inset: Iceland		
France	1:3 150 000	72-3
Germany & the Alps	1:3 150 000	74-5
Eurasia–Physical	1:44 000 000	76-7
Insets: Annual Rainfall, Build & Minerals	1:110 000 000	
Eurasia–Vegetation	1:44 000 000	78-9
Insets: Rainfall, Pressure & Winds May-October, November-April	1:110 000 000	
Eurasia–Population & Communications	1:44 000 000	80-1
Insets: Political, Land Use	1:110 000 000	
U.S.S.R.	1:25 000 000	82-3
Western U.S.S.R.	1:12 500 000	84-5
Middle East	1:12 500 000	86-7
Inset: Cairo–Beirut	1:4 000 000	
India, Pakistan, Bangladesh & Sri Lanka	1:12 600 000	88
Inset: Sri Lanka	1:7 750 000	
Indian Ocean	1:63 000 000	89
Far East	1:19 000 000	90-1
Mainland Southeast Asia	1:12 500 000	92
Japan	1:6 250 000	93
Insets: Tokyo, Kobe–Nagoya	1:2 000 000	
Eastern China	1:6 250 000	94-5
Australasia–Vegetation	1:44 000 000	96
Insets: Annual Rainfall, Physical	1:132 000 000	
Australasia–Physical	1:44 000 000	
Insets: Build, Minerals	1:44 000 000	
Australasia–Land Use	1:44 000 000	97
Australasia–Population & Communications	1:44 000 000	
Australasia	1:22 000 000	98-9
Eastern Australia	1:6 250 000	100-1
South West Australia	1:6 250 000	
Pacific Ocean	1:63 000 000	102-3
New Zealand	1:6 250 000	104
Africa–Physical	1:44 000 000	105
Insets: Build, Annual Rainfall	1:190 000 000	
Africa–Population & Communications	1:44 000 000	106
Inset: Land Use	1:190 000 000	
Africa–Vegetation	1:44 000 000	107
Inset: Tsetse Fly		
North Africa	1:19 000 000	108-9
Inset: Suez Canal	1:1 500 000	
Southern Africa	1:19 000 000	110
South Africa	1:12 500 000	111
London	1:400 000	112
Paris, Berlin	1:400 000	113
Tokyo, Peking, Moscow	1:400 000	114
Sydney, Delhi, Calcutta	1:400 000	115

Title	Representative fraction (R/f) (approx.)	Page
World–Relief	1:88 000 000	116-17
Insets: Antarctic, Arctic	1:50 000 000	
World–Climate	1:220 000 000	118-19
World–Seasonal Climate	1:88 000 000	120-1
World–Economic Geology	1:88 000 000	122-3
Inset: Plate Tectonics		
World–Energy	1:88 000 000	124-5
Insets: Eastern U.S.A.	1:29 000 000	
Europe & the Mediterranean	1:44 000 000	
Japan	1:29 000 000	
World–Iron Ore/Steel	1:88 000 000	126-7
Insets: Eastern U.S.A.	1:13 000 000	
British Isles	1:22 700 000	
W. Europe	1:22 000 000	
Japan	1:13 000 000	
World–Economic Regions	1:88 000 000	128-9
World–Political	1:88 000 000	130-1
World–Population Distribution & Growth	1:88 000 000	132-3
World–Nutrition	1:88 000 000	134-5
Insets: Calories, Protein		
World–Crude Birth Rate	1:180 000 000	136
–Crude Death Rate	1:180 000 000	
ABBREVIATIONS		137
GAZETTEER OF CANADA		138
GAZETTEER OF THE WORLD		149

Canada: Statistics on Population, Production, & Trade

List of Tables and Graphs

1. Land Area and Density of Population iv
2. Percentage of Population in Urban Areas iv
3. Growth Components of Canada's Population v
4. Components of Population Change by Province v
5. Vital Statistics Rates vi
6. Immigration to and Emigration from Canada vi
7. Age Groups and Sex Ratio of Canada's Population vi
8. Ethnic Origin of Canada's Population vii
9. Immigration to Canada by Country or Region of Last Permanent Residence vii
10. Population and Other Characteristics of Census Metropolitan Areas viii
11. Unemployment Rates viii
12. Census-Farms—Population, Number, Use of Land, and Capital Value ix
13. Average Size of Census-farms ix
14. Farm Characteristics by Province x
15. Leading World Producers of Wheat x
16. Canadian Wheat Statistics xi
17. Census-farms with Sales of $2 500 or More Classified by Type of Product xi
18. Area, Production, and Values of Major Field Crops by Provinces xii
19. Value of Mineral Production xiv
20. Value of Production of Principal Minerals xv
21. Petroleum Supply and Demand xvi
22. Marketable Gas Supply and Demand xvi
23. Installed Generating Capacity xvii
24. Electricity Supply and Demand xvii
25. Coal Supply and Demand xvii
26. Lumber Production and Shipments and Value of All Shipments of the Sawmill and Planing Industry xviii
27. Estimated World Newsprint Production and Exports by Leading Countries xviii
28. Pulp Production xviii
29. Pulp Production and Imports and Exports by Leading Countries xix
30. Quantity and Value of Sea and Inland Fish Landed and Persons Employed xix
31. St. Lawrence Seaway: Type of Traffic xix
32. Water-Borne Cargo Loaded and Unloaded for Six Largest Ports xx
33. St. Lawrence Seaway Traffic by Classification and Direction—Montreal–Lake Ontario Section xx
34. St. Lawrence Seaway Traffic by Classification and Direction—Welland Canal Section xxi
35. Regional Shares of Selected National Manufacturing Statistics xxii
36. Percentage of Domestic and Foreign Control of Principal Canadian Manufacturing Industries xxii
37. Principal Manufacturing Industries: National and Provincial Areas Ranked by Value Added xxiii
38. Major Import Commodities xxiv
39. Major Export Commodities xxiv
40. Imports: Principal Nations xxiv
41. Exports: Principal Nations xxiv

Canada: Statistics on Population, Production, & Trade

1. Land Area and Density of Population, 1951, 1961, 1971, and 1976

		POPULATION 1951		POPULATION 1961		POPULATION 1971		POPULATION 1976		AVERAGE ANNUAL GROWTH RATE	
PROVINCE OR TERRITORY	LAND AREA[1] km²	TOTAL	/km²	TOTAL	/km²	TOTAL	/km²	TOTAL	/km²	1966–71 %	1971–76 %
NEWFOUNDLAND (incl. Labrador)........	370 487	361 416	0.98	457 853	1.24	522 104	1.41	548 789	1.48	1.1	1.0
PRINCE EDWARD ISLAND...............	5 657	98 429	17.40	104 629	18.50	111 641	19.74	116 251	20.55	0.6	0.8
NOVA SCOTIA........	52 841	642 584	12.16	737 007	13.95	788 960	14.94	812 127	15.37	0.9	0.6
NEW BRUNSWICK....	72 093	515 697	7.15	597 936	8.29	634 557	8.80	664 525	9.22	0.6	0.9
QUÉBEC...............	1 356 797	4 055 681	2.99	5 259 211	3.88	6 027 764	4.44	6 141 491	4.53	0.8	0.4
ONTARIO.............	891 198	4 597 542	5.16	6 236 092	7.00	7 703 106	8.64	8 131 618	9.12	2.0	1.1
MANITOBA...........	548 497	776 541	1.42	921 686	1.68	988 247	1.80	1 005 953	1.83	0.5	0.4
SASKATCHEWAN......	570 271	831 728	1.46	925 181	1.62	926 242	1.62	907 650	1.59	−0.6	−0.4
ALBERTA.............	644 392	939 501	1.46	1 331 944	2.07	1 627 874	2.53	1 799 771	2.79	2.2	2.1
BRITISH COLUMBIA..	930 533	1 165 210	1.25	1 629 082	1.75	2 184 021	2.35	2 406 212	2.59	3.1	2.0
YUKON TERRITORY...	531 846	9 096	0.017	14 628	0.028	18 388	0.034	21 392	0.040	5.6	3.3
NORTHWEST TERRITORIES.........	3 246 404	16 004	0.005	22 998	0.007	34 807	0.011	42 237	0.013	4.2	4.3
CANADA............	**9 221 016**	**14 009 429**	**1.52**	**18 238 247**	**1.98**	**21 568 310**	**2.34**	**22 598 016**	**2.45**	**1.5**	**1.0**

[1]Includes only land area excluding fresh water.

Sources: *Canada Year Book 1970–71*; *1976 Census of Canada*, Statistics Canada.

2. Percentage of Population in Urban Areas, 1851 to 1971[1]

PROVINCE	1851	1871	1891	1911	1931	1951	1961	1971
NEWFOUNDLAND.............	—	—	—	—	—	43.3	50.7	57.2
PRINCE EDWARD ISLAND.......................	—	9.4	13.1	16.0	19.5	25.1	32.4	38.3
NOVA SCOTIA................	7.5	8.3	19.4	36.7	46.6	54.5	54.3	56.7
NEW BRUNSWICK............	14.0	17.6	19.9	26.7	35.4	42.8	46.5	56.9
QUÉBEC......................	14.9	19.9	28.6	44.5	59.5	66.8	74.3	80.6
ONTARIO......................	14.0	20.6	35.0	49.5	63.1	72.5	77.3	82.4
MANITOBA...................	—	—	23.3	39.3	45.2	56.0	63.9	69.5
SASKATCHEWAN..............	—	—	—	16.1	20.3	30.4	43.0	53.0
ALBERTA......................	—	—	—	29.4	31.8	47.6	63.3	73.5
BRITISH COLUMBIA...........	—	9.0	42.6	50.9	62.3	68.6	72.6	75.7
CANADA.....................	**13.1**	**18.3**	**29.8**	**41.8**	**52.5**	**62.4**	**69.7**	**76.1**

[1]The percentage of the population classified as urban, rural farm, and rural non-farm in 1971 is shown on the various provincial maps in the *Atlas*.

Sources: *Urban Development in Canada* by Leroy O. Stone, *1961 Census Monograph*; *1971 Census of Canada*.

3. Growth Components of Canada's Population, 1851 to 1971

PERIOD	TOTAL POPULATION GROWTH 000	BIRTHS 000	DEATHS 000	NATURAL INCREASE 000	RATIO OF NATURAL INCREASE TO TOTAL GROWTH %	IMMIGRATION 000	EMIGRATION 000	NET MIGRATION 000	RATIO OF NET MIGRATION TO TOTAL GROWTH %
1851–1861	793	1 281	670	611	77.0	352	170	182	23.0
1861–1871	460	1 370	760	610	132.6	260	410	−150	−32.6
1871–1881	636	1 480	790	690	108.5	350	404	−54	−8.5
1881–1891	508	1 524	870	654	128.7	680	826	−146	−28.7
1891–1901	538	1 548	880	668	124.2	250	380	−130	−24.2
1901–1911	1 835	1 925	900	1 025	55.9	1 550	740	810	44.1
1911–1921	1 581	2 340	1 070	1 270	80.3	1 400	1 089	311	19.7
1921–1931	1 589	2 420	1 060	1 360	85.5	1 200	970	230	14.5
1931–1941	1 130	2 294	1 072	1 222	108.1	149	241	−92	−8.1
1941–1951[1]	2 503	3 212	1 220	1 992	92.3	548	382	166	7.7
1951–1961	4 228	4 468	1 320	3 148	74.5	1 543	463	1 080	25.5
1961–1971	3 330	4 105	1 497	2 608	78.3	1 429	707	722	21.7

[1]Includes Newfoundland in 1951 but not in 1941.

Source: *Canada Year Book 1975.*

4. Components of Population Change by Province, 1961 to 1966 and 1966 to 1971

PROVINCE OR TERRITORY	TOTAL POPULATION CHANGE		NATURAL INCREASE		NET MIGRATION	
	1961–66	1966–71	1961–66	1966–71	1961–66	1966–71
NEWFOUNDLAND	35 543	28 708	59 577	49 096	−24 034	−20 388
PRINCE EDWARD ISLAND	3 906	3 106	8 506	5 207	−4 600	−2 101
NOVA SCOTIA	19 032	32 921	59 526	37 418	−40 494	−4 497
NEW BRUNSWICK	18 852	17 769	53 229	35 233	−34 377	−17 464
QUÉBEC	521 634	246 919	457 717	288 727	63 917	−41 808
ONTARIO	724 778	742 236	487 852	373 072	236 926	369 164
MANITOBA	41 380	25 181	70 340	49 260	−28 960	−24 079
SASKATCHEWAN	30 163	−29 102	75 691	50 867	−45 528	−79 969
ALBERTA	131 259	164 671	134 607	105 293	−3 348	59 378
BRITISH COLUMBIA	244 592	310 947	104 103	88 494	140 489	222 453
YUKON TERRITORY & NORTHWEST TERRITORIES	5 494	10 075	6 745	6 720	−1 251	3 355
CANADA	**1 776 633**	**1 553 431**	**1 517 893**	**1 089 387**	**258 740**	**464 044**

Source: *Canada Year Book 1975.*

5. Vital Statistics Rates,1930 to 1976

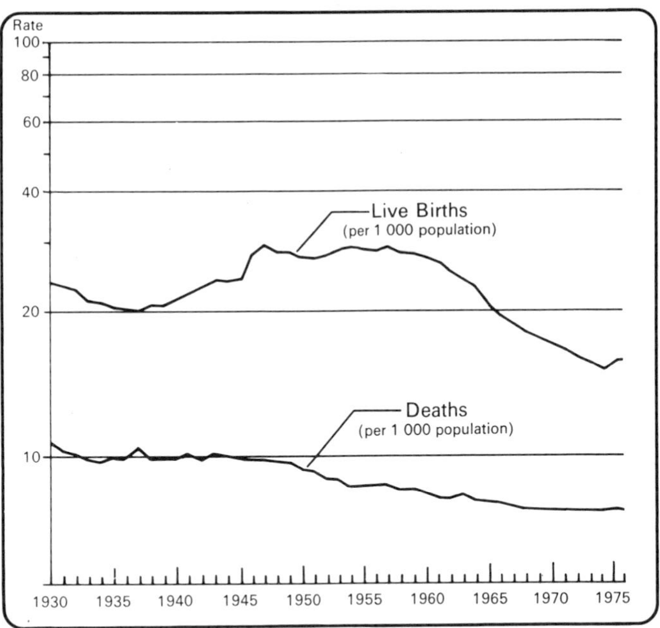

Source: *Quarterly Vital Statistics*, December 1976, Statistics Canada.

6. Immigration to and Emigration from Canada, 1952 to 1976

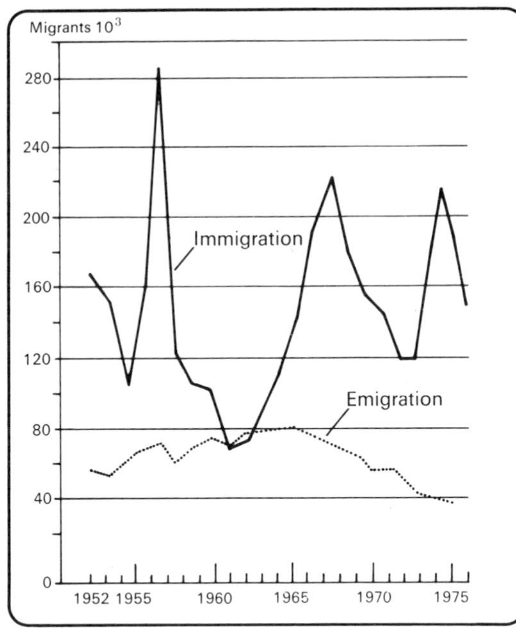

Sources: *Canada Year Book 1974; Canadian Statistical Review*, July 1976, Statistics Canada; *Immigration Statistics Canada*, 1976.

7. Age Groups and Sex Ratio of Canada's Population, Census Years, 1901 to 1971[1]

AGE GROUP	PER CENT OF TOTAL POPULATION							
	1901	1911	1921	1931	1941	1951	1961	1971
0–4	12.0	12.3	12.0	10.4	9.1	12.3	12.4	8.4
5–9	11.5	10.9	12.0	10.9	9.1	10.0	11.4	10.5
10–14	10.8	9.7	10.4	10.4	9.6	8.1	10.2	10.7
15–19	10.4	9.5	9.2	10.0	9.7	7.6	7.9	9.8
20–24	9.6	9.9	8.1	8.8	9.0	7.8	6.5	8.8
25–34	14.9	17.0	15.3	14.4	15.7	15.5	13.6	13.4
35–44	11.7	12.0	13.2	12.9	12.5	13.3	13.1	11.7
45–54	8.3	8.6	9.1	10.4	10.7	10.0	10.3	10.6
55–64	5.7	5.5	5.9	6.4	7.9	7.7	7.1	8.0
65–69	2.0	1.8	2.0	2.2	2.7	3.1	2.7	2.9
70+	3.1	2.8	2.8	3.3	4.0	4.7	5.0	5.2
Total	100.0	100.0	100.0	100.0	100.0	100.0	100.0	100.0
Median age[2]	22.7	23.8	24.0	24.7	27.0	27.7	26.3	26.3
Sex ratio[3]	105.0	112.9	106.4	107.4	105.3	102.4	102.2	100.2

[1]Excluding Newfoundland in censuses prior to 1951.

[2]Fifty per cent of the population lies below the median age, which is given in years and fractions of years.

[3]Males per 100 females.

Source: *Canadian Urban Trends, National Perspective*, Vol. I. Printed with the permission of the Ministry of State for Urban Affairs and Copp Clark Publishing.

8. Ethnic Origin of Canada's Population, Census Years, 1901 to 1971[1]

ETHNIC GROUP	PER CENT OF TOTAL POPULATION							
	1901	1911	1921	1931	1941	1951	1961	1971
BRITISH ISLES	57.0	55.5	55.4	51.9	49.7	47.9	43.8	44.6
FRENCH	30.7	28.6	27.9	28.2	30.3	30.8	30.4	28.7
OTHER EUROPEAN	8.5	13.1	14.2	17.6	17.8	18.3	22.6	23.0
Austrian	0.2	0.6	1.2	0.5	0.3	0.2	0.6	0.2
German	5.8	5.6	3.4	4.6	4.0	4.4	5.7	6.1
Greek	v.s.	0.1	0.1	0.1	0.1	0.1	0.3	0.6
Hungarian	v.s.	0.2	0.1	0.4	0.5	0.4	0.7	0.6
Italian	0.2	0.6	0.8	0.9	1.0	1.1	2.5	3.4
Jewish	0.3	1.1	1.4	1.5	1.5	1.5	1.4	1.4
Netherlands	0.6	0.8	1.3	1.4	1.8	1.9	2.4	2.0
Polish	0.1	0.5	0.6	1.4	1.5	1.5	1.6	1.5
Russian	0.4	0.6	1.1	0.8	0.7	0.6	0.5	0.3
Scandinavian	0.6	1.6	1.9	2.2	2.1	2.0	2.1	1.8
Ukrainian	0.1	1.0	1.2	2.2	2.7	2.8	2.6	2.7
Other	0.2	0.5	1.0	1.4	1.4	1.5	1.9	2.0
ASIAN	0.4	0.6	0.8	0.8	0.6	0.5	0.7	1.3
Chinese and Japanese	0.4	0.5	0.6	0.7	0.5	0.4	0.5	0.7
Other	v.s.	0.1	0.1	0.1	0.1	0.1	0.2	0.6
NATIVE INDIAN and ESKIMO	2.4	1.5	1.3	1.2	1.4	1.2	1.2	1.4
OTHER and NOT STATED	0.9	0.7	0.5	0.3	0.3	1.3	1.3	1.0
TOTAL	100.0	100.0	100.0	100.0	100.0	100.0	100.0	100.0

v.s. Very small.

[1]Excluding Newfoundland in censuses prior to 1951.

Source: *Canadian Urban Trends, National Perspective*, Vol. I. Printed with the permission of the Ministry of State for Urban Affairs and Copp Clark Publishing.

9. Immigration to Canada by Country or Region of Last Permanent Residence, 1946 to 1950, 1963 to 1967, and 1975

COUNTRY	ANNUAL AVERAGE 1946–50	ANNUAL AVERAGE 1963–67	1975
ASIA	1 061	11 150	47 382
BRITISH ISLES	32 081	42 946	36 076
UNITED STATES	8 777	15 199	21 055
WEST INDIES	446	3 993	17 800
PORTUGAL	22	6 495	8 547
ITALY	4 010	24 360	5 978
GREECE	568	6 523	4 062
FRANCE	956	6 266	3 891
GERMANY (WEST)	1 996	8 541	3 469
NETHERLANDS	5 193	2 905	1 448
OTHERS	31 537	26 363	29 646
Total	**86 078**	**154 027**	**187 881**

Sources: *Immigration and Population Statistics*, Manpower and Immigration; *Canadian Statistical Review*, July 1976, Statistics Canada.

10. Population and Other Characteristics of Census Metropolitan Areas, 1971 and 1976

CENSUS METROPOLITAN AREAS	POPULATION	AVERAGE ANNUAL POPULATION CHANGE		IMMIGRANTS	POPULATION BORN OUT OF PROVINCE	LABOUR FORCE IN MANUFACTURING	COMPONENT MUNICIPALITIES	PREDOMINANT LANGUAGE (MOTHER TONGUE)
	1976	1966–71 %	1971–76 %	1971 %	1971 %	1971 %	1971 No.	1971 %
MONTRÉAL, Qué.	2 758 780	1.3	0.2	14.8	20.5	28.4	103	F66
TORONTO, Ont.	2 753 112	3.0	1.2	34.0	44.2	27.5	29	E74
VANCOUVER, B.C.	1 135 774	3.2	1.0	26.5	53.9	18.4	22	E82
OTTAWA-HULL, Ont.	668 853	2.8	1.6	12.5	34.8	8.7	25	E57
WINNIPEG, Man.	570 725	1.2	0.8	19.9	34.4	19.7	14	E71
EDMONTON, Alta.	542 845	3.3	1.9	18.3	39.3	12.6	10	E76
QUÉBEC, Qué.	534 193	2.0	1.3	2.2	4.3	13.8	36	F95
HAMILTON, Ont.	525 222	1.8	0.9	26.7	36.0	37.5	12	E80
CALGARY, Alta.	457 828	4.4	2.7	20.5	49.8	12.1	1	E84
ST. CATHARINES-NIAGARA FALLS, Ont.	298 129	1.3	0.9	22.9	33.0	36.4	4	E76
KITCHENER, Ont.	269 828	3.6	2.6	21.8	31.3	42.0	9	E81
LONDON, Ont.	264 639	2.5	0.9	20.0	28.6	24.4	9	E88
HALIFAX, N.S.	261 366	1.8	0.9	7.2	26.0	8.9	7	E94
WINDSOR, Ont.	243 289	1.7	−0.4	21.5	28.8	36.0	12	E74
VICTORIA, B.C.	212 466	2.3	1.7	24.7	54.4	9.8	8	E91
SUDBURY, Ont.	155 013	2.7	−0.3	12.4	25.9	14.3	11	E54
REGINA, Sask.	148 965	1.3	1.2	13.1	26.0	10.3	2	E82
ST. JOHN'S, Nfld.	140 883	2.4	1.4	3.0	6.8	7.8	14	E99
OSHAWA, Ont.	133 959	n.a.	2.3	19.9	30.0	42.1	3	E84
SASKATOON, Sask.	132 291	1.8	0.9	13.9	28.1	10.6	1	E79
CHICOUTIMI-JONQUIÈRE, Qué.	127 181	0.1	0.1	1.4	3.9	28.4	13	F96
THUNDER BAY, Ont.	117 988	0.8	0.6	21.1	33.6	17.7	3	E74
SAINT JOHN, N.B.	109 700	0.5	0.6	4.9	17.2	17.9	15	E92

Source: *Census of Canada, 1971* and *1976*.

11. Unemployment Rates, 1961 to 1976

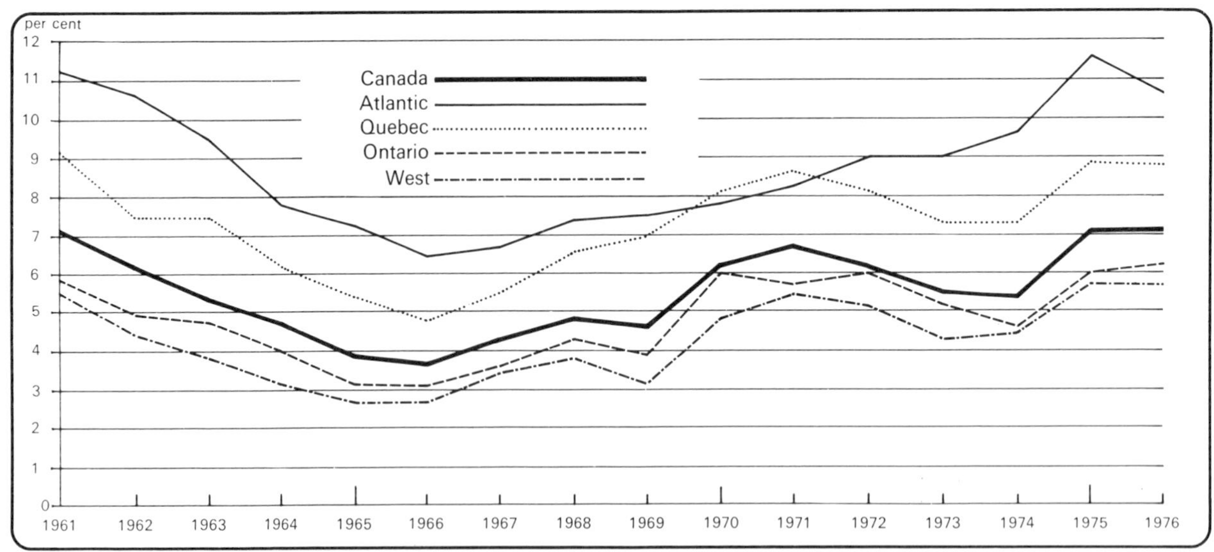

Sources: *Climate for Regional Development*, DREE, 1976; *Labour Force*, December 1976, Statistics Canada.

12. Census-farms[1]—Population, Number, Use of Land, and Capital Value, 1931, 1951, 1961, and 1971

	Unit	1931	1951	1961	1971
POPULATION ON CENSUS-FARMS	no.	3 289 140	2 911 996	2 128 400	1 489 565
Percentage of total Canadian population living on census-farms	%	31.7	20.8	11.7	6.9
NUMBER OF CENSUS-FARMS	no.	728 623	623 091	480 903	366 128
AREA IN CENSUS-FARMS	ha	65 245 614	69 618 662	69 020 420	67 867 446
Percentage of total land area of Canada in census-farms	%	7.5	7.7	7.6	7.5
USE OF AGRICULTURAL LAND:					
Improved land	ha	34 292 869	38 741 130	41 361 370	43 259 551
Under crops	ha	23 335 979	24 884 859	24 974 214	27 506 271
Pasture	ha	3 204 686	4 002 050	4 099 158	4 090 186
Summer fallow	ha	6 802 911	8 812 824	11 297 354	10 696 291
Other improved land	ha	949 292	1 041 396	990 644	996 803
Unimproved land	ha	30 952 745	30 877 531	27 659 050	24 607 895
Woodland	ha	10 658 112	9 111 978	6 898 956	4 605 668
Other unimproved land	ha	20 294 632	21 765 554	20 760 094	20 002 226
Total capital value	$	5 247 753 468	9 470 876 372	13 171 221 700	24 067 857 000
Land and buildings	$	4 053 282 300	5 527 207 155	8 622 641 300	16 936 043 000
Machinery and equipment	$	650 664 000	1 933 312 262	2 568 631 500	3 909 184 700
Livestock and poultry	$	543 807 168	2 010 356 955	1 979 948 900	3 221 285 970

[1]A census-farm was defined in the 1971 Census as an agricultural holding of one or more acres (0.4 ha) with sales of $50 or more of agricultural products in the year prior to the census.

Sources: *1966 Census of Canada*, Vol. III (3–1), June 1968; *1971 Census of Canada*, Statistics Canada.

13. Average Size of Census-farms, 1931, 1941, 1951, 1961, and 1971

PROVINCE OR TERRITORY	HECTARES (ha)					AVERAGE ANNUAL RATE OF INCREASE	
	1931	1941	1951	1961	1971	1951–61 %	1961–71 %
NEWFOUNDLAND	n.a.	n.a.	9.2	12.4	24.0	3.5	9.4
PRINCE EDWARD ISLAND	37.2	38.4	43.2	52.4	68.4	2.1	3.1
NOVA SCOTIA	43.6	46.4	54.0	71.2	88.4	3.2	2.4
NEW BRUNSWICK	48.8	49.6	52.4	74.8	97.6	4.3	3.1
QUÉBEC	50.8	46.8	50.0	59.2	70.4	1.8	1.9
ONTARIO	47.6	50.4	55.6	61.2	67.6	1.0	1.1
MANITOBA	111.6	116.4	135.2	168.0	217.2	2.4	2.9
SASKATCHEWAN	163.2	172.8	220.0	274.4	338.0	2.5	2.3
ALBERTA	160.0	173.6	210.8	258.0	316.0	2.2	2.3
BRITISH COLUMBIA	54.4	61.2	71.2	90.4	126.8	2.7	4.0
CANADA[1]	—	—	**111.6**	**143.6**	**185.2**	**2.9**	**2.9**

n.a. Not available.

[1]Includes data for Yukon and Northwest Territories.

Sources: *Agricultural Trends in Canada, 1966 Census of Canada,* Special Bulletin S-403, September 1969; *Selected Statistical Information on Agriculture in Canada,* October 1969, Economics Branch, Canadian Department of Agriculture; and *1971 Census of Canada,* Statistics Canada,

14. Farm Characteristics by Province, 1971

	CANADA	NFLD.	P.E.I.	N.S.	N.B.	QUÉ.	ONT.	MAN.	SASK.	ALTA.	B.C.
Total number of census farms	**366 128**	**1 042**	**4 543**	**6 008**	**5 485**	**61 257**	**94 722**	**34 981**	**76 970**	**62 702**	**18 400**
AVERAGES FOR CENSUS-FARMS											
Area (hectares per farm)	185	24	68	88	98	70	68	217	338	316	127
Improved land (as a % of total farm area)	64%	30%	64%	29%	37%	60%	68%	67%	71%	58%	30%
Improved pasture (as a % of total farm area)	6%	13%	15%	8%	7%	16%	15%	4%	3%	6%	7%
Under crops (as a % of total farm area)	41%	13%	46%	18%	24%	40%	49%	48%	42%	37%	19%
Summer fallow (as a % of total farm area)	16%	2%	1%	1%	1%	1%	2%	14%	25%	14%	3%
Value of machinery and equipment ($ per farm)	10 677	3 934	8 425	6 636	7 402	6 979	9 396	11 762	13 336	13 834	8 868
Total capital value[1] ($ per farm)	65 759	30 201	35 636	34 301	31 579	35 919	72 819	58 764	71 353	83 606	87 333
Value of all crops sold ($ per farm)	3 760	1 208	3 651	1 967	3 476	1 186	4 207	3 799	5 386	3 953	3 329
Value of all livestock and poultry sold ($ per farm)	5 236	2 049	3 477	3 350	2 330	2 986	6 920	4 712	3 452	8 349	4 007
Value of other products sold (dairy, eggs, forest products) ($ per farm)	2 332	4 511	1 516	4 214	2 741	4 510	3 404	1 140	356	976	4 053

[1]Includes land, buildings, machinery, equipment, and livestock.

Source: *1971 Census of Canada*, Statistics Canada.

15. Leading World Producers of Wheat, 1974

	PRODUCTION 10^3 t	EXPORTS 10^3 t
USSR	83 849	4 700 (1970)
USA	48 806	25 133
CHINA	27 700	n.a.
INDIA	22 072	260
FRANCE	18 905	7 384
CANADA	14 221	10 122
AUSTRALIA	11 700	3 827

n.a. Not available.

Source: *Statistical Yearbook*, United Nations, 1975.

16. Canadian Wheat Statistics, 1965 to 1976

	1965	1966	1967	1968	1969	1970	1971	1972	1973	1974	1975	1976
Hectares seeded (10^3)	11 320	11 877	12 049	11 770	9 985	4 993	7 763	8 540	9 464	8 831	9 369	11 012
Yield (kg/ha)	1 539	1 875	1 324	1 486	1 808	1 788	1 835	1 681	1 687	1 486	1 802	2 111
Production (10^6 t)	17.67	22.51	16.13	17.69	18.26	9.02	14.41	14.51	16.15	13.29	17.07	23.52
Exports (10^6 t)	15.91	14.02	9.14	8.32	9.43	11.84	13.71	15.69	11.41	10.73	12.25	n.a.
Domestic use (10^6 t)	4.28	4.36	4.25	4.48	4.56	4.65	4.79	4.76	4.59	4.60	4.78	n.a.
Carry-over at the beginning of crop year (10^6 t)	13.96	11.43	15.56	18.30	23.18	27.45	19.98	15.88	9.94	10.08	8.03	8.07

n.a. Not available.

Source: Agriculture Division, Statistics Canada.

17. Census-farms with Sales of $2 500 or More Classified by Type of Product, 1971[1]

PROVINCE	FARMS WITH SALES OF $2 500 OR MORE	TYPE AND NUMBER OF FARMS									
		Dairy	Cattle, hogs, sheep	Poultry	Wheat	Small grains[3]	Other field crops[4]	Fruits and vegetables	Forestry	Miscellaneous specialty	Mixed combinations
NEWFOUNDLAND	282	70	40	54	—	—	30	58	5	5	20
PRINCE EDWARD ISLAND	2 780	629	980	21	—	11	616	26	6	8	483
NOVA SCOTIA	2 568	1 019	655	169	—	9	76	250	114	109	167
NEW BRUNSWICK	2 603	821	535	111	—	4	670	98	119	26	219
QUÉBEC	40 932	28 646	5 183	1 561	20	342	1 124	1 472	331	423	1 830
ONTARIO	65 667	17 718	28 129	1 912	313	5 189	4 593	3 856	165	1 606	2 186
MANITOBA	25 336	1 614	9 829	519	2 738	7 249	376	65	16	209	2 721
SASKATCHEWAN	62 930	701	15 913	210	26 516	13 900	112	14	3	128	5 443
ALBERTA	46 533	2 490	25 843	413	3 893	9 105	814	40	28	320	3 587
BRITISH COLUMBIA	8 625	1 633	2 501	644	166	390	387	1 948	162	571	223
CANADA[2]	**258 259**	**55 341**	**89 610**	**5 615**	**33 646**	**36 199**	**8 798**	**7 827**	**949**	**3 405**	**16 869**

[1]A criterion of 51% or more total sales was used to determine in which category a farm was placed.
[2]Includes data for Yukon and Northwest Territories.
[3]Includes oats, barley, rye, mixed grains, buckwheat, corn, field peas and beans, flaxseed, soybeans, etc
[4]Includes hay and fodder crops, potatoes, sugar beets, tobacco, etc.

Source: *1971 Census of Canada*, Statistics Canada.

18. Area, Production, and Values of Major Field Crops by Province[1], Various Years

FIELD CROP AND PROVINCE	AREA			TOTAL PRODUCTION			GROSS FARM VALUE		
	Average 1945–49	Average 1963–67	1974	Average 1945–49	Average 1963–67	1974	Average 1945–49	Average 1963–67	1972
	10³ ha	10³ ha	10³ ha	10³ t	10³ t	10³ t	$000	$000	$000
Wheat	**9 823.0**	**11 630.0**	**9 391.0**	**9 873.0**	**18 473.2**	**14 220.4**	**587 412**	**1 145 512**	**993 349**
Prince Edward Island	0.8	1.2	4.0	1.5	2.2	12.8	84	141	530
Nova Scotia	0.4	0.4	1.2	0.6	1.0	3.3	34	62	286
New Brunswick	0.8	1.2	0.8	1.3	2.6	3.9	77	164	253
Québec	4.8	9.2	24.0	5.6	16.3	41.8	313	1 024	1 524
Ontario									
Winter	248.0	159.0	168.0	492.6	433.3	519.0	28 358	27 547	27 310
Spring	16.0	8.0	4.0	22.4	14.4	8.2	1 287	915	738
Manitoba	968.0	1 324.0	1 200.0	1 306.3	2 144.6	1 714.6	79 827	132 286	128 340
Saskatchewan	5 775.0	7 575.0	6 160.0	5 034.8	11 523.0	8 872.3	301 085	719 844	612 880
Alberta	2 766.0	2 509.0	1 800.0	2 939.3	4 261.9	2 993.7	171 983	259 464	217 120
British Columbia	42.0	44.0	28.0	71.2	73.9	51.7	4 365	4 064	4 368
Oats	**4 605.0**	**3 284.0**	**2 442.0**	**5 034.4**	**5 773.2**	**3 928.7**	**219 370**	**261 224**	**266 733**
Prince Edward Island	44.0	35.0	20.0	62.8	67.4	43.3	3 113	3 559	2 399
Nova Scotia	26.0	11.0	7.6	34.3	19.6	14.2	1 891	1 138	796
New Brunswick	71.0	32.0	20.0	94.6	53.4	35.4	4 799	2 891	1 775
Québec	550.0	430.0	250.0	508.3	654.4	367.2	26 716	36 992	25 029
Ontario	601.0	547.0	198.0	875.5	1 117.9	361.1	42 078	56 534	27 134
Manitoba	584.0	633.0	480.0	755.7	1 045.6	663.2	31 402	45 526	49 500
Saskatchewan	1 634.0	718.0	760.0	1 480.5	1 258.4	1 156.6	60 134	51 872	70 310
Alberta	1 058.0	849.0	680.0	1 156.7	1 505.2	1 233.8	46 148	60 542	87 360
British Columbia	37.0	28.0	26.0	69.9	51.3	54.0	3 088	2 169	2 430
Barley	**2 628.0**	**2 670.0**	**4 600.0**	**3 073.6**	**5 042.0**	**8 584.6**	**133 431**	**226 867**	**646 184**
Prince Edward Island	2.0	5.0	8.0	3.7	11.8	22.8	172	585	1 606
Nova Scotia	2.0	1.2	2.4	3.3	2.6	5.9	172	149	465
New Brunswick	4.0	2.0	4.0	6.8	4.1	9.7	346	228	432
Québec	34.0	6.0	21.0	40.7	12.5	35.9	2 006	688	1 869
Ontario	94.0	79.0	136.0	162.8	195.2	336.8	7 148	10 391	22 556
Manitoba	706.0	282.0	720.0	914.4	500.8	1 153.9	40 907	23 118	107 100
Saskatchewan	942.0	775.0	1 600.0	936.2	1 463.1	2 786.9	39 813	66 146	217 710
Alberta	835.0	1 462.0	2 040.0	979.8	2 760.7	4 093.2	42 121	121 832	289 800
British Columbia	8.0	57.0	68.0	15.9	91.2	139.3	746	3 730	4 646
Soybeans	**29.0**	**103.0**	**178.0**	**40.6**	**202.0**	**300.4**	**3 492**	**20 886**	**53 703**
Ontario	29.0	103.0	178.0	40.6	202.0	300.4	3 492	20 886	53 703
Mixed Grains	**490.0**	**646.0**	**724.0**	**998.9**	**1 726.2**	**1 831.3**	**36 988**	**68 250**	**103 257**
Prince Edward Island	19.0	19.0	30.0	42.6	55.9	98.8	1 590	2 269	4 010
Nova Scotia	1.6	4.0	3.0	3.1	9.9	8.3	135	473	422
New Brunswick	1.2	4.0	1.2	2.1	8.7	5.7	79	397	351
Québec	76.0	40.0	50.0	111.6	90.2	106.0	4 852	4 590	5 960

Table 18 continued

FIELD CROP AND PROVINCE	AREA			TOTAL PRODUCTION			GROSS FARM VALUE		
	Average 1945–49	Average 1963–67	1974	Average 1945–49	Average 1963–67	1974	Average 1945–49	Average 1963–67	1972
	10³ ha	10³ ha	10³ ha	10³ t	10³ t	10³ t	$000	$000	$000
Ontario	366.0	320.0	328.0	803.7	998.0	993.4	29 194	39 415	51 442
Manitoba	7.0	61.0	80.0	11.2	128.6	136.1	364	4 943	13 500
Saskatchewan	5.0	49.0	80.0	5.8	102.8	145.1	192	3 652	8 460
Alberta	13.0	148.0	148.0	16.7	327.5	331.1	512	12 286	18 700
British Columbia	0.8	1.6	2.4	1.9	4.5	6.8	70	225	412
Flaxseed	**466.0**	**713.0**	**600.0**	**241.3**	**518.1**	**363.2**	**37 188**	**57 799**	**70 863**
Ontario	16.0	7.0	0.0	11.8	7.3	0.0	1 879	787	53
Manitoba	180.0	397.0	300.0	108.4	263.1	180.3	16 732	29 182	24 190
Saskatchewan	210.0	177.0	220.0	85.3	135.6	119.4	12 872	15 170	35 820
Alberta	58.0	122.0	80.0	34.9	102.1	63.5	5 555	11 501	10 800
Rapeseed	**16.0**	**468.0**	**1 304.0**	**672.7**	**429.5**	**1 199.7**	**1 746**	**44 595**	**181 086**
Manitoba	—	47.0	200.0	—	40.9	192.8	—	4 262	26 350
Saskatchewan	16.0	192.0	600.0	672.7	194.8	544.3	1 746	20 252	79 856
Alberta	—	229.0	480.0	—	193.8	442.2	—	20 082	74 880
Shelled Corn	**98.0**	**291.0**	**584.0**	**280.4**	**1 467.8**	**2 588.5**	**14 056**	**77 233**	**164 100**
Québec	—	—	66.0	—	—	292.6	—	—	14 359
Ontario	92.0	286.0	516.0	272.6	1 449.8	2 291.1	13 726	76 198	148 656
Manitoba	5.0	2.0	2.0	7.7	4.4	4.8	330	233	1 085
Potatoes	**167.0**	**118.0**	**112.0**	**1 801.0**	**2 182.7**	**2 427.4**	**72 522**	**100 208**	**160 356**
Prince Edward Island	18.0	18.0	18.4	271.8	402.7	467.4	7 746	16 071	33 212
Nova Scotia	6.0	2.0	1.6	80.2	37.4	28.9	3 436	1 787	1 910
New Brunswick	24.0	23.0	23.2	396.0	551.2	607.7	13 241	20 944	45 548
Québec	47.0	29.0	21.0	406.2	389.4	382.2	17 485	18 153	17 017
Ontario	37.0	20.0	17.0	363.1	427.0	368.3	16 877	20 957	32 857
Manitoba	8.0	9.0	14.0	63.7	119.4	222.3	2 371	5 571	7 500
Saskatchewan	10.0	4.0	1.6	55.8	31.8	24.0	2 570	1 909	1 662
Alberta	9.0	9.0	9.2	76.1	136.4	181.4	3 706	8 495	11 275
British Columbia	6.0	4.0	5.6	88.0	87.4	145.2	5 089	6 321	9 375
Tame Hay	**4 214.0**	**5 121.0**	**5 355.0**	**15 176.0**	**21 368.0**	**23 604.0**	**250 847**	**430 464**	**552 356**
Prince Edward Island	88.0	72.0	51.0	302.0	296.0	204.0	4 620	4 410	4 019
Nova Scotia	161.0	90.0	60.0	634.0	429.0	288.0	11 773	7 668	6 099
New Brunswick	214.0	100.0	64.0	678.0	430.0	251.0	11 849	7 305	5 596
Québec	1 584.0	1 345.0	1 070.0	5 013.0	5 495.0	4 518.0	87 681	109 928	122 431
Ontario	1 348.0	1 354.0	1 080.0	5 559.0	6 701.0	5 733.0	86 292	146 814	147 226
Manitoba	130.0	407.0	500.0	504.0	1 571.0	2 177.0	6 021	28 198	40 000
Saskatchewan	192.0	467.0	800.0	617.0	1 579.0	2 903.0	9 029	28 077	52 250
Alberta	376.0	1 114.0	1 480.0	1 243.0	3 949.0	6 078.0	19 053	75 507	132 060
British Columbia	121.0	174.0	250.0	624.0	917.0	1 451.0	14 530	22 558	42 675

Continued overleaf

Table 18 continued

FIELD CROP AND PROVINCE	AREA			TOTAL PRODUCTION			GROSS FARM VALUE		
	Average 1945–49	Average 1963–67	1974	Average 1945–49	Average 1963–67	1974	Average 1945–49	Average 1963–67	1972
	10^3 ha	10^3 ha	10^3 ha	10^3 t	10^3 t	10^3 t	$000	$000	$000
Fodder Corn	**162.0**	**212.0**	**419.0**	**3 183.0**	**5 594.0**	**10 043.0**	**17 951**	**38 877**	**79 129**
Québec	28.0	26.0	64.0	549.0	705.0	1 855.0	4 172	5 506	16 338
Ontario	123.0	166.0	336.0	2 531.0	4 579.0	7 697.0	12 910	30 828	58 691
Manitoba	6.0	15.0	11.0	53.0	213.0	190.0	422	1 599	1 600
British Columbia	2.0	2.0	7.0	38.0	77.0	299.0	309	677	2 500

[1]Excluding Newfoundland.

[2]Because of rounding and omissions, columns may not always add up to the totals indicated.

Sources: *Canada Year Book 1961, 1970–71*, and *1975*; *Quarterly Bulletin of Agricultural Statistics 1971*.

19. Value of Mineral Production, 1970 and 1976

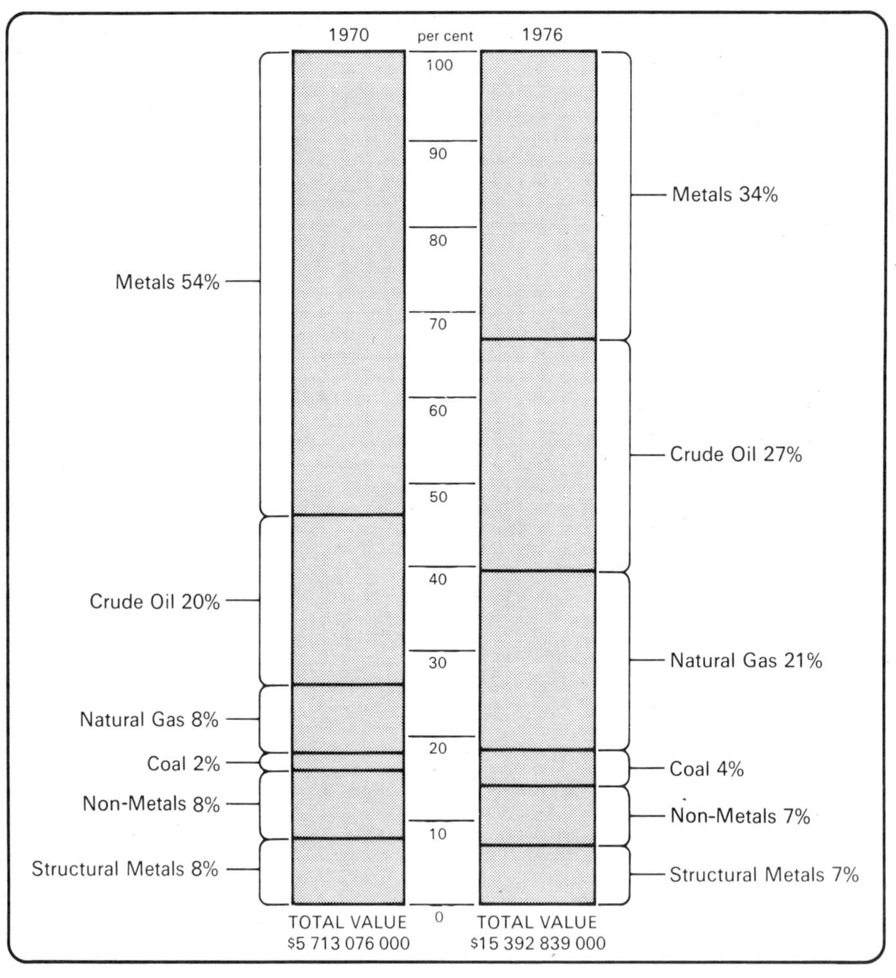

Source: *Canada's Mineral Production, Preliminary Estimate*, Statistics Canada, 1970 and 1976.

20. Value of Production of Principal Minerals, 1976*

Metals	NFLD. $000	N.S. $000	N.B. $000	QUÉ. $000	ONT. $000	MAN. $000	SASK. $000	ALTA. $000	B.C. $000	Y.T. & N.W.T. $000	CANADA $000
COBALT	—	—	—	—	9 679	2 090	—	—	—	—	11 769
COPPER	10 194	—	14 587	181 500	390 361	85 444	14 463	—	412 308	17 299	1 126 156
GOLD	1 596	—	460	58 460	90 414	5 674	2 342	—	21 820	27 030	207 796
IRON ORE	643 455	—	—	324 607	264 111	—	—	—	9 090	—	1 241 263
IRON, remelt	—	—	—	65 086	—	—	—	—	—	—	65 086
LEAD	4 621	—	30 808	460	3 186	137	—	—	44 264	45 912	129 388
MOLYBDENUM	—	—	—	2 946	—	—	—	—	88 927	—	91 873
NICKEL	—	—	—	—	993 704	238 439	—	—	—	—	1 232 143
PLATINUM GROUP	—	—	—	—	48 790	—	—	—	—	—	48 790
SILVER	2 194	—	21 497	15 794	67 000	3 817	1 387	—	35 108	28 331	175 128
URANIUM (U_3O_8)†	—	—	—	—	3 892 kg	—	2 166 kg	—	—	—	6 058 kg
ZINC	37 833	—	142 432	101 960	265 426	51 367	6 755	—	93 940	162 583	862 296
Total—All Metals	**699 919**	—	**217 945**	**765 699**	**2 153 488**	**387 330**	**25 116**	—	**710 487**	**281 167**	**5 241 151**
Non-Metallics											
ASBESTOS	33 383	—	—	343 164	3 797	—	—	—	30 719	34 460	445 523
GYPSUM	2 436	13 804	177	—	2 658	203	—	—	3 628	—	22 906
PEAT	—	500	5 800	7 800	870	2 470	400	1 100	3 560	—	22 500
POTASH (K_2O)	—	—	—	—	—	—	361 442	—	—	—	361 442
QUARTZ	218	231	—	5 075	5 400	1 517	168	1 125	161	—	13 895
SALT	—	17 632	—	—	44 272	161	7 833	5 793	—	—	75 691
SODIUM SULPHATE	—	—	—	—	—	—	22 221	2 657	—	—	24 878
SULPHUR, in smelter gas	—	—	781	2 575	7 318	—	—	—	4 780	—	15 454
SULPHUR, elemental	—	—	—	—	35	15	293	62 280	716	—	63 339
TITANIUM DIOXIDE, &C.	—	—	—	74 410	—	—	—	—	—	—	74 410
Total—All Non-metallics	**38 699**	**32 927**	**6 758**	**439 174**	**75 742**	**4 366**	**392 357**	**72 955**	**45 078**	**34 460**	**1 142 516**
Fuels											
COAL	—	54 500	6 300	—	—	—	12 900	223 800	306 500	—	604 000
NATURAL GAS	—	—	59	2	5 760	—	8 250	2 302 235	130 137	20 178	2 466 621
NATURAL GAS BY-PRODUCTS	—	—	—	—	—	—	5 787	772 414	16 124	—	794 325
PETROLEUM, CRUDE	—	—	24	—	6 028	32 995	435 675	3 531 100	114 272	8 364	4 128 485
Total—All Fuels	—	**54 500**	**6 383**	**2**	**11 788**	**32 995**	**462 612**	**6 829 549**	**567 033**	**28 542**	**7 993 404**
Structural Materials											
CLAY PRODUCTS	475	3 915	2 464	14 243	50 926	1 318	3 098	8 727	6 944	—	92 110
CEMENT	5 014	7 059	8 967	88 733	116 162	22 606	15 171	36 948	38 499	—	339 159
LIME	—	—	1 440	20 570	24 236	2 805	—	4 093	955	—	54 099
SAND AND GRAVEL	9 200	14 400	4 100	75 900	95 200	25 200	10 200	42 100	42 800	—	320 800
STONE	2 700	4 400	7 000	117 000	66 500	1 500	—	1 200	9 300	—	209 600
Total—All Structural Materials	**17 389**	**29 774**	**23 971**	**316 446**	**353 024**	**53 429**	**28 469**	**93 068**	**98 498**	—	**1 015 768**
Grand Totals 1976	**756 007**	**117 201**	**255 057**	**1 521 321**	**2 594 042**	**478 120**	**908 554**	**6 995 572**	**1 421 096**	**344 169**	**15 392 839**
Grand Totals 1968	**309 712**	**56 928**	**88 451**	**728 784**	**1 355 629**	**209 626**	**357 174**	**1 091 749**	**389 311**	**137 002**	**4 725 341**

*Based on rounded figures shown.

†Value of uranium production not available.

Source: *Canada's Mineral Production, Preliminary Estimate*, Statistics Canada, 1976.

21. Petroleum Supply and Demand, 1960, 1965, 1970, 1973, and 1975

	1960	1965	1970	1973	1975
			10^3 t		
SUPPLY					
Production					
Crude and equivalent[1]	32 605	55 356	88 571	126 969	106 814
Imports					
Crude	20 586	23 703	34 135	53 024	50 673
Refined Products	5 771	9 749	11 600	7 417	2 778
Total Supply	**58 962**	**88 808**	**134 306**	**187 410**	**160 265**
DEMAND					
Domestic Demand	51 604	68 678	87 983	102 678	104 908
Exports	7 377	19 517	45 782	83 808	55 079
Total Demand	**58 981**	**88 195**	**133 765**	**186 486**	**159 987**

[1]Includes plant liquefied petroleum gases.

Source: *An Energy Strategy for Canada*, Energy, Mines and Resources, 1976.

22. Marketable Gas Supply and Demand, 1960, 1965, 1970, 1973, and 1975

	1960	1965	1970	1973	1975
			10^9 m^3		
SUPPLY					
Production	12.53	29.74	52.88	71.34	71.32
Imports	0.15	0.50	0.31	0.42	0.31
Total	**12.68**	**30.24**	**53.19**	**71.76**	**71.63**
DEMAND					
Net Sales	9.08	16.29	26.15	35.05	38.17
Pipeline uses[1]	0.32	1.56	3.36	3.68	2.88
Exports[2]	3.11	11.45	22.08	29.09	26.80
Reprocessing	—	0.61	0.83	2.29	2.41
Stock change	0.19	0.34	0.77	1.65	1.38
Total	**12.70**	**30.25**	**53.19**	**71.76**	**71.64**

[1]Includes pipeline fuel consumed in Canada to move gas for export.

[2]Includes pipeline fuel consumed in USA to move gas to central Canada.

Source: *An Energy Strategy for Canada*, Energy, Mines and Resources, 1976.

23. Installed Generating Capacity by Type and Region, 1960, 1970, and 1975

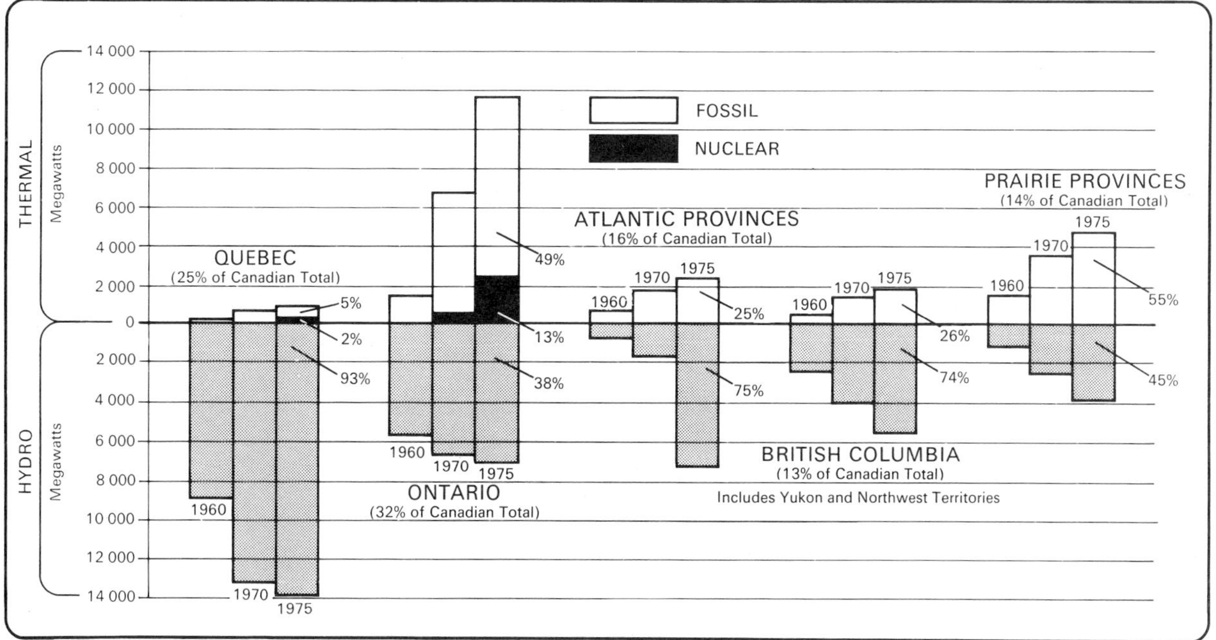

Source: *Electrical Power in Canada*, Department of Energy, Mines and Resources, 1975.

24. Electricity Supply and Demand, 1960, 1965, and 1970 to 1975

	1960	1965	1970	1971	1972	1973	1974	1975
				10^9 kW·h				
Canadian production	114	144	205	216	240	263	279	273
Imports	1	4	3	3	2	2	2	4
Domestic demand	109	144	202	213	232	248	266	266
Exports	6	4	6	7	11	17	15	11

Source: *An Energy Strategy for Canada*, Energy, Mines and Resources, 1976.

25. Coal Supply and Demand, 1960, 1965, and 1970 to 1975

	1960	1965	1970	1971	1972	1973	1974	1975
				10^6 t				
Canadian production	10.0	10.4	15.1	16.7	18.8	20.5	21.1	25.1
Imports[1]	11.5	15.1	18.0	16.7	17.6	15.7	13.0	16.4
Domestic demand	20.4	23.4	25.7	25.3	24.2	25.0	24.9	25.4
Exports[1]	0.9	1.2	4.3	7.3	8.8	10.6	10.8	12.2

[1]Includes coke.

Source: *An Energy Strategy for Canada*, Energy, Mines and Resources, 1976.

26. Lumber Production and Shipments and Value of All Shipments of the Sawmill and Planing Industry, 1968 and 1973

PROVINCE OR TERRITORY	PRODUCTION		QUANTITY SHIPPED		VALUE OF SHIPMENTS	
	1968	1973	1968	1973	1968	1973
	m³	m³	m³	m³	$000	$000
NEWFOUNDLAND	17 310	45 859	25 213	44 583	931	3 203
PRINCE EDWARD ISLAND	6 563	2 279	2 305	2 279	73	120
NOVA SCOTIA	511 294	375 911	439 751	376 107	15 572	24 059
NEW BRUNSWICK	627 963	658 859	663 549	689 052	24 886	48 117
QUÉBEC	3 801 653	5 497 449	3 631 322	5 590 304	135 075	323 735
ONTARIO	1 985 433	2 445 160	1 736 936	2 361 517	76 824	163 533
MANITOBA	79 890	184 861	68 055	176 451	1 849	9 742
SASKATCHEWAN	199 185	394 238	251 602	455 443	8 767	23 599
ALBERTA	805 896	1 363 278	909 442	1 454 906	29 950	83 808
BRITISH COLUMBIA	17 317 436	23 823 777	18 171 589	23 522 533	707 896	1 546 889
YUKON & NORTHWEST TERRITORIES	17 296	7 266	18 646	7 266	584	351
CANADA	**25 369 913**	**34 798 930**	**25 918 404**	**34 680 461**	**1 002 407**	**2 227 156**

Sources: *Canada Year Book 1970–71*; *Canadian Forestry Statistics*, Statistics Canada, 1973.

27. Estimated World Newsprint Production and Exports by Leading Countries, 1966, 1969, and 1974

COUNTRY	1966		1969		1974	
	Production	Exports	Production	Exports	Production	Exports
	10³ t	10³ t	10³ t	10³ t	10³ t	10³ t
CANADA	8 419	7 764	8 758	8 033	8 661	7 892
UNITED STATES	2 408	99	3 232	117	2 924	v.s.
JAPAN	1 301	26	1 779	4	2 233	v.s.
USSR	972	197	1 358	273	1 334	v.s.
FINLAND	1 330	1 210	1 212	1 108	1 219	1 137
SWEDEN	760	474	964	659	1 210	944
BRITAIN	825	3	876	2	383	v.s.
WORLD	18 275		20 850		22 655	

v.s. Very small.
Sources: *Statistical Yearbook*, United Nations, 1975; *Yearbook of International Trade Statistics*, United Nations, 1974.

28. Pulp Production, 1964, 1969, and 1973

	1964	1969	1973
	10³ t	10³ t	10³ t
QUÉBEC	4 720	5 938	5 590
BRITISH COLUMBIA	2 564	4 425	5 336
ONTARIO	3 009	3 593	3 668
OTHER PROVINCES	2 170	2 905	3 965
Total Production	**12 464**	**16 861**	**18 559**

Sources: *Canada Year Book 1972*; *Canadian Forestry Statistics*, Statistics Canada, 1973.

29. Pulp Production and Imports and Exports by Leading Countries, 1973

COUNTRY	PRODUCTION	EXPORTS	IMPORTS
	10³ t	$US millions	$US millions
UNITED STATES	43 388	1 007	1 112
CANADA	18 559	1 919	44
JAPAN	10 086	12	266
SWEDEN	9 462	1 318	11
USSR	7 767	80	48
FINLAND	6 678	349	1

Sources: *Statistical Yearbook*, United Nations, 1975; *Yearbook of International Trade Statistics*, United Nations, 1974.

30. Quantity and Value of Sea and Inland Fish Landed, 1962, 1968, and 1972 and Persons Employed, 1968 and 1972

PROVINCE OR TERRITORY	QUANTITY			VALUE			PERSONS EMPLOYED	
	1962	1968	1972	1962	1968	1972	1968	1972
	t	t	t	$000	$000	$000		
NEWFOUNDLAND	249 127	435 972	295 135	17 222	28 007	35 723	19 355	14 452
PRINCE EDWARD ISLAND	17 065	21 312	25 780	4 361	7 399	9 540	3 301	3 210
NOVA SCOTIA	197 682	360 719	286 856	30 928	52 250	66 375	13 108	11 735
NEW BRUNSWICK	92 746	247 205	162 144	9 182	15 581	19 923	5 942	5 161
QUÉBEC	60 512	92 751	83 210	5 534	8 544	11 138	4 945	5 843
ONTARIO	28 924	25 263	19 589	5 341	5 968	8 119	2 044	2 097
MANITOBA	16 374	11 670	11 101	4 229	3 276	4 523	4 018	1 827
SASKATCHEWAN	6 822	4 976	4 864	1 478	1 382	1 634	2 348	1 800
ALBERTA	4 093	5 389	2 202	714	917	727	4 758	1 547
BRITISH COLUMBIA	311 517	121 193	153 060	49 067	57 274	75 128	12 133	9 902
YUKON & NORTHWEST TERRITORIES	2 968	1 948	1 625	859	781	866	401	201
Totals	**987 813**	**1 328 403**	**1 045 566**	**128 915**	**181 379**	**233 696**	**72 353**	**57 775**

Sources: *Canada Year Book 1969, 1970–71*, and *1975*; *Fishery Statistics of Canada*, 1971.

31. St. Lawrence Seaway: Type of Traffic, 1975[1]

DOMESTIC	UPBOUND		DOWNBOUND	
	No. of Transits	Cargo tonnes	No. of Transits	Cargo tonnes
Canada to Canada	1 275	5 851 957	1 531	15 327 411
Canada to United States	1 301	12 050 055	33	239 130
United States to Canada	51	98 173	1 022	15 234 567
United States to United States	97	140 933	100	245 773

FOREIGN		UPBOUND		DOWNBOUND	
		No. of Transits	Cargo tonnes	No. of Transits	Cargo tonnes
Canada	Import	180	508 413	—	—
	Export	—	—	196	1 204 205
United States	Import	655	3 381 100	—	—
	Export	—	—	658	6 392 947

[1] Combines Montreal-Lake Ontario and Welland Canal Sections.

Source: *Traffic Report of the St. Lawrence Seaway*, St. Lawrence Seaway Authority, 1975.

32. Water-Borne Cargo Loaded and Unloaded for Six Largest Ports, 1973

PORT & COMMODITY	INTERNATIONAL Loaded	INTERNATIONAL Un-loaded	COASTWISE Loaded	COASTWISE Un-loaded	TOTAL
	t	t	t	t	t
Vancouver (205-115)[2]	**24 671 201**	**3 549 504**	**2 749 659**	**4 516 125**	**35 486 490**
Wheat	5 146 171	—	—	—	5 146 171
Coal	9 084 196	—	—	—	9 084 196
Sept Îles-Pointe Noire (12-92)	**21 840 735**	**568 236**	**859 564**	**505 059**	**23 773 594**
Iron ore and concentrates	21 816 884	—	840 635	—	22 657 519
Montréal (211-155)	**5 579 172**	**4 716 805**	**4 069 285**	**4 844 381**	**19 209 644**
Wheat	1 750 700	148 822	—	—	1 899 522
Fuel oil	916 237	1 479 529	2 443 058	299 203	5 138 027
Containerized freight	915 080	654 994	—	—	1 570 073
Thunder Bay (41-105)	**3 658 080**	**238 276**	**13 584 692**	**765 157**	**18 246 205**
Wheat	69 886	—	7 897 143	—	7 967 029
Iron ore and concentrates	2 282 065	—	2 891 255	—	5 173 319
Port Cartier (10-21)	**11 942 246**	**2 017 260**	**22 101**	**1 646 307**	**15 627 913**
Iron ore and concentrates	8 764 774	—	9 077	—	8 773 851
Wheat	1 984 063	900 862	10 563	1 252 613	4 148 101
Québec (117-55)	**4 865 635**	**5 718 461**	**1 013 272**	**2 844 690**	**14 442 058**
Fuel oil	1 298 197	522 930	747 963	655 405	3 224 495
Crude petroleum	—	3 941 017	—	85 326	4 026 343

[1] Bold figures represent total tonnage and include commodities not listed.

[2] The two figures in parenthesis indicate approximately the total number of international (left-hand figure) and coastwise (right-hand figure) commodities handled by the port in 1971.

Source: *Shipping Report*, Parts II and III, Statistics Canada, 1973.

33. St. Lawrence Seaway Traffic by Classification and Direction—Montreal-Lake Ontario Section—1975

Principal Commodities	Upbound 10^3 t	Upbound %	Downbound 10^3 t	Downbound %	Principal sources and destinations of commodities
Wheat	—	—	11 260	47.6	Can → Can [66%] USA → Foreign [16%] USA → Can [14%]
Corn	—	—	2 907	12.3	USA → Foreign [48%] USA → Canada [45%]
Oats	—	—	427	1.8	Can → Can [47%] USA → Foreign [28%]
Barley	—	—	2 231	9.4	Can → Can [89%]
Soybeans	—	—	1 157	4.9	USA → Foreign [62%] USA → Can [38%]
Total Agricultural Products	**29**	**0.1**	**19 408**	**82.1**	
Bituminous Coal	173	0.9	225	1.0	USA → Can [50%] Can → Can [43%]
Coke	311	1.6	522	2.2	USA → Can [45%] USA → Foreign [13%] Foreign → USA [33%]
Iron Ore	13 143	66.1	14	0.1	Can → USA [82%] Can → Can [18%]
Salt	20	0.1	760	3.2	Can → Can [59%] USA → Can [38%]
Total Mine Products	**14 499**	**72.9**	**2 029**	**8.6**	

Continued

Table 33 continued

Principal Commodities	Upbound 10³ t	Upbound %	Downbound 10³ t	Downbound %	Principal sources and destinations of commodities
Fuel Oil	1 545	7.7	224	1.0	Can → Can [47%] Can → USA [35%]
Iron and Steel Products	2 171	10.9	188	0.6	Foreign → USA [80%] Foreign → Can [8%]
Total Manufactures and Miscellaneous	**5 292**	**26.6**	**2 015**	**8.5**	
Grand Total	**19 896**	**100.0**	**23 650**	**100.0**	

Source: *Traffic Report of the St. Lawrence Seaway*, St. Lawrence Seaway Authority, 1975.

34. St. Lawrence Seaway Traffic by Classification and Direction—Welland Canal Section—1975

Principal Commodities	Upbound 10³ t	Upbound %	Downbound 10³ t	Downbound %	Principal sources and destinations of commodities
Wheat	—	—	11 870	31.9	Can → Can [69%] USA → Foreign [16%] USA → Can [14%]
Corn	—	—	3 124	8.4	USA → Foreign [44%] USA → Can [46%] Can → Can [10%]
Oats	—	—	450	1.2	Can → Can [49%] USA → Foreign [26%]
Barley	—	—	2 345	6.3	Can → Can [88%] USA → Can [5%]
Soybeans	—	—	1 558	4.2	USA → Foreign [46%] USA → Can [52%]
Total Agricultural Products	**11**	—	**20 767**	**55.9**	
Bituminous Coal	—	—	7 699	20.7	USA → Can [94%]
Coke	304	1.8	499	1.3	USA → Can [49%] Foreign → USA [35%]
Iron Ore	11 121	64.8	3 817	10.3	Can → USA [74%] Can → Can [9%] USA → Can [16%]
Stone, Ground or Crushed	972	5.7	106	0.3	Can → USA [91%]
Salt	20	0.1	1 336	3.6	Can → Can [51%] USA → Can [45%]
Total Mine Products	**12 899**	**75.3**	**13 999**	**37.7**	
Fuel Oil	547	3.2	485	1.3	Can → Can [70%]
Iron and Steel, Manufactured	2 012	11.8	112	0.3	Foreign → USA [91%]
Scrap Iron and Steel	—	—	559	1.6	USA → Foreign [99%]
Package Freight—Domestic	241	1.4	39	0.1	Can → Can [100%]
Total Manufactures and Miscellaneous	**3 953**	**23.1**	**2 182**	**5.9**	
Grand Total	**17 134**	**100.0**	**37 149**	**100.0**	

Source: *Traffic Report of the St. Lawrence Seaway*, St. Lawrence Seaway Authority, 1975.

35. Regional Shares of Selected National Manufacturing Statistics, Selected Years, 1926 to 1973

Total Employees	1926 %	1933 %	1942 %	1951 %	1961 %	1971 %	1973 %
ATLANTIC PROVINCES	6.4	5.2	4.8	5.3	4.8	4.6	4.9
QUÉBEC	31.3	33.6	34.6	33.2	33.5	31.2	30.0
ONTARIO	48.5	48.0	47.1	47.6	46.8	49.1	49.2
PRAIRIE PROVINCES	5.9	7.1	5.7	6.5	7.2	7.1	7.1
BRITISH COLUMBIA	8.0	6.1	7.8	7.4	7.7	7.9	8.7
CANADA[1]	100.0	100.0	100.0	100.0	100.0	100.0	100.0
	558 861	468 366	1 150 616	1 258 375	1 264 946	1 628 404	1 772 109
Salaries and Wages[2]							
ATLANTIC PROVINCES	4.3	4.4	4.1	4.3	3.9	3.7	3.9
QUÉBEC	29.2	30.9	31.9	30.7	31.1	28.5	27.4
ONTARIO	51.5	50.6	50.0	51.0	49.7	52.2	52.2
PRAIRIE PROVINCES	6.7	7.6	5.2	6.0	7.0	6.6	6.8
BRITISH COLUMBIA	8.3	6.5	8.8	8.0	8.4	9.1	9.7
CANADA[1]	100.0	100.0	100.0	100.0	100.0	100.0	100.0
	$625 416	$435 908	$1 681 150	$3 276 281	$5 231 447	$12 129 897	$15 217 314
Census Value Added[2]							
ATLANTIC PROVINCES	4.3	4.3	3.6	4.3	3.7	3.3	3.8
QUÉBEC	29.5	31.3	32.0	30.0	30.0	27.6	26.2
ONTARIO	51.9	50.6	50.5	51.4	50.8	54.1	53.3
PRAIRIE PROVINCES	7.0	7.4	5.6	5.7	7.3	6.7	6.9
BRITISH COLUMBIA	7.2	6.4	8.3	8.6	8.1	8.2	9.8
CANADA[1]	100.0	100.0	100.0	100.0	100.0	100.0	100.0
	$1 281 021	$918 923	$3 305 495	$6 940 947	$10 682 138	$23 187 881	$30 890 503

[1]Canada shown total.
[2]Total Salaries and Wages and total Census Value Added × $000.

Source: *Canadian Urban Trends, National Perspective*, Vol. I. Printed with the permission of the Ministry of State for Urban Affairs and Copp Clark Publishing.

36. Percentage of Domestic and Foreign Control of Principal Canadian Manufacturing Industries, 1970

INDUSTRY	NUMBER OF ESTABLISHMENTS %			PRODUCTION & RELATED WORKERS %			VALUE ADDED[1] %		
	U.S.A.	Other Foreign	Canada	U.S.A.	Other Foreign	Canada	U.S.A.	Other Foreign	Canada
Food and beverages	6.4	2.4	91.2	21.8	10.7	67.5	28.1	11.8	60.1
Textiles	8.7	3.9	87.4	28.9	9.0	62.1	40.3	10.0	49.7
Paper and related products	22.8	9.4	67.7	32.6	15.0	52.4	35.1	14.1	50.8
Primary metals	19.2	8.4	72.5	35.4	7.3	57.3	40.1	6.6	53.3
Transportation equipment	18.7	2.8	78.6	66.8	6.6	26.6	77.6	5.4	17.0
Printing and publishing	1.4	0.8	97.9	5.2	3.3	91.5	8.2	3.0	88.8
Metal fabricating	9.3	2.1	88.7	26.5	5.1	68.4	33.5	5.3	61.2
Electrical products	36.5	6.3	57.2	51.7	9.4	38.9	55.0	10.8	34.2
Chemicals and chemical products	34.6	12.1	53.3	50.1	22.5	27.4	62.8	21.2	16.0
Total	9.1	2.8	88.1	32.4	8.1	59.5	40.8	10.1	49.1

[1]Value added refers to the value of manufactured goods shipped less cost of materials and supplies used including fuel and electricity.

Source: *Domestic and Foreign Control of Manufacturing Establishments in Canada*, 1969 and 1970, Statistics Canada, March 1976.

37. Principal Manufacturing Industries: National and Provincial Areas Ranked by Value Added, 1973[1]

CANADA		ATLANTIC PROVINCES	
Motor vehicles and parts	7.2[2]	Pulp and paper	20.5[2]
Pulp and paper	6.3	Fish products	11.9
Sawmills and planing mills	4.4	Sawmills and planing mills	4.6
Iron and steel mills	4.0	Dairy products	2.6
Misc. machinery and equipment	2.8	Breweries	2.4
Smelting and refining	2.2	Fabricated structural metals	1.8
Commercial printing	2.1	Industrial chemicals	1.5
Publishing and printing	2.1	Meat processing	1.2
Communications equipment	2.0	Read-mix concrete	0.8
Petroleum refining	1.9	Machine shops	0.8
Total value added ($000)	**28 825 008**	**Total value added ($000)**	**1 110 712**

QUÉBEC		ONTARIO	
Pulp and paper	7.4[2]	Motor vehicles and parts	12.9[2]
Smelting and refining	4.5	Iron and steel mills	6.4
Sawmills and planing mills	2.8	Misc. machinery and equipment	3.4
Women's clothing	2.5	Pulp and paper	3.0
Misc. machinery and equipment	2.3	Communications equipment	2.6
Petroleum refining	2.2	Commercial printing	2.2
Men's clothing	2.2	Rubber products	2.2
Commercial printing	2.2	Publishing and printing	1.9
Pharmaceuticals and medicines	1.9	Metal stamping and pressing	1.9
Dairy products	1.8	Electrical industrial equipment	1.8
Total value added ($000)	**7 672 770**	**Total value added ($000)**	**15 055 448**

PRAIRIE PROVINCES		BRITISH COLUMBIA	
Meat processing	7.6[2]	Sawmills and planing mills	28.1[2]
Publishing and printing	4.3	Pulp and paper	16.4
Pulp and paper	3.7	Veneer and plywood	5.1
Sawmills and planing mills	3.4	Fish products	3.2
Dairy products	3.1	Misc. machinery and equipment	2.7
Fabricated structural metals	2.5	Publishing and printing	2.2
Commercial printing	2.3	Shipbuilding and repair	1.9
Agricultural implements	2.3	Fabricated structural metals	1.4
Breweries	2.3	Dairy products	1.4
Bakeries	1.9	Commercial printing	1.2
Total value added ($000)	**2 048 771**	**Total value added ($000)**	**2 934 260**

[1]Value added refers to the value of manufactured goods shipped less cost of materials and supplies used including fuel and electricity.

[2]All figures refer to per cent of total value added by manufacturing for national or provincial areas.

Source: *Manufacturing Industries of Canada: National and Provincial Areas*, 1973, Statistics Canada, April 1976.

38. Major Import Commodities, 1976

		$000
1	Motor vehicle parts, except engines	4 302 964
2	Crude petroleum	3 272 033
3	Passenger automobiles and chassis	2 804 140
4	Trucks, truck tractors, chassis and other motor vehicles	1 177 694
5	Telecommunication and related equipment	1 089 795
6	Motor vehicle engines and parts	979 123
7	Electronic computers and other office machines	738 722
8	Outerwear	603 974
9	Coal	544 285
10	Miscellaneous equipment and tools	539 559
11	Plastic film, sheet and other materials	478 073
12	Wheel tractors, new	443 214
13	Organic chemicals	411 706
14	Photographic goods	391 255
15	Paper and paperboard	333 259
16	Meat, fresh, chilled or frozen	329 206
17	Tractor engines and tractor parts	264 453
18	Raw sugar	253 758
19	Coffee	249 546
	Total—All Imports	**37 390 942**

Source: *Summary of External Trade*, December 1976, Statistics Canada.

39. Major Export Commodities, 1976

		$000
1	Passenger automobiles and chassis	3 629 229
2	Crude petroleum	2 287 976
3	Motor vehicle parts, except engines	2 181 868
4	Wood pulp and similar pulp	2 172 057
5	Newsprint paper	1 993 026
6	Wheat	1 705 489
7	Natural gas	1 616 490
8	Lumber, softwood	1 605 418
9	Trucks, truck tractors and chassis	1 395 248
10	Iron ores and concentrates	916 544
11	Motor vehicle engines and parts	774 785
12	Coal and other crude bitumin substances	560 980
13	Petroleum and coal products	557 168
14	Fertilizers and fertilizer materials	547 224
15	Barley	542 362
16	Agricultural machinery and tractors	538 269
17	Nickel in ores, concentrates and scrap	523 577
18	Copper and alloys	515 864
19	Asbestos, unmanufactured	471 419
20	Aluminum, including alloys	464 551
21	Nickel and alloys	443 609
	Total—All Exports	**37 212 853**

Source: *Summary of External Trade*, December 1976, Statistics Canada.

40. Imports: Principal Nations, 1976

		$000
1	United States	25 661 677
2	Japan	1 523 727
3	Venezuela	1 295 110
4	United Kingdom	1 153 318
5	West Germany	817 855
6	Iran	695 426
7	Saudi Arabia	481 614
8	France	437 721
9	Italy	365 369
10	Australia	340 836
11	South Korea	303 251
12	Taiwan	292 061
	All Countries	**37 390 942**

Source: *Summary of External Trade*, December 1976, Statistics Canada.

41. Exports: Principal Nations, 1976

		$000
1	United States	25 122 901
2	Japan	2 386 190
3	United Kingdom	1 826 797
4	West Germany	694 778
5	Italy	547 917
6	USSR	535 224
7	Belgium & Luxembourg	472 154
8	Netherlands	442 327
9	France	393 464
10	Australia	359 067
11	Venezuela	355 317
12	Brazil	327 588
	All Countries	**37 212 853**

Source: *Summary of External Trade*, December 1976, Statistics Canada.

Canada: Population

Canada's population of 21 568 000 (1971) is composed of: (a) Indians and Inuit or Eskimos (only 1.5%); (b) descendants of the early French colonists (29%), primarily in the province of Québec; (c) Canadians of British origin(45%)–the first large influx was during and after the American War of Independence (1775-83) and there has been a fairly steady flow from the British Isles ever since ; and (d) Canadians of other origins (25%,mainly from Europe), who arrived in well-defined surges,especially during the opening up of the Prairies(1901–15) and after the Second World War(1945).

Canada is essentially a nation of city dwellers. In 1971,76.1% of Canadians lived in, or on the fringes of, cities and towns, while approximately 6.6% lived on farms and were classified as rural. The remaining 17.3%, described as rural non-farm, included such diverse groups as people who commute to work-places within urban centres and miners, forest workers, fishermen, etc. The urban proportion of the population has been steadily increasing (from approximately 69.5% in 1961) and will likely continue to do so, as urban areas, particularly the large cities,will be absorbing most of the future increase in Canada's population. Much of the land of Canada cannot support a large population; important industries like forestry, mining, and the generation of power do not employ great numbers.

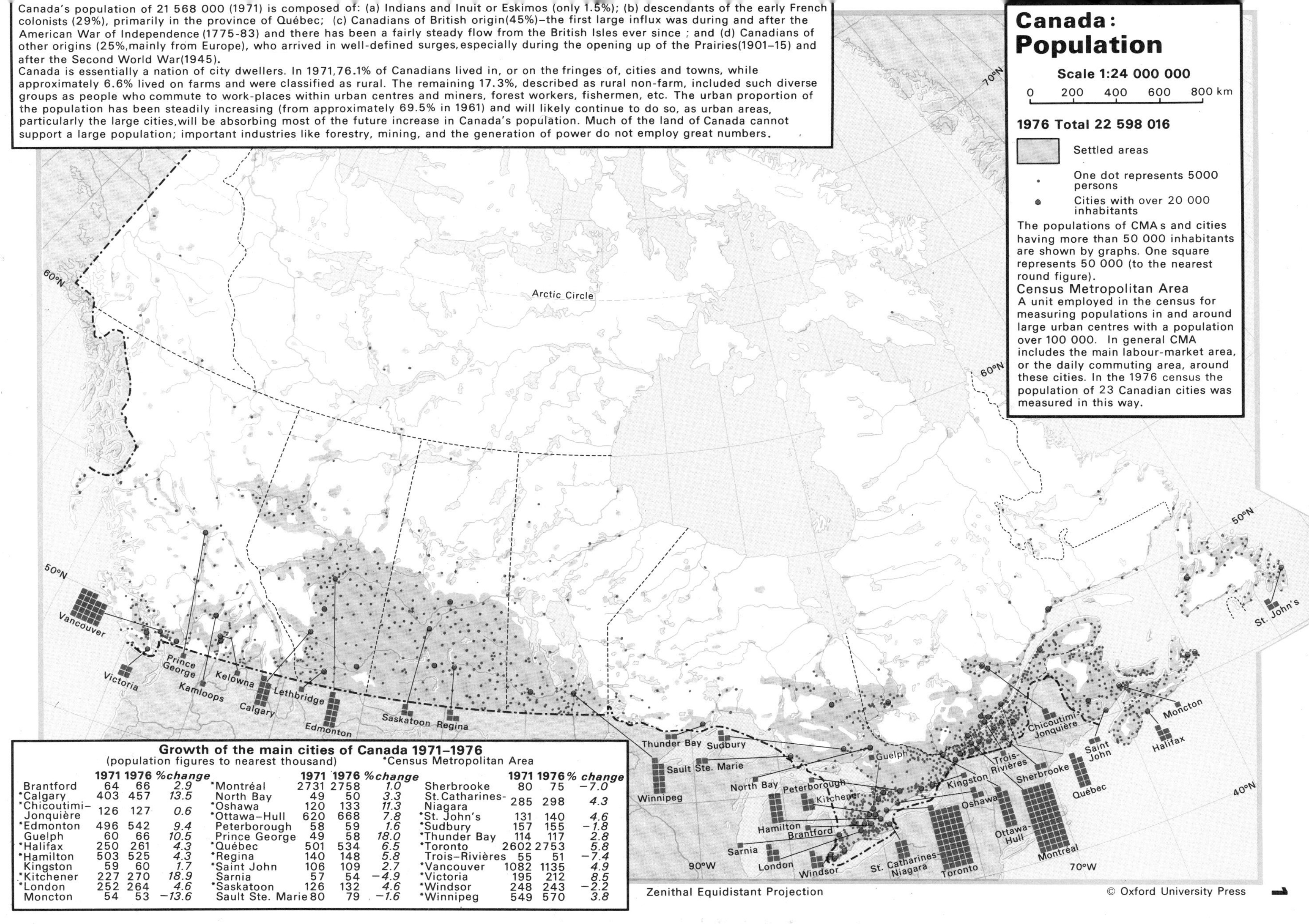

The populations of CMA s and cities having more than 50 000 inhabitants are shown by graphs. One square represents 50 000 (to the nearest round figure).

Census Metropolitan Area
A unit employed in the census for measuring populations in and around large urban centres with a population over 100 000. In general CMA includes the main labour-market area, or the daily commuting area, around these cities. In the 1976 census the population of 23 Canadian cities was measured in this way.

Growth of the main cities of Canada 1971–1976
(population figures to nearest thousand) *Census Metropolitan Area

	1971	1976	% change
Brantford	64	66	2.9
*Calgary	403	457	13.5
*Chicoutimi–Jonquière	126	127	0.6
*Edmonton	496	542	9.4
Guelph	60	66	10.5
*Halifax	250	261	4.3
*Hamilton	503	525	4.3
Kingston	59	60	1.7
*Kitchener	227	270	18.9
*London	252	264	4.6
Moncton	54	53	−13.6
*Montréal	2731	2758	1.0
North Bay	49	50	3.3
*Oshawa	120	133	11.3
*Ottawa–Hull	620	668	7.8
Peterborough	58	59	1.6
Prince George	49	58	18.0
*Québec	501	534	6.5
*Regina	140	148	5.8
*Saint John	106	109	2.7
Sarnia	57	54	−4.9
*Saskatoon	126	132	4.6
Sault Ste. Marie	80	79	−1.6
Sherbrooke	80	75	−7.0
St. Catharines-Niagara	285	298	4.3
*St. John's	131	140	4.6
*Sudbury	157	155	−1.8
*Thunder Bay	114	117	2.8
*Toronto	2602	2753	5.8
Trois–Rivières	55	51	−7.4
*Vancouver	1082	1135	4.9
*Victoria	195	212	8.5
*Windsor	248	243	−2.2
*Winnipeg	549	570	3.8

Canada: Physiographic Regions

Scale 1:24 000 000

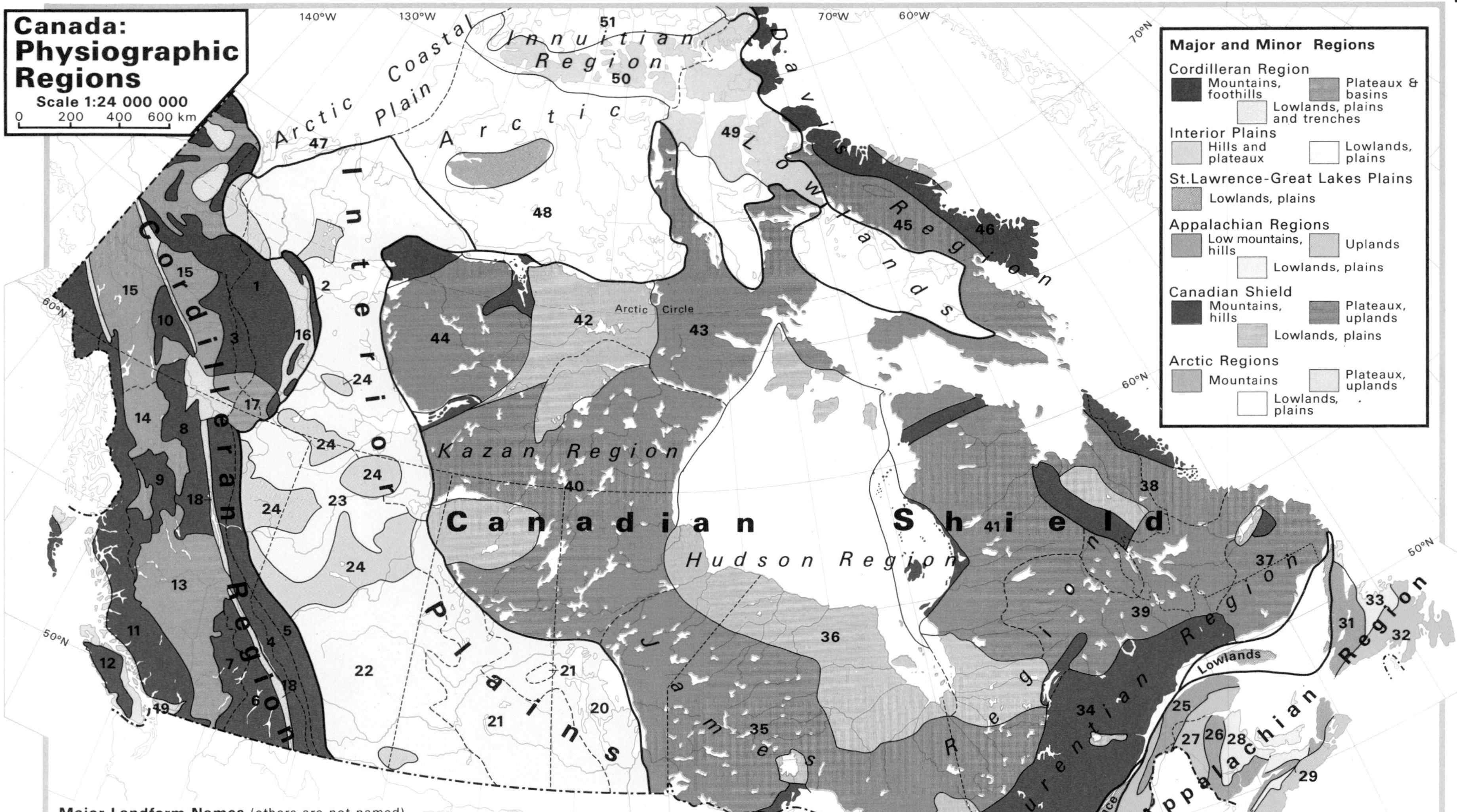

0 200 400 600 km

Major and Minor Regions

Cordilleran Region
- Mountains, foothills
- Plateaux & basins
- Lowlands, plains and trenches

Interior Plains
- Hills and plateaux
- Lowlands, plains

St.Lawrence-Great Lakes Plains
- Lowlands, plains

Appalachian Regions
- Low mountains, hills
- Uplands
- Lowlands, plains

Canadian Shield
- Mountains, hills
- Plateaux, uplands
- Lowlands, plains

Arctic Regions
- Mountains
- Plateaux, uplands
- Lowlands, plains

Major Landform Names (others are not named)

Cordilleran Region
1 Mackenzie Mountains
2 Franklin Mountains
3 Selwyn Mountains
4 Rocky Mountains
5 Foothills
6 Columbia Mountains
7 Columbia Highlands
8 Cassiar-Omineca Mts.
9 Skeena Mountains
10 Pelly Mountains
11 Coast Mountains
12 Vancouver Is. Ranges
13 Fraser-Nechako Plateaux
14 Stikine Plateau
15 Yukon Plateau
16 Mackenzie Plain
17 Liard Plain
18 Rocky Mountain Trench
19 Fraser Lowland

Interior Plains
20 Manitoba Plain
21 Saskatchewan Plain
22 Alberta Plain
23 Fort-Nelson-Peace River Lowland
24 Alberta Plateau

Appalachian Region
25 Notre Dame Mountains
26 New Brunswick Highlands
27 Chaleur Uplands
28 Maritime Plain
29 Atlantic Uplands
30 Annapolis Lowland
31 Newfoundland Highlands
32 Atlantic Uplands
33 Newfoundland Lowlands

Canadian Shield
34 Laurentian Highland
35 Abitibi-Severn Uplands
36 Hudson Bay Lowland
37 Mecatina Plateau
38 George Plateau
39 Lake Plateau
40 Kazan Upland
41 Larch Plateau
42 Back Plateau
43 Wager Plateau
44 Bear-Slave Upland
45 Baffin Upland
46 Davis Highland

Arctic Region
47 Mackenzie Delta
48 Victoria Lowland
49 Lancaster Plateau
50 Parry Plateau
51 Sverdrup Lowland

Source: *The National Atlas of Canada* (4th ed., pp. 5–6), published by the Macmillan Company of Canada Limited.

Zenithal Equidistant Projection

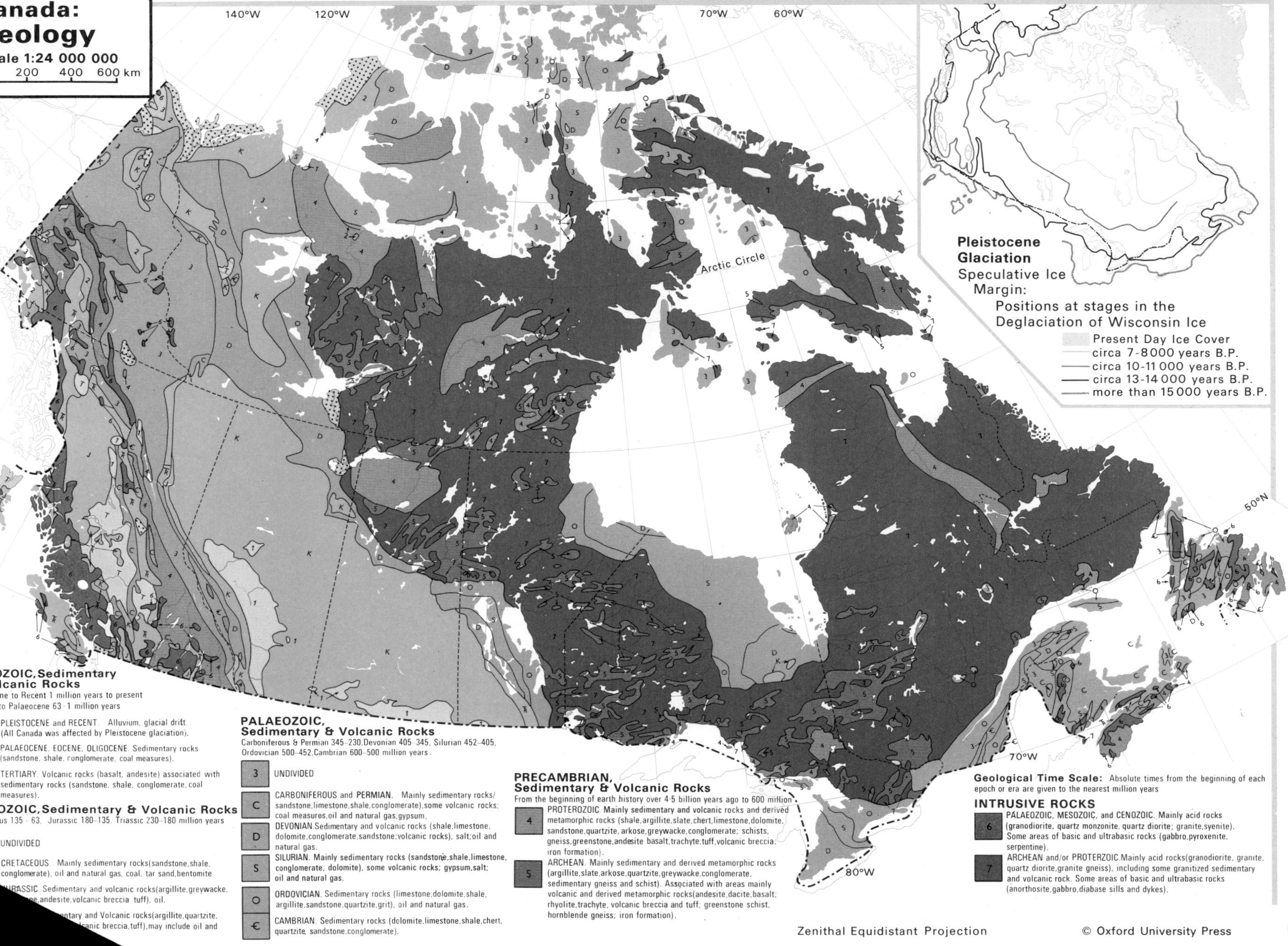

Canada:
Geology
Scale 1:24 000 000
0 200 400 600 km
140°W
120°W
70°W
60°W
60°N
50°N
50°N
70°W
80°W
Arctic Circle
Pleistocene
Glaciation
Speculative Ice
Margin:
Positions at stages in the
Deglaciation of Wisconsin Ice
Present Day Ice Cover
circa 7-8000 years B.P.
circa 10-11 000 years B.P.
circa 13-14 000 years B.P.
more than 15 000 years B.P.
CENOZOIC, Sedimentary & Volcanic Rocks
Pleistocene to Recent 1 million years to present
Tertiary to Palaeocene 63·1 million years
PLEISTOCENE and RECENT. Alluvium, glacial drift. (All Canada was affected by Pleistocene glaciation).
1 PALAEOCENE, EOCENE, OLIGOCENE. Sedimentary rocks (sandstone, shale, conglomerate, coal measures).
T TERTIARY. Volcanic rocks (basalt, andesite) associated with sedimentary rocks (sandstone, shale, conglomerate, coal measures).
MESOZOIC, Sedimentary & Volcanic Rocks
Cretaceous 135 - 63, Jurassic 180–135, Triassic 230–180 million years
2 UNDIVIDED
K CRETACEOUS. Mainly sedimentary rocks(sandstone,shale, conglomerate), oil and natural gas, coal, tar sand,bentonite
JURASSIC. Sedimentary and volcanic rocks(argillite,greywacke, andesite,volcanic breccia tuff), oil.
ntary and Volcanic rocks(argillite,quartzite, canic breccia,tuff),may include oil and
PALAEOZOIC, Sedimentary & Volcanic Rocks
Carboniferous & Permian 345–230, Devonian 405–345, Silurian 452–405, Ordovician 500–452, Cambrian 600–500 million years.
3 UNDIVIDED
C CARBONIFEROUS and PERMIAN. Mainly sedimentary rocks/ sandstone,limestone,shale,conglomerate),some volcanic rocks; coal measures,oil and natural gas,gypsum.
D DEVONIAN. Sedimentary and volcanic rocks (shale,limestone, dolomite,conglomerate,sandstone;volcanic rocks), salt;oil and natural gas.
S SILURIAN. Mainly sedimentary rocks (sandstone,shale,limestone, conglomerate, dolomite), some volcanic rocks; gypsum,salt; oil and natural gas.
O ORDOVICIAN. Sedimentary rocks (limestone,dolomite,shale, argillite,sandstone,quartzite,grit), oil and natural gas.
€ CAMBRIAN. Sedimentary rocks (dolomite,limestone,shale,chert, quartzite, sandstone,conglomerate).
PRECAMBRIAN, Sedimentary & Volcanic Rocks
From the beginning of earth history over 4·5 billion years ago to 600 million
4 PROTEROZOIC. Mainly sedimentary and volcanic rocks and derived metamorphic rocks (shale,argillite,slate,chert,limestone,dolomite, sandstone,quartzite, arkose,greywacke,conglomerate; schists, gneiss,greenstone,andesite basalt,trachyte,tuff,volcanic breccia; iron formation).
5 ARCHEAN. Mainly sedimentary and derived metamorphic rocks (argillite,slate,arkose,quartzite,greywacke,conglomerate, sedimentary gneiss and schist). Associated with areas mainly volcanic and derived metamorphic rocks(andesite,dacite,basalt; rhyolite,trachyte, volcanic breccia and tuff; greenstone schist, hornblende gneiss; iron formation).
Geological Time Scale: Absolute times from the beginning of each epoch or era are given to the nearest million years
INTRUSIVE ROCKS
6 PALAEOZOIC, MESOZOIC, and CENOZOIC. Mainly acid rocks (granodiorite, quartz monzonite, quartz diorite; granite,syenite). Some areas of basic and ultrabasic rocks (gabbro,pyroxenite, serpentine).
7 ARCHEAN and/or PROTERZOIC. Mainly acid rocks(granodiorite, granite, quartz diorite,granite gneiss), including some granitized sedimentary and volcanic rock. Some areas of basic and ultrabasic rocks (anorthosite,gabbro,diabase sills and dykes).
Zenithal Equidistant Projection
© Oxford University Press

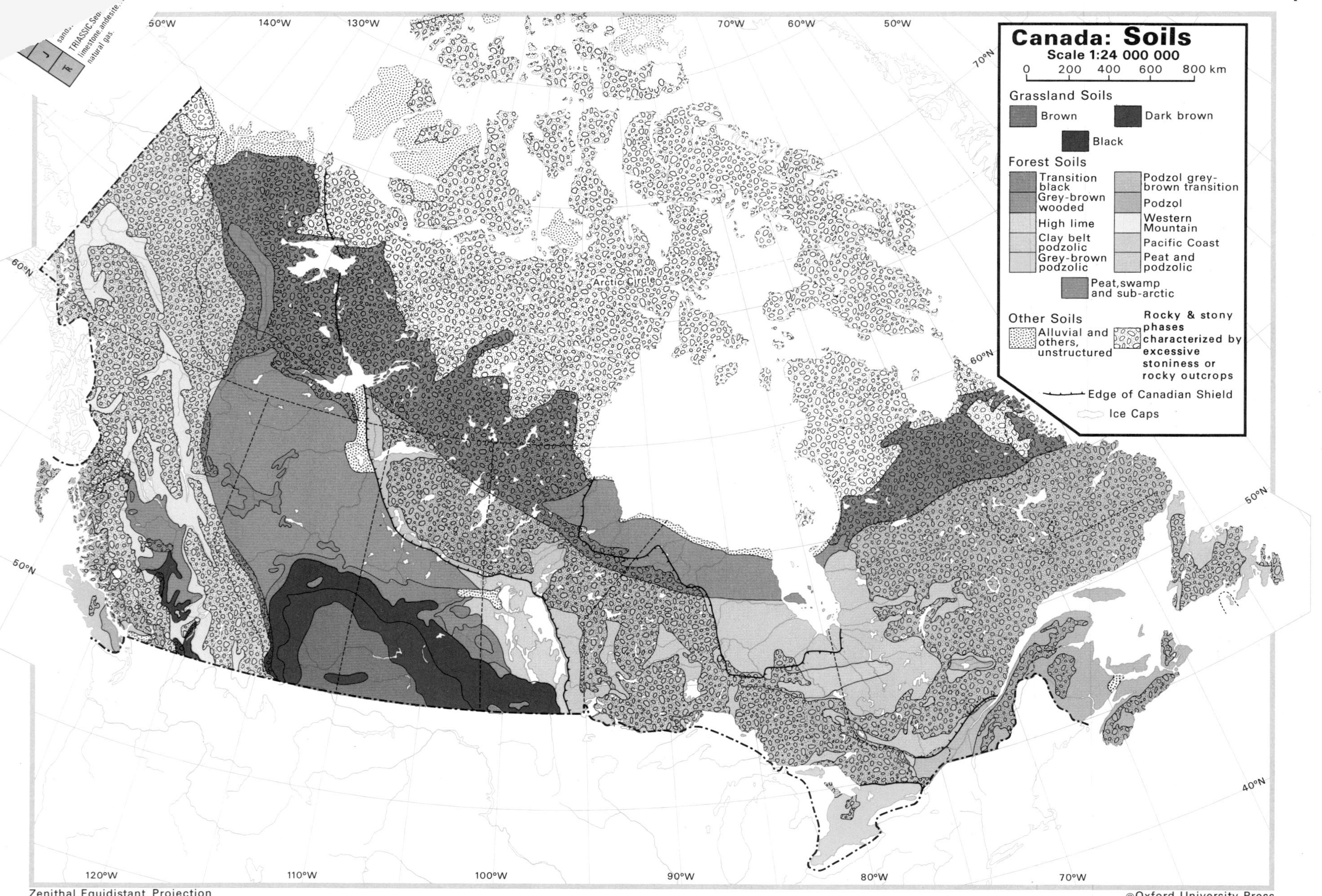
Canada: Soils
Scale 1:24 000 000
0 200 400 600 800 km
Grassland Soils
Brown
Dark brown
Black
Forest Soils
Transition black
Grey-brown wooded
High lime
Clay belt podzolic
Grey-brown podzolic
Podzol grey-brown transition
Podzol
Western Mountain
Pacific Coast
Peat and podzolic
Peat, swamp and sub-arctic
Other Soils
Alluvial and others, unstructured
Rocky & stony phases characterized by excessive stoniness or rocky outcrops
Edge of Canadian Shield
Ice Caps
Arctic Circle
150°W
140°W
130°W
70°W
60°W
50°W
70°N
60°N
50°N
40°N
120°W
110°W
100°W
90°W
80°W
Zenithal Equidistant Projection
©Oxford University Press

Canada: Climate

Scale 1:44 000 000

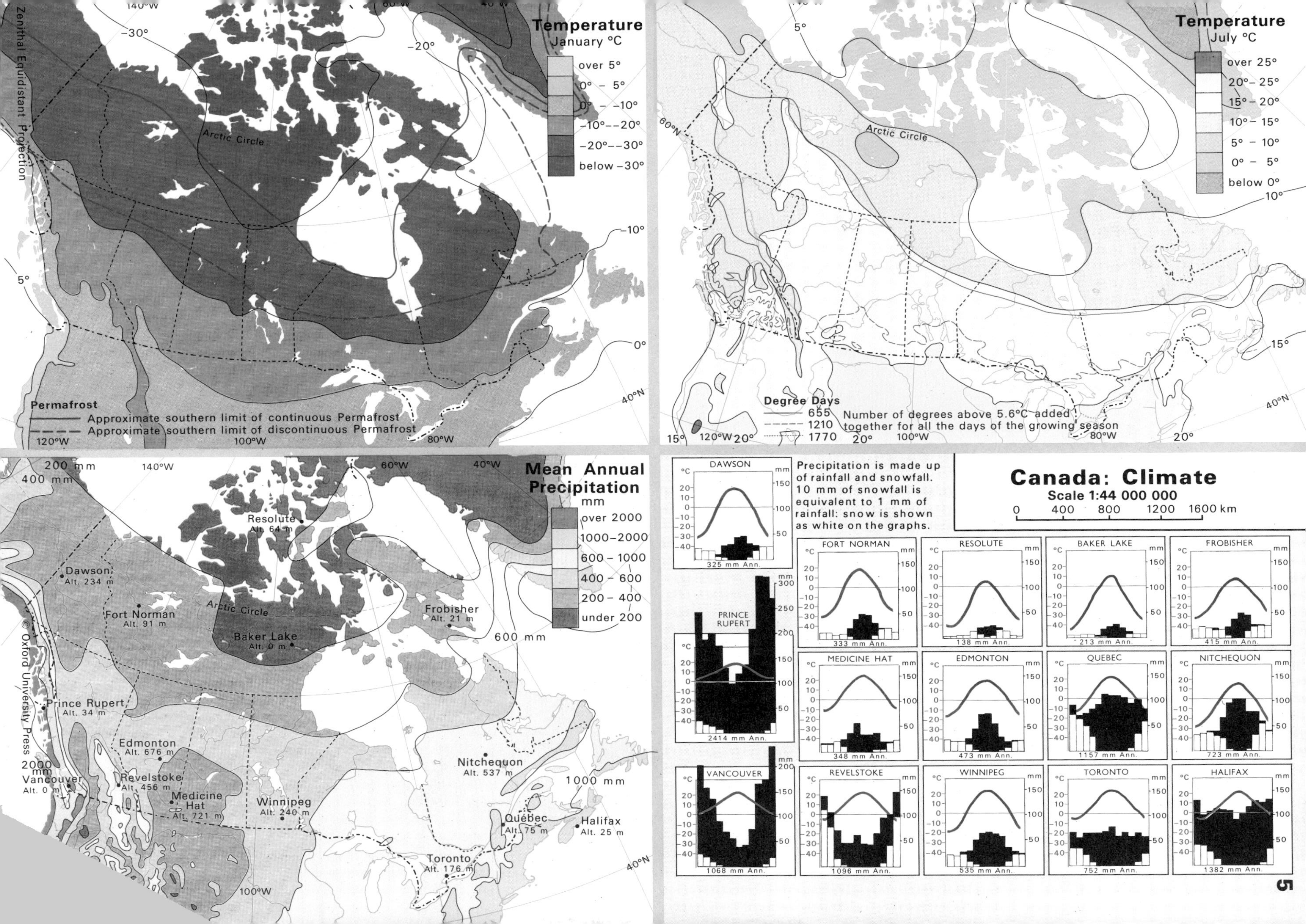

Canada: Agriculture and Forestry

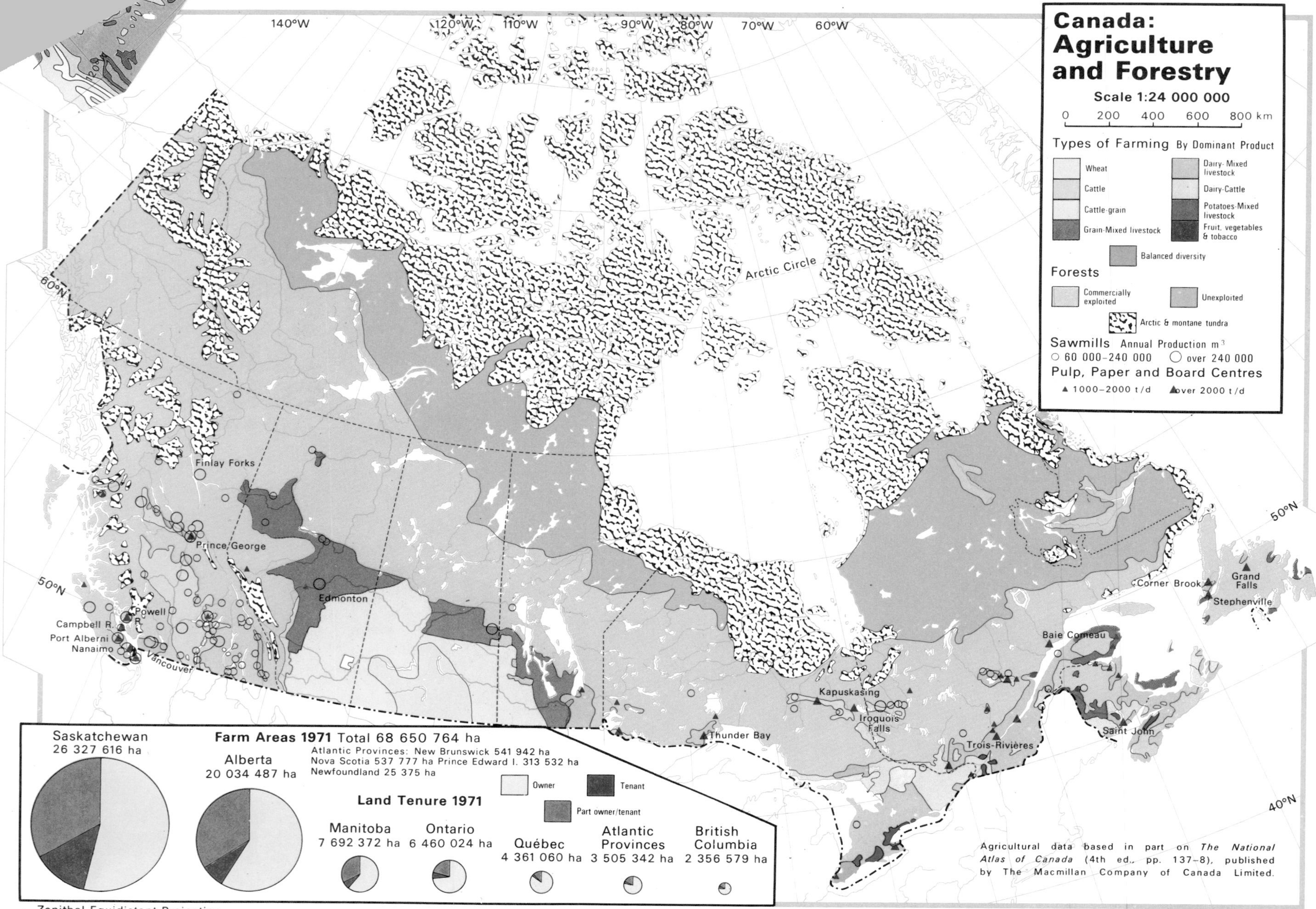

Scale 1:24 000 000

0 200 400 600 800 km

Types of Farming By Dominant Product

- Wheat
- Cattle
- Cattle-grain
- Grain-Mixed livestock
- Dairy-Mixed livestock
- Dairy-Cattle
- Potatoes-Mixed livestock
- Fruit, vegetables & tobacco
- Balanced diversity

Forests

- Commercially exploited
- Unexploited
- Arctic & montane tundra

Sawmills Annual Production m^3

○ 60 000–240 000 ○ over 240 000

Pulp, Paper and Board Centres

▲ 1000–2000 t/d ▲ over 2000 t/d

140°W 120°W 110°W 90°W 80°W 70°W 60°W

60°N 50°N 40°N

Arctic Circle

Finlay Forks
Prince George
Edmonton
Powell R.
Campbell R.
Port Alberni
Nanaimo
Vancouver
Thunder Bay
Kapuskasing
Iroquois Falls
Trois-Rivières
Baie Comeau
Saint John
Corner Brook
Grand Falls
Stephenville

Farm Areas 1971 Total 68 650 764 ha

Atlantic Provinces: New Brunswick 541 942 ha
Nova Scotia 537 777 ha Prince Edward I. 313 532 ha
Newfoundland 25 375 ha

Land Tenure 1971

Owner · Part owner/tenant · Tenant

Saskatchewan 26 327 616 ha
Alberta 20 034 487 ha
Manitoba 7 692 372 ha
Ontario 6 460 024 ha
Québec 4 361 060 ha
Atlantic Provinces 3 505 342 ha
British Columbia 2 356 579 ha

Agricultural data based in part on *The National Atlas of Canada* (4th ed., pp. 137–8), published by The Macmillan Company of Canada Limited.

Zenithal Equidistant Projection

Canada: Water Resources and Electrical Power

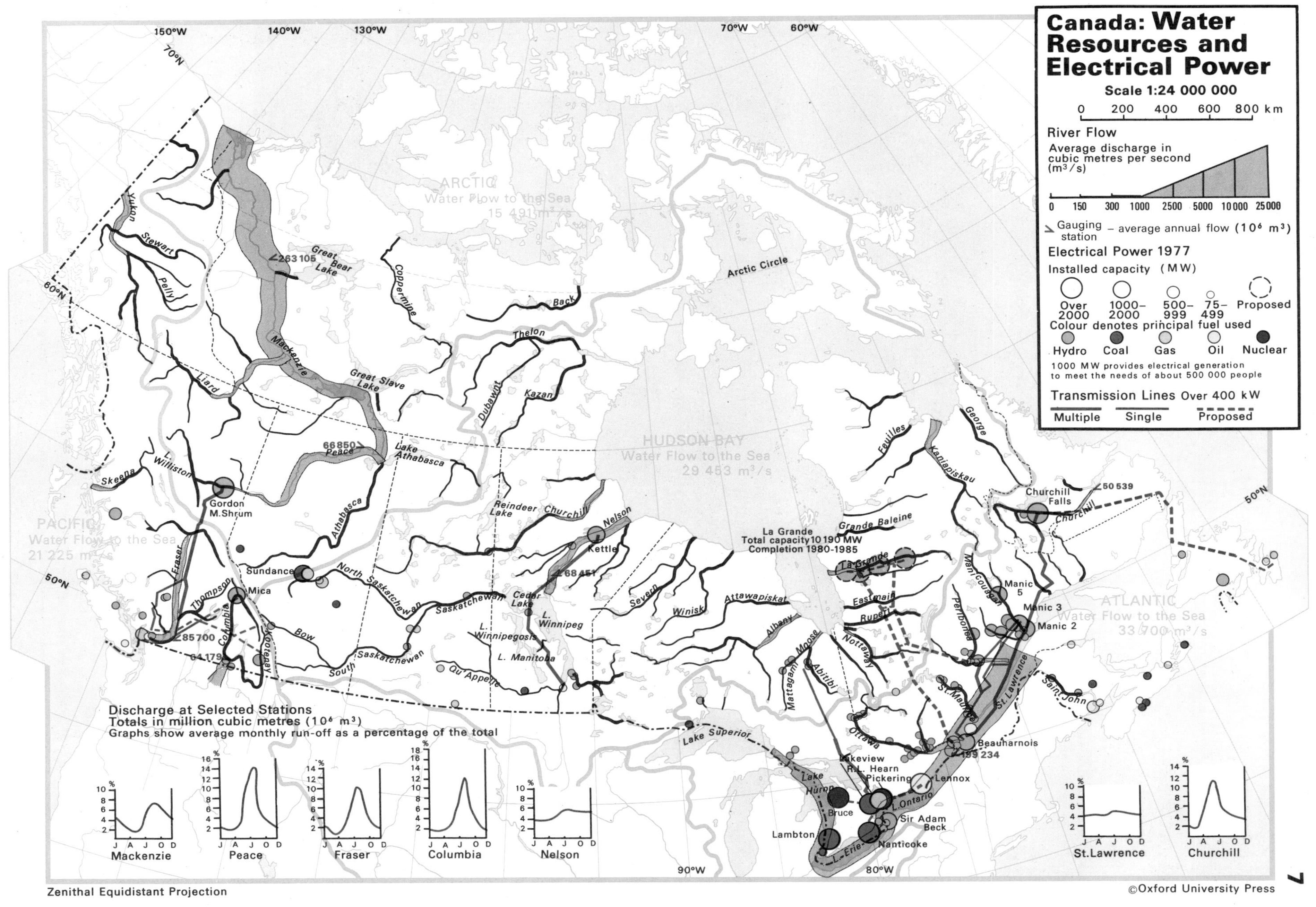

Zenithal Equidistant Projection

Conical Orthomorphic Projection

Canada: Natural Resources and Native Peoples
Scale 1:19 000 000
0 150 300 450 600 750 km
Native Peoples
Estimated Population 1971 Eskimo 12 000 Indian 20 000
Settlement
Major settlement
Major reserve
Minerals Resources 1974
Mining centres Major Minor
1 Petroleum 2 Natural Gas 3 Aluminum 4 Nickel 5 Copper 6 Iron 7 Zinc 8 Coal 9 Potash 10 Gold 11 Asbestos 12 Silver 13 Lead 14 Molybdenum 15 Platinum 16 Cobalt 17 Uranium 18 Tungsten 19 Mercury
The minerals are listed in order of value.
Most minerals are extracted from composite ores which is why most centres have several numbers.
Production 12 Exceptionally large 9 Major 5 Minor
Italic numbers mean that the mineral is obtained as a by-product.
See pp. 10–11 Canada: Manufacturing for smelters, refineries and iron pelletizing plants.
BYLOT IS. BIRD SANCTUARY
AUYUITTUQ NATIONAL PARK
DEWEY SOPER BIRD SANCTUARY
Arctic Circle
Prawns
Cod and Redfish
Capelin
Baleen Whale
Redfish
Beluga
Putunig
Sperm Whale
Shrimps
Crab
Schefferville
Carol Lake
Wabush
Gagnon
Baie Verte
Buchans
Murdochville
Ste.Anne des Monts
CAPE BRETON HIGHLANDS N. P.
Glace Bay
Bathurst
Newcastle
Minto
Chibougamau
Chapais
CHICOUTIMI PROVINCIAL PARK
LAURENTIDES PROVINCIAL PARK
Thompson
Wabowden
Red Lake
Uchi Lake
Sturgeon Lake
Manitouwadge
Atikokan
Shebandowan
Virginiatown
Matagami
Kirkland Lake
Noranda
South Porcupine
Joutel
Timmins
Val d'Or
Schumacher
Pamour
Temagami
Cobalt
Malartic
MONT TREMBLANT P.P.
East Broughton
Thetford Mines
Black Lake
Asbestos
Wawa
Shawville
Falconbridge
Sudbury
Elliot Lake
ALGONQUIN P.P.
Whitefish
Lake Trout
Goldeneye
Pickerel
Herring
Haddock
Witch
Hake
Lobster
Flounder
Alewife
60°N
55°N
50°N
45°N
40°N
95°W
90°W
85°W
80°W
75°W
70°W
65°W

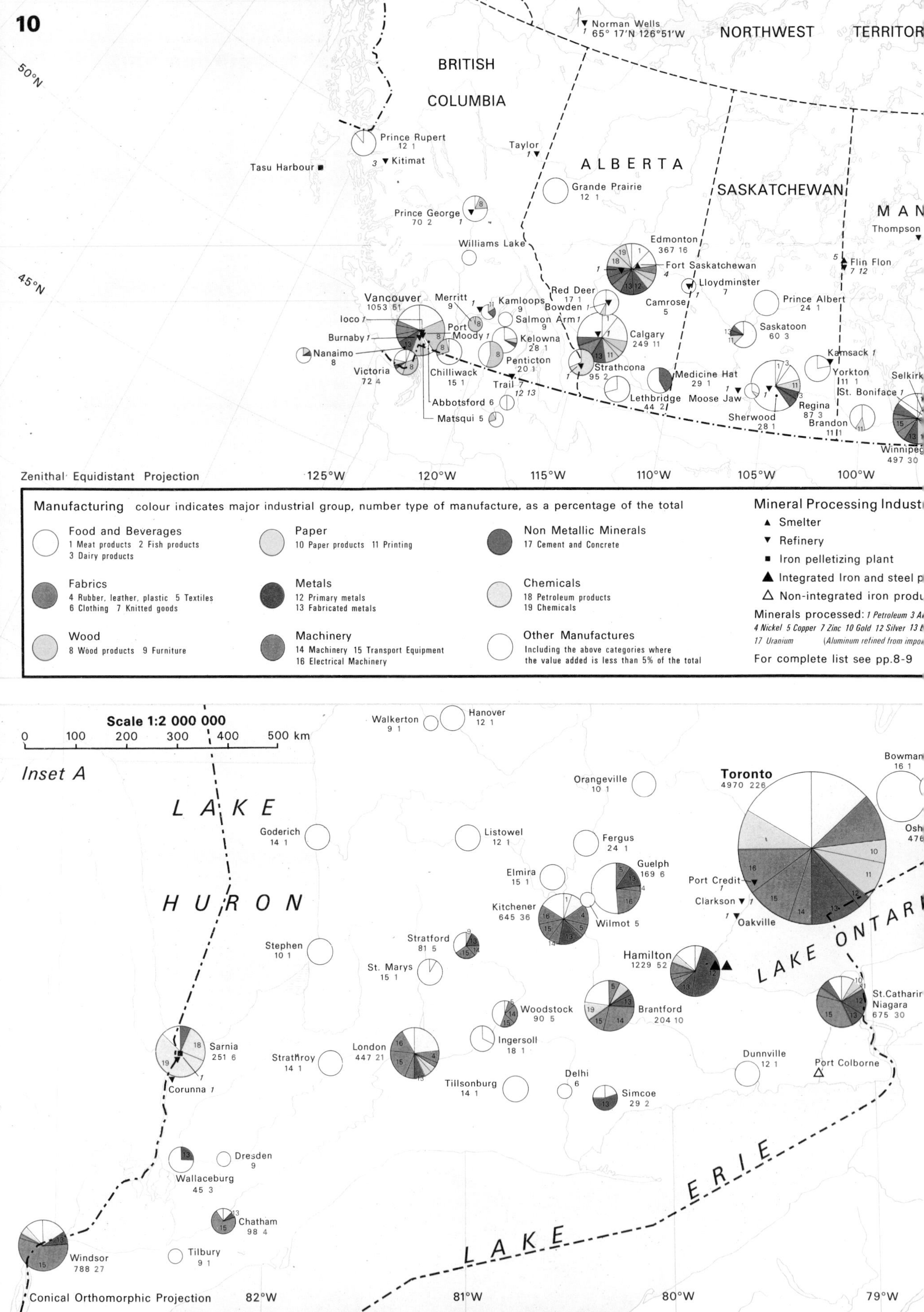

50°N
45°N
Norman Wells
1 65° 17'N 126°51'W
NORTHWEST TERRITOR
BRITISH
COLUMBIA
ALBERTA
SASKATCHEWAN
MAN
Prince Rupert
12 1
3 Kitimat
Tasu Harbour
Taylor
1
Grande Prairie
12 1
Prince George
70 2
Williams Lake
Edmonton
367 16
Fort Saskatchewan
Lloydminster
7
Thompson
Flin Flon
7 12
Red Deer
17 1
Bowden
Camrose
5
Prince Albert
24 1
Vancouver
1053 51
Merritt
9
Kamloops
9
Salmon Arm
9
Ioco
Burnaby
Port Moody
Kelowna
28 1
Calgary
249 11
Saskatoon
60 3
Nanaimo
8
Penticton
20 1
Strathcona
95 2
Kamsack
Victoria
72 4
Chilliwack
15 1
Trail
12 13
Medicine Hat
29 1
Yorkton
11 1
Selkirk
St. Boniface
Lethbridge
44 2
Moose Jaw
Regina
87 3
Abbotsford 6
Matsqui 5
Sherwood
28 1
Brandon
11 1
Winnipeg
497 30
Zenithal Equidistant Projection
125°W
120°W
115°W
110°W
105°W
100°W
Manufacturing colour indicates major industrial group, number type of manufacture, as a percentage of the total
Food and Beverages
1 Meat products 2 Fish products
3 Dairy products
Paper
10 Paper products 11 Printing
Non Metallic Minerals
17 Cement and Concrete
Fabrics
4 Rubber, leather, plastic 5 Textiles
6 Clothing 7 Knitted goods
Metals
12 Primary metals
13 Fabricated metals
Chemicals
18 Petroleum products
19 Chemicals
Wood
8 Wood products 9 Furniture
Machinery
14 Machinery 15 Transport Equipment
16 Electrical Machinery
Other Manufactures
Including the above categories where
the value added is less than 5% of the total
Mineral Processing Indust
Smelter
Refinery
Iron pelletizing plant
Integrated Iron and steel p
Non-integrated iron produ
Minerals processed: 1 Petroleum 3 A
4 Nickel 5 Copper 7 Zinc 10 Gold 12 Silver 13
17 Uranium (Aluminum refined from impo
For complete list see pp.8-9
Scale 1:2 000 000
0 100 200 300 400 500 km
Inset A
LAKE
HURON
Walkerton
9 1
Hanover
12 1
Bowman
16 1
Toronto
4970 226
Orangeville
10 1
Goderich
14 1
Listowel
12 1
Fergus
24 1
Osh
476
Elmira
15 1
Guelph
169 6
Port Credit
Clarkson
Kitchener
645 36
Wilmot 5
Oakville
LAKE ONTAR
Stephen
10 1
Stratford
81 5
Hamilton
1229 52
St. Marys
15 1
St.Catharir
Niagara
675 30
Woodstock
90 5
Brantford
204 10
Ingersoll
18 1
Sarnia
251 6
London
447 21
Strathroy
14 1
Dunnville
12 1
Port Colborne
Corunna
Delhi
6
Tillsonburg
14 1
Simcoe
29 2
Dresden
9
Wallaceburg
45 3
Chatham
98 4
LAKE ERIE
Windsor
788 27
Tilbury
9 1
Conical Orthomorphic Projection
82°W
81°W
80°W
79°W

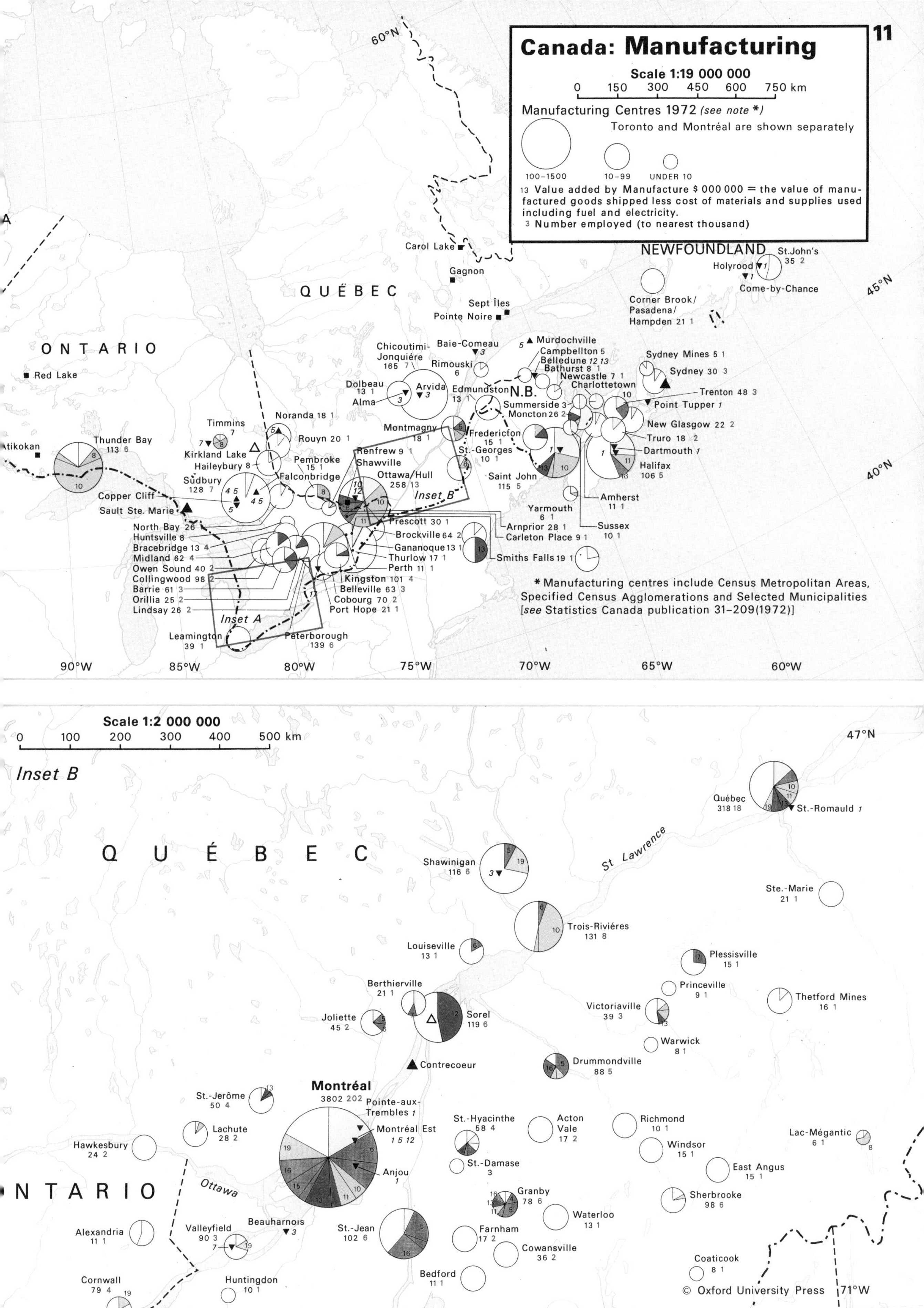
Canada: Manufacturing
Scale 1:19 000 000
0 150 300 450 600 750 km
Manufacturing Centres 1972 (see note *)
Toronto and Montréal are shown separately
100–1500
10–99
UNDER 10
13 Value added by Manufacture $ 000 000 = the value of manufactured goods shipped less cost of materials and supplies used including fuel and electricity.
3 Number employed (to nearest thousand)
60°N
QUÉBEC
ONTARIO
NEWFOUNDLAND
N.B.
Carol Lake
Gagnon
Sept Îles
Pointe Noire
St.John's 35 2
Holyrood 1
Come-by-Chance 1
Corner Brook/ Pasadena/ Hampden 21 1
Red Lake
Atikokan
Thunder Bay 113 6
Timmins 7
Kirkland Lake
Haileybury 8
Noranda 18 1
Rouyn 20 1
Sudbury 128 7
Copper Cliff
Sault Ste. Marie
Falconbridge
Pembroke 15 1
Renfrew 9 1
Shawville
Ottawa/Hull 258 13
Inset B
Montmagny 18 1
Chicoutimi-Jonquière 165 7
Dolbeau 13 1
Alma
Arvida 3
Baie-Comeau 3
Rimouski 6
Edmundston 13 1
Murdochville 5
Campbellton 5
Belledune 12 13
Bathurst 8 1
Newcastle 7 1
Charlottetown 10
Summerside 3
Moncton 26 2
Fredericton 15 1
St.-Georges 10 1
Saint John 115 5
Sydney Mines 5 1
Sydney 30 3
Trenton 48 3
Point Tupper 1
New Glasgow 22 2
Truro 18 2
Dartmouth 1
Halifax 106 5
Amherst 11 1
Yarmouth 6 1
Sussex 10 1
North Bay 26
Huntsville 8
Bracebridge 13 4
Midland 62 4
Owen Sound 40 2
Collingwood 98 2
Barrie 61 3
Orillia 25 2
Lindsay 26 2
Inset A
Leamington 39 1
Peterborough 139 6
Prescott 30 1
Brockville 64 2
Gananoque 13 1
Thurlow 17 1
Perth 11 1
Kingston 101 4
Belleville 63 3
Cobourg 70 2
Port Hope 21 1
Arnprior 28 1
Carleton Place 9 1
Smiths Falls 19 1
* Manufacturing centres include Census Metropolitan Areas, Specified Census Agglomerations and Selected Municipalities [see Statistics Canada publication 31–209(1972)]
45°N
40°N
90°W
85°W
80°W
75°W
70°W
65°W
60°W
Scale 1:2 000 000
0 100 200 300 400 500 km
Inset B
47°N
QUÉBEC
ONTARIO
St Lawrence
Ottawa
Québec 318 18
St.-Romauld 1
Shawinigan 116 6
Ste.-Marie 21 1
Trois-Riviéres 131 8
Louiseville 13 1
Plessisville 15 1
Princeville 9 1
Thetford Mines 16 1
Berthierville 21 1
Joliette 45 2
Sorel 119 6
Victoriaville 39 3
Warwick 8 1
Contrecoeur
Drummondville 88 5
St.-Jerôme 50 4
Montréal 3802 202
Pointe-aux-Trembles 1
Montréal Est 15 12
Anjou 1
Lachute 28 2
Hawkesbury 24 2
St.-Hyacinthe 58 4
Acton Vale 17 2
Richmond 10 1
Windsor 15 1
Lac-Mégantic 6 1
St.-Damase 3
East Angus 15 1
Granby 78 6
Sherbrooke 98 6
Waterloo 13 1
Alexandria 11 1
Valleyfield 90 3
Beauharnois 3
St.-Jean 102 6
Farnham 17 2
Cowansville 36 2
Coaticook 8 1
Cornwall 79 4
Huntingdon 10 1
Bedford 11 1
71°W

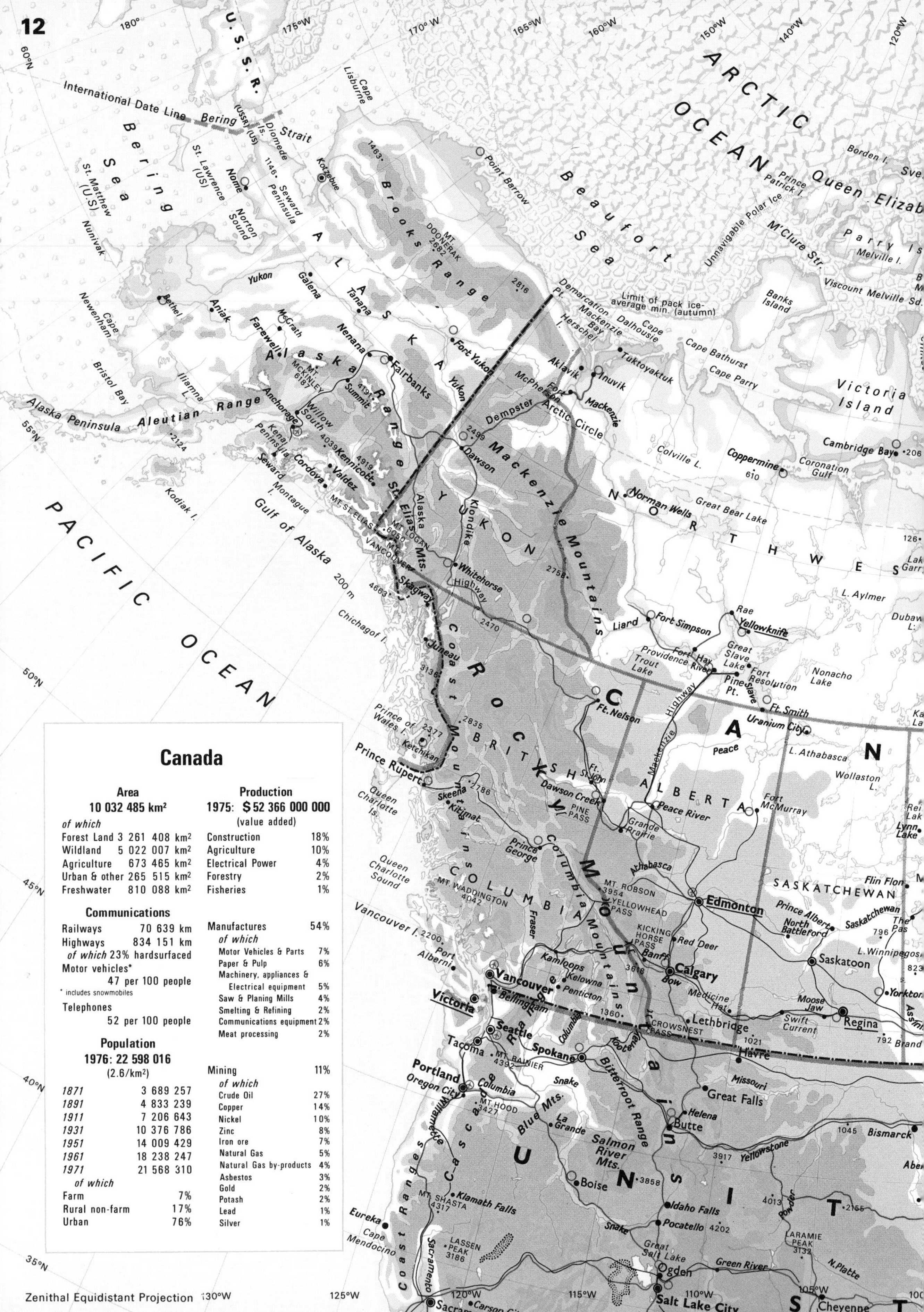

Canada

Area	
10 032 485 km²	
of which	
Forest Land	3 261 408 km²
Wildland	5 022 007 km²
Agriculture	673 465 km²
Urban & other	265 515 km²
Freshwater	810 088 km²

Communications

Railways	70 639 km
Highways	834 151 km
of which 23% hardsurfaced	
Motor vehicles*	47 per 100 people
Telephones	52 per 100 people

* includes snowmobiles

Population

1976: 22 598 016 (2.6/km²)

1871	3 689 257
1891	4 833 239
1911	7 206 643
1931	10 376 786
1951	14 009 429
1961	18 238 247
1971	21 568 310
of which	
Farm	7%
Rural non-farm	17%
Urban	76%

Production

1975: **$52 366 000 000** (value added)

Construction	18%
Agriculture	10%
Electrical Power	4%
Forestry	2%
Fisheries	1%
Manufactures	54%
of which	
Motor Vehicles & Parts	7%
Paper & Pulp	6%
Machinery, appliances & Electrical equipment	5%
Saw & Planing Mills	4%
Smelting & Refining	2%
Communications equipment	2%
Meat processing	2%
Mining	11%
of which	
Crude Oil	27%
Copper	14%
Nickel	10%
Zinc	8%
Iron ore	7%
Natural Gas	5%
Natural Gas by-products	4%
Asbestos	3%
Gold	2%
Potash	2%
Lead	1%
Silver	1%

Canada
Scale 1:19 000 000
0 200 400 600 km
Provincial capitals are underlined
GREENLAND (Denmark)
Baffin Bay
Baffin Island
Davis Strait
Foxe Basin
Hudson Bay
Détroit d'Hudson
Péninsule d'Ungava
Baie James
NEWFOUNDLAND
LABRADOR
QUÉBEC
ONTARIO
NORTHWEST TERRITORIES
ATLANTIC OCEAN
Montréal
Québec
Ottawa
Toronto
Winnipeg
Thunder Bay
Halifax
St. John's
Fredericton
Charlottetown
New York
Boston
Philadelphia
Chicago
Detroit
© Oxford University Press

Québec

Area	
1 540 733 km²	
(15.3% of Canada)	
Forestland	696 075 km²
Wildland	566 641 km²
Agriculture	36 864 km²
Urban & other	8 236 km²
Freshwater	232 917 km²

Communications

Railways	8 705 km
Highways	106 400 km
of which 40% hardsurfaced	
Motor Vehicles *	
45 per 100 people	
* includes snowmobiles	
Telephones	
50 per 100 people	

Population 1976: 6 141 491 (3.98 / km²)	
1871	1 191 516
1891	1 488 535
1911	2 005 776
1931	2 874 662
1951	4 055 681
1961	5 259 211
1971	6 027 765
of which	
Farm	5%
Rural non-farm	14%
Urban	81%
1976 * Census Metropolitan Area	
*Montréal	2 758 780
*Ottawa-Hull	668 853
*Québec	534 193
*Chicoutimi-Jonquière	127 181
Sherbrooke	75 137
Trois-Rivières	51 772
St.-Hyacinthe	36 832

Production 1973: $11 639 000 000 (Value added)	
Construction	18%
Electrical Power	6%
Agriculture	5%
Forestry	2%
Manufactures	65%
of which	
Textiles & Knitting	8%
Paper & Pulp	7%
Clothing	7%
Publishing & Printing	5%
Smelting & Refining	4%
Saw & Planing Mills	3%
Pharmaceuticals	2%
Dairy products	2%
Mining	4%
of which	
Copper	22%
Asbestos	19%
Iron Ore	14%
Zinc	8%
Gold	5%

Newfoundland

Area	
403 661 km²	
(4.0% of Canada)	
Labrador	292 219 km²
Island	111 442 km²
Forest Land	127 492 km²
Wildland	235 672 km²
Agriculture*	65 km²
Urban & other*	826 km²
Freshwater	39 696 km²
*Island only	

Communications

Railways	409 km
Highways	11 177 km
of which 32% hardsurfaced	
Motor Vehicles	
28 per 100 people	
Telephones	
32 per 100 people	

Population 1976: 548 789 (1.35 / km²)	
1871	152 500
1891	202 040
1911	242 619
1931	281 500
1951	361 416
1961	457 853
1971	522 105
of which	
Farm	1%
Rural Non-farm	42%
Urban	57%
1976 *Census Metropolitan Area	
*St. John's	140 883
Corner Brook	24 789
Labrador City	11 877
Happy Valley-Goose Bay	8 114

Production 1973: $763 000 000 (Value added)	
Construction	31%
Electrical Power	12%
Fisheries	6%
Forestry	5%
Manufacture	22%
of which	
Paper & Pulp	30%
Fish products	27%
Publishing & Printing	3%
Concrete manufacture	2%
Mining	24%
of which	
Iron ore	84%
Asbestos	5%
Copper	3%

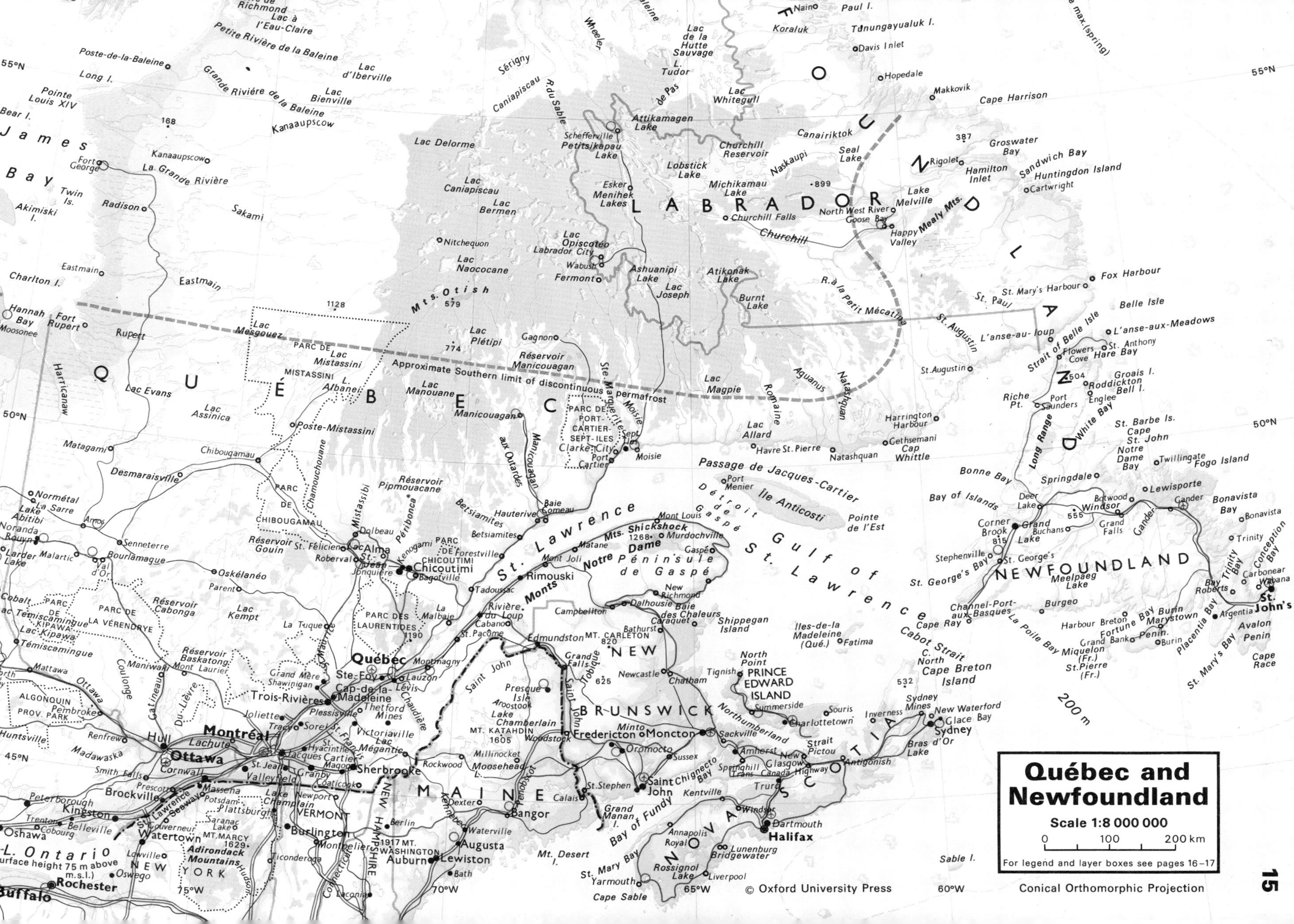

Québec and Newfoundland
Scale 1:8 000 000
0 100 200 km
For legend and layer boxes see pages 16–17
Conical Orthomorphic Projection
© Oxford University Press
QUÉBEC
LABRADOR
NEWFOUNDLAND
NEW BRUNSWICK
NOVA SCOTIA
PRINCE EDWARD ISLAND
MAINE
NEW HAMPSHIRE
VERMONT
NEW YORK
James Bay
Gulf of St. Lawrence
St. Lawrence
Approximate Southern limit of discontinuous permafrost
Passage de Jacques-Cartier
Détroit de Gaspé
Île Anticosti
Péninsule de Gaspé
Mts. Notre Dame
Mts. Shickshock
Monts Notre Dame
Mts. Otish
Mealy Mts.
Long Range
Cabot Strait
Strait of Belle Isle
Bay of Fundy
Baie des Chaleurs
Northumberland
L. Ontario
(Surface height 75 m above m.s.l.)
Québec
Montréal
Ottawa
Trois-Rivières
Sherbrooke
Chicoutimi
Rimouski
Halifax
Fredericton
Moncton
Saint John
Charlottetown
Sydney
St. John's
Corner Brook
Gander
Churchill Falls
Labrador City
Schefferville
Goose Bay
Sept-Îles
Hull
Kingston
Rochester
Buffalo
Burlington
Augusta
Bangor
Lewiston
Auburn
55°N
50°N
45°N
75°W
70°W
65°W
60°W
200 m

Atlantic Provinces

Scale 1:5 000 000

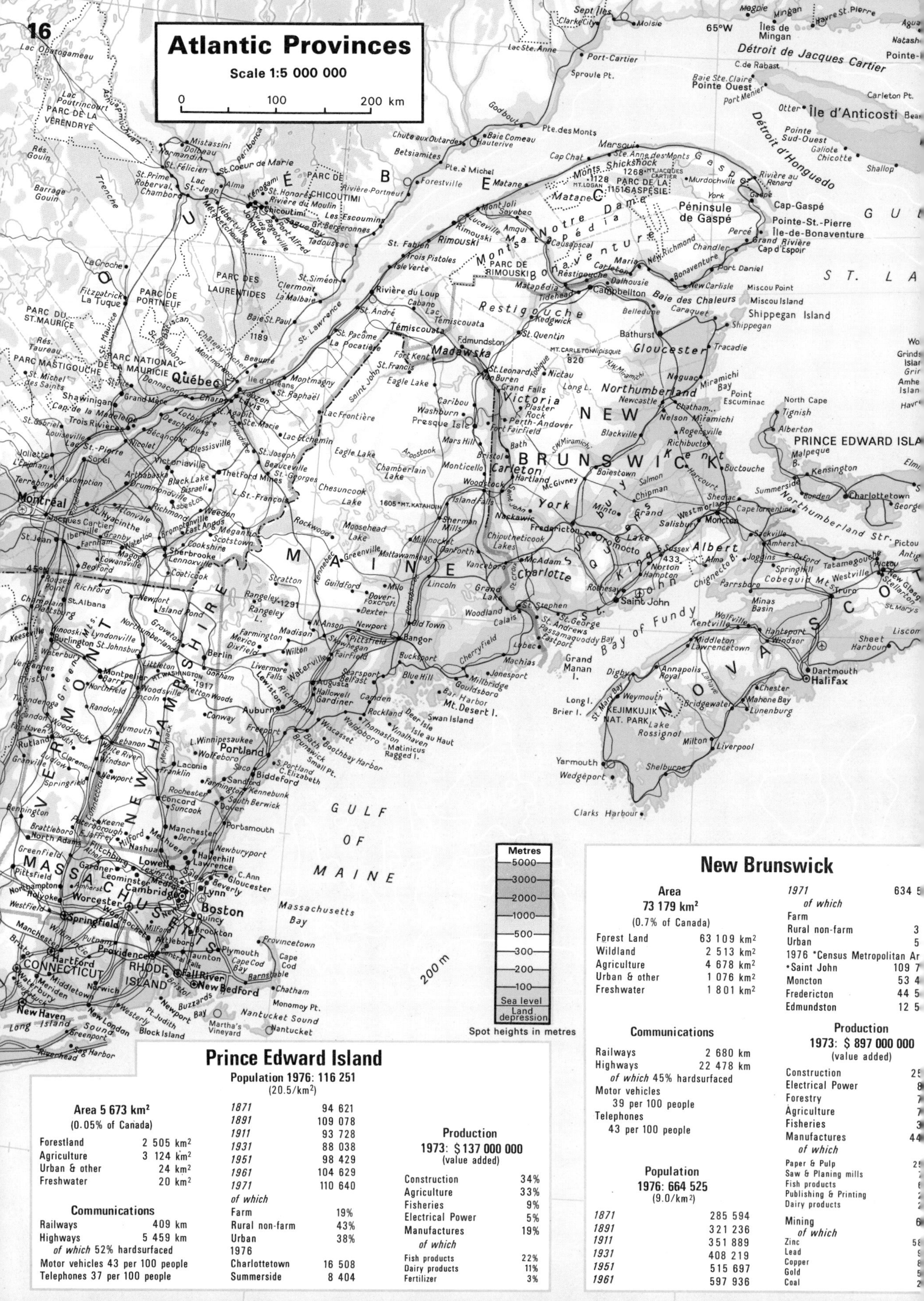

Prince Edward Island

Population 1976: 116 251
(20.5/km²)

Area 5 673 km²
(0.05% of Canada)

Forestland	2 505 km²
Agriculture	3 124 km²
Urban & other	24 km²
Freshwater	20 km²

Communications

Railways	409 km
Highways	5 459 km
of which 52% hardsurfaced	
Motor vehicles 43 per 100 people	
Telephones 37 per 100 people	

1871	94 621
1891	109 078
1911	93 728
1931	88 038
1951	98 429
1961	104 629
1971	110 640
of which	
Farm	19%
Rural non-farm	43%
Urban	38%
1976	
Charlottetown	16 508
Summerside	8 404

Production
1973: $137 000 000
(value added)

Construction	34%
Agriculture	33%
Fisheries	9%
Electrical Power	5%
Manufactures	19%
of which	
Fish products	22%
Dairy products	11%
Fertilizer	3%

New Brunswick

Area
73 179 km²
(0.7% of Canada)

Forest Land	63 109 km²
Wildland	2 513 km²
Agriculture	4 678 km²
Urban & other	1 076 km²
Freshwater	1 801 km²

Communications

Railways	2 680 km
Highways	22 478 km
of which 45% hardsurfaced	
Motor vehicles	
39 per 100 people	
Telephones	
43 per 100 people	

Population
1976: 664 525
(9.0/km²)

1871	285 594
1891	321 236
1911	351 889
1931	408 219
1951	515 697
1961	597 936
1971	634 5
of which	
Farm	
Rural non-farm	3
Urban	5
1976 *Census Metropolitan Ar	
*Saint John	109 7
Moncton	53 4
Fredericton	44 5
Edmundston	12 5

Production
1973: $ 897 000 000
(value added)

Construction	2
Electrical Power	8
Forestry	7
Agriculture	7
Fisheries	3
Manufactures	44
of which	
Paper & Pulp	2
Saw & Planing mills	
Fish products	
Publishing & Printing	
Dairy products	
Mining	6
of which	
Zinc	5
Lead	
Copper	
Gold	5
Coal	2

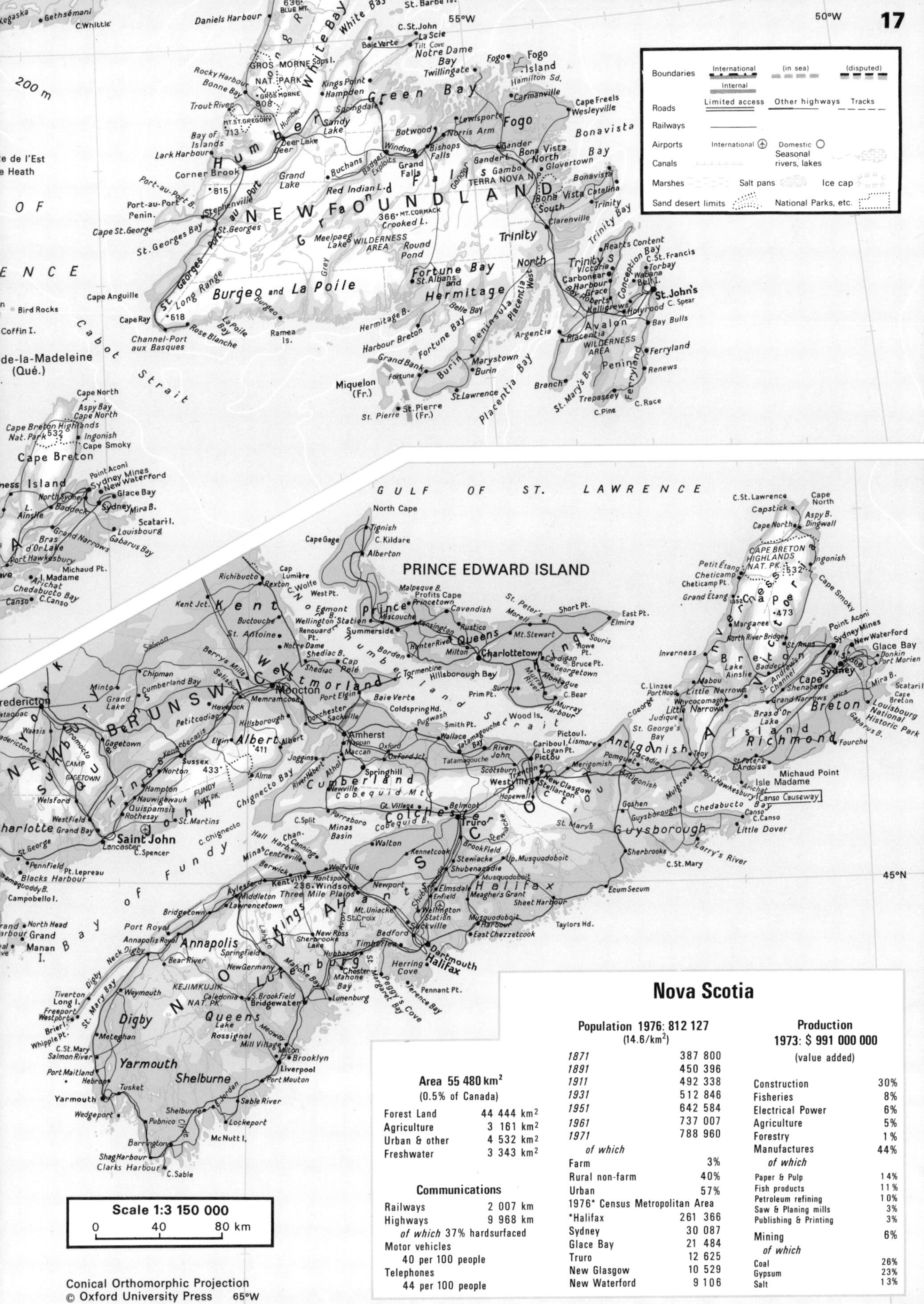

Nova Scotia

Area 55 480 km²
(0.5% of Canada)

Forest Land	44 444 km²
Agriculture	3 161 km²
Urban & other	4 532 km²
Freshwater	3 343 km²

Communications

Railways	2 007 km
Highways	9 968 km
of which 37% hardsurfaced	
Motor vehicles	
40 per 100 people	
Telephones	
44 per 100 people	

Population 1976: 812 127
(14.6/km²)

1871	387 800
1891	450 396
1911	492 338
1931	512 846
1951	642 584
1961	737 007
1971	788 960
of which	
Farm	3%
Rural non-farm	40%
Urban	57%
1976* Census Metropolitan Area	
*Halifax	261 366
Sydney	30 087
Glace Bay	21 484
Truro	12 625
New Glasgow	10 529
New Waterford	9 106

Production
1973: $ 991 000 000
(value added)

Construction	30%
Fisheries	8%
Electrical Power	6%
Agriculture	5%
Forestry	1%
Manufactures	44%
of which	
Paper & Pulp	14%
Fish products	11%
Petroleum refining	10%
Saw & Planing mills	3%
Publishing & Printing	3%
Mining	6%
of which	
Coal	26%
Gypsum	23%
Salt	13%

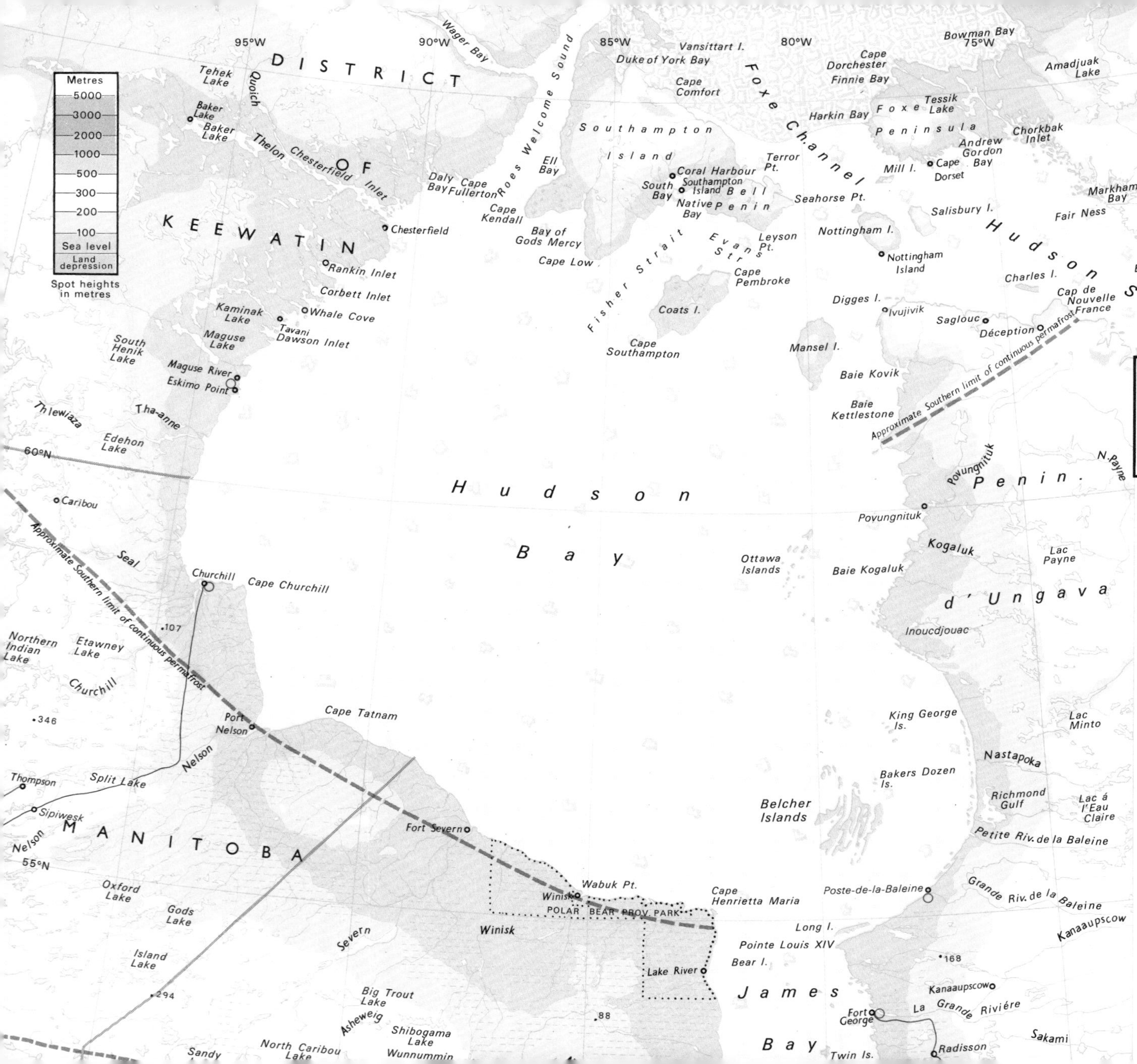

Ontario

Scale 1:8 000 000

0 100 200 300 km

For legend see page 24

Ontario

Area

1 061 651 km²
(10.5% of Canada)

Forest Land	432 232 km²
Wildland	371 623 km²
Agriculture	52 038 km²
Urban & other	28 874 km²
Freshwater	176 884 km²

Communications

Railways	15 894 km
Highways	158 673 km
of which 36% hardsurfaced	
Motor vehicles*	48 per 100 people
Telephones	57 per 100 people

* includes snowmobiles

Population

1976: 8 131 618
(7.7/km²)

1871	1 620 851
1891	2 114 321
1911	2 527 292
1931	3 431 683
1951	4 597 542
1961	6 236 092
1971	7 703 105
of which	
Farm	5%
Rural non-farm	13%

1976 *Census Metropolitan Area

*Toronto	2 753 112
*Ottawa-Hull	668 853
*Hamilton	525 222
*St Catharines-Niagara	298 129
*Kitchener	269 828
*London	264 639
*Windsor	243 289
*Sudbury	155 013
*Oshawa	133 959
*Thunder Bay	117 988

Production

1973: $1 543 000 000
(value added)

Construction	16%
Agriculture	6%
Electrical Power	4%
Manufactures	70%
of which	
Motor Vehicles & Parts	14%
Fabricated metals	9%
Electrical products	8%
Chemicals	7%
Iron & Steel mills	6%
Publishing & Printing	4%
Paper & Pulp	3%
Rubber products	2%
Mining	4%
of which	
Nickel	31%
Copper	20%
Zinc	12%
Iron ore	8%
Gold	5%
Silver	3%

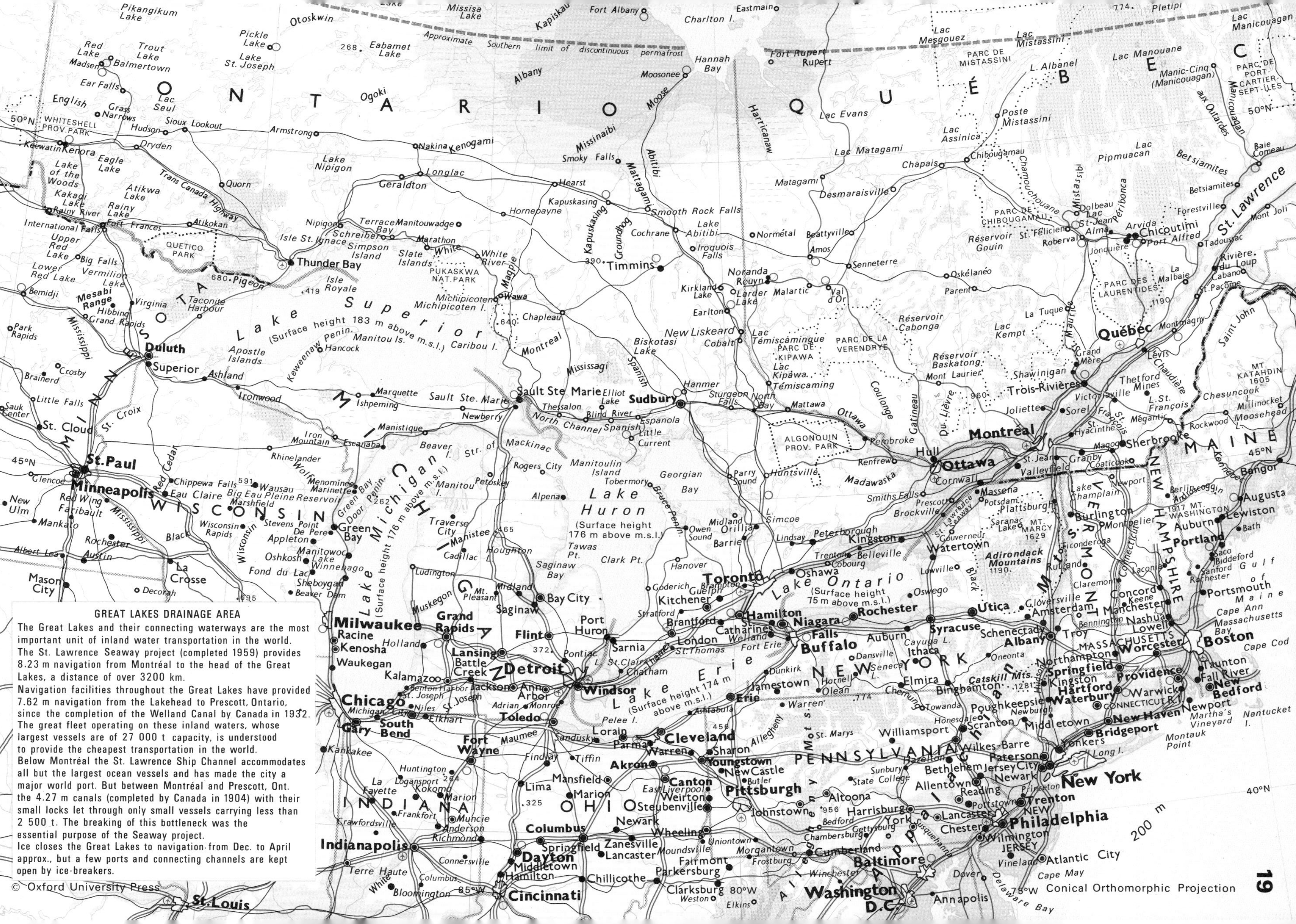

GREAT LAKES DRAINAGE AREA

The Great Lakes and their connecting waterways are the most important unit of inland water transportation in the world.

The St. Lawrence Seaway project (completed 1959) provides 8.23 m navigation from Montréal to the head of the Great Lakes, a distance of over 3200 km.

Navigation facilities throughout the Great Lakes have provided 7.62 m navigation from the Lakehead to Prescott, Ontario, since the completion of the Welland Canal by Canada in 1932. The great fleet operating on these inland waters, whose largest vessels are of 27 000 t capacity, is understood to provide the cheapest transportation in the world.

Below Montréal the St. Lawrence Ship Channel accommodates all but the largest ocean vessels and has made the city a major world port. But between Montréal and Prescott, Ont. the 4.27 m canals (completed by Canada in 1904) with their small locks let through only small vessels carrying less than 2 500 t. The breaking of this bottleneck was the essential purpose of the Seaway project.

Ice closes the Great Lakes to navigation from Dec. to April approx., but a few ports and connecting channels are kept open by ice-breakers.

20
83°W
80°W
45°N
O N T A R I O
Q
Vére
N E W
Y O R K
LAKE ONTARIO
Mean surface height 75 m above m.s.l.
146
73
LAKE HURON
Mean surface height 176 m above m.s.l.
146
73
LAKE ERIE
Mean surface height 174 m above m.s.l.
GEORGIAN BAY
73
Lake Superior Prov. Park
Algoma
Sudbury
Timiskaming
Nipissing
Parry Sound
Muskoka
Haliburton
Mississagi Provincial Forest
Timagami Provincial Forest
Temiscamingue
Parc de Kipawa
Algonquin Provincial Park
Goulais River Game Preserve
Manitoulin
Manitoulin Island
North Channel
Lucas Channel
Bruce Peninsula
Thirty Thousand Islands
Saginaw Bay
Lake St. Clair
Long Point Bay
Bruce
Grey
Simcoe
Dufferin
Peel
York
Durham
Victoria
Peterborough
Northumberland
Hastings
Lennox and
Huron
Perth
Waterloo
Wellington
Halton
Hamilton-Wentworth
Oxford
Brant
Middlesex
Lambton
Elgin
Kent
Essex
Norfolk
Haldimand
Niagara
Michipicoten
Wawa
Chapleau
Sault Ste. Marie
Elliot Lake
Blind River
Espanola
Sudbury
North Bay
Timmins
Kirkland Lake
New Liskeard
Haileybury
Cobalt
Mattawa
Huntsville
Bracebridge
Gravenhurst
Orillia
Barrie
Owen Sound
Collingwood
Goderich
Kincardine
Stratford
London
Sarnia
Windsor
Detroit
Toronto
Mississauga
Hamilton
Cambridge
Kitchener
Guelph
Brantford
St. Catharines
Niagara Falls
Buffalo
Rochester
Erie
Cleveland
Toledo
Flint
Saginaw
Bay City
Pontiac
Port Huron
Alpena
Cheboygan
Peterborough
Belleville
Oshawa
Cobourg
Jamestown
Olean
Noranda
Rouyn
Val d'Or
Amos
Témiscaming
Mt. Sinclair 488
Collins Mtn. 519
Mt. Batchawana 640
Mamainse Hill 597
Blue Mt. 541
777
544
419

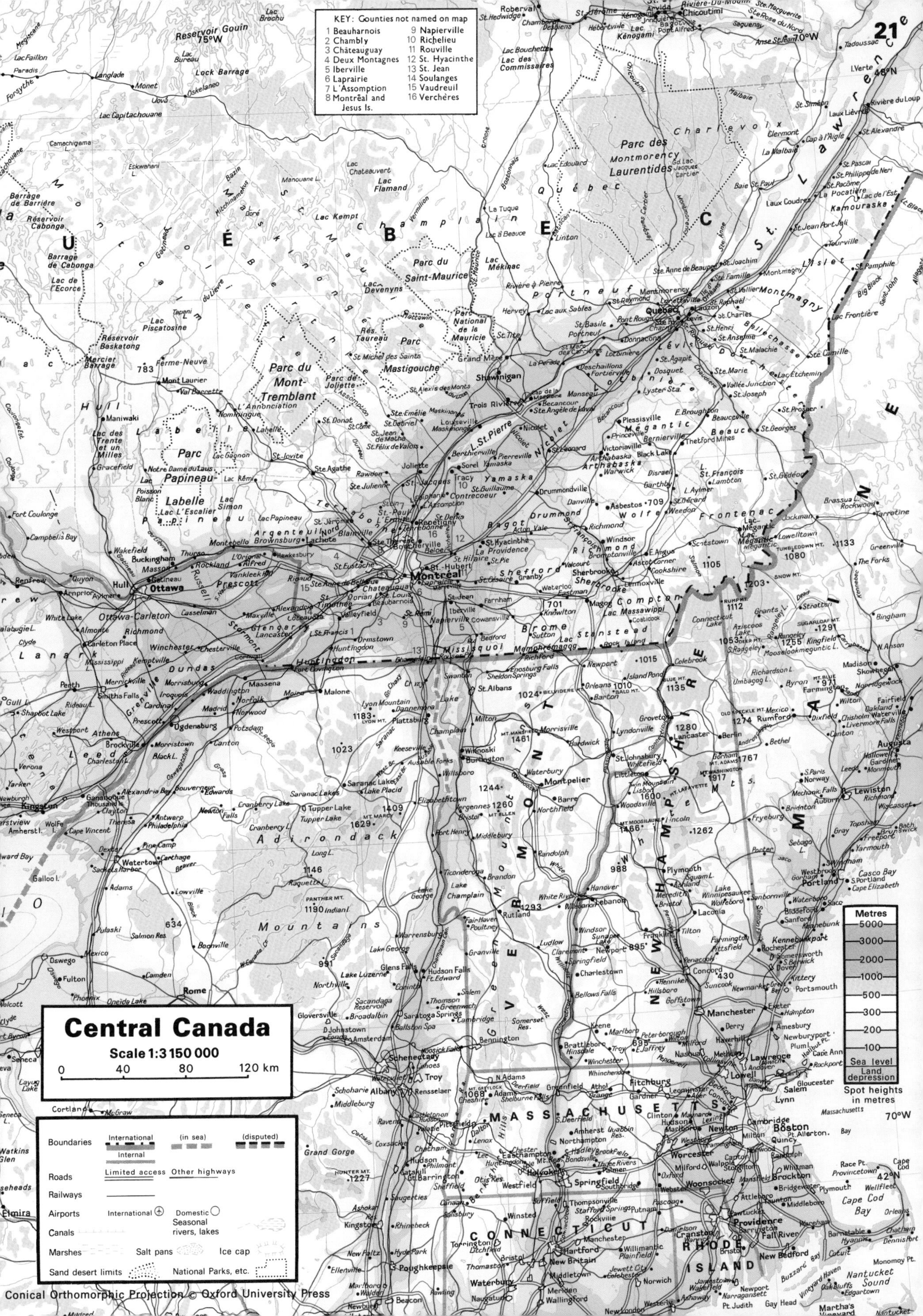
KEY: Counties not named on map
1 Beauharnois
2 Chambly
3 Châteauguay
4 Deux Montagnes
5 Iberville
6 Laprairie
7 L'Assomption
8 Montrêal and Jesus Is.
9 Napierville
10 Richelieu
11 Rouville
12 St. Hyacinthe
13 St. Jean
14 Soulanges
15 Vaudreuil
16 Verchères
Central Canada
Scale 1:3 150 000
0 40 80 120 km
Boundaries International (in sea) (disputed)
Internal
Roads Limited access Other highways
Railways
Airports International Domestic
Canals Seasonal rivers, lakes
Marshes Salt pans Ice cap
Sand desert limits National Parks, etc.
Metres
5000
3000
2000
1000
500
300
200
100
Sea level
Land depression
Spot heights in metres
75°W
70°W
48°N
42°N
Q U É B E C
Ottawa
Montréal
Québec
MAINE
NEW HAMPSHIRE
VERMONT
MASSACHUSETTS
CONNECTICUT
RHODE ISLAND
Adirondack Mountains
Green Mountains
White Mts
St. Lawrence
Conical Orthomorphic Projection © Oxford University Press

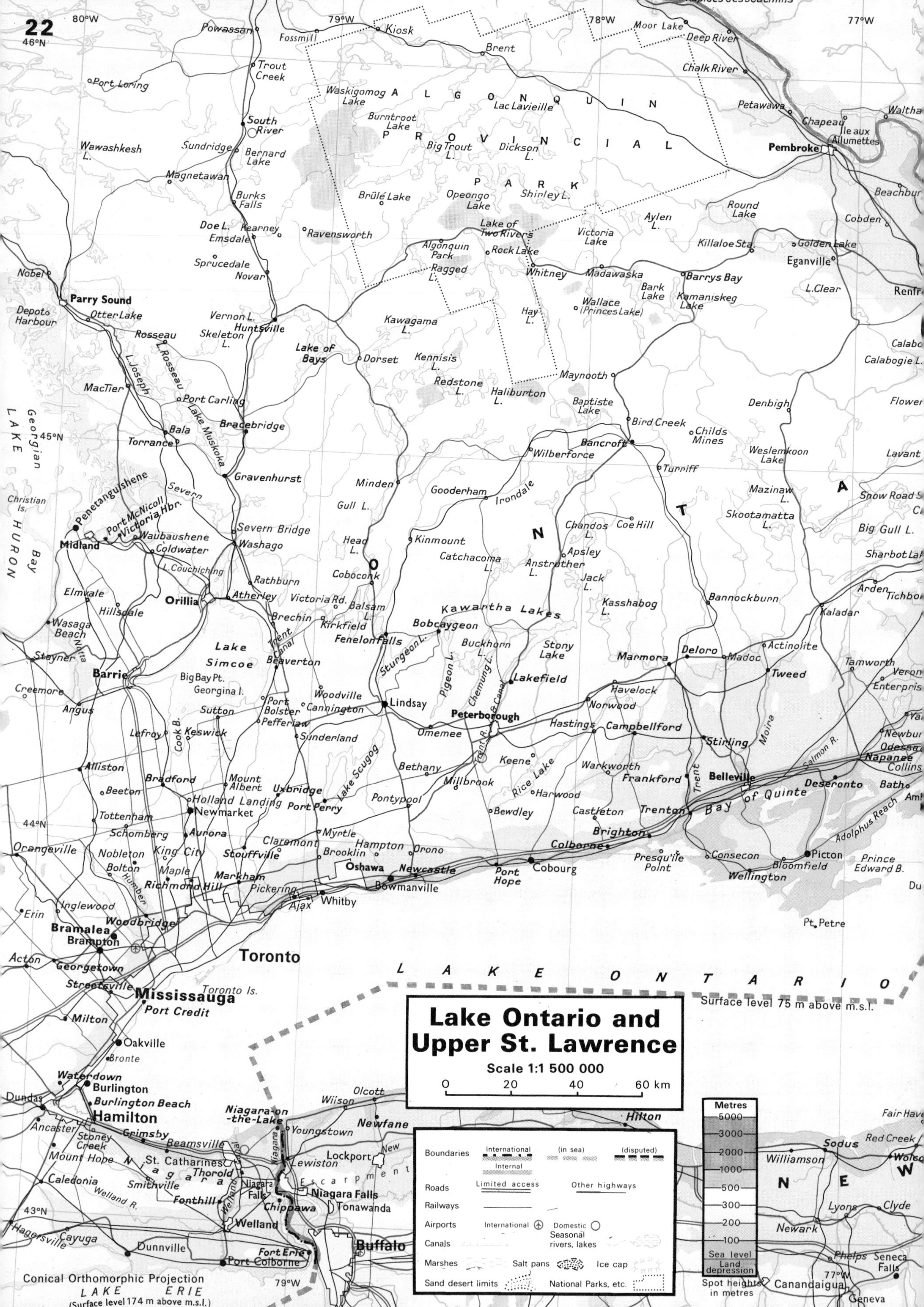
Lake Ontario and Upper St. Lawrence
Scale 1:1 500 000
0 20 40 60 km
Conical Orthomorphic Projection
Boundaries International (in sea) (disputed)
Internal
Roads Limited access Other highways
Railways
Airports International Domestic
Canals
Seasonal rivers, lakes
Marshes Salt pans Ice cap
Sand desert limits National Parks, etc.
Metres
5000
3000
2000
1000
500
300
200
100
Sea level
Land depression
Spot heights in metres
80°W
79°W
78°W
77°W
46°N
45°N
44°N
43°N
LAKE ONTARIO
Surface level 75 m above m.s.l.
LAKE ERIE
(Surface level 174 m above m.s.l.)
ALGONQUIN PROVINCIAL PARK
ONTARIO
NEW
Georgian Bay
LAKE HURON
Lake Simcoe
Kawartha Lakes
Bay of Quinte
Niagara Escarpment
Rapides des Joachims
Powassan
Fossmill
Kiosk
Moor Lake
Deep River
Brent
Trout Creek
Chalk River
Port Loring
Waskigomog Lake
Lac Lavieille
Petawawa
Waltham
Chapeau
Ile aux Allumettes
Burntroot Lake
South River
Big Trout L.
Dickson L.
Pembroke
Wawashkesh L.
Sundridge
Bernard Lake
Magnetawan
Brûlé Lake
Opeongo Lake
Shirley L.
Beachburg
Burks Falls
Round Lake
Cobden
Aylen L.
Doe L.
Kearney
Ravensworth
Lake of Two Rivers
Victoria Lake
Emsdale
Algonquin Park
Rock Lake
Killaloe Sta.
Golden Lake
Eganville
Sprucedale
Ragged L.
Whitney
Madawaska
Barrys Bay
Nobel
Novar
Bark Lake
Kamaniskeg Lake
L.Clear
Renfrew
Parry Sound
Wallace (Princes Lake)
Depot Harbour
Otter Lake
Vernon L.
Huntsville
Kawagama L.
Hay L.
Rosseau
Skeleton L.
Lake of Bays
Calabogie L.
L. Rosseau
L. Joseph
Dorset
Kennisis L.
Maynooth
MacTier
Redstone L.
Haliburton L.
Port Carling
Lake Muskoka
Baptiste Lake
Denbigh
Flower
Bala
Bracebridge
Bird Creek
Childs Mines
Torrance
Bancroft
Wilberforce
Weslemkoon Lake
Lavant
Gravenhurst
Turriff
Christian Is.
Penetanguishene
Severn
Minden
Gooderham
Irondale
Mazinaw L.
Snow Road
Port McNicoll
Victoria Hbr.
Gull L.
Skootamatta L.
Coe Hill
Severn Bridge
Chandos L.
Big Gull L.
Midland
Waubaushene
Kinmount
Coldwater
Washago
Head L.
Catchacoma L.
Apsley
Sharbot Lake
L. Couchiching
Anstruther L.
Jack L.
Coboconk
Rathburn
Arden
Tichborne
Elmvale
Orillia
Atherley
Victoria Rd.
Balsam L.
Kasshabog L.
Bannockburn
Kaladar
Hillsdale
Wasaga Beach
Brechin
Kirkfield
Bobcaygeon
Nottawa
Fenelon Falls
Trent Canal
Buckhorn L.
Stony Lake
Actinolite
Stayner
Marmora
Deloro
Madoc
Tamworth
Barrie
Beaverton
Sturgeon L.
Pigeon L.
Chemung L.
Lakefield
Tweed
Enterprise
Big Bay Pt.
Georgina I.
Havelock
Creemore
Woodville
Angus
Port Bolster
Cannington
Lindsay
Norwood
Sutton
Peterborough
Pefferlaw
Hastings
Campbellford
Lefroy
Cook B.
Keswick
Omemee
Moira
Newburgh
Sunderland
Stirling
Odessa
Salmon R.
Alliston
Keene
Warkworth
Napanee
Collins
Lake Scugog
Bethany
Bradford
Mount Albert
Millbrook
Rice Lake
Frankford
Belleville
Deseronto
Bath
Beeton
Holland Landing
Uxbridge
Harwood
Port Perry
Pontypool
Newmarket
Bewdley
Castleton
Trenton
Tottenham
Adolphus Reach
Schomberg
Aurora
Myrtle
Brighton
Claremont
Hampton
Orono
Colborne
Orangeville
Nobleton
King City
Stouffville
Brooklin
Presqu'ile Point
Consecon
Picton
Prince Edward B.
Bolton
Maple
Oshawa
Newcastle
Port Hope
Cobourg
Bloomfield
Wellington
Humber
Richmond Hill
Markham
Pickering
Bowmanville
Inglewood
Ajax
Whitby
Erin
Bramalea
Woodbridge
Pt. Petre
Brampton
Toronto
Acton
Georgetown
Streetsville
Toronto Is.
Mississauga
Port Credit
Milton
Oakville
Bronte
Waterdown
Burlington
Olcott
Dundas
Burlington Beach
Wilson
Hamilton
Niagara-on-the-Lake
Newfane
Hilton
Fair Haven
Ancaster
Stoney Creek
Grimsby
Youngstown
Beamsville
Lockport
Sodus
Red Creek
Mount Hope
St. Catharines
Lewiston
Williamson
Wolcott
Niagara
Thorold
Welland Canal
Caledonia
Smithville
Welland R.
Niagara Falls
Fonthill
Chippawa
Tonawanda
Lyons
Clyde
Welland
Newark
Hagersville
Cayuga
Dunnville
Buffalo
Fort Erie
Port Colborne
Phelps
Seneca Falls
Canandaigua
Geneva

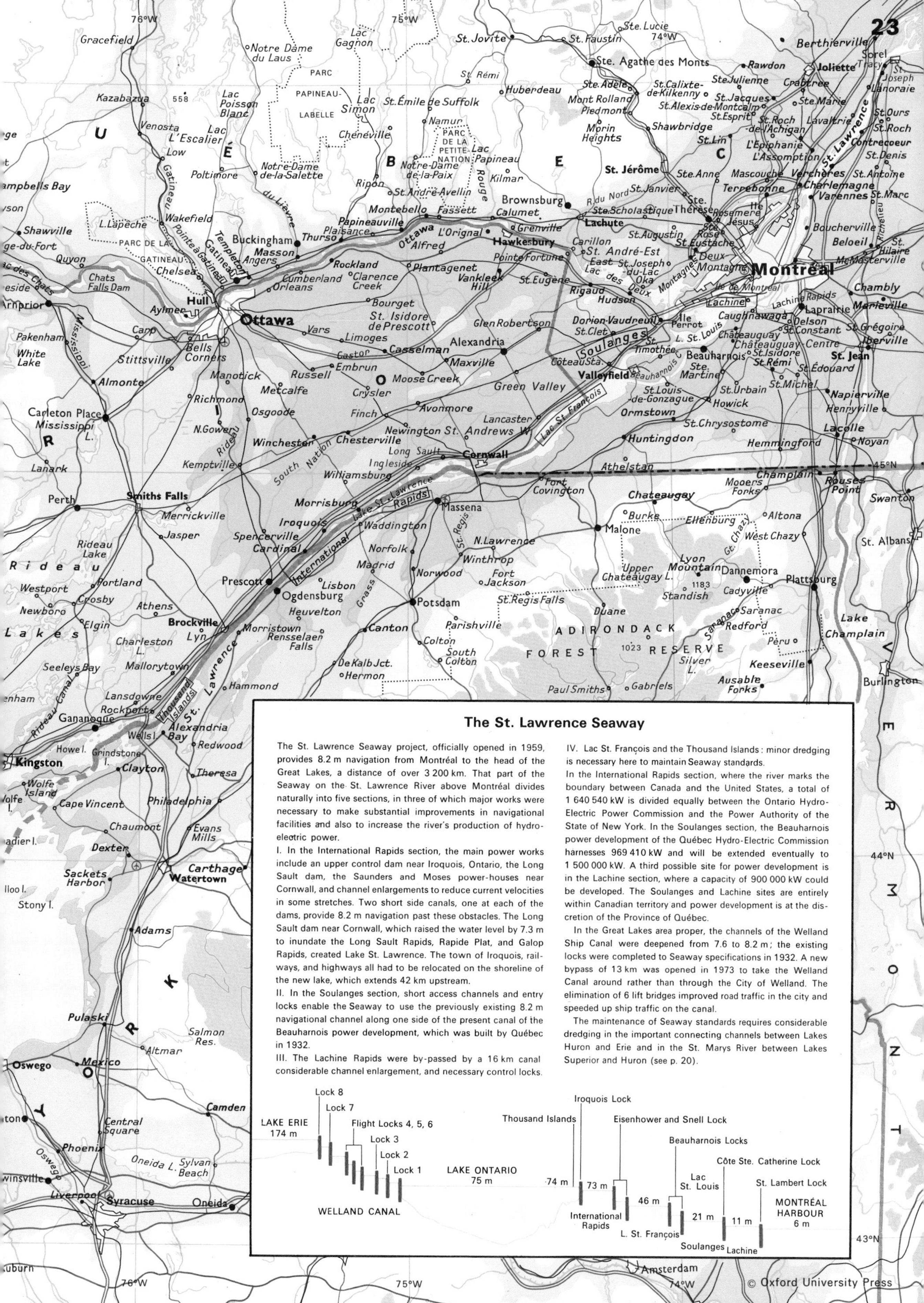

The St. Lawrence Seaway

The St. Lawrence Seaway project, officially opened in 1959, provides 8.2 m navigation from Montréal to the head of the Great Lakes, a distance of over 3 200 km. That part of the Seaway on the St. Lawrence River above Montréal divides naturally into five sections, in three of which major works were necessary to make substantial improvements in navigational facilities and also to increase the river's production of hydro-electric power.

I. In the International Rapids section, the main power works include an upper control dam near Iroquois, Ontario, the Long Sault dam, the Saunders and Moses power-houses near Cornwall, and channel enlargements to reduce current velocities in some stretches. Two short side canals, one at each of the dams, provide 8.2 m navigation past these obstacles. The Long Sault dam near Cornwall, which raised the water level by 7.3 m to inundate the Long Sault Rapids, Rapide Plat, and Galop Rapids, created Lake St. Lawrence. The town of Iroquois, railways, and highways all had to be relocated on the shoreline of the new lake, which extends 42 km upstream.

II. In the Soulanges section, short access channels and entry locks enable the Seaway to use the previously existing 8.2 m navigational channel along one side of the present canal of the Beauharnois power development, which was built by Québec in 1932.

III. The Lachine Rapids were by-passed by a 16 km canal considerable channel enlargement, and necessary control locks.

IV. Lac St. François and the Thousand Islands: minor dredging is necessary here to maintain Seaway standards.

In the International Rapids section, where the river marks the boundary between Canada and the United States, a total of 1 640 540 kW is divided equally between the Ontario Hydro-Electric Power Commission and the Power Authority of the State of New York. In the Soulanges section, the Beauharnois power development of the Québec Hydro-Electric Commission harnesses 969 410 kW and will be extended eventually to 1 500 000 kW. A third possible site for power development is in the Lachine section, where a capacity of 900 000 kW could be developed. The Soulanges and Lachine sites are entirely within Canadian territory and power development is at the discretion of the Province of Québec.

In the Great Lakes area proper, the channels of the Welland Ship Canal were deepened from 7.6 to 8.2 m; the existing locks were completed to Seaway specifications in 1932. A new bypass of 13 km was opened in 1973 to take the Welland Canal around rather than through the City of Welland. The elimination of 6 lift bridges improved road traffic in the city and speeded up ship traffic on the canal.

The maintenance of Seaway standards requires considerable dredging in the important connecting channels between Lakes Huron and Erie and in the St. Marys River between Lakes Superior and Huron (see p. 20).

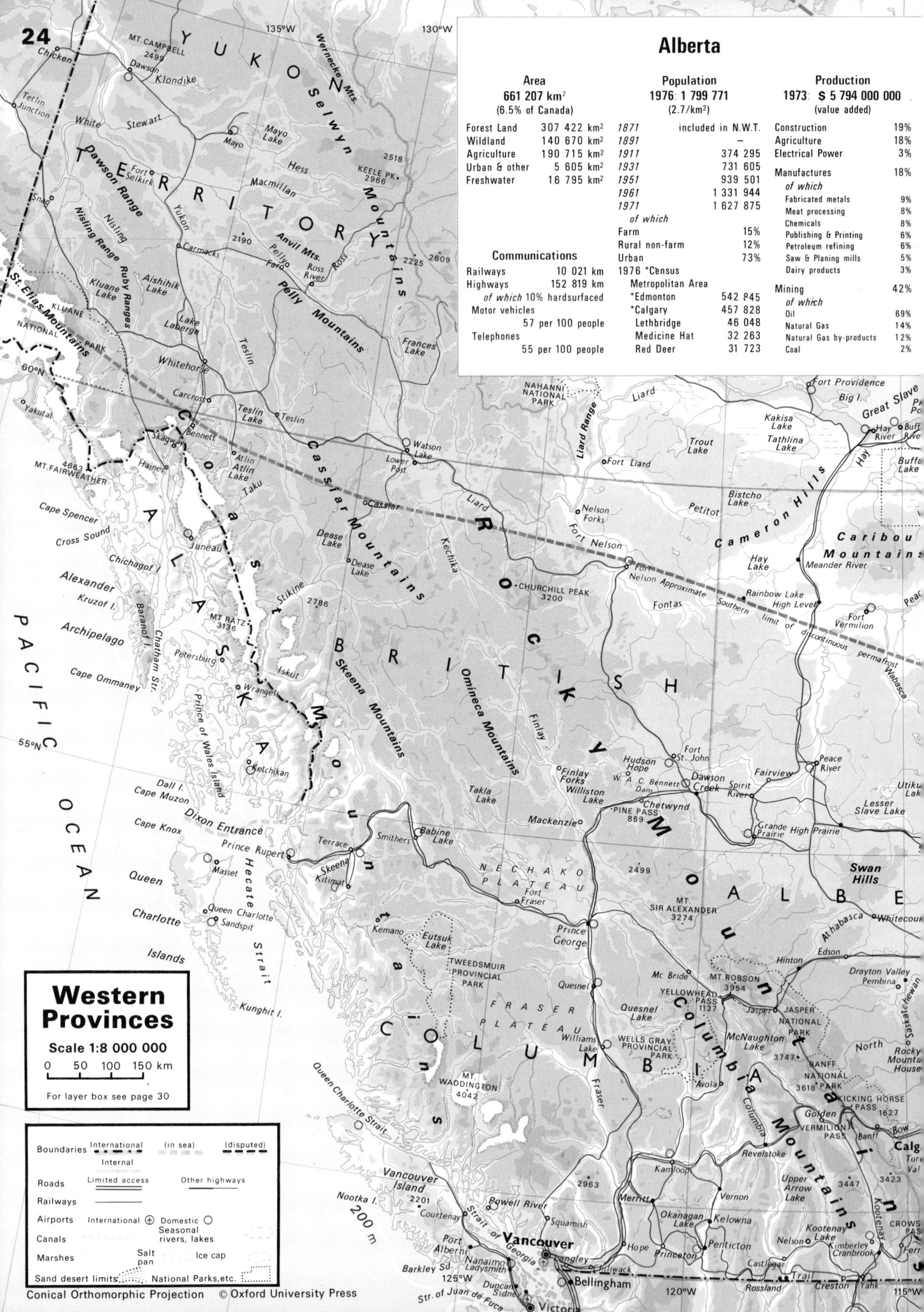

Alberta

Area		Population		Production	
661 207 km² (6.5% of Canada)		1976: 1 799 771 (2.7/km²)		1973: $ 5 794 000 000 (value added)	
Forest Land	307 422 km²	*1871*	included in N.W.T.	Construction	19%
Wildland	140 670 km²	*1891*	–	Agriculture	18%
Agriculture	190 715 km²	*1911*	374 295	Electrical Power	3%
Urban & other	5 605 km²	*1931*	731 605	Manufactures	18%
Freshwater	16 795 km²	*1951*	939 501	*of which*	
		1961	1 331 944	Fabricated metals	9%
		1971	1 627 875	Meat processing	8%
		of which		Chemicals	8%
		Farm	15%	Publishing & Printing	6%
		Rural non-farm	12%	Petroleum refining	6%
Communications		Urban	73%	Saw & Planing mills	5%
Railways	10 021 km	1976 *Census Metropolitan Area		Dairy products	3%
Highways	152 819 km	*Edmonton	542 845	Mining	42%
of which 10% hardsurfaced		*Calgary	457 828	*of which*	
Motor vehicles	57 per 100 people	Lethbridge	46 048	Oil	69%
Telephones	55 per 100 people	Medicine Hat	32 263	Natural Gas	14%
		Red Deer	31 723	Natural Gas by-products	12%
				Coal	2%

Saskatchewan

Area
651 923 km²
(6.4% of Canada)

est Land	128 201 km²
ldland	179 043 km²
riculture	264 269 km²
an & other	8 774 km²
shwater	71 636 km²

Communications

lways	13 784 km
hways	207 033 km
of which 8% hardsurfaced	
tor vehicles*	
	60 per 100 people
cludes snowmobiles	
lephones	
	46 per 100 people

Population
1976: 907 650
(1.4/km²)

1871	included in N.W.T.
1891	
1911	492 432
1931	921 785
1951	831 728
1961	925 181
1971	926 240
of which	
Farm	25%
Rural non-farm	22%
Urban	53%
1976 *Census Metropolitan Area	
* Regina	148 965
* Saskatoon	132 291
Moose Jaw	31 884
Prince Albert	28 240
Swift Current	14 523

Production
1973: $ 2 474 000 000
(value added)

Agriculture	54%
Construction	13%
Electrical Power	3%
Forestry)	
Fisheries)	1%
Trapping)	
Manufactures	12%
of which	
Meat processing	8%
Petroleum refining	7%
Agricultural implements	5%
Publishing & Printing	5%
Dairy products	4%
Mining	17%
of which	
Oil	51%
Potash	38%
Zinc	5%
Copper	3%

Manitoba

Area
650 090 km²
(6.4% of Canada)

Forest Land	135 472 km²
Wildland	121 191 km²
Agriculture	85 283 km²
Urban & other	204 577 km²
Freshwater	103 566 km²

Communications

Railways	7 633 km
Highways	75 920 km
of which 14% hardsurfaced	
Motor vehicles	
	47 per 100 people
Telephones	
	51 per 100 people

Population
1976: 1 005 953
(1.5/km²)

1871	25 228
1891	152 506
1911	461 394
1931	700 139
1951	776 541
1961	921 686
1971	988 245
of which	
Farm	13%
Rural non-farm	17%
Urban	70%
1976 *Census Metropolitan Area	
*Winnipeg	570 725
Brandon	34 481
Portage la Prairie	11 719
Flin Flon	8 431

Production
1973: $ 2 021 000 000
(value added)

Agriculture	27%
Construction	20%
Electrical Power	5%
Forestry)	
Fisheries)	1%
Trapping)	
Manufactures	36%
of which	
Clothing	9%
Publishing & Printing	7%
Meat processing	6%
Aircraft & Parts	4%
Agricultural implements	4%
Mining	11%
of which	
Nickel	54%
Zinc	32%
Copper	4%
Oil	4%

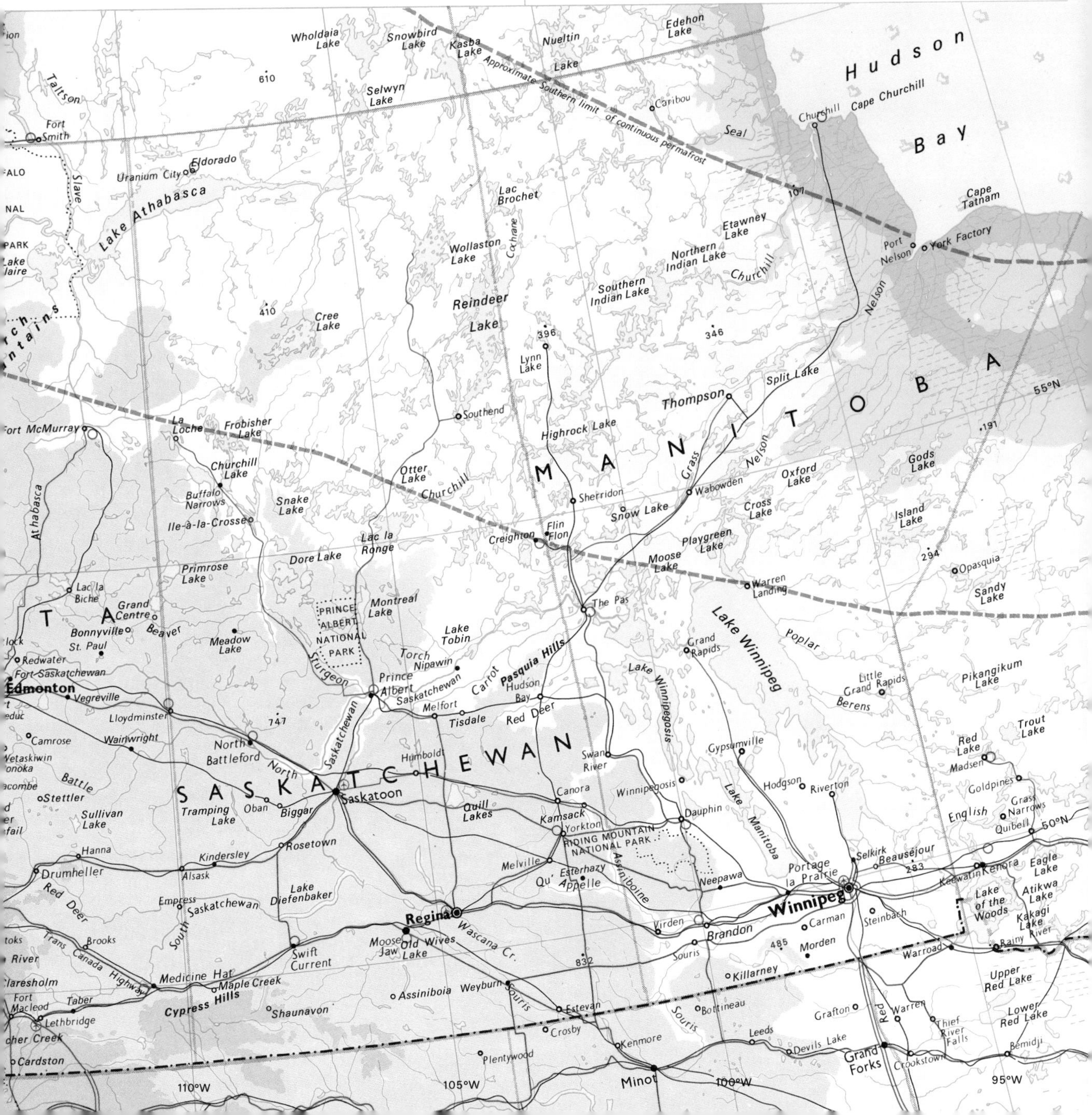

Hudson Bay
MANITOBA
SASKATCHEWAN
Approximate Southern limit of continuous permafrost
Lake Athabasca
Reindeer Lake
Wollaston Lake
Lake Winnipeg
Lake Winnipegosis
Lake Manitoba
Churchill
Cape Churchill
Cape Tatnam
Port Nelson
York Factory
Thompson
Lynn Lake
Flin Flon
The Pas
Prince Albert
Saskatoon
Regina
Moose Jaw
Swift Current
Yorkton
Brandon
Winnipeg
Portage la Prairie
Kenora
Edmonton
Medicine Hat
Lethbridge
Minot
Grand Forks
PRINCE ALBERT NATIONAL PARK
RIDING MOUNTAIN NATIONAL PARK
Trans Canada Highway
Cypress Hills
Pasquia Hills
110°W
105°W
100°W
95°W
55°N
50°N

Prairie Provinces
Scale 1:5 000 000
0 50 100 150 200 km
Boundaries International (in sea) (disputed)
Internal
Roads Limited access Other highways Tracks
Railways
Airports International Domestic
Seasonal rivers, lakes
Canals
Marshes
Salt pan
Ice cap
Sand desert limits
National Parks,etc.
Conical Orthomorphic Projection © Oxford University Press
120°W
115°W
110°W
55°N
ALBERTA
SASKA
Wood Buffalo National Park
Caribou Mts.
Birch Mts.
Buffalo Head Hills
Pelican Mts.
Swan Hills
Firebag Hills
Mostoos Hills
Clear Hills
Cypress Hills
Great Sand Hills
Rocky Mts.
Selkirk Mts.
Jasper National Park
Banff National Park
Willmore Wilderness Prov. Park
Hamber Provincial Park
Mount Robson Prov. Pk.
Meadow Lake Provincial Park
Waterton Lakes N.P.
Lake Athabasca
Lesser Slave Lake
Lake Claire
Peace
Hay
Chinchaga
Fontas
Beatton
Smoky
Wapiti
Little Smoky
Athabasca
Clearwater
Christina
Richardson
Firebag
Wabasca
Mikkwa
Slave
William
McFarlane
Mudjatik
Beaver
Pembina
Brazeau
N. Saskatchewan
Red Deer
Bow
Oldman
Belly
Milk
South Saskatchewan
North Saskatchewan
Battle
Sounding L.
Ft. Fitzgerald
Fort Chipewyan
Uranium City
Eldorado
Gunnar
Fond du Lac
Tazin L.
Charles L.
Meander River
Hay L.
Habay
Chateh
Rainbow Lake
High Level
Fort Vermilion
Paddle Prairie
Margaret L.
Manning
Eureka River
Deer Hill
Hines Creek
Fairview
Grimshaw
Berwyn
Peace River
Cecil Lake
Fort St. John
Taylor
Pine Valley
Dawson Creek
Pouce Coupé
Spirit River
Wanham
Falher
McLennan
Beaverlodge
Hythe
Sexsmith
Wembley
Grande Prairie
High Prairie
Valleyview
Sturgeon L.
Slave Lake
Smith
Calling Lake
Utikuma L.
Lubicon L.
Peerless Lake
N. Wabasca Lake
Desmarais
Fort McMurray
Conklin
Winefred L.
Gordon L.
Methy L.
La Loche
Turnor L.
Frobisher Lake
Peter Pond Lake
Churchill Lake
Buffalo Narrows
Île à la Crosse
Lac Île à la Crosse
Canoe L.
Beauval
Lac la Plonge
Primrose Lake
Cold L.
Cold Lake
Grand Centre
Bonnyville
Goodsoil
Waterhen
Meadow Lake
Loon Lake
Frog L.
St. Paul
Elk Point
Two Hills
Myrnam
Frenchman Butte
St. Walburg
Lloydminster
Vermilion
Mannville
Lac la Biche
Boyle
Athabasca
Thorhild
Smoky Lake
Redwater
Andrew
Bruderheim
Morinville
Fort Saskatchewan
Mundare
Vegreville
Beaverhill L.
Tofield
Edmonton
Stony Plain
Devon
Leduc
Calmar
Camrose
Holden
Viking
Westlock
Barrhead
Mayerthorpe
Whitecourt
Blue Ridge
Swan Hills
Fox Creek
Grand Cache
Hinton
Edson
Rosevear
Chip L.
Wildwood
Evansburg
Golden Spike
Thorsby
Drayton Valley
Pigeon Lake
Millet
Wetaskiwin
Rimbey
Gull L.
Ponoka
Lacombe
Bentley
Rocky Mountain House
Blackfalds
Sylvan Lake
Red Deer
Penhold
Innisfail
Bowden
Olds
Sundre
Didsbury
Carstairs
Trochu
Three Hills
Alix
Bashaw
Buffalo Lake
Stettler
Castor
Coronation
Sullivan Lake
Consort
Dowling Lake
Forestburg
Hardisty
Daysland
Killam
Irma
Wainwright
Provost
Macklin
Unity
Wilkie
Luseland
Tramping Lake
Kerrobert
Kirkpatrick L.
Dodsland
Hanna
Drumheller
Beiseker
Crossfield
Airdrie
Cochrane
Calgary
Canmore
Strathmore
Forest Lawn
Bowness
Black Diamond
Turner Valley
Okotoks
High River
Nanton
Vulcan
Claresholm
Lake McGregor
Lake Newell
Bassano
Brooks
Wardlow
Oyen
Alsask
Eatonia
Kindersley
Rosetown
Elrose
Eston
Leader
Prelate
Burstall
Fox Valley
Cabri
Big Stick L.
Gull Lake
Ralston
Redcliff
Medicine Hat
Crane L.
Maple Creek
Cypress Hills Park
Swift Current
Shaunavon
Eastend
Ponteix
Gravelbourg
Hodgeville
Morse
Herbert
Kyle
Lake Diefenbaker
Outlook
Delisle
Saskatoon
Biggar
Perdue
Oban
Langham
Warman
Dalmeny
Radisson
Redberry L.
North Battleford
Battleford
Cutknife
Manito L.
Maidstone
Lashburn
Turtleford
Big River
Leoville
Neeb
Picture Butte
Coaldale
Lethbridge
Taber
Vauxhall
Bow Island
Fort Macleod
Pincher Creek
Cowley
Coleman
Michel
Blairmore
Bellevue
Crowsnest Pass
Coal Creek
Elko
Cardston
St. Mary
Magrath
Raymond
Stirling
Warner
Milk River
Nemiskam Park
Foremost
Pakowki Lake
Coutts
Sweetgrass
Writing on Stone Park
Sunburst
Kettle Falls
Colville
Priest Lake
St. Mary Lakes
Jasper
Dunster
Shere
Lucerne
Valemount
Blue River
Avola
Beavermouth
Field
L. Louise
Kicking Horse Pass
Adams Lake
Columbia
Kettle
Mt. Robson 3954
Mt. Chown 3331
Yellowhead Pass
Mt. Sir Wilfrid Laurier 3581
Mt. Evans 3188
Mt. Brazeau 3470
Mt. Columbia 3747
Gordon Horne Pk. 2914
Mt. Forbes 3628
Pukeashun Mt. 2252
Mt. Lyall 2950
Tornado Mt. 3100
3160
2862
3618
3422
1357
1392
1117
2205
425
527
876
Pinto Butte 1021
Kotcho L.
Davy L.
Mayson L.
Forrest L.
Lloyd L.
Cree
Black Birch Lake
Wasekamio L.
Porter L.
Snake Lake
Doré L.
Ordale
Shellbrook
Blaine Lake
Central Butte
Gardiner Dam
Qu'Appelle Arm
Sutherland

Metres
5000
3000
2000
1000
500
300
200
100
Sea level
Land depression
Spot heights in metres
105°W
100°W
95°W
55°N
50°N
M A N I T O B A
CHEWAN
Churchill
C. Churchill
Hubbart Pt.
Caribou
Nejanilini Lake
North River
Button B.
Seal
N. Knife
S. Knife
North Knife L.
Etawney L.
Stony L.
Tadoule L.
Lac Brochet
Cochrane
N. Seal
Black Lake
Fond du Lac
Wollaston Lake
Waterbury L.
Close L.
Brochet
S. Seal
Big Sand Lake
Northern Indian L.
McClintock
Owl
Port Nelson
York Factory
Nelson
Hayes
Gods
Shamattawa
Amery
Kettle Rapids
Gillam
Split Lake
Ilford
Split L.
Gauer Lake
Southern Indian Lake
South Indian Lake
346
249
Baldock L.
Barrington Lake
Co-op Point
Reindeer Lake
655
Lynn Lake
Geikie
Wheeler
Nokomis L.
Watheman
Upper Foster Lake
Lower Foster Lake
Macoun Lake
Southend
Reindeer
Churchill
Granville Lake
Granville Falls
Moak L.
Mystery L.
Thompson
Grass
Arnot
Pikwitonei
Highrock
Highrock Lake
Rat
Nelson House
Pukatawagan
The Two Rivers
Island Falls
Sandy Bay
Kipahigan L.
Otter Lake
Burntwood
Sipiwesk
Thicket Portage
Utik L.
Sipiwesk Lake
Bear L.
Oxford House
Knee L.
Edmund L.
Kistigan L.
Gods L.
Gods Lake
Oxford L.
Carrot
Lac la Ronge
Lac la Ronge Prov. Park
Pelican Narrows
Kississing Lake
Sherridon
Wabowden
Chisel Lake
Snow Lake
Wekusko L.
Cross Lake
Wapawekka Lake
Wapawekka Hills
Deschambault Lake
Flin Flon
Creighton
Amisk Lake
Grass River Prov. Park
Cranberry Portage
Wekusko
Ross
Island
Playgreen Lake
Norway House
Molson L.
Beaverhill L.
Red Sucker L.
Lindman Lake
Sachigo L.
St. Theresa Point
Island L.
Island Lake
Bigstone L.
Sturgeon Landing
Cormorant L.
Cormorant
Wanless
Clearwater L. Provincial Park
Moose Lake
Cumberland Lake
The Pas
Warren Landing
Gunisao
Nipawin Prov. Pk.
Montreal Lake
Candle Lake
Squaw Rapids Hydro Dam
Saskatchewan
Tobin Lake
Torch
Choiceland
Nipawin
Foxford
Carrot
Carrot River
Pasquia Hills
Arborfield
Gronlid
Albert
Birch Hills
Kinistino
Tisdale
Melfort
Star City
Cedar Lake
Grand Rapids
Mukutawa
Opasquia
Sandy Lake
Sandy L.
Severn
Favourable Lake
Long Pt.
Lake Winnipeg
Poplar
Weaver L.
Wrong L.
Charron L.
Deer Lake
MacDowell L.
Red Deer Lake
Dawson Bay
Pelican Bay
Lake Winnipegosis
Hudson Bay
Red Deer
Porcupine Plain
Greenwater Lake Provincial Park
Porcupine Hills
Reindeer Island
Berens River
Berens
Pigeon Bay
Sturgeon Bay
Fishing Lake
Little Grand Rapids
Stout L.
Poplar Hill
McInnes L.
Barton L.
Moar L.
Pikangikum L.
Basin L.
Lenore L.
Naicam
Cudworth
Rose Valley
Kelvington
Humboldt
Watson
Nut Mountain
NUT MT.
Preeceville
Sturgis
Quill Lake
Quill Lakes
Wadena
Norquay
Pelican L.
Swan Lake
Duck Bay
Swan River
Minitonas
Benito
Camperville
Waterhen Lake
Skownan
Dauphin R.
Family L.
Cairns L.
Nungesser L.
Bloodvein
Sasaginnigak L.
Swain Post
Little Vermilion L.
Larus L.
Trout L.
Lanigan
Wynyard
Canora
Duck Mountain Provincial Park
Duck Mtn.
831
Winnipegosis
Ethelbert
Lake St. Martin
Washow Bay
Hecla Prov. Park
Red L.
McKenzie Island
Red Lake
Madsen
Pakwash L.
Watrous
Nokomis
Foam Lake
Raymore
Kamsack
Assiniboine
Sifton
Rorketon
Magnet
Lake Manitoba
Portage B.
Grindstone Prov. Park
Black I.
Hecla I.
Donald L.
Manigotagan L.
Kelliher
Yorkton
Roblin
Ashville
Dauphin Lake
Ashern
Riverton
Arborg
Goldpines
Last Mountain Lake
Strasbourg
Ituna
Goodeve
Saltcoats
Grandview
Gilbert Plains
Dauphin
Ste. Rose du Lac
Dog L.
Lundar
Gimli
L. Winnipeg
Sydney L.
Penzance
Southey
Cupar
Lipton
Balcarres
Melville
Churchbridge
Langenburg
Russell
Riding Mountain National Park
Riding Mtn.
Winnipeg Beach
Pine Falls
Powderview
Lac du Bonnet
Winnipeg R.
Umfreville L.
English
Grassy Narrows
Perrault L.
Fort Qu'Appelle
Qu'Appelle
Neudorf
Esterhazy
Shoal Lakes
Teulon
Lac du Bonnet
Pinawa
Whiteshell
Tetu L.
Sand L.
Lumsden
Regina
Indian Head
Wolseley
Grenfell
Birtle
Shoal Lake
Gladstone
Selkirk
Beausejour
Molson
Whitemouth
Whiteshell Prov. Park
Minaki
Reddit
Vermilion Bay
Moose Jaw
Pasqua
Balgonie
Broadview
Montmartre
Whitewood
Wapella
Hamiota
Minnedosa
Neepawa
Stonewall
Stony Mountain
Keewatin
Kenora
Eagle L.
Rouleau
Wascana Cr.
Kipling
Moosomin
Kennedy
Arrow River
Portage la Prairie
MacGregor
Spruce Woods Prov. Park
Winnipeg
Atikwa L.
Dunkirk
Milestone
Wawota
Moose Mountain Park
Elkhorn
Rivers
Virden
Brandon
Carberry
Assiniboine
Ste. Anne
Niverville
Aulneau Penin.
Kakagi L.
Yellow Grass
Weyburn
Stoughton
Maryfield
Carlyle
Oak L.
Souris
Glenboro
Treherne
Carman
Steinbach
St. Pierre
Shoal L.
Whitemouth L.
Lake of the Rivers
Arcola
Redvers
Reston
Hartney
Somerset
Morris
St. Malo
Red
Lake of the Woods
Radville
Souris
Midale
Boissevain
Manitou
Winkler
Altona
Roseau
Williams
Bengough
Willowbunch L.
Lampman
Melita
Killarney
Pilot Mound
Morden
Plum Coulee
Gretna
Emerson
Warroad
Rainy River
Fort Frances
Carnduff
Oxbow
Deloraine
100°W
Pembina
Hannah
Walhalla
Neche
Hallock
Badger
Greenbush
Emo
International Falls
Fife L.
Estevan
Bienfait
International Peace Garden
St. John
Sarles
Rolla
Rock Lake
Langdon
Cavalier
Big Muddy L.
Portal
Sherwood
Antler
Westhope
Bottineau
Karlstad
Thief L.

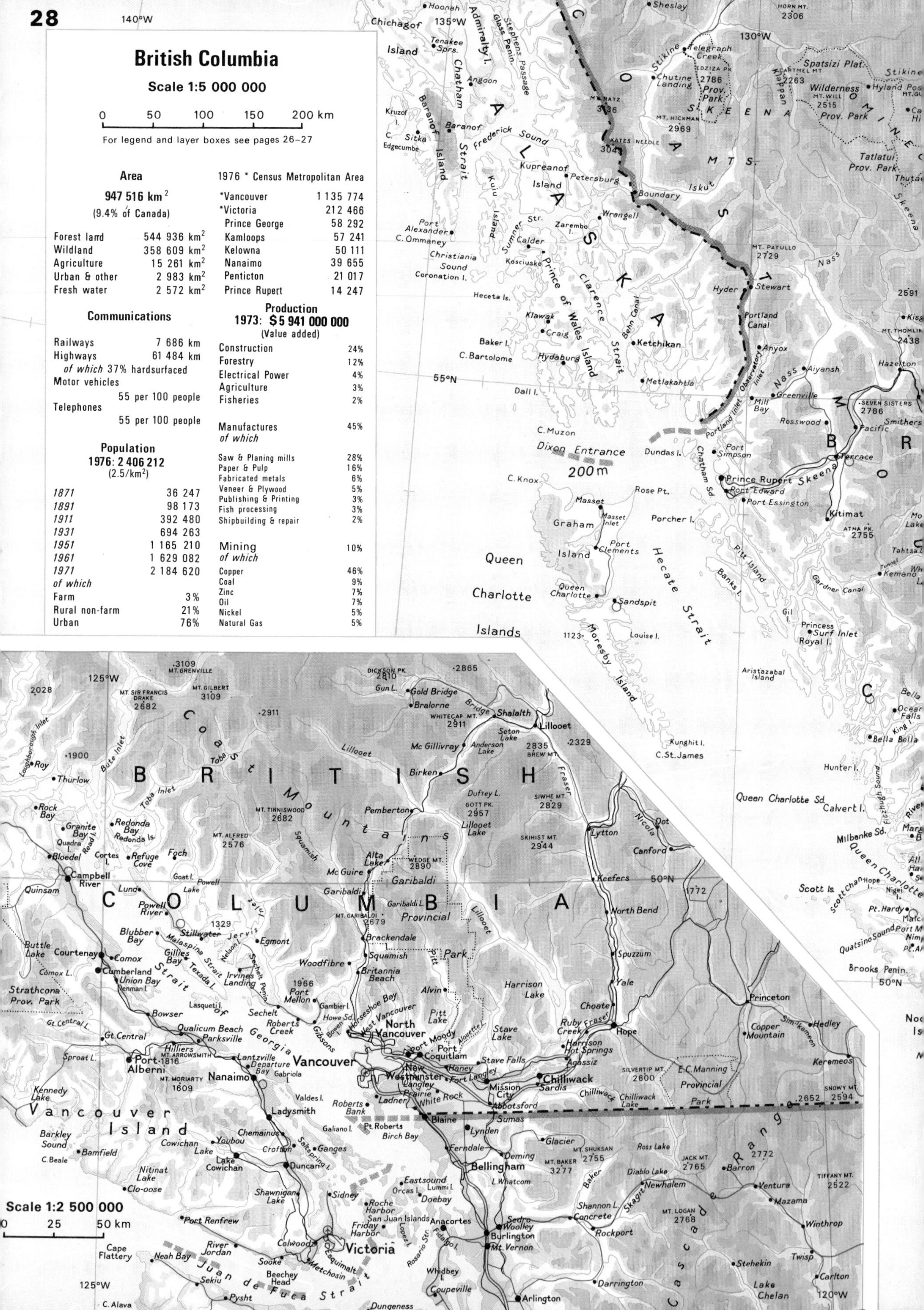

British Columbia

Scale 1:5 000 000

0 50 100 150 200 km

For legend and layer boxes see pages 26–27

Area

947 516 km²

(9.4% of Canada)

Forest land	544 936 km²
Wildland	358 609 km²
Agriculture	15 261 km²
Urban & other	2 983 km²
Fresh water	2 572 km²

Communications

Railways	7 686 km
Highways	61 484 km
of which 37% hardsurfaced	
Motor vehicles	55 per 100 people
Telephones	55 per 100 people

Population

1976: 2 406 212

(2.5/km²)

1871	36 247
1891	98 173
1911	392 480
1931	694 263
1951	1 165 210
1961	1 629 082
1971	2 184 620
of which	
Farm	3%
Rural non-farm	21%
Urban	76%

1976 * Census Metropolitan Area

*Vancouver	1 135 774
*Victoria	212 466
Prince George	58 292
Kamloops	57 241
Kelowna	50 111
Nanaimo	39 655
Penticton	21 017
Prince Rupert	14 247

Production

1973: $5 941 000 000

(Value added)

Construction	24%
Forestry	12%
Electrical Power	4%
Agriculture	3%
Fisheries	2%
Manufactures *of which*	45%
Saw & Planing mills	28%
Paper & Pulp	16%
Fabricated metals	6%
Veneer & Plywood	5%
Publishing & Printing	3%
Fish processing	3%
Shipbuilding & repair	2%
Mining *of which*	10%
Copper	46%
Coal	9%
Zinc	7%
Oil	7%
Nickel	5%
Natural Gas	5%

onical Orthomorphic Projection

The Territories
Yukon: North West Territories

Area

Yukon: 558 396 km²
(5.5% of Canada)

Forest Land	232 366 km²
Wildland	310 528 km²
Agriculture	11 012 km²
Freshwater	44 800 km²

N.W.T.: 3 422 904 km²
(34.1% of Canada)

Forest Land	547 130 km²
Wildland	2 735 485 km²
Agriculture	6 989 km²
Freshwater	133 300 km²

Communications

Railways: *Yukon*	93 km
N.W.T.	208 km
Highways	5 477 km

of which 2% hardsurfaced

Motor vehicles *Yukon* 56
N.W.T. 34 per 100 people
includes snowmobiles

Telephones *Yukon* 46
N.W.T. 34 per 100 people

Population

1976: Yukon 21 392
(0.04/km² : 1/2.5 km²)
N.W.T. 42 237
0.01/km² : 1/80 km²)

	Yukon	*N.W.T.*
1871		56 446*
1891		98 967
1911	8 512	6 507
1931	4 230	9 316
1951	9 096	16 004
1961	14 628	22 998
1971	18 390	34 805

*includes Saskatchewan & Alberta

of which		
Rural non-farm	39%	52%
Urban	61%	48%

1976

Yukon:	Whitehorse	13 045
N.W.T.:	Yellowknife	8 195
	Hay River	3 222
	Inuvik	3 039
	Fort Smith	2 268

Production

1973: $ 166 000 000
(value added)

Electrical Power	8%
Trapping	1%
Manufactures	2%
of which	
Paper & Pulp	30%
Food & Beverages	13%
Wood products	7%
Mining	89%
of which	
Yukon	
Zinc	40%
Lead	25%
Silver	10%
Copper	10%
Asbestos	9%
N.W.T.	
Zinc	53%
Lead	19%
Gold	15%
Silver	8%

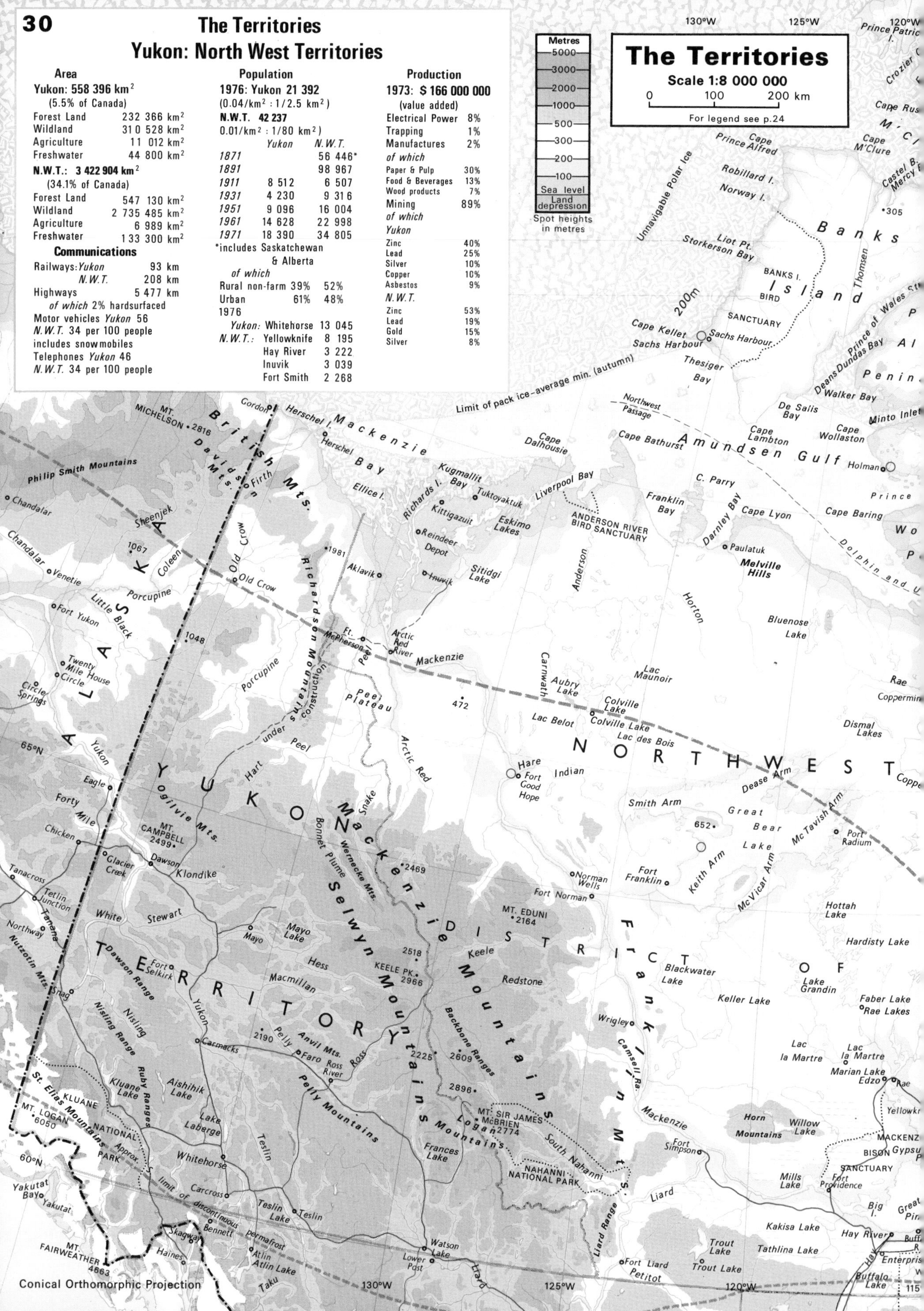

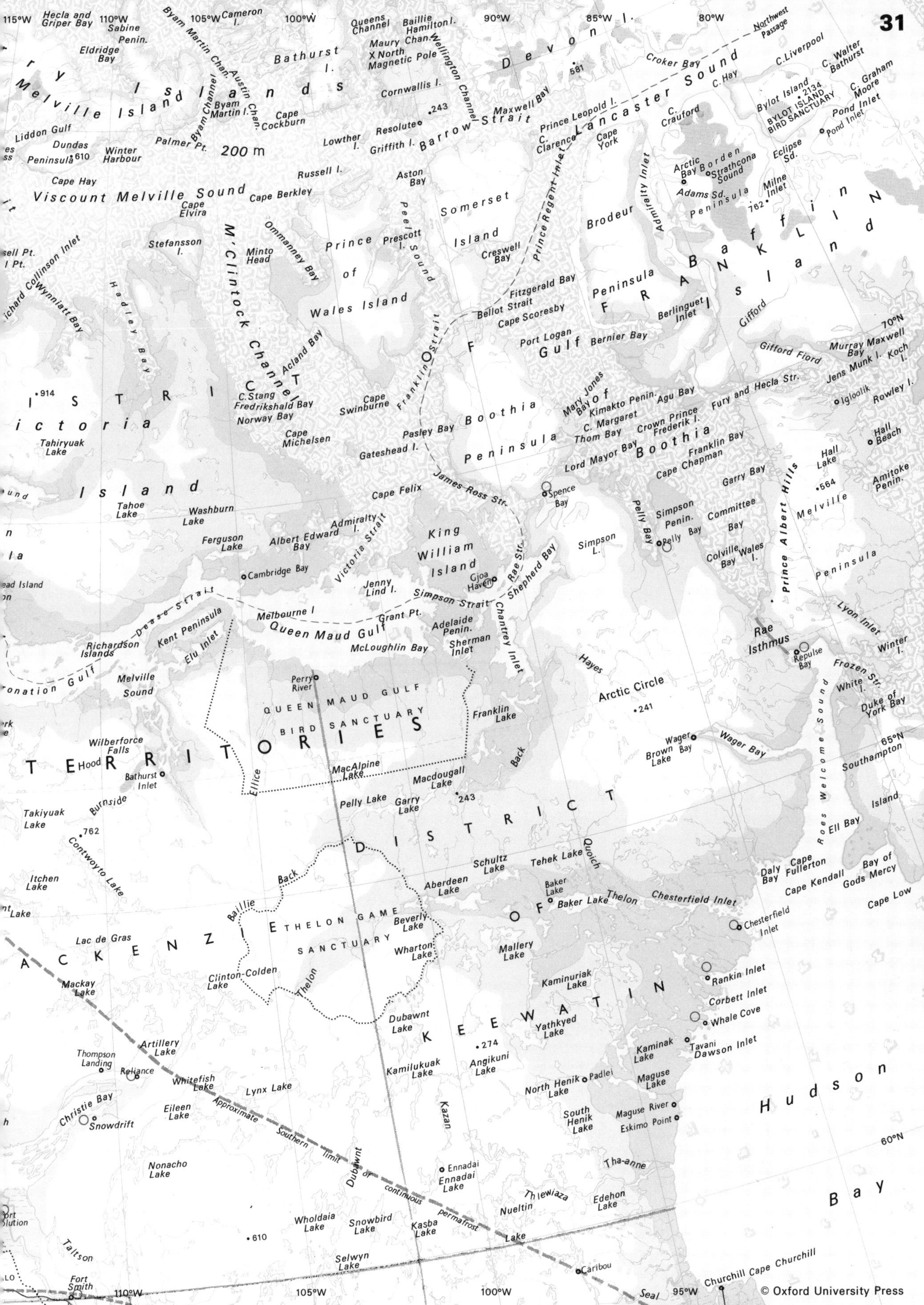
115°W
Hecla and Griper Bay
110°W
Sabine Penin.
105°W
Cameron I.
100°W
Queens Channel
Baillie Hamilton I.
Maury Chan.
North Magnetic Pole
Wellington Channel
90°W
85°W
Devon I.
80°W
Northwest Passage
Byam Martin Chan.
Austin Chan.
Eldridge Bay
Bathurst I.
Croker Bay
581
C. Liverpool
C. Walter Bathurst
Melville Island
Islands
Byam Channel
Byam Martin I.
Cornwallis I.
Lancaster Sound
C. Hay
Bylot Island
2134
BYLOT ISLAND BIRD SANCTUARY
C. Graham Moore
Pond Inlet
Liddon Gulf
Cape Cockburn
Resolute
243
Maxwell Bay
Barrow Strait
Prince Leopold I.
C. Clarence
C. Crauford
Dundas Peninsula
610
Winter Harbour
Palmer Pt.
200 m
Lowther I.
Griffith I.
Cape York
Eclipse Sd.
Cape Hay
Russell I.
Aston Bay
Admiralty Inlet
Arctic Bay
Borden
Strathcona Sound
Adams Sd.
Peninsula
Milne Inlet
762
Viscount Melville Sound
Cape Berkley
Cape Elvira
Somerset Island
Prince Regent Inlet
Brodeur
Baffin
M'Clintock Channel
Ommanney Bay
Prince of Wales Island
Prescott I.
Peel Sound
Stefansson I.
Minto Head
Creswell Bay
Franklin
Island
Collinson Inlet
Wynniatt Bay
Hadley Bay
Fitzgerald Bay
Bellot Strait
Cape Scoresby
Peninsula
Berlinguet Inlet
Gifford
Port Logan
Gulf
Bernier Bay
70°N
Gifford Fiord
Murray Maxwell Bay
Acland Bay
Franklin Strait
Jens Munk I.
Koch I.
914
District
Victoria
C. Stang
Fredrikshald Bay
Norway Bay
Cape Swinburne
Boothia
Mary Jones Bay of
Kimakto Penin.
Agu Bay
Fury and Hecla Str.
Igloolik
Rowley I.
C. Margaret
Thom Bay
Crown Prince Frederik I.
Tahiryuak Lake
Cape Michelsen
Gateshead I.
Pasley Bay
Peninsula
Lord Mayor Bay
Boothia
Franklin Bay
Hall Beach
Cape Chapman
Hall Lake
James Ross Str.
Spence Bay
Garry Bay
564
Amitoke Penin.
Island
Cape Felix
Melville
Tahoe Lake
Washburn Lake
Simpson Penin.
Committee Bay
Admiralty I.
King William Island
Pelly Bay
Ferguson Lake
Albert Edward Bay
Victoria Strait
Simpson L.
Shepherd Bay
Rae Str.
Colville Bay
Wales I.
Prince Albert Hills
Cambridge Bay
Gjoa Haven
Peninsula
Jenny Lind I.
Simpson Strait
Dease Strait
Melbourne I
Grant Pt.
Adelaide Penin.
Chantrey Inlet
Lyon Inlet
Kent Peninsula
Queen Maud Gulf
Sherman Inlet
Rae Isthmus
Richardson Islands
Elu Inlet
McLoughlin Bay
Repulse Bay
Winter I.
Hayes
Frozen Str.
Melville Sound
Perry River
Arctic Circle
White I.
QUEEN MAUD GULF BIRD SANCTUARY
241
Duke of York Bay
Franklin Lake
Wilberforce Falls
TERRITORIES
Wager Bay
Brown Lake
Wager Bay
65°N
Southampton Island
Hood
Bathurst Inlet
Back
MacAlpine Lake
Macdougall Lake
Roes Welcome Sound
Ellice
Pelly Lake
Garry Lake
243
Takiyuak Lake
Burnside
DISTRICT
Ell Bay
762
Contwoyto Lake
Quoich
Schultz Lake
Tehek Lake
Cape Fullerton
Bay of Gods Mercy
Itchen Lake
Back
Aberdeen Lake
Baker Lake
Thelon
Daly Bay
Cape Kendall
Chesterfield Inlet
Cape Low
OF
Baillie
THELON GAME SANCTUARY
Beverly Lake
Chesterfield Inlet
Lac de Gras
MACKENZIE
Wharton Lake
Mallery Lake
Mackay Lake
Clinton-Colden Lake
Thelon
Kaminuriak Lake
Rankin Inlet
KEEWATIN
Corbett Inlet
Dubawnt Lake
Whale Cove
Artillery Lake
Yathkyed Lake
274
Kaminak Lake
Tavani
Dawson Inlet
Thompson Landing
Reliance
Whitefish Lake
Kamilukuak Lake
Angikuni Lake
Hudson
Lynx Lake
North Henik Lake
Padlei
Maguse Lake
Christie Bay
Eileen Lake
Approximate southern limit of continuous permafrost
Kazan
Maguse River
Snowdrift
South Henik Lake
Eskimo Point
60°N
Nonacho Lake
Dubawnt
Ennadai
Ennadai Lake
Tha-anne
Thlewiaza
Edehon Lake
Bay
Nueltin Lake
Wholdaia Lake
Snowbird Lake
Kasba Lake
610
Taltson
Selwyn Lake
Caribou
Churchill
Cape Churchill
Fort Smith
110°W
105°W
100°W
Seal
95°W

Urban Land Use

These urban land use maps show only a simplified land use pattern. Their primary intent is to illustrate the overall relationships of land use and transportation systems. Therefore, much detail has been omitted.

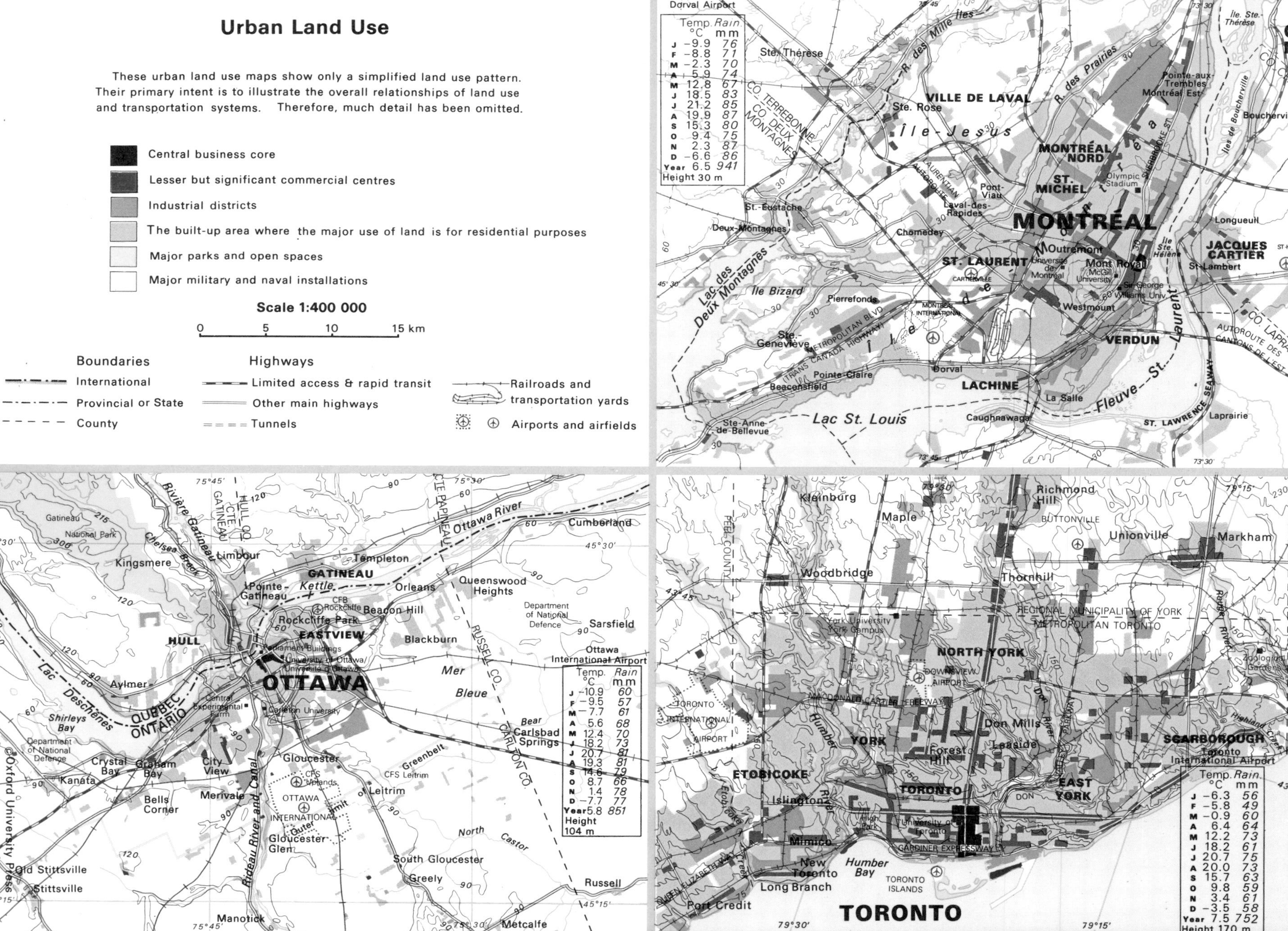

Dorval Airport

	Temp. °C	Rain mm
J	−9.9	76
F	−8.8	71
M	−2.3	70
A	5.9	74
M	12.8	67
J	18.5	83
J	21.2	85
A	19.9	87
S	15.3	80
O	9.4	75
N	2.3	87
D	−6.6	86
Year	6.5	941

Height 30 m

Ottawa International Airport

	Temp. °C	Rain mm
J	−10.9	60
F	−9.5	57
M	−7.7	61
A	5.6	68
M	12.4	70
J	18.2	73
J	20.7	81
A	19.3	81
S	14.6	79
O	8.7	66
N	1.4	78
D	−7.7	77
Year	5.8	851

Height 104 m

Toronto International Airport

	Temp. °C	Rain mm
J	−6.3	56
F	−5.8	49
M	−0.9	60
A	6.4	64
M	12.2	73
J	18.2	61
J	20.7	75
A	20.0	73
S	15.7	63
O	9.8	59
N	3.4	61
D	−3.5	58
Year	7.5	752

Height 170 m

Winnipeg International Airport

	Temp. °C	Rain mm
J	−18.3	24
F	−15.7	19
M	−8.1	26
A	3.3	37
M	10.6	57
J	16.5	80
J	19.7	80
A	18.7	74
S	12.6	53
O	6.6	35
N	−4.4	27
D	−13.7	23
Year	2.3	535

Height 240 m

City Airport

	J	F	M	A	M	J	J	A	S	O	N	D	Year
Temp. °C	−3.8	−3.3	1.1	8.3	14.4	20.0	22.7	21.6	17.7	11.6	4.4	−1.6	9.4
Rain mm	53	53	60	68	83	83	81	71	66	60	73	55	806

Height 189 m

Washington Airport

	Temp. °C	Rain mm
J	2.2	66
F	3.3	66
M	7.2	83
A	13.3	71
M	18.9	99
J	23.3	86
J	25.6	106
A	25.0	122
S	21.1	78
O	15.0	71
N	8.9	76
D	3.3	76
Year	13.9	1101

Height 3 m

Gen. Logan International Airport

	J	F	M	A	M	J	J	A	S	O	N	D	Year
Temp. °C	−1.6	−1.6	2.7	8.3	14.4	19.4	22.2	21.6	17.7	12.2	6.1	0.0	10.1
Rain mm	91	86	96	91	81	78	81	91	81	81	99	91	1047

Height 4.5 m

Greater Pittsburgh Airport

	J	F	M	A	M	J	J	A	S	O	N	D	Year
Temp. °C	-0.5	-0.5	4.4	10.5	16.6	21.6	23.8	22.7	19.4	12.7	6.1	1.1	11.5
Rain. mm	73	63	83	78	83	93	101	81	66	63	60	68	912

Height 347 m

Midway Airport

	Temp. °C	Rain. mm
J	-3.3	48
F	-2.2	40
M	2.2	68
A	9.4	76
M	15.5	93
J	21.6	101
J	23.8	86
A	23.3	81
S	18.8	68
O	12.7	73
N	4.4	55
D	-1.6	73
Year	10.5	814

Height 185 m

For legend see page 32

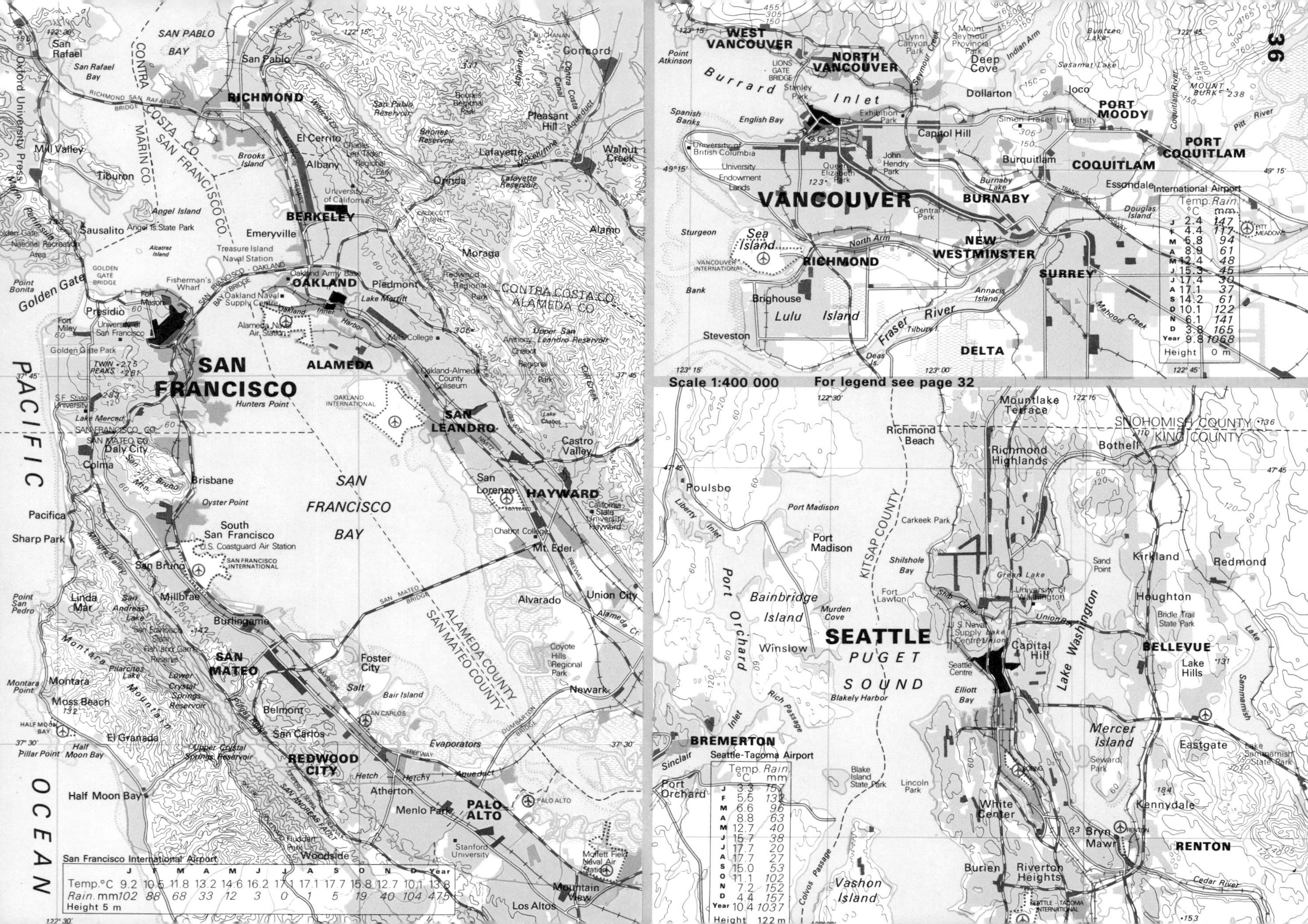

San Francisco International Airport

	J	F	M	A	M	J	J	A	S	O	N	D	Year
Temp. °C	9.2	10.5	11.8	13.2	14.6	16.2	17.1	17.1	17.7	15.8	12.7	10.1	13.8
Rain. mm	102	88	68	33	12	3	0	1	5	19	40	104	475

Height 5 m

Vancouver International Airport

	Temp. °C	Rain mm
J	2.4	147
F	4.4	117
M	5.8	94
A	8.9	61
M	12.4	48
J	15.3	45
J	17.4	30
A	17.1	37
S	14.2	61
O	10.1	122
N	6.1	141
D	3.8	165
Year	9.8	1068
Height	0 m	

Seattle-Tacoma Airport

	Temp. °C	Rain mm
J	3.3	157
F	5.5	132
M	6.6	96
A	8.8	63
M	12.7	40
J	15.7	38
J	17.7	20
A	17.7	27
S	15.0	53
O	11.1	102
N	7.2	152
D	4.4	157
Year	10.4	1037
Height	122 m	

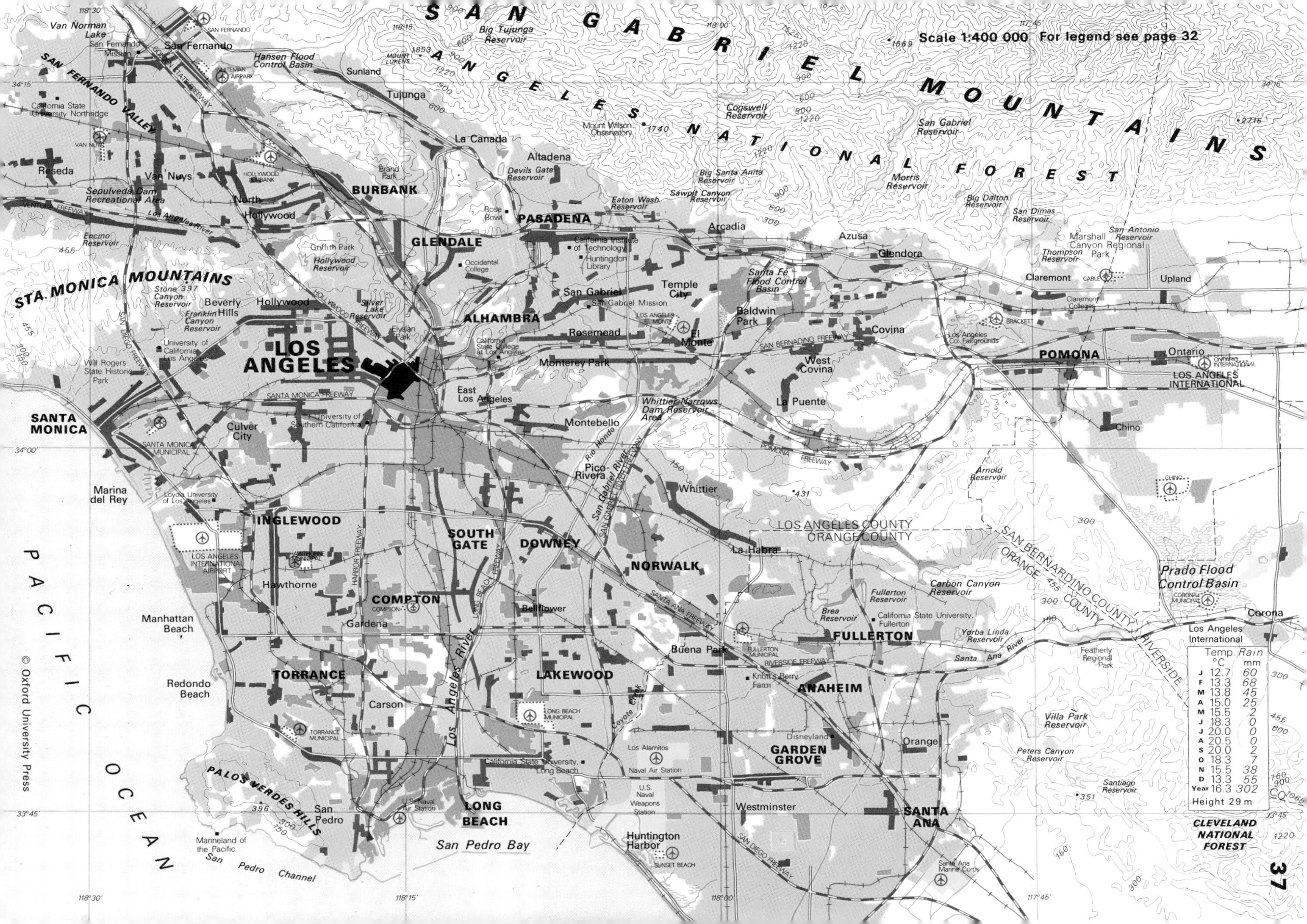

Los Angeles International

	Temp. °C	Rain mm
J	12.7	60
F	13.3	68
M	13.8	45
A	15.0	25
M	15.5	2
J	18.3	0
J	20.0	0
A	20.5	0
S	20.0	2
O	18.3	7
N	15.5	38
D	13.3	55
Year	16.3	302

Height 29 m

North and South America: Physical
Scale 1:44 000 000
0
1000
2000 km
Metres
5000
3000
2000
1000
500
300
200
100
Sea level
Land depression
200
3000
4000
5000
6000
Spot heights in metres
NORTH PACIFIC OCEAN
NORTH ATLANTIC OCEAN
Arctic Ocean
Polar Ice
Queen Elizabeth Islands
Banks Island
Victoria Island
GREENLAND
Baffin Bay
Baffin Island
ICELAND
UNITED KINGDOM
IRELAND
Arctic Circle
Limit of pack ice–min.
Limit of pack ice – max.
Reykjanes Ridge
West European Basin
PEAKE DEEP 5944
Azores
Mid Atlantic Ridge
Cape Verde Basin
Tropic of Cancer
Labrador Basin
Nova Scotia Basin
Northwest Atlantic Basin
BERMUDA (Br.)
Sargasso Sea
6995
6095
CANADA
Hudson Bay
Ungava Pen.
Labrador Peninsula
Newfoundland
St. Lawrence
Lake Winnipeg
Great Lakes
Peace
Mackenzie
Yukon
ALASKA (U.S.A.)
Bering Sea
Aleutian Islands
Kodiak Island
Gulf of Alaska
Queen Charlotte Is.
Vancouver I.
Fraser
Columbia
Snake
Rocky Mountains
UNITED STATES
Missouri
Platte
Colorado
Mississippi
Hudson
Maximum extent of Glaciation
Appalachian Mts.
Rio Grande
MEXICO
Gulf of Mexico
Guadaloupe
Tropic of Cancer
Revilla Gigedo Is.
BAHAMAS
CUBA
JAMAICA
HAITI
DOMINICAN REPUBLIC
PUERTO RICO
Puerto Rico Trench
Leeward Is.
Yucatan Basin
BELIZE
GUATEMALA
HONDURAS
EL SALVADOR
Middle America
Caribbean Sea
Guiana
60°N
75°N
45°N
30°N
120°W
90°W
60°W
30°W

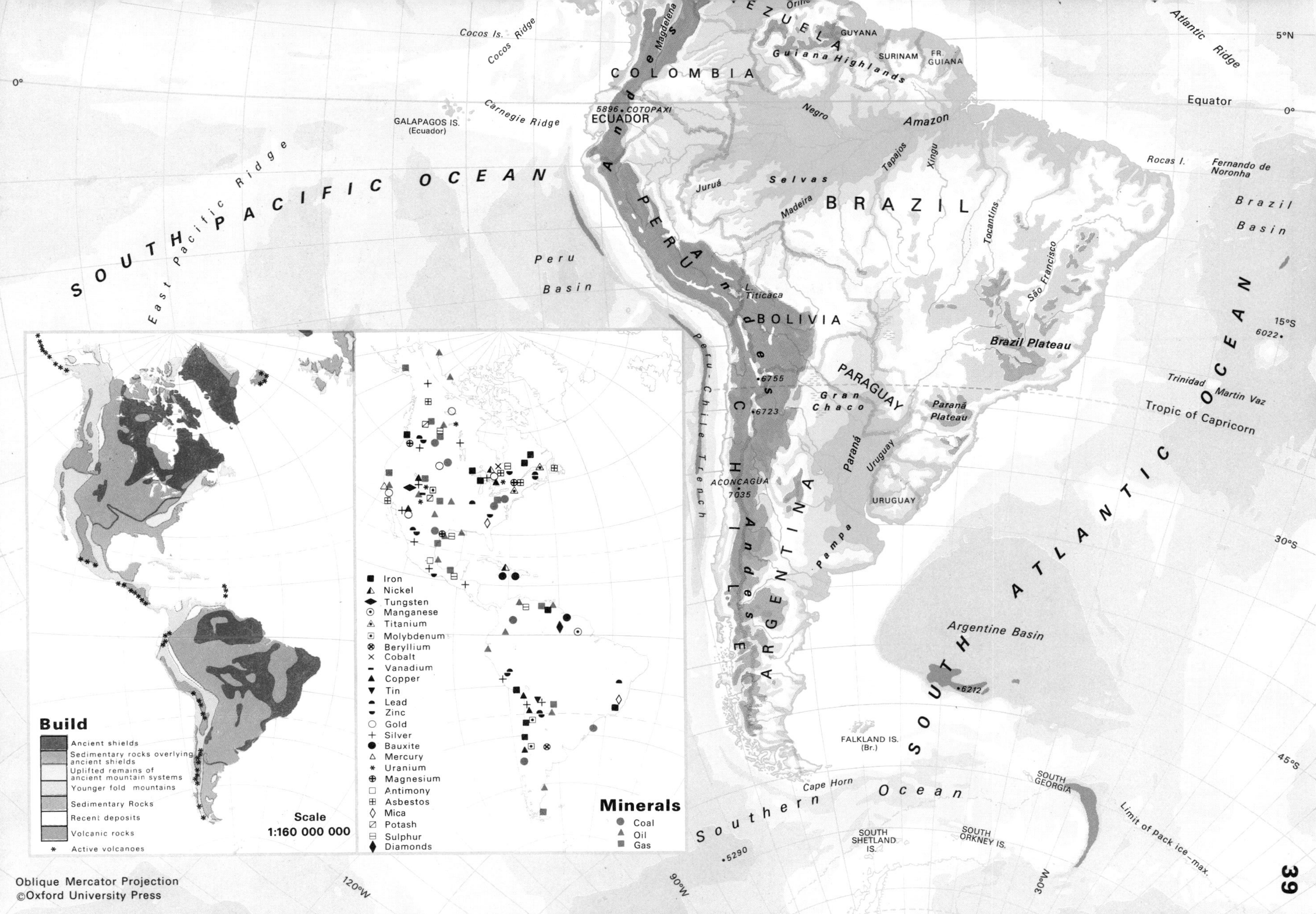

Oblique Mercator Projection

North and South America: Vegetation

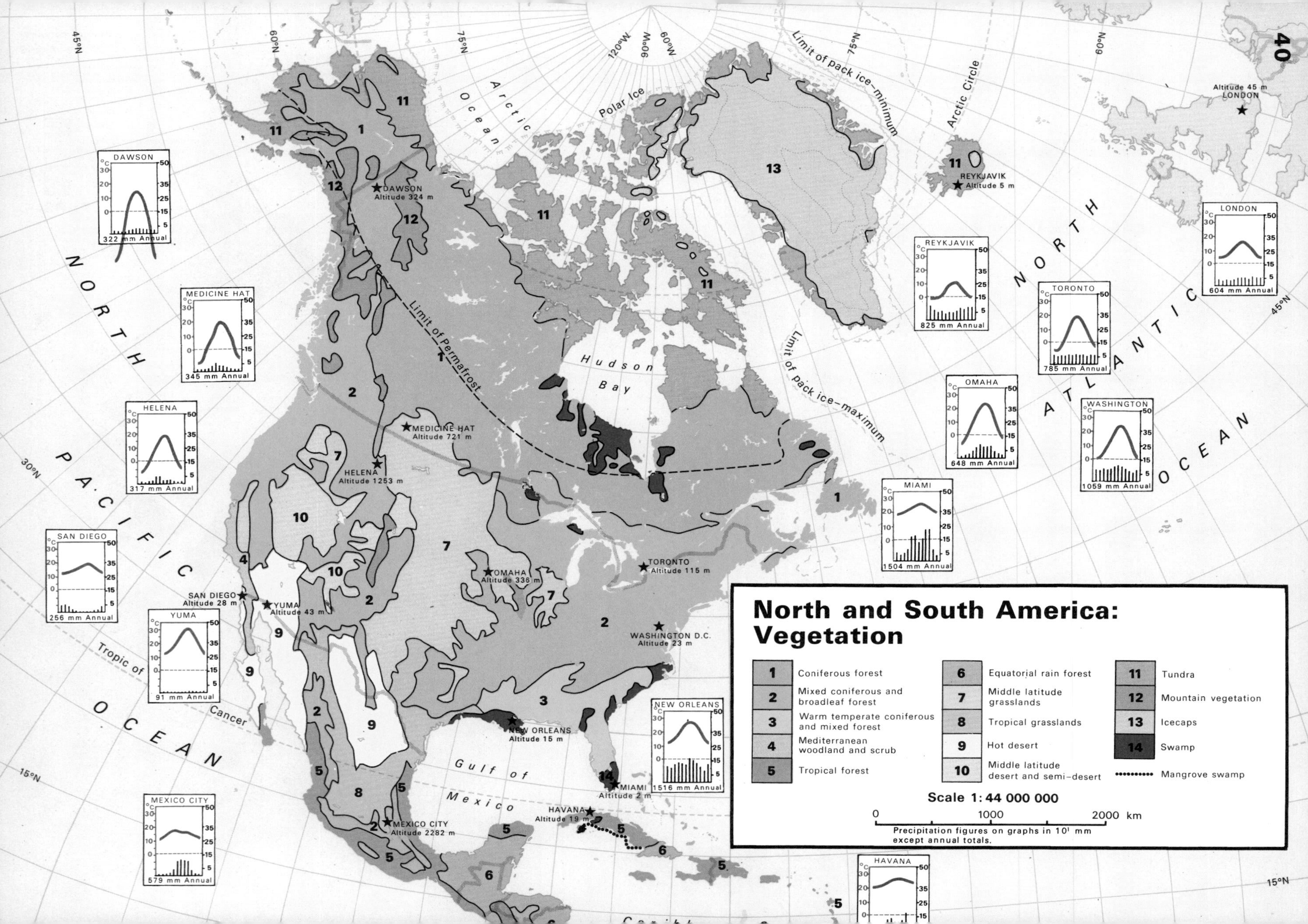

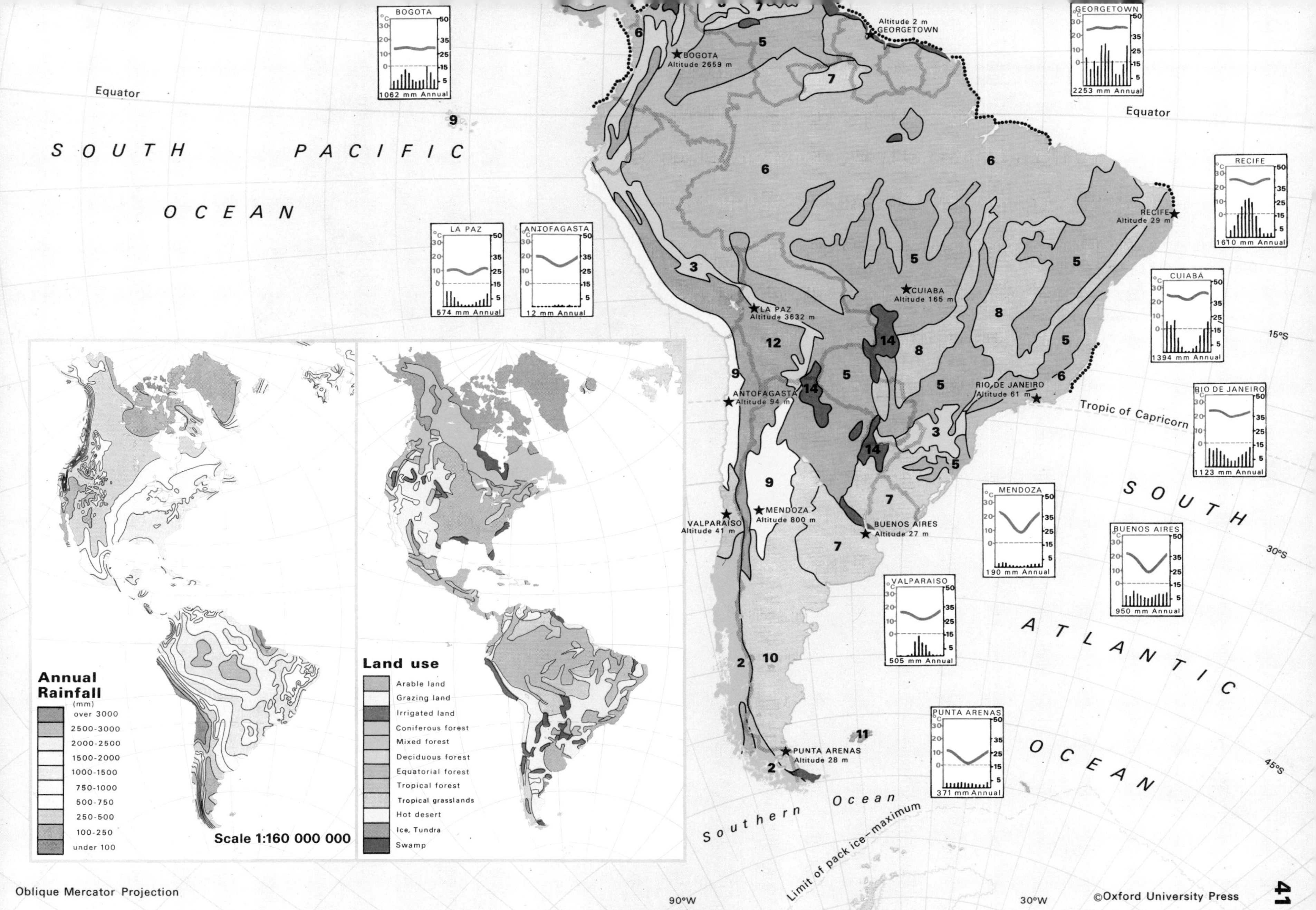
SOUTH PACIFIC OCEAN
SOUTH ATLANTIC OCEAN
Southern Ocean
Equator
Tropic of Capricorn
Limit of pack ice–maximum
15°S
30°S
45°S
90°W
30°W
BOGOTA Altitude 2659 m
GEORGETOWN Altitude 2 m
RECIFE Altitude 29 m
CUIABA Altitude 165 m
LA PAZ Altitude 3632 m
ANTOFAGASTA Altitude 94 m
RIO DE JANEIRO Altitude 61 m
MENDOZA Altitude 800 m
VALPARAISO Altitude 41 m
BUENOS AIRES Altitude 27 m
PUNTA ARENAS Altitude 28 m
BOGOTA 1062 mm Annual
GEORGETOWN 2253 mm Annual
RECIFE 1610 mm Annual
CUIABA 1394 mm Annual
LA PAZ 574 mm Annual
ANTOFAGASTA 12 mm Annual
RIO DE JANEIRO 1123 mm Annual
MENDOZA 190 mm Annual
BUENOS AIRES 950 mm Annual
VALPARAISO 505 mm Annual
PUNTA ARENAS 371 mm Annual
Annual Rainfall (mm)
over 3000
2500-3000
2000-2500
1500-2000
1000-1500
750-1000
500-750
250-500
100-250
under 100
Land use
Arable land
Grazing land
Irrigated land
Coniferous forest
Mixed forest
Deciduous forest
Equatorial forest
Tropical forest
Tropical grasslands
Hot desert
Ice, Tundra
Swamp
Scale 1:160 000 000
Oblique Mercator Projection

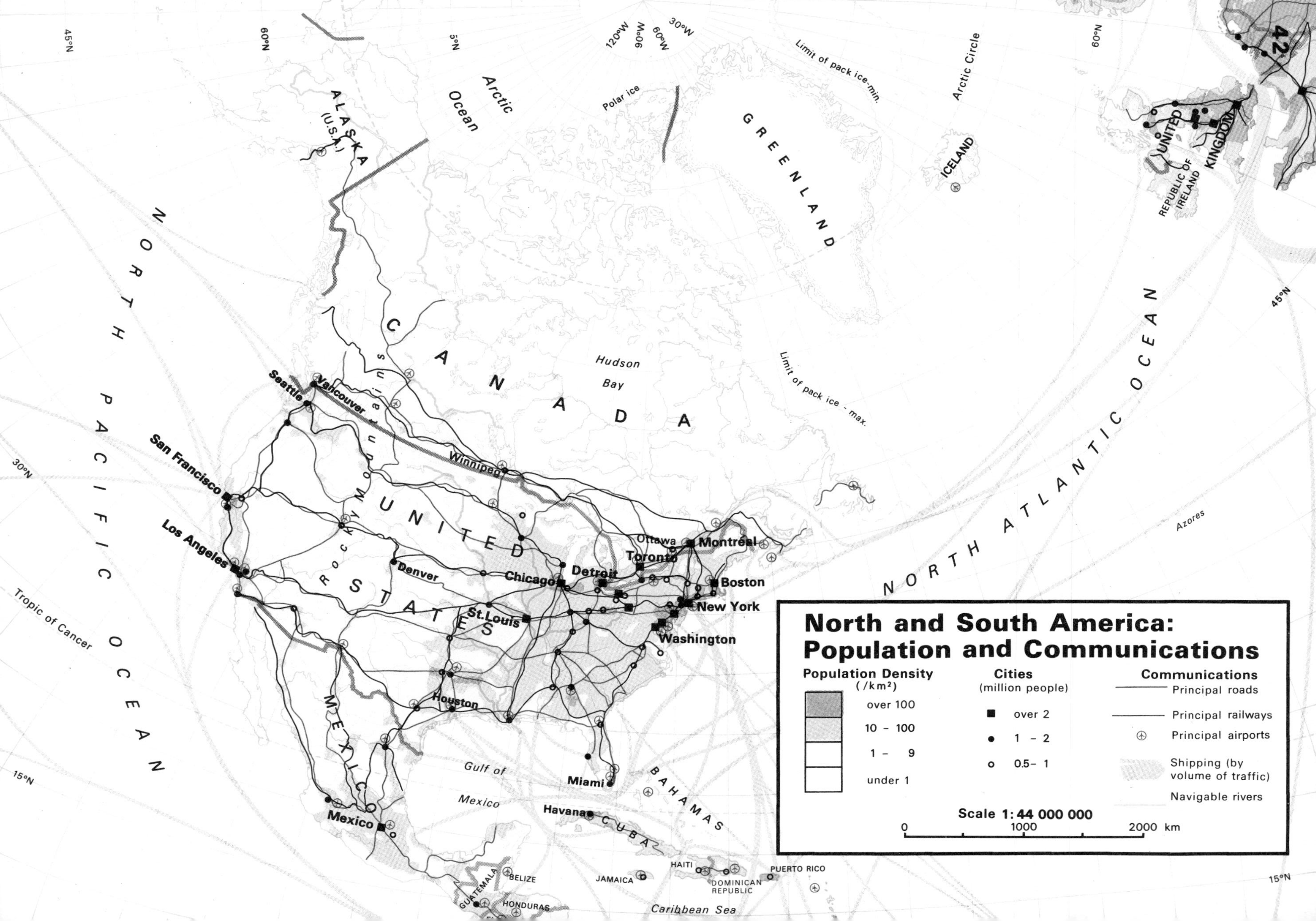

North and South America:
Population and Communications
Population Density (/km²)
over 100
10 - 100
1 - 9
under 1
Cities (million people)
over 2
1 - 2
0.5 - 1
Communications
Principal roads
Principal railways
Principal airports
Shipping (by volume of traffic)
Navigable rivers
Scale 1: 44 000 000
0
1000
2000 km
42
ALASKA (U.S.A.)
Arctic Ocean
Polar ice
GREENLAND
Limit of pack ice-min.
Arctic Circle
ICELAND
UNITED KINGDOM
REPUBLIC OF IRELAND
CANADA
Hudson Bay
Limit of pack ice - max.
NORTH ATLANTIC OCEAN
Azores
NORTH PACIFIC OCEAN
Tropic of Cancer
Rocky Mountains
UNITED STATES
MEXICO
Seattle
Vancouver
Winnipeg
San Francisco
Los Angeles
Denver
Chicago
Detroit
St.Louis
Houston
Ottawa
Toronto
Montreal
Boston
New York
Washington
Miami
Havana
Mexico
Gulf of Mexico
BAHAMAS
CUBA
JAMAICA
HAITI
DOMINICAN REPUBLIC
PUERTO RICO
Caribbean Sea
BELIZE
GUATEMALA
HONDURAS
45°N
60°N
75°N
30°N
15°N
120°W
90°W
60°W
30°W

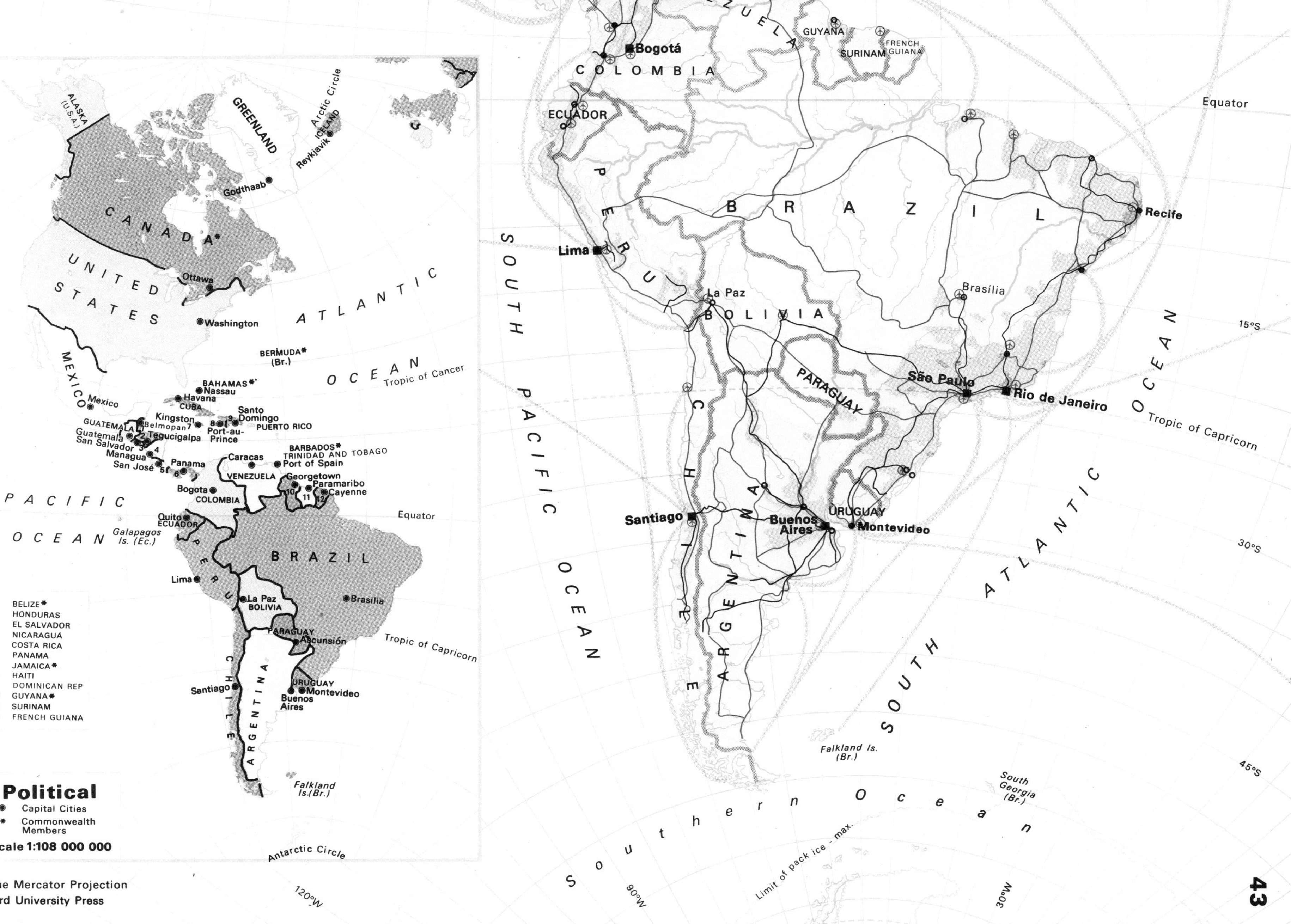
Political
Capital Cities
* Commonwealth Members
Scale 1:108 000 000
1 BELIZE*
2 HONDURAS
3 EL SALVADOR
4 NICARAGUA
5 COSTA RICA
6 PANAMA
7 JAMAICA*
8 HAITI
9 DOMINICAN REP
10 GUYANA*
11 SURINAM
12 FRENCH GUIANA
ALASKA (U.S.A.)
GREENLAND
ICELAND
Reykjavik
Arctic Circle
Godthaab
CANADA*
Ottawa
UNITED STATES
Washington
ATLANTIC OCEAN
BERMUDA* (Br.)
Tropic of Cancer
MEXICO
Mexico
BAHAMAS*
Nassau
Havana
CUBA
Kingston
Santo Domingo
Port-au-Prince
PUERTO RICO
GUATEMALA
Belmopan
Guatemala
Tegucigalpa
San Salvador
Managua
San José
Panama
BARBADOS*
TRINIDAD AND TOBAGO
Port of Spain
Caracas
VENEZUELA
Georgetown
Paramaribo
Cayenne
Bogota
COLOMBIA
PACIFIC OCEAN
Quito
ECUADOR
Galapagos Is. (Ec.)
Equator
BRAZIL
PERU
Lima
La Paz
BOLIVIA
Brasilia
PARAGUAY
Asuncíon
Tropic of Capricorn
CHILE
Santiago
ARGENTINA
URUGUAY
Montevideo
Buenos Aires
Falkland Is.(Br.)
Antarctic Circle
120°W
Oblique Mercator Projection
© Oxford University Press
COLOMBIA
Bogotá
GUYANA
SURINAM
FRENCH GUIANA
ECUADOR
Equator
BRAZIL
Recife
PERU
Lima
La Paz
BOLIVIA
Brasilia
15°S
PARAGUAY
São Paulo
Rio de Janeiro
Tropic of Capricorn
ATLANTIC OCEAN
SOUTH PACIFIC OCEAN
CHILE
Santiago
ARGENTINA
Buenos Aires
URUGUAY
Montevideo
30°S
SOUTH ATLANTIC
Falkland Is. (Br.)
45°S
South Georgia (Br.)
Southern Ocean
90°W
Limit of pack ice - max.
30°W

U.S.A. and Central America
Scale 1:19 000 000
0 200 400 600 km
Boundaries International (in sea) (disputed)
Internal
Highways
Railways
Airports International Domestic
Canals
Seasonal rivers, lakes
Marshes
Salt pans
Ice cap
Sand desert limits
National Parks, etc.
Zenithal Equidistant Projection
The United States
Alabama 23, Arizona 44, Arkansas 30, California 48, Colorado 40, Connecticut 6, Delaware 10,
Florida 17, Georgia 16, Idaho 42, Illinois 28, Indiana 20, Iowa 27, Kansas 35, Kentucky 21,
Louisiana 31, Maine 1, Maryland 11, Massachusetts 4, Michigan 18, Minnesota 26,
Mississippi 24, Missouri 29, Montana 38, Nebraska 34, Nevada 47, New Hampshire 2,
New Jersey 8, New Mexico 41, New York 7, North Carolina 14, North Dakota 32,
Ohio 19, Oklahoma 36, Oregon 46, Pennsylvania 9, Rhode Island 5, South Carolina 15,
South Dakota 33, Tenessee 22, Texas 37, Utah 43, Vermont 3, Virginia 13,
Washington 45, West Virginia 12, Wisconsin 25, Wyoming 39,
Alaska became a state on January 3,1959 and Hawaii on August 21,1959
UNITED STATES
CANADA
MEXICO
PACIFIC OCEAN
Gulf of Mexico
Bay of Campeche
Gulf of California
Gulf of Tehuantepec
Isthmus of Tehuantepec
LOWER CALIFORNIA
GUATEMALA
EL SALVADOR
Rocky Mountains
Cascade Ra.
Coast Ra.
Sierra Nevada
Wasatch Ra.
Bitterroot Range
Blue Mts.
Salmon River Mts.
Colorado Plateau
Llano Estacado
Edwards Plateau
Ozark Plateau
Mexican Plateau
Sierra Madre Occidental
Western Sierra Madre
Eastern Sierra Madre
Southern Sierra Madre
Prairies
Middle West
Tropic of Cancer
40°N
35°N
30°N
25°N
115°W
110°W
105°W
100°W
95°W
90°W
Portland
Oregon City
Spokane
Grand Coulee Dam
Lethbridge
Regina
Winnipeg
Lake Winnipeg
L. Manitoba
Assiniboine
Havre
Missouri
Fort Peck Dam
Fort Peck Reservoir
Great Falls
Helena
Butte
Yellowstone
Powder
Bismarck
Fargo
Grand Forks
Duluth
Mesabi Range
Iron Mo
Thund
Red
Aberdeen
Pierre
The Badlands
Minneapolis
St. Paul
Mississippi
Sioux Falls
Madiso
Milwa
Chic
Cedar Rapids
Des Moines
Omaha
Lincoln
Platte
Peoria
Illinois
Springfield
St. Joseph
Kansas City
Topeka
St.
Wichita
Ozark
Springfield
Paduca
Tulsa
Oklahoma City
Fort Smith
Memphis
Little Rock
Arkansas
Mississippi
Shreveport
Jacks
Baton Rouge
Mob
New Orleans
Port
Galveston
Houston
San Antonio
Austin
Dallas
Fort Worth
Red
Canadian
Amarillo
Colorado
Pecos
Rio Grande
Corpus Christi
Laredo
Brownsville
Monterrey
Saltillo
Torreón
Chihuahua
Jiménez
Hidalgo del Parral
Durango
Fresnillo
Zacatecas
San Luis Potosí
León
Guadalajara
Lake Chapala
Santiago
Tampico
Tuxpan
Mexico City
Puebla
Orizaba
Veracruz
V. POPOCATEPETL 5452
ORIZABA 5700
Balsas
Inter-American Highway
Acapulco
Manzanillo
Tomatlán
Banderas Bay
Mazatlán
Topolobampo
La Paz
Guaymas
Hermosillo
Angel de la Guarda
Guadalupe (Mex.)
San Benito Islands
Mexicali
Yuma
Ajo
Gila
Tucson
Phoenix
Miami
Globe
Imperial Dam
San Diego
Los Angeles
Hollywood
Bakersfield
Las Vegas
L. Mead
Hoover Dam
Grand Canyon
Colorado
Fresno
MT. WHITNEY 4418
Oakland
San Francisco
Sacramento
Reno
Carson City
LASSEN PEAK 3131
MT. SHASTA 4316
Shasta Dam
Eureka
Cape Mendocino
Klamath Falls
Willamette
Bonneville Dam
MT. HOOD 3428
MT. RAINIER 4392
La Grande
Boise
Snake
Idaho Falls
Pocatello
Great Salt Lake
Ogden
Salt Lake City
Green River
Laramie
LARAMIE PEAK 3289
N. Platte
Cheyenne
LONGS PEAK 4345
Denver
PIKES PEAK 4301
Los Alamos
Santa Fe
Albuquerque
Carlsbad
El Paso
Mérida
Chichen Itzá
Uxmal
Progreso
Suchiate
Antigua
Guatemala
San Salvador
200m

85°W
Moosonee
80°W
75°W
Lac Mistassini
Sept Îles
Gaspé
Gaspé Peninsula
Gulf of St. Lawrence
Channel-Port aux Basques
Miquelon (Fr.)
Placentia Bay
C. Race
55°W
50°W
45°W
Magdalen Is.
Cabot Strait
Cape Breton I.
Sydney Mines
Sydney
PRINCE EDWARD I.
Kapuskasing
Gouin Res.
L. St. Jean
Tadoussac
Edmundston
L. Abitibi
S. Porcupine
Timmins
Kirkland Lake
Cobalt
Quebec
Charlottetown
Pictou
Canso
NOVA SCOTIA
Fredericton
Moncton
Saint John
Halifax
40°N
Sault Ste. Marie
Sudbury
Ottawa
Montreal
Trois Rivières
St. Lawrence
Thetford Mines
Bangor
Bay of Fundy
Cape Sable
200 m
Georgian Bay
Midland
Ottawa
Kingston
L. Champlain
Burlington
MT. WASHINGTON
Portland
Lake Huron
Toronto
L. Ontario
Rochester
Utica
Albany
Manchester
Boston
Grand Rapids
Flint
Hamilton
Niagara Falls
Buffalo
Syracuse
Hartford
Providence
Cape Cod
Fall River
Detroit
Windsor
Lake Erie
Scranton
New Haven
Long Island
Toledo
Cleveland
New York
Fort Wayne
Pittsburgh
Jersey City
Trenton
Philadelphia
Indianapolis
Columbus
Wilmington
Baltimore
Washington
Delaware Bay
Cincinnati
Ohio
Louisville
Lexington
Charleston
Richmond
James
Newport News
Chesapeake Bay
Norfolk
Nashville
Bristol
Knoxville
MT. MITCHELL 2036
Winston-Salem
Raleigh
Cape Hatteras
Chattanooga
Charlotte
Columbia
Wilmington
Gadsden
Atlanta
Augusta
Birmingham
Macon
Charleston
Columbus
Montgomery
Savannah
Jacksonville
Daytona Beach
Cape Canaveral
Melbourne
Tampa
Lake Okeechobee
Palm Beach
Everglades
Miami
Grand Bahama
Great Abaco
Nassau
Eleuthera
Key West
Florida Keys
Andros
Straits of Florida
Cat I.
THE BAHAMAS
San Salvador (Watling)
Long. I.
Tropic of Cancer
BERMUDA
ATLANTIC OCEAN
Metres
5000
3000
2000
1000
500
300
200
100
Sea level
Land depression
Spot heights in metres
35°N
Gaillard Cut (Culebra)
Maximum elevation 95m
Minimum depth 12 m
ATLANTIC
PACIFIC
Sea level
Sea level
0 15 30 45 60 75 km
Gatun Locks 3 pairs
Length 305 m
Width 34 m
Total Lift 26 m
Pedro Miguel Locks 1 pair
Length 305 m
Width 34 m
Total Lift 9.3 m
Miraflores Locks 2pairs
Length 305 m
Width 34 m
Total Lift 16.6 m
Panama Canal
1 cm to 15 km approx.
ATLANTIC OCEAN
80°W
Colón
Gatun Locks
Gatun Lake
CANAL ZONE
PANAMÁ
Pedro Miguel Locks
Miraflores Locks
Balboa
Panama
9°N
PACIFIC OCEAN
PANAMA: The canal, opened in 1914, is 80 km long, including approaches (actual canal 64 km). Minimum depth 12 m, minimum width 152 m (Gaillard Cut). Time of passage 8 hours. In 1974 14 033 vessels used the canal, carrying 150 000 000 t of cargo. In 1974 the United States relinquished its claim to sovereignty and agreed to negotiate.
Havana
Matanzas
Santa Clara
Pinar del Rio
Cienfuegos
Camagüey
CUBA
Yucatan Channel
Acklins I.
Caicos Islands (Br.)
Turks Is. (Br.)
Great Inagua
WEST INDIES
Guantánamo
Windward Passage
Santiago de Cuba
Cap-Haïtien
HAITI
Santiago
DOMINICAN REPUBLIC
La Romana
Mona Passage
San Juan
Ponce
PUERTO RICO
Virgin Is.
Anegada (Br.)
St. Thomas (U.S.)
St. Croix (U.S.)
Sombrero
Sombrero Passage
Anguilla
St. Martin (Fr. & Neth.)
St. Christophers (St. Kitts)
Nevis
Barbuda
Antigua
Montserrat
Guadeloupe (Fr.)
Basse-Terre
Marie-Galante (Fr.)
Dominica
Les Saintes
Leeward Islands
Fort de France
Martinique (Fr.)
St. Lucia
St. Vincent
BARBADOS
Bridgetown
Grenadines
Grenada
Windward Islands
Lesser Antilles
15°N
Cayman Is.
Montego Bay
JAMAICA
Kingston
Spanish Town
Port-au-Prince
Les Cayes
Hispaniola
Santo Domingo
Greater Antilles
Caribbean Sea
Trujillo
C. Gracias a Dios
Segovia
Tegucigalpa
NICARAGUA
Managua
200 m
Lake Nicaragua
COSTA RICA
San José
Puerto Limón
Panama Canal
Portobello
Colón
Panamá
PANAMA
Aruba (Neth.)
Curaçao (Neth.)
Bonaire (Neth.)
Pt. de Gallinas
Gulf of Venezuela
Puerto Cabello
Margarita Is.
Tobago
Port of Spain
TRINIDAD & TOBAGO
San Fernando
10°N
Sta. Marta
Barranquilla
Cartagena
Magdalena
Maracaibo
Cabimas
Lake of Maracaibo
Valencia
Maracay
La Guaira
Caracas
Cumaná
Barcelona
Maturín
Tucupita
Barquisimeto
Calabozo
Ciudad Bolívar
GUYANA
Georgetown
Mackenzie
G. of Darien
COLOMBIA
Cucuta
Cord. de Mérida
VENEZUELA
Orinoco
85°W
70°W
65°W
60°W

Eastern
United States
Scale 1:8 000 000
0 100 200 km
Boundaries International (in sea) (disputed) Internal
Roads Limited access Other highways Tracks
Railways
Airports International Domestic
Canals Seasonal rivers, lakes
Marshes Salt Pan Ice cap
Sand desert limits National Parks etc.
Conical Orthomorphic Projection
105°W
100°W
95°W
40°N
35°N
30°N
NEBRASKA
IOWA
COLORADO
KANSAS
MISSOURI
OKLAHOMA
ARKANSAS
NEW MEXICO
TEXAS
LOUISIANA
ROCKY MOUNTAINS
Llano Estacado
Edwards Plateau
Ozark Plateau
Gulf of
200 m
Denver
Cheyenne
Fort Collins
Greeley
Boulder
Colorado Springs
Pueblo
La Junta
Trinidad
Santa Fe
Las Vegas
Los Alamos
Amarillo
Lubbock
Roswell
Carlsbad
Hobbs
Midland
Odessa
Big Spring
Abilene
San Angelo
Fort Worth
Dallas
Waco
Temple
Austin
San Antonio
Houston
Beaumont
Port Arthur
Galveston
Corpus Christi
Laredo
Nuevo Laredo
McAllen
Harlingen
Brownsville
Matamoros
Reynosa
Piedras Negras
Del Rio
Ciudad Acuña
Victoria
Wichita Falls
Lawton
Oklahoma City
Tulsa
Muskogee
Enid
Wichita
Hutchinson
Salina
Topeka
Kansas City
St. Joseph
Lawrence
Joplin
Springfield
Fort Smith
Fayetteville
Little Rock
N. Little Rock
Hot Springs
Pine Bluff
Texarkana
Shreveport
Monroe
Alexandria
Lake Charles
Lafayette
Baton Rouge
Omaha
Council Bluffs
Lincoln
Grand Island
Kearney
North Platte
Sioux City
Des Moines
Ames
Fort Dodge
Waterloo
Cedar Rapids
Dubuque
Mason City
Columbia
Jefferson City
St. Louis
Garden City
Dodge City
Liberal
Tucumcari
Santa Rosa
MT. ELBERT 4399
MT. LIVERMORE 2555
SUE PEAKS 1785
EMORY PEAK 2388
WHITE SANDS N.P.
CARLSBAD CAVERNS N.P.
GUADALUPE MTS N.P.
ROCKY MTNS. N.P.
Rio Grande
Arkansas
Red
Canadian
Colorado
Brazos
Pecos
Missouri
Platte
Mississippi
Matagorda Bay
Padre Island
Laguna Madre

Milwaukee
Grand Rapids
Flint
Port Huron
Sarnia
London
Buffalo
NEW YORK
Waukesha
Racine
Holland
Kenosha
Janesville
Lansing
Battle Creek
Detroit
Pontiac
Chatham
Port Stanley
Dunkirk
Jamestown
Hornell
Olean
Elmira
Chemung
Towanda
Poughkeepsie
Catskill Mts.
Hudson
Newburgh
New Haven
Bridgeport
75°W
Lake Erie
(Surface height 174m above m.s.l.)
Kalamazoo
Jackson
Ann Arbor
Windsor
Pelee I.
Erie
Warren
Honesdale
Scranton
Middletown
Rockford
Benton Harbor
St. Joseph
Adrian
Monroe
Ashtabula
Williamsport
Wilkes-Barre
Yonkers
De Kalb
Chicago
Michigan City
Niles
Elkhart
Toledo
Lorain
Cleveland
Sharon
Allegheny
St. Marys
PENNSYLVANIA
Hazelton
Bethlehem
Paterson
Newark
Long I.
New York
Joliet
Gary
South Bend
Fort Wayne
Maumee
Sandusky
Parma
Warren
Youngstown
New Castle
Butler
Sunbury
State College
Allentown
Jersey City
Princeton
Trenton
40°N
Ottawa
Kankakee
Huntington
Findlay
Tiffin
Mansfield
Akron
Canton
East Liverpool
Weirton
Pittsburgh
Altoona
Reading
Pottstown
Lancaster
NEW JERSEY
Philadelphia
La Fayette
Logansport
Kokomo
Marion
Lima
Marion
OHIO
Steubenville
Johnstown
Harrisburg
York
Chester
Wilmington
Bloomington
INDIANA
Muncie
Anderson
Richmond
Columbus
Newark
Wheeling
Uniontown
Morgantown
Bedford
Chambersburg
Gettysburg
Cumberland
Hagerstown
Susquehanna
Vineland
Atlantic City
Danville
Champaign
Frankfort
Crawfordsville
Springfield
Zanesville
Lancaster
Moundsville
Fairmont
Frostburg
Baltimore
DELAWARE
Dover
Delaware Bay
Cape May
Decatur
Indianapolis
Connersville
Dayton
Middletown
Hamilton
Chillicothe
Parkersburg
Winchester
Wheaton
Washington D.C.
Annapolis
Cambridge
Cape Henlopen
Charleston
Terre Haute
Mattoon
Clarksburg
Weston
Elkins
Seaford
Salisbury
Kaskaskia
Bloomington
Bedford
Columbus
Cincinnati
Little Kanawha
MARYLAND
Pocomoke City
Portsmouth
Madison
WEST
Harrisonburg
Fredericksburg
Chesapeake Bay
Vincennes
Washington
Charleston
Richwood
Staunton
Waynesboro
Charlottesville
Centralia
Mount Vernon
Wabash
Louisville
Frankfort
Lexington
Licking
Ashland
Huntington
VIRGINIA
Richmond
Cape Charles
Evansville
Owensboro
Winchester
Paintsville
Logan
Beckley
Williamson
Covington
James
Lynchburg
Hopewell
Hampton
Cape Henry
Carbondale
Henderson
Elizabethtown
Richmond
Pikeville
Bluefield
Salem
Roanoke
Petersburg
Newport News
Portsmouth
Norfolk
KENTUCKY
Richlands
Pulaski
South Boston
Kerr Res.
Emporia
Suffolk
Madisonville
Lake Cumberland
Somerset
Bowling Green
Glasgow
Norton
MT. ROGERS 1743
Galax
Martinsville
Danville
Rapids
Roanoke
Elizabeth City
Albemarle Sound
Paducah
Mayfield
Hopkinsville
Middlesboro
CUMBERLAND GAP
Kingsport
Bristol
Elizabethton
Reidsville
Winston-Salem
Greensboro
Burlington
Henderson
Rocky Mount
Clarksville
Livingston
Lebanon
Plateau
Johnson City
Morristown
Durham
Washington
Kentucky Lake
Greenfield
Nashville
Oak Ridge
Greenville
Statesville
High Point
Raleigh
Wilson
Pamlico Sound
Cape Hatteras
35°N
TENNESSEE
Maryville
Knoxville
Kannapolis
NORTH CAROLINA
Neuse
Jackson
Murfreesboro
CLINGMANS DOME
GT.SMOKY MTNS. 2024 N.P.
Asheville
Concord
Sanford
Kinston
New Bern
Raleigh Bay
Columbia
Shelbyville
Athens
Gastonia
Charlotte
Fayetteville
Morehead City
Cape Lookout
Tennessee
Savannah
Tullahoma
Cumberland
Cleveland
Gaffney
Rock Hill
Clinton
Cape Fear
Florence
Wheeler Lake
Huntsville
Chattanooga
1457
Spartanburg
Greenville
Cheraw
Lumberton
Onslow Bay
Corinth
Sheffield
Guntersville Lake
Dalton
BRASSTOWN BALD
Toccoa
Easley
Anderson
SOUTH CAROLINA
Wilmington
Decatur
Rome
Lake Sidney Lanier
Greenwood
Florence
Conway
Cape Fear
Tupelo
Haleyville
Cullman
Gainesville
Columbia
Pee Dee
Long Bay
Houston
Coosa
Gadsden
Athens
Clark Hill Res.
Sumter
Kingstree
Jasper
Atlanta
Aiken
Marion
Orangeburg
Georgetown
Cape Romain
Tombigbee
Fayette
Birmingham
Bessemer
Anniston
CHEAHA MT.
Talladega
Newnan
Thomson
Augusta
Columbus
Tuscaloosa
Sylacauga
GEORGIA
Griffin
Milledgeville
Charleston
ALABAMA
Alexander City
La Grange
Macon
Oconee
Swainsboro
Savannah
Beaufort
St. Helena Sound
Opelika
Auburn
Phenix City
Columbus
Dublin
Statesboro
Meridian
Selma
Montgomery
Americus
Cordele
McRae
Ocmulgee
Altamaha
Savannah
Sea Islands
Thomasville
Alabama
Troy
Greenville
Eufaula
Chattahoochee
Albany
Jesup
Waycross
200 m
Laurel
Ellisville
Monroeville
Enterprise
Conecuh
Flint
Moultrie
Homerville
Brunswick
Hattiesburg
Brewton
Andalusia
Dothan
Bainbridge
Valdosta
30°N
Pascagoula
Prichard
Crestview
Choctawhatchee
Thomasville
Madison
Jacksonville
Jacksonville Beach
Mobile
Niceville
Chattahoochee
Tallahassee
Lake City
St. Augustine
Biloxi
Mississippi Sd.
Pascagoula
Pensacola
Panama City
Apalachicola
Apalachee Bay
FLORIDA
Suwannee
Gainesville
St. Johns
Palatka
Port St Joe
Cape San Blas
Breton Sound
Port Sulphur
Cape St. George
Ocala
Oklawaha
Daytona Beach
Waccasassa Bay
Sanford
Orlando
Cape Canaveral
Brooksville
Cocoa
Melbourne
Lakeland
Tampa
Winter Haven
Clearwater
St.Petersburg
Barlow
Fort Pierce
Kissimmee
Tampa Bay
Bradenton
Sarasota
MYAKKA R.N.P.
Lake Okeechobee
Belle Glade
West Palm Beach
Little Bahama Bank
Charlotte Harbour
Fort Myers
Delray Beach
Grand Bahama
Great Abaco Island
Pine Island Sound
Everglades
Fort Lauderdale
Northwest Providence Channel
Northeast Providence Channel
Mexico
Hollywood
Miami Beach
THE BAHAMAS
Cape Romano
Ten Thousand Islands
Miami
Coral Gables
Bimini Islands
Berry Is.
Eleuthera
Homestead
Key Largo
25°N
EVERGLADES NAT. PARK
Cape Sable
Nassau
New Providence
Andros
Florida Bay
Florida Keys
Str. of Florida
Pine Is.
Key West
85°W
80°W
ATLANTIC OCEAN
Metres
5000
3000
2000
1000
500
300
200
100
Sea level
Land depression
Spot heights in metres

125°W
120°W
115°W
110°W
45°N
40°N
35°N
Cape Flattery
Bellingham
NORTH CASCADES N.P.
Victoria
Anacortes
Mount Vernon
Port Angeles
OLYMPIC NAT. PARK
Seattle
Bremerton
Everett
WASHINGTON
Castlegar
Trail
Okanogan
Franklin D. Roosevelt Lake
Colville
Columbia
Grand Coulee
Spokane
Sandpoint
Pend Oreille Lake
Coeur d'Alene
Wenatchee
Grays Harbor
Hoquiam
Aberdeen
Tacoma
Olympia
Willapa Bay
Raymond
MT. RAINIER 4392
Ellensburg
Centralia
Moses Lake
Yakima
Longview
Kelso
Astoria
Saint Helens
Richland
Prosser
Pasco
Kennewick
Walla Walla
Colfax
Pullman
Moscow
Elk River
Lewiston
Snake
Vancouver
Columbia
Portland
Oregon City
The Dalles
3428 MT. HOOD
Silverton
Salem
Willamette
Pendleton
Grande Ronde
La Grande
Blue Mountains
John Day
3142
Baker
Corvallis
Albany
Lebanon
Toledo
3199
Eugene
Springfield
Bend
OREGON
2759 STRAWBERRY MT.
Cascade Range
North Bend
Roseburg
Cape Blanco
Harney Basin
Burns
Malheur
Malheur L.
Owyhee Res.
CRATER LAKE NATIONAL PARK
Grants Pass
Medford
Ashland
Upper Klamath L.
Klamath Falls
Crescent City
Klamath
Yreka
Goose L.
Weed
MT. SHASTA 4316
Pit
Alturas
Arcata
Eureka
Weaverville
Redding
Shasta L.
LASSEN PEAK 3190
Westwood
Red Bluff
Sacramento
Chico
Willows
Ukiah
Clear L.
Cloverdale
Healdsburg
Woodland
Yuba City
Nevada City
Roseville
Santa Rosa
Napa
Vallejo
Point Reyes
Sacramento
Berkeley
Lodi
San Francisco
Oakland
Stockton
Santa Clara
San Jose
Oakdale
Modesto
Turlock
MT. RITTER 4009
YOSEMITE N.P.
Merced
Santa Cruz
Monterey Bay
Watsonville
Gilroy
Pacific Grove
Salinas
Monterey
San Joaquin
Madera
Clovis
Fresno
Hanford
Visalia
Tulare
4418 MT. WHITNEY
KINGS CANYON N.P.
SEQUOIA N.P.
Sierra Nevada
CALIFORNIA
Estero Bay
San Luis Obispo
San Luis Obispo Bay
Delano
Kern
Bakersfield
Santa Maria
Point Arguello
Point Conception
Santa Barbara
Santa Barbara Channel
San Miguel
Santa Rosa
Santa Cruz
Santa Barbara Islands
Santa Barbara
San Nicolas
San Clemente
Santa Paula
Oxnard
Hollywood
Pasadena
Los Angeles
Long Beach
Santa Ana
Santa Catalina
Gulf of Santa Catalina
Oceanside
Escondido
San Diego
Tijuana
Ensenada
Guadalupe
Sierra de Juarez
PACIFIC OCEAN
200 m
Mojave
Mojave Desert
Barstow
Ludlow
San Bernardino
Riverside
Aqueduct
JOSHUA TREE N.M.
Blythe
ANZA-BORREGO DESERT S.P.
Calipatria
Brawley
El Centro
Calexico
Mexicali
Yuma
San Luis
Needles
Trona
Owens L.
Death Valley
-86
DEATH VALLEY NATIONAL MONUMENT
3620
LAKE MEAD NAT. RECREATION AREA
Las Vegas
Henderson
Boulder City
Lake Mead
Virgin
Caliente
MT. GRANT 3445
Hawthorne
NEVADA
Carson Sink
Austin
Eureka
Ely
Carson City
Lake Tahoe
Reno
Sparks
Pyramid Lake
Winnemucca L.
Humboldt
Winnemucca
Battle Mountain
Palisade
Elko
Wells
Wendover
Lucin
Great Salt Lake Desert
Great Salt Lake
Tooele
Yakima
Lethbridge
Cypress Hills
WATERTON LAKES N.P.
Yahk
Eureka
GLACIER INTERNATIONAL PEACE PARK
Cut Bank
Shelby
Libby
Whitefish
Kalispell
Flathead Lake
Hungry Horse Res.
Conrad
Havre
Milk
Malta
Glasgow
Great Falls
Winifred
Fort Peck Reservoir
3069
Missoula
Bitterroot Range
Missouri
Helena
MONTANA
Lewistown
Roundup
Deer Lodge
Anaconda
Butte
Grangeville
Salmon
Warren
Salmon River Mountains
Salmon River
3139
Twin Bridges
Bozeman
Livingston
Billings
Laurel
Yellowstone
Forsyth
Hardin
Bighorn
Dillon
3232
3860
ROCKY
Absaroka Range
YELLOWSTONE NATIONAL PARK
Yellowstone Lake
Powell
Cody
Bighorn Mountains
Weiser
Payette
IDAHO
3917
Caldwell
Nampa
Boise
Arrowrock Res.
CRATERS OF THE MOON N.M.
Idaho Falls
Rexburg
Ashton
GRAND TETON N.P.
Worland
Thermopolis
Wind
Wind River Range
WYOMING
Mountain Home
Big Wood
Blackfoot
American Falls Res.
Pocatello
Alameda
Lander
Casper
IRON MTN. 2386
Owyhee
Twin Falls
Burley
Bear Lake
Logan
Brigham
2156
Ogden
Pathfinder Res.
Seminoe Res.
Rock Springs
Green River
Rawlins
Evanston
Flaming Gorge Res.
Salt Lake City
Uinta Mts.
Little Snake
Vernal
3502
Orem
Provo
Utah Lake
Duchesne
Yampa
Price
Green
Colorado
UTAH
MT. ELBERT
Grand Junction
Delta
Gunnison
Montrose
Richfield
ARCHES NAT. MON.
3989 MT. PEALE
3710 DELANO PEAK
Dolores
CAPITOL REEF N.M.
CANYONLANDS N.P.
Cedar City
BRYCE CANYON N.P.
Lake Powell
San Juan
Silverton
San Juan Mountains
St. George
LION N.P.
MESA VERDE N.P.
Durango
Farmington
Colorado Plateau
GRAND CANYON NATIONAL PARK
Grand Canyon
CANYON DE CHELLY NAT. MON.
Kingman
Gallup
Flagstaff
Winslow
Mogollon Plateau
Little Colorado
PETRIFIED FOREST N.P.
Zuni
Albuquerque
San Jose
Belen
Prescott
Verde
ARIZONA
NEW
Socorro
Phoenix
Glendale
Mesa
Miami
Globe
Gila
Gila Bend
Florence
Hayden
San Pedro
San Francisco
Safford
Truth or Consequences
Caballo Res.
Silver City
WHITE SANDS N.
Tucson
Ajo
ORGAN PIPE CACTUS N.P.
Sonoyta
Puerto Penasco
Bisbee
Deming
El Paso
Ciudad Juarez
Metres
5000
3000
2000
1000
500
300
200
100
Sea level
Land depression
Spot heights in metres
Conical Orthomorphic Projection

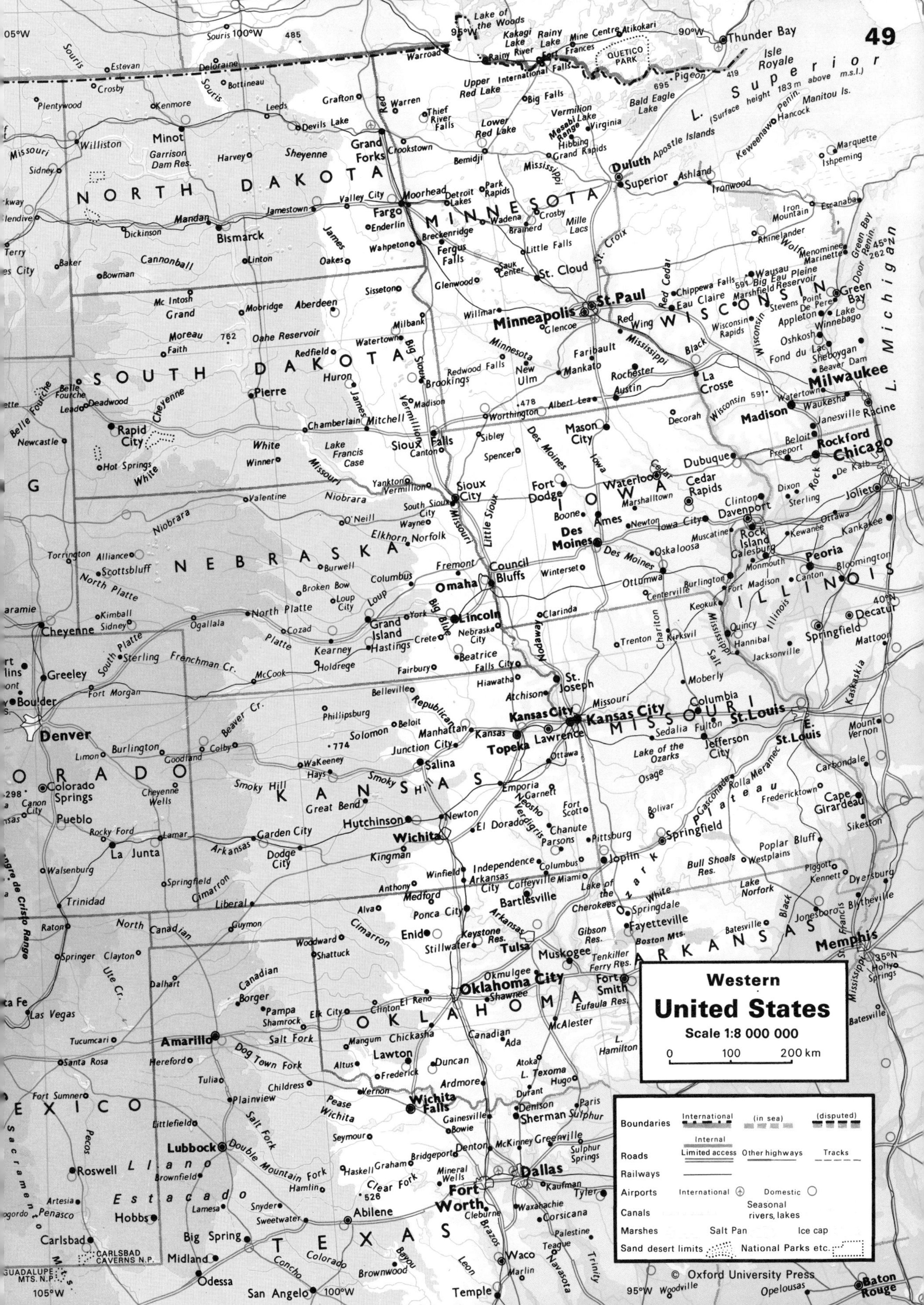
Western
United States
Scale 1:8 000 000
0
100
200 km
Boundaries
International
(in sea)
(disputed)
Internal
Roads
Limited access
Other highways
Tracks
Railways
Airports
International
Domestic
Canals
Seasonal rivers, lakes
Marshes
Salt Pan
Ice cap
Sand desert limits
National Parks etc.
© Oxford University Press
NORTH DAKOTA
SOUTH DAKOTA
NEBRASKA
KANSAS
OKLAHOMA
TEXAS
MINNESOTA
IOWA
MISSOURI
ILLINOIS
WISCONSIN
ARKANSAS
L. Superior
(Surface height 183 m above m.s.l.)
L. Michigan
Lake of the Woods
Thunder Bay
Isle Royale
QUETICO PARK
Kakagi Lake
Rainy Lake
Rainy River
Fort Frances
International Falls
Mine Centre
Atikokari
Warroad
Souris
100°W
485
95°W
90°W
105°W
Pigeon
419
695
Estevan
Deloraine
Bottineau
Crosby
Plentywood
Kenmore
Leeds
Devils Lake
Grafton
Warren
Thief River Falls
Upper Red Lake
Lower Red Lake
Big Falls
Vermilion Lake
Mesabi Range
Virginia
Hibbing
Grand Rapids
Bald Eagle Lake
Manitou Is.
Keweenaw Penin.
Hancock
Apostle Islands
Marquette
Ishpeming
Duluth
Superior
Ashland
Tronwood
Williston
Minot
Garrison Dam Res.
Harvey
Sheyenne
Grand Forks
Crookstown
Bemidji
Mississippi
Missouri
Sidney
Valley City
Moorhead
Detroit Lakes
Park Rapids
Jamestown
Fargo
Enderlin
Mandan
Bismarck
Dickinson
Glendive
Terry
Baker
Bowman
Cannonball
Linton
Oakes
James
Wahpeton
Breckenridge
Fergus Falls
Wadena
Crosby
Brainerd
Mille Lacs
Little Falls
St. Croix
Iron Mountain
Escanaba
Rhinelander
Wolf
Menominee
Marinette
Green Bay
Door Penin.
262
45°N
Sauk Center
St. Cloud
Red Cedar
Chippewa Falls
Wausau
591
Big Eau Pleine
Marshfield Reservoir
Eau Claire
Stevens Point
De Pere
Green Bay
Lake Winnebago
Appleton
Oshkosh
Fond du Lac
Sheboygan
Beaver Dam
Milwaukee
Glenwood
Sisseton
Mc Intosh
Grand
Mobridge
Aberdeen
Willmar
Minneapolis
St. Paul
Glencoe
Red Wing
Milbank
Moreau
762
Oahe Reservoir
Faith
Redfield
Watertown
Big Sioux
Minnesota
Faribault
Black
Wisconsin Rapids
Wisconsin
Mankato
Rochester
La Crosse
Huron
Redwood Falls
New Ulm
Brookings
Austin
Belle Fourche
Deadwood
Lead
Pierre
Cheyenne
Madison
•478
Albert Lea
Watertown
Waukesha
Racine
Janesville
Madison
Rapid City
Chamberlain
Mitchell
Vermillion
Worthington
Mason City
Decorah
Newcastle
Sibley
Des Moines
Iowa
Beloit
Freeport
Rockford
Chicago
White
Winner
Lake Francis Case
Sioux Falls
Canton
Spencer
Cedar
Dubuque
De Kalb
Hot Springs
Yankton
Vermillion
Sioux City
Fort Dodge
Waterloo
Cedar Rapids
Marshalltown
Dixon
Rock
Sterling
Joliet
Valentine
Niobrara
South Sioux City
Wayne
Little Sioux
Boone
Ames
Newton
Iowa City
Clinton
Davenport
Ottawa
Kankakee
O'Neill
Elkhorn
Norfolk
Des Moines
Muscatine
Rock Island
Kewanee
Galesburg
Peoria
Bloomington
Torrington
Alliance
Scottsbluff
North Platte
Burwell
Fremont
Council Bluffs
Winterset
Oskaloosa
Monmouth
Canton
Broken Bow
Columbus
Omaha
Ottumwa
Burlington
Fort Madison
Loup City
Loup
Centerville
Keokuk
Laramie
Kimball
Sidney
Cheyenne
Ogallala
North Platte
Grand Island
York
Lincoln
Clarinda
Chariton
Kirksvil
Quincy
Illinois
Decatur
40°N
Cozad
Platte
Kearney
Hastings
Crete
Nebraska City
Nodaway
Trenton
Hannibal
Springfield
Mattoon
Jacksonville
Salt
Sterling
South Platte
Frenchman Cr.
Holdrege
Beatrice
Falls City
Greeley
McCook
Fairbury
Hiawatha
St. Joseph
Moberly
Kaskaskia
Fort Morgan
Boulder
Atchison
Belleville
Republican
Missouri
Columbia
Denver
Beaver Cr.
Phillipsburg
Kansas City
Beloit
Solomon
Manhattan
Kansas
Topeka
Lawrence
Sedalia
Fulton
St. Louis
E. St. Louis
Mount Vernon
Burlington
Colby
•774
Junction City
Limon
Goodland
WaKeeney
Hays
Salina
Lake of the Ozarks
Jefferson City
Smoky Hill
Ottawa
Osage
Carbondale
Colorado Springs
Cheyenne Wells
Emporia
Garnett
Gasconade
Rolla
Meramec
Plateau
Fredericktown
Cape Girardeau
Canon City
Great Bend
Neosho
Fort Scott
Bolivar
Pueblo
Hutchinson
Newton
El Dorado
Verdigris
Chanute
Sikeston
Rocky Ford
Lamar
Garden City
Wichita
Parsons
Pittsburg
Springfield
Poplar Bluff
La Junta
Arkansas
Dodge City
Kingman
Independence
Columbus
Joplin
Ozark
Bull Shoals Res.
Westplains
Walsenburg
Springfield
Cimarron
Winfield
Arkansas City
Coffeyville
Miami
Piggott
Kennett
Dyersburg
Trinidad
Anthony
Liberal
Medford
Bartlesville
Lake of the Cherokees
Springdale
White
Lake Norfolk
Black
Blytheville
Alva
Ponca City
Fayetteville
Batesville
Jonesboro
Raton
North Canadian
Guymon
Cimarron
Enid
Keystone Res.
Gibson Res.
Boston Mts.
Woodward
Stillwater
Tulsa
Memphis
35°N
Springer
Clayton
Shattuck
Muskogee
Tenkiller Ferry Res.
Holly Springs
Ute Cr.
Dalhart
Canadian
Okmulgee
Oklahoma City
Fort Smith
Shawnee
Santa Fe
Las Vegas
Borger
Pampa
Shamrock
Elk City
Clinton
El Reno
Eufaula Res.
McAlester
Batesville
Tucumcari
Amarillo
Salt Fork
Mangum
Chickasha
Canadian
Ada
L. Hamilton
Santa Rosa
Hereford
Dog Town Fork
Altus
Lawton
Duncan
Atoka
L. Texoma
Hugo
Tulia
Childress
Frederick
Ardmore
Fort Sumner
Plainview
Pease
Vernon
Wichita Falls
Durant
Paris
Wichita
Gainesville
Denison
Sherman
Sulphur
Pecos
Littlefield
Salt Fork
Seymour
Bowie
Lubbock
Double Mountain Fork
Denton
McKinney
Greenville
Sulphur Springs
Bridgeport
Graham
Haskell
Mineral Wells
Dallas
Roswell
Llano Estacado
Brownfield
Hamlin
Clear Fork
•526
Fort Worth
Kaufman
Tyler
Artesia
Penasco
Lamesa
Snyder
Abilene
Waxahachie
Corsicana
Hobbs
Sweetwater
Cleburne
Brazos
Palestine
Carlsbad
CARLSBAD CAVERNS N.P.
Big Spring
Colorado
Teague
Trinity
Midland
Concho
Bayou
Leon
Waco
Navasota
GUADALUPE MTS. N.P.
Odessa
Brownwood
Marlin
San Angelo
Temple
Woodville
Opelousas
Baton Rouge
Sangre de Cristo Range
Sacramento Mts.

NEW YORK
PENNSYLVANIA
MARYLAND
WEST VIRGINIA
VIRGINIA
DELAWARE
APPALACHIAN MOUNTAINS
ALLEGHENY MTS.
BLUE MTN.
JACKS MTN.
SOUTH BRANCH MTN.
Wilson
Newfane
Lyndonville
Hilton
Middleport
Albion
Medina
Lewiston
Lockport
Niagara Falls
Tonawanda
Brockport
Rochester
Irondequoit
Webster
Sodus
Williamson
Wolcott
N Rose
Marion
Penfield
East Rochester
Pittsford
Fairport
Palmyra
Oakfield
NEW YORK STATE THRUWAY
Clarence
Williamsville
Fort Erie
Buffalo
Lancaster
Depew
Alden
Batavia
Le Roy
Caledonia
Scottsville
Victor
Honeoye Falls
Avon
Lima
Attica
Retsof
Canandaigua
Manchester
Phelps
Lyons
Clyde
Newark
Geneva
Seneca Falls
Waterloo
Port Byron
Weedsport
Oswego
Mexico
Oswego R.
Fulton
Phoenix
Baldwinsville
Lake Oneida
State Barge Canal
Syracuse
Jordan
Marcellus
Skaneateles
Auburn
Skaneateles Lake
Owasco Lake
497
Camden
Delta Res.
Hinckley Res.
W. Canada Cr.
Rome
Oriskany
Oneida
Canastota
E. Syracuse
Fayetteville
Manlius
Sherrill
Whitesboro
Utica
New Hartford
Clinton
Ilion
Herkimer
Little Falls
Dolgeville
Cazenovia
Morrisville
Waterville
Richfield Springs
Canajoharie
Hamilton
Earlville
Sherburne
Cooperstown
Otsego L.
Blasdell
Wanakah
Hamburg
East Aurora
Warsaw
643
Eden
Angola
North Collins
Castile
Mount Morris
Letchworth State Pk.
Hemlock
Canandaigua Lake
Gorham
Rushville
Penn Yan
Seneca Lake
Cayuga Lake
Moravia
Homer
Cortland
McGraw
Springville
Gowanda
Cattaraugus Cr.
Dayton
Arcade
Nunda
Genesee R.
Wayland
Naples
Dansville
Keuka Lake
669
Dundee
Groton
Ludlowville
Trumansburg
Ithaca
Tioughnioga R.
New Berlin
Norwich
Oxford
Oneonta
Cattaraugus
Ellicottville
Little Valley
Franklinville
Hornell
Cohocton R.
Hammondsport
Watkins Glen
Bath
Montour Falls
Greene
Bainbridge
Unadilla
Sidney
Susquehanna R.
Franklin
Delhi
Salamanca
Randolph
Allegany State Pk.
747
Allegany
Cuba
Belmont
Friendship
Canisteo
Canisteo R.
734
Andover
Wellsville
Corning
Van Etten
Candor
Newark Valley
Olean
Portville
Bolivar
Addison
Horseheads
Elmira Heights
Elmira
Endwell
Johnson City
Binghamton
Walton
Owego
Endicott
Pepacton Res.
Downsville
Bradford
Eldred
Shinglehouse
Cowanesque R.
Elkland
Tioga R.
Wellsburg
Waverly
Sayre
Deposit
908
655
Kinzua
760
Westfield
Hallstead
Susquehanna
Hancock
Morrison
Smethport
781
Port Allegany
Allegheny R.
Coudersport
Mansfield
Thompson
Delaware R.
725
Sheffield
Kane
Mount Jewett
Clermont
Galeton
Wellsboro
748
Covington
Troy
Towanda
Montrose
Liberty
Blossburg
Canton
Susquehanna R.
793
Austin
Nicholson
Forest City
White Lake
Johnsonburg
Emporium
732
729
Tunkhannock
Waymart
Honesdale
Ridgway
St. Marys
704
Dalton
Carbondale
Hawley
Clarion R.
English Center
Pine Cr.
Peckville
Lake Ariel
Scranton
Hamlin
Dunmore
Renovo
North Bend
Loyalsock Cr.
Old Forge
Lake Wallenpaupack
Port Jervis
Brockway
Dallas
Pittston
Moscow
Allens Mills
Williamsport
West Branch Susquehanna R.
716
Jersey Shore
Avis
Montgomery
Hughesville
Muncy
Kingston
Wilkes-Barre
Milford
Falls Creek
Du Bois
Reynoldsville
728
Mill Hall
Lock Haven
Nanticoke
Shickshinny
Glen Lyon
Ashley
Mountaintop
Thornhurst
Sussex
Sykesville
Clearfield
351
Watsontown
Berwick
White Haven
Punxsutawney
Curwensville
Grassflat
Moshannon
Milton
Bloomsburg
Freeland
Newton
Rossiter
Philipsburg
Bellefonte
Pleasant Gap
Lewisburg
Danville
Catawissa
596
Hazleton
Stroudsburg
Blairstown
Osceola Mills
Mifflinburg
Northumberland
Weatherly
Jim Thorpe
Delaware Water Gap
Houtzdale
Old Fort
State College
Hummels Wharf
Selinsgrove
Sunbury
Shamokin
Mt. Carmel
Shenandoah
McAdoo
Nesquehoning
Lehighton
Pen Argyl
Bangor
Windgap
Hackettstown
Budd Lake
Belvidere
Morristown
Barnesboro
Coalport
802
Hastings
Patton
Middleburg
Beavertown
Trevorton
Gordon
Ashland
Mahanoy City
Summit Hill
Palmerton
Slatington
Tamaqua
Washington
Nazareth
Mendham
Spangler
Tyrone
Milroy
660
728
Carrolltown
Bellwood
Lewistown
St. Clair
Minersville
Pottsville
Valley View
McKeansburg
Bath
Easton
Phillipsburg
Plainfield
Colver
Ebensburg
Belleville
Williamstown
Tremont
Schuylkill Haven
Allentown
Bethlehem
Alpha
High Bridge
Somerville
Vintondale
Gallitzin
Altoona
Cresson
Huntingdon
Granville
Juniata R.
Elizabethville
Lykens
Tower City
Pine Grove
Hamburg
Kutztown
Hellertown
Lilly
Hollidaysburg
Williamsburg
Reeds Gap
Ickesburg
Halifax
Shoemakersville
Emmaus
Topton
Frenchtown
Coopersburg
Flemington
S. Fork
Portage
Duncansville
Mount Union
Honey Grove
Duncannon
Newport
Fleetwood
Quakertown
New Brunswick
Johnstown
Roaring Spring
Martinsburg
Greenpark
Clarks Ferry
Lebanon
Myerstown
Temple
Laureldale
Pennsburg
Perkasie
Lambertville
Hopewell
956
Claysburg
Marysville
Annville
Womelsdorf
Reading
Sellersville
Pennington
Windber
Saxton
Raystown Br.
706
Harrisburg
Palmyra
Hershey
Robesonia
Boyertown
Baumstown
Doylestown
Fairless Hills
Levittown
Princeton
Hooversville
Mechanicsburg
Steelton
Cornwall
Pottstown
Souderton
Lansdale
Hatboro
Trenton
Morrisville
Robbinsville
PENNSYLVANIA TURNPIKE
Carlisle
Middletown
Landisville
Denver
Royersford
Fort Washington
Central City
Newville
Elizabethtown
Manheim
Lititz
Ephrata
Akron
318
Norristown
Langhorne
Oakford
Bordentown
Bedford
Everett
Dickinson
Mt. Holly Springs
Dillsburg
Florin
Marietta
Columbia
New Holland
Phoenixville
Conshohocken
Eddington
Burlington
Shippensburg
Manchester
Wrightsville
Lancaster
Exton
Downingtown
Swedeland
Beverly
Delanco
McConnellsburg
643
Millersville
Strasburg
Coatesville
Malvern
Chambersburg
Biglerville
York
Dallastown
Windsor
Red Lion
Christiana
Parkesburg
W. Chester
Moorestown
Camden
Mount Holly
Hyndman
Mercersburg
Conococheague Cr.
New Oxford
Gettysburg
Susquehanna R.
Quarryville
Philadelphia
Chester
Maple Shade
Medford
Greencastle
Waynesboro
Hanover
Glenville
Glen Rock
Stewartstown
W. Grove
Oxford
Wilmington
Claymont
Paulsboro
Westville
Glassboro
Gibbstown
Swedesboro
Mullica R.
Mt. Savage
Hancock
Emmitsburg
Littlestown
New Freedom
Delta
Penns Gr.
Pitman
Cumberland
Hagerstown
Thurmont
Taneytown
Prettyboy Res.
Newark
Collins Park
New Castle
Pennsville
Williamstown
Hammonton
Pinto
Gt. Cacapon
Berkeley Springs
578
Woodstown
Elmer
Malaga
Westminster
Port Deposit
Elkton
Bel Air
Cacapon St. Pk.
Williamsport
Gambrill St. Pk.
Monocacy R.
Salem
Newfield
Buena
Martinsburg
Boonsboro
Havre de Grace
Aberdeen
Egg Harbor
S. Br. Potomac R.
Shepherdstown
Patapsco Res.
Reisterstown
Seabrook
Romney
Frederick
Middletown
Bridgeton
Vineland
Absecon
Harpers Ferry
Towson
Greenwich
Millville
Pleasantville
Charles Town
Brunswick
Mount Airy
Potomac R.
Damascus
Baltimore
Essex
Cedarville
Linwood
Somers Pt.
Lost R.
Winchester
Shenandoah R.
Ellicott City
132
Dundalk
Smyrna
Newport
Port Norris
Ocean City
Berryville
Purcellville
Glen Burnie
Sparrows Point
Chestertown
Woodbine
Stephens City
Leesburg
Gaithersburg
Laurel
Savage
Orchard Beach
Dover
Delaware Bay
Cape May Court House
Rockville
26
Wyoming
Strasburg
78°W
Silver Spr.
Odenton
Queenstown
Centreville
76°W
Avalon
Stone Harbor
Washington D.C.
Annapolis
Front Royal
Greensboro
Ridgely
Villas
75°W
Wildwood

Northeastern
United States
Scale 1:2 000 000
0 20 40 60 km
Metres
5000
3000
2000
1000
500
300
200
100
Sea level
Land depression
Spot heights in metres
Boundaries
International
(in sea)
(disputed)
Internal
Roads
Limited Access
Other Highways
Railways
Airports
International
Domestic
Canals
Seasonal rivers, lakes
Marshes
Salt pans
Ice cap
Sand desert limits
National Parks, etc.
Conical Orthomorphic Projection
©Oxford University Press
43°N
42°N
41°N
40°N
39°N
74°W
73°W
72°W
71°W
VERMONT
NEW HAMPSHIRE
MAINE
MASSACHUSETTS
CONNECTICUT
RHODE ISLAND
New York
ATLANTIC OCEAN
Long Island Sound
Long Island
Massachusetts Bay
Cape Cod Bay
Cape Cod
Nantucket Sound
Buzzards Bay
Martha's Vineyard
Nantucket I.
Elizabeth Islands
Block I.
Fishers I.
Montauk Pt.
Cape Ann
Green Mts.
Hudson R.
Connecticut R.
Boston
Cambridge
Quincy
Worcester
Springfield
Providence
Hartford
New Haven
Bridgeport
Stamford
Albany
Schenectady
Troy
Concord
Manchester
Nashua
Portsmouth
Lowell
Lawrence
Brockton
Fall River
New Bedford
Pawtucket
Newport
Norwich
New London
Waterbury
New Britain
Pittsfield
Fitchburg
Holyoke
Chicopee
Poughkeepsie
Kingston
Newburgh
Yonkers
Jersey City
Long Branch
Asbury Park
Point Pleasant
Atlantic City
Fire Island Nat. Seashore
Cape Cod Nat. Seashore
Island Beach State Pk.

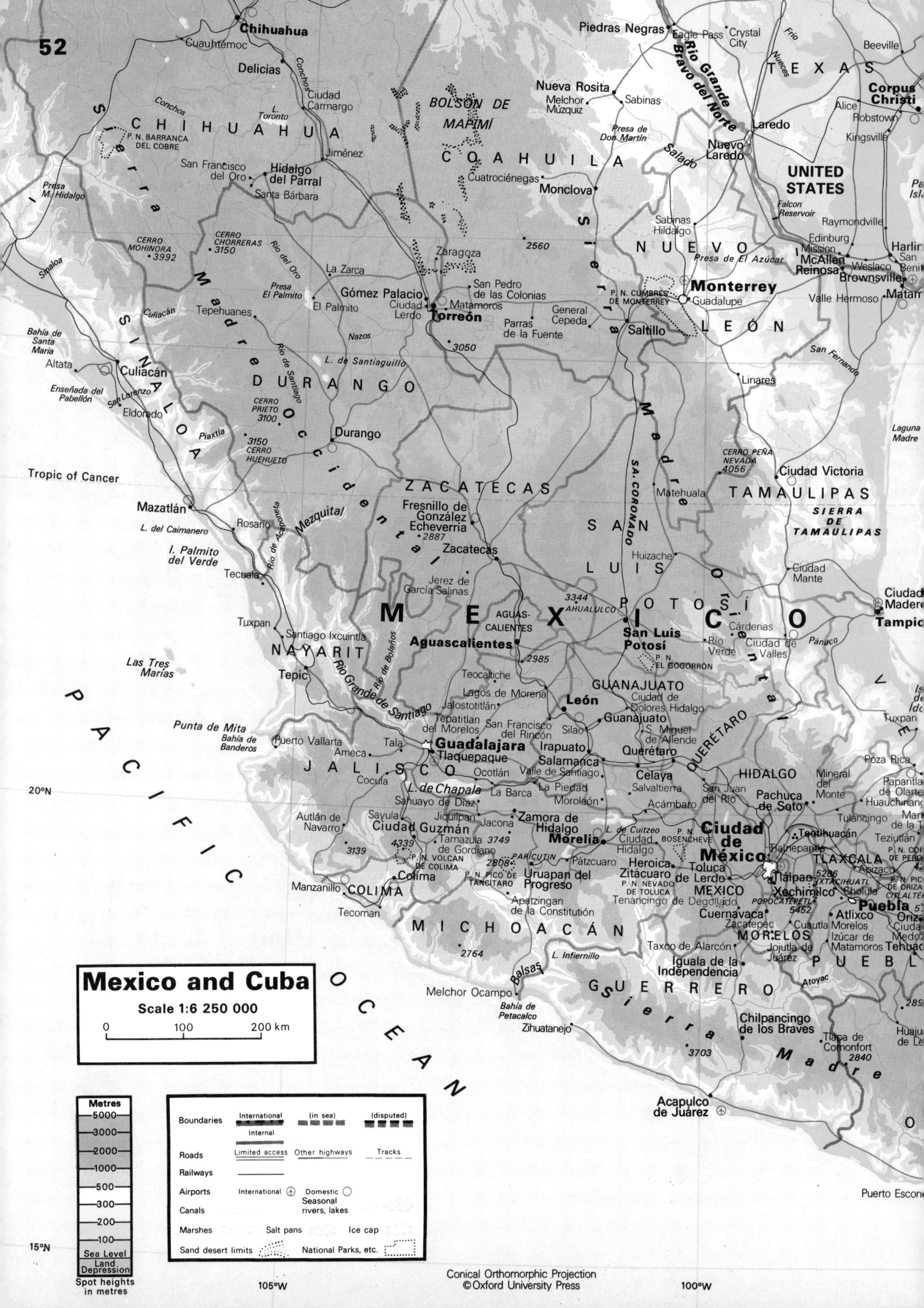
Mexico and Cuba
Scale 1:6 250 000
0 100 200 km
Metres
5000
3000
2000
1000
500
300
200
100
Sea Level
Land Depression
Spot heights in metres
Boundaries International (in sea) (disputed)
Internal
Roads Limited access Other highways Tracks
Railways
Airports International Domestic
Canals
Seasonal rivers, lakes
Marshes
Salt pans
Ice cap
Sand desert limits
National Parks, etc.
Conical Orthomorphic Projection
©Oxford University Press
105°W
100°W
20°N
15°N
Tropic of Cancer
PACIFIC OCEAN
UNITED STATES
TEXAS
MEXICO
CHIHUAHUA
COAHUILA
NUEVO LEÓN
TAMAULIPAS
SINALOA
DURANGO
ZACATECAS
SAN LUIS POTOSÍ
NAYARIT
AGUAS-CALIENTES
JALISCO
GUANAJUATO
QUERÉTARO
HIDALGO
MEXICO
TLAXCALA
MORELOS
COLIMA
MICHOACÁN
GUERRERO
PUEBLA
Sierra Madre Occidental
Sierra Madre Oriental
Sierra Madre
SIERRA DE TAMAULIPAS
SA. CORONADO
BOLSÓN DE MAPIMÍ
Rio Grande
Bravo del Norte
Conchos
Nueces
Frio
Salado
San Fernando
Rio del Oro
Rio de Santiago
Rio Grande de Santiago
Rio de Bolaños
Rio de Acaponeta
Mezquital
Piaxtla
Sinaloa
Culiacán
San Lorenzo
Pánuco
Balsas
Atoyac
L. Toronto
L. de Santiaguillo
L. de Chapala
L. de Cuitzeo
L. Infiernillo
L. del Caimanero
Laguna Madre
Presa M. Hidalgo
Presa El Palmito
Presa de Don Martín
Presa de El Azúcar
Falcon Reservoir
Bahía de Santa María
Ensenada del Pabellón
Bahía de Banderos
Bahía de Petacalco
Punta de Mita
Las Tres Marías
I. Palmito del Verde
P. N. BARRANCA DEL COBRE
P. N. CUMBRES DE MONTERREY
P. N. EL GOGORRÓN
P. N. VOLCAN DE COLIMA
P. N. PICO DE TANCÍTARO
P. N. NEVADO DE TOLUCA
P. N. BOSENCHEVE
CERRO MOHINORA 3992
CERRO CHORRERAS 3150
CERRO PRIETO 3100
3150 CERRO HUEHUETO
CERRO PEÑA NEVADA 4056
3344 AHUALULCO
PARÍCUTIN
POPOCATÉPETL 5452
IXTACIHUATL 5286
CITLALTÉPETL
2560
3050
2887
2985
4339
3139
3749
2808
2764
3703
2840
Chihuahua
Cuauhtémoc
Delicias
Ciudad Camargo
Jiménez
Hidalgo del Parral
San Francisco del Oro
Santa Bárbara
La Zarca
El Palmito
Tepehuanes
Gómez Palacio
Ciudad Lerdo
Torreón
Matamoros
San Pedro de las Colonias
Parras de la Fuente
General Cepeda
Saltillo
Monterrey
Guadalupe
Zaragoza
Cuatrociénegas
Monclova
Nueva Rosita
Melchor Múzquiz
Sabinas
Piedras Negras
Eagle Pass
Crystal City
Beeville
Corpus Christi
Alice
Robstown
Kingsville
Laredo
Nuevo Laredo
Raymondville
Sabinas Hidalgo
Edinburg
Mission
McAllen
Reinosa
Weslaco
Harlingen
San Benito
Brownsville
Matamoros
Valle Hermoso
Linares
Ciudad Victoria
Matehuala
Huizache
Ciudad Mante
Ciudad Madero
Tampico
Cárdenas
Rio Verde
Ciudad de Valles
Nazos
Culiacán
Altata
Eldorado
Durango
Mazatlán
Rosario
Tecuala
Tuxpan
Santiago Ixcuintla
Tepic
Fresnillo de González Echeverria
Zacatecas
Jerez de García Salinas
Aguascalientes
San Luis Potosí
Teocaltiche
Lagos de Moreno
Jalostotitlán
Tepatitlan del Morelos
San Francisco del Rincón
León
Silao
Guanajuato
Ciudad de Dolores Hidalgo
S. Miguel de Allende
Querétaro
Irapuato
Salamanca
Valle de Santiago
Celaya
Salvaltierra
San Juan del Rio
Acámbaro
Puerto Vallarta
Ameca
Tala
Guadalajara
Tlaquepaque
Cocula
Ocotlán
La Barca
La Piedad
Moroleón
Sahuayo de Díaz
Jiquilpan
Jacona
Zamora de Hidalgo
Sayula
Ciudad Guzmán
Autlán de Navarro
Tamazula de Gordiano
Colima
Manzanillo
Tecoman
Morelia
Pátzcuaro
Uruapan del Progreso
Apatzingan de la Constitución
Ciudad Hidalgo
Heroica Zitácuaro
Toluca de Lerdo
Tenancingo de Degollado
Ciudad de México
Tlalnepantla
Teotihuacán
Tlalpan
Xochimilco
Cuernavaca
Zacatepec
Cuautla Morelos
Jojutla de Juárez
Taxco de Alarcón
Iguala de la Independencia
Pachuca de Soto
Mineral del Monte
Tulancingo
Poza Rica
Papantla de Olarte
Huauchinango
Teziutlán
Apizaco
Cholula
Puebla
Atlixco
Izúcar de Matamoros
Tuxpan
Chilpancingo de los Braves
Tlapa de Comonfort
Acapulco de Juárez
Zihuatanejo
Melchor Ocampo
Puerto Escondido

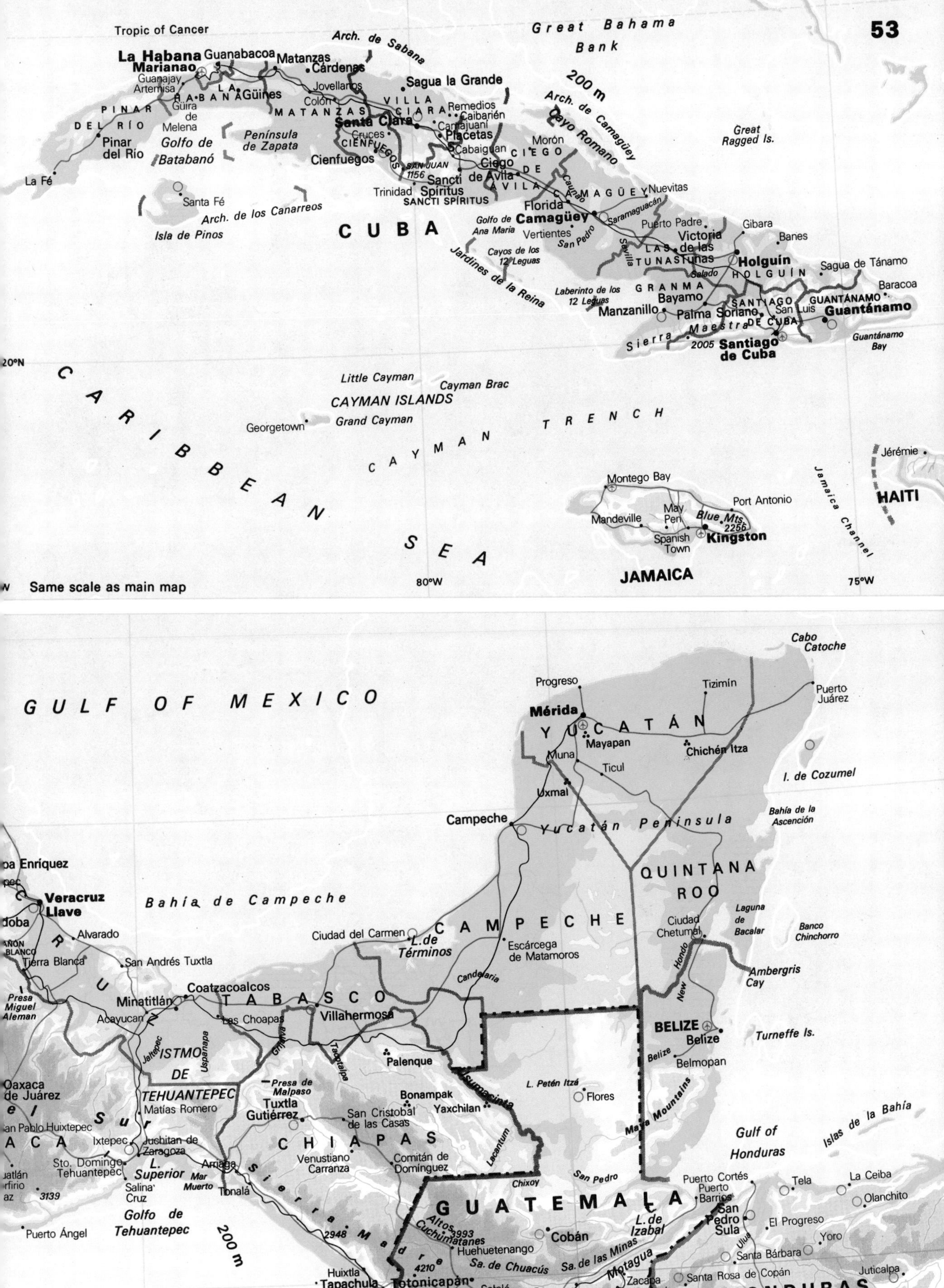
Tropic of Cancer
Great Bahama Bank
200 m
La Habana
Marianao
Guanabacoa
Matanzas
Cárdenas
Arch. de Sabana
Sagua la Grande
Santa Clara
Cienfuegos
Placetas
Remedios
Caibarién
Península de Zapata
Golfo de Batabanó
Pinar del Río
La Fé
Santa Fé
Isla de Pinos
Arch. de los Canarreos
Arch. de Camagüey
Cayo Romano
Great Ragged Is.
Morón
Ciego de Avila
Sancti Spíritus
Trinidad
CUBA
Camagüey
Florida
Nuevitas
Puerto Padre
Victoria de las Tunas
Gibara
Banes
Holguín
Sagua de Tánamo
Baracoa
Bayamo
Manzanillo
Palma Soriano
San Luis
Guantánamo
Guantánamo Bay
Santiago de Cuba
Sierra Maestra
2005
Jardines de la Reina
Golfo de Ana Maria
Cayos de los 12 Leguas
Laberinto de los 12 Leguas
20°N
CARIBBEAN SEA
Little Cayman
Cayman Brac
CAYMAN ISLANDS
Grand Cayman
Georgetown
CAYMAN TRENCH
Montego Bay
Mandeville
May Pen
Spanish Town
Kingston
Port Antonio
Blue Mts. 2256
JAMAICA
Jamaica Channel
Jérémie
HAITI
Same scale as main map
80°W
75°W
GULF OF MEXICO
Cabo Catoche
Progreso
Mérida
Tizimín
Puerto Juárez
YUCATÁN
Mayapan
Chichén Itza
Muna
Ticul
Uxmal
I. de Cozumel
Campeche
Yucatán Peninsula
Bahía de la Ascención
QUINTANA ROO
Laguna de Bacalar
Banco Chinchorro
Ciudad Chetumal
Veracruz Llave
Bahía de Campeche
Alvarado
Tierra Blanca
San Andrés Tuxtla
Ciudad del Carmen
L. de Términos
CAMPECHE
Escárcega de Matamoros
Candelaria
Ambergris Cay
Coatzacoalcos
Minatitlán
Acayucan
Las Choapas
TABASCO
Villahermosa
ISTMO DE TEHUANTEPEC
Presa Miguel Aleman
BELIZE
Belize
Belmopan
Turneffe Is.
Palenque
Oaxaca de Juárez
Presa de Malpaso
Bonampak
Yaxchilan
L. Petén Itzá
Flores
Maya Mountains
Matías Romero
Tuxtla Gutiérrez
San Cristobal de las Casas
CHIAPAS
Islas de la Bahía
Gulf of Honduras
Ixtepec
Juchitan de Zaragoza
Sto. Domingo Tehuantepec
L. Superior
Mar Muerto
Arriaga
Tonalá
Salina Cruz
Venustiano Carranza
Comitán de Domínguez
Sierra Madre
3139
Chixoy
San Pedro
Puerto Cortés
Puerto Barrios
Tela
La Ceiba
Olanchito
Golfo de Tehuantepec
200 m
Puerto Ángel
2948
GUATEMALA
Altos Cuchumatanes
3993
Huehuetenango
Cobán
L. de Izabal
San Pedro Sula
El Progreso
Yoro
4210
Sa. de Chuacús
Sa. de las Minas
Motagua
Santa Bárbara
Huixtla
Tapachula
Totonicapán
Sololá
El Progreso
Zacapa
Chiquimula
Santa Rosa de Copán
Juticalpa
HONDURAS
Quezaltenango
Antigua
Guatemala
2858
Comayagua
95°W

Equator
Tropic of Capricorn
ATLANTIC OCEAN
PACIFIC OCEAN
Caribbean Sea
200m
Mouth of the Amazon
I. of Marajó
Fernando de Noronha
C. de São Roque
VENEZUELA
COLOMBIA
ECUADOR
PERU
BOLIVIA
BRAZIL
PARAGUAY
CHILE
GUYANA
SURINAM
FRENCH GUIANA
PANAMA
COSTA RICA
NICARAGUA
Managua
San José
Puerto Limón
Colón
Panama
Panama Canal
Gulf of Panama
Gulf of Darien
Cocos Is. (C.R.)
Malpelo I. (Col.)
BARBADOS
TRINIDAD AND TOBAGO
Port of Spain
ST. LUCIA
GRENADA
Martinique (Fr.)
St. Vincent (Br.)
Windward Islands
Grenadines
Margarita I.
Aruba (Neth.)
Curaçao (Neth.)
Gulf of Venezuela
Gulf of Maracaibo
Pt. de Gallinas
Caracas
Maracaibo
Barranquilla
Cartagena
Sta. Marta
Medellín
Manizales
Ibagué
Cali
Buenaventura
Bogotá
Bucaramanga
Cúcuta
Tunja
Neiva
Florencia
Pasto
Tumaco
San Lorenzo
Valencia
Barquisimeto
Barcelona
Cumaná
Maturín
Tucupita
Ciudad Bolívar
San Cristóbal
Arauca
Pto. Ayacucho
Orinoco
Caroni
Casiquiare
Angel Falls
RORAIMA
Kaieteur Falls
Georgetown
Mackenzie
Essequibo
Paramaribo
Moengo
Cayenne
Boa Vista
Branco
Guiana Highlands
Serro do Navio
Macapá
Belém
Pará
Óbidos
Manaus
Amazon
Negro
Madeira
Purús
Juruá
Selvas
Xingu
Tocantins
Araguaia
Tapajós
Juruena
Fordlândia
Canudos
São Luís
Parnaíba
Camocim
Fortaleza
Teresina
Floriano
Natal
João Pessoa
Recife
Campina Grande
Maceió
Aracajú
Salvador (Bahia)
Ilhéus
Itabuna
Poções
Paulistana
Paulo Afonso Falls
Feira de Santana
São Francisco
Angical
Carolina
Caravelas
Vitória
Colatina
ESPIRITO SANTO
Belo Horizonte
Diamantina
Juiz de Fora
Petrópolis
Niterói
Rio de Janeiro
Volta Redonda
Campinas
Santos
São Paulo
Curitiba
Brasília
Goiânia
Anápolis
Goiás
Goiás Massif
Uberaba
Ribeirão Prêto
Campo Grande
Cuiabá
Corumbá
Plateau of Mato Grosso
Serra dos Parecis
Brazilian Highlands
Brazil Plateau
Paraná Plateau
Porto Velho
Santo Antônio
Guajará-mirim
Rio Branco
Cruzeiro do Sul
Riberalta
Beni
Leticia
Iquitos
Putumayo
Amazon (Solimões)
Mitú
Vaupés
Marañón
Ucayali
Huallaga
Quito
COTOPAXI 5896
CHIMBORAZO 6267
Riobamba
Guayaquil
Gulf of Guayaquil
Manta
Loja
Talara
Piura
Sechura Desert
Chiclayo
Trujillo
Chimbote
Lima
Callao
Huancayo
Huancavelica
Cerro de Pasco
Ica
Cuzco
Puno
Arequipa
Mollendo
LA MONTAÑA
Titicaca
La Paz
ILLIMANI 6882
Oruro
L. Poopó
Cochabamba
Sucre
Potosí
Santa Cruz
Llanos de Guarayos
Chiquitos Plateau
Tacna
Arica
Iquique
Antofagasta
Chañaral
Caldera
Copiapó
Potrerillos
OJOS DEL SALADO
Atacama Desert
Uyuni
Yacuiba
Chuquicamata
Jujuy
Salta
Tucumán
Asunción
Concepción
Paraguay
Pilcomayo
Gran Chaco
Corrientes
Resistencia
Posadas
Ponta Porã
Paraná
Uruguay
Félix I.

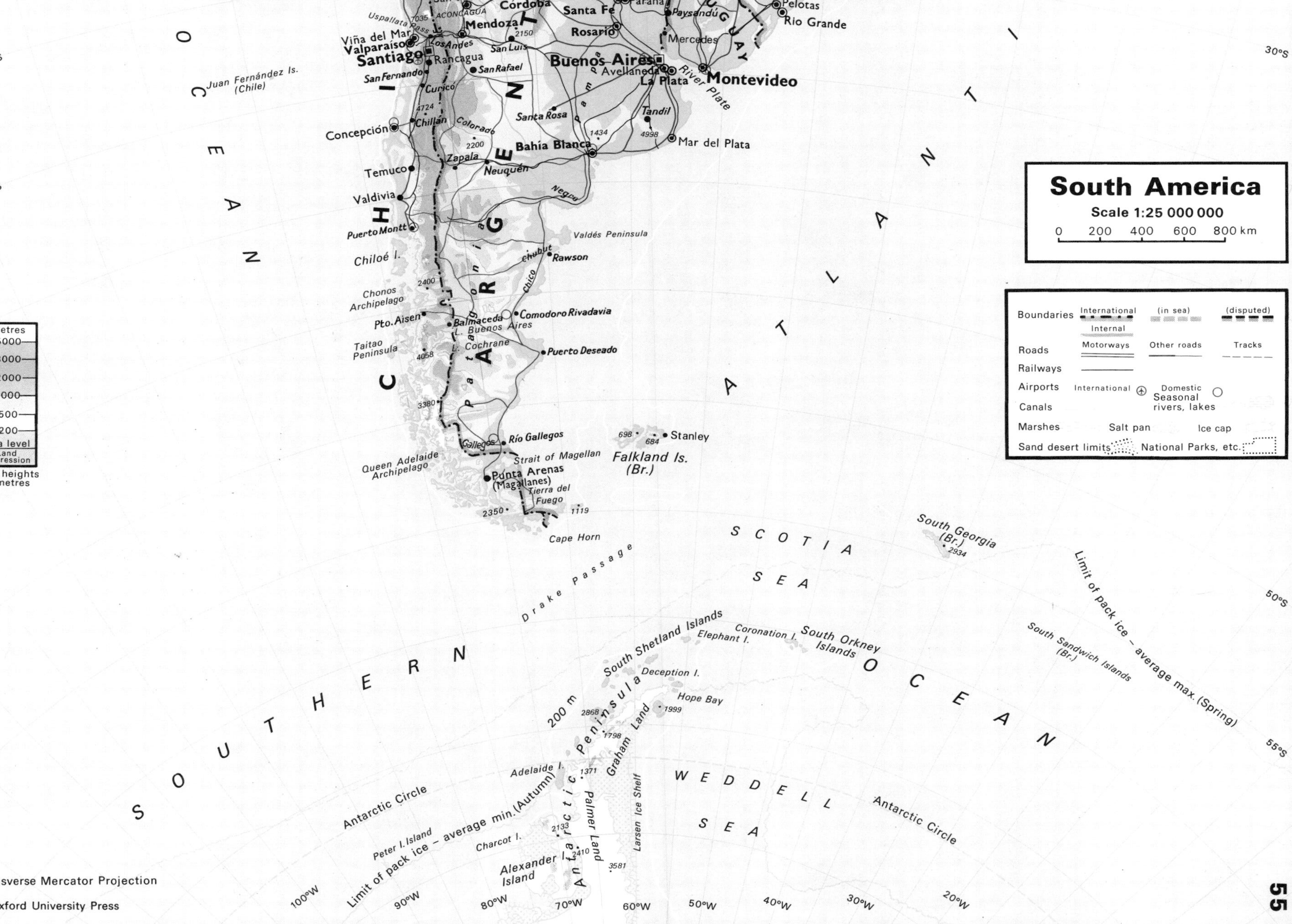
South America
Scale 1:25 000 000
0 200 400 600 800 km
Boundaries International (in sea) (disputed)
Internal
Roads Motorways Other roads Tracks
Railways
Airports International Domestic
Canals Seasonal rivers, lakes
Marshes Salt pan Ice cap
Sand desert limits National Parks, etc.
Metres
5000
3000
2000
1000
500
200
Sea level
Land depression
Spot heights in metres
San Juan
Córdoba
Santa Fe
Paraná
Paysandú
Pelotas
Rio Grande
Uspallata Pass
7035
ACONCAGUA
Mendoza
2150
Rosario
Mercedes
Viña del Mar
Valparaíso
Los Andes
San Luis
Santiago
Rancagua
Buenos Aires
Avellaneda
La Plata
River Plate
Montevideo
San Fernando
San Rafael
Juan Fernández Is. (Chile)
Curicó
4724
Chillán
Colorado
Santa Rosa
Tandil
4998
Concepción
2200
1434
Bahía Blanca
Mar del Plata
Zapala
Neuquén
Temuco
Negro
Valdivia
Puerto Montt
Valdés Peninsula
Chiloé I.
Chubut
Rawson
Chico
2400
Chonos Archipelago
Pto. Aisen
Balmaceda
L. Buenos Aires
Comodoro Rivadavia
Taitao Peninsula
4058
L. Cochrane
Puerto Deseado
3380
Río Gallegos
Gallegos
698
684
Stanley
Falkland Is. (Br.)
Queen Adelaide Archipelago
Strait of Magellan
Punta Arenas (Magallanes)
Tierra del Fuego
2350
1119
Cape Horn
OCEAN
ATLANTIC
CHILE
ARGENTINA
Pampa
Patagonia
URUGUAY
SCOTIA SEA
South Georgia (Br.)
2934
Drake Passage
Limit of pack ice – average max. (Spring)
South Shetland Islands
Elephant I.
Coronation I.
South Orkney Islands
South Sandwich Islands (Br.)
Deception I.
Hope Bay
1999
200 m
2868
Peninsula
Graham Land
1798
Adelaide I.
1371
Antarctic Circle
WEDDELL SEA
Larsen Ice Shelf
Palmer Land
Antarctic
Peter I. Island
Limit of pack ice – average min. (Autumn)
Charcot I.
2133
2410
3581
Alexander I. Island
SOUTHERN OCEAN
30°S
35°S
50°S
55°S
100°W
90°W
80°W
70°W
60°W
50°W
40°W
30°W
20°W
Transverse Mercator Projection

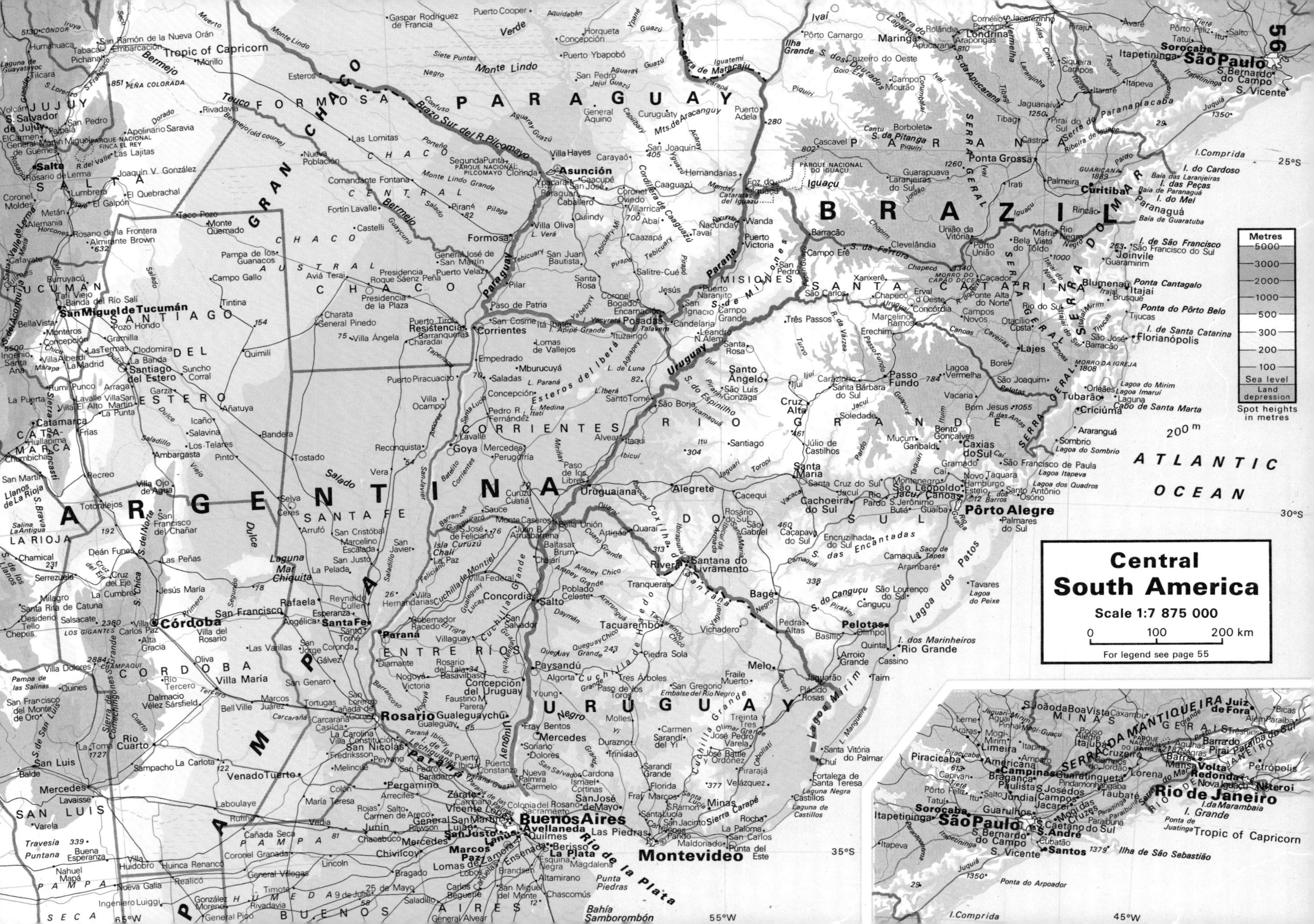

Central
South America
Scale 1:7 875 000
0
100
200 km
For legend see page 55
Metres
5000
3000
2000
1000
500
300
200
100
Sea level
Land depression
Spot heights in metres
ATLANTIC
OCEAN
200 m
BRAZIL
PARAGUAY
URUGUAY
ARGENTINA
GRAN CHACO
PAMPA
Tropic of Capricorn
25°S
30°S
35°S
65°W
55°W
45°W
Asunción
Montevideo
Buenos Aires
Pôrto Alegre
Curitiba
Florianópolis
São Paulo
Rio de Janeiro
Santos
Córdoba
Rosario
Santa Fe
Paraná
San Miguel de Tucumán
Salta
Corrientes
Resistencia
Posadas
Formosa
Santiago del Estero
Catamarca
La Plata
Mar Chiquita
Lagoa dos Patos
Lagoa Mirim
Río de la Plata
Paraná
Uruguay
Paraguay
Bermejo
Salado
Pilcomayo
Iguaçu
Ponta Grossa
Londrina
Maringá
Pelotas
Rio Grande
Santa Maria
Passo Fundo
Lajes
Joinvile
Blumenau
Caxias do Sul
Uruguaiana
Alegrete
Salto
Paysandú
Concordia
Goya
Jujuy
Tucumán
Santiago del Estero
Chaco
Corrientes
Misiones
Entre Ríos
Santa Fe
San Luis
La Rioja
Buenos Aires
Santa Catarina
Rio Grande do Sul
Serra Geral
Serra do Mar
Serra da Mantiqueira

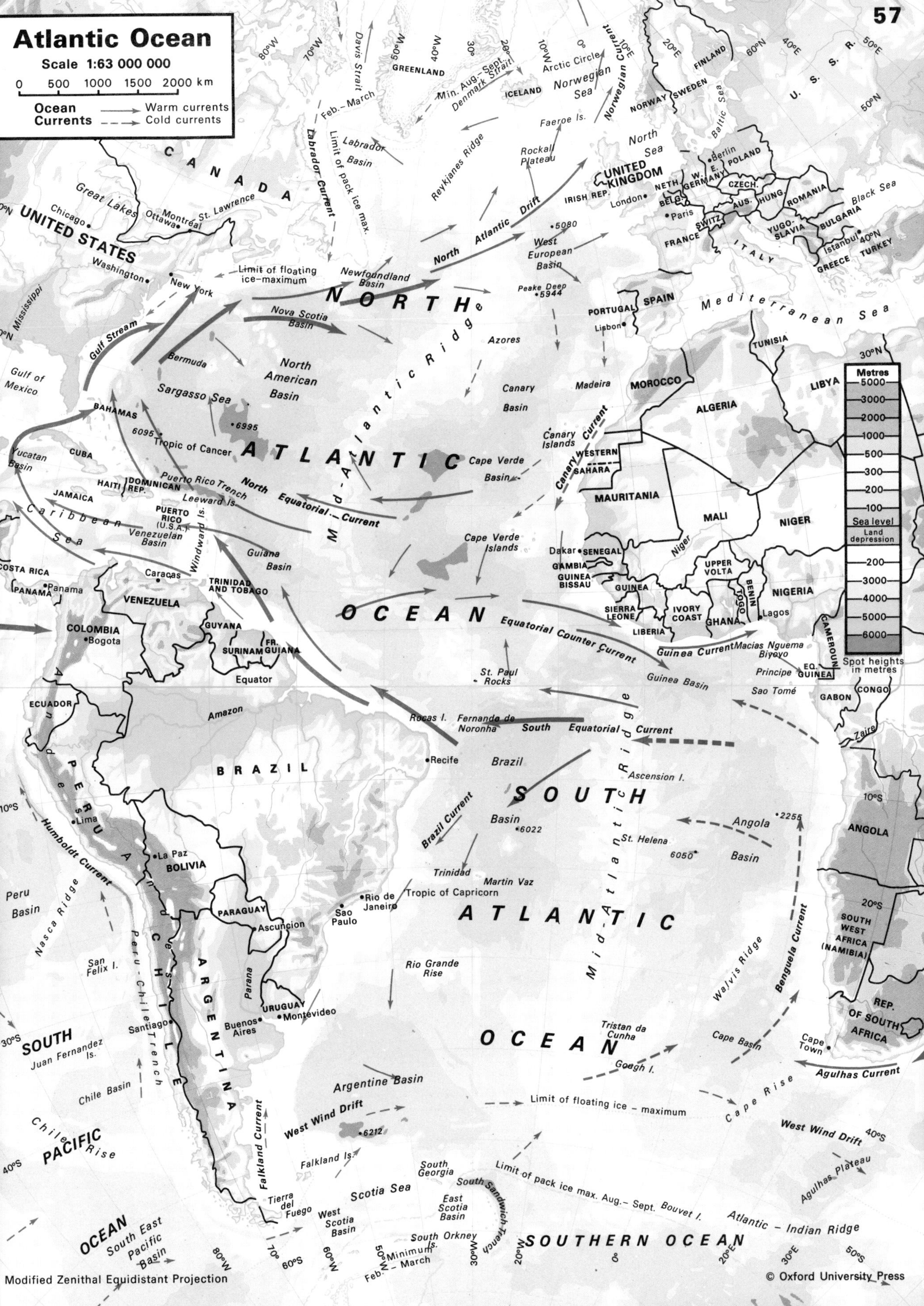
Atlantic Ocean
Scale 1:63 000 000
0 500 1000 1500 2000 km
Ocean Currents
Warm currents
Cold currents
Metres
5000
3000
2000
1000
500
300
200
100
Sea level
Land depression
200
3000
4000
5000
6000
Spot heights in metres
NORTH ATLANTIC OCEAN
SOUTH ATLANTIC OCEAN
SOUTHERN OCEAN
PACIFIC OCEAN
CANADA
UNITED STATES
GREENLAND
ICELAND
Norwegian Sea
North Sea
UNITED KINGDOM
IRISH REP.
Gulf Stream
North Atlantic Drift
Labrador Current
Canary Current
North Equatorial Current
Equatorial Counter Current
Guinea Current
South Equatorial Current
Brazil Current
Benguela Current
Humboldt Current
Falkland Current
West Wind Drift
Agulhas Current
Norwegian Current
Mid-Atlantic Ridge
Sargasso Sea
Caribbean Sea
Mediterranean Sea
Black Sea
Baltic Sea
Scotia Sea
Gulf of Mexico
BRAZIL
ARGENTINA
CHILE
PERU
BOLIVIA
COLOMBIA
VENEZUELA
ECUADOR
PARAGUAY
URUGUAY
GUYANA
SURINAM
FR. GUIANA
MOROCCO
ALGERIA
LIBYA
TUNISIA
MAURITANIA
MALI
NIGER
NIGERIA
ANGOLA
SOUTH WEST AFRICA (NAMIBIA)
REP. OF SOUTH AFRICA
SPAIN
PORTUGAL
FRANCE
ITALY
U. S. S. R.
Modified Zenithal Equidistant Projection

Europe : Physical

Scale 1:19 000 000

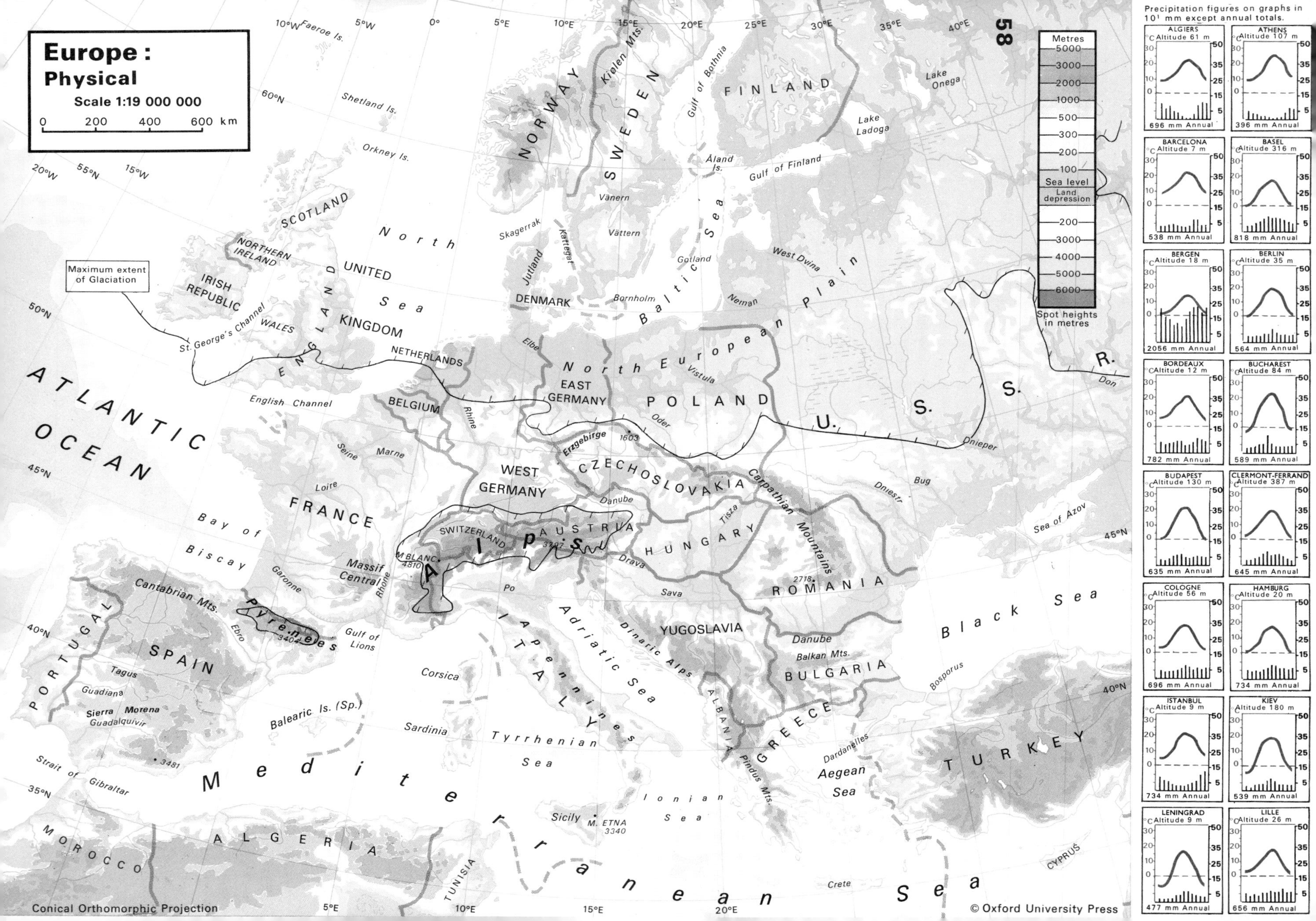

Conical Orthomorphic Projection

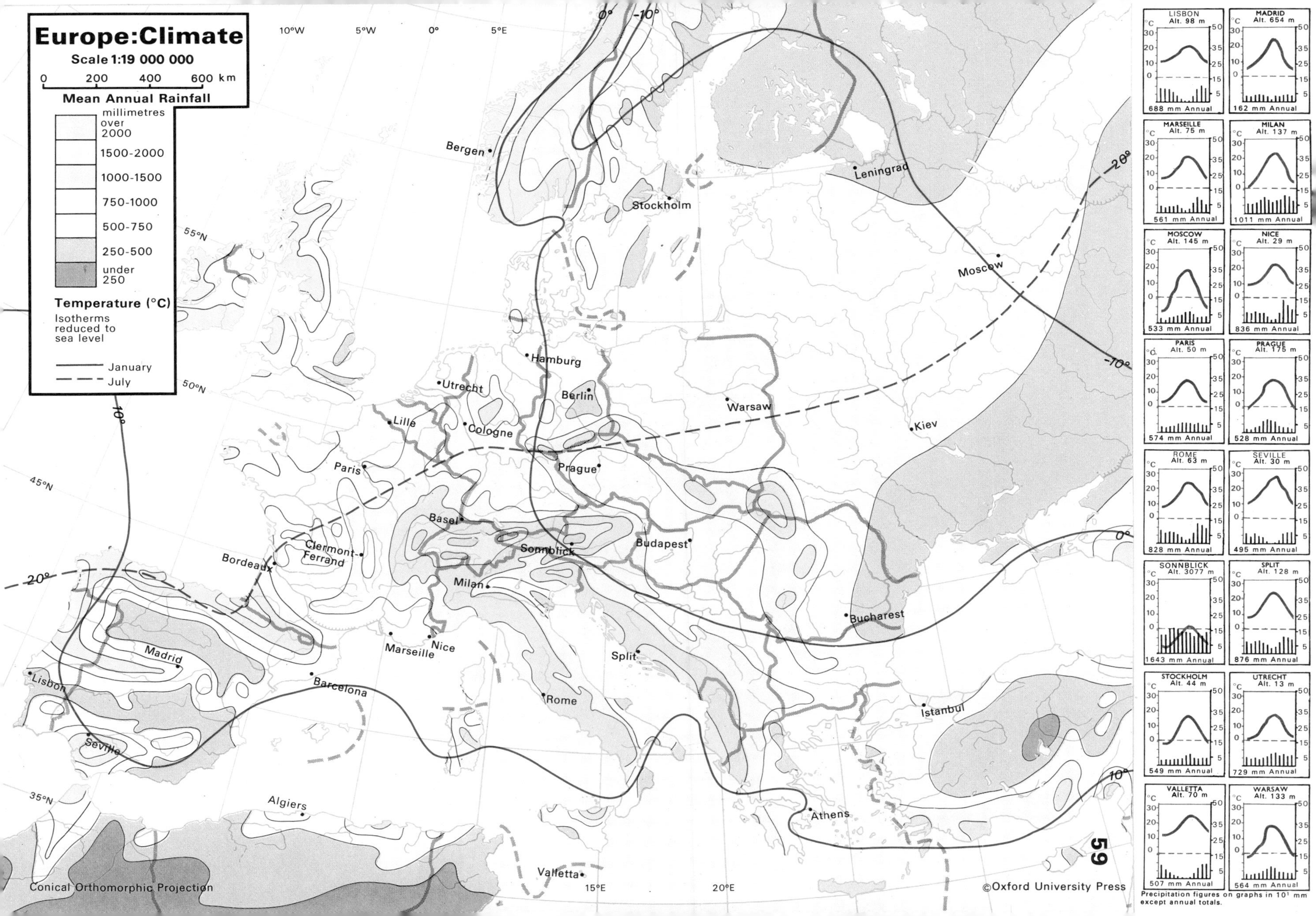
Europe:Climate
Scale 1:19 000 000
0 200 400 600 km
Mean Annual Rainfall
millimetres
over 2000
1500-2000
1000-1500
750-1000
500-750
250-500
under 250
Temperature (°C)
Isotherms reduced to sea level
January
July
10°W
5°W
0°
5°E
15°E
20°E
55°N
50°N
45°N
35°N
0°
-10°
-20°
10°
20°
Bergen
Stockholm
Leningrad
Moscow
Hamburg
Utrecht
Berlin
Warsaw
Lille
Cologne
Kiev
Paris
Prague
Basel
Clermont-Ferrand
Sonnblick
Budapest
Bordeaux
Milan
Bucharest
Madrid
Marseille
Nice
Split
Lisbon
Barcelona
Rome
Istanbul
Seville
Algiers
Athens
Valletta
Conical Orthomorphic Projection
©Oxford University Press
LISBON Alt. 98 m
688 mm Annual
MADRID Alt. 654 m
162 mm Annual
MARSEILLE Alt. 75 m
561 mm Annual
MILAN Alt. 137 m
1011 mm Annual
MOSCOW Alt. 145 m
533 mm Annual
NICE Alt. 29 m
836 mm Annual
PARIS Alt. 50 m
574 mm Annual
PRAGUE Alt. 175 m
528 mm Annual
ROME Alt. 63 m
828 mm Annual
SEVILLE Alt. 30 m
495 mm Annual
SONNBLICK Alt. 3077 m
1643 mm Annual
SPLIT Alt. 128 m
876 mm Annual
STOCKHOLM Alt. 44 m
549 mm Annual
UTRECHT Alt. 13 m
729 mm Annual
VALLETTA Alt. 70 m
507 mm Annual
WARSAW Alt. 133 m
564 mm Annual
Precipitation figures on graphs in 10¹ mm except annual totals.

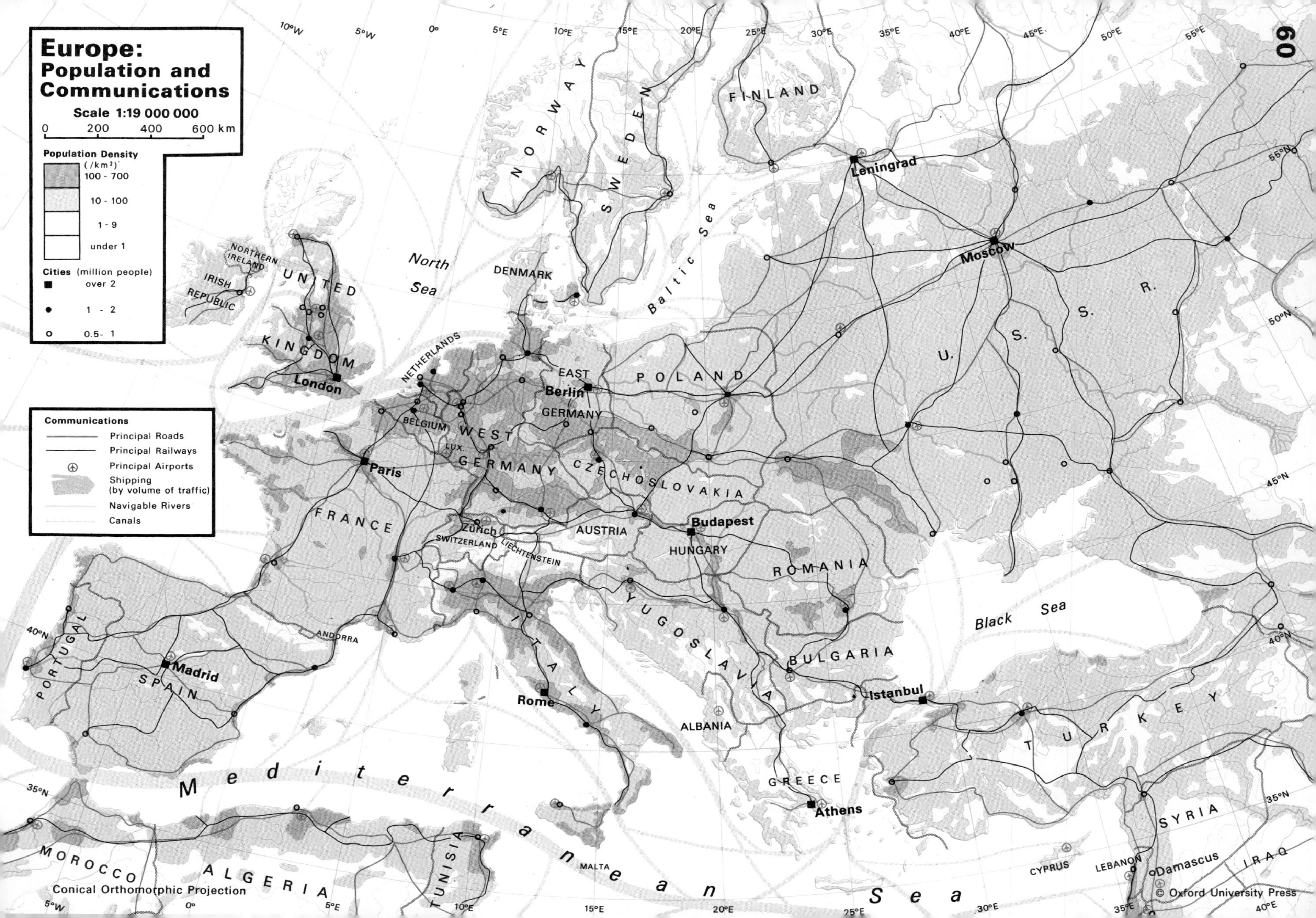
Europe:
Population and Communications
Scale 1:19 000 000
0 200 400 600 km
Population Density (/km²)
100 - 700
10 - 100
1 - 9
under 1
Cities (million people)
over 2
1 - 2
0.5 - 1
Communications
Principal Roads
Principal Railways
Principal Airports
Shipping (by volume of traffic)
Navigable Rivers
Canals
Conical Orthomorphic Projection
© Oxford University Press
NORWAY
SWEDEN
FINLAND
DENMARK
UNITED KINGDOM
NORTHERN IRELAND
IRISH REPUBLIC
NETHERLANDS
BELGIUM
LUX.
WEST GERMANY
EAST GERMANY
POLAND
CZECHOSLOVAKIA
AUSTRIA
SWITZERLAND
LIECHTENSTEIN
HUNGARY
ROMANIA
YUGOSLAVIA
BULGARIA
ALBANIA
GREECE
TURKEY
SYRIA
IRAQ
LEBANON
CYPRUS
MALTA
FRANCE
ANDORRA
SPAIN
PORTUGAL
ITALY
MOROCCO
ALGERIA
TUNISIA
U. S. S. R.
North Sea
Baltic Sea
Black Sea
Mediterranean Sea
London
Paris
Berlin
Zürich
Budapest
Madrid
Rome
Athens
Istanbul
Leningrad
Moscow
Damascus
10°W
5°W
0°
5°E
10°E
15°E
20°E
25°E
30°E
35°E
40°E
45°E
50°E
55°E
55°N
50°N
45°N
40°N
35°N

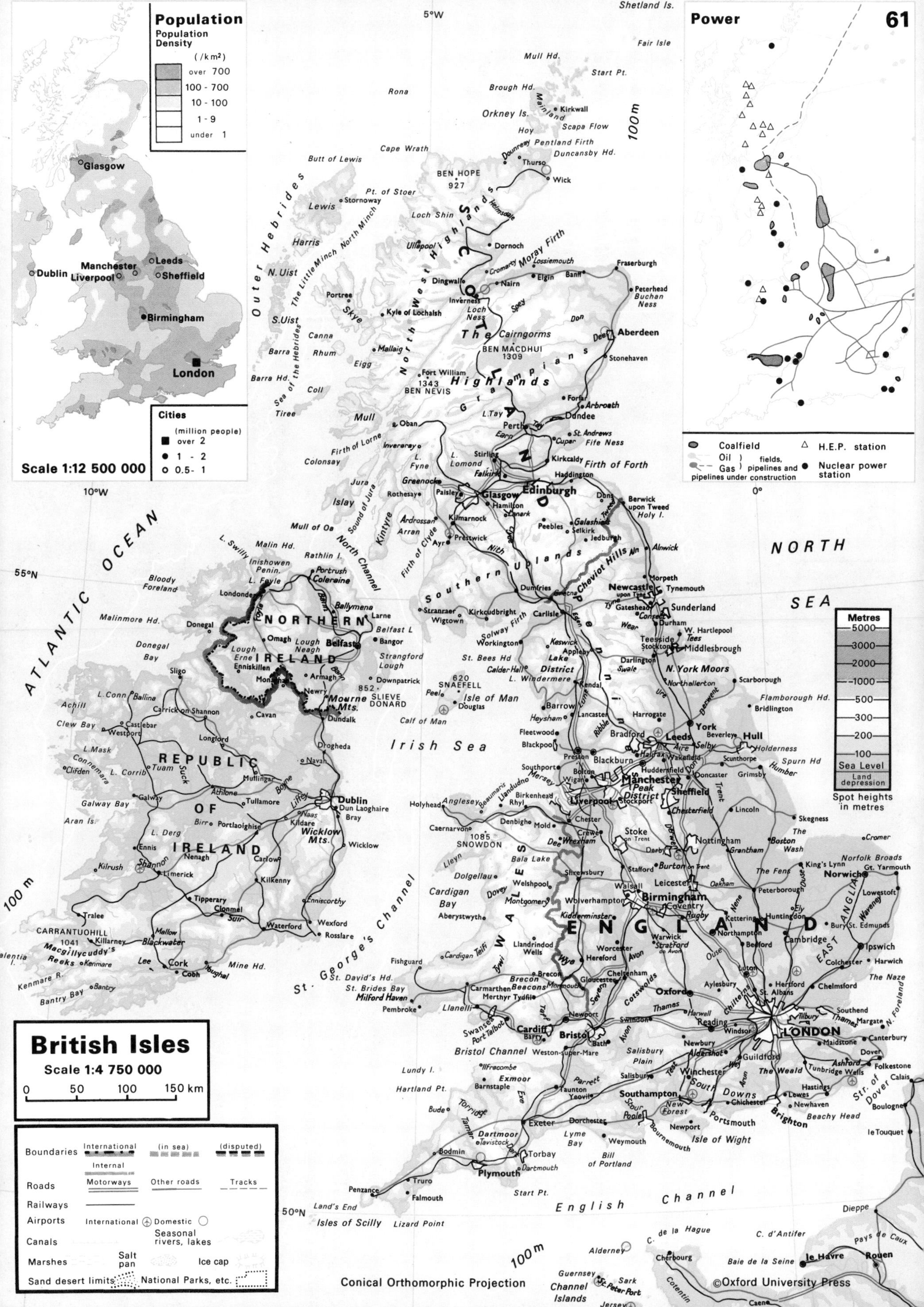
British Isles
Scale 1:4 750 000
0 50 100 150 km
Conical Orthomorphic Projection
Population
Population Density
(/km²)
over 700
100 - 700
10 - 100
1 - 9
under 1
Glasgow
Dublin
Manchester
Liverpool
Leeds
Sheffield
Birmingham
London
Cities
(million people)
over 2
1 - 2
0.5 - 1
Scale 1:12 500 000
Power
Coalfield
Oil) fields,
Gas) pipelines and
pipelines under construction
H.E.P. station
Nuclear power station
Metres
5000
3000
2000
1000
500
300
200
100
Sea Level
Land depression
Spot heights in metres
Boundaries
International
(in sea)
(disputed)
Internal
Roads
Motorways
Other roads
Tracks
Railways
Airports
International
Domestic
Canals
Seasonal rivers, lakes
Marshes
Salt pan
Ice cap
Sand desert limits
National Parks, etc.
5°W
10°W
0°
55°N
50°N
100 m
ATLANTIC OCEAN
NORTH SEA
Irish Sea
English Channel
St. George's Channel
Bristol Channel
North Channel
Shetland Is.
Fair Isle
Orkney Is.
Kirkwall
Mainland
Hoy
Scapa Flow
Pentland Firth
Duncansby Hd.
Mull Hd.
Start Pt.
Brough Hd.
Rona
Cape Wrath
Butt of Lewis
Dounreay
Thurso
Wick
BEN HOPE 927
Outer Hebrides
Lewis
Stornoway
Pt. of Stoer
Loch Shin
Harris
N. Uist
S. Uist
Barra
Barra Hd.
The Little Minch
North Minch
Sea of the Hebrides
Skye
Portree
Kyle of Lochalsh
Canna
Rhum
Eigg
Mallaig
Coll
Tiree
Mull
Colonsay
Islay
Jura
Sound of Jura
Kintyre
Mull of Oa
Ullapool
Dornoch
Moray Firth
Cromarty
Lossiemouth
Elgin
Banff
Fraserburgh
Peterhead
Buchan Ness
Dingwall
Nairn
Inverness
Loch Ness
Spey
Don
Dee
Aberdeen
Stonehaven
The Cairngorms
BEN MACDHUI 1309
Grampians
Fort William
1343
BEN NEVIS
North West Highlands
Highlands
SCOTLAND
Forfar
Arbroath
Dundee
L. Tay
Tay
Perth
Earn
St. Andrews
Fife Ness
Cupar
Oban
Firth of Lorne
Inveraray
L. Fyne
L. Lomond
Stirling
Falkirk
Kirkcaldy
Firth of Forth
Haddington
Edinburgh
Greenock
Paisley
Glasgow
Rothesay
Hamilton
Lanark
Kilmarnock
Ardrossan
Arran
Prestwick
Ayr
Firth of Clyde
Dunbar
Berwick upon Tweed
Holy I.
Tweed
Peebles
Galashiels
Selkirk
Jedburgh
Southern Uplands
Nith
Cheviot Hills
Dumfries
Gretna
Stranraer
Wigtown
Kirkcudbright
Solway Firth
Carlisle
Alnwick
Morpeth
Tynemouth
Newcastle upon Tyne
Gateshead
Sunderland
Consett
Durham
W. Hartlepool
Tees
Teesside
Stockton
Middlesbrough
Darlington
Swale
N. York Moors
Northallerton
Scarborough
Flamborough Hd.
Bridlington
Malin Hd.
Inishowen Penin.
L. Swilly
Rathlin I.
Portrush
Coleraine
Bloody Foreland
L. Foyle
Londonderry
Bann
Ballymena
Larne
NORTHERN IRELAND
Belfast L.
Belfast
Bangor
Malinmore Hd.
Donegal
Donegal Bay
Omagh
Lough Neagh
Lough Erne
Enniskillen
Strangford Lough
Armagh
Downpatrick
Newry
852 SLIEVE DONARD
Mourne Mts.
Monaghan
Sligo
L. Conn
Ballina
Achill
Clew Bay
Castlebar
Westport
Carrick-on-Shannon
Cavan
Dundalk
L. Mask
Longford
Drogheda
Connemara
Clifden
L. Corrib
Tuam
Suck
REPUBLIC OF IRELAND
Navan
Mullingar
Boyne
Galway
Galway Bay
Athlone
Tullamore
Liffey
Dublin
Dun Laoghaire
Bray
Naas
Kildare
Aran Is.
Birr
Portlaoighise
Wicklow Mts.
Wicklow
L. Derg
Ennis
Shannon
Nenagh
Carlow
Kilrush
Limerick
Kilkenny
Tipperary
Clonmel
Enniscorthy
Suir
Waterford
Wexford
Rosslare
Tralee
CARRANTUOHILL 1041
Killarney
Macgillycuddy's Reeks
Kenmare
Blackwater
Mallow
Cork
Cobh
Youghal
Lee
Mine Hd.
Kenmare R.
Bantry
Bantry Bay
Valentia I.
620 SNAEFELL
Isle of Man
Peel
Douglas
Calf of Man
Workington
St. Bees Hd
Keswick
Appleby
Lake District
Calder Hall
L. Windermere
Kendal
Lune
Barrow
Heysham
Lancaster
Fleetwood
Blackpool
Ribble
Harrogate
York
Derwent
Ure
Leeds
Bradford
Aire
Selby
Beverley
Hull
Holderness
Spurn Hd
Humber
Scunthorpe
Grimsby
Halifax
Wakefield
Huddersfield
Doncaster
Don
Trent
Preston
Blackburn
Southport
Bolton
Wigan
Mersey
Manchester
Peak District
Sheffield
Stockport
Liverpool
Birkenhead
Chesterfield
Lincoln
Skegness
Holyhead
Anglesey
Beaumaris
Llandudno
Rhyl
Denbigh
Mold
Chester
Caernarvon
1085 SNOWDON
Crewe
Wrexham
Dee
Stoke on Trent
Nottingham
Derby
Derwent
Boston
The Wash
Grantham
Cromer
Lleyn
Bala Lake
Shrewsbury
Stafford
Burton on Trent
Oakham
King's Lynn
Norfolk Broads
Norwich
Gt. Yarmouth
The Fens
Dolgellau
Welshpool
Walsall
Leicester
Peterborough
Ouse
Lowestoft
Cardigan Bay
Dovey
Montgomery
Wolverhampton
Birmingham
Coventry
Nene
Ely
Waveney
EAST ANGLIA
Aberystwyth
Kidderminster
Rugby
Kettering
Huntingdon
Bury St. Edmunds
WALES
ENGLAND
Llandrindod Wells
Worcester
Warwick
Stratford on Avon
Northampton
Bedford
Cambridge
Ipswich
Harwich
Fishguard
Cardigan
Teifi
Hereford
Avon
Wye
Colchester
The Naze
Tywi
Brecon Beacons
Brecon
Monmouth
Gloucester
Cheltenham
Severn
Cotswolds
Oxford
Chilterns
Luton
Aylesbury
Hertford
St. Albans
Chelmsford
St. David's Hd.
St. Brides Bay
Milford Haven
Pembroke
Carmarthen
Merthyr Tydfil
Llanelli
Swansea
Port Talbot
Taff
Cardiff
Barry
Newport
Bristol
Bath
Swindon
Thames
Harwell
Reading
Windsor
LONDON
Tilbury
Southend
Margate
N. Foreland
Canterbury
Maidstone
Dover
Folkestone
Ashford
Weston-super-Mare
Salisbury Plain
Newbury
Aldershot
Guildford
The Weald
Tunbridge Wells
Str. of Dover
Lundy I.
Ilfracombe
Exmoor
Barnstaple
Hartland Pt.
Parrett
Taunton
Yeovil
Salisbury
Test
Winchester
Wey
Arun
South Downs
Chichester
Lewes
Hastings
Newhaven
Brighton
Beachy Head
Bude
Torridge
Tamar
Exe
Exeter
Southampton
Stour
New Forest
Poole
Bournemouth
Portsmouth
Newport
Isle of Wight
Dorchester
Weymouth
Lyme Bay
Bill of Portland
Dartmoor
Tavistock
Dart
Torbay
Dartmouth
Bodmin
Plymouth
Start Pt.
Truro
Falmouth
Penzance
Land's End
Lizard Point
Isles of Scilly
Alderney
Guernsey
Sark
St. Peter Port
Channel Islands
Jersey
C. de la Hague
Cherbourg
Cotentin
C. d'Antifer
Baie de la Seine
Le Havre
Rouen
Pays de Caux
Dieppe
le Touquet
Boulogne
Calais
Caen
©Oxford University Press

Great Britain
Scale 1:2 200 000
0 35 70 km
Metres
5000
3000
2000
1000
500
300
200
100
Sea level
Land depression
Spot heights in metres
Boundaries
International
Internal
(in sea)
(disputed)
Roads
Motorways
Other roads
Railways
Airports
International
Domestic
Canals
Seasonal rivers, lakes
Marshes
Salt pans
Ice cap
Sand desert limits
National Parks, etc.
North Sea
Irish Sea
North Channel
Inner Hebrides
Grampian Mountains
Southern Uplands
Pennines
Cheviot Hills
Lake District
Yorkshire Dales
North York Moors
Firth of Forth
Firth of Clyde
Solway Firth
Firth of Lorne
Sound of Jura
Loch Linnhe
Loch Fyne
Isle of Man
Arran
Mull
Jura
Islay
Northern Ireland
Aberdeen
Dundee
Perth
Stirling
Glasgow
Edinburgh
Dumfries
Carlisle
Newcastle upon Tyne
Sunderland
Middlesbrough
York
Leeds
Bradford
Huddersfield
Blackburn
Bolton
Hull
Belfast
Bergen & Oslo
Hamburg
Caledonian Canal
BEN NEVIS 1343
BEN MACDHUI 1309
Cairngorm Mts.
Monadhliath Mts.
CENTRAL
FIFE
TAYSIDE
GRAMPIAN
LOTHIAN
BORDERS
STRATHCLYDE
DUMFRIES & GALLOWAY
NORTHUMBERLAND
TYNE & WEAR
DURHAM
CLEVELAND
CUMBRIA
NORTH YORKSHIRE
WEST YORKSHIRE
HUMBERSIDE
LANCS
ANTRIM
DOWN
ARMAGH
LOUTH
MEATH
Spurn Hd.
Flamborough Hd.
Mull of Kintyre
Mull of Galloway
Mull of Oa
St. Abb's Head
Fife Ness
Buddon Ness
55°N
100 m

LONDON
English Channel
Bristol Channel
St. George's Channel
Cardigan Bay
Strait of Dover
Meridian of Greenwich
FRANCE
Channel Islands
Jersey
Guernsey
Alderney
Sark
Isle of Wight
Norfolk Broads
The Wash
The Fens
Cambrian Mountains
Black Mountains
Dartmoor
Exmoor
Bodmin Moor
Salisbury Plain
Mendip Hills
North Downs
South Downs
The Weald
Chiltern Hills
Birmingham
Bristol
Cardiff
Plymouth
Southampton
Portsmouth
Brighton
Oxford
Cambridge
Norwich
Ipswich
Northampton
Nottingham
Leicester
Coventry
Derby
Swansea
Exeter
Torbay
Bournemouth
Poole
Le Havre
Dieppe
Boulogne
Fécamp
Land's End
Isles of Scilly
Lizard Pt.
Hartland Pt.
Start Pt.
Bill of Portland
Transverse Mercator Projection

Europe
Scale 1:12 500 000
0 100 200 300 400 km
Boundaries International (in sea) (disputed) Internal
Roads Motorways Other roads Tracks
Railways
Airports International Domestic
Canals
Seasonal rivers, lakes
Marsh
Salt pan
Ice cap
Sand Desert limits
National Parks, etc.
ATLANTIC OCEAN
North Sea
UNITED KINGDOM
SCOTLAND
NORTHERN IRELAND
IRISH REPUBLIC
WALES
ENGLAND
Irish Sea
English Channel
Bay of Biscay
FRANCE
SPAIN
PORTUGAL
MOROCCO
ALGERIA
Mediterranean
NETHERLANDS
Balearic Islands
Corsica (Fr.)
Sardinia (It.)
Pyrenees
Cantabrian Mts.
Massif Central
Sierra Morena
Sierra Nevada
Er Rif
High Atlas
Saharan Atlas
Tell Atlas
NORTH RHINE WESTPHALIA
Scale 1:1 000 000
0 10 20 km
Motorways
Other roads
Metres
5000
3000
2000
1000
500
300
200
100
Sea level
Land depression
Spot heights in metres
Conical Orthomorphic Projection
5° W
0°
5°E
50°N
35°N

Gulf of Finland
Tallinn
Novgorod
Msta
Rybinsk
Yaroslavl'
Ivanovo
Gor'kiy
Dzerzhinsk
P'yana
Åland Is.
Uppsala
Malaren
Stockholm
Karlstad
Örebro
Vänern
Norrköping
Linköping
Vättern
Borås
Göteborg
SWEDEN
Visby
Gotland
Kalmar
Halmstad
Hälsingborg
Karlskrona
Malmö
Bornholm
Baltic Sea
Lake Peipus
Tartu
L. Il'men
Kalinin
Vladimir
Arzamas
Alatyr
Gulf of Riga
Lovat
Volga
Moscow
Moksha
Sura
Kolomna
Ryazan
Riga
West Dvina
Velikiye Luki
Rzhev
Dnieper
Serpukhov
Novomoskovsk
Penza
Tula
R.
Liepāja
Daugavpils
Vitebsk
Smolensk
Oka
Don
Tsna
Tambov
Voronezh
Klaipeda
Kaunas
Vilnius
Mogilev
Orel
S.
Lipetsk
Balashov
Borisoglebsk
Kaliningrad
Minsk
Berezina
Bryansk
Besed
Desna
Voronezh
Rügen
Gdańsk
Grodno
Neman
Bobruysk
S.
Seym
Kursk
Rostock
Białystok
Narew
U.
Gomel'
Don
Szczecin
Bydgoszcz
Vistula
Pinsk
Pripet
Chernigov
EAST
Oder
Warta
Havel
Berlin
Poznań
Warsaw
Brest Litovskiy
Kharkov
Oskol
Elbe
Braunschweig
Łódź
Sluch
Kiev
Sula
Poltava
Donets
Kramatorsk
Lugansk
Magdeburg
GERMANY
POLAND
Lublin
Rovno
Vorskla
Dnieper
Leipzig
Dresden
Erfurt
Neisse
Wrocław
Pilica
Vistula
Bug
Zhitomir
Cherkassy
Dnepropetrovsk
Donetsk
Don
Sal
Erzgebirge
Sudeten Mts.
Gliwice
Katowice
Cracow
L'vov
Kirovograd
Krivoy Rog
Zaporozh'ye
Taganrog
Rostov-na-Donu
Manych
Elbe
Prague
Ostrava
Zhdanov
CZECHOSLOVAKIA
Plzen
Brno
Vah
Košice
Mukachevo
Carpathians
Chernovtsy
Dniester
Bug
Dnieper
Melitopol'
Sea of Azov
Kuban
Vltava
Morava
Tatra
2043
Kherson
Nikolayev
Passau
Linz
Vienna
Bratislava
Miskolc
Satu-Mare
Kishinev
Iaşi
Odessa
Kerch'
Krasnodar
Salzburg
Gyor
Tisza
Debrecen
CRIMEA
AUSTRIA
Budapest
Cluj
Siretul
Simferopol'
3797
Graz
HUNGARY
ROMANIA
C. Tarkhankut
Sevastopol'
1545
200 m
Bolzano
Klagenfurt
2556
Pécs
Szeged
Mureşul
Oltul
Braşov
Braila
Ljubljana
Subotica
Timişoara
Ploeşti
Black Sea
Trieste
Zagreb
2529
Constanţa
Venice
Rijeka
Sava
Danube
Novi Sad
Jiutul
Bucharest
Padua
Una
Craiova
Belgrade
Morava
Danube
Ruse
Varna
Samsun
Bologna
YUGOSLAVIA
Drina
Pleven
BULGARIA
SAN MARINO
Dinaric Alps
Sarajevo
Niš
Balkan Mts
Burgas
Zonguldak
Devrez
Sivas
Florence
Split
2522
Sofiya
Bosporus
Kizilirmak
Adriatic Sea
2924
Plovdiv
Maritsa
Assisi
Dubrovnik
Skopje
Struma
Istanbul
Sakarya
Ankara
Delice
2921
Tiber
ALBANIA
Vardar
Bursa
Eskisehir
Kizil
Kayseri
Rome
C. Gargano
Tirane
Drin
Kavalla
TURKEY
Thessalonica
Dardanelles
Balikesir
L. Tuz
Bari
Vlorë
Pindus Mts.
Afyonkarahisar
Naples
Taranto
2574
Mitilini
L. Eğridir
Konya
Ceyhan
Tyrrhenian Sea
Ioannina
Larisa
Aegean Sea
Gediz
2734
Adana
İzmir
L. Beyşehir
GREECE
Menderes
Aksu
Antakya
Ionian Sea
Athens
Muğla
Antalya
Pátrai
Piraieus
3086
Latakia
SYRIA
Palermo
Messina
C. Gelidonya
Sicily
3340
Catania
Rhodes
Rodos
Nicosia
Kalamai
CYPRUS
LEBANON
Beirut
C. Bon
C. Matapan
C. Passero
Khania
Iráklion
Tyre
Pantelleria (It)
2148
Crete
Haifa
MALTA
Valletta
Sousse
Tel Aviv-Jaffa
ISRAEL
Mediterranean Sea
Gulf of Gabès
Port Said
200 m
Beida
Alexandria
Tanta
EGYPT
Tarabulus
Barce
LIBYA
LIBYA
Cairo
Suez
15°E
20°E
25°E

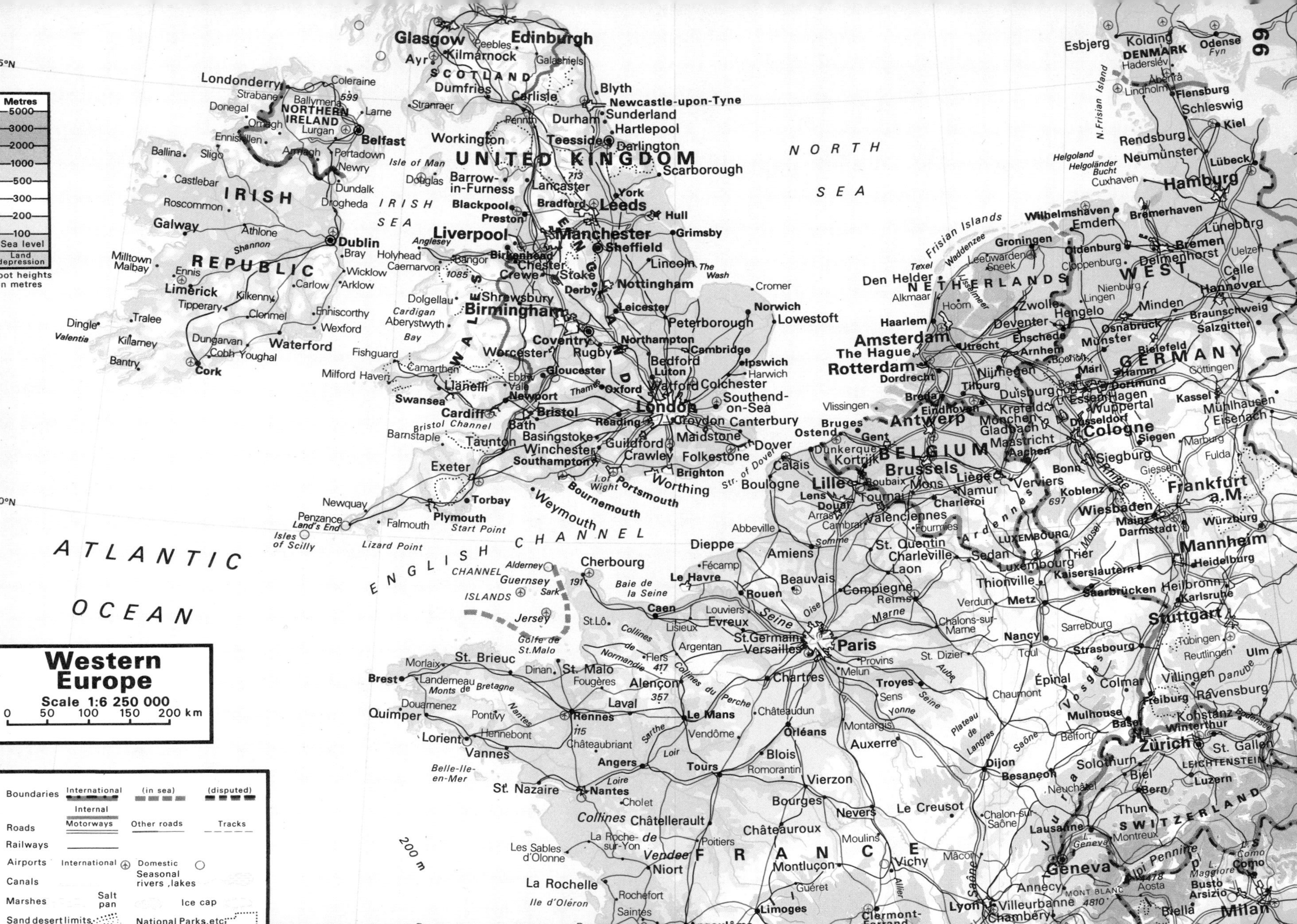
Western Europe
Scale 1:6 250 000
0 50 100 150 200 km
Metres
5000
3000
2000
1000
500
300
200
100
Sea level
Land depression
Spot heights in metres
Boundaries
International
Internal
(in sea)
(disputed)
Roads
Motorways
Other roads
Tracks
Railways
Airports
International
Domestic
Canals
Seasonal rivers, lakes
Marshes
Salt pan
Ice cap
Sand desert limits
National Parks, etc.
55°N
50°N
ATLANTIC
OCEAN
NORTH
SEA
IRISH
SEA
ENGLISH
CHANNEL
CHANNEL
ISLANDS
200 m
IRISH
REPUBLIC
NORTHERN
IRELAND
SCOTLAND
UNITED KINGDOM
ENGLAND
WALES
FRANCE
BELGIUM
NETHERLANDS
WEST
GERMANY
DENMARK
LUXEMBOURG
SWITZERLAND
LEICHTENSTEIN
Glasgow
Edinburgh
Peebles
Ayr
Kilmarnock
Galashiels
Dumfries
Carlisle
Blyth
Newcastle-upon-Tyne
Sunderland
Durham
Hartlepool
Teesside
Darlington
Stranraer
Workington
Barrow-in-Furness
Lancaster
Scarborough
York
Leeds
Bradford
Blackpool
Preston
Hull
Liverpool
Manchester
Grimsby
Sheffield
Birkenhead
Chester
Crewe
Stoke
Lincoln
The Wash
Derby
Nottingham
Shrewsbury
Leicester
Birmingham
Coventry
Northampton
Peterborough
Norwich
Cromer
Lowestoft
Rugby
Cambridge
Ipswich
Harwich
Worcester
Gloucester
Bedford
Luton
Watford
Colchester
Oxford
London
Southend-on-Sea
Reading
Croydon
Canterbury
Maidstone
Dover
Folkestone
Guildford
Crawley
Brighton
Worthing
Portsmouth
Southampton
Winchester
Basingstoke
Bournemouth
Weymouth
I. of Wight
Bath
Bristol
Newport
Cardiff
Swansea
Llanelli
Carmarthen
Fishguard
Milford Haven
Aberystwyth
Cardigan Bay
Dolgellau
Bangor
Caernarvon
Holyhead
Anglesey
Bristol Channel
Barnstaple
Taunton
Exeter
Torbay
Plymouth
Start Point
Falmouth
Lizard Point
Newquay
Penzance
Land's End
Isles of Scilly
Isle of Man
Douglas
Londonderry
Coleraine
Strabane
Ballymena
Donegal
Omagh
Larne
Enniskillen
Lurgan
Belfast
Armagh
Portadown
Newry
Ballina
Sligo
Castlebar
Dundalk
Roscommon
Drogheda
Galway
Athlone
Dublin
Shannon
Bray
Milltown Malbay
Ennis
Wicklow
Limerick
Carlow
Arklow
Kilkenny
Tipperary
Enniscorthy
Clonmel
Wexford
Dingle
Tralee
Valentia
Killarney
Dungarvan
Waterford
Cobh
Youghal
Bantry
Cork
Strait of Dover
Calais
Boulogne
Dunkerque
Lille
Lens
Douai
Arras
Cambrai
Abbeville
Amiens
Dieppe
Fécamp
Le Havre
Rouen
Beauvais
Compiègne
Cherbourg
Baie de la Seine
Caen
Lisieux
Evreux
Louviers
Seine
Oise
Paris
St. Germain
Versailles
Argentan
Flers
Alençon
Chartres
Collines de Normandie
Collines du Perche
St. Lô
Alderney
Guernsey
Sark
Jersey
Golfe de St. Malo
St. Malo
Dinan
St. Brieuc
Morlaix
Brest
Landerneau
Monts de Bretagne
Douarnenez
Quimper
Pontivy
Lorient
Hennebont
Vannes
Belle-Ile-en-Mer
Rennes
Fougères
Laval
Le Mans
Châteaubriant
Angers
Nantes
St. Nazaire
Cholet
Collines de Vendée
La Roche-sur-Yon
Les Sables d'Olonne
La Rochelle
Ile d'Oléron
Rochefort
Saintes
Niort
Châtellerault
Poitiers
Tours
Vendôme
Châteaudun
Orléans
Blois
Romorantin
Vierzon
Bourges
Châteauroux
Montluçon
Guéret
Limoges
Angoulême
Nevers
Moulins
Vichy
Clermont-Ferrand
Montargis
Auxerre
Melun
Provins
Troyes
Sens
Yonne
Marne
Reims
Laon
St. Quentin
Charleville
Sedan
Verdun
Chalons-sur-Marne
St. Dizier
Aube
Chaumont
Plateau de Langres
Dijon
Le Creusot
Chalon-sur-Saône
Mâcon
Saône
Lyon
Villeurbanne
Chambéry
Annecy
Besançon
Belfort
Mulhouse
Colmar
Vosges
Épinal
Nancy
Toul
Metz
Thionville
Strasbourg
Sarrebourg
Valenciennes
Fourmies
Ardennes
Den Helder
Texel
Alkmaar
Haarlem
Amsterdam
The Hague
Rotterdam
Dordrecht
Utrecht
Hoorn
IJsselmeer
Leeuwarden
Sneek
Groningen
Waddenzee
Frisian Islands
Zwolle
Deventer
Enschede
Hengelo
Arnhem
Nijmegen
Tilburg
Breda
Eindhoven
Vlissingen
Bruges
Ostend
Gent
Antwerp
Kortrijk
Roubaix
Tournai
Brussels
Mons
Charleroi
Namur
Liège
Maastricht
Verviers
Aachen
Mönchen Gladbach
Krefeld
Duisburg
Essen
Dortmund
Hamm
Hagen
Wuppertal
Düsseldorf
Cologne
Bonn
Siegburg
Siegen
Koblenz
Rhine
Mosel
Trier
Luxembourg
Kaiserslautern
Saarbrücken
Wiesbaden
Mainz
Darmstadt
Frankfurt a.M.
Würzburg
Mannheim
Heidelberg
Heilbronn
Karlsruhe
Stuttgart
Tübingen
Reutlingen
Ulm
Danube
Villingen
Ravensburg
Freiburg
Konstanz
Bodensee
Basel
Winterthur
Zürich
St. Gallen
Luzern
Solothurn
Biel
Bern
Neuchâtel
Thun
Jura
Lausanne
Montreux
L. Geneva
Geneva
Mont Blanc
4810
Alpi Pennine
4478
Aosta
Biella
L. Maggiore
L. Como
Como
Busto Arsizio
Milan
Giessen
Marburg
Fulda
Kassel
Mühlhausen
Eisenach
Göttingen
Münster
Bielefeld
Osnabrück
Minden
Hannover
Celle
Braunschweig
Salzgitter
Nienburg
Lingen
Cloppenburg
Oldenburg
Delmenhorst
Bremen
Uelzen
Lüneburg
Emden
Wilhelmshaven
Bremerhaven
Cuxhaven
Hamburg
Lübeck
Neumünster
Rendsburg
Kiel
Schleswig
Flensburg
Helgoland
Helgoländer Bucht
N. Frisian Island
Esbjerg
Kolding
Haderslev
Odense
Fyn
Lindholm
599
713
1085
697
191
417
357
115

BISCAY
MEDITERRANEAN SEA
SPAIN
PORTUGAL
MOROCCO
ALGERIA
ITALY
CÔTE D'AZUR
Golfe du Lion
Golfo de Valencia
Balearic Islands (Sp.)
Golfo de Cadiz
Costa del Sol
Costa Brava
Str. of Gibraltar
Cordillera Cantabrica
Pyrenees
Sistema Ibérico
Cordillera Central
Septentrional
Meseta
Montes de Toledo
Sierra Morena
Meridional
Cordilleras Béticas
Sierra Nevada
Algarve
Er Rif Mts
Atlas Mountains
Tell Atlas
Monts du Hodna
Central
Cévennes
Alpes Maritimes
Les Landes
El Ferrol del Caudillo
La Coruña
Santiago de Compostela
C. Finisterre
Ortigueira
Villalba
Ribadeo
Avilés
Gijón
Oviedo
Sama de Langreo
Mieres
Santander
Torrelavega
Lugo
1960
Pontevedra
Ponferrada
León
Vigo
Orense
Ribadavia
2124
2188
La Guardia
Viana do Castelo
Braga
Bragança
Vila Real
Oporto
Vila Nova de Gaia
Douro
Duero
Viseu
Aveiro
Coimbra
Guarda
Covilhã
40°N
Caldas da Rainha
Tagus
Castelo Branco
Santarém
Portalegre
Lisbon
Almada
Barreiro
Setúbal
Evora
Guadiana
Beja
Portimão
C. de São Vicente
Faro
Olhão
Ayamonte
Órbigo
Benavente
Zamora
Salamanca
Ávila
2592
Tietar
Alberche
Palencia
Valladolid
Segovia
2430
Burgos
Miranda de Ebro
Vitoria
Bilbao
Haro
Logroño
Calahorra
Soria
El Burgo
Sigüenza
Guadalajara
Tajo
Alcalá de Henares
Madrid
Talavera de la Reina
Toledo
Cáceres
Mérida
Badajoz
Jerez de los Caballeros
Alcázar de San Juan
Ciudad Real
Almadén
Puertollano
Peñarroya
Valdepeñas
Tomelloso
Andújar
Linares
Córdoba
Guadalquivir
Jaén
Sevilla
Huelva
Écija
Lucena
Utrera
Loja
Antequera
Granada
2269
Baza
2381
Sanlúcar de Barremeda
Cádiz
San Fernando
Jerez
Ronda
Málaga
Motril
Adra
Almeria
C. de Gata
Algeciras
La Línea
GIBRALTAR (U.K.)
Tangier
Ceuta (Sp.)
Tetuan
Asilah
Larache
Ksar-el-Kebir
Al Hoceima
Nador
Melilla (Sp.)
5°W
35°N
Arcachon
Bayonne
Biarritz
San Sebastián
Pamplona
Tudela
Ebro
Zaragoza
Calatayud
Teruel
2204
Mijares
Cuenca
Cabriel
Júcar
Albacete
Mundo
Segura
Hellin
Elche
Alicante
Orihuela
Murcia
Lorca
Cartagena
Águilas
C. de Palos
Alcira
Alcoy
C. de la Nao
Valencia
Sagunto
Castellón de la Plana
Benicarló
Vinaroz
Tortosa
Tarragona
Reus
Lérida
Sabadell
Manresa
Barcelona
Hospitalet
Gerona
San Feliú de Guixols
Ter
Sègre
C. Creus
Huesca
Jaca
2504
3404
ANDORRA
2785
Pau
Lourdes
Tarbes
St. Gaudens
Pamiers
Perpignan
Narbonne
Bordeaux
Garonne
Dordogne
Marmande
Lot
Cahors
Villeneuve-sur-Lot
Agen
Mont-de-Marsan
Adour
Montauban
Toulouse
Albi
Castres
Carcassonne
Aveyron
Rodez
Millau
Béziers
Montpellier
Sète
Nîmes
Alès
Rhône
Montélimar
Orange
Avignon
Arles
Aix-en-Provence
Marseille
Toulon
Hyères
Durance
Verdon
Digne
Gap
Draguignan
Grasse
Cannes
Antibes
Nice
St. Tropez
MONACO
San Remo
Imperia
Cuneo
3297
Savona
Genoa
Menorca
Mahón
Mallorca
Palma de Mallorca
Ibiza
Formentera
200 m
10°E
Leghorn
Piombino
I. d'Elba
C. Corse
Bastia
Calvi
2710
Corte
Corsica (Fr.)
Ajaccio
Sartène
Porto-Vecchio
Bonifacio
Str. of Bonifacio
La Maddalena
Tempio Pausania
Olbia
Porto Torres
Sassari
Alghero
Nuoro
Sardinia (It.)
40°N
Monti del Gennargentu
1834
Tirso
Oristano
Iglesias
Carbonia
Cágliari
Golfo di Cágliari
C. Spartivento
Same scale
Algiers
Cherchell
Ténès
Blida
Médéa
Tizi Ouzou
1810
Ksar el Boukhari
Bejaïa
Djidjelli
Skikda
Annaba
Constantine
Souk Ahras
Sétif
El Eulma
El Asnam
Chéliff
Mostaganem
Oran
Ighil Izane
Mohammadia
Mascara
Tiaret
Bou Saâda
Sidi-bel-Abbès
Beni-Saf
Aïn Témouchent
Tlemcen
0°
5°E
Conical Orthomorphic Projection
© Oxford University Press

BALTIC SEA
SWEDEN
DENMARK
WEST GERMANY
EAST GERMANY
POLAND
CZECHOSLOVAKIA
HUNGARY
AUSTRIA
SWITZ.
LIECHTENSTEIN
R.S.F.S.R.
LITHUANIAN S.S.R.
BYELORUSSIAN S.S.R.
UKRAINIAN S.S.R.
MOLDAVIAN S.S.R.
U. S. S. R.
Copenhagen
Karlskrona
Kristianstad
Malmö
Lund
Hälsingborg
Helsingør
Bornholm
Zealand
Jutland
Odense
Esbjerg
Kolding
Vejle
Horsens
Flensburg
Kiel
Lübeck
Hamburg
Bremen
Hannover
Osnabrück
Bielefeld
Kassel
Göttingen
Braunschweig
Magdeburg
Berlin
Potsdam
Rostock
Stralsund
Schwerin
Wismar
Neubrandenburg
Frankfurt a.d.O.
Cottbus
Leipzig
Halle
Dessau
Dresden
Karl-Marx-Stadt
Zwickau
Plauen
Erfurt
Weimar
Jena
Gera
Frankfurt a.M.
Darmstadt
Würzburg
Nürnberg
Regensburg
Stuttgart
Ulm
Augsburg
Munich
Ingolstadt
Heilbronn
Reutlingen
Szczecin
Gorzów Wielkopolski
Poznań
Bydgoszcz
Toruń
Gdańsk
Gdynia
Sopot
Elbląg
Olsztyn
Warsaw
Łódź
Płock
Radom
Kielce
Lublin
Białystok
Wrocław
Opole
Częstochowa
Katowice
Cracow
Tarnów
Rzeszów
Przemyśl
Prague
Plzeň
Ústí
Liberec
Hradec Králové
Pardubice
Jihlava
České Budějovice
Brno
Olomouc
Ostrava
Žilina
Banská Bystrica
Prešov
Košice
Bratislava
Nitra
Trnava
Vienna
Linz
Salzburg
Graz
Innsbruck
Klagenfurt
Villach
Budapest
Debrecen
Miskolc
Eger
Győr
Szeged
Pécs
Kecskemét
Szolnok
Nyíregyháza
Kaliningrad
Klaipeda
Sovetsk
Kaunas
Vilnius
Šiauliai
Panevėžys
Daugavpils
Grodno
Lida
Minsk
Brest
Pinsk
Bobruysk
Gomel'
Mogilev
Vitebsk
Orsha
Polotsk
Borisov
Mozyr'
Kiev
Zhitomir
Vinnitsa
Rovno
Lutsk
Kovel'
L'vov
Ternopol'
Chernovtsy
Khmel'nitskiy
Uman'
Kishinev
Tiraspol'
Bendery
Iaşi
Suceava
Botoşani
Cluj
Oradea
Satu-Mare
Baia-Mare
Arad
Tîrgu Mureş
Bacău
Roman
Bolzano
Merano
Trento
Udine
Gorizia
Ljubljana
Maribor
Bergamo
Vistula
Oder
Elbe
Danube
Dnestr
Prut
Bug
Pripet
Dvina
Neman
Tatry 2655
Bohemian Forest
Erzgebirge
Sudeten Mts.
Carnic Alps
Dolomites
Gulf of Gdansk
Pomeranian Bay
L. Balaton
L. Neusiedler
Brenner Pass
55°N
50°N

© Oxford University Press

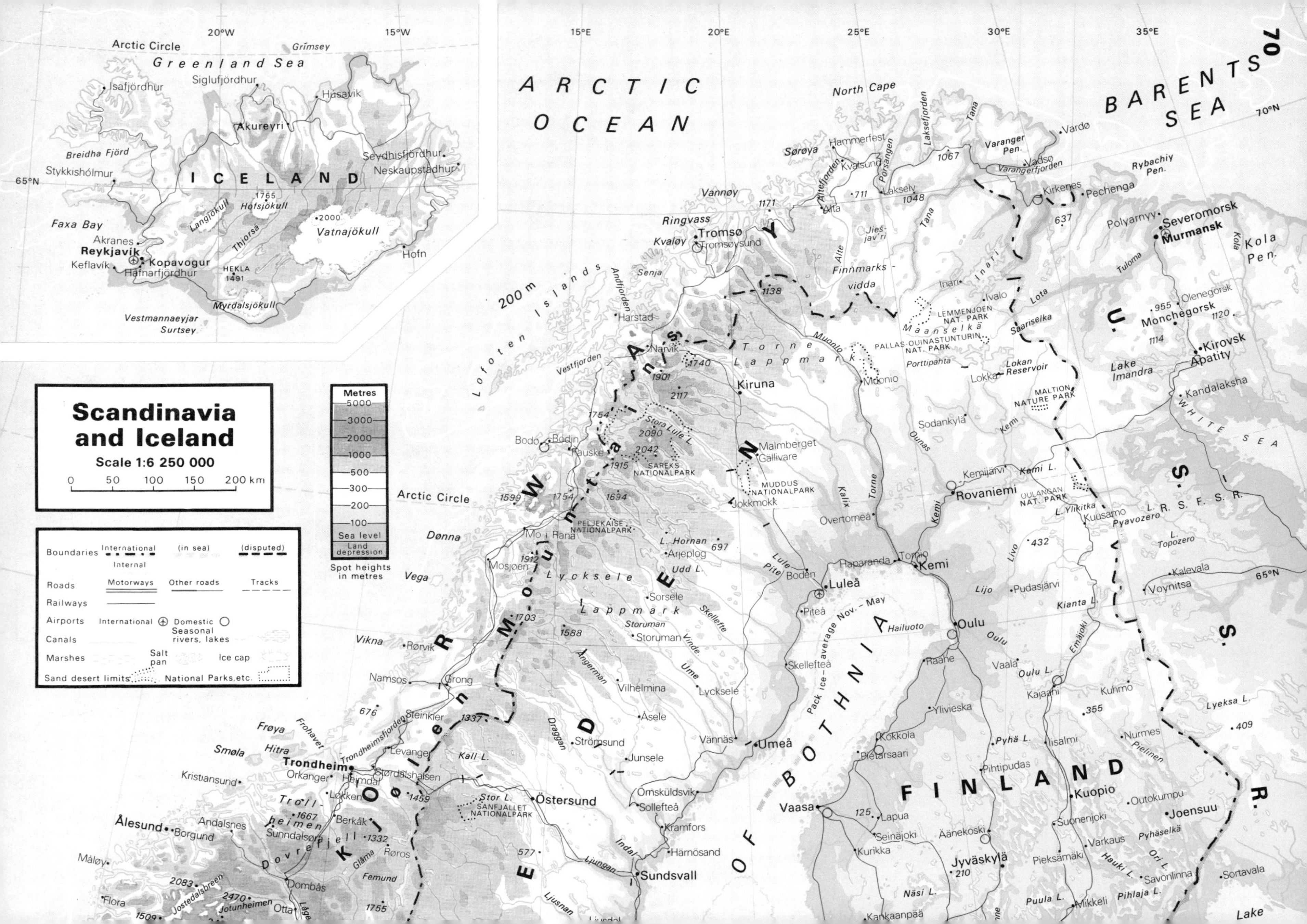

Scandinavia and Iceland
Scale 1:6 250 000
0 50 100 150 200 km
Metres
5000
3000
2000
1000
500
300
200
100
Sea level
Land depression
Spot heights in metres
Boundaries International (in sea) (disputed)
Internal
Roads Motorways Other roads Tracks
Railways
Airports International Domestic
Canals Seasonal rivers, lakes
Marshes Salt pan Ice cap
Sand desert limits National Parks,etc.
ARCTIC OCEAN
BARENTS SEA
WHITE SEA
GULF OF BOTHNIA
Greenland Sea
ICELAND
FINLAND
SWEDEN
NORWAY
U.S.S.R.
R.S.F.S.R.
Kjølen Mountains
Arctic Circle
North Cape
Lofoten Islands
200 m
Pack ice - average Nov. - May
Reykjavík
Kopavogur
Hafnarfjördhur
Keflavík
Akranes
Faxa Bay
Stykkishólmur
Breidha Fjörd
Isafjördhur
Siglufjördhur
Akureyri
Húsavík
Grímsey
Seydhisfjördhur
Neskaupstadhur
Hofn
Vatnajökull
Hofsjökull
Langjökull
Mýrdalsjökull
Thjórsá
HEKLA 1491
Vestmannaeyjar
Surtsey
Tromsø
Hammerfest
Narvik
Kiruna
Bodø
Mo i Rana
Luleå
Umeå
Sundsvall
Östersund
Trondheim
Ålesund
Kemi
Oulu
Rovaniemi
Vaasa
Kuopio
Jyväskylä
Joensuu
Murmansk
Severomorsk
Kirovsk
Apatity
Monchegorsk
Kandalaksha
Kola Pen.
Rybachiy Pen.
Varanger Pen.
Kirkenes
Vardø
Vadsø
Pechenga
Finnmarksvidda
Torne Lappmark
Lycksele Lappmark
Dovrefjell
Trollheimen
SAREKS NATIONALPARK
MUDDUS NATIONALPARK
PELJEKAISE NATIONALPARK
SANFJÄLLET NATIONALPARK
LEMMENJOEN NAT. PARK
PALLAS-OUNASTUNTURIN NAT. PARK
OULANGAN NAT. PARK
MALTION NATURE PARK
Maanselkä
Lake Imandra
Gulf of Bothnia
15°E
20°E
25°E
30°E
35°E
20°W
15°W
65°N
70°N

NORTH SEA
Skagerrak
Kattegat
BALTIC SEA
GULF OF FINLAND
Gulf of Riga
ESTONIAN S.S.R.
LATVIAN S.S.R.
LITHUANIAN S.S.R.
BYELORUSSIAN S.S.R.
R. S. F. S. R.
DENMARK
POLAND
EAST GERMANY
WEST GERMANY
NETHERLANDS
Oslo
Stockholm
Helsinki (Helsingfors)
Leningrad
Tallinn
Riga
Vilnius
Minsk
Warsaw
Copenhagen
Berlin
Hamburg
Göteborg
Gdańsk
Kaliningrad
Klaipeda
Kaunas
Pskov
Łódź
Poznań
Szczecin
Leipzig
Dresden
Hanover
Cologne
Bergen
Stavanger
Kristiansand
Malmö
Aarhus
Ålborg
Uppsala
Turku
Pack ice - average max. Feb. - March
200 m
55°N
60°N
Modified Conical Orthomorphic Projection

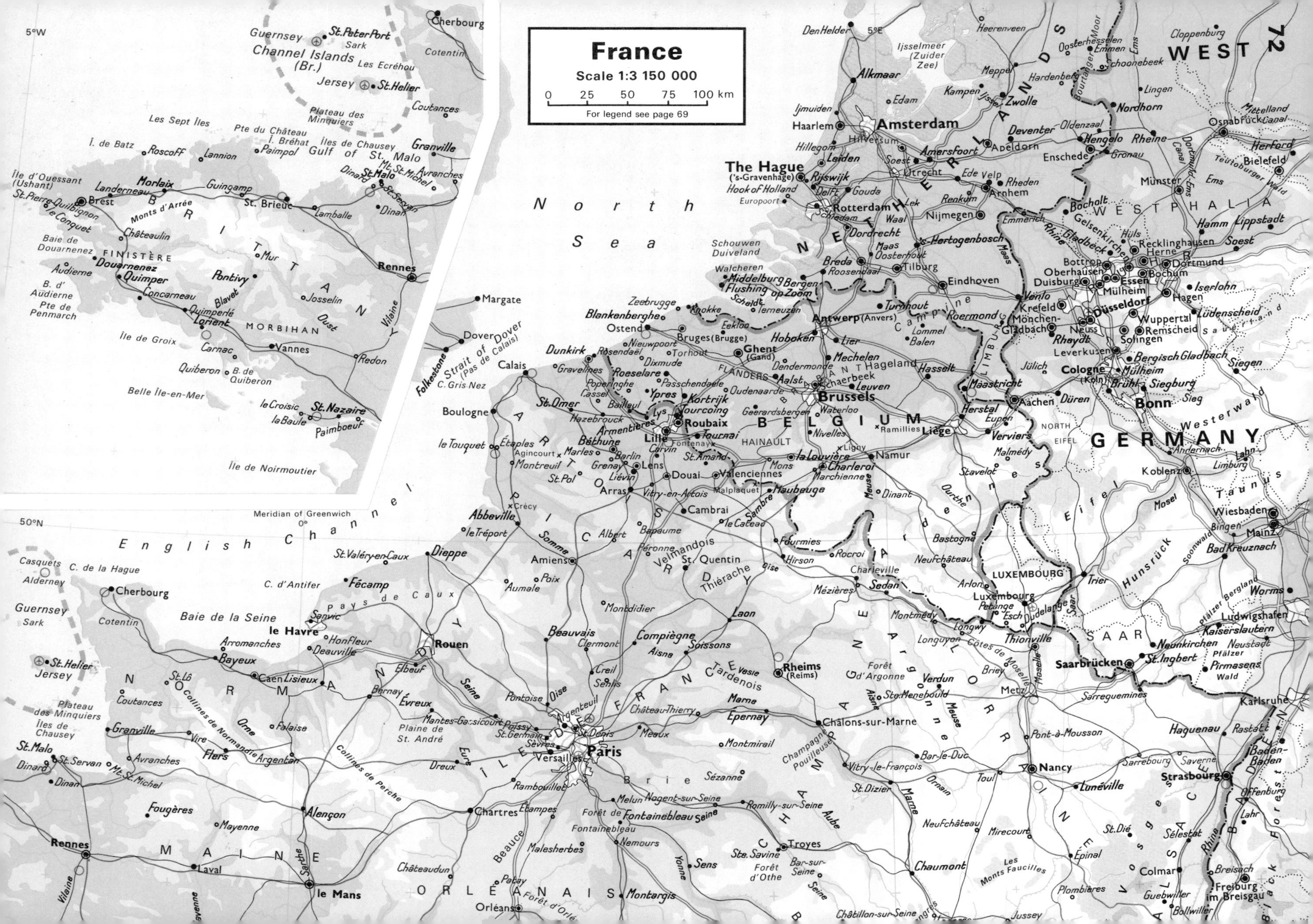

France
Scale 1:3 150 000
0 25 50 75 100 km
For legend see page 69
5°W
5°E
50°N
Meridian of Greenwich 0°
North Sea
English Channel
Strait of Dover (Pas de Calais)
Channel Islands (Br.)
Guernsey
St.Peter Port
Sark
Jersey
St.Helier
Alderney
Gulf of St. Malo
Baie de la Seine
NETHERLANDS
BELGIUM
LUXEMBOURG
WEST GERMANY
BRITTANY
NORMANDY
PICARDY
ÎLE DE FRANCE
CHAMPAGNE
LORRAINE
ALSACE
MAINE
ORLÉANAIS
WESTPHALIA
SAAR
FLANDERS
HAINAULT
FINISTÈRE
MORBIHAN
Paris
Versailles
Rouen
le Havre
Cherbourg
Caen
Rennes
le Mans
Chartres
Orléans
Amiens
Lille
Roubaix
Calais
Boulogne
Dunkirk
Dieppe
Rheims (Reims)
Troyes
Nancy
Metz
Strasbourg
Brussels
Antwerp (Anvers)
Ghent (Gand)
Liège
Namur
Amsterdam
Rotterdam
The Hague ('s-Gravenhage)
Utrecht
Eindhoven
Cologne (Köln)
Bonn
Düsseldorf
Essen
Dortmund
Koblenz
Wiesbaden
Mainz
Saarbrücken
Trier
Luxembourg
Aachen
Maastricht
Brest
Quimper
Lorient
Vannes
St. Brieuc
St.Malo
St.Nazaire
Dover
Folkestone
Margate
Ardennes
Argonne
Vosges
Eifel
Hunsrück
Taunus
Westerwald
Black Forest
Seine
Marne
Oise
Somme
Meuse
Moselle
Rhine
Maas
Aisne
Sambre
Yonne
Aube
Sarthe
Vilaine

Metres
5000
3000
2000
1000
500
300
200
100
Sea level
Land depression
Spot heights in metres
FRANCE
SWITZ.
SPAIN
ANDORRA
MONACO
Bay of Biscay
Gulf of Lions
Côte d'Azur
Massif Central
Auvergne
Limousin
Aquitaine
Gascony
Languedoc
Provence
Dauphiné
Burgundy
Franche-Comté
Lyonnais
Poitou
Saintonge
Angoumois
Aunis
Marche
Bourbonnais
Nivernais
Berry
Touraine
Vendée
Béarn
Foix
Roussillon
Savoy
Cévennes
Périgord
Agenais
Médoc
Les Landes
Pyrenees
Maritime Alps
Graian Alps
Pennine Alps
Bernese Alps
Cottian Alps
Provence Alps
Dauphiné Alps
The Jura
Morvan
Limagne
Monts du Forez
Monts de la Margeride
Monts d'Aubrac
Monts Garrigues
Montagnes du Plantaurel
Corbières
PYRÉNÉES OCCIDENTALES
M. BLANC 4810
M. PELVOUX
MATTERHORN 4478
WEISSHORN 4454
DOM 4545
JUNGFRAU 4158
ALETSCHHORN 4195
PUY DE SANCY 1886
PLOMB DU CANTAL 1858
PIC D'ESTATS 3141
PIC DE MONTVALIER 2840
ANETO 3404
MONT PERDU 3352
GT. ST. BERNARD P.
LT. ST. BERNARD P.
M. CENIS P.
SIMPLON P.
MADDALENA P.
TENDA P.
Nantes
Tours
Bourges
Nevers
Dijon
Besançon
Bern
Geneva
Lausanne
Poitiers
Limoges
Clermont-Ferrand
Lyons
St. Étienne
Grenoble
Valence
Bordeaux
Toulouse
Montpellier
Avignon
Marseilles
Toulon
Nice
Cannes
Perpignan
Narbonne
Carcassonne
Bayonne
Pau
Tarbes
Lourdes
45°N
5°E
Meridian of Greenwich 0°
Conical Orthomorphic Projection

North Sea
Heligoland Bight
East Frisian Islands
West Frisian Islands
Wadden Zee
Terschelling
Texel
Borkum
Juist
Norderney
Baltrum
Langeoog
Spiekeroog
Wangerooge
Cuxhaven
Kiel Canal
HOLSTEIN
Plön
Neumünster
Lübeck Bay
Lübeck
Elmshorn
Altona
Hamburg
Harburg Wilhelmsburg
Wismar
Schwerin
MECKLENBURG
Rostock
Greifswald
Demmin
Neubrandenburg
Neustrelitz
Parchim
Ludwigslust
Pomeranian Bay
Świnoujście
POLAND
Szczecin (Stettin)
Odra Oder
Kostrzyn Odrz. (Küstrin)
Frankfurt an der Oder
Eisenhuttenstadt
Gubin
Nysa Neisse
Spree
Cottbus
Norden
Bensersiel
Wilhelmshaven
Aurich
Emden
Leer
Hoch Moor
Bremerhaven
Nordenham
Blumenthal
Bremen
Oldenburg
Delmenhorst
Cloppenburg
Lüneburg
Lüneburg Heath
Elbe
Uelzen
Wittenberge
Eberswalde
Oranienburg
Stendal
Rathenow
Spandau
Brandenburg
Potsdam
Berlin
WEST
EAST
Leeuwarden
Harlingen
FRIESLAND
Groningen
Hoogezand
Veendam
Assen
Onstwedde
Heerenveen
Den Helder
IJsselmeer (Zuider Zee)
Alkmaar
Edam
Meppel
Kampen
IJssel
Zwolle
Hardenberg
Oosterhesselen
Emmen
Schoonebeek
Bourtanger Moor
Ems
Lingen
Nordhorn
Nienburg
Celle
Weser
IJmuiden
Haarlem
Amsterdam
Hilversum
Hillegom
Leiden
The Hague ('s-Gravenhage)
Hook of Holland
Europoort
Rijswijk
Delft
Gouda
Soest
Utrecht
Amersfoort
Deventer
Oldenzaal
Apeldoorn
Hengelo
Enschede
Gronau
Rheine
Osnabrück
Mittelland Canal
Minden
Hanover
Lehrte
Peine
Wolfsburg
Haldensleben
Brunswick (Braunschweig)
Wolfenbüttel
Magdeburg
Luckenwalde
Rotterdam
Schiedam
Lek
Ede
Velp
Rheden
Renkum
Arnhem
Waal
Nijmegen
Dordrecht
Maas
Oosterhout
's-Hertogenbosch
NETHERLANDS
Schouwen Duiveland
Walcheren
Middelburg
Flushing
Bergen op Zoom
Scheldt
Breda
Roosendaal
Tilburg
Eindhoven
Terneuzen
Eekloo
Dortmund-Ems Canal
Münster
Herford
Bielefeld
Teutoburger Wald
Wesergebirge
Hameln
Hildesheim
Salzgitter
HARZ
Goslar
Halberstadt
Wernigerode
Quedlinburg
Stassfurt
Saale
Dessau
Köthen
Bitterfeld
Torgau
Emmerich
Rhine
Bocholt
WESTPHALIA
Gladbeck
Gelsenkirchen
Hüls
Recklinghausen
Herne
Bottrop
Oberhausen
Duisburg
Mülheim
Essen
Bochum
Dortmund
Hamm
Lippstadt
Soest
Paderborn
Clausthal-Zellerfeld
BROCKEN 1142
Mansfeld
Nordhausen
Halle
Eilenburg
Antwerp (Anvers)
Turnhout
Campine
Hoboken
Lier
Venlo
Roermond
Krefeld
Mönchen-Gladbach
Iserlohn
Hagen
Arnsberger Wald
Warburg
Göttingen
Kassel
Merseburg
Leipzig
Ghent (Gand)
FLANDERS
Dendermonde
Mechelen
Lommel
Balen
Aalst
Oudenaarde
Schaerbeek
Hageland
BRABANT
LIMBURG
Neuss
Rheydt
Düsseldorf
Wuppertal
Remscheid
Solingen
Lüdenscheid
Sauerland
Eschwege
Mühlhausen
Langensalza
GERMANY
Meissen
Bautzen
Dresden
Geeraardsbergen
Brussels
Leuven
Hasselt
Waterloo
Maastricht
Jülich
Leverkusen
Cologne (Köln)
Mülheim
Bergisch Gladbach
Brühl
Siegburg
Siegen
Eisenach
Gotha
Weimar
Erfurt
Zeitz
Altenburg
Jena
Gera-Glauchau
Zittau
BELGIUM
HAINAULT
Nivelles
Ramillies
Ligny
Liège
Herstal
Eupen
Aachen
Düren
Bonn
Sieg
Marburg
THURINGIA
Thüringer Wald
Schmalkalden
Zella Mehlis
Ilmenau
Meiningen
Saalfeld
Zwickau
Karl-Marx-Stadt (Chemnitz)
Děčín
Mons
La Louvière
Charleroi
Marchienne
Namur
Sambre
Maubeuge
Meuse
Dinant
Verviers
NORTH EIFEL
Malmédy
Stavelot
Ourthe
Westerwald
Andernach
Lahn
Limburg
Koblenz
HIGH TAUNUS
Taunus
Wetzlar
Giessen
Fulda
Hohe Rhön
Annaberg
Plauen
Erzgebirge
Jáchymov
Ústí nad Labem (Aussig)
Labe
Most
Ohře (Eger)
Ardennes
Eifel
Mosel
Hunsrück
Soonwald
Bingen
Wiesbaden
Mainz
Frankfurt am Main
Offenbach
Spessart
Aschaffenburg
Darmstadt
Main
Bad Kissingen
Schweinfurt
Coburg
Kulmbach
Hof
Fichtelgebirge
Bayreuth
Cheb
Karlovy Vary (Karlsbad)
Mariánské Lázně (Marienbad)
Prague (Praha)
CZECH.
Rocroi
Charleville
Mézières
Sedan
Bastogne
Neufchâteau
Arlon
LUXEMBOURG
Luxembourg
Pétange
Esch
Dudelange
Montmédy
Longwy
Longuyon
Côtes de Moselle
Thionville
Trier
Saar
SAAR
Pfälzer Bergland
Bad Kreuznach
Worms
Ludwigshafen
Kaiserslautern
Mannheim
Heidelberg
Odenwald
BERGSTRASSE ODENWALD
Würzburg
Steigerwald
Bamberg
Erlangen
Weiden
Plzeň (Plzen)
Vltava (Moldau)
Forêt d'Argonne
Argonne
LORRAINE
Verdun
Briey
Metz
Moselle
Aisne
Ste. Menehould
Châlons-sur-Marne
Champagne
Saarbrücken
St. Ingbert
Neunkirchen
Neustadt
Pfälzer Wald
Pirmasens
Sarreguemines
Speyer
Bruchsal
Karlsruhe
Neckar
Mosbach
Heilbronn
Rothenburg
Ansbach
Dinkelsbühl
Frankenhöhe
Fürth
Nuremberg (Nürnberg)
Franconian Jura
Amberg
Schwandorf
BAVARIAN FOREST
Bavaria
Regensburg
Domažlice
Klatovy
Písek
5°E
50°N
Metres
5000
3000
2000
1000
500
300
200
100
Sea level
Land depression
Spot heights in metres

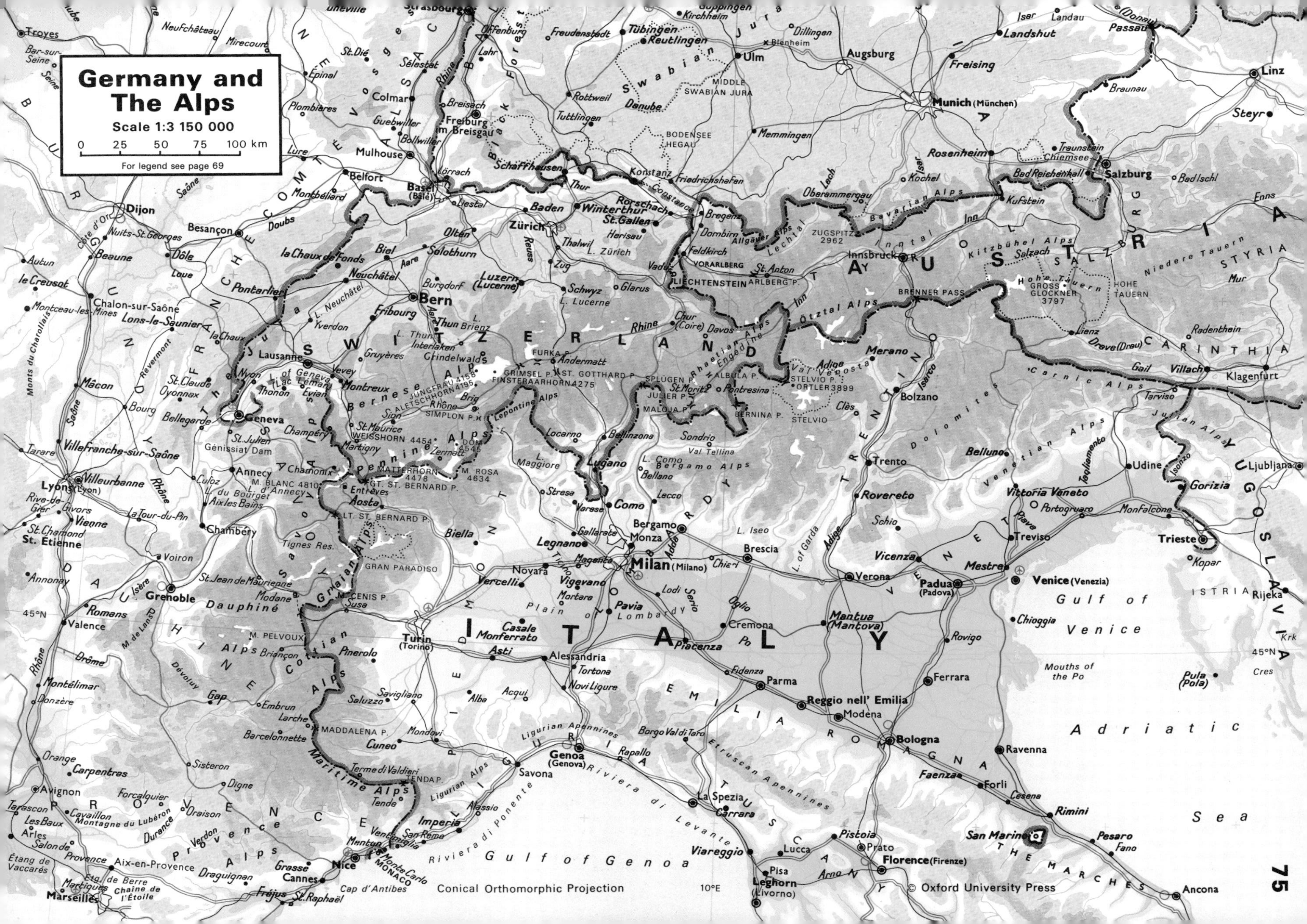
Germany and The Alps
Scale 1:3 150 000
0 25 50 75 100 km
For legend see page 69
Conical Orthomorphic Projection
© Oxford University Press
10°E
45°N
SWITZERLAND
AUSTRIA
ITALY
YUGOSLAVIA
LIECHTENSTEIN
MONACO
San Marino
Adriatic Sea
Gulf of Venice
Gulf of Genoa
Riviera di Levante
Riviera di Ponente
Mouths of the Po
Plain of Lombardy
Swabian Jura
Black Forest
Vosges
Jura
Bavarian Alps
Allgäuer Alps
Kitzbühel Alps
Hohe Tauern
Niedere Tauern
Carnic Alps
Julian Alps
Dolomites
Ötztal Alps
Rhaetian Alps
Bernese Alps
Pennine Alps
Lepontine Alps
Bergamo Alps
Graian Alps
Cottian Alps
Maritime Alps
Ligurian Alps
Ligurian Apennines
Etruscan Apennines
Alsace
Franche Comté
Burgundy
Savoy
Dauphiné
Provence
Piedmont
Lombardy
Trentino
Venetia
Emilia
Romagna
Tuscany
The Marches
Salzburg
Carinthia
Styria
Vorarlberg
Istria
Zugspitze 2962
Gross Glockner 3797
Ortler 3899
M. Rosa 4634
Finsteraarhorn 4275
Jungfrau 4158
Aletschhorn 4195
Weisshorn 4454
Matterhorn 4478
Dom 4545
M. Blanc 4810
Brenner Pass
Arlberg P.
Furka P.
Grimsel P.
St. Gotthard P.
Splügen P.
Albula P.
Julier P.
Maloja P.
Bernina P.
Stelvio P.
Simplon P.
Gt. St. Bernard P.
Lt. St. Bernard P.
M. Cenis P.
Maddalena P.
Tenda P.
Gran Paradiso
M. Pelvoux
Munich (München)
Augsburg
Ulm
Salzburg
Innsbruck
Linz
Klagenfurt
Villach
Ljubljana
Trieste
Rijeka
Venice (Venezia)
Padua (Padova)
Verona
Vicenza
Trento
Bolzano
Merano
Milan (Milano)
Bergamo
Brescia
Como
Turin (Torino)
Genoa (Genova)
Bologna
Florence (Firenze)
Pisa
Leghorn (Livorno)
Parma
Modena
Ravenna
Rimini
Ancona
Zürich
Bern
Basel (Bâle)
Luzern (Lucerne)
Geneva
Lausanne
Neuchâtel
Fribourg
Lugano
Chur (Coire)
St. Gallen
Konstanz
Freiburg im Breisgau
Mulhouse
Colmar
Besançon
Dijon
Lyons (Lyon)
Grenoble
Chambéry
Annecy
St. Etienne
Valence
Avignon
Marseilles
Nice
Cannes
Aix-en-Provence

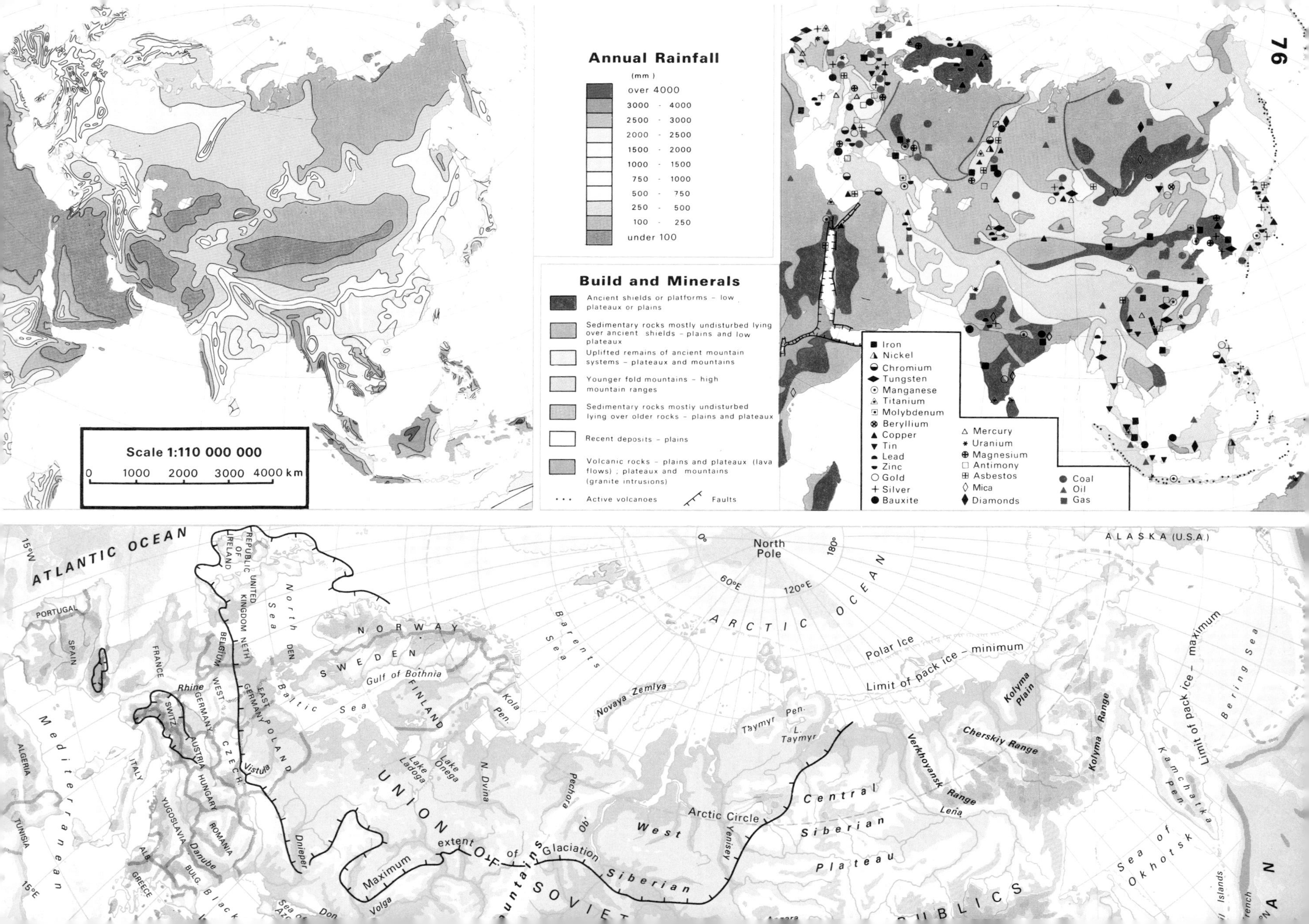
Annual Rainfall
(mm)
over 4000
3000 - 4000
2500 - 3000
2000 - 2500
1500 - 2000
1000 - 1500
750 - 1000
500 - 750
250 - 500
100 - 250
under 100
Scale 1:110 000 000
0 1000 2000 3000 4000 km
Build and Minerals
Ancient shields or platforms – low plateaux or plains
Sedimentary rocks mostly undisturbed lying over ancient shields – plains and low plateaux
Uplifted remains of ancient mountain systems – plateaux and mountains
Younger fold mountains – high mountain ranges
Sedimentary rocks mostly undisturbed lying over older rocks – plains and plateaux
Recent deposits – plains
Volcanic rocks – plains and plateaux (lava flows); plateaux and mountains (granite intrusions)
Active volcanoes
Faults
Iron
Nickel
Chromium
Tungsten
Manganese
Titanium
Molybdenum
Beryllium
Copper
Tin
Lead
Zinc
Gold
Silver
Bauxite
Mercury
Uranium
Magnesium
Antimony
Asbestos
Mica
Diamonds
Coal
Oil
Gas
ATLANTIC OCEAN
15°W
PORTUGAL
SPAIN
FRANCE
REPUBLIC OF IRELAND
UNITED KINGDOM
NETH
BELGIUM
WEST GERMANY
EAST GERMANY
Rhine
SWITZ
AUSTRIA
CZECH.
POLAND
Vistula
HUNGARY
ROMANIA
YUGOSLAVIA
Danube
BULG.
ALB
GREECE
ITALY
ALGERIA
TUNISIA
15°E
Mediterranean
North Sea
DEN
NORWAY
SWEDEN
Gulf of Bothnia
Baltic Sea
FINLAND
Kola Pen.
Lake Ladoga
Lake Onega
N. Dvina
Dnieper
Volga
Don
UNION OF SOVIET
Maximum extent of Glaciation
Pechora
Ob'
West Siberian
Barents Sea
Novaya Zemlya
ARCTIC OCEAN
North Pole
0°
60°E
120°E
180°
Polar Ice
Limit of pack ice – minimum
Taymyr Pen.
L. Taymyr
Arctic Circle
Yenisey
Central Siberian Plateau
Verkhoyansk Range
Lena
Cherskiy Range
Kolyma Plain
Kolyma Range
Limit of pack ice – maximum
Bering Sea
ALASKA (U.S.A.)
Kamchatka Pen.
Sea of Okhotsk

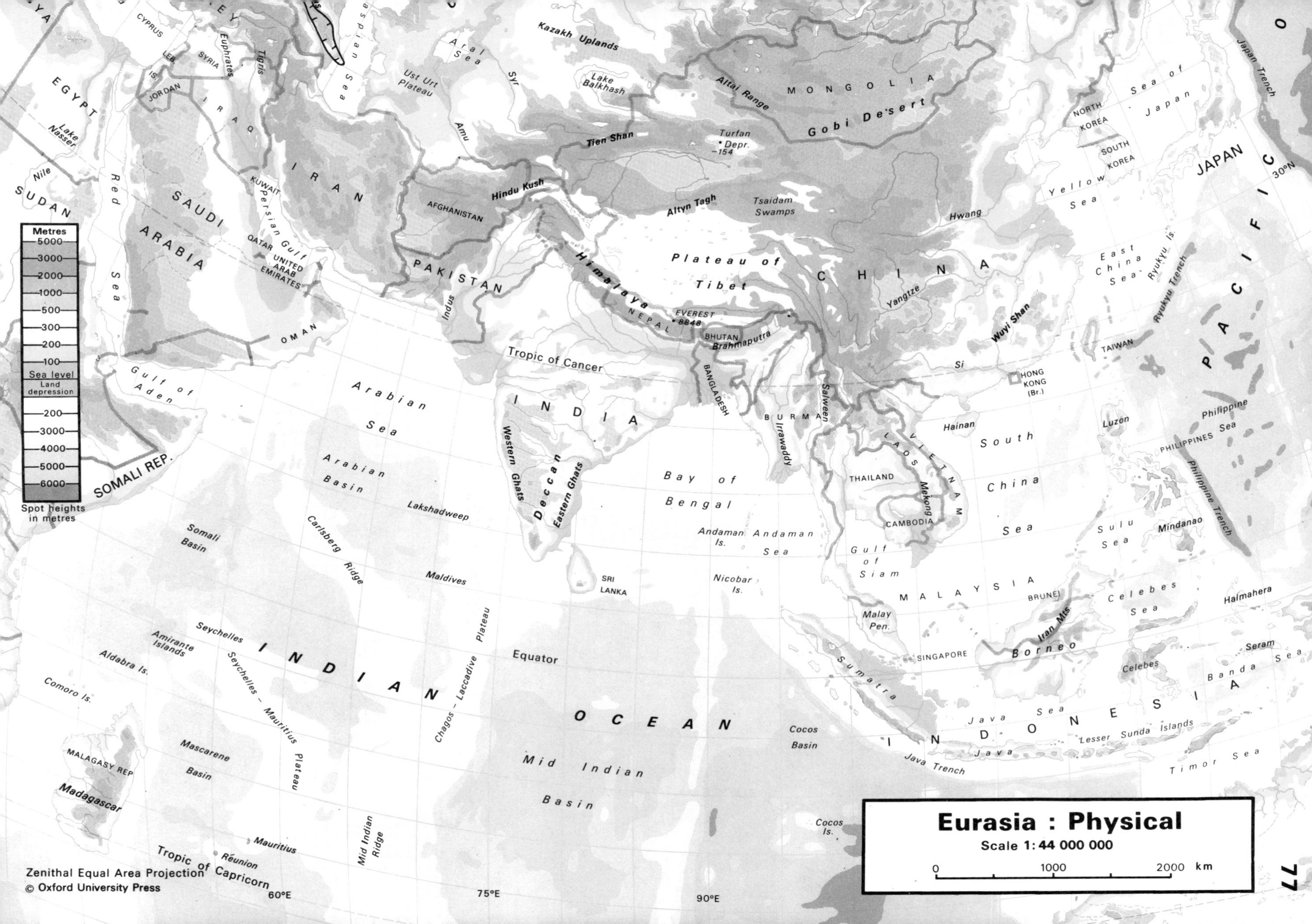

Eurasia : Physical
Scale 1: 44 000 000
0
1000
2000 km
Zenithal Equal Area Projection
© Oxford University Press
Metres
5000
3000
2000
1000
500
300
200
100
Sea level
Land depression
200
3000
4000
5000
6000
Spot heights in metres
CYPRUS
LEB.
IS.
JORDAN
SYRIA
Euphrates
Tigris
EGYPT
Lake Nasser
Nile
SUDAN
Red Sea
I R A Q
I R A N
SAUDI ARABIA
KUWAIT
Persian Gulf
QATAR
UNITED ARAB EMIRATES
OMAN
Gulf of Aden
SOMALI REP.
Caspian Sea
Aral Sea
Ust Urt Plateau
Amu
Syr
Kazakh Uplands
Lake Balkhash
Tien Shan
Altai Range
M O N G O L I A
Gobi Desert
Turfan Depr. -154
AFGHANISTAN
Hindu Kush
Altyn Tagh
Tsaidam Swamps
PAKISTAN
Indus
Plateau of Tibet
Himalaya
NEPAL
EVEREST 8848
BHUTAN
Brahmaputra
BANGLADESH
C H I N A
Hwang
Yangtze
Wuyi Shan
Si
HONG KONG (Br.)
NORTH KOREA
SOUTH KOREA
Sea of Japan
JAPAN
30°N
Japan Trench
Yellow Sea
East China Sea
Ryukyu Is.
Ryukyu Trench
TAIWAN
P A C I F I C
Tropic of Cancer
I N D I A
Western Ghats
Deccan
Eastern Ghats
Arabian Sea
Arabian Basin
Lakshadweep
Carlsberg Ridge
Somali Basin
Maldives
SRI LANKA
Bay of Bengal
Andaman Is.
Andaman Sea
Nicobar Is.
BURMA
Irrawaddy
Salween
THAILAND
LAOS
VIETNAM
Mekong
CAMBODIA
Gulf of Siam
Hainan
South China Sea
Luzon
PHILIPPINES
Philippine Sea
Philippine Trench
Mindanao
Sulu Sea
MALAYSIA
BRUNEI
Iran Mts
Borneo
Celebes Sea
Halmahera
Celebes
Seram
Banda Sea
Malay Pen.
SINGAPORE
Sumatra
Java Sea
I N D O N E S I A
Java
Lesser Sunda Islands
Timor Sea
Java Trench
Equator
Seychelles
Amirante Islands
Aldabra Is.
Comoro Is.
I N D I A N
O C E A N
Seychelles – Mauritius Plateau
Chagos – Laccadive Plateau
Mascarene Basin
MALAGASY REP.
Madagascar
Mid Indian Basin
Cocos Basin
Cocos Is.
Mid Indian Ridge
Mauritius
Réunion
Tropic of Capricorn
60°E
75°E
90°E

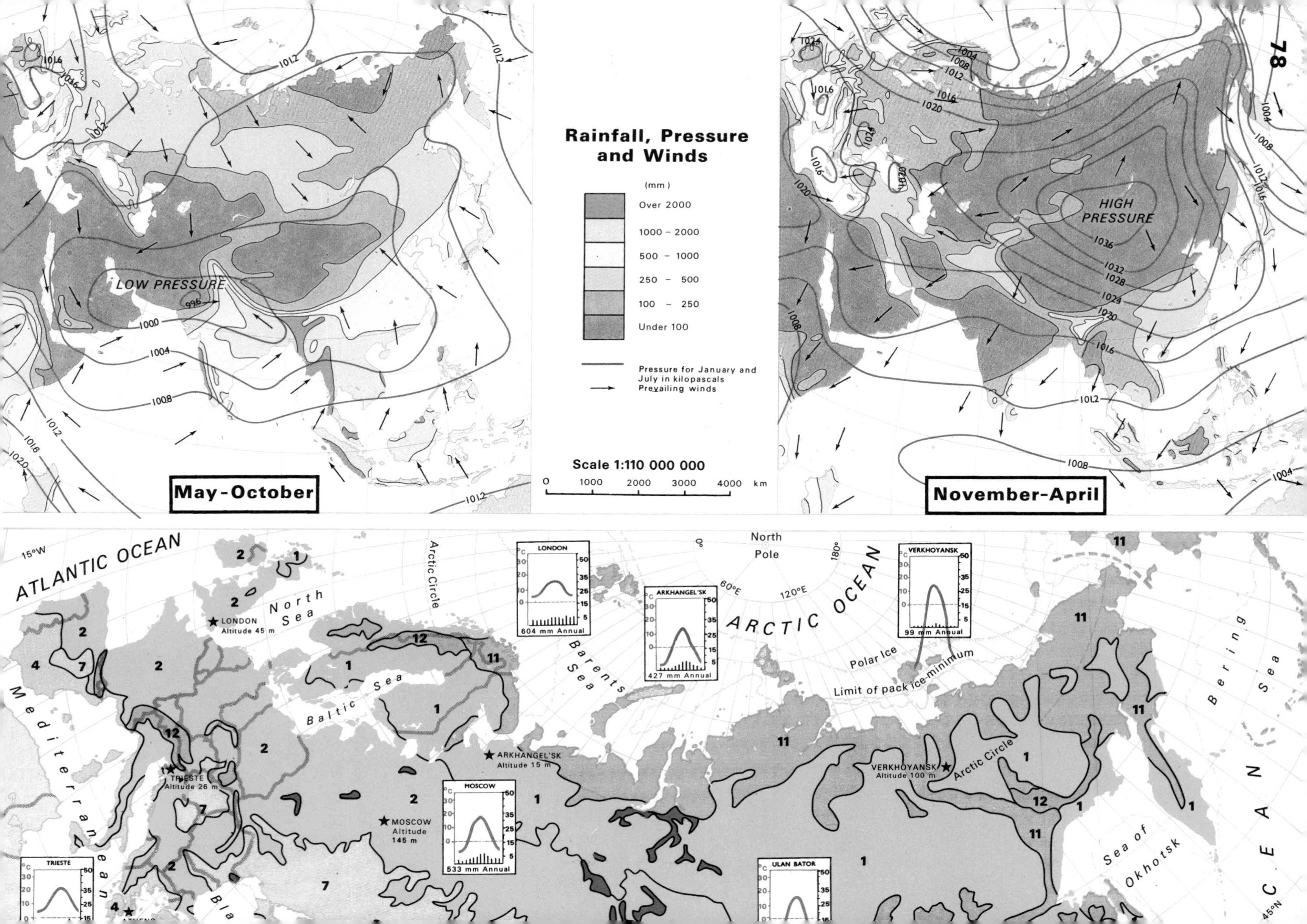
Rainfall, Pressure and Winds
(mm)
Over 2000
1000 – 2000
500 – 1000
250 – 500
100 – 250
Under 100
Pressure for January and July in kilopascals
Prevailing winds
Scale 1:110 000 000
0 1000 2000 3000 4000 km
May-October
LOW PRESSURE
November-April
HIGH PRESSURE
ATLANTIC OCEAN
North Sea
Baltic Sea
Barents Sea
Arctic Circle
North Pole
ARCTIC OCEAN
Polar Ice
Limit of pack ice-minimum
Bering Sea
Sea of Okhotsk
Mediterranean
LONDON Altitude 45 m
TRIESTE Altitude 26 m
MOSCOW Altitude 145 m
ARKHANGEL'SK Altitude 15 m
VERKHOYANSK Altitude 100 m
LONDON 604 mm Annual
ARKHANGEL'SK 427 mm Annual
VERKHOYANSK 99 mm Annual
MOSCOW 533 mm Annual
TRIESTE
ULAN BATOR

Eurasia : Vegetation

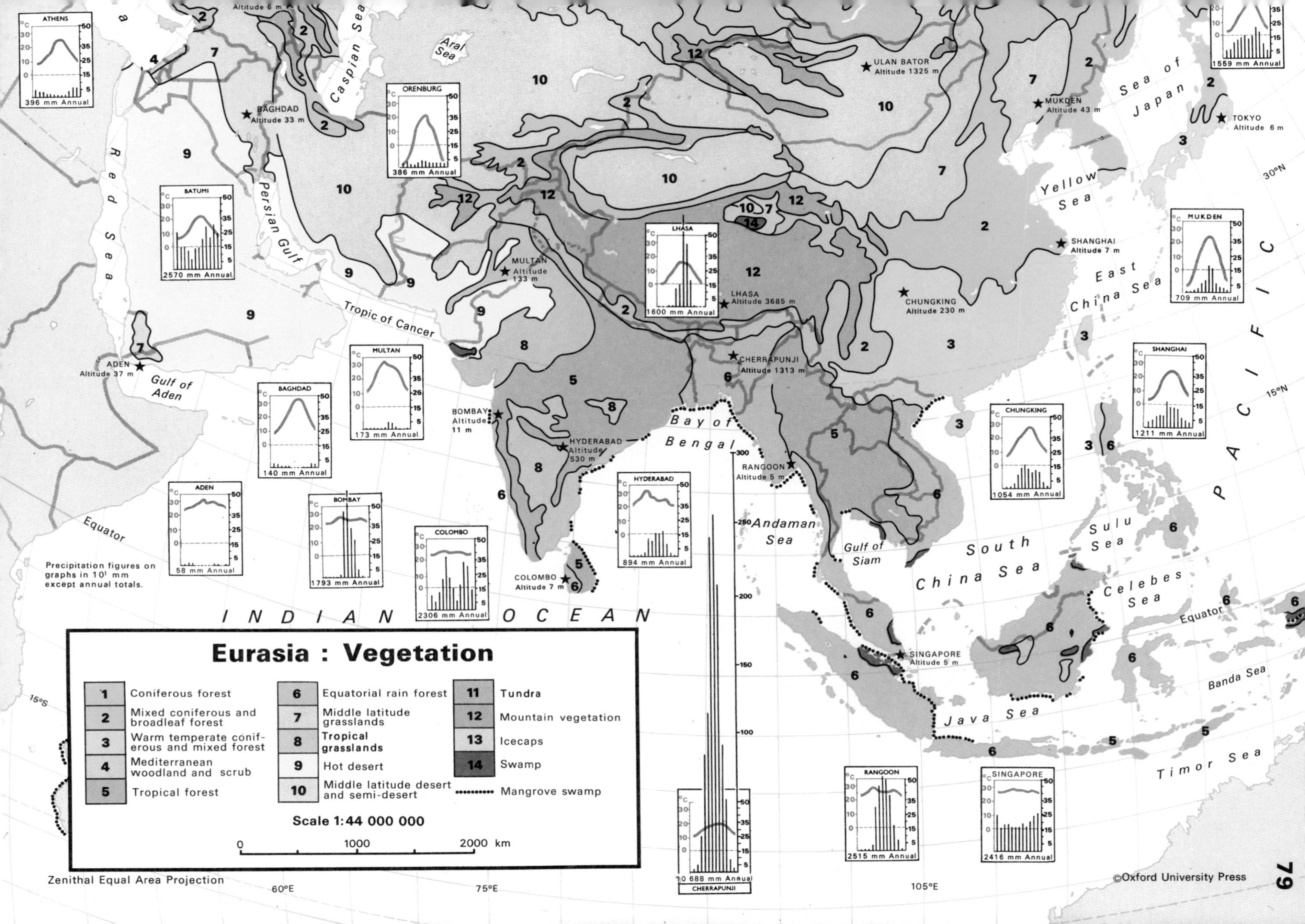

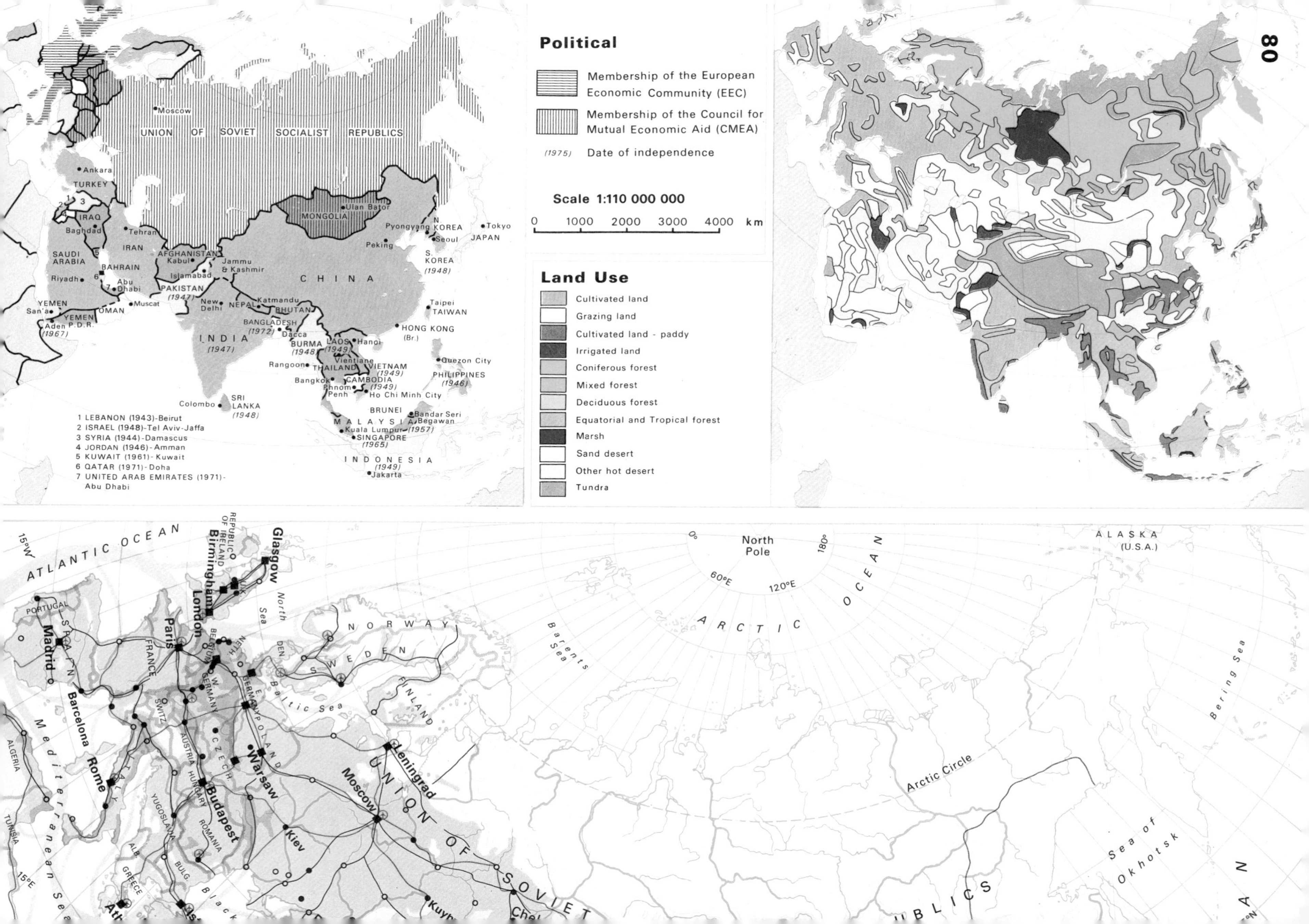

Political
Membership of the European Economic Community (EEC)
Membership of the Council for Mutual Economic Aid (CMEA)
(1975) Date of independence
Scale 1:110 000 000
0 1000 2000 3000 4000 km
Land Use
Cultivated land
Grazing land
Cultivated land - paddy
Irrigated land
Coniferous forest
Mixed forest
Deciduous forest
Equatorial and Tropical forest
Marsh
Sand desert
Other hot desert
Tundra
UNION OF SOVIET SOCIALIST REPUBLICS
Moscow
Ankara
TURKEY
IRAQ
Baghdad
Tehran
IRAN
SAUDI ARABIA
BAHRAIN
Riyadh
Abu Dhabi
OMAN
Muscat
YEMEN
San'a
YEMEN P.D.R.
Aden
(1967)
AFGHANISTAN
Kabul
Islamabad
Jammu & Kashmir
PAKISTAN
(1947)
New Delhi
NEPAL
Katmandu
BHUTAN
BANGLADESH
(1972)
Dacca
INDIA
(1947)
Colombo
SRI LANKA
(1948)
MONGOLIA
Ulan Bator
CHINA
Peking
Pyongyang
N. KOREA
Seoul
S. KOREA
(1948)
Tokyo
JAPAN
Taipei
TAIWAN
HONG KONG
(Br.)
BURMA
(1948)
Rangoon
LAOS
(1949)
Hanoi
Vientiane
THAILAND
Bangkok
VIETNAM
(1949)
CAMBODIA
(1949)
Phnom Penh
Ho Chi Minh City
Quezon City
PHILIPPINES
(1946)
BRUNEI
Bandar Seri Begawan
MALAYSIA
Kuala Lumpur
(1957)
SINGAPORE
(1965)
INDONESIA
(1949)
Jakarta
1 LEBANON (1943)-Beirut
2 ISRAEL (1948)-Tel Aviv-Jaffa
3 SYRIA (1944)-Damascus
4 JORDAN (1946)-Amman
5 KUWAIT (1961)-Kuwait
6 QATAR (1971)-Doha
7 UNITED ARAB EMIRATES (1971)-Abu Dhabi
ATLANTIC OCEAN
15°W
REPUBLIC OF IRELAND
Glasgow
U.K.
Birmingham
London
North Sea
PORTUGAL
SPAIN
Madrid
Barcelona
FRANCE
Paris
BELGIUM
NETH.
W. GERMANY
SWITZ.
ITALY
Rome
DEN.
NORWAY
SWEDEN
Baltic Sea
FINLAND
E. GERMANY
POLAND
Warsaw
CZECH.
AUSTRIA
HUNGARY
Budapest
YUGOSLAVIA
ROMANIA
ALB.
GREECE
BULG.
Black
Mediterranean Sea
ALGERIA
TUNISIA
15°E
Leningrad
Moscow
Kiev
UNION OF SOVIET
Kuyb
Chel
Barents Sea
0°
North Pole
60°E
120°E
180°
ARCTIC OCEAN
Arctic Circle
ALASKA (U.S.A.)
Bering Sea
Sea of Okhotsk

Eurasia: Population & Communications

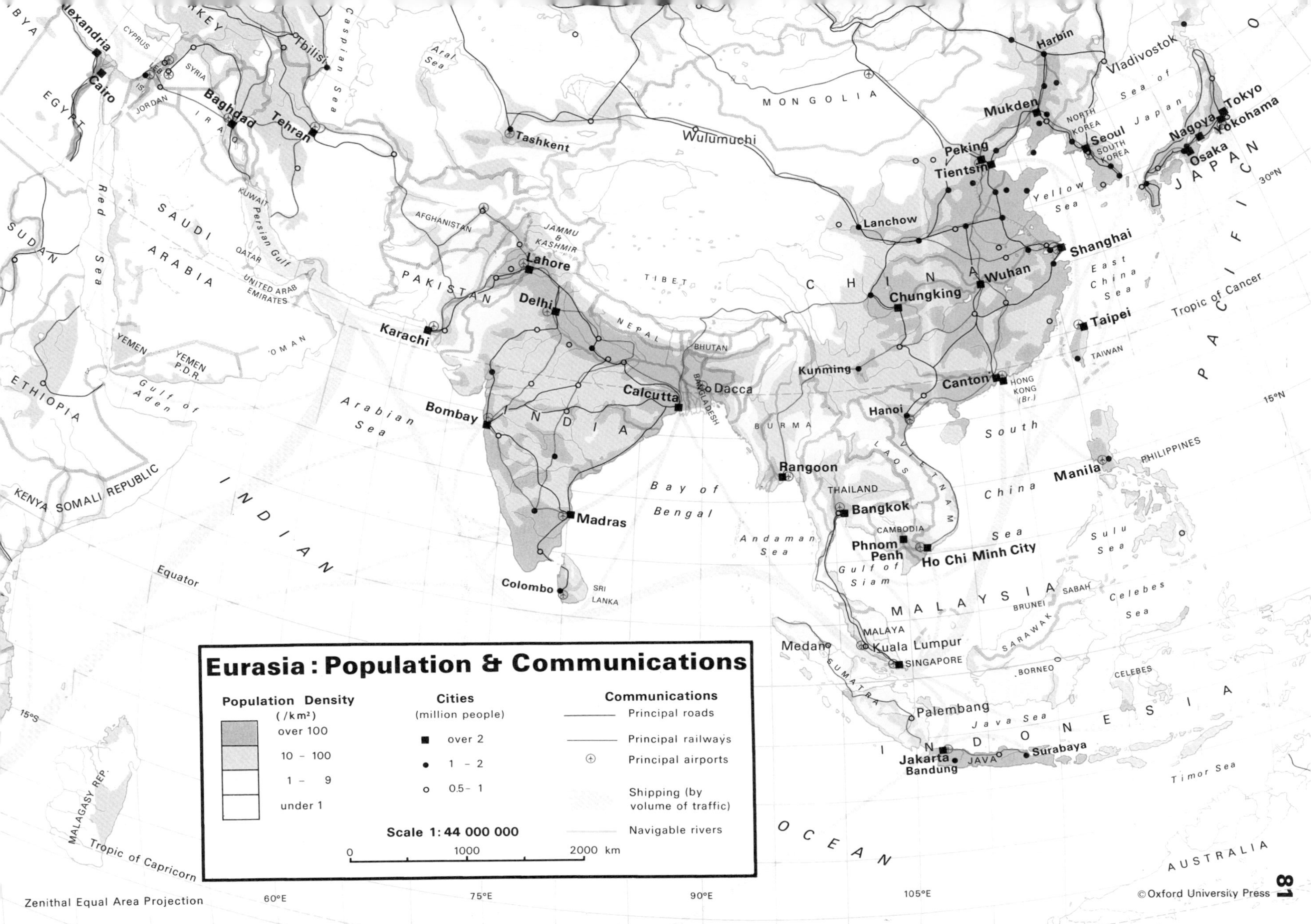

Population Density (/km²)
- over 100
- 10 – 100
- 1 – 9
- under 1

Cities (million people)
- ■ over 2
- ● 1 – 2
- ○ 0.5 – 1

Communications
- Principal roads
- Principal railways
- Principal airports
- Shipping (by volume of traffic)
- Navigable rivers

Scale 1: 44 000 000

0 1000 2000 km

Zenithal Equal Area Projection

U.S.S.R.
Scale 1:25 000 000
0 200 400 600 800 km
ATLANTIC OCEAN
Arctic Circle
GREENLAND (DENMARK)
ICELAND
Greenwich Meridian
Limit of Pack Ice-average maximum (spring)
Spitsbergen (Svalbard) (Norway)
Bear I.
Faeroe Is.
Shetland Is.
Orkney Is.
Scilly Is.
IRELAND
NORTHERN IRELAND
SCOTLAND
WALES
UNITED KINGDOM
Glasgow
Edinburgh
Dublin
Birmingham
Liverpool
London
English Channel
Bay of Biscay
North Sea
FRANCE
Paris
Loire
Rhône
Rhine
Marseille
Corsica
Amsterdam
NETH.
Brussels
BELG.
LUX.
Bonn
WEST GERMANY
EAST GERMANY
Hamburg
Elbe
Berlin
DENMARK
Copenhagen
Göteborg
Oslo
Bergen
Trondheim
NORWAY
Narvik
North Cape
SWEDEN
Stockholm
Luleå
Gulf of Bothnia
Gotland
Baltic Sea
FINLAND
Helsinki
Lapland
Gulf of Finland
Tallinn
ESTONIAN S.S.R.
Riga
LATVIAN S.S.R.
LITHUANIAN S.S.R.
Vilnius
Kaliningrad
Gdańsk
Szczecin
Oder
Vistula
POLAND
Warsaw
Wrocław
Kraków
SWITZ.
Bern
Turin
Milan
AUSTRIA
Vienna
Prague
CZECHOSLOVAKIA
HUNGARY
Budapest
ITALY
Rome
Naples
Adriatic Sea
YUGOSLAVIA
Belgrade
Sava
ALBANIA
GREECE
Athens
Aegean Sea
Crete
BULGARIA
Sofiya
ROMANIA
Bucharest
Galati
Danube
Prut
Dnestr
MOLD. S.S.R.
Kishinev
Odessa
L'vov
UKRAINIAN S.S.R.
Kiev
Bug
Dnieper
Khar'kov
Dnepropetrovsk
Nikopol
Nikolayev
Simferopol'
Sevastopol'
Zhdanov
Kerch'
Sea of Azov
DONBASS
Donets
Voroshilovgrad
Rostov
BYELORUSSIAN S.S.R.
Pinsk
Pripet Marshes
Minsk
Vitebsk
Smolensk
Gomel'
Orel'
Kursk
Leningrad
L. Ladoga
L. Onega
Petrozavodsk
Novgorod
Volga
Yaroslavl'
Kalinin
Moscow
Vologda
Ivanovo
Gorki
Tula
Ryazan'
Voronezh
Tambov
Penza
Saratov
Volgograd
Tsimlyansk Res.
Don
Astrakhan'
Kazan'
Kuybyshev
Izhevsk
Kama
Perm
Kirov
Kotlas
Vychegda
Arkhangel'sk
N. Dvina
White Sea
Kola Penin.
Murmansk
C. Kanin
Barents Sea
C. Speedwell
Novaya Zemlya
Kara Sea
Vaygach I.
Pechora
Naryan-Mar
Vorkuta
Kara
Usa
Izhma
Ob'
Salekhard
N. Sos'va
U.S.S.R.
RUSSIAN SOVIET
Ural Mountains
West Siberian Plain
Serov
Nizhniy-Tagil
Sverdlovsk
Tobolsk
Tyumen'
Irtysh
Chelyabinsk
Kurgan
Petukhovo
Petropavlovsk
Ishim
Tobol'
Omsk
Ufa
Belaya
Magnitogorsk
Orenburg
Ural
Uralsk
Orsk
Guryev
Emba
KAZAKH S.S.R.
Steppes
Turgay
Tselinograd
Karaganda
Pavlodar
Aralsk
Aral Sea
Kiyakty
L.Balkhash
Balkhash
Mangyshlak Penin.
Shevchenko
Ust-Urt Plateau
Kara Bogaz Gol
Kungrad
UZBEK S.S.R.
Kyzyl Kum
Khiva
Syr-Darya
Muyun Kum
Chu
Chimkent
Tashkent
Frunze
Alma-Ata
ili
KIRGIZ S.S.R.
Samarkand
Bukhara
Fergana
Dushanbe
TADZHIK S.S.R.
COMMUNISM PEAK 7495
Pamirs
Kashgar
Yarkand
Hindu Kush
Kabul
AFGHANISTAN
Herat
TURKMEN S.S.R.
Kara Kum
Ashkhabad
Mary
Mashhad
Bander-e Shah
Krasnovodsk
Caspian Sea
Baku
Kura
AZERBAYDZHAN S.S.R.
Makhachkala
Grozny
Caucasus Mts.
GEORGIAN S.S.R.
Tbilisi
ARMENIAN S.S.R.
Yerevan
Batumi
Krasnodar
Armavir
Novorossiysk
Black Sea
Istanbul
Zonguldak
Ankara
Izmir
TURKEY
Adana
Erzurum
Lake Van
Lake Urmia
Tabriz
Tehrān
Shāhrūd
Hamadān
Isfahan
Dasht-e-Kavir
IRAN
Kermān
Shīrāz
Bushire
Abadan
Persian Gulf
Kuwait
KUWAIT
Basra
Baghdad
Tigris
Euphrates
Mosul
IRAQ
SYRIA
Aleppo
Damascus
Beirut
LEBANON
CYPRUS
ISRAEL
Jerusalem
Amman
JORDAN
Aqaba
Port Said
Suez
Cairo
Alexandria
Mediterranean Sea
SAUDI ARABIA
Medina
Riyadh
Conical Orthomorphic Projection
©Oxford University Press

North Pole
Metres
5000
3000
2000
1000
500
300
200
100
Sea level
Land depression
Spot heights in metres
Boundaries
International
(in sea)
(disputed)
Internal
Roads
Motorways
Other roads
Tracks
Railways
Airports
International
Domestic
Canals
Seasonal rivers, lakes
Marshes
Salt Pan
Ice cap
Sand desert limits
National Parks etc.
A L A S K A
Seward Penin.
Nome
Norton Sound
Bering Strait
St.Lawrence (U.S.)
Diomede Is. (U.S.S.R.) (U.S.)
Chukchi Sea
C.Lisburne
G. of Kolyuchin
Kivak
International Date Line
Bering Sea
Wrangel I.
East Siberian Sea
Anadyr'
Gulf of Anadyr'
C. Navarin
Ayon I.
Ambarchik
Ostrovnoye
Markovo
Kavacha
Kamenskoye
Komandor Is.
Kamchatka Bay
Kronotskiy Bay
Kamchatka
Petropavlovsk-Kamchatskiy
Severnaya Zemlya
Wiese I. (Vize)
Bol'shevik I.
C. Chelyuskin
Unnavigable Polar Ice
Novosibirskiye Ostrova
Lyakhov Islands
Laptev Str.
Laptev Sea
O C E A N
Pack Ice-average minimum (autumn)
Taymyr Penin.
L. Taymyr
Nordvik
Tiksi
Kazachiye
Indigirka
Kolyma Plain
Kolyma
Yukagir Plateau
Range
(Kolyma)
Gydan
Shelekov Bay
C.Tolstoy
Cherskiy Range
Susuman
Magadan
Okhotsk
Verkhoyansk
Verkhoyansk Range
Sangar
Lena
Olenek
Anabar
Khatanga
G.of Yenisey
Gyda Penin.
Karaul
Dudinka
Noril'sk
Putoran Mts.
Igarka
Central Siberian Plateau
Vilyuy
Yakutsk
Amga
Aldan
R.
Sea of Okhotsk
Paramushir
Onekotan
Sakhalin Bay
Nikolayevsk
Aleksandrovsk-Sakhalinskiy
Sakhalin
G.of Tartary
Tarpeniya Bay
Yuzhno Sakhalinsk
Aniva Bay
Kholmsk
Wakkanai
Hokkaido
Sapporo
Muroran
Hakodate
Aomori
Tarko-Sale
Taz
Pur
Lower Tunguska
Yenisey
Stony Tunguska
Elgyay
Olekminsk
Buyaga
Dzherba
Vitim
Korshunova
FEDERATED SOCIALIST REPUBLIC
S.
Amgun
Amur
Komsomolsk-na-Amur
Soviet Harbour
Khabarovsk
Zeya
Tygda
Never
Chekunda
Blagoveshchensk
Bureya
Birobidzhan
Sikhote Alin' Range
Ob'
Yeniseysk
Angara
Chuna
Ust'-Kut
Bratsk
Tayshet
Krasnoyarsk
Tomsk
Kemerovo
Novosibirsk
Prokop'yevsk
Abakan
Minusinsk
Novokuznetsk
Shelym
Biysk
Kyzyl
Zhigalovo
Lake Baykal
Irkutsk
Usol'ye
Cheremknovo
Ulan-Ude
Chita
Mogocha
Bukachacha
Shilka
Sretensk
Nerchinsk
Sherlovaya Gora
Aksha
Erentsab
Hulun
Shihchan
Nunkiang
Tsitsihar (Lungkiang)
Harbin (Pinkiang)
Ussuri
L. Khanka
Ussuriysk
Partizansk
Vladivostok
Sea of Japan
Mutankiang
Chuho
Kirin
Sungari Res.
Great Khingan Mts.
Ulanhoto
Uldza
Choibalsan
Tamsag Bulag
Semipalatinsk
Leninogorsk
Ulan Gom
Selenga
Bulagan
Ulan Bator
Hovd
Uliastay
Altai Range
MONGOLIA
Sayn Shanda
Gobi Desert
Changchun
Cheonyangchen
Mukden (Shenyang)
Anshan
NORTH KOREA
Pyongyang
Nampo
Yingkow
Lü-ta
Seoul
SOUTH KOREA
Pusan
Kyoto
Kobe
Honshu
JAPAN
Hiroshima
Shimonoseki
Kitakyushu
Nagasaki
Kyushu
Shikoku
Wulumuchi (Urumchi)
Turfan depr.
Hami (Qomul)
Chengteh (Jehol)
Changkiakow (Kalgan)
Peking (Peiping)
Huhehot
Paotow
Tientsin
Po Hai (G.of Chihli)
Yentai
Tsingtao
Shihkiachwang
Tsinan
Taiyuan
Yellow Sea
Ala Shan
Yinchwan (Ninghsia)
Ansi
Anyang
Hwang
Loyang
Süchow (Tungshan)
Nanking
Shanghai
East China Sea
Ryukyu Is.
Sining
Lanchow (Kaolan)
Tsaidam Swamps
Altyn Tagh
UIGHUR
REGION
INNER MONGOLIA
CHINA
85°E
90°E
100°E
110°E
115°E
120°E
60°N
65°N
70°N
75°N
80°N
140°E
180°

Baltic Sea
Helsinki
Leningrad
Moscow
RUSSIAN SOVIET FEDER
Gulf of Finland
Lake Ladoga
Lake Onega
ESTONIAN S.S.R.
LATVIAN S.S.R.
LITHUANIAN S.S.R.
BYELORUSSIAN S.S.R.
UKRAINIAN S.S.R.
POLAND
ROMANIA
BULGARIA
TURKEY
SYRIA
LEBANON
ISRAEL
CYPRUS
IRAN
'IRAQ
GEORGIAN S.S.R.
ARMENIAN S.S.R.
AZERBAYDZHAN S.S.R.
MOLD. S.S.R.
Black Sea
Sea of Azov
Caspian Sea
Surface height 28 m below m.s.l.
Caspian Lowlands
Caucasus Mountains
Pontic Mountains
Taurus Mts.
Elburz Mts.
Valdai Hills
Volga Hills
Pripet Marshes
DONBASS
CRIMEA
Kiev
Warsaw
Minsk
Bucharest
Istanbul
Ankara
Tbilisi
Baku
Tehran
Volgograd
Rostov
Kharkov
Odessa
Riga
Vilnius
Tallinn
Kazan'
Gor'kiy
Kuybyshev
Saratov
Astrakhan'
Metres
5000
3000
2000
1000
500
300
200
100
Sea level
Land depression
Spot heights in metres
Conical Orthomorphic Projection

Western
U.S.S.R.
Scale 1:12 500 000
0 100 200 300 400 km
Boundaries
International
(in sea)
(disputed)
Internal
Roads
Motorways
Other roads
Tracks
Railways
Airports
International
Domestic
Canals
Seasonal rivers, lakes
Marshes
Salt Pan
Ice cap
Sand desert limits
National Parks etc.
© Oxford University Press
West Siberian Plain
ED SOCIALIST REPUBLIC
R S F S R
KAZAKH S.S.R.
Steppes
Kazakh Uplands
Hunger Steppe
Turgay
Berezovo
Faktoriye
Vakh
Surgut
Khanty-Mansiysk
Polunochnoye
Ivdel'
Vasyugan
Severoural'sk
Serov
Sos'va
Tavda
Tobol'sk
Kushva
Alapayevsk
Nizhniy-Tagil
Artemovskiy
Kamyshlov
Tyumen'
Sverdlovsk
Kamensk-Uralskiy
Omutinskoye
Irtysh
Tara
Kuybyshev
Tatarsk
Novonazyvayevka
Omsk
Kalachinsk
Lake Chany
Novosibirsk
Kolyvan'
Ob'
Barnaul
Biysk
Shalym
Gorno-Altaysk
Asino
Chulym
Tomsk
Mariinsk
Achinsk
Krasnoyarsk
Kansk
Tayshet
Yeniseysk
Angara
Yenisey
Anzhero-Sudzhensk
Kemerovo
Leninsk-Kuznetskiy
Prokop'yevsk
Novo-kuznetsk
KUZBASS
Chernogorsk
Minusinsk
Abakan
Western Sayan Mts.
Kasli
Zlatoust
Chelyabinsk
Kurgan
Makushino
Petukhovo
Petropavlovsk
Troitsk
Ust'Uyskoye
Magnitogorsk
Kartaly
Kustanay
Ishim
Kokchetav
Lake Selety-Tengiz
Danilovka
Semiozernoye
Bredy
Dzhetygara
Baymak
Mednogorsk
Orsk
Spasskoye
Atbasar
Tselinograd
Temir-Tau
Karaganda
Lake Tengiz
Khrom-Tau
Turgay
Okt'abr'sk
Emba
Ulu-Tau
Marganets
Atasuskiy
Uspenskiy
Dzhezkazgan
Baykonur
L.Chelkar-Tengiz
Aral'sk
Kazalinsk
Mointy
Kounradskiy
Balkhash
Lake Balkhash
L.Kulundinskoye
Kulunda Steppe
Pavlodar
Rubtsovsk
Kolyvan'
Leninogorsk
Belousovka
Zyryanovsk
Semipalatinsk
Ust'-Kamenogorsk
Cherdoyak
L.Zaysan
Black Irtysh
Zharma
Ulyungur Nor
Ayaguz
Chuguchak
Yamatu
Ala Kul
Andreyevka
Dzungarian Gate
Dzungaria
Ebi Nor
Tekely
Ili
Alma-Ata
Chu
Kzyl-Orda
Suzak
Muyun-Kum
Kara-Tau
Aral Sea
Surface height 48 m above m.s.l.
Syr Darya (Jaxartes)
Turkestan
Chulak-Tau
Dzhambul
Frunze
Issyk-Kul'
Rybach'ye
KIRGIZ S.S.R.
Tien Shan
KHAN TENGRI 7200
Tarim
Arys'
Chimkent
Kyzyl-Kum
UZBEK S.S.R.
Turanian Plain
Kungrad
Khodzheyli
Khiva
Tashkent
Namangan
Andizhan
Osh
Angren
Kokand
Fergana
Leninabad
Begovat
Alai Range
LENIN PEAK 7127
MT.COMMUNISM 7495
TADZHIK S.S.R.
Bukhara
Samarkand
Dyushanbe
Khorog
Pamirs
Chardzhou
Kara Kum
TURKMEN S.S.R.
Amu Darya (Oxus)
Kerki
Termez
Faizabad
Kishm
Mary (Merv)
Kirovsk
Ashkhabad
Kopeh Dāgh
Mashhad
Mazar-i-Sharif
Maimana
Hindu Kush
Chitral
AFGHANISTAN
Kabul
Jalalabad
Peshawar
Abbottabad
PAKISTAN
Indus
KASHMIR
TIBET
CHINA
MONGOLIA
Kosh-Agach
Altai Ra.
Kushka
60°E
65°E
70°E
75°E
80°E
85°E
90°E
95°E
60°N
55°N
50°N
45°N
40°N
35°N

Middle East
Scale 1:12 500 000
0 100 200 300 400 km
Scale 1:4 000 000
0 20 40 60 km
Boundaries International (in sea)
Internal
Ceasefire lines, 1967
Roads Motorways Other roads Tracks
Railways
Oilfields
Airports International Domestic
Canals
Seasonal rivers, lakes
Marshes salt pans
Ice cap
Sand desert limits
National Parks, etc.
Mediterranean Sea
Tyrrhenian Sea
Aegean Sea
LIBYA
EGYPT
TURKEY
CYPRUS
LEBANON
ISRAEL
SYRIA
JORDAN
SUDAN
GREECE
ITALY
MALTA
Sinai
Eastern Desert
Red Sea Hills
Nubian Desert
Lake Nasser
Tropic of Cancer
Cairo
Alexandria
Athens
İstanbul
Ankara
Beirut
Damascus
Jerusalem
Amman
Tel Aviv-Jaffa
Khartoum
Tarabulus
Benghazi
Plateau of El Tih
Negeb
Galilee
Samaria
Judaea
Gilead
Dead Sea
Sea of Galilee
Biblical names in red
© Oxford University Press

U. S. S. R.
GEORGIAN S.S.R.
ARMENIAN S.S.R.
AZERBAYDZHAN S.S.R.
TURKMEN S.S.R.
Batumi
Trabzon
3937
Leninakan
Kura
Kirovabad
Sumgait
Baku
Krasnovodsk
Nebit Dag
Kara Kum
Çoruh
L. Sevan
Yerevan
Erzurum
MT. ARARAT 5165
Araxe
Caspian
Sea
Erzincan
3449
3650
Divrigi
Elâzig
Muş
Malatya
Van
L. Van
L. Urmia
Tabrīz
3700
4811
Astara
Ardabīl
Ashkhabad
Mary
Atrak
Koppet Dagh
3048
3147
Tedzhen
Murghab
Gasan-Kuli
Bandar-e Shāh
Gurgan
Mashhad
Diyarbakır
Siirt
Kurdistan
4168
Rezā'iyeh
Mianeh
Rasht
Elburz Mts.
Shāhrud
Khurasan
Mardin
Urfa
Nuseybin
Gaziantep
Nineveh
Mosul
Erbil
Qazvīn
DAMAVEND 5601
Tehrān
Semnan
35°N
Hari
Herat
Kirkuk
Kirkūk
Tigris
Sanandaj
Dasht-e-Kavir
2850
2886
Deir ez Zor
Euphrates
Hamadān
Qum
Bīrjand
SYRIA
Kermānshāh
Kāshān
AFGHANISTAN
Pipeline
Khanaqin
Naft-e Shāh
Zagros Mountains
Luristan
IRAN
2992
Hadītha
Samarra
IRAQ
Baghdād
4070
Isfahan
Nehbandān
Dasht-e-Lut
Habbaniya
4547
3972
Shahrezā
Yazd
Zabul
Karbalā
Babylon
Al Kūt
Sistan
Najaf
Hilla
4075
30°N
Syrian
Amara
Haft-Gel
Kermān
Baluchistan
Wadian
Ahwaz
Khuzistan
Agha Jari
4276
Zāhedān
Nasriyah
Khorramshahr
Bandar-e Shāhpūr
4419
Urx
Gachsaran
4040
Desert
Hajara
Basra
Abādān
Rumaylah
Shīrāz
3962
KUWAIT
Kuwait
Persian Gulf
Fars
3862
Sakaka
Jauf
3489
Kharg
Bushire
3280
Laristan
Bandar Abbās
Maktan
2164
Oil Pipeline
Safaniyah
2161
Nafud
Str. of Hormuz
Hasa
OMAN
Jask
Hail
BAHRAIN
Manama
25°N
Jabal Shammar
Dhahran
Gulf of Oman
Summan
Dahna
QATAR
Sharjah
Dubai
Buraid
Abqaiq
Doha
Anaiza
Jabal
Hufhuf
Zakum
Abu Dhabi
UNITED ARAB EMIRATES
Buraimi
Matrah
Muscat
1829
Najd
Riyadh
Haradh
J. AKHDHAR
3109
Ras al Hadd
Medina
Quwaiiya
Tuwaiq
Yanbu
Hejaz
Hauta
SAUDI ARABIA
Umm Samim
OMAN
Laila
Masira
Rub' al Khali
20°N
Jidda
Mecca
Taif
Sabkha Minjora
Ras al Madraka
Tihama
2598
Asir
Red Sea
Port Sudan
Suakin
Qunfidha
Kuria Muria Is.
Abha
Salala
YEMEN P.D.R.
Najran
2780
Farasan Is.
Hadramaut
Saiwūn
W. al-Masilah
Ras Fartak
ERITREA
Dahlak Arch.
YEMEN
Shabwah
Arabian Sea
Agordat
Massawa
Kamaran Is.
San'a
3760
Asmara
Hodeida
Mukallā
Aduwa
3267
Hadibu (Tamridah)
Socotra (Yemen P.D.R.)
ETHIOPIA
Ta'iz
Medinat-ash-Sha'b
Aden
Gulf of Aden
Abd al Kuri
4620 RAS DASHAN
40°E
Assab
50°E
Metres
5000
3000
2000
1000
500
300
200
100
Sea level
Land depression
Spot heights in metres
Conical Orthomorphic Projection

India, Pakistan, Bangladesh and Sri Lanka
Scale 1:12 500 000
0 100 200 300 400 km
Boundaries International (in sea) (disputed)
Internal
Roads Roads Tracks
Railways Metre Broad Narrow
Airports International Domestic
Canals
Seasonal rivers, lakes
Marshes
Salt pan
Ice cap
Sand desert limits
National Parks, etc.
Conical Orthomorphic Projection
Same scale
Sri Lanka
Scale 1:7 750 000
AFGHANISTAN
PAKISTAN
INDIA
CHINA
TIBET
NEPAL
BALUCHISTAN
SIND
PUNJAB
RAJASTHAN
MADHYA PRADESH
UTTAR PRADESH
BIHAR
ORISSA
MAHARASHTRA
HYDERABAD
ANDHRA PRADESH
KARNATAKA
TAMIL NADU
KERALA
GUJERAT
KATHIAWAR
JAMMU and KASHMIR
HIMACHAL PRADESH
HARIYANA
WEST BENGAL
BERAR
SIKKIM
SRI LANKA
MAKRAN
Hindu Kush
KUNLUN MTS
Karakoram Pass
Great Himalaya Range
Kailas Range
Ladakh Range
Pangong Range
Sulaiman Range
Salt Range
Thal
Thar Desert
Vindhya Range
Satpura Range
Western Ghats
Eastern Ghats
Arabian Sea
Mouths of the Indus
Rann of Kutch
Tropic of Cancer
G. of Kutch
G. of Cambay
Laccadive Sea
Coromandel Coast
Malabar Coast
Palk Str.
Adam's Bridge
G. of Manaar
C. Comorin
Kabul
Kandahar
Quetta
Karachi
Hyderabad
Peshawar
Rawalpindi
Islamabad
Srinagar
Lahore
Multan
Amritsar
Simla
Delhi
New Delhi
Agra
Jaipur
Kanpur
Lucknow
Varanasi
Patna
Calcutta
Ahmedabad
Bhopal
Indore
Nagpur
Bombay
Poona
Hyderabad
Bangalore
Madras
Mysore
Madurai
Trivandrum
Katmandu
Mt. Everest 8848
Kangchenjunga 8586
Annapurna 8078
K2 8611
Gasherbrum 8068
Nanga Parbat 8126
Nanda Devi 7816
Kamet 7756
Darjeeling
Jaffna
Trincomalee
Anuradhapura
Kandy
Colombo
Nuwara Eliya
Galle
Matara
Dondra Head
Batticaloa
35°N
30°N
25°N
20°N
15°N
10°N
6°N
65°E
75°E
80°E
85°E

Indian Ocean

	km
Karachi to Aden	2750
" " Basra	2750
" " Bombay	900
" " Chittagong	4800
" " Colombo	2400
" " Durban	7200
" " Fremantle	8300
" " Hong Kong	8150
" " Jidda	4050
" " Mombasa	4450
" " Rangoon	4800
" " Singapore	5350
" " Suez	5150

	km
Chittagong to Aden	6300
" " Bombay	4050
" " Calcutta	550
" " Colombo	2400
" " Durban	9050
" " Fremantle	6850
" " Hong Kong	5700
" " Jidda	7600
" " Madras	2000
" " Mombasa	7000
" " Rangoon	1100
" " Singapore	2950
" " Suez	8700

	km
Aden to Colombo	3850
" " Jakarta	7200
" " Durban	5900
" " Mombasa	2950
" " Suez	2400
Durban to Bombay	7200
" " Fremantle	7750
" " Mombasa	3300
" " Shanghai	12 950
Colombo to Hong Kong	5500
Madras to Rangoon	1800
Mombasa to Singapore	7600
" " Fremantle	8850

Far East
Scale 1:19 000 000
0 150 300 450 600 km
Boundaries International Internal (in sea) (disputed)
Roads Motorways Other roads
Railways
Airports International Domestic
Canals Seasonal rivers, lakes
Marshes Salt pans Ice cap
Sand desert limits National Parks, etc.
U. S. S. R.
MONGOLIA
CHINA
MANCHURIA
INNER MONGOLIA
NORTH KOREA
SOUTH KOREA
JAPAN
TAIWAN
INDIA
BURMA
Sea of Japan
Yellow Sea
East China Sea
Gulf of Tartary
Limit of pack ice average maximum Jan-Mar
Ryukyu (Nánsei) Islands
200 m
Tropic of Cancer
Gobi Desert
Altai Range
Sikhote Alin Range
Great Khingan Mts
Yin Shan
Ala Shan
Ordos Plateau
Great Wall
Nan Shan
Tsaidam Swamps
Tsinling Shan
Tapa Shan
Red Basin
Yunkwei Plateau
Nan Ling
Wu Yi Shan Min
Formosa Strait
Shantung Peninsula
Kwantung Peninsula
Po Hai (G. of Chihli)
Hokkaido
Honshu
Shikoku
Kyushu
Inland Sea
Ulan Bator
Ulan-Ude
Wulumuchi (Urumchi)
Lanchow (Kaolan)
Paotow
Changkiakow (Kalgan)
Peking (Peiping)
Tientsin
Tangshan
Taiyuan (Yangku)
Shihkiachwang
Sian (Changan)
Kaifeng
Chengchow
Suchow (Tungshan)
Nanking
Shanghai
Hangchow
Wuhan
Chungking
Chengtu
Kweiyang (Kweichu)
Kunming (Yunnanfu)
Changsha
Nanchang
Foochow
Amoy
Swatow
Canton
HONG KONG (Br.)
Victoria
Macao (Port.)
Nanning (Yungning)
Hanoi
Tai-Pei
Kao-hsiung
Harbin (Pinkiang)
Changchun
Kirin
Mukden (Shen-Yang)
Fushun
Anshan
Lü-ta
Tsingtao
Pyongyang
Seoul (Kyongsong)
Pusan
Vladivostok
Khabarovsk
Tokyo
Yokohama
Nagoya
Kyoto
Osaka
Kobe
Hiroshima
Shimonoseki
Nagasaki
Sapporo
Hakodate
Sendai
Mandalay

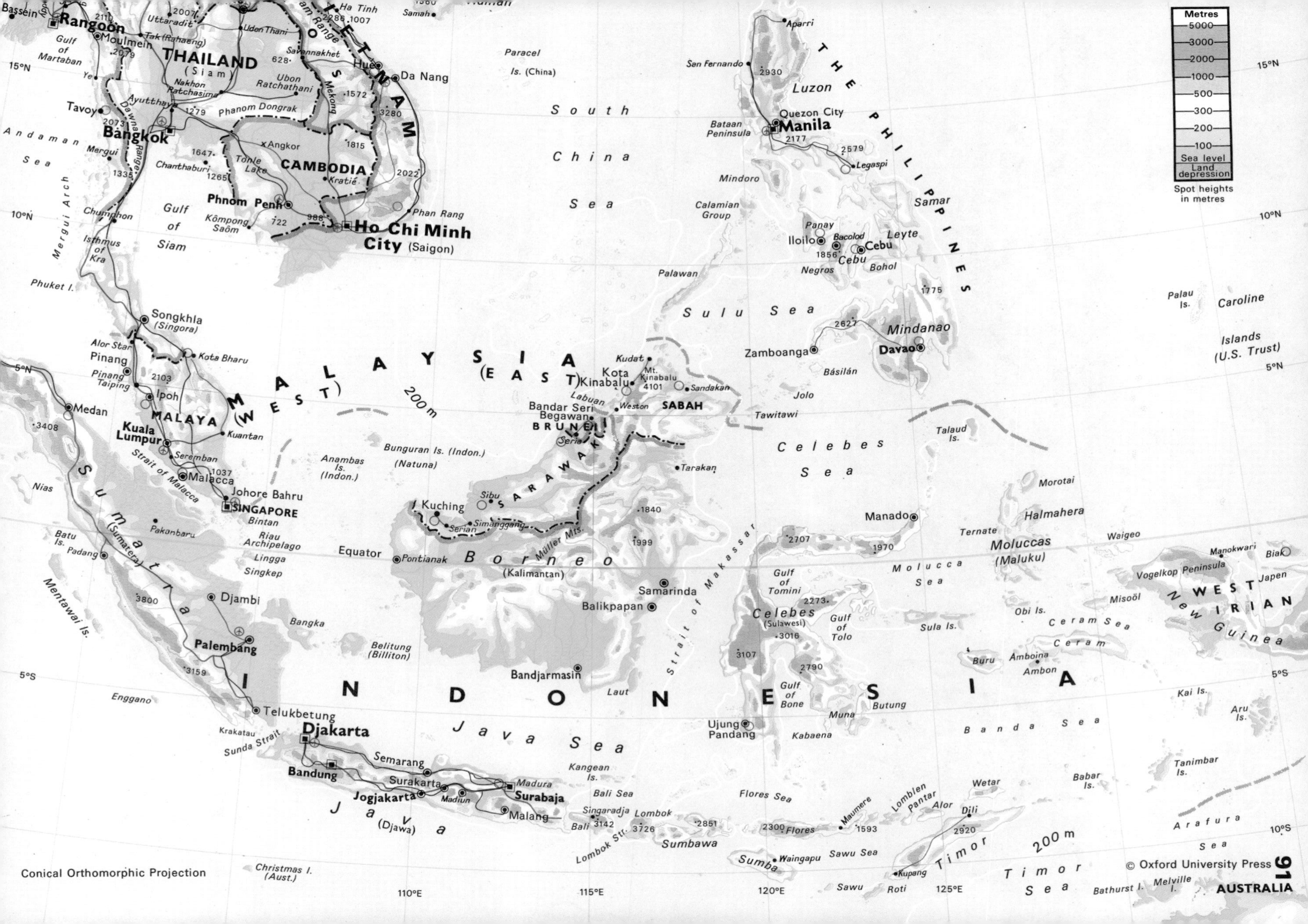

© Oxford University Press

Mainland Southeast Asia
Scale 1:12 500 000
0 100 200 300 400 km
For legend see page 93
Metres
4000
3000
2000
1000
500
300
150
Sea level
Spot heights in metres
Transverse Mercator Projection
© Oxford University Press
95°E
105°E
110°E
25°N
20°N
15°N
10°N
5°N
200 m
INDIA
CHINA
BURMA
LAOS
VIETNAM
THAILAND
CAMBODIA
MALAYSIA
INDONESIA
SINGAPORE
ASSAM
NAGA-LAND
MANIPUR
MIZORAM
KACHIN
SAGAING
CHIN
ARAKAN
MAGWE
MANDALAY
SHAN STATES
PEGU
IRRAWADDY
TENASSERIM
SZECHWAN
YUNNAN
KWEICHOW
HUNAN
KWANGSI
KWANGTUNG
MALAYA
SUMATRA
SARAWAK
Tezpur
Sibsagar
Jorhat
Rangia
Gauhati
Golaghat
Shillong
Kohima
Sylhet
Silchar
Imphal
Aijal
Chittagong
Akyab
Kyaukpyu
Ramree
Sandoway
Bassein
Henzada
Rangoon
Pegu
Prome
Toungoo
Thayetmyo
Magwe
Minbu
Pakokku
Myingyan
Meiktila
Mandalay
Maymyo
Sagaing
Monywa
Shwebo
Myitkyina
Bhamo
Lashio
Taunggyi
Kengtung
Yamethin
Pyinmana
Taungdwingyi
Thaton
Moulmein
Ye
Tavoy
Mergui
Kunming
Tali
Paoshan
Tengchung
Tsuyung
Chaotung
Kweiyang
Anshun
Tsuni
Chuking
Hsingi
Mengtsz
Wenshan
Nanning
Liuchow
Kweilin
Wuchow
Canton
Kongmoon
Macao (Port.)
Yulin
Hoppo
Peihai
Kaochow
Shaokuan
Hengyang
Shaoyang
Hunkiang
Chihkiang
Haikow
Kiungshan
Hainan
Hainan Strait
Gulf of Tonkin
Paracel Is.
Hanoi
Haiphong
Nam Dinh
Thanh Hoa
Vinh
Ha Tinh
Dong Hoi
Quang Tri
Hué
Da Nang
Quang Ngai
Kontum
Qui Nhon
Tuy Hòa
Ban Me Thuot
Nha Trang
Cam Ranh
Da Lat
Phan Rang
Phan Thiet
Ho Chi Minh City (Saigon)
Cholon
My Tho
Vung Tau
Vinh Long
Can Tho
Vinh Loi
Quan Long
Rach Gia
Long Xuyen
Mekong Delta
Lang Son
Cao Bang
Ha Giang
Lao Cai
Lai Chau
Dien Bien Phu
Son La
Phong Saly
Luang Prabang
Sam Neua
Vientiane
Thakhek
Savannakhet
Saravane
Pakse
Attopeu
Annam Highlands
Chiang Rai
Chiang Mai
Lampang
Nan
Phitsanulok
Nakhon Sawan
Udon Thani
Nong Khai
Khon Kaen
Nakhon Ratchasima
Ubon Ratchathani
Ayutthaya
Bangkok
Kanchanaburi
Suphan Buri
Phet Buri
Chanthaburi
Battambang
Siem Reap
Tonle Sap
Kompong Cham
Kompong Chhnang
Kratie
Stung Treng
Phnom Penh
Kampot
Kompong Som
Gulf of Siam
Isthmus of Kra
Chumphon
Ranong
Surat Thani
Nakhon Si Thammarat
Phuket
Songkhla
Hat Yai
Pattani
Trang
Alor Setar
Kota Bahru
George Town
Butterworth
Taiping
Ipoh
Kuala Terengganu
Kuantan
Kuala Lumpur
Kelang
Seremban
Melaka
Johor Bahru
Banda Aceh
Medan
Pematang Siantar
Sibolga
Padangsidimpuan
Pakanbaru
Bukittinggi
Kuching
Sibu
Pontianak
Singkawang
Sintang
Andaman Is. (India)
Port Blair
Little Andaman
Coco Is.
Nicobar Is.
Great Nicobar
ANDAMAN SEA
Mergui Arch.
INDIAN OCEAN
SOUTH CHINA SEA
Natuna Is.
Anambas Is.
Simeulue
Nias
Batu Is.
Strait of Malacca

Scale 1:2 000 000
0 20 40 60 km
KYOTO
SHIGA
MIE
NARA
OSAKA
AICHI
Fukuchiyama
Ayabe
Ikuno
Kaibara
Sannan
Naka
Ichikawa
Fukuzaki
Nishiwaki
Kasai
Sasayama
Sonobe
Kameoka
Keihoku
Kyoto
Otsu
Shiga
Chuzu
Yasu
Omi-hachiman
Notogawa
Hikone
Takashima
Adogawa
Ado
Nagahama
Biwa-ko
Ogaki
Kisogawa
Inuyama
Mizunami
Toki
Tajimi
Hashima
Bisai
Konan
Komaki
Ichinomiya
Sobue
Inazawa
Saori
Tsushima
Kasugai
Nagoya
Mino-mikawa-kogen
Toyota
Kuwana
Komono
Yokosuka
Ueno
Obu
Chiryu
Okazaki
Chita
Yokkaichi
Moriyama
Kusatsu
Yokaichi
Hino
Minakuchi
Shigaraki
Suzuka
Kameyama
Tokoname
Handa
Hekinan
Gamagori
Toyohashi
Toyokawa
Atsumi-wan
Atsumi-Hanto
Ise-wan
Tsu
Hisai
Karasu
Ureshino
Matsusaka
Irago-suido
Obata
Ise
Toba
ISE-SHIMA-Shima-Hanto
KOKURITSU-KOEN
Yoroi-zaki
Ago
Daio-zaki
Shima
137°E
Nanto
Nagashima
Himeji
Ono
Miki
Kakogawa
Takasago
Nishinomiya
Kobe
Akashi
Toyonaka
Itami
Suita
Amagasaki
Takatsuki
Ibaraki
Hirakata
Neyagawa
Kadoma
Nagaoka
Muko
Uji
Joyo
Inagawa
Sanda
Osaka
Sakai
Higashiosaka
Yao
Nara
Kashiwara
Habikino
Yamato-koriyama
Sakurai
Kashihara
Yamato-takada
Izumi
Izumi-otsu
Takaishi
Kishiwada
Kaizuka
Izumi-sano
Sennan
Kawachi-nagano
Gose
Yoshino
Oyodo
Gojo
Hashimoto
Katsuragi
Koyaguchi
Iwade
Kainan
Wakayama
135°E
Awaji
Hokudan
Osaka-wan
SETO-NAIKAI KRK.
Awaji-shima
Tsuna
Sumoto
Seidan
Nandan
Tomioka
Fujioka
Honjo
Tatebayashi
140°E
Makabe
Shimotsuma
Ishioka
Ogawa
Hokota
Tomioka
Shimonita
Oniishi
Kumagaya
Fukaya
Hanyu
Koga
Kurihashi
Kanto Heiya
IBARAKI
Tsukuba
Tsuchiura
Mamba
Gyoda
Kazo
Ogawa
SAITAMA
Konosu
Satte
Sugito
Yatabe
Ami
Kasumigaura
SUIGO TSUKUBA KRK.
Kitaura
Ogano
Chichibu
Ageo
Kasukabe
Mitsukaido
Kawagoe
Omiya
Noda
Fujishiro
Edosaki
Itako
Kashima
Kashimanada
CHICHIBU TAMA KRK
Agano
Hanno
Izumi-otsu
Sayama
Yono
Urawa
Kosigaya
Toride
Ryugasaki
Sawara
Omigawa
Tokorozawa
Kawaguchi
Kashiwa
Tone
Okutama
Ome
TOKYO
Kodaira
Matsudo
Inzai
Narita
Hasaki
Akijima
Musashino
Ichikawa
Imbanuma
Sakura
Asahi
Choshi
Enzan
Katsunuma
Tachikawa
Hachioji
Fuchu
Mitaka
Chofu
Tokyo
Funabashi
CHIBA
Yokaichiba
Inubozaki
Otsuki
Uenohara
Tokyo-wan
Yachimata
Naruto
Yokoshiba
Sagamihara
Chiba
Togane
Tsuru
Machida
Oamishirasato
Fujiyoshida
Yamato
Kawasaki
Yokohama
Ichihara
Atsugi
Mobara
Fujisan
3776
FUJI HAKONE IZU KRK.
Hadano
Hiratsuka
Kisarazu
Nanso
Ichinomiya
Fujisawa
Kimitsu
Gotenba
Oiso
Kamakura
Kazusa
Boso Hanto
Otaki
Odawara
Chigasaki
Zushi
Yokosuka
Ohara
Hakone
Kiyosumiyama
Mishima
Manazuru
Yugawara
Miura
MINAMIBOSO KRK.
Katsuura
Hatimanzaki
Numazu
Atami
Sagaminada
Kyonan
Kominato
Kamogawa
Wada
Heta
Ohito
Ito
Tateyama
35°N
Shuzenji
Tikura
Toi
Yugashima
Nojimazaki
Sirahama
Hokkaido
Haboro
Nayoro
Shibetsu
Rumoi
Asahigawa
Akabira
Takikawa
Sunagawa
Ishikari-wan
Utashinai
Bibai
Mikasa
Yoichi
Otaru
Ebetsu
Yubari
Iwanai
Sapporo
Chitose
SHIKOTSU-TOYA KOKURITSU-KOEN
Tomakomai
1520
KARIBA-YAMA
Shiraoi
Shizunai
Uchiura-wan
Noboribetsu
Muroran
Yakumo
Mori
Okushiri-shima
Kamiiso
Hakodate
Tsugaru-kaikyo
Ohata
Mutsu
Teppi-zaki
Mutsu-wan
Aomori
TOWADA HACHIMANTAI KOKURITSU-KOEN
Misawa
Hachinohe
Hirosaki
Odate
Noshiro
Ou-sammyaku
IWATE-SAN 2041
40°N
Oga
Oga-Hanto
Morioka
Akita
Dewa-kyuryo
Miyako
Kamaishi
Yokote
Ofunato
Kesennuma
Ichinoseki
Sakata
Shinjo
Tsuruoka
GAS-SAN 1980
Ishinomaki
Ojika-Hanto
Shiogama
Yamagata
Sendai
Iwanuma
Sado
Niigata
BANDAI-ASAHI KOKURITSU-KOEN
Fukushima
Sado-kaikyo
Honshu
Sanjo
Nagaoka
Aizu-wakamatsu
Koriyama
Sukagawa
Suzu-misaki
Kashiwazaki
Wajima
Noto-Hanto
Naoetsu
Shirakawa
Iwaki
Takada
NIKKO KOKURITSU-KOEN
Kitaibaraki
Nanao
Toyama-wan
Himi
Uozu
2026
Hitachi
Takaoka
Nagano
Kiryu
Utsunomiya
Kanazawa
Toyama
Maebashi
Mito
Nakaminato
CHUBU-SANGAKU KOKURITSU-KOEN
YARIGA-TAKE 3180
Ashikaga
Tsuchiura
Oki-gunto
Sea of Japan
Ueda
Matsumoto
Kumagaya
Fukui
HAKU-SAN KOKURITSU-KOEN
Okaya
Suwa
Kawagoe
Urawa
Choshi
SOUTH KOREA
Pohang
Ulsan
200 m
Kyoga-saki
Tsuruga
MINAMI-ALPS KOKURITSU-KOEN
Tokyo
Yokohama
Chiba
Kisarazu
Matsue
Sakai-minato
Tottori
Maizuru
Ryohaku-Sanchi
Kofu
FUJI-SAN 3776
Mobara
Yonago
DAI-SEN-OKI KOKURITSU-KOEN
Ayabe
Nagahama
Hikone
Ogaki
Gifu
Ichinomiya
Iida
Yokosuka
Oda
Biwa-ko
Odawara
Sagami-nada
35°N
Hamada
1126
Chugoku-Sanchi
Tsuyama
Kyoto
Otsu
Nagoya
Toyota
Okazaki
Shimizu
Numazu
Shizuoka
Tateyama
O-shima
Masuda
Kurashiki
Fukuyama
Himeji
Kobe
Suzuka
Handa
Hamamatsu
FUJI-HAKONE-IZU-KOKURITSU-KOEN
Okayama
Akashi
Tsu
Yokkaichi
Toyohashi
1339
Mihara
Kasaoka
Nara
Matsuzaka
Tsushima
Nagato
Hagi
naikai
Osaka
Nii-shima
Tsushima-kaikyo
Hibiki-nada
Hiroshima
Kure
Takamatsu
Sumoto
Kishiwada
Ise
Izu-Shoto
Shimonoseki
Tokuyama
Iwakuni
Seto-
Kanonji
Naruto
Kii-suido
Wakayama
Daio-zaki
Kozu-shima
Miyake-jima
Kitakyushu
Ube
Imabari
Niihama
Tokushima
1915
HAKKEN-SAN
Mikura-jima
Fukuoka
Suo-nada
Iyo-nada
Matsuyama
Anan
Iizuka
Nakatsu
Kochi
Tanabe
Shingu
Usa
Ozu
Saga
Beppu
Yawatahama
Tosa-wan
Shiono-zaki
Kurume
Oita
Sasebo
Omuta
Usuki
Uwajima
Tsukumi
Muroto-zaki
Shikoku
Nagasaki
Saeki
Bungo-suido
Kumamoto
Nobeoka
Yatsushiro
Ashizuri-zaki
Kyushu-Sanchi
Hyuga
Minamata
Kyushu
Sendai
Miyazaki
Koshiki-retto
Kagoshima
Miyakonojo
Makurazaki
Kanoya
130°E
PACIFIC OCEAN
140°E
Japan
Scale 1:6 250 000
0 50 100 150 200 km
Zenithal Equidistant Projection
135°E ©Oxford University Press
Boundaries
International
(in sea)
(disputed)
Internal
Roads
Motorways
Other roads
Tracks
Railways
Airports
International
Domestic
Canals
Seasonal rivers, lakes
Marshes
Salt pans
Ice cap
Sand desert limits
National Parks, etc.
Metres
5000
3000
2000
1000
500
300
200
100
Sea level
Land depression
Spot heights in metres

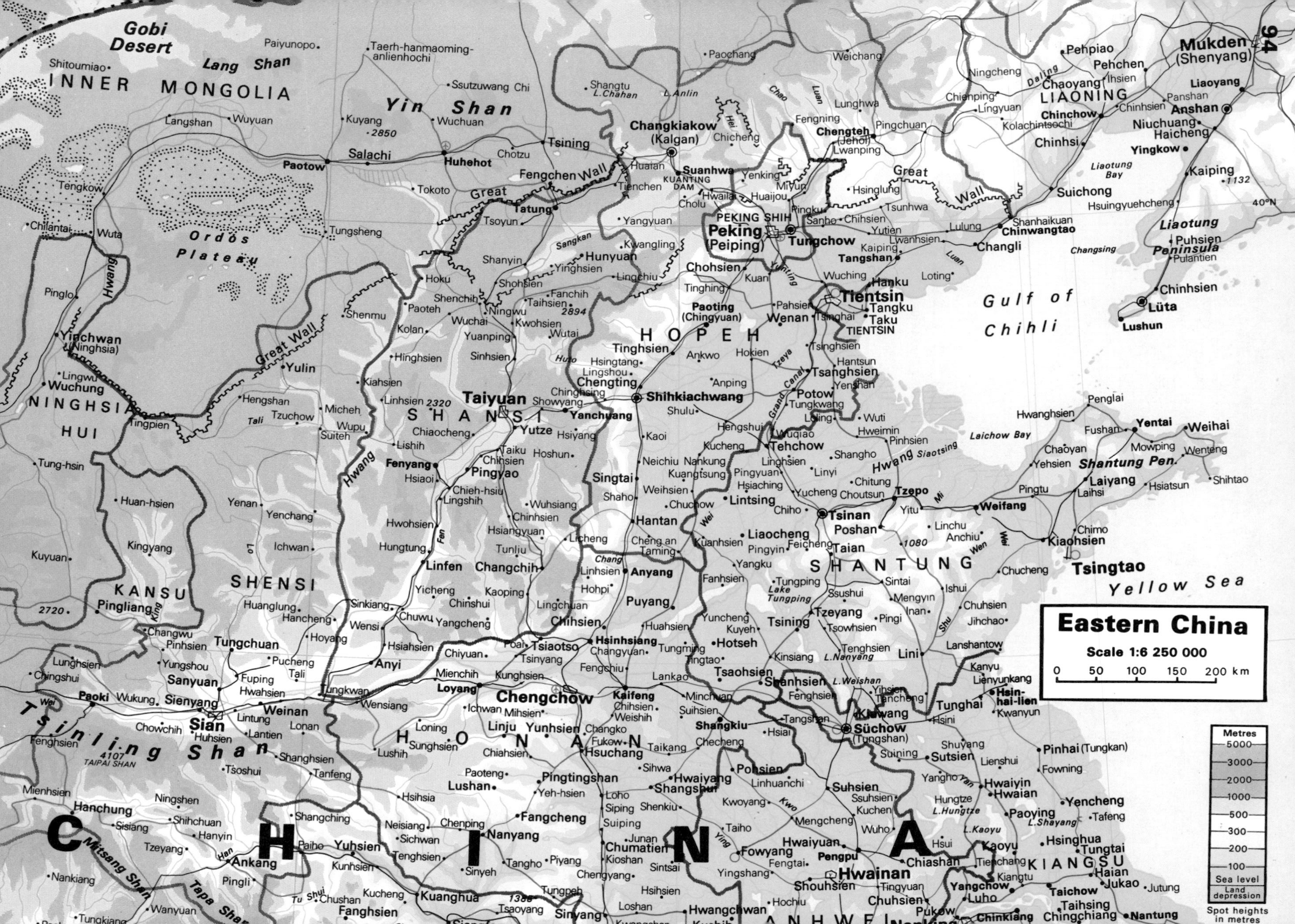
Eastern China
Scale 1:6 250 000
0 50 100 150 200 km
Metres
5000
3000
2000
1000
500
300
200
100
Sea level
Land depression
Spot heights in metres
Gobi Desert
INNER MONGOLIA
Lang Shan
Yin Shan
Ordos Plateau
LIAONING
HOPEH
SHANSI
SHENSI
KANSU
NINGHSIA HUI
HONAN
SHANTUNG
KIANGSU
ANHWEI
CHINA
Gulf of Chihli
Yellow Sea
Laichow Bay
Liaotung Bay
Liaotung Peninsula
Shantung Pen.
Tsinling Shan
Mitsang Shan
Tapa Shan
Great Wall
Grand Canal
Hwang
Wei
Fen
Luan
Mukden (Shenyang)
Anshan
Lüta
Lushun
Chinchow
Chinwangtao
Changkiakow (Kalgan)
Peking (Peiping)
PEKING SHIH
Tientsin
Tangshan
Paoting (Chingyuan)
Shihkiachwang
Taiyuan
Tatung
Huhehot
Paotow
Yinchwan (Ninghsia)
Sian
Loyang
Chengchow
Kaifeng
Tsinan
Tsingtao
Yentai
Weifang
Süchow (Tungshan)
Hwainan
Pengpu
Nanyang
Hsinhsiang
Anyang
Hantan
Linfen
Changchih
Yangchow
Nantung
40°N

SZECHWAN

HUPEH

HUNAN

KIANGSI

CHEKIANG

FUKIEN

KWEICHOW

KWANGSI CHUANG

KWANGTUNG

TAIWAN (FORMOSA)

East China Sea

South China Sea

Formosa Strait

Gulf of Tonkin

Tropic of Cancer

Boundaries	International	(in sea)	(disputed)
	Internal		
Roads	Motorways	Other roads	Tracks
Railways			
Airports	International	Domestic	
Canals		Seasonal rivers, lakes	
Marshes	Salt pan	Ice cap	
Sand desert limits		National Parks, etc.	

Conical Orthomorphic Projection

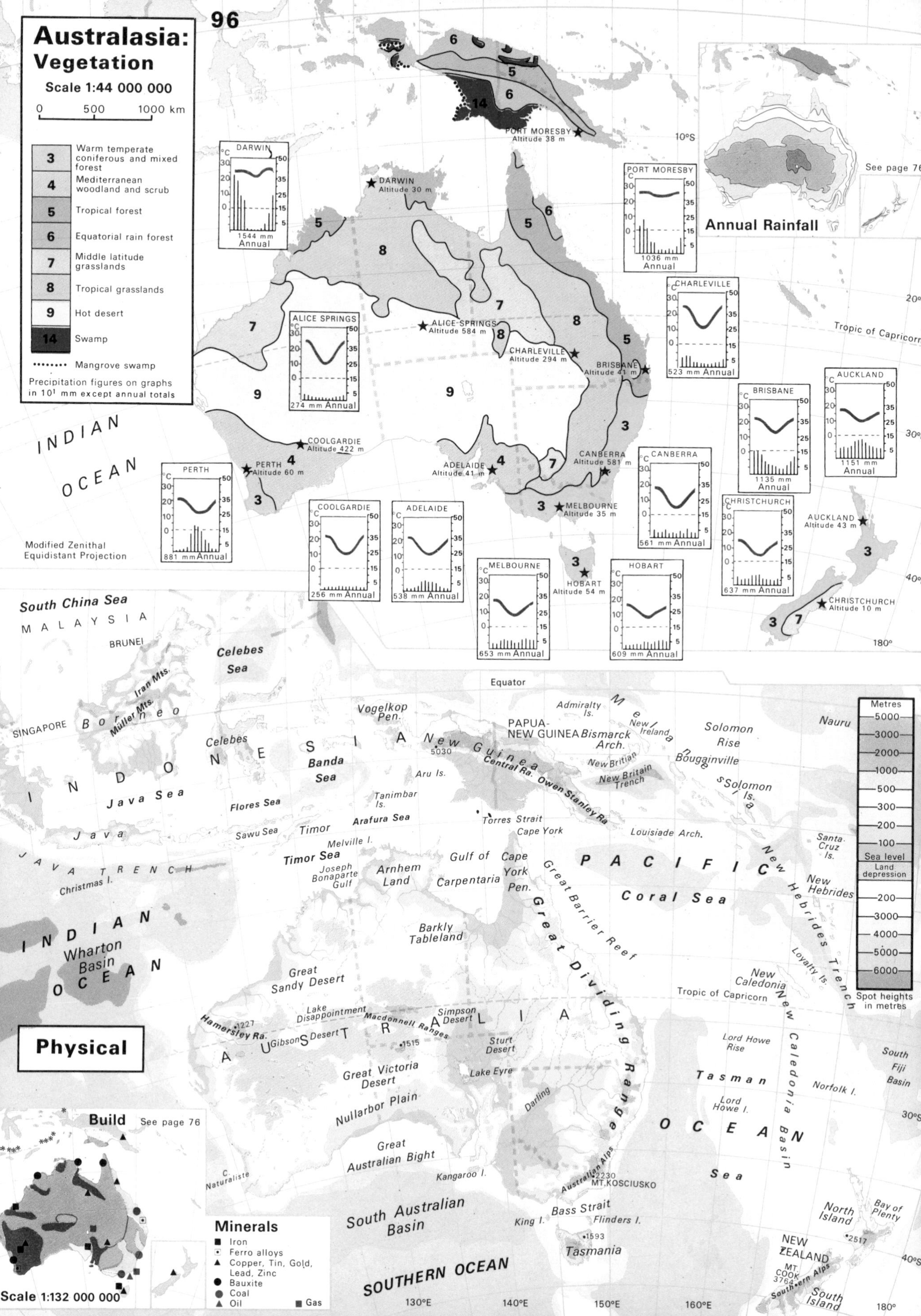
Australasia: Vegetation
Scale 1:44 000 000
0 500 1000 km
3 Warm temperate coniferous and mixed forest
4 Mediterranean woodland and scrub
5 Tropical forest
6 Equatorial rain forest
7 Middle latitude grasslands
8 Tropical grasslands
9 Hot desert
14 Swamp
Mangrove swamp
Precipitation figures on graphs in 10¹ mm except annual totals
Modified Zenithal Equidistant Projection
INDIAN OCEAN
PORT MORESBY Altitude 38 m
DARWIN Altitude 30 m
ALICE SPRINGS Altitude 584 m
CHARLEVILLE Altitude 294 m
BRISBANE Altitude 41 m
COOLGARDIE Altitude 422 m
PERTH Altitude 60 m
ADELAIDE Altitude 41 m
CANBERRA Altitude 581 m
MELBOURNE Altitude 35 m
HOBART Altitude 54 m
AUCKLAND Altitude 43 m
CHRISTCHURCH Altitude 10 m
DARWIN 1544 mm Annual
PORT MORESBY 1036 mm Annual
CHARLEVILLE 523 mm Annual
ALICE SPRINGS 274 mm Annual
BRISBANE 1135 mm Annual
AUCKLAND 1151 mm Annual
PERTH 881 mm Annual
COOLGARDIE 256 mm Annual
ADELAIDE 538 mm Annual
CANBERRA 561 mm Annual
CHRISTCHURCH 637 mm Annual
MELBOURNE 653 mm Annual
HOBART 609 mm Annual
Annual Rainfall
See page 76
10°S
20°S
Tropic of Capricorn
30°S
40°S
180°
Physical
South China Sea
MALAYSIA
BRUNEI
SINGAPORE
Borneo
Iran Mts.
Müller Mts.
Celebes Sea
Celebes
INDONESIA
Java Sea
Java
Banda Sea
Flores Sea
Sawu Sea
Timor
Timor Sea
Arafura Sea
JAVA TRENCH
Christmas I.
INDIAN OCEAN
Wharton Basin
Vogelkop Pen.
New Guinea
5030
Central Ra.
Owen Stanley Ra.
Aru Is.
Tanimbar Is.
Torres Strait
Cape York
Melville I.
Joseph Bonaparte Gulf
Arnhem Land
Gulf of Carpentaria
Cape York Pen.
Barkly Tableland
Great Sandy Desert
Lake Disappointment
Hamersley Ra.
1227
Gibson Desert
Macdonnell Ranges
1515
Simpson Desert
AUSTRALIA
Sturt Desert
Lake Eyre
Great Victoria Desert
Nullarbor Plain
Great Australian Bight
C. Naturaliste
Kangaroo I.
Darling
Great Dividing Range
Great Barrier Reef
Australian Alps
2230 MT. KOSCIUSKO
Bass Strait
King I.
Flinders I.
1593
Tasmania
South Australian Basin
SOUTHERN OCEAN
Equator
Admiralty Is.
PAPUA-NEW GUINEA
Bismarck Arch.
New Ireland
Melanesia
New Britain
New Britain Trench
Solomon Rise
Bougainville
Solomon Is.
Louisiade Arch.
Nauru
Santa Cruz Is.
PACIFIC
Coral Sea
New Hebrides
New Hebrides Trench
Loyalty Is.
New Caledonia
New Caledonia Basin
Tropic of Capricorn
Lord Howe Rise
Lord Howe I.
Tasman Sea
OCEAN
Norfolk I.
South Fiji Basin
North Island
Bay of Plenty
2517
NEW ZEALAND
MT. COOK 3764
Southern Alps
South Island
30°S
40°S
180°
130°E
140°E
150°E
160°E
Metres
5000
3000
2000
1000
500
300
200
100
Sea level
Land depression
200
3000
4000
5000
6000
Spot heights in metres
Build
See page 76
Scale 1:132 000 000
Minerals
Iron
Ferro alloys
Copper, Tin, Gold, Lead, Zinc
Bauxite
Coal
Oil
Gas

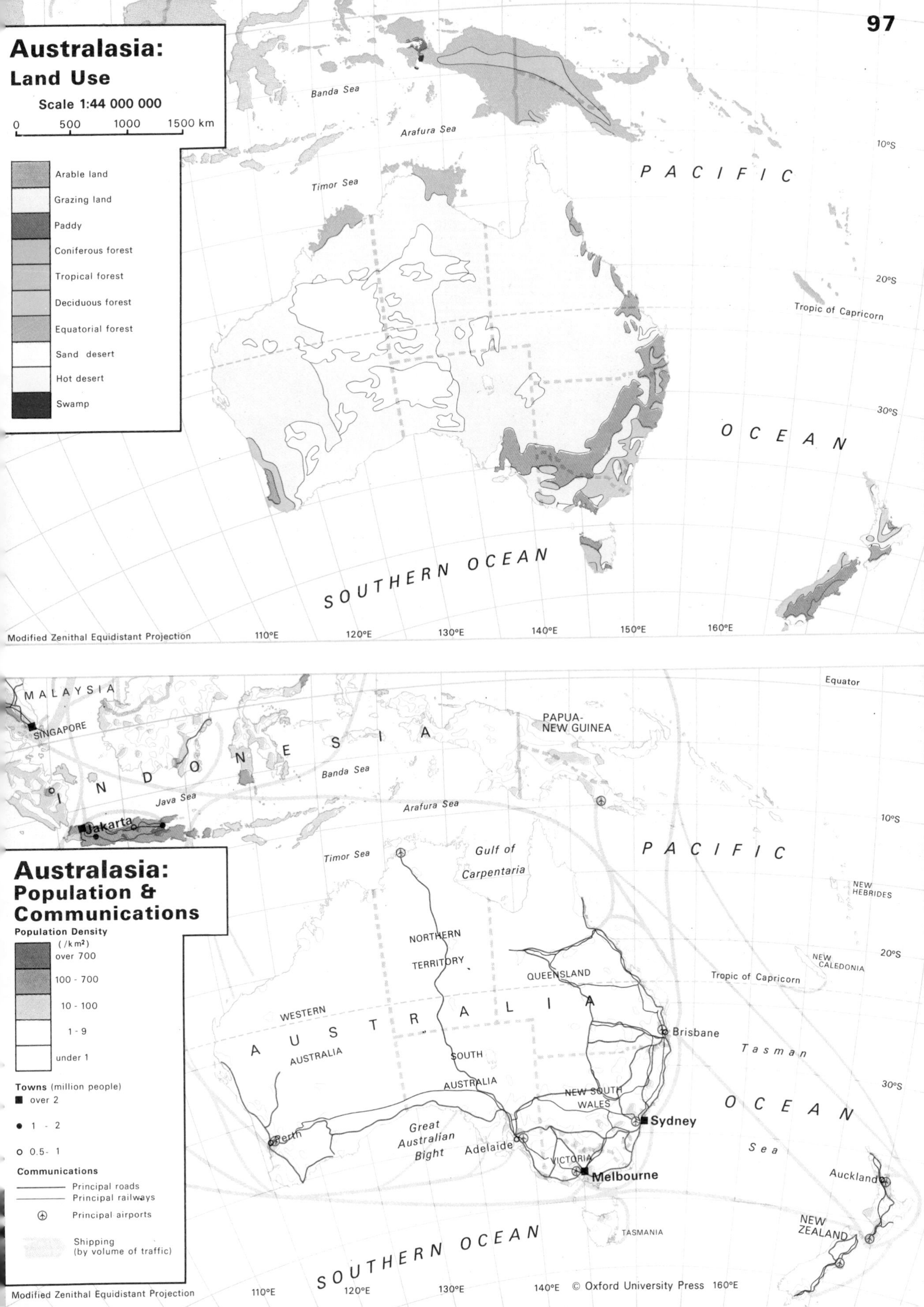

Australasia:
Land Use
Scale 1:44 000 000
0
500
1000
1500 km
Arable land
Grazing land
Paddy
Coniferous forest
Tropical forest
Deciduous forest
Equatorial forest
Sand desert
Hot desert
Swamp
Banda Sea
Arafura Sea
Timor Sea
PACIFIC
OCEAN
10°S
20°S
30°S
Tropic of Capricorn
SOUTHERN OCEAN
Modified Zenithal Equidistant Projection
110°E
120°E
130°E
140°E
150°E
160°E
Australasia:
Population & Communications
Population Density
(/km²)
over 700
100 - 700
10 - 100
1 - 9
under 1
Towns (million people)
over 2
1 - 2
0.5 - 1
Communications
Principal roads
Principal railways
Principal airports
Shipping
(by volume of traffic)
MALAYSIA
SINGAPORE
INDONESIA
Jakarta
Java Sea
Banda Sea
Arafura Sea
Timor Sea
Equator
PAPUA-
NEW GUINEA
Gulf of
Carpentaria
PACIFIC
NEW
HEBRIDES
NEW
CALEDONIA
Tropic of Capricorn
NORTHERN
TERRITORY
QUEENSLAND
WESTERN
AUSTRALIA
AUSTRALIA
SOUTH
AUSTRALIA
NEW SOUTH
WALES
Brisbane
Sydney
Tasman
Sea
OCEAN
Perth
Great
Australian
Bight
Adelaide
VICTORIA
Melbourne
Auckland
NEW
ZEALAND
TASMANIA
SOUTHERN OCEAN
10°S
20°S
30°S
Modified Zenithal Equidistant Projection
110°E
120°E
130°E
140°E
160°E

Australasia
Scale 1:22 000 000
0 350 700 km
Boundaries International (in sea) (disputed) Internal
Roads
Railways
Airports International Domestic
Canals
Seasonal rivers, lakes
Marshes
Salt pans
Ice cap
Sand desert limits
National Parks, etc.
Metres
5000
3000
2000
1000
500
300
200
100
Sea level
Land depression
Spot heights in metres
MALAYSIA
INDONESIA
AUSTRALIA
INDIAN OCEAN
THE PHILIPPINES
BRUNEI
SINGAPORE
Borneo (Kalimantan)
Celebes (Sulawesi)
Java
Sumatra
Celebes Sea
Java Sea
Flores Sea
Banda Sea
Arafura Sea
Timor Sea
Molucca Sea
Great Australian Bight
WESTERN AUSTRALIA
NORTHERN TERRITORY
SOUTH AUSTRALIA
Great Sandy Desert
Gibson Desert
Great Victoria Desert
Nullarbor Plain
Perth
Darwin
Jakarta
Alice Springs
Zenithal Equidistant Projection

PACIFIC OCEAN
Coral Sea
Tasman Sea
PAPUA-NEW GUINEA
QUEENSLAND
NEW SOUTH WALES
VICTORIA
TASMANIA
NEW ZEALAND
NORTH ISLAND
SOUTH ISLAND
Equator
Tropic of Capricorn
Solomon Islands
New Hebrides (Br.-Fr. Condominium)
Loyalty Is. (Fr.)
New Caledonia (Fr.)
Nouméa
Fiji Is.
Tuvalu
Gilbert Islands (Br.)
Nauru
Ocean I. (Br.)
Brisbane
Sydney
Canberra
Melbourne
Hobart
Newcastle
Wollongong
Auckland
Wellington
Christchurch
Dunedin
Great Barrier Reef
Great Dividing Range
Bass Strait
Cook Strait
Southern Alps
MT. KOSCIUSKO 2230
MT. COOK 3764
Norfolk I. (Austl.)

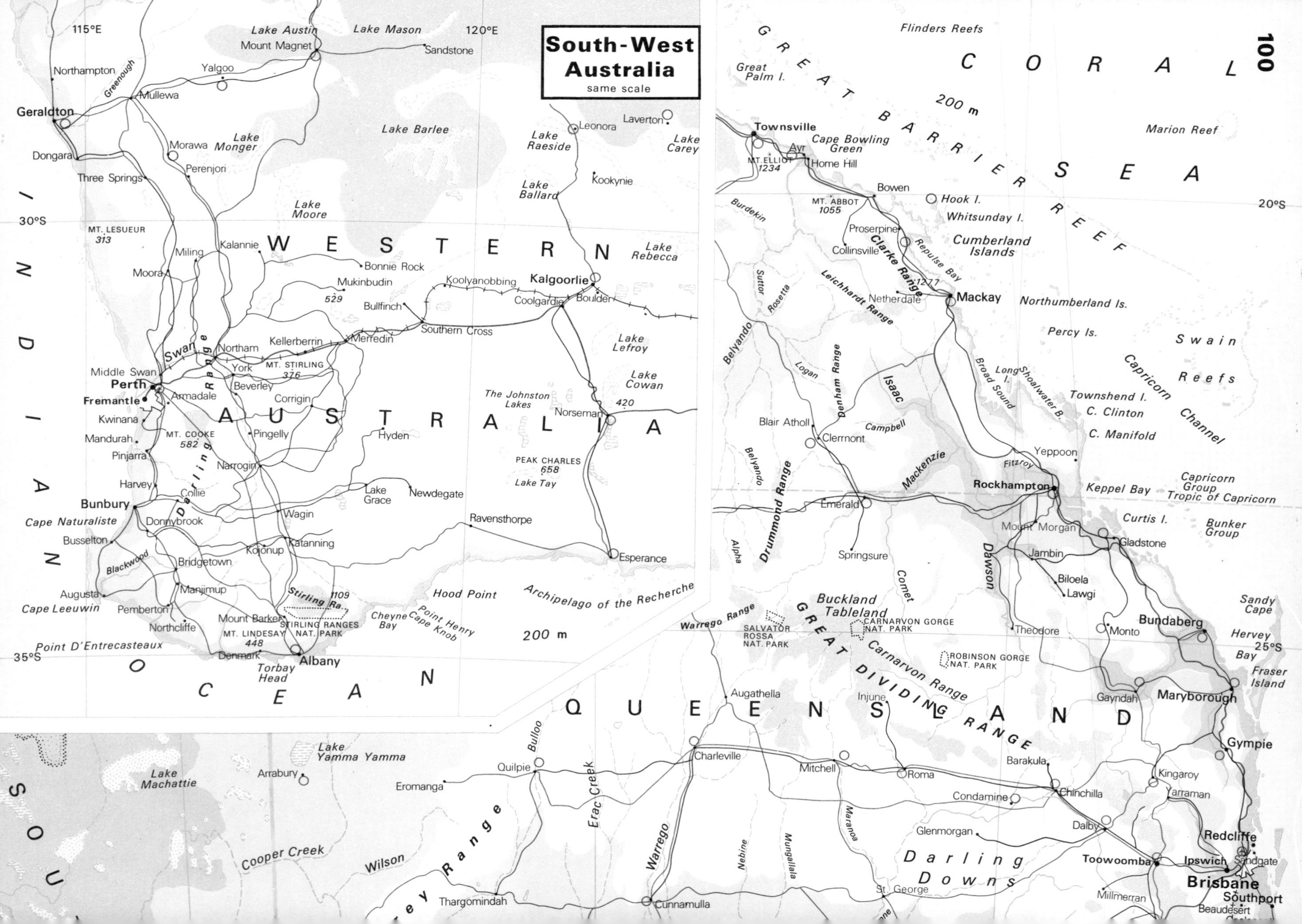

South-West Australia
same scale
115°E
120°E
30°S
35°S
20°S
25°S
Lake Austin
Lake Mason
Mount Magnet
Sandstone
Northampton
Greenough
Yalgoo
Mullewa
Geraldton
Lake Barlee
Leonora
Laverton
Lake Raeside
Lake Carey
Morawa
Lake Monger
Dongara
Perenjori
Three Springs
Kookynie
Lake Ballard
Lake Moore
MT. LESUEUR 313
Kalannie
WESTERN AUSTRALIA
Lake Rebecca
Miling
Bonnie Rock
Moora
Mukinbudin
529
Koolyanobbing
Kalgoorlie
Boulder
Coolgardie
Bullfinch
Southern Cross
Swan
Range
Northam
Kellerberrin
Merredin
Lake Lefroy
MT. STIRLING 376
York
Middle Swan
Perth
Beverley
Lake Cowan
Armadale
Fremantle
Corrigin
The Johnston Lakes
420
Norseman
Kwinana
Mandurah
MT. COOKE 582
Pingelly
Hyden
Darling
Pinjarra
Narrogin
PEAK CHARLES 658
Lake Tay
Harvey
Collie
Lake Grace
Newdegate
Bunbury
Cape Naturaliste
Donnybrook
Wagin
Ravensthorpe
Busselton
Katanning
Kojonup
Esperance
Blackwood
Bridgetown
Augusta
Manjimup
Stirling Ra.
1109
Hood Point
Archipelago of the Recherche
Cape Leeuwin
Pemberton
Mount Barker
STIRLING RANGES NAT. PARK
Cheyne Bay
Point Henry
Cape Knob
Northcliffe
MT. LINDESAY 448
200 m
Point D'Entrecasteaux
Denmark
Albany
Torbay Head
INDIAN OCEAN
Flinders Reefs
CORAL SEA
GREAT BARRIER REEF
Great Palm I.
200 m
Marion Reef
Townsville
Cape Bowling Green
Ayr
MT. ELLIOT 1234
Home Hill
Bowen
Hook I.
MT. ABBOT 1055
Whitsunday I.
Burdekin
Proserpine
Cumberland Islands
Collinsville
Clarke Range
Repulse Bay
Leichhardt Range
1277
Suttor
Rosetta
Netherdale
Mackay
Northumberland Is.
Percy Is.
Swain Reefs
Belyando
Logan
Denham Range
Isaac
Broad Sound
Long I.
Shoalwater B.
Townshend I.
Capricorn Channel
C. Clinton
Blair Atholl
Campbell
Clermont
C. Manifold
Yeppoon
Belyando
Mackenzie
Fitzroy
Capricorn Group
Drummond Range
Rockhampton
Keppel Bay
Tropic of Capricorn
Emerald
Curtis I.
Bunker Group
Mount Morgan
Gladstone
Jambin
Alpha
Springsure
Dawson
Comet
Biloela
Lawgi
Buckland Tableland
Sandy Cape
Bundaberg
Warrego Range
SALVATOR ROSSA NAT. PARK
CARNARVON GORGE NAT. PARK
Theodore
Monto
Hervey Bay
GREAT DIVIDING RANGE
Carnarvon Range
ROBINSON GORGE NAT. PARK
Fraser Island
Augathella
Injune
Gayndah
Maryborough
QUEENSLAND
Bulloo
Gympie
Lake Yamma Yamma
Charleville
Barakula
Lake Machattie
Arrabury
Quilpie
Mitchell
Roma
Kingaroy
Eromanga
Condamine
Chinchilla
Yarraman
Erac Creek
Maranoa
Dalby
Nebine
Mungallala
Glenmorgan
Redcliffe
Range
Warrego
Darling Downs
Toowoomba
Ipswich
Sandgate
Cooper Creek
Wilson
Brisbane
Southport
St. George
Millmerran
Thargomindah
Cunnamulla
Beaudesert
SOU

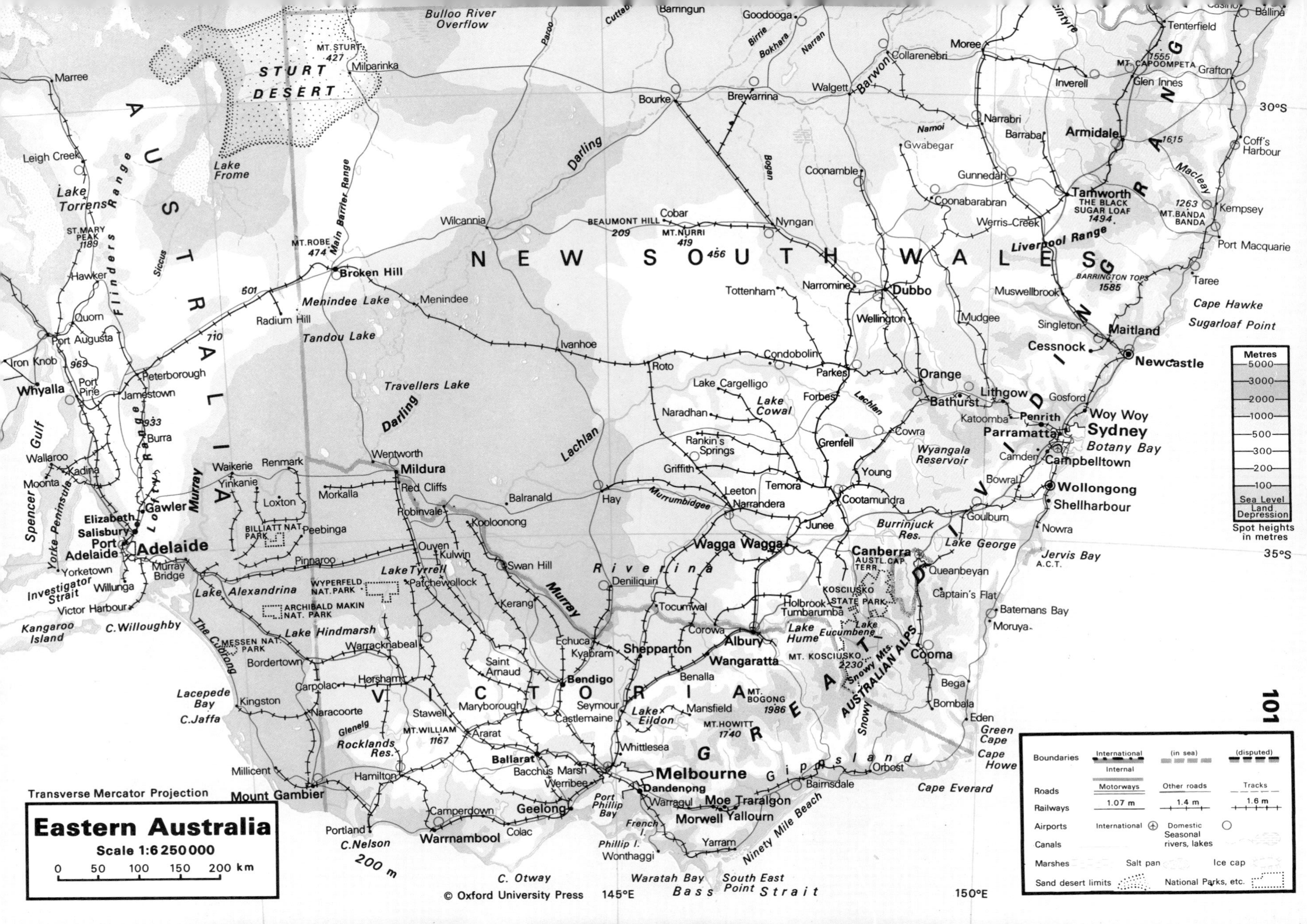
Eastern Australia
Scale 1:6 250 000
0 50 100 150 200 km
Transverse Mercator Projection
Metres
5000
3000
2000
1000
500
300
200
100
Sea Level
Land Depression
Spot heights in metres
Boundaries
International
(in sea)
(disputed)
Internal
Roads
Motorways
Other roads
Tracks
Railways
1.07 m
1.4 m
1.6 m
Airports
International
Domestic
Canals
Seasonal rivers, lakes
Marshes
Salt pan
Ice cap
Sand desert limits
National Parks, etc.
30°S
35°S
145°E
150°E
NEW SOUTH WALES
VICTORIA
AUSTRALIA
GREAT DIVIDING RANGE
STURT DESERT
Bulloo River Overflow
Sydney
Melbourne
Adelaide
Canberra
Newcastle
Wollongong
Broken Hill
Mildura
Dubbo
Bendigo
Ballarat
Geelong
Albury
Wagga Wagga
Tamworth
Armidale
Orange
Bathurst
Lithgow
Parramatta
Penrith
Campbelltown
Maitland
Cessnock
Goulburn
Cooma
Queanbeyan
Shepparton
Wangaratta
Warrnambool
Mount Gambier
Whyalla
Port Augusta
Port Pirie
Port Adelaide
Gawler
Elizabeth
Salisbury
Murray Bridge
Bourke
Cobar
Wilcannia
Menindee
Ivanhoe
Hay
Deniliquin
Griffith
Leeton
Narrandera
Cootamundra
Young
Cowra
Parkes
Forbes
Condobolin
Narromine
Nyngan
Moree
Walgett
Narrabri
Gunnedah
Inverell
Glen Innes
Tenterfield
Grafton
Ballina
Coff's Harbour
Kempsey
Port Macquarie
Taree
Gosford
Woy Woy
Katoomba
Camden
Bowral
Shellharbour
Nowra
Batemans Bay
Moruya
Bega
Bombala
Eden
Orbost
Bairnsdale
Sale
Traralgon
Morwell
Yallourn
Moe
Warragul
Dandenong
Wonthaggi
Yarram
Werribee
Bacchus Marsh
Colac
Camperdown
Portland
Hamilton
Horsham
Stawell
Ararat
Maryborough
Castlemaine
Seymour
Benalla
Mansfield
Whittlesea
Echuca
Kyabram
Kerang
Swan Hill
Ouyen
Kulwin
Patchewollock
Robinvale
Red Cliffs
Wentworth
Balranald
Tocumwal
Corowa
Holbrook
Tumbarumba
Junee
Temora
Grenfell
Wellington
Mudgee
Muswellbrook
Singleton
Werris Creek
Coonabarabran
Coonamble
Gwabegar
Barraba
Collarenebri
Brewarrina
Goodooga
Barringun
Tottenham
Lake Cargelligo
Naradhan
Rankin's Springs
Roto
Milparinka
Marree
Leigh Creek
Hawker
Quorn
Iron Knob
Peterborough
Jamestown
Burra
Radium Hill
Renmark
Waikerie
Yinkanie
Loxton
Morkalla
Peebinga
Pinnaroo
Kooloonong
Bordertown
Kingston
Naracoorte
Carpolac
Warracknabeal
Millicent
Wallaroo
Kadina
Moonta
Yorketown
Willunga
Victor Harbour
Darling
Murray
Lachlan
Murrumbidgee
Barwon
Namoi
Bogan
Macleay
Paroo
Narran
Bokhara
Birrie
Siccus
Glenelg
Snowy
Lake Torrens
Lake Frome
Menindee Lake
Tandou Lake
Travellers Lake
Lake Cowal
Lake Tyrrell
Lake Hindmarsh
Lake Alexandrina
Lake Hume
Lake Eildon
Lake Eucumbene
Lake George
Burrinjuck Res.
Wyangala Reservoir
Rocklands Res.
Flinders Range
Main Barrier Range
Liverpool Range
Lofty Range
AUSTRALIAN ALPS
Snowy Mts.
Riverina
Gippsland
Ninety Mile Beach
The Coorong
Spencer Gulf
Yorke Peninsula
Investigator Strait
Kangaroo Island
C. Willoughby
Lacepede Bay
C. Jaffa
C. Nelson
C. Otway
200 m
Port Phillip Bay
Phillip I.
French I.
Waratah Bay
South East Point
Bass Strait
Cape Everard
Cape Howe
Green Cape
Jervis Bay A.C.T.
Botany Bay
Cape Hawke
Sugarloaf Point
AUSTL. CAP. TERR.
KOSCIUSKO STATE PARK
MT. KOSCIUSKO 2230
MT. BOGONG 1986
MT. HOWITT 1740
MT. WILLIAM 1167
MT. STURT 427
MT. ROBE 474
MT. NURRI 419
BEAUMONT HILL 209
ST. MARY PEAK 1189
MT. CAPOOMPETA 1555
THE BLACK SUGAR LOAF 1494
MT. BANDA BANDA 1263
BARRINGTON TOPS 1585
1615
456
501
710
933
969
WYPERFELD NAT. PARK
ARCHIBALD MAKIN NAT. PARK
BILLIATT NAT. PARK
MESSEN NAT. PARK

Pacific Ocean
Scale 1:63 000 000
0 500 1000 1500 2000 km
Ocean Currents
Warm currents
Cold currents
Metres
5000
3000
2000
1000
500
300
200
100
Sea Level
Land depression
200
3000
4000
5000
6000
Spot heights in metres
NORTH PACIFIC
INDIAN OCEAN
SOUTH
SOUTHERN
U. S. S. R.
CHINA
Plateau of Tibet
Himalaya
NEPAL
INDIA
BANGLADESH
BURMA
LAOS
VIETNAM
THAILAND
CAMBODIA
MALAYSIA
SINGAPORE
INDONESIA
PHILIPPINES
BRUNEI
PAPUA-NEW GUINEA
AUSTRALIA
NEW ZEALAND
JAPAN
NORTH KOREA
SOUTH KOREA
TAIWAN
HONG KONG (Br.)
FIJI
TONGA
WESTERN SAMOA
MICRONESIA
MELANESIA
Sea of Okhotsk
Sea of Japan
Yellow Sea
East China Sea
South China Sea
Philippine Sea
Celebes Sea
Banda Sea
Arafura Sea
Timor Sea
Coral Sea
Tasman Sea
Bering Sea
Kuro Siwo
Oya Siwo
Northwest Pacific Basin
North Central Pacific Basin
North Equatorial Current
South Equatorial Current
East Australian Current
West Wind Drift
Limit of pack ice max. Feb. - March
Limit of icebergs - average max.
Limit of pack ice max. Aug. - Sept.
International Date line
Tropic of Cancer
Tropic of Capricorn
Arctic Circle
Equator
JULY
JANUARY
Modified Zenithal Equidistant Projection

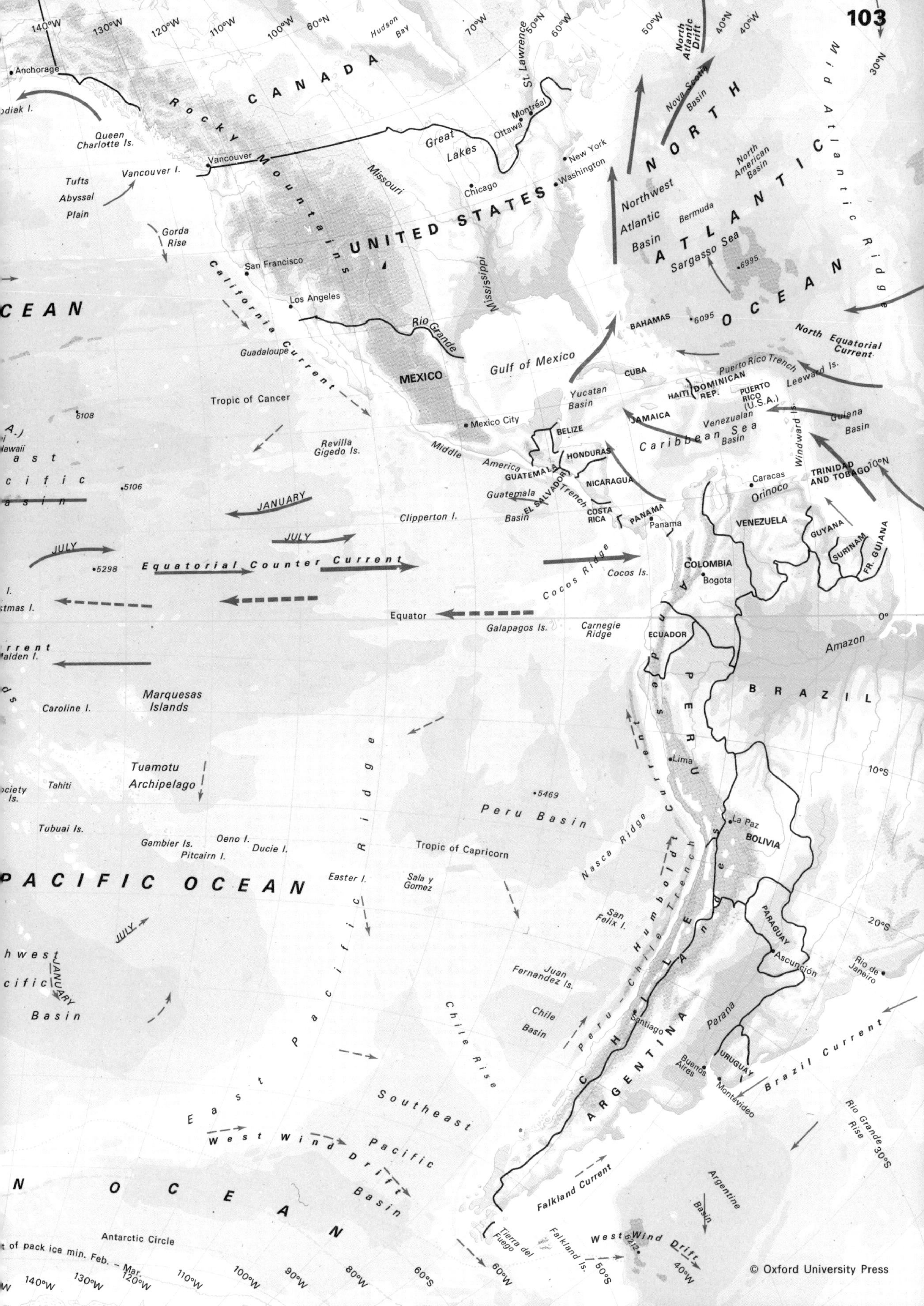
CANADA
Rocky Mountains
UNITED STATES
MEXICO
Anchorage
Queen Charlotte Is.
Vancouver
Vancouver I.
Tufts Abyssal Plain
Gorda Rise
San Francisco
Los Angeles
California Current
Guadaloupe
Tropic of Cancer
Hudson Bay
St. Lawrence
Montréal
Ottawa
Great Lakes
New York
Washington
Chicago
Missouri
Mississippi
Rio Grande
Gulf of Mexico
Mexico City
Revilla Gigedo Is.
Middle America Trench
Guatemala Basin
Clipperton I.
JANUARY
JULY
Equatorial Counter Current
Equator
Galapagos Is.
Cocos Ridge
Cocos Is.
Carnegie Ridge
Marquesas Islands
Caroline I.
Tuamotu Archipelago
Tahiti
Tubuai Is.
Gambier Is.
Oeno I.
Pitcairn I.
Ducie I.
Easter I.
Sala y Gomez
PACIFIC OCEAN
Peru Basin
Tropic of Capricorn
Nasca Ridge
San Felix I.
Juan Fernandez Is.
Chile Basin
Chile Rise
East Pacific Ridge
Southeast Pacific Basin
West Wind Drift
Antarctic Circle
Limit of pack ice min. Feb. – Mar.
NORTH ATLANTIC OCEAN
North Atlantic Drift
Nova Scotia Basin
Northwest Atlantic Basin
North American Basin
Bermuda
Sargasso Sea
Mid Atlantic Ridge
North Equatorial Current
BAHAMAS
CUBA
HAITI
DOMINICAN REP.
PUERTO RICO (U.S.A.)
Puerto Rico Trench
Leeward Is.
Windward Is.
Yucatan Basin
JAMAICA
BELIZE
HONDURAS
GUATEMALA
EL SALVADOR
NICARAGUA
COSTA RICA
PANAMA
Panama
Caribbean Sea
Venezuelan Basin
Guiana Basin
Caracas
TRINIDAD AND TOBAGO
Orinoco
VENEZUELA
GUYANA
SURINAM
FR. GUIANA
COLOMBIA
Bogota
ECUADOR
PERU
Lima
Andes
BRAZIL
Amazon
BOLIVIA
La Paz
PARAGUAY
Asunción
Rio de Janeiro
CHILE
Santiago
ARGENTINA
Parana
URUGUAY
Buenos Aires
Montevideo
Peru – Chile Trench
Humboldt Current
Peru Current
Brazil Current
Rio Grande Rise
Argentine Basin
Falkland Current
Falkland Is.
Tierra del Fuego
6108
5106
5298
5469
6995
6095
6212
140°W
130°W
120°W
110°W
100°W
90°W
80°W
70°W
60°W
50°W
40°W
60°N
50°N
40°N
30°N
10°N
0°
10°S
20°S
30°S
50°S
60°S

New Zealand

Scale 1:6 250 000

0 50 100 150 200 km

Boundaries	International	(in sea)	(disputed)
Roads	Motorways	Other roads	Tracks
Railways			
Airports	International	Domestic	
Canals	Seasonal rivers, lakes		
Marshes	Salt Pan	Ice cap	
Sand desert limits	National Parks etc.		

170°E 175°E 35°S 40°S 45°S

Three Kings Is.
C. Maria Van Diemen
North Cape
Kaitaia 751
Waitangi
Bay of Islands
Russell
Kaikohe
461
NORTHLAND
Hokianga Harbour
771
Whangarei
Dargaville
Great Barrier I.
221
Kaipara Harbour
Hauraki Gulf
Helensville
Devonport
Auckland
819
Papakura
Thames
Coromandel Ra.
Pukekohe
Paeroa
404
Huntly
WAIKATO
953
NORTH ISLAND
Bay of Plenty
Hamilton
Tauranga
Cambridge
Karapiro
Whakatane
Raukumara Ra.
East Cape
962
Te Awamutu
Kawerau
Opotiki
1754
Waikato
Rotorua
822
Te Kuiti
Kinleith
808
Volcanic Plateau
Rangitaiki
Murupara
1213
200 m
Wairakei
Taupo
1087
Waikaremoana
Gisborne
Poverty Bay
Taumarunui
UREWERA N.P.
New Plymouth
Waitara
L. Taupo
1383
Wairoa
TARANAKI
NGAURUHOE 2291
MT. EGMONT N.P.
TONGARIRO N.P.
2517
RUAPEHU 2797
Kaimanawa Mts.
Hawke Bay
Mahia Penin.
Opunake
Stratford
Ohakune
Wanganui
Napier
Hawera
743
Taihape
Hastings
Wanganui
Ruahine Ra.
Waipawa
Marton
Feilding
Dannevirke
Palmerston North
Woodville
803
C. Turnagain
C. Farewell
Golden Bay
Takaka
ABEL TASMAN N.P.
1213
Tasman Bay
D'Urville I.
Tasman Mts.
Motueka
The Sounds
Tararua Ra.
1571
Masterton
Nelson
Cook Strait
Petone
Rimutaka Tunnel
536
Hutt
663
Picton
1760
Wairau
Blenheim
Wellington
C. Palliser
MT. OWEN 1876
Westport
BULLER
C. Foulwind
Buller
NELSON LAKES N.P.
Spenser Mts.
TAPUAENUKU 2885
2338
Kaikoura Ra.
1501
Reefton
LEWIS P.
1875
Kaikoura
Greymouth
965
Waiau
Waiau
ARTHURS PASS N.P.
Hokitika
Hurunui
Otira Tunnel
ARTHURS PASS
2400
Waipara
1935
WESTLAND
Pegasus Bay
MT. TASMAN 3498
MT. ARROWSMITH 2795
Plains
Christchurch
Southern Alps
Rakaia
2330
Riccarton
Lyttelton
WESTLAND N.P.
1951
MT. COOK 3764 N.P.
Hermitage
Akaroa
Banks Peninsula
Jackson Bay
Haast
Canterbury
Ashburton
2508
HAAST P.
1322
Canterbury Bight
MT. ASPIRING 3035
Timaru
SOUTH ISLAND
Milford Sound
Waitaki
Kurow
L. Wanaka
1871
FIORDLAND N.P.
Queenstown
Oamaru
1855
L. Wakatipu
Cromwell
945
Doubtful Sound
L. Te Anau
1679
Alexandra
1449
OTAGO
Kingston
Roxburgh
L. Manapouri
200 m
1694
777
1067
Lumsden
Port Chalmers
FIORDLAND
Edievale
Otago Peninsula
Dusky Sound
Ohai
Clutha
1018
Dunedin
SOUTHLAND
Gore
C. Providence
Tuatapere
869
Balclutha
Mataura
720
Kaitangata
Invercargill
Bluff
Foveaux Strait
980
Stewart Island
Southwest Cape
Tasman Sea
SOUTH PACIFIC OCEAN

Metres
5000
3000
2000
1000
500
300
200
100
Sea level
Land depression

Spot heights in metres

Conical Orthomorphic Projection

170°E 175°E

Bounty Is. (N.Z.)

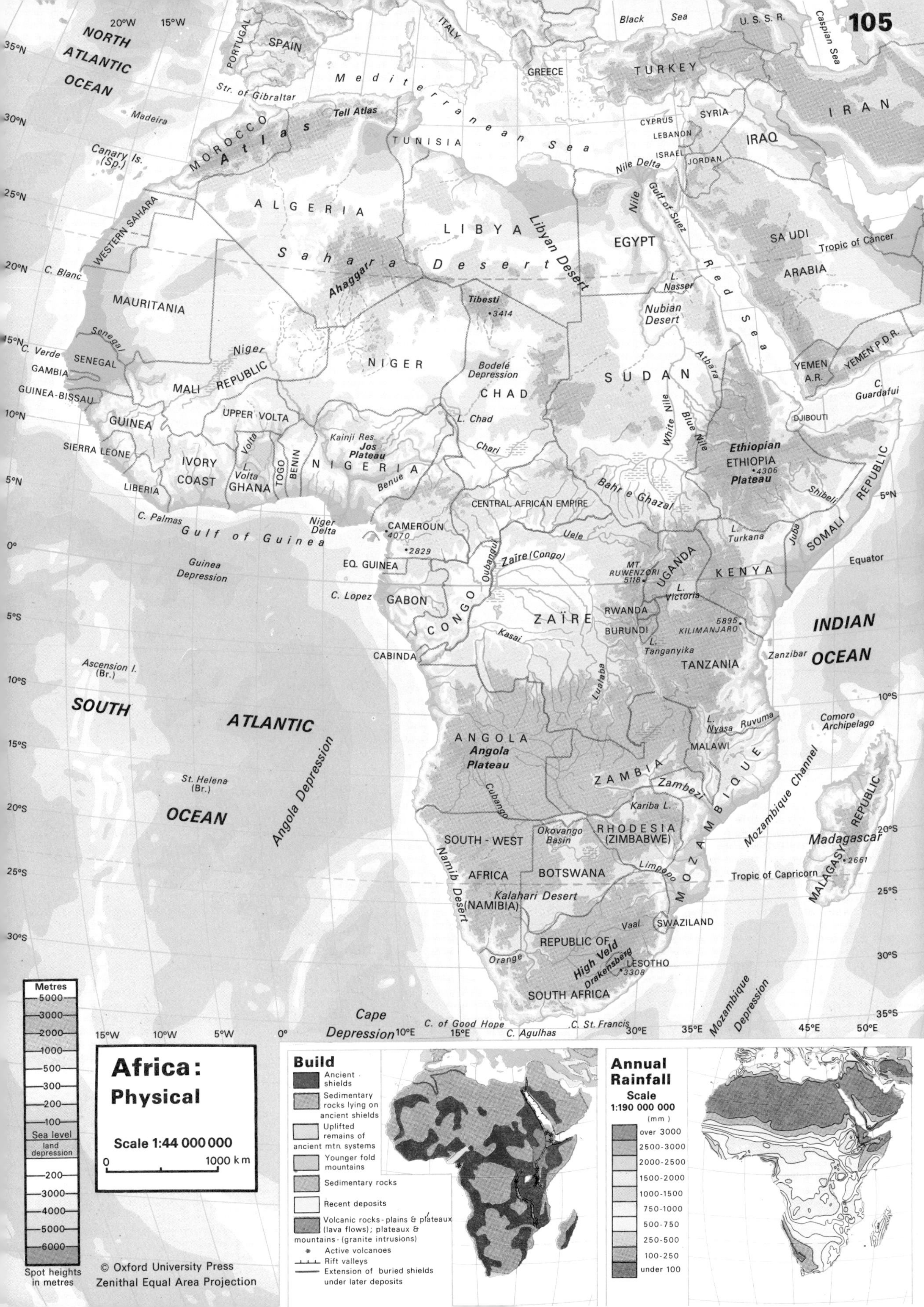
Africa: Physical
Scale 1:44 000 000
0
1000 km
Zenithal Equal Area Projection
Metres
5000
3000
2000
1000
500
300
200
100
Sea level
land depression
200
3000
4000
5000
6000
Spot heights in metres
NORTH ATLANTIC OCEAN
SOUTH ATLANTIC OCEAN
INDIAN OCEAN
Mediterranean Sea
Black Sea
Caspian Sea
Red Sea
Gulf of Guinea
Guinea Depression
Angola Depression
Cape Depression
Mozambique Depression
Mozambique Channel
PORTUGAL
SPAIN
ITALY
GREECE
TURKEY
U. S. S. R.
IRAN
IRAQ
SYRIA
CYPRUS
LEBANON
ISRAEL
JORDAN
SAUDI ARABIA
YEMEN A.R.
YEMEN P.D.R.
Str. of Gibraltar
Madeira
Canary Is. (Sp.)
MOROCCO
Atlas
Tell Atlas
TUNISIA
ALGERIA
LIBYA
EGYPT
Nile Delta
Nile
Gulf of Suez
Libyan Desert
Sahara Desert
Ahaggar
Tibesti
3414
WESTERN SAHARA
C. Blanc
MAURITANIA
Senegal
C. Verde
SENEGAL
GAMBIA
GUINEA-BISSAU
GUINEA
SIERRA LEONE
LIBERIA
IVORY COAST
MALI REPUBLIC
Niger
UPPER VOLTA
Volta
L. Volta
GHANA
TOGO
BENIN
NIGERIA
Kainji Res.
Jos Plateau
Benue
NIGER
Bodelé Depression
CHAD
L. Chad
Chari
L. Nasser
Nubian Desert
SUDAN
Atbara
White Nile
Blue Nile
Bahr e Ghazal
Ethiopian Plateau
ETHIOPIA
4306
DJIBOUTI
C. Guardafui
Shibeli
SOMALI REPUBLIC
Juba
L. Turkana
KENYA
UGANDA
MT. RUWENZORI 5118
L. Victoria
RWANDA
BURUNDI
5895 KILIMANJARO
L. Tanganyika
TANZANIA
Zanzibar
C. Palmas
Niger Delta
CAMEROUN
4070
2829
EQ. GUINEA
C. Lopez
GABON
CONGO
CENTRAL AFRICAN EMPIRE
Uele
Oubangui
Zaïre (Congo)
ZAÏRE
Kasai
Lualaba
CABINDA
Ascension I. (Br.)
St. Helena (Br.)
ANGOLA
Angola Plateau
Cubango
ZAMBIA
Zambezi
Kariba L.
L. Nyasa
Ruvuma
MALAWI
MOZAMBIQUE
Comoro Archipelago
Madagascar
MALAGASY REPUBLIC
2661
RHODESIA (ZIMBABWE)
Okovango Basin
SOUTH-WEST AFRICA (NAMIBIA)
Namib Desert
BOTSWANA
Kalahari Desert
Limpopo
Vaal
SWAZILAND
Orange
REPUBLIC OF SOUTH AFRICA
High Veld
Drakensberg
LESOTHO
3308
C. of Good Hope
C. Agulhas
C. St. Francis
Tropic of Cancer
Equator
Tropic of Capricorn
35°N
30°N
25°N
20°N
15°N
10°N
5°N
0°
5°S
10°S
15°S
20°S
25°S
30°S
35°S
20°W
15°W
10°W
5°W
0°
10°E
15°E
30°E
35°E
45°E
50°E
Build
Ancient shields
Sedimentary rocks lying on ancient shields
Uplifted remains of ancient mtn. systems
Younger fold mountains
Sedimentary rocks
Recent deposits
Volcanic rocks - plains & plateaux (lava flows); plateaux & mountains - (granite intrusions)
Active volcanoes
Rift valleys
Extension of buried shields under later deposits
Annual Rainfall
Scale 1:190 000 000
(mm)
over 3000
2500-3000
2000-2500
1500-2000
1000-1500
750-1000
500-750
250-500
100-250
under 100

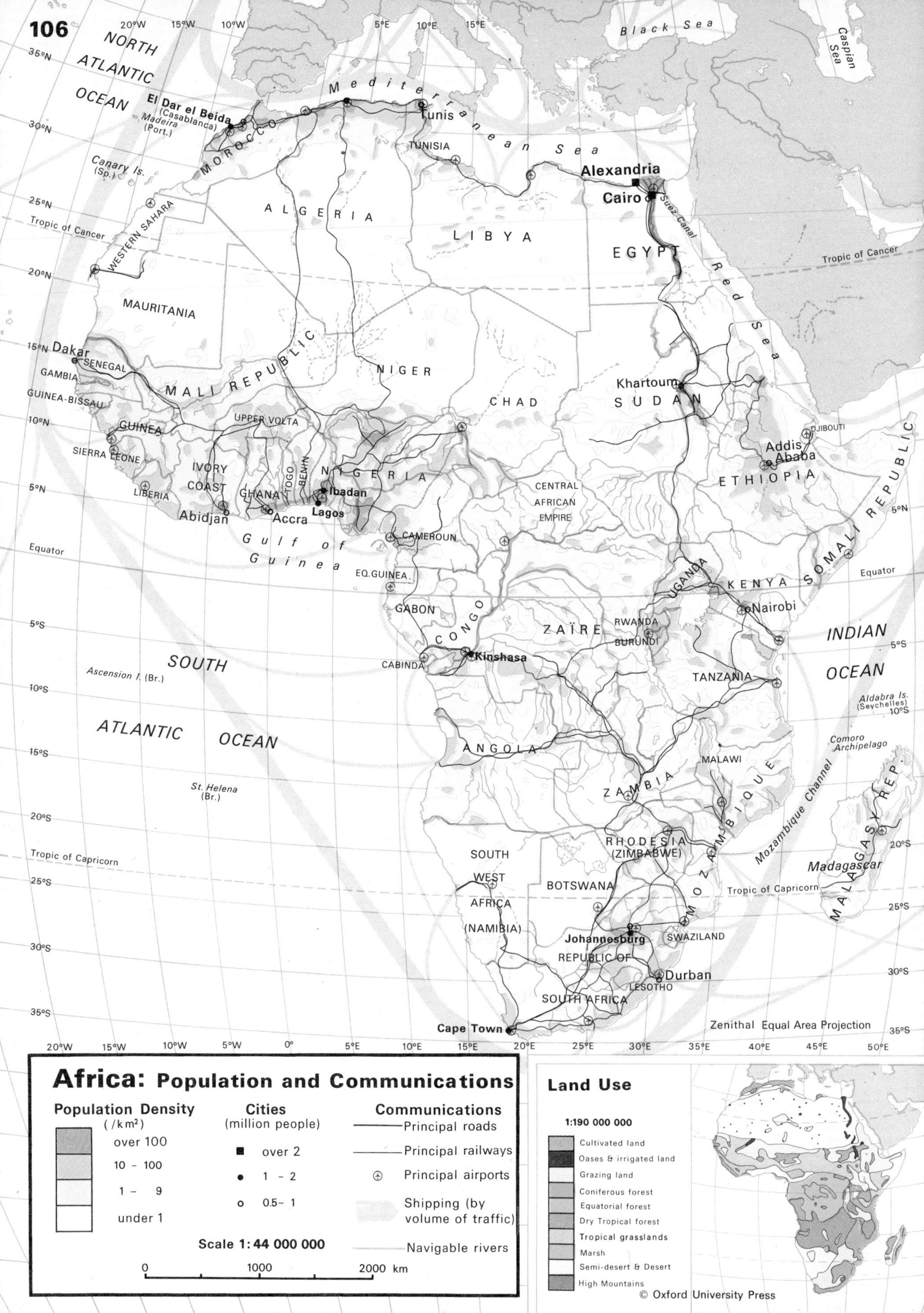

Africa: Population and Communications
Population Density
(/km²)
over 100
10 - 100
1 - 9
under 1
Cities
(million people)
over 2
1 - 2
0.5 - 1
Scale 1: 44 000 000
0
1000
2000 km
Communications
Principal roads
Principal railways
Principal airports
Shipping (by volume of traffic)
Navigable rivers
Land Use
1:190 000 000
Cultivated land
Oases & irrigated land
Grazing land
Coniferous forest
Equatorial forest
Dry Tropical forest
Tropical grasslands
Marsh
Semi-desert & Desert
High Mountains
© Oxford University Press
Zenithal Equal Area Projection
NORTH ATLANTIC OCEAN
SOUTH ATLANTIC OCEAN
INDIAN OCEAN
Mediterranean Sea
Black Sea
Caspian Sea
Red Sea
Suez Canal
Gulf of Guinea
Mozambique Channel
Tropic of Cancer
Tropic of Capricorn
Equator
Madeira (Port.)
Canary Is. (Sp.)
Ascension I. (Br.)
St. Helena (Br.)
Aldabra Is. (Seychelles)
Comoro Archipelago
Madagascar
El Dar el Beida (Casablanca)
Tunis
Alexandria
Cairo
Dakar
Khartoum
Addis Ababa
Abidjan
Accra
Ibadan
Lagos
Kinshasa
Nairobi
Johannesburg
Durban
Cape Town
MOROCCO
ALGERIA
TUNISIA
LIBYA
EGYPT
WESTERN SAHARA
MAURITANIA
SENEGAL
GAMBIA
GUINEA-BISSAU
GUINEA
SIERRA LEONE
LIBERIA
MALI REPUBLIC
UPPER VOLTA
IVORY COAST
GHANA
TOGO
BENIN
NIGERIA
NIGER
CHAD
SUDAN
ETHIOPIA
DJIBOUTI
SOMALI REPUBLIC
CENTRAL AFRICAN EMPIRE
CAMEROUN
EQ. GUINEA
GABON
CONGO
CABINDA
ZAÏRE
UGANDA
KENYA
RWANDA
BURUNDI
TANZANIA
ANGOLA
ZAMBIA
MALAWI
MOZAMBIQUE
RHODESIA (ZIMBABWE)
SOUTH WEST AFRICA (NAMIBIA)
BOTSWANA
SWAZILAND
LESOTHO
REPUBLIC OF SOUTH AFRICA
MALAGASY REP.
35°N
30°N
25°N
20°N
15°N
10°N
5°N
5°S
10°S
15°S
20°S
25°S
30°S
35°S
20°W
15°W
10°W
5°W
0°
5°E
10°E
15°E
20°E
25°E
30°E
35°E
40°E
45°E
50°E

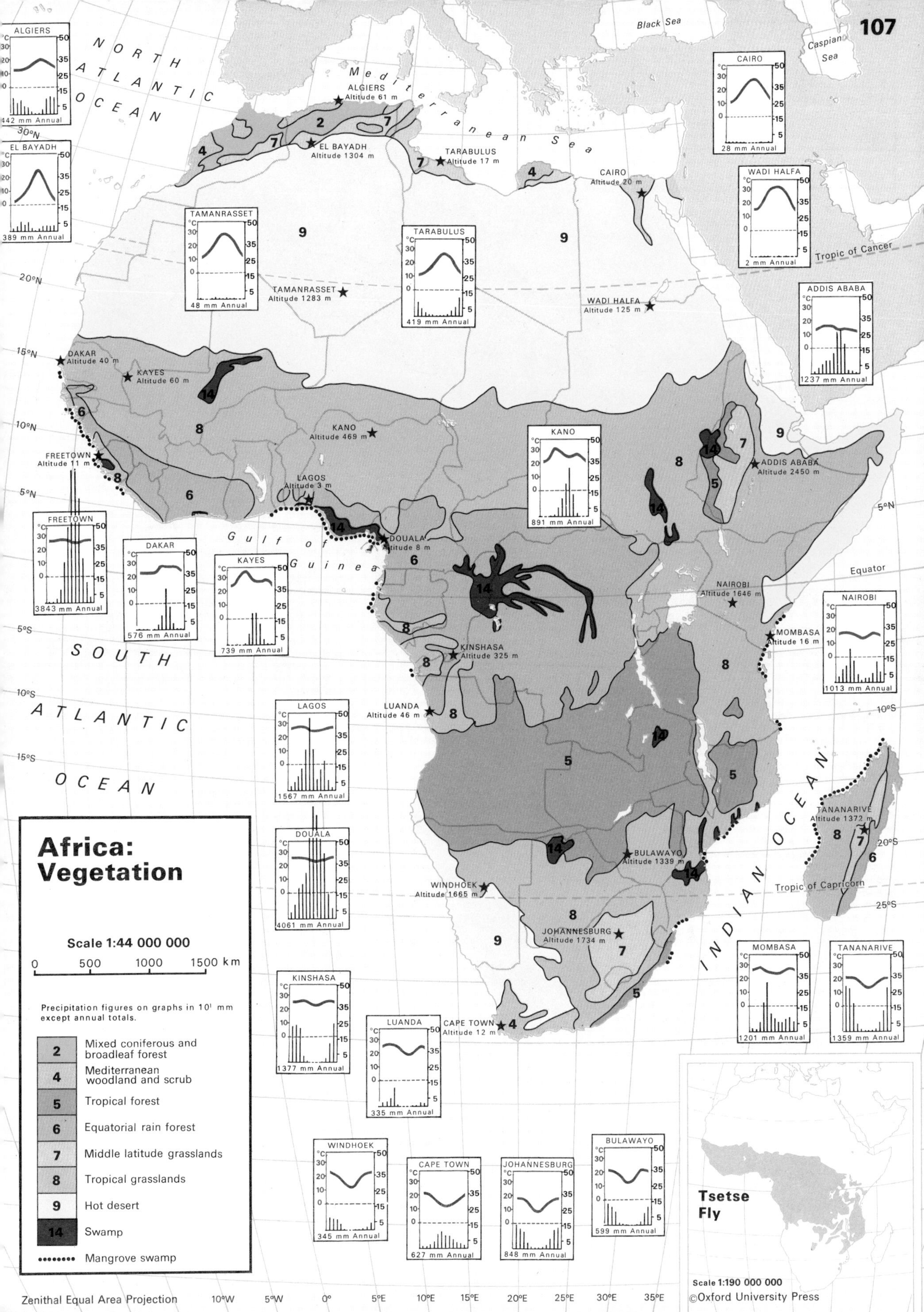
Africa: Vegetation
Scale 1:44 000 000
0 500 1000 1500 km
Precipitation figures on graphs in 10¹ mm except annual totals.
2 Mixed coniferous and broadleaf forest
4 Mediterranean woodland and scrub
5 Tropical forest
6 Equatorial rain forest
7 Middle latitude grasslands
8 Tropical grasslands
9 Hot desert
14 Swamp
Mangrove swamp
NORTH ATLANTIC OCEAN
SOUTH ATLANTIC OCEAN
INDIAN OCEAN
Mediterranean Sea
Black Sea
Caspian Sea
Gulf of Guinea
Tropic of Cancer
Equator
Tropic of Capricorn
ALGIERS Altitude 61 m
EL BAYADH Altitude 1304 m
TARABULUS Altitude 17 m
CAIRO Altitude 20 m
TAMANRASSET Altitude 1283 m
WADI HALFA Altitude 125 m
DAKAR Altitude 40 m
KAYES Altitude 60 m
KANO Altitude 469 m
FREETOWN Altitude 11 m
LAGOS Altitude 3 m
DOUALA Altitude 8 m
ADDIS ABABA Altitude 2450 m
NAIROBI Altitude 1646 m
MOMBASA Altitude 16 m
KINSHASA Altitude 325 m
LUANDA Altitude 46 m
TANANARIVE Altitude 1372 m
BULAWAYO Altitude 1339 m
WINDHOEK Altitude 1665 m
JOHANNESBURG Altitude 1734 m
CAPE TOWN Altitude 12 m
ALGIERS 442 mm Annual
EL BAYADH 389 mm Annual
TAMANRASSET 48 mm Annual
TARABULUS 419 mm Annual
CAIRO 28 mm Annual
WADI HALFA 2 mm Annual
ADDIS ABABA 1237 mm Annual
KANO 891 mm Annual
FREETOWN 3843 mm Annual
DAKAR 576 mm Annual
KAYES 739 mm Annual
NAIROBI 1013 mm Annual
LAGOS 1567 mm Annual
DOUALA 4061 mm Annual
KINSHASA 1377 mm Annual
LUANDA 335 mm Annual
MOMBASA 1201 mm Annual
TANANARIVE 1359 mm Annual
WINDHOEK 345 mm Annual
CAPE TOWN 627 mm Annual
JOHANNESBURG 848 mm Annual
BULAWAYO 599 mm Annual
Tsetse Fly
Scale 1:190 000 000
Zenithal Equal Area Projection

Boundaries
International
(in sea)
(disputed)
Internal
Roads
Motorways
Other roads
Tracks
Railways
Airports
International
Domestic
Canals
Seasonal rivers, lakes
Marshes
Salt pan
Ice cap
Sand desert limits
National Parks etc.
ATLANTIC OCEAN
Madeira
Funchal
Canary Islands (Sp.)
Sta.Cruz de Tenerife
Tenerife
Gran Canaria
Las Palmas
Alegranza
Lanzarote
Fuerteventura
C. Juby
3707
C. Finisterre
Oporto
Lisbon
PORTUGAL
Madrid
SPAIN
Seville
Cape St. Vincent
Tagus
Ebro
Pyrenees
3402
Toulouse
FRANCE
Gulf of Lions
Marseille
Barcelona
Valencia
Balearic Is. (Sp.)
Majorca
Corsica (Fr.)
2710
Sardinia (It.)
Rome
ITALY
Naples
Tyrrhenian Sea
Adriatic
Palermo
Sicily
MALTA
Mediterranean
1738
2018
902
3480
Gibraltar (Br.)
Str. of Gibraltar
Tangier
Tetuán
C.de Gata
Melilla (Sp.)
Oran
Arzew
Gas Pipeline
Algiers
Bejaia
Skikda
Annaba
Tunis
Constantine
Tell Atlas
1729
Sousse
Sfax
Gulf of Gabès
Gabès
Djerba I.
TUNISIA
Tozeur
Kenitra
Er Rif Mts
Rabat
El Dar el Beida (Casablanca)
Fès
Mèknes
Middle Atlas
Oujda
Mascara
Djelfa
El Bayadh
Saharan Atlas
Ain Sefra
Laghouat
Biskra
Oil Pipeline
Safi
Essaouira
Marrakesh
High Atlas
MOROCCO
4165
4070
Tafilalet Oasis
Agadir
Béchar
651
Abadla
Dra
630
750
Great Western Erg
Ghardaia
Ouargla
Hassi Messaoud
Touggourt
230
Great Eastern Erg
Gadames
Tarabulus
Homs
Zuara
Garian
Jofra Oasis
Soda Mts
Sebha Oasis
El Aaiun
C. Bojador
WESTERN SAHARA
Dakhla
Tropic of Cancer
F'Dérik
C. Blanc
Nouadhibou
Nouakchott
MAURITANIA
ALGERIA
Sahara Desert
834
Edjelé
Tassili-n-Ajjer
1680
2359
1455
Tanezrouft
3002
Ahaggar
376
950
1798
Aïr
NIGER
402
St. Louis
Senegal
Linguère
Dakar
Touba
SENEGAL
Banjul
GAMBIA
Gambia
Kayes
Nema
Lake Faguibine
Tombouctou (Timbuktu)
Bamba
Lake Haogoundou
MALI
Niger
GUINEA-BISSAU
Bissau
Bolama
1515
Bamako
Tillabéry
Niamey
UPPER VOLTA
Ouagadougou
White Volta
Bobo-Dioulasso
Boké
GUINEA
785
Conakry
Kankan
SIERRA LEONE
Freetown
Makeni
Bo
200m
1280
Pendembu
LIBERIA
1850
Monrovia
Buchanan
701
IVORY COAST
527
Black Volta
Tamale
GHANA
Blitta
592
Kumasi
Volta Lake
649
Volta Dam
Akosombo
Abidjan
Sekondi-Takoradi
Accra
C. Palmas
C. Three Points
TOGO
1050
Palime
Lomé
C. St. Paul
BENIN
Kandi
Parakou
Gaya
Cotonou
Porto Novo
Kebbi
Sokoto
Kaura Namoda
Kano
Nguru
Bosso
Lake Chad
Maiduguri
N'Djamena
Lake Chad Basin
854
Kaduna
Kainji Dam
Zaria
Jos Plateau
Jos
1982
Jebba
NIGERIA
Benue
Garoua
Niger
Oshogbo
Baro
Ibadan
Abeokuta
Lagos
2021
Enugu
1650
N'Gaoundéré
1600
2679
1420
Port Harcourt
CAMEROUN
Douala
Yaoundé
4070
Macias Nguema Biyogo (Eq.Guinea)
Bight of Benin
Gulf of Guinea
Bight of Bonny
750
720
35°N
30°N
25°N
20°N
15°N
10°N
5°N
Metres
5000
3000
2000
1000
500
300
200
100
Sea level
Land depression
Spot heights in metres
Zenithal Equal Area Projection
5°W
Greenwich Meridian 0°
© Oxford University Press
10°E
15°E

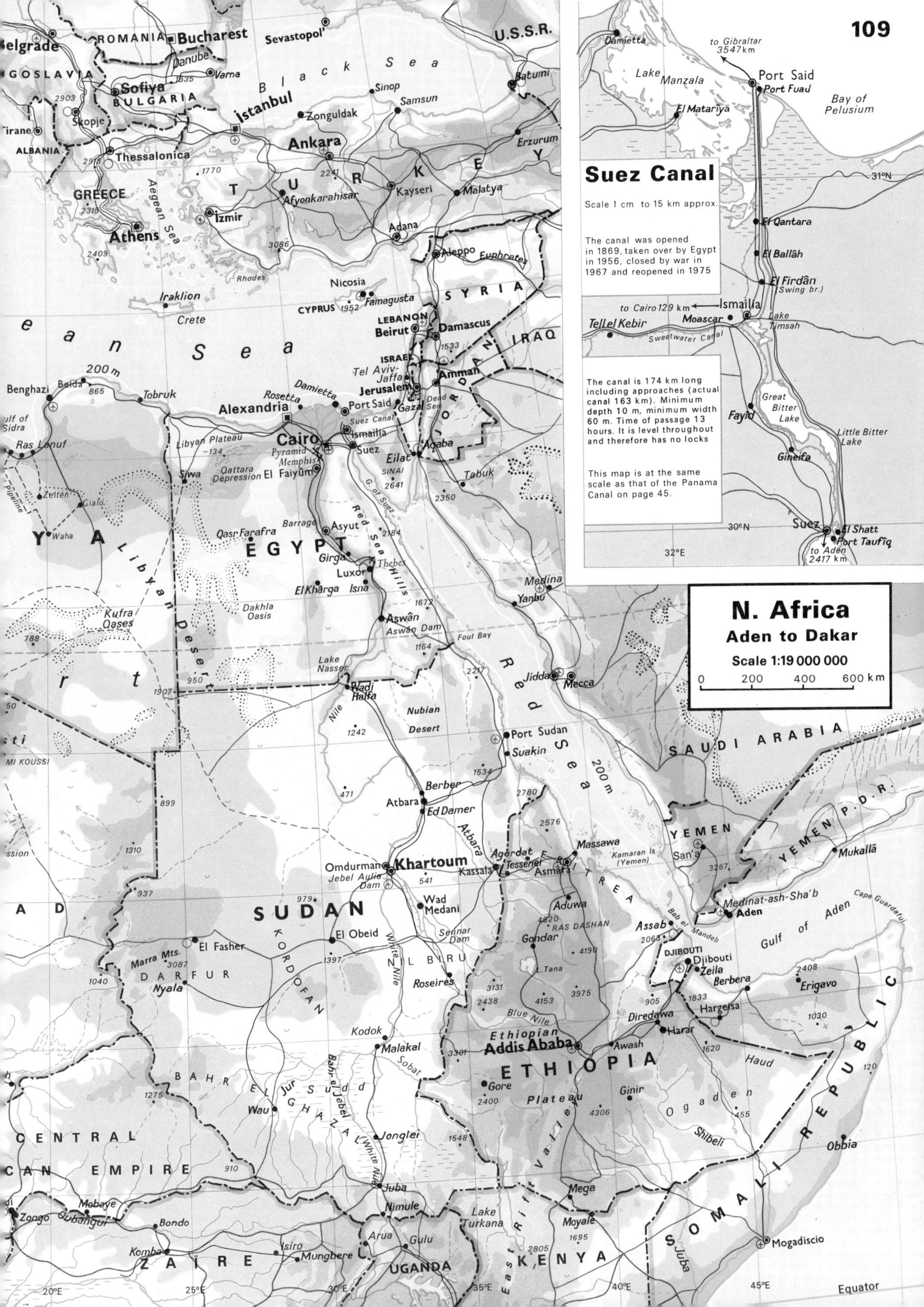
N. Africa
Aden to Dakar
Scale 1:19 000 000
0 200 400 600 km
Suez Canal
Scale 1 cm to 15 km approx.
The canal was opened in 1869, taken over by Egypt in 1956, closed by war in 1967 and reopened in 1975
The canal is 174 km long including approaches (actual canal 163 km). Minimum depth 10 m, minimum width 60 m. Time of passage 13 hours. It is level throughout and therefore has no locks
This map is at the same scale as that of the Panama Canal on page 45.
Damietta
to Gibraltar 3547 km
Port Said
Port Fuad
Lake Manzala
Bay of Pelusium
El Matarîya
31°N
El Qantara
El Ballâh
El Firdân
(Swing br.)
Ismailia
to Cairo 129 km
Moascar
Lake Timsah
Tell el Kebir
Sweetwater Canal
Great Bitter Lake
Fayid
Little Bitter Lake
Gineifa
30°N
Suez
El Shatt
Port Taufîq
to Aden 2417 km
32°E
Belgrade
ROMANIA
Bucharest
Sevastopol'
U.S.S.R.
Danube
Varna
Black Sea
Batumi
Sofiya
BULGARIA
Sinop
Samsun
İstanbul
Zonguldak
Skopje
Tirane
ALBANIA
Thessalonica
Ankara
Erzurum
TURKEY
GREECE
Aegean Sea
Afyonkarahisar
Kayseri
Malatya
İzmir
Athens
Adana
Aleppo
Euphrates
Rhodes
Nicosia
Iraklion
Crete
Famagusta
CYPRUS
SYRIA
LEBANON
Beirut
Damascus
IRAQ
ISRAEL
Tel Aviv-Jaffa
Jerusalem
Amman
JORDAN
Dead Sea
Gaza
Benghazi
Beida
Tobruk
Rosetta
Damietta
Port Said
Alexandria
Suez Canal
Ismailia
Cairo
Suez
Eilat
Aqaba
Gulf of Sidra
Ras Lanuf
Libyan Plateau
Pyramid
Memphis
Qattara Depression
El Faiyûm
SINAI
Tabuk
Siwa
G. of Suez
Zelten
Gialo
Pipeline
Waha
Barrage
Asyut
Red Sea Hills
Qasr Farafra
EGYPT
Girga
Thebes
Luxor
El Khârga
Isna
Libyan Desert
Medina
Yanbu
Dakhla Oasis
Kufra Oases
Aswân
Aswân Dam
Foul Bay
Lake Nasser
Jidda
Mecca
Red Sea
Wadi Halfa
Nile
Nubian Desert
Port Sudan
Suakin
SAUDI ARABIA
MI KOUSSI
Berber
Atbara
Ed Damer
YEMEN
YEMEN P.D.R.
Mukallā
Massawa
Kamaran Is (Yemen)
San'a
Omdurman
Khartoum
Kassala
Agordat
Tessenei
Asmara
ERITREA
Jebel Aulia Dam
Wad Medani
Medinat-ash-Sha'b
Aden
Cape Guardafui
SUDAN
El Obeid
Sennar Dam
Aduwa
RAS DASHAN
Assab
Bab el Mandeb
Gulf of Aden
El Fasher
Marra Mts.
KORDOFAN
Gondar
DJIBOUTI
Djibouti
Zeila
Berbera
Erigavo
DARFUR
Nyala
NIL BIRU
White Nile
Roseires
L.Tana
Hargeisa
Blue Nile
Diredawa
Harar
Kodok
Malakal
Ethiopian
Addis Ababa
Awash
ETHIOPIA
Sobat
Haud
BAHR EL GHAZAL
Jur
Sudd
Bahr el Jebel
Gore
Plateau
Ginir
Ogaden
Wau
Rift Valley
Shibeli
SOMALI REPUBLIC
CENTRAL AFRICAN EMPIRE
Jonglei
Obbia
Juba
Mega
Nimule
Lake Turkana
Moyale
Mobaye
Zongo
Oubangui
Bondo
Arua
Gulu
East Rift
Juba
Mogadiscio
Isiro
Komba
Mungbere
ZAÏRE
UGANDA
KENYA
20°E
25°E
30°E
35°E
40°E
45°E
Equator

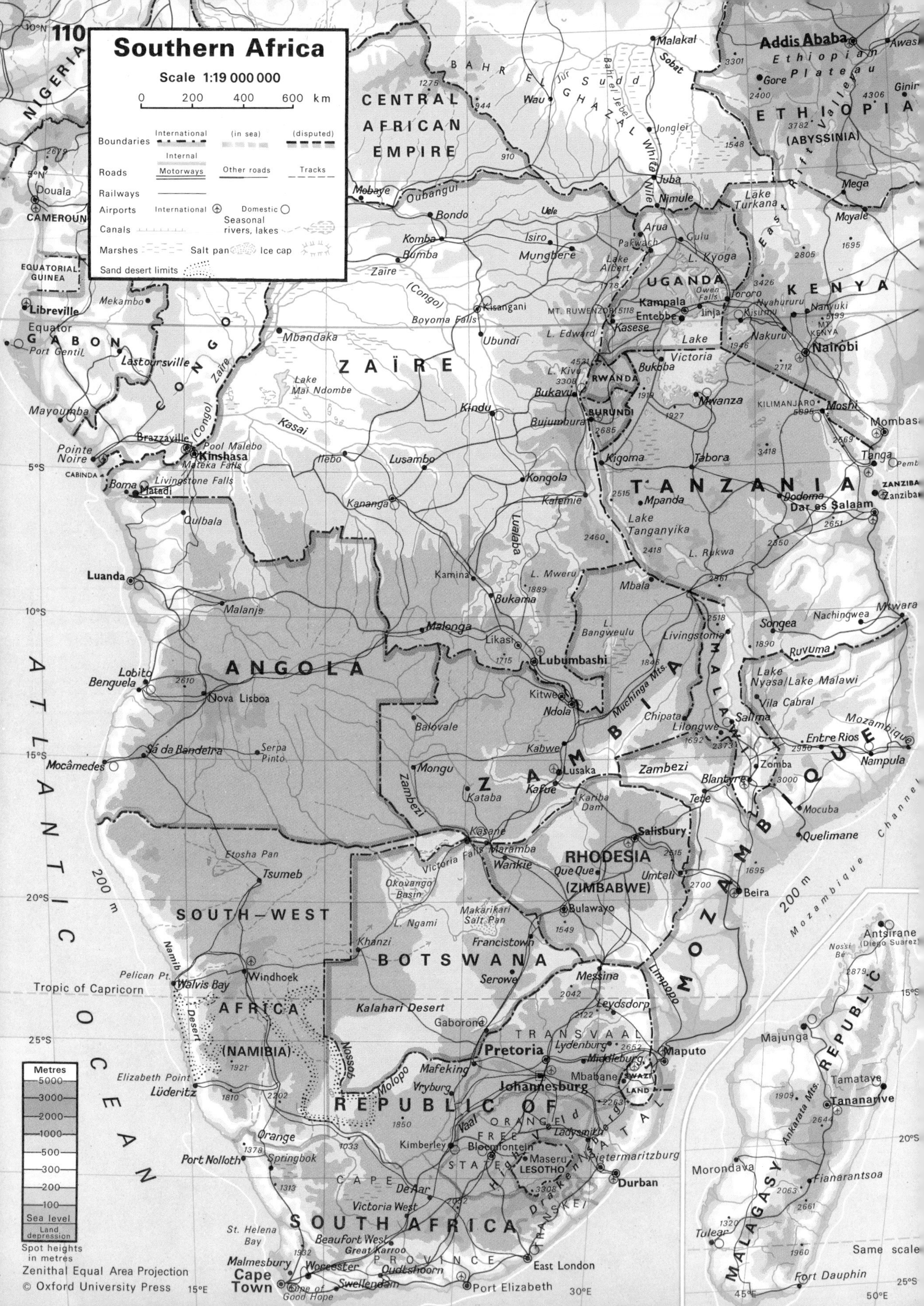
Southern Africa
Scale 1:19 000 000
0 200 400 600 km
Boundaries International (in sea) (disputed)
Internal
Roads Motorways Other roads Tracks
Railways
Airports International Domestic
Canals
Seasonal rivers, lakes
Marshes
Salt pan
Ice cap
Sand desert limits
Metres
5000
3000
2000
1000
500
300
200
100
Sea level
Land depression
Spot heights in metres
Zenithal Equal Area Projection
© Oxford University Press
NIGERIA
CAMEROUN
Douala
EQUATORIAL GUINEA
Libreville
Equator
GABON
Port Gentil
Lastoursville
Mekambo
Mayoumba
CONGO
Pointe Noire
CABINDA
Brazzaville
Kinshasa
Pool Malebo
Mateka Falls
Livingstone Falls
Boma
Matadi
CENTRAL AFRICAN EMPIRE
Mobaye
Oubangui
Bondo
Uele
Komba
Bumba
Isiro
Mungbere
Zaïre
(Congo)
Kisangani
Boyoma Falls
Ubundi
Mbandaka
ZAÏRE
Lake Mai Ndombe
Kasai
Kindu
Ilebo
Lusambo
Kananga
Kongola
Kalemie
Lualaba
Kamina
Bukama
Malonga
Likasi
Lubumbashi
L. Mweru
Bukavu
Bujumbura
Quibala
Luanda
Malanje
ANGOLA
Lobito
Benguela
Nova Lisboa
Sá da Bandeira
Serpa Pinto
Moçâmedes
BAHR EL GHAZAL
Wau
Jur
Sudd
Bahr el Jebel
White Nile
Malakal
Sobat
Jonglei
Juba
Nimule
Addis Ababa
Ethiopian Plateau
Gore
ETHIOPIA
(ABYSSINIA)
Awash
Ginir
East Rift Valley
Mega
Moyale
Lake Turkana
Arua
Pakwach
Gulu
L. Kyoga
Lake Albert
UGANDA
MT. RUWENZORI 5118
Kampala
Entebbe
Owen Falls
Jinja
Tororo
Kasese
L. Edward
Kisumu
Nyahururu
Nanyuki
MT. KENYA
KENYA
Nakuru
Nairobi
Lake Victoria
Bukoba
L. Kivu
RWANDA
BURUNDI
Mwanza
KILIMANJARO 5895
Moshi
Mombasa
Tanga
Kigoma
Tabora
TANZANIA
Mpanda
Lake Tanganyika
Dodoma
Dar es Salaam
ZANZIBAR
Zanzibar
L. Rukwa
Mbala
L. Bangweulu
Livingstonia
Songea
Nachingwea
Mtwara
Ruvuma
Lake Nyasa/Lake Malawi
Vila Cabral
MALAWI
Salima
Lilongwe
Chipata
Muchinga Mts.
ZAMBIA
Kitwe
Ndola
Kabwe
Lusaka
Kafue
Balovale
Mongu
Zambezi
Kataba
Kariba Dam
Zomba
Blantyre
Tete
Entre Rios
Nampula
Mozambique
Mocuba
Quelimane
MOZAMBIQUE
Mozambique Channel
Beira
Kasane
Victoria Falls
Maramba
Wankie
Salisbury
RHODESIA
(ZIMBABWE)
Que Que
Umtali
Bulawayo
Okovango Basin
Makarikari Salt Pan
L. Ngami
Francistown
Khanzi
BOTSWANA
Serowe
Kalahari Desert
Gaborone
Messina
Limpopo
Leydsdorp
TRANSVAAL
Pretoria
Lydenburg
Middleburg
Maputo
Mbabane
SWAZILAND
Johannesburg
Mafeking
Vryburg
Molopo
Nossob
Etosha Pan
Tsumeb
SOUTH-WEST AFRICA
(NAMIBIA)
Namib Desert
Windhoek
Pelican Pt.
Walvis Bay
Tropic of Capricorn
Elizabeth Point
Lüderitz
Orange
Port Nolloth
Springbok
REPUBLIC OF SOUTH AFRICA
Vaal
ORANGE FREE STATE
Kimberley
Bloemfontein
Maseru
LESOTHO
Ladysmith
Pietermaritzburg
Durban
Drakensberg
NATAL
TRANSKEI
CAPE PROVINCE
De Aar
Victoria West
St. Helena Bay
Beaufort West
Great Karroo
Malmesbury
Cape Town
Worcester
Oudtshoorn
Swellendam
Cape of Good Hope
Port Elizabeth
East London
ATLANTIC OCEAN
200 m
Antsirane
(Diego Suarez)
Nossi Bé
Majunga
MALAGASY REPUBLIC
Tamatave
Tananarive
Ankarata Mts.
Morondava
Fianarantsoa
Tulear
Fort Dauphin
Same scale
10°N
5°N
5°S
10°S
15°S
20°S
25°S
15°E
30°E
45°E
50°E

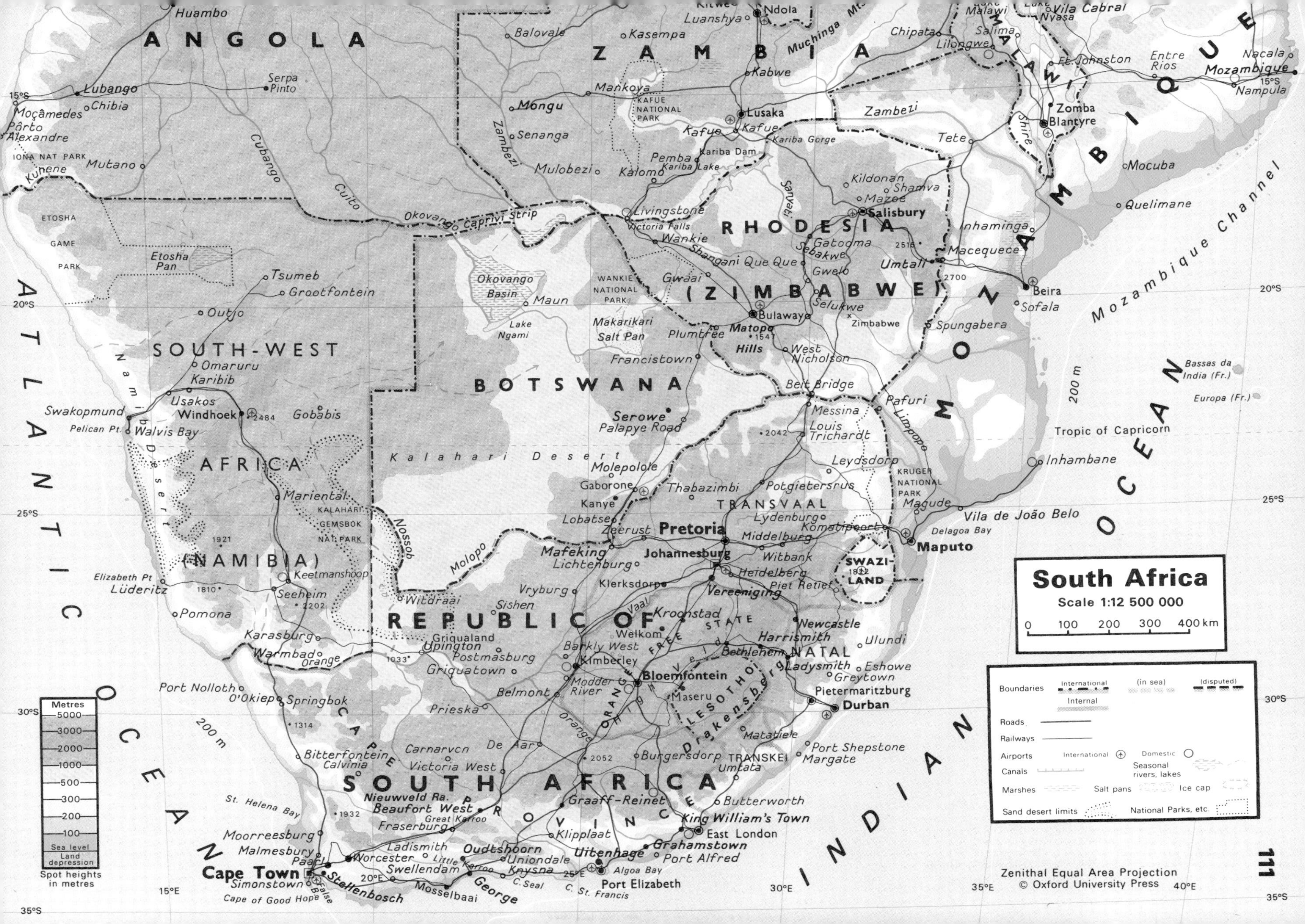
South Africa
Scale 1:12 500 000
0 100 200 300 400 km
Boundaries International (in sea) (disputed)
Internal
Roads
Railways
Airports International Domestic
Canals
Seasonal rivers, lakes
Marshes
Salt pans
Ice cap
Sand desert limits
National Parks, etc.
Zenithal Equal Area Projection
© Oxford University Press
Metres
5000
3000
2000
1000
500
300
200
100
Sea level
Land depression
Spot heights in metres
ANGOLA
ZAMBIA
MALAWI
MOZAMBIQUE
RHODESIA (ZIMBABWE)
BOTSWANA
SOUTH-WEST AFRICA (NAMIBIA)
REPUBLIC OF SOUTH AFRICA
TRANSVAAL
ORANGE FREE STATE
NATAL
CAPE PROVINCE
LESOTHO
SWAZILAND
TRANSKEI
ATLANTIC OCEAN
INDIAN OCEAN
Mozambique Channel
Tropic of Capricorn
Kalahari Desert
Namib Desert
Huambo
Lubango
Serpa Pinto
Moçâmedes
Chibia
Pôrto Alexandre
Mutano
Cubango
Cuito
Kunene
IONA NAT PARK
ETOSHA GAME PARK
Etosha Pan
Tsumeb
Grootfontein
Outjo
Omaruru
Karibib
Usakos
Windhoek
Gobabis
Swakopmund
Pelican Pt.
Walvis Bay
Mariental
KALAHARI GEMSBOK NAT PARK
Keetmanshoop
Seeheim
Elizabeth Pt
Lüderitz
Pomona
Karasburg
Warmbad
Balovale
Kasempa
Mankoya
KAFUE NATIONAL PARK
Mongu
Senanga
Zambezi
Mulobezi
Kalomo
Pemba
Kafue
Lusaka
Kariba Dam
Kariba Lake
Kariba Gorge
Kabwe
Ndola
Luanshya
Kitwe
Muchinga Mts
Chipata
Lilongwe
Salima
Ft. Johnston
Zomba
Blantyre
Shire
Vila Cabral
Nyasa
Entre Rios
Nacala
Mozambique
Nampula
Tete
Mocuba
Quelimane
Inhaminga
Macequece
Beira
Sofala
Spungabera
Bassas da India (Fr.)
Europa (Fr.)
Inhambane
Vila de João Belo
Delagoa Bay
Maputo
Magude
KRUGER NATIONAL PARK
Pafuri
Limpopo
Livingstone
Victoria Falls
Wankie
WANKIE NATIONAL PARK
Gwaai
Shangani
Que Que
Sanyati
Kildonan
Shamva
Mazoe
Salisbury
Gatooma
Sebakwe
Gwelo
Umtali
Selukwe
Zimbabwe
Bulawayo
Matopo Hills
Plumtree
West Nicholson
Beit Bridge
Okovango
Caprivi Strip
Okovango Basin
Maun
Lake Ngami
Makarikari Salt Pan
Francistown
Serowe
Palapye Road
Molepolole
Gaborone
Kanye
Lobatse
Zeerust
Mafeking
Lichtenburg
Molopo
Nossob
Witdraai
Messina
Louis Trichardt
Leydsdorp
Potgietersrus
Thabazimbi
Pretoria
Johannesburg
Lydenburg
Middelburg
Komatipoort
Witbank
Heidelberg
Piet Retief
Vereeniging
Klerksdorp
Vryburg
Sishen
Kroonstad
Welkom
Vaal
Newcastle
Harrismith
Bethlehem
Ladysmith
Ulundi
Eshowe
Greytown
Pietermaritzburg
Durban
Barkly West
Kimberley
Bloemfontein
Maseru
Modder River
Belmont
Griqualand
Upington
Postmasburg
Griquatown
Orange
High Veld
Drakensberg
Matatiele
Port Shepstone
Margate
Umtata
Port Nolloth
O'Okiep
Springbok
Prieska
De Aar
Carnarvon
Victoria West
Bitterfontein
Calvinia
Burgersdorp
Nieuwveld Ra.
Beaufort West
Great Karroo
Graaff-Reinet
Butterworth
King William's Town
East London
Fraserburg
St. Helena Bay
Moorreesburg
Malmesbury
Paarl
Worcester
Ladismith
Little Karroo
Oudtshoorn
Uniondale
Klipplaat
Grahamstown
Port Alfred
Uitenhage
Algoa Bay
Port Elizabeth
Cape Town
Simonstown
Cape of Good Hope
False Bay
Stellenbosch
Swellendam
Mosselbaai
George
Knysna
C. Seal
C. St. Francis
200 m
2484
1921
1810
2202
1033
1314
1932
2052
2042
1547
2516
2700
1862
15°S
20°S
25°S
30°S
35°S
15°E
20°E
25°E
30°E
35°E
40°E

Scale 1:400 000 For legend see page 32

	Temp. °C	Rain mm
J	4.2	53
F	4.4	40
M	6.6	37
A	9.3	38
M	12.4	46
J	15.8	46
J	17.6	56
A	17.2	59
S	14.8	50
O	10.8	57
N	7.2	64
D	5.2	48
Year	10.5	594

Height 5 m

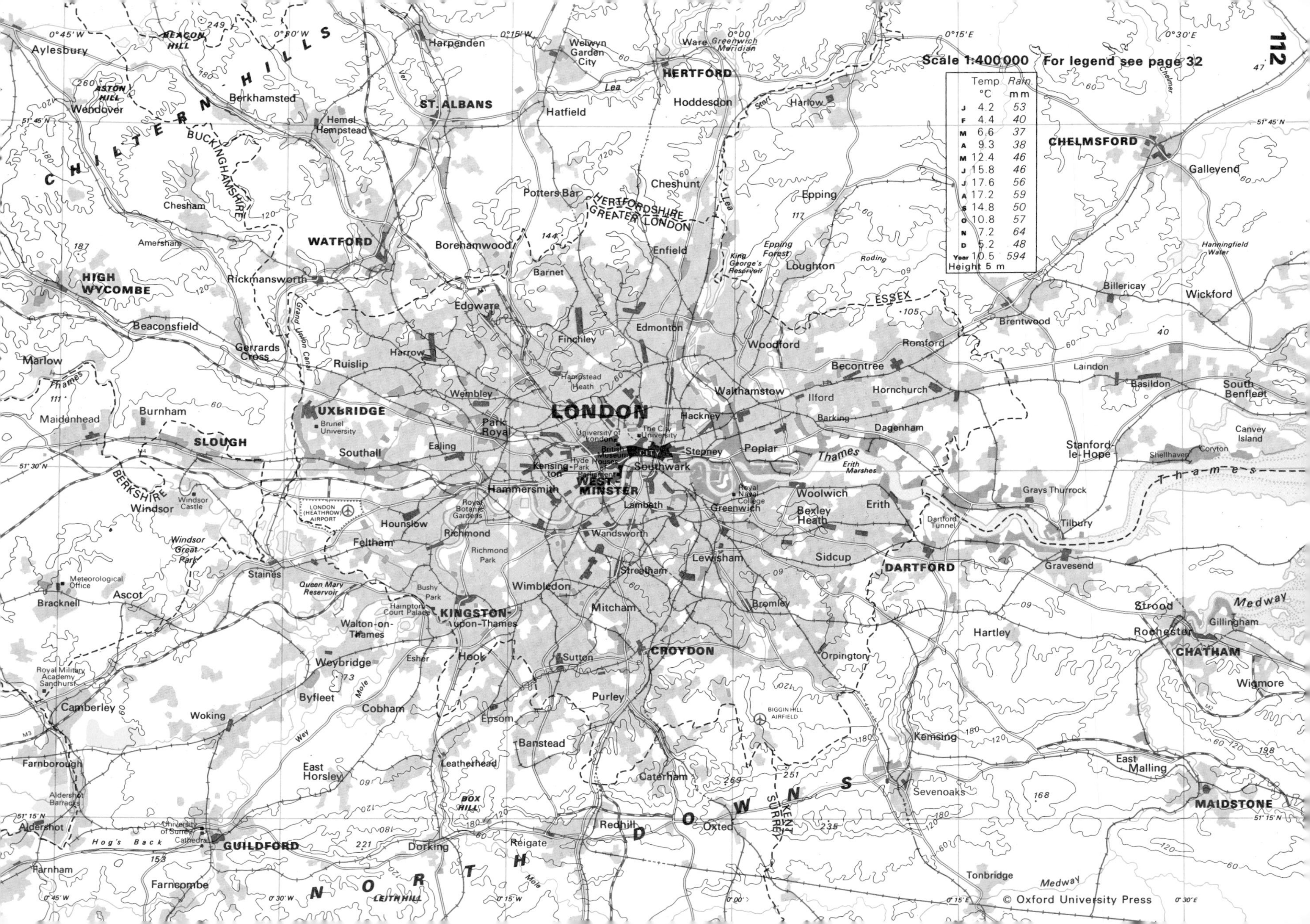

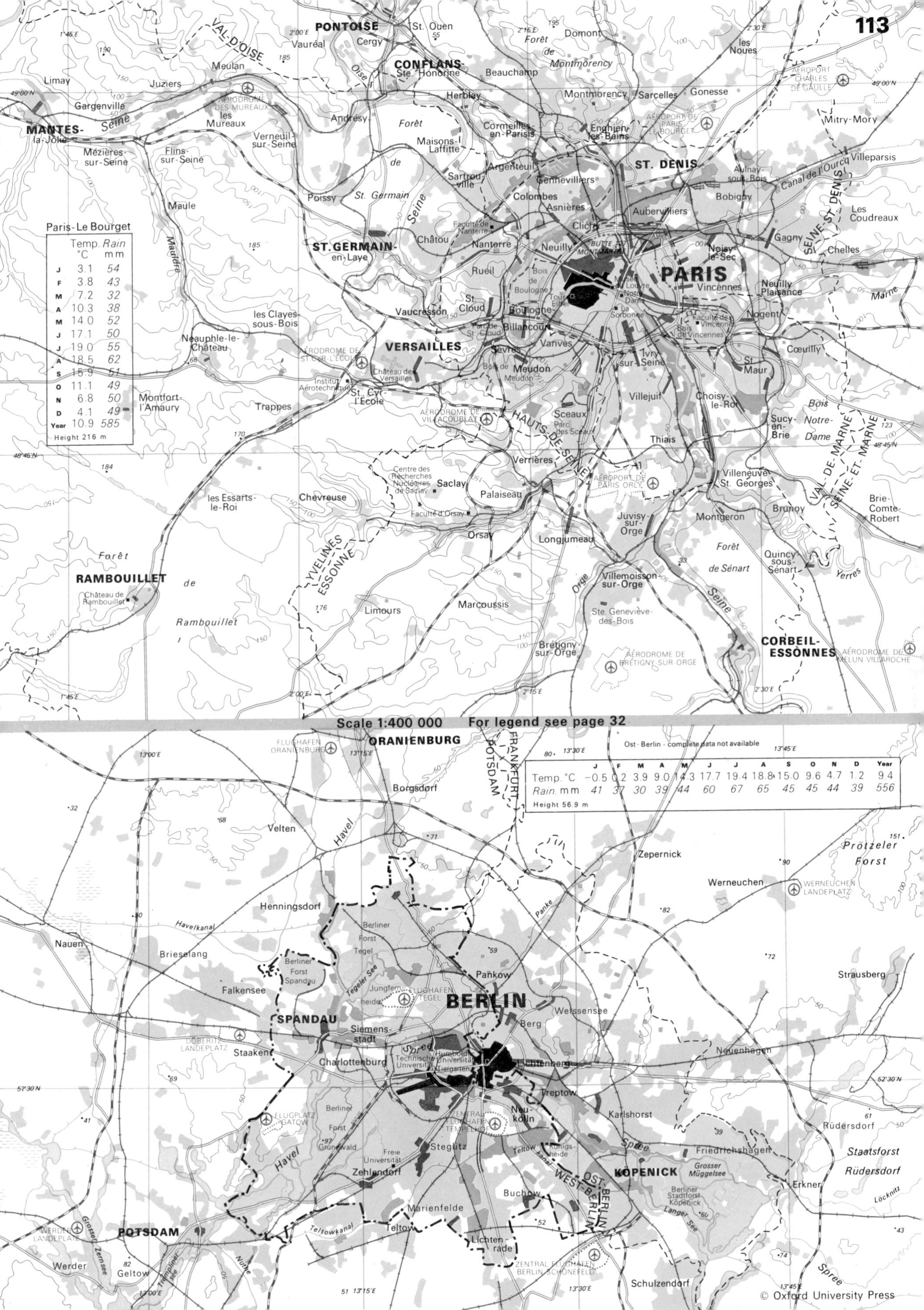

Paris-Le Bourget

	Temp. °C	Rain mm
J	3.1	54
F	3.8	43
M	7.2	32
A	10.3	38
M	14.0	52
J	17.1	50
J	19.0	55
A	18.5	62
S	15.9	51
O	11.1	49
N	6.8	50
D	4.1	49
Year	10.9	585

Height 216 m

Ost-Berlin - complete data not available

	J	F	M	A	M	J	J	A	S	O	N	D	Year
Temp. °C	−0.5	0.2	3.9	9.0	14.3	17.7	19.4	18.8	15.0	9.6	4.7	1.2	9.4
Rain. mm	41	37	30	39	44	60	67	65	45	45	44	39	556

Height 56.9 m

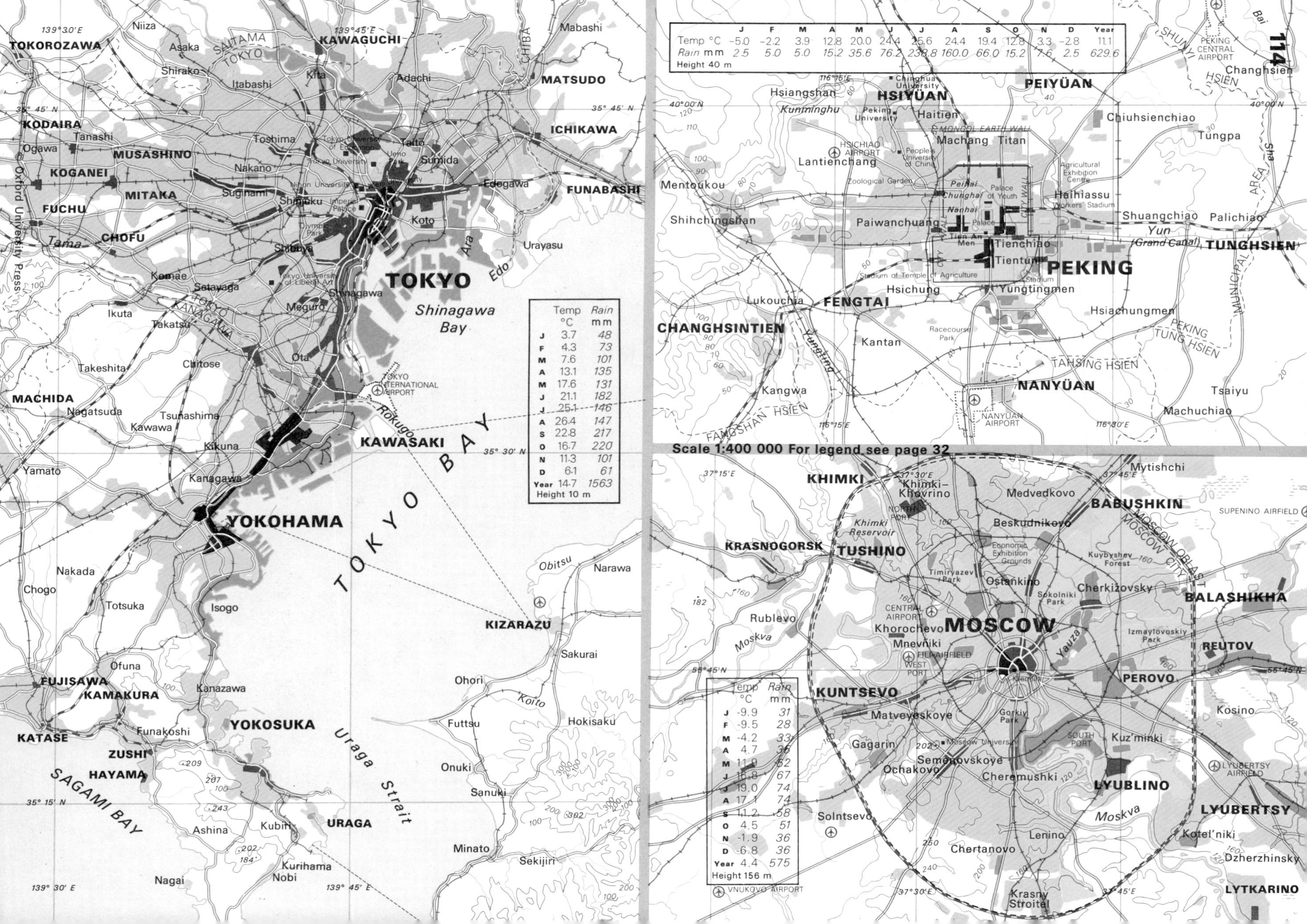

	J	F	M	A	M	J	J	A	S	O	N	D	Year
Temp °C	-5.0	-2.2	3.9	12.8	20.0	24.4	25.6	24.4	19.4	12.8	3.3	-2.8	11.1
Rain mm	2.5	5.0	5.0	15.2	35.6	76.2	238.8	160.0	66.0	15.2	7.6	2.5	629.6

Height 40 m

	Temp °C	*Rain* mm
J	3.7	48
F	4.3	73
M	7.6	101
A	13.1	135
M	17.6	131
J	21.1	182
J	25.1	146
A	26.4	147
S	22.8	217
O	16.7	220
N	11.3	101
D	6.1	61
Year	14.7	1563

Height 10 m

	Temp °C	*Rain* mm
J	-9.9	31
F	-9.5	28
M	-4.2	33
A	4.7	35
M	11.9	52
J	16.8	67
J	19.0	74
A	17.1	74
S	11.2	58
O	4.5	51
N	-1.9	36
D	-6.8	36
Year	4.4	575

Height 156 m

Scale 1:400 000 For legend see page 32

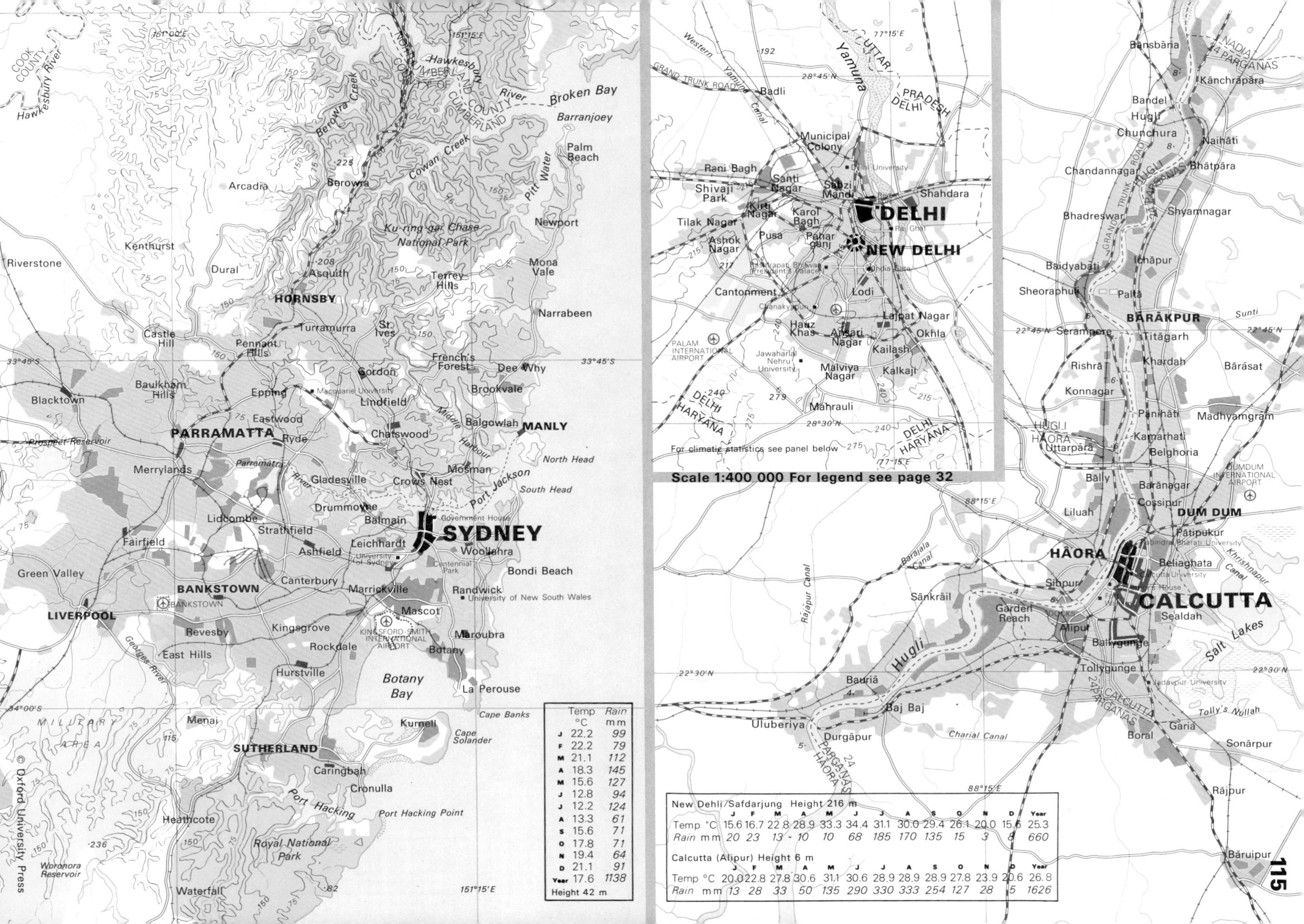

Scale 1:400 000 For legend see page 32

	Temp °C	Rain mm
J	22.2	99
F	22.2	79
M	21.1	112
A	18.3	145
M	15.6	127
J	12.8	94
J	12.2	124
A	13.3	61
S	15.6	71
O	17.8	71
N	19.4	64
D	21.1	91
Year	17.6	1138

Height 42 m

New Dehli/Safdarjung Height 216 m

	J	F	M	A	M	J	J	A	S	O	N	D	Year
Temp °C	15.6	16.7	22.8	28.9	33.3	34.4	31.1	30.0	29.4	26.1	20.0	15.6	25.3
Rain mm	20	23	13	10	10	68	185	170	135	15	3	8	660

Calcutta (Alipur) Height 6 m

	J	F	M	A	M	J	J	A	S	O	N	D	Year
Temp °C	20.0	22.8	27.8	30.6	31.1	30.6	28.9	28.9	28.9	27.8	23.9	20.6	26.8
Rain mm	13	28	33	50	135	290	330	333	254	127	28	5	1626

World: Relief

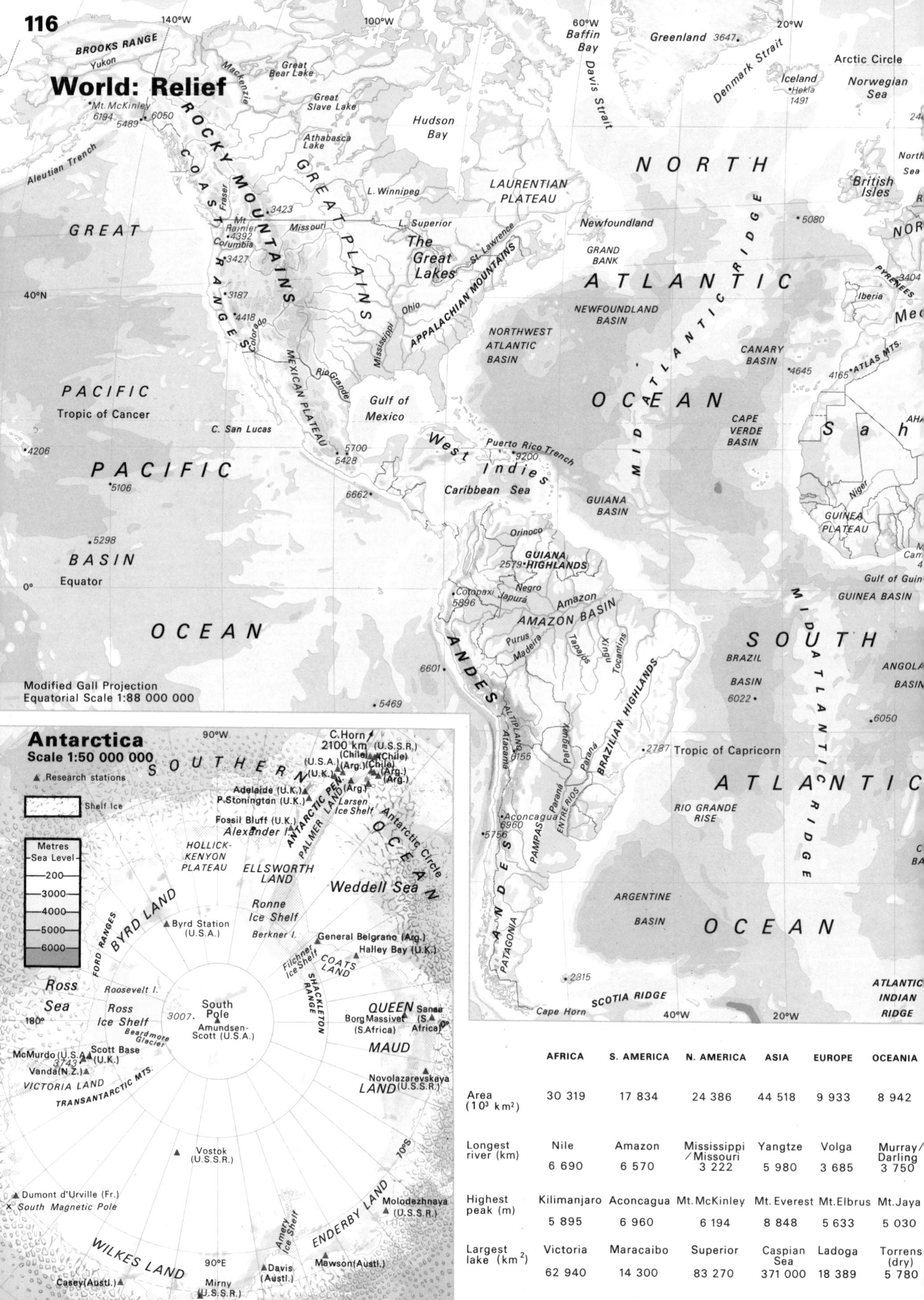

	AFRICA	S. AMERICA	N. AMERICA	ASIA	EUROPE	OCEANIA
Area (10^3 km^2)	30 319	17 834	24 386	44 518	9 933	8 942
Longest river (km)	Nile 6 690	Amazon 6 570	Mississippi/Missouri 3 222	Yangtze 5 980	Volga 3 685	Murray/Darling 3 750
Highest peak (m)	Kilimanjaro 5 895	Aconcagua 6 960	Mt. McKinley 6 194	Mt. Everest 8 848	Mt. Elbrus 5 633	Mt. Jaya 5 030
Largest lake (km^2)	Victoria 62 940	Maracaibo 14 300	Superior 83 270	Caspian Sea 371 000	Ladoga 18 389	Torrens (dry) 5 780

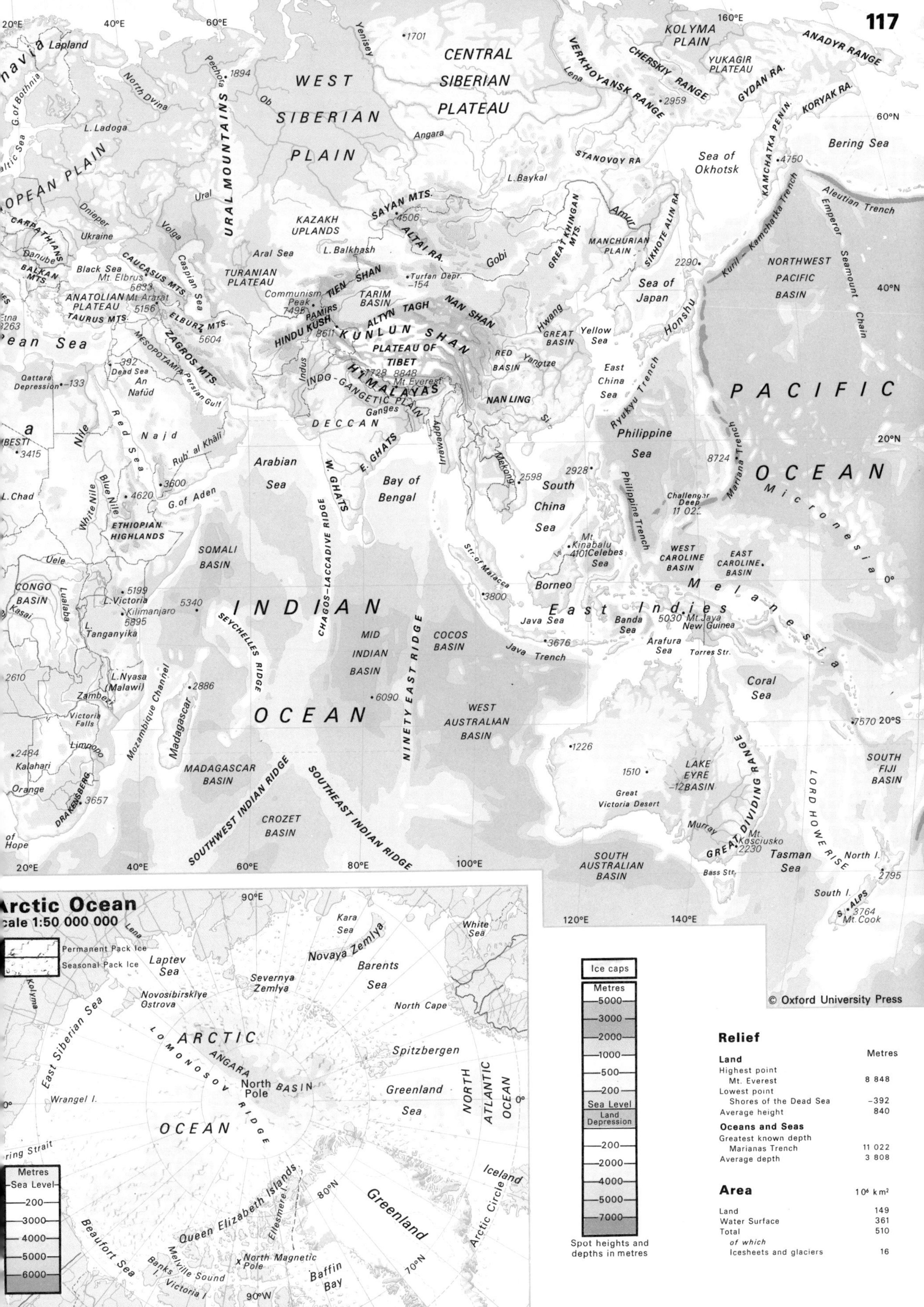

20°E
40°E
60°E
160°E
Lapland
G. of Bothnia
L. Ladoga
Baltic Sea
EUROPEAN PLAIN
North Dvina
Pechora
1894
URAL MOUNTAINS
Ob
WEST
SIBERIAN
PLAIN
Yenisey
1701
CENTRAL
SIBERIAN
PLATEAU
Angara
KOLYMA
PLAIN
YUKAGIR
PLATEAU
VERKHOYANSK RANGE
CHERSKIY RANGE
2959
Lena
ANADYR RANGE
GYDAN RA.
KORYAK RA.
KAMCHATKA PENIN.
4750
60°N
Bering Sea
Sea of
Okhotsk
STANOVOY RA
L. Baykal
Aleutian Trench
Emperor
Seamount
Chain
Kuril – Kamchatka Trench
GREAT KHINGAN MTS.
Amur
SIKHOTE ALIN RA
MANCHURIAN
PLAIN
2290
NORTHWEST
PACIFIC
BASIN
40°N
Sea of
Japan
Honshu
CARPATHIANS
Dnieper
Ukraine
Danube
BALKAN
MTS
Ural
Volga
KAZAKH
UPLANDS
SAYAN MTS.
4506
ALTAI RA.
L. Balkhash
Aral Sea
Gobi
Black Sea
Mt. Elbrus
5633
CAUCASUS MTS.
Caspian Sea
TURANIAN
PLATEAU
Turfan Depr.
–154
TIEN SHAN
Communism
Peak
7495
PAMIRS
TARIM
BASIN
ALTYN TAGH
NAN SHAN
ANATOLIAN
PLATEAU
Mt. Ararat
5156
TAURUS MTS.
ELBURZ MTS.
5604
HINDU KUSH
8611
KUNLUN SHAN
PLATEAU OF
TIBET
Hwang
GREAT
BASIN
Yellow
Sea
Etna
3263
Mediterranean Sea
ZAGROS MTS.
MESOPOTAMIA
–392
Dead Sea
An
Nafūd
Persian Gulf
Indus
HIMALAYAS
7728
8848
Mt. Everest
INDO-GANGETIC PLAIN
Ganges
RED
BASIN
Yangtze
East
China
Sea
Ryukyu Trench
PACIFIC
Qattara
Depression
–133
NAN LING
DECCAN
Nile
Red Sea
Najd
Rub' al Khālī
TIBESTI
3415
Arabian
Sea
W. GHATS
E. GHATS
Bay of
Bengal
Irrawaddy
Mekong
Philippine
Sea
20°N
8724
Mariana Trench
OCEAN
2598
2928
South
China
Sea
Philippine Trench
Challenger
Deep
11 022
Micronesia
L. Chad
White Nile
Blue Nile
3600
4620
G. of Aden
ETHIOPIAN
HIGHLANDS
CHAGOS–LACCADIVE RIDGE
SOMALI
BASIN
Str. of Malacca
Mt.
Kinabalu
4101
Celebes
Sea
WEST
CAROLINE
BASIN
EAST
CAROLINE
BASIN
Uele
CONGO
BASIN
Lualaba
Kasai
5199
L. Victoria
Kilimanjaro
5895
5340
INDIAN
3800
Borneo
0°
Melanesia
L.
Tanganyika
SEYCHELLES RIDGE
MID
INDIAN
BASIN
NINETY EAST RIDGE
COCOS
BASIN
Java Sea
East Indies
Banda
Sea
5030
Mt. Jaya
New Guinea
Java Trench
3676
Arafura
Sea
Torres Str.
2610
L. Nyasa
(Malawi)
Zambezi
Mozambique Channel
2886
Madagascar
6090
OCEAN
Coral
Sea
Victoria
Falls
WEST
AUSTRALIAN
BASIN
7570
20°S
Limpopo
2484
Kalahari
Orange
1226
LAKE
EYRE
BASIN
–12
1510
GREAT DIVIDING RANGE
SOUTH
FIJI
BASIN
LORD HOWE RISE
MADAGASCAR
BASIN
SOUTHWEST INDIAN RIDGE
SOUTHEAST INDIAN RIDGE
DRAKENSBERG
3657
Great
Victoria Desert
C. of Good Hope
CROZET
BASIN
Murray
Mt.
Kosciusko
2230
Tasman
Sea
North I.
2795
20°E
40°E
60°E
80°E
100°E
SOUTH
AUSTRALIAN
BASIN
Bass Str.
South I.
S. ALPS
3764
Mt. Cook
120°E
140°E
Arctic Ocean
Scale 1:50 000 000
Permanent Pack Ice
Seasonal Pack Ice
90°E
Lena
Kara
Sea
White
Sea
Novaya Zemlya
Laptev
Sea
Barents
Sea
Kolyma
Severnya
Zemlya
Novosibirsklye
Ostrova
North Cape
East Siberian Sea
ARCTIC
LOMONOSOV RIDGE
ANGARA
BASIN
Spitzbergen
North
Pole
Greenland
Sea
NORTH
ATLANTIC
OCEAN
0°
Wrangel I.
OCEAN
Bering Strait
Metres
Sea Level
200
3000
4000
5000
6000
Iceland
Queen Elizabeth Islands
Ellesmere I.
80°N
Greenland
Arctic Circle
Beaufort Sea
Banks I.
Melville Sound
North Magnetic
Pole
Victoria I.
Baffin
Bay
70°N
90°W
Ice caps
Metres
5000
3000
2000
1000
500
200
Sea Level
Land
Depression
200
2000
4000
5000
7000
Spot heights and
depths in metres
© Oxford University Press
Relief
Metres
Land
Highest point
Mt. Everest 8 848
Lowest point
Shores of the Dead Sea –392
Average height 840
Oceans and Seas
Greatest known depth
Marianas Trench 11 022
Average depth 3 808
Area
10⁶ km²
Land 149
Water Surface 361
Total 510
of which
Icesheets and glaciers 16

Rainfall
and other forms of precipitation

Temperature
(actual)
and Ocean Currents

Air Masses Pressure and Winds

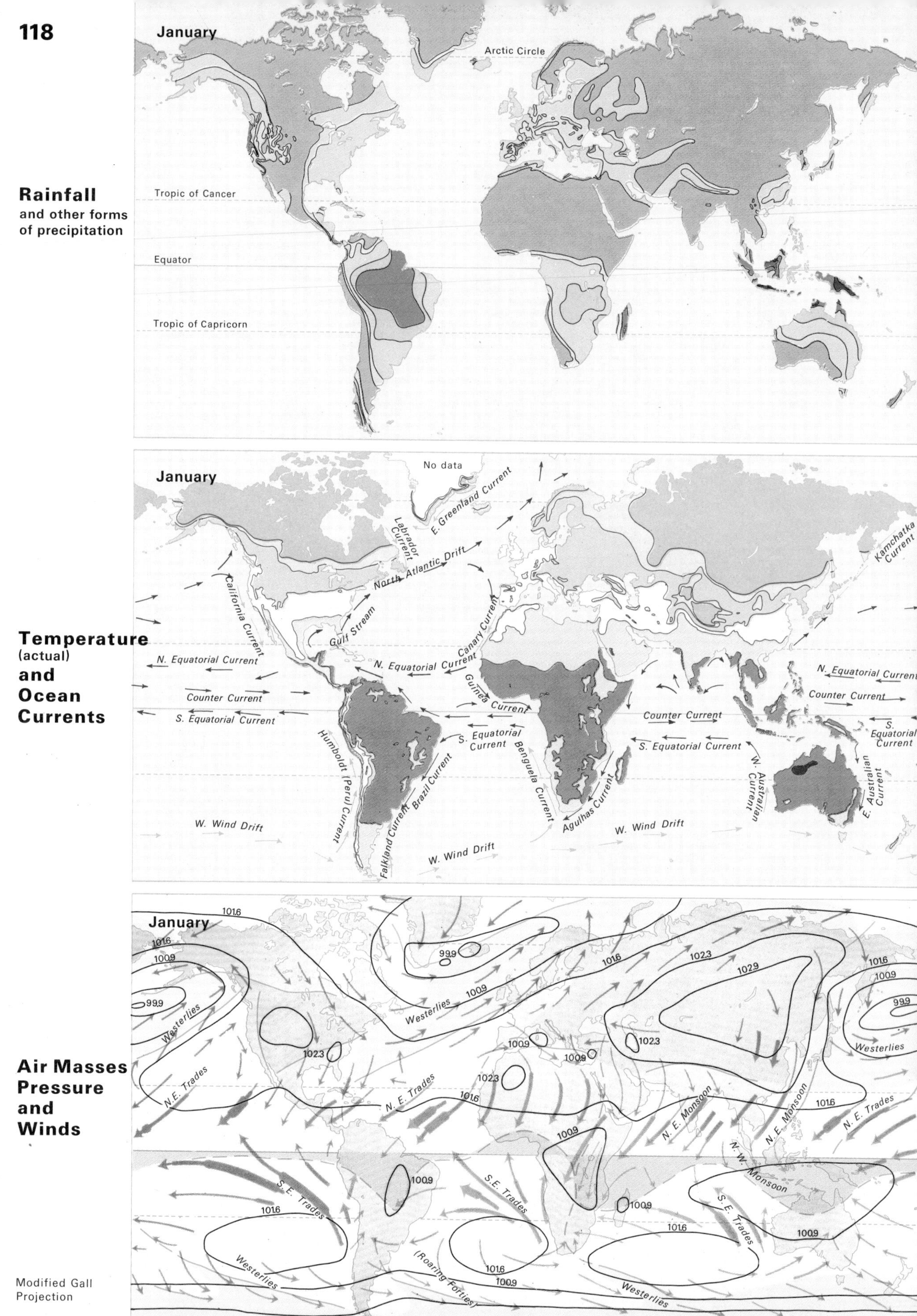

Modified Gall Projection

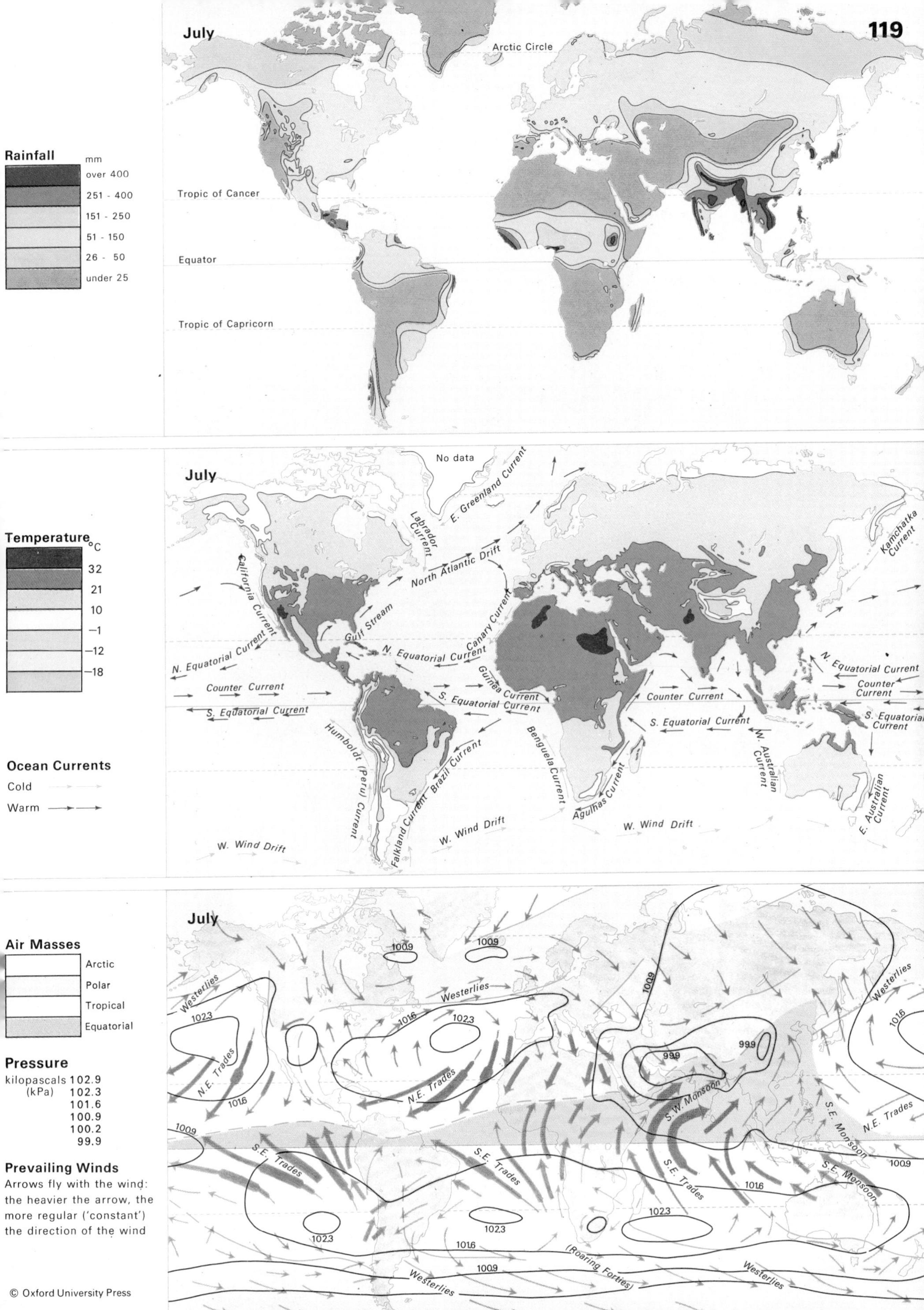
July
Rainfall
mm
over 400
251 - 400
151 - 250
51 - 150
26 - 50
under 25
Arctic Circle
Tropic of Cancer
Equator
Tropic of Capricorn
July
Temperature °C
32
21
10
–1
–12
–18
Ocean Currents
Cold
Warm
No data
E. Greenland Current
Labrador Current
North Atlantic Drift
California Current
Gulf Stream
Canary Current
N. Equatorial Current
Counter Current
S. Equatorial Current
Guinea Current
Humboldt (Peru) Current
Brazil Current
Falkland Current
Benguela Current
Agulhas Current
W. Wind Drift
W. Australian Current
E. Australian Current
Kamchatka Current
July
Air Masses
Arctic
Polar
Tropical
Equatorial
Pressure
kilopascals (kPa)
102.9
102.3
101.6
100.9
100.2
99.9
Prevailing Winds
Arrows fly with the wind: the heavier the arrow, the more regular ('constant') the direction of the wind
Westerlies
N.E. Trades
S.E. Trades
S.W. Monsoon
S.E. Monsoon
(Roaring Forties)

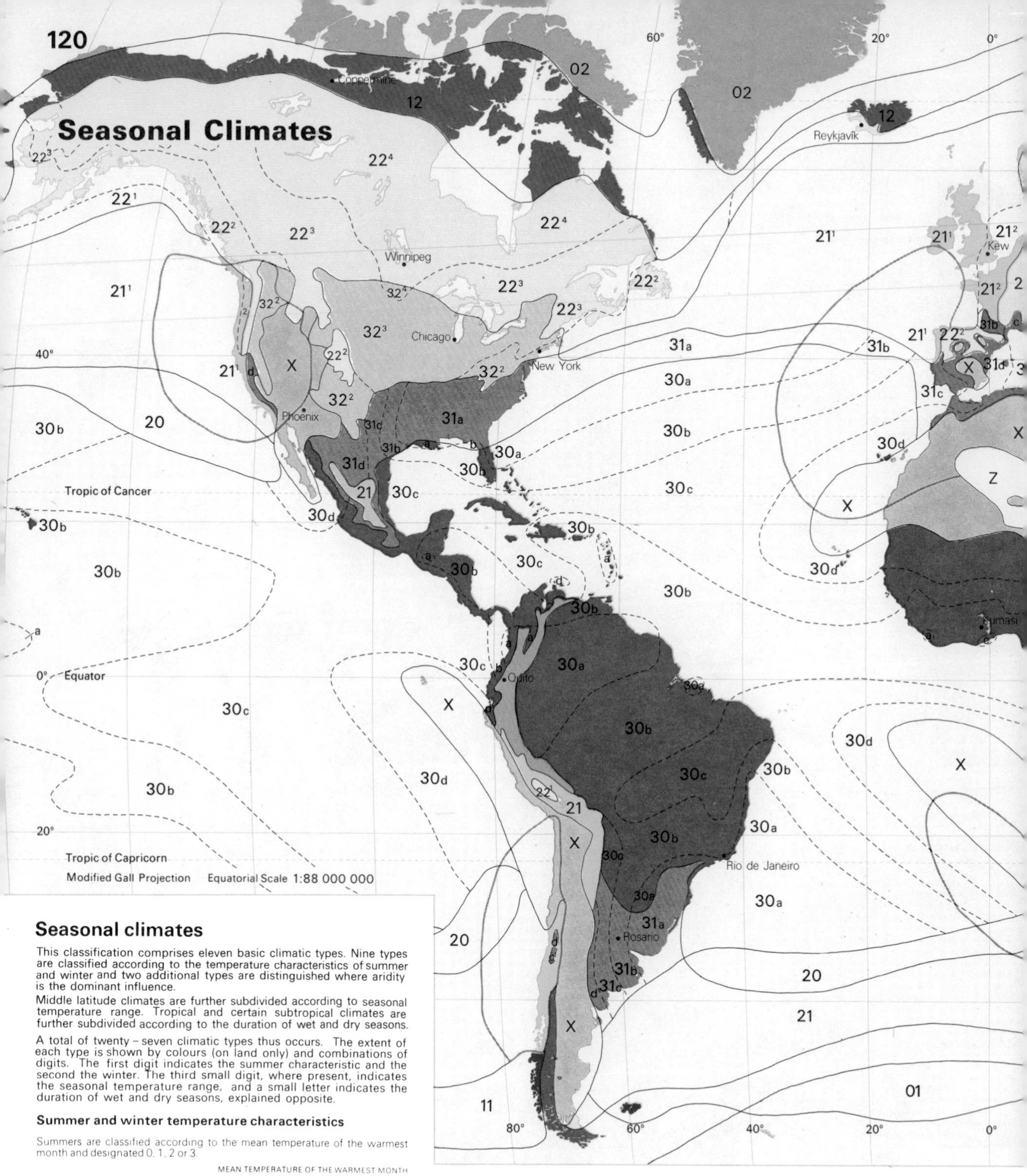

Seasonal Climates

Modified Gall Projection Equatorial Scale 1:88 000 000

Seasonal climates

This classification comprises eleven basic climatic types. Nine types are classified according to the temperature characteristics of summer and winter and two additional types are distinguished where aridity is the dominant influence.

Middle latitude climates are further subdivided according to seasonal temperature range. Tropical and certain subtropical climates are further subdivided according to the duration of wet and dry seasons.

A total of twenty-seven climatic types thus occurs. The extent of each type is shown by colours (on land only) and combinations of digits. The first digit indicates the summer characteristic and the second the winter. The third small digit, where present, indicates the seasonal temperature range, and a small letter indicates the duration of wet and dry seasons, explained opposite.

Summer and winter temperature characteristics

Summers are classified according to the mean temperature of the warmest month and designated 0, 1, 2 or 3.

		MEAN TEMPERATURE OF THE WARMEST MONTH
0	No summer	6°C and under.
1	Very cool summer	6-10°C
2	Cool summer	10-20°C
3	Full summer	over 20°C

Winters are classified according to the mean temperature of the coldest month and designated 0, 1 or 2.

		MEAN TEMPERATURE OF THE COLDEST MONTH
0	No winter	over 13°C
1	Mild winter	2-13°C
2	Cold winter	below 2°C

Combinations of summer and winter conditions are used to indicate climatic types. These are shown on land areas by colour and by figures and on sea areas by figures only. The digit for summer is always given first. Thus 02 indicates no summer, cold winter.

Combinations of summer and winter conditions

Code	Conditions	Code	Conditions
02	No summer, Cold winter	20	Cool summer, No winter
12	Very cool summer, Cold winter	32	Full summer, Cold winter
11	Very cool summer, Mild winter	31	Full summer, Mild winter
22	Cool summer, Cold winter	30	Full summer, No winter
21	Cool summer, Mild winter		

Arid climates

X	Arid

Arid climates are those climates in middle and low latitudes in which no month receives as much as 50 mm rainfall.

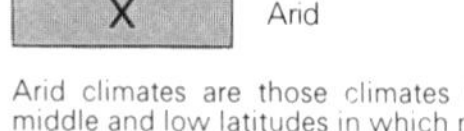

Z	Extremely arid

Extremely arid climates are perennially rainless with no more than 2.5 mm rainfall per month for at least 10 months of the year.

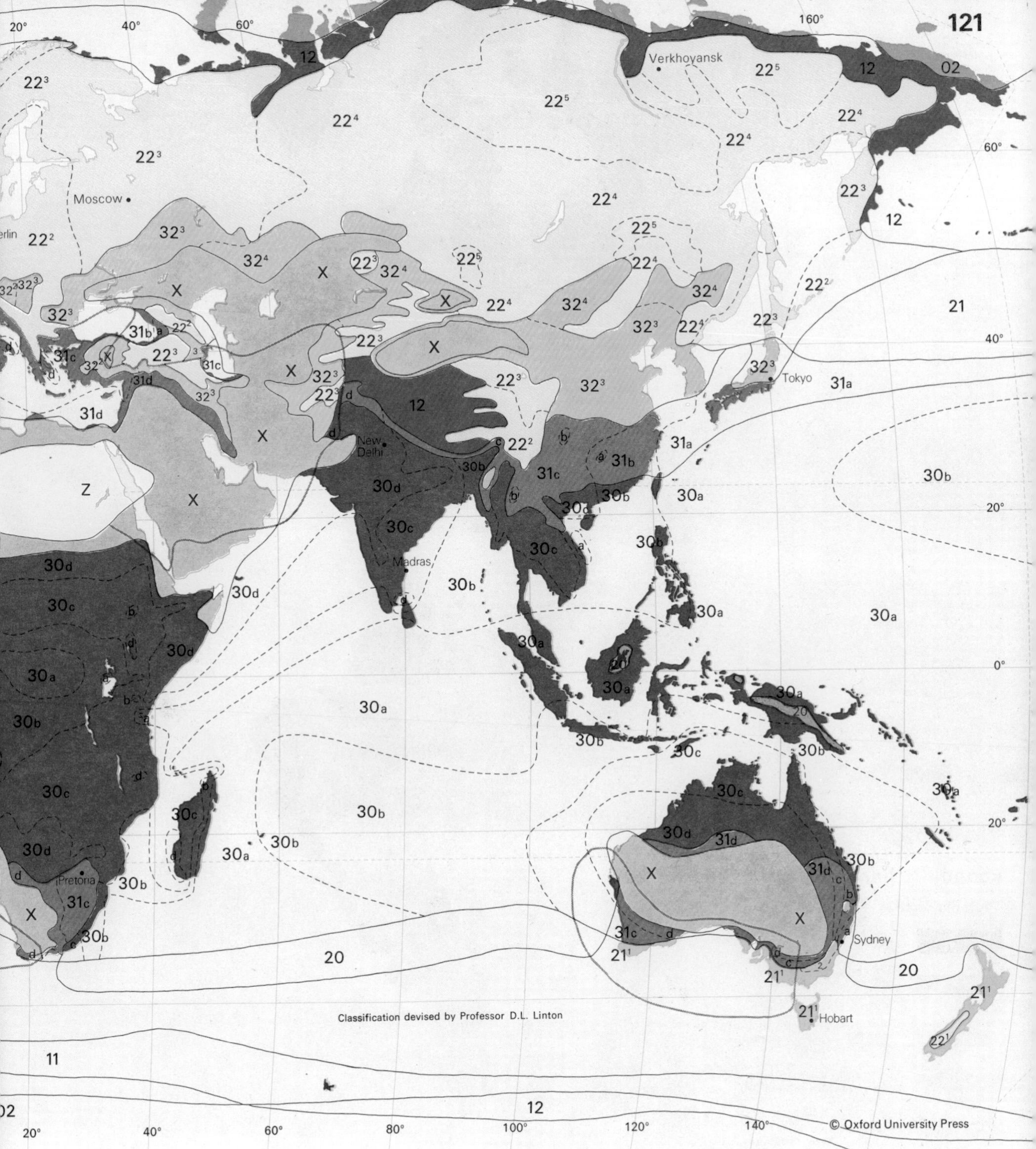

Seasonal temperature range

For areas 21, 22 and 32 outside the tropics

1 Oceanic
Seasonal range under 12°C

2 Sub Continental
Seasonal range 12-24°C

3 Continental
Seasonal range 24-36°C

4 Very Continental
Seasonal range 36-48°C

5 Extremely Continental
Seasonal range over 48°C

Duration of wet and dry seasons

For areas 30 and 31 only

a All months rainy
i.e. with over 50 mm rainfall

b Rainy season predominant
8-11 months with over 50 mm

c Rainy and dry seasons approx. equal
5, 6 or 7 months with over 50 mm

d Dry season predominant
1-4 months with over 50 mm

Winter rain regions

Boundary of region where rainfall occurs predominantly in winter

Mean monthly temperatures for January and July

Selected stations *(with altitude in metres)*

	Jan. °C	July °C		Jan. °C	July °C
Coppermine *(0)*	–28.6	9.3	**Chicago** *(190)*	–3.3	24.3
Verkhoyansk *(137)*	–46.8	15.7	**New York** *(16)*	0.9	24.9
Winnipeg *(240)*	–17.7	20.2	**Sydney** *(42)*	21.9	12.3
Moscow *(156)*	–9.9	19.0	**Rosario** *(27)*[1]	23.8	9.9
Berlin *(50)*	–0.5	19.4	**Pretoria** *(1400)*[2]	21.0	10.3
Reykjavík *(16)*	–0.4	11.2	**Rio de Janeiro** *(27)*	26.0	20.8
Kew *(5)*	4.2	17.6	**Kumasi** *(293)*[1]	25.2	24.2
Hobart *(54)*	16.3	7.8	**Madras** *(16)*	24.5	30.7
Quito *(2812)*	13.0	12.9	**New Delhi** *(216)*[1]	14.3	31.2
Tokyo *(6)*	3.7	25.1	**Phoenix** *(337)*	10.4	32.9

Temperatures decrease with increasing altitude at a rate of about 2°C for every 300 m
Location, season and time of day all influence the actual rate.

[1] 1941-60 [2] 1951-60

Economic Geology

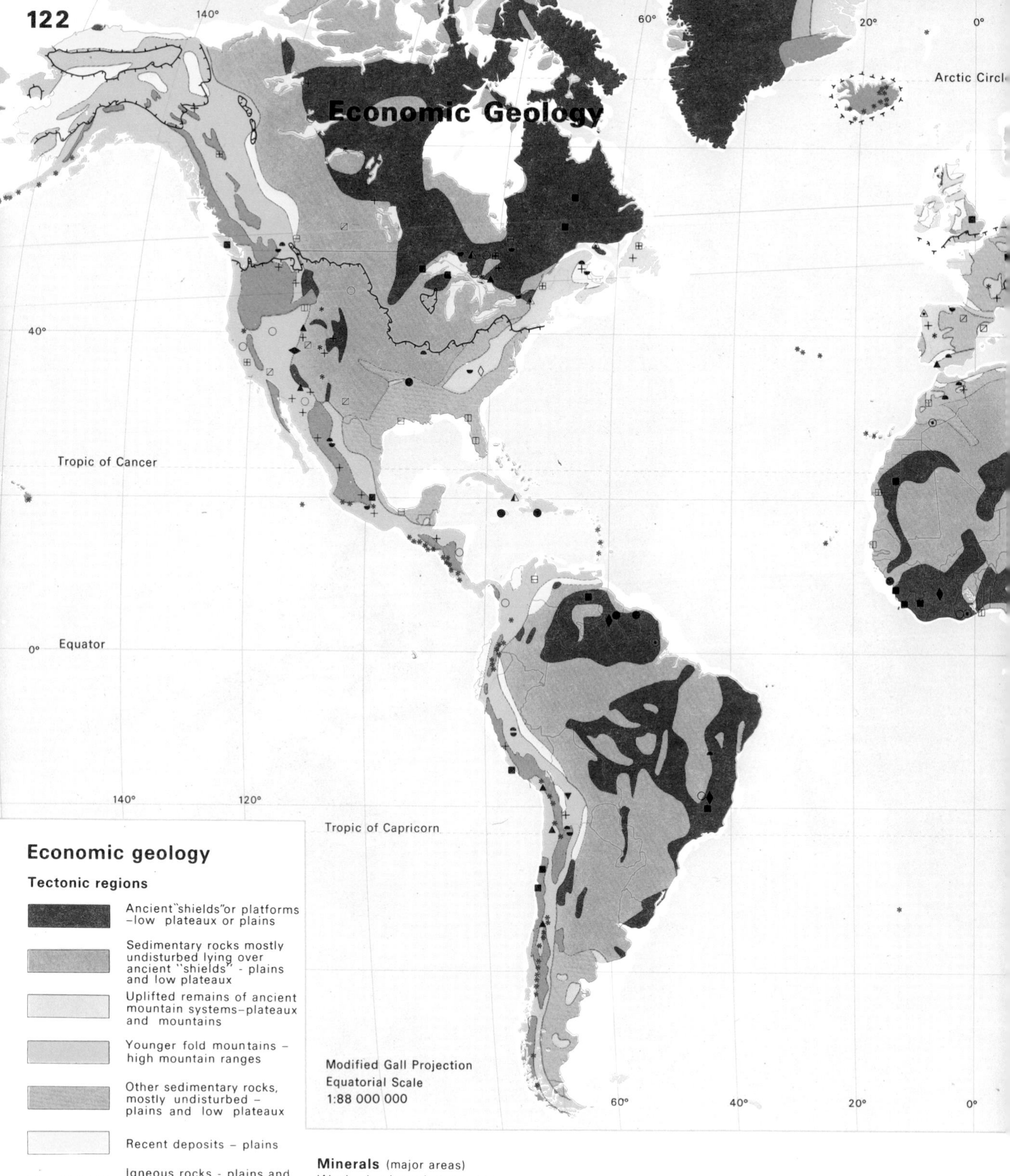

Economic geology

Tectonic regions

- Ancient "shields" or platforms – low plateaux or plains
- Sedimentary rocks mostly undisturbed lying over ancient "shields" – plains and low plateaux
- Uplifted remains of ancient mountain systems – plateaux and mountains
- Younger fold mountains – high mountain ranges
- Other sedimentary rocks, mostly undisturbed – plains and low plateaux
- Recent deposits – plains
- Igneous rocks – plains and plateaux (lava flows); plateaux and mountains (granite intrusions)

* * * * * Active volcanoes

Volcanoes which have shown no major activity during this century are not shown

Continental shelf/ocean shallows

White areas represent those regions lying between 0 and 200 m below sea level

Pleistocene glaciation

Approximate limit of maximum extent of Pleistocene glaciation

Minerals (major areas)
Worked mineral deposits

○ gold	■ iron	⊞ asbestos
+ silver	nickel	◆ diamond
▲ copper	chrome	◊ mica
▼ tin	manganese	phosphate
lead	titanium	potash
zinc	* uranium	sulphur
● bauxite		

The distribution of Fossil Fuels is shown on pages 124–5

The map gives a general indication of the distribution of worked mineral deposits and their relationship with the structure of the earth's crust. Only the major areas of worked deposits of a selection of minerals are indicated.
It is important to note that lack of mineral workings does not necessarily indicate lack of deposits. Some areas remain unworked either because of insufficient knowledge of the geology or inaccessibility of deposits, or because the deposits are uneconomical to work given present day levels of technology

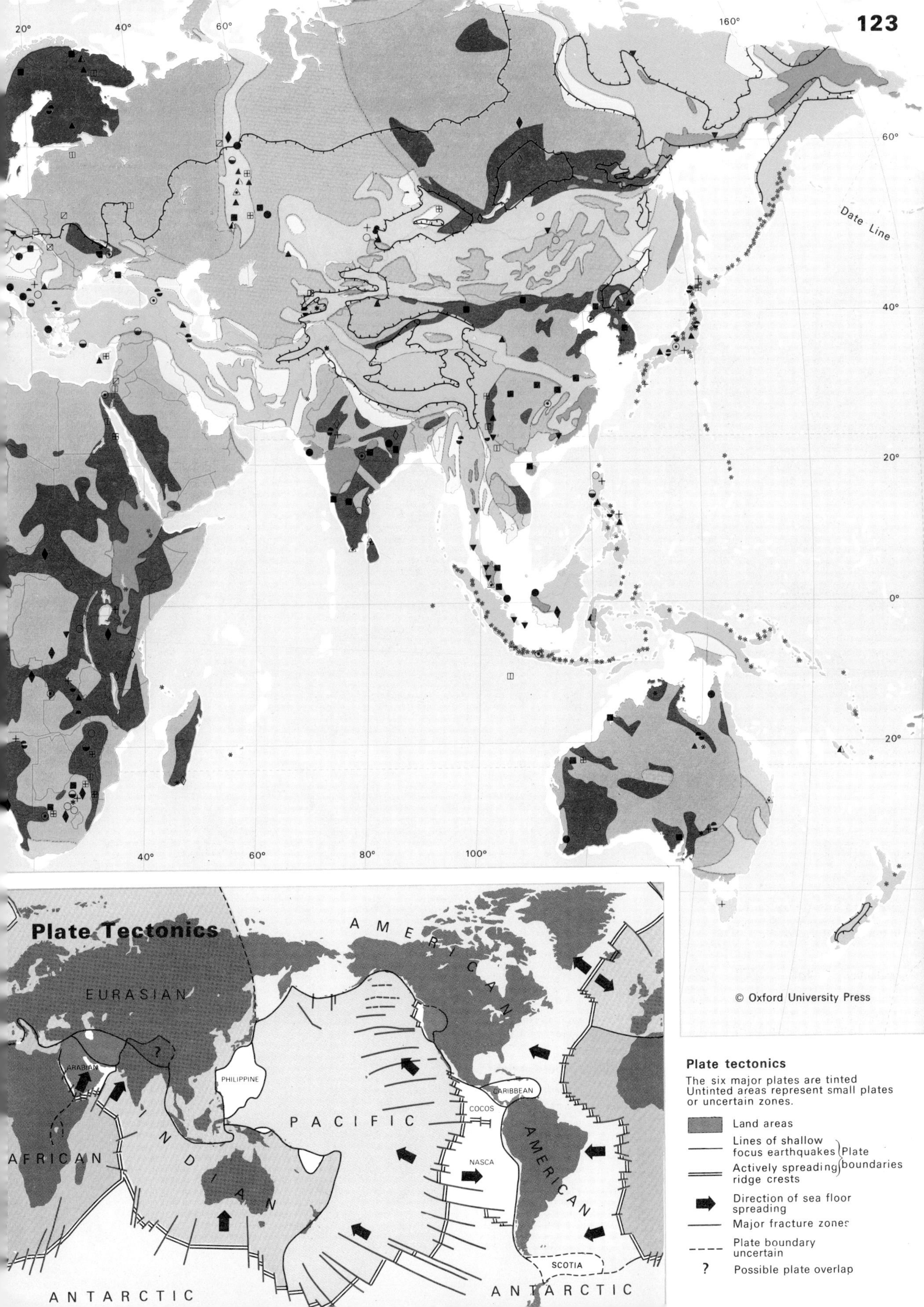

Plate tectonics

The six major plates are tinted
Untinted areas represent small plates or uncertain zones.

- Land areas
- Lines of shallow focus earthquakes } Plate boundaries
- Actively spreading ridge crests } Plate boundaries
- Direction of sea floor spreading
- Major fracture zones
- Plate boundary uncertain
- ? Possible plate overlap

Energy

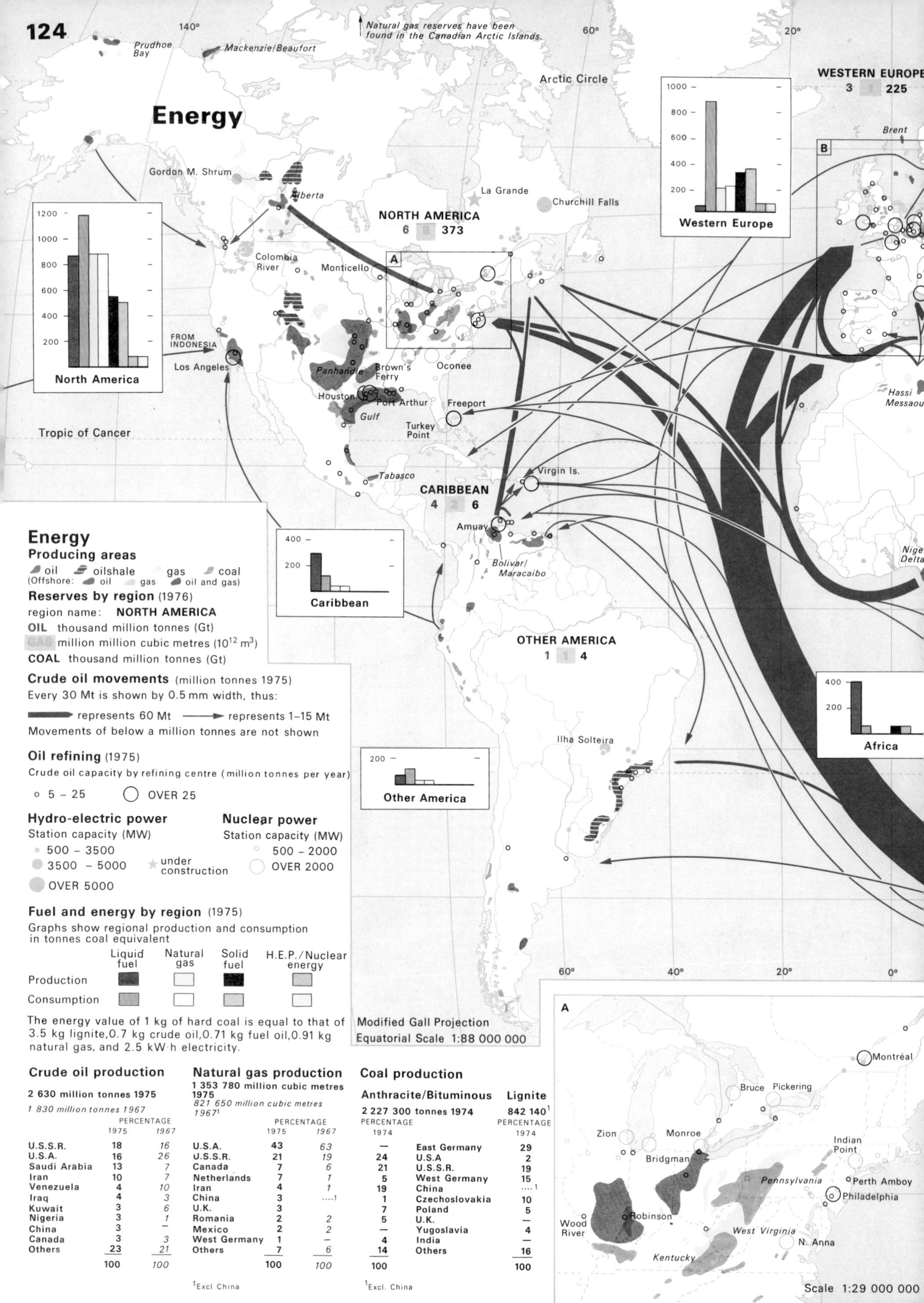

Crude oil production

2 630 million tonnes 1975

1 830 million tonnes 1967

	PERCENTAGE 1975	*1967*
U.S.S.R.	18	*16*
U.S.A.	16	*26*
Saudi Arabia	13	*7*
Iran	10	*7*
Venezuela	4	*10*
Iraq	4	*3*
Kuwait	3	*6*
Nigeria	3	*1*
China	3	–
Canada	3	*3*
Others	23	*21*
	100	*100*

Natural gas production

1 353 780 million cubic metres 1975

821 650 million cubic metres 1967[1]

	PERCENTAGE 1975	*1967*
U.S.A.	43	*63*
U.S.S.R.	21	*19*
Canada	7	*6*
Netherlands	7	*1*
Iran	4	*1*
China	3	....[1]
U.K.	3	
Romania	2	*2*
Mexico	2	*2*
West Germany	1	–
Others	7	*6*
	100	*100*

[1] Excl China

Coal production

Anthracite/Bituminous 2 227 300 tonnes 1974 PERCENTAGE 1974		Lignite 842 140[1] PERCENTAGE 1974
—	East Germany	29
24	U.S.A	2
21	U.S.S.R.	19
5	West Germany	15
19	China	....[1]
1	Czechoslovakia	10
7	Poland	5
5	U.K.	—
—	Yugoslavia	4
4	India	—
14	Others	16
100		100

[1] Excl. China

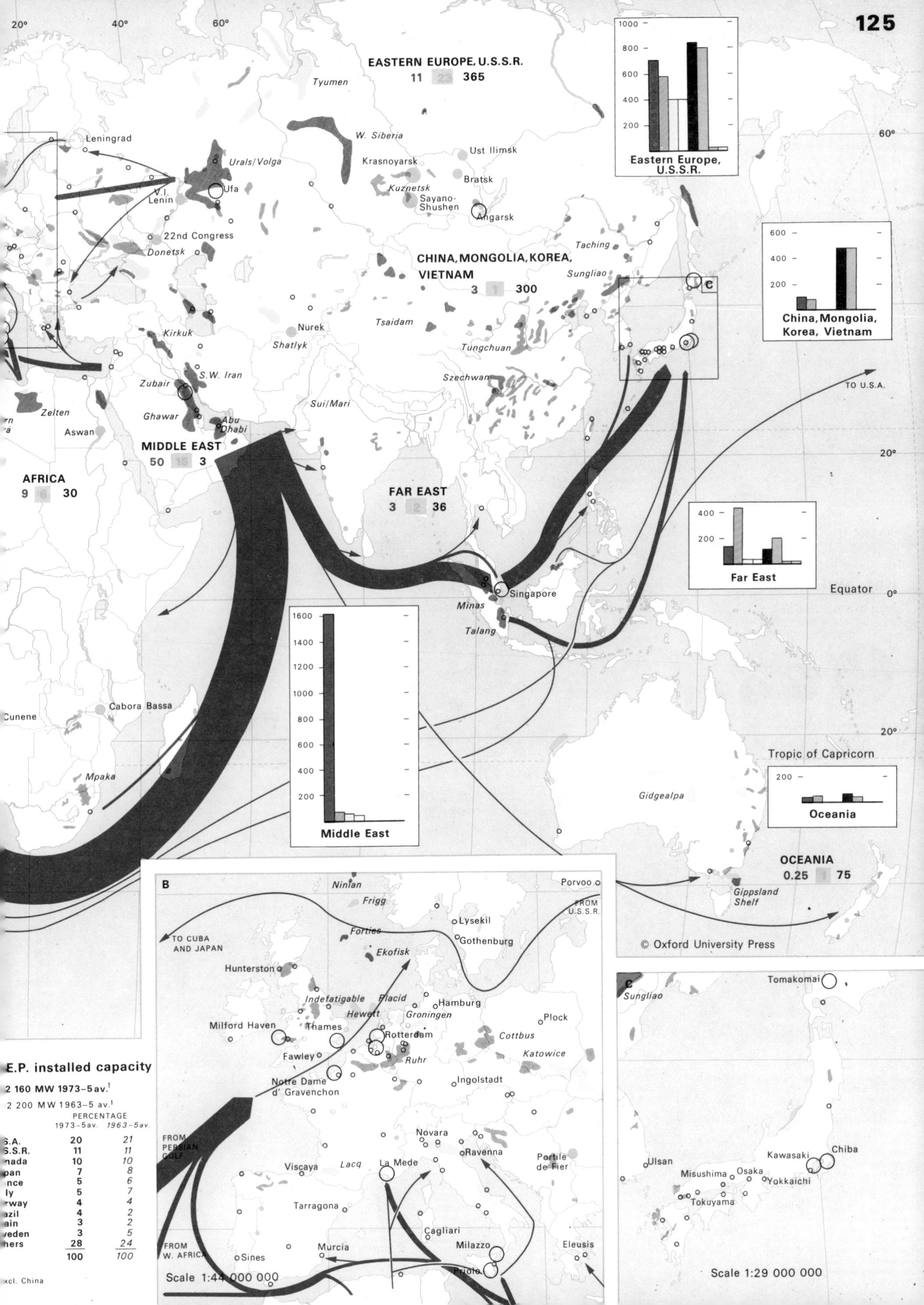

E.P. installed capacity

2 160 MW 1973–5 av.[1]

2 200 MW 1963–5 av.[1]

	PERCENTAGE 1973–5 av.	*1963–5 av.*
S.A.	20	*21*
S.S.R.	11	*11*
nada	10	*10*
pan	7	*8*
nce	5	*6*
ly	5	*7*
rway	4	*4*
azil	4	*2*
ain	3	*2*
veden	3	*5*
hers	28	*24*
	100	*100*

xcl. China

Iron and Steel

140° 60° 20° 0°

Trondheimsfj

Tasu Harbour
Edmonton
Regina
Bruce Lake
Steep Rock Lake
Marquette Range
Scheffersville
Labrador City
Wabash
Gagnon
Selkirk
Mesabi Range
Iron Mt.
Wawa
Sault St. Marie
Kirkland Lake
Timagami & Moose Mt.
Montreal
Sydney
Seattle
Portland
McMinnville
Norfolk
Peoria
Bridgeport
Sayreville
40°
Geneva
Kansas City
Union City
Pueblo
Fontana
Sand Springs
Granite City
Gadsden
Roanoke
Georgetown
Los Angeles
Eagle Mt.
Tempe
Fort Worth
Lone Star
Atlanta
Birmingham
Ciudad Camargo
Houston
Tampa
Indiantown
Monclova
Monterrey
Victoria de Durango
Pihuamo
Tropic of Cancer
Pena Colorado
Las Truchas
Mexico City
Veracruz
Haulbowline
Mondeville
Bilbao
<u>Aviles/Oviedo</u>
Madrid
Fos's Mer
Seixal
Sagur Men.
Nadar
Annaba
Ouen Bou Kha
Fort-Gouraud
Caracas
Boyaca
El Pao
Cerro Bolivar
Belencito
Conakry
Marampo
Nimba
Mano River
Mt. Klahoyo
Bomi Hills
Bong
0°
Chimbote
Marcona
Acari
Belo Horizonte/Itabira
20°
Belo Horizonte
Juiz de Fora
Piracicaba
Barra Mansa
Palpalá
Zapla
São Paulo
Rio de Janeiro
Atacama
El Romeral
Algarrobo
Rosario
Sapucaia do Sul
San Nicolas de los Arroyos
Buenos Aires
Huachipato
40°

Iron and steel

Iron ore production (1972–4av.)

thousand tonnes iron content

25 000 AND OVER	15 000 – 25 000	5 000 – 15 000	2 500 – 5 000	1 000 – 2 500	100 – 1 000

+ Data not available for known producing centres, but where regional data are known the appropriate symbol is enclosed in a box

☆ Major area of development

Steel production centres (1976)

thousand tonnes crude steel capacity

32 000 AND OVER	16 000 – 32 000	8 000 – 16 000	4 000 – 8 000	2 000 – 4 000	1 000 – 2 000	150 – 1 000

Where iron ore mine and steel works are coincident the locational name is underlined, for example <u>Maanshan</u>

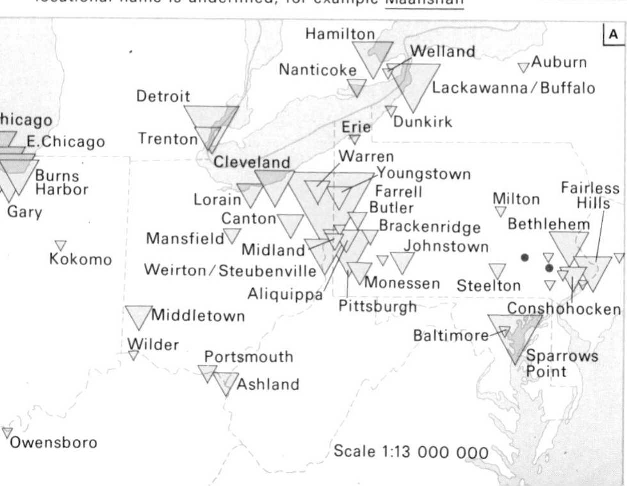

20° 0°

Modified Gall Projection
Equatorial Scale 1:88 000 000

Iron ore production[1]			**Steel production**	
477 533 000*		**tonnes 1972–4av.**	**674 067 000***	
*309 707 000**		*1963–5av.*	*428 044 000**	
PERCENTAGE			PERCENTAGE	
1963–5av.	1972–4av.		1972–4av	1963–5av.
28	**25**	U.S.S.R.	**19**	*20*
15	**10**	U.S.A.	**19**	*26*
—	—	Japan [2]	**16**	*9*
1	**10**	Australia [2]	**1**	*1*
3	**8**	Brazil [2]	**1**	*1*
1	—	W. Germany [2]	**7**	*8*
8	**7**	China*	**4**	*3*
6	**6**	Canada [2]	**2**	*2*
6	**3**	France*[2]	**4**	*4*
32	**31**	Others	**27**	*26*
100	**100**		**100**	*100*

*Estimate [1] Iron content. [2] The inclusion of countries whose ratings for the commodity are not greybacked, is based on their production of the other commodity.

0°
Glasgow
Motherwell
Glengarnock
Consett
Hartlepool
Middlesborough
Manchester
Scunthorpe
Birkenhead
Deeside
Wrexham
Sheffield
Stoke
Wolverhampton
Corby
Ebbw Vale
Llanelli
Llanwern
Port Talbot
Cardiff
Sheerness
Scale 1:22 000 000

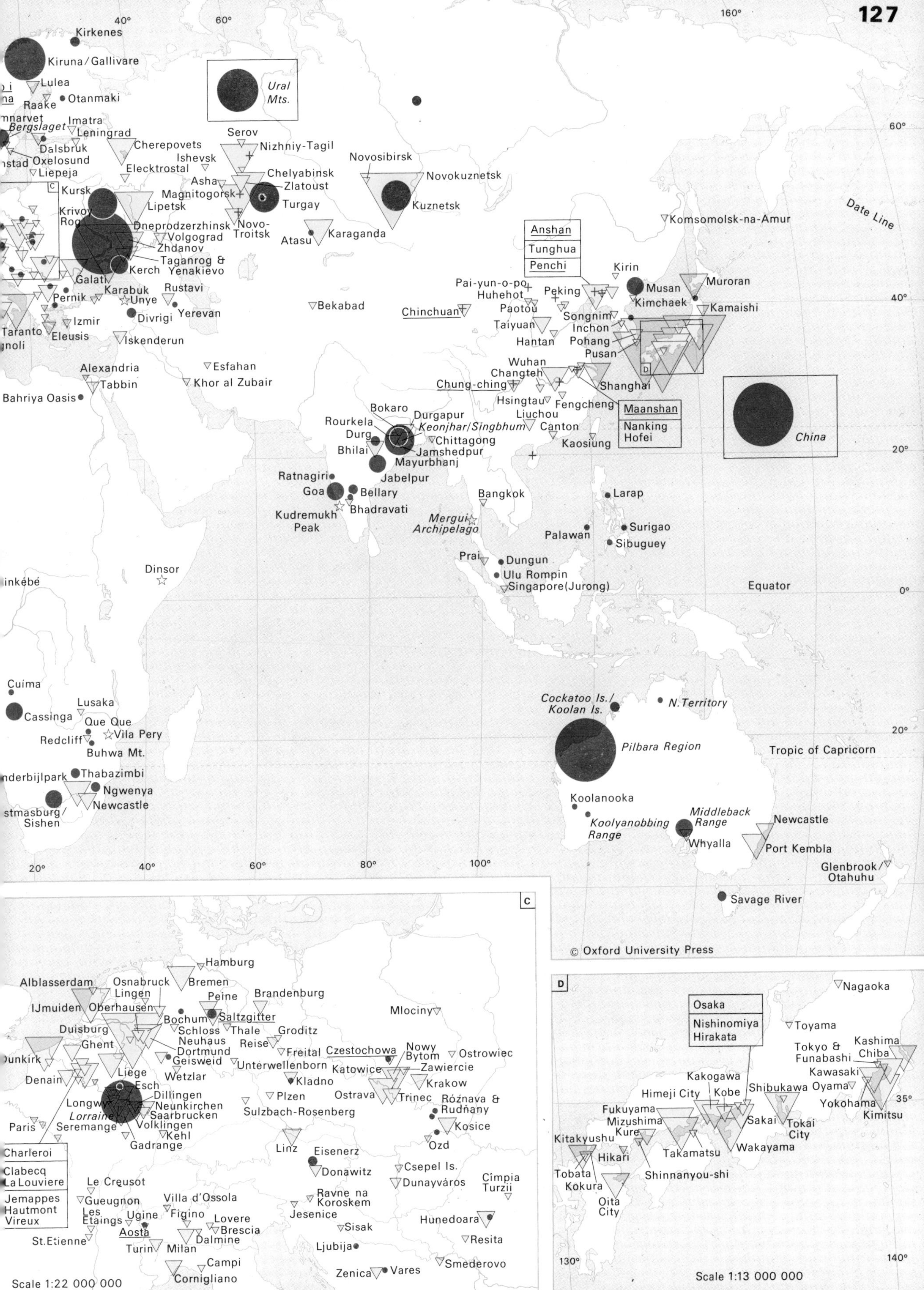

40°
60°
160°
Kirkenes
Kiruna/Gallivare
Lulea
Otanmaki
Raake
Imatra
Bergslaget
Leningrad
Dalsbruk
Oxelosund
Liepeja
Cherepovets
Ishevsk
Elecktrostal
Serov
Nizhniy-Tagil
Ural Mts.
Novosibirsk
Novokuznetsk
Kuznetsk
Chelyabinsk
Zlatoust
Asha
Magnitogorsk
Turgay
Kursk
Lipetsk
Krivoy Rog
Dneprodzerzhinsk
Novo-Troitsk
Volgograd
Zhdanov
Taganrog & Yenakievo
Kerch
Galati
Karabuk
Unye
Pernik
Rustavi
Yerevan
Divrigi
Izmir
Taranto
Eleusis
Iskenderun
Atasu
Karaganda
Bekabad
Komsomolsk-na-Amur
Date Line
60°
Anshan
Tunghua
Penchi
Kirin
Musan
Muroran
Kimchaek
Kamaishi
Pai-yun-o-po
Huhehot
Paotou
Peking
Chinchuan
Taiyuan
Hantan
Songnim
Inchon
Pohang
Pusan
40°
D
Alexandria
Tabbin
Bahriya Oasis
Esfahan
Khor al Zubair
Wuhan
Changteh
Chung-ching
Shanghai
Hsingtau
Liuchou
Fengcheng
Canton
Kaosiung
Maanshan
Nanking
Hofei
China
Bokaro
Rourkela
Durgapur
Durg
Keonjhar/Singbhum
Chittagong
Bhilai
Jamshedpur
Mayurbhanj
Jabelpur
Ratnagiri
Goa
Bellary
Bhadravati
Kudremukh Peak
20°
Bangkok
Mergui Archipelago
Larap
Palawan
Surigao
Sibuguey
Prai
Dungun
Ulu Rompin
Singapore(Jurong)
Equator
0°
Dinsor
Cuima
Cassinga
Lusaka
Que Que
Vila Pery
Redcliff
Buhwa Mt.
Thabazimbi
Ngwenya
Newcastle
Sishen
Cockatoo Is./Koolan Is.
N.Territory
Pilbara Region
20°
Tropic of Capricorn
Koolanooka
Koolyanobbing Range
Middleback Range
Whyalla
Newcastle
Port Kembla
Glenbrook/Otahuhu
Savage River
20°
40°
60°
80°
100°
C
Hamburg
Alblasserdam
Osnabruck
Bremen
Lingen
Peine
Brandenburg
IJmuiden
Oberhausen
Bochum
Saltzgitter
Mlociny
Duisburg
Schloss
Thale
Groditz
Ghent
Neuhaus
Reise
Dortmund
Freital
Czestochowa
Nowy Bytom
Ostrowiec
Dunkirk
Geisweid
Unterwellenborn
Katowice
Zawiercie
Denain
Liege
Wetzlar
Kladno
Krakow
Esch
Dillingen
Plzen
Ostrava
Trinec
Róznava & Rudňany
Longwy
Neunkircehn
Lorraine
Saarbrucken
Sulzbach-Rosenberg
Paris
Seremange
Volklingen
Kosice
Kehl
Gadrange
Linz
Ozd
Charleroi
Eisenerz
Clabecq
La Louviere
Donawitz
Csepel Is.
Le Creusot
Dunayváros
Cîmpia Turzii
Jemappes
Hautmont
Vireux
Gueugnon
Villa d'Ossola
Ravne na Koroskem
Les Etaings
Ugine
Figino
Lovere
Jesenice
Aosta
Brescia
Hunedoara
St.Etienne
Dalmine
Sisak
Turin
Milan
Resita
Ljubija
Campi
Zenica
Vares
Smederovo
Cornigliano
Scale 1:22 000 000
D
Nagaoka
Osaka
Nishinomiya
Hirakata
Toyama
Tokyo & Funabashi
Kashima
Chiba
Kawasaki
Kakogawa
Himeji City
Kobe
Shibukawa
Oyama
Fukuyama
Yokohama
35°
Mizushima
Kimitsu
Kure
Sakai
Tokai City
Kitakyushu
Hikari
Takamatsu
Wakayama
Tobata
Shinnanyou-shi
Kokura
Oita City
130°
140°
Scale 1:13 000 000

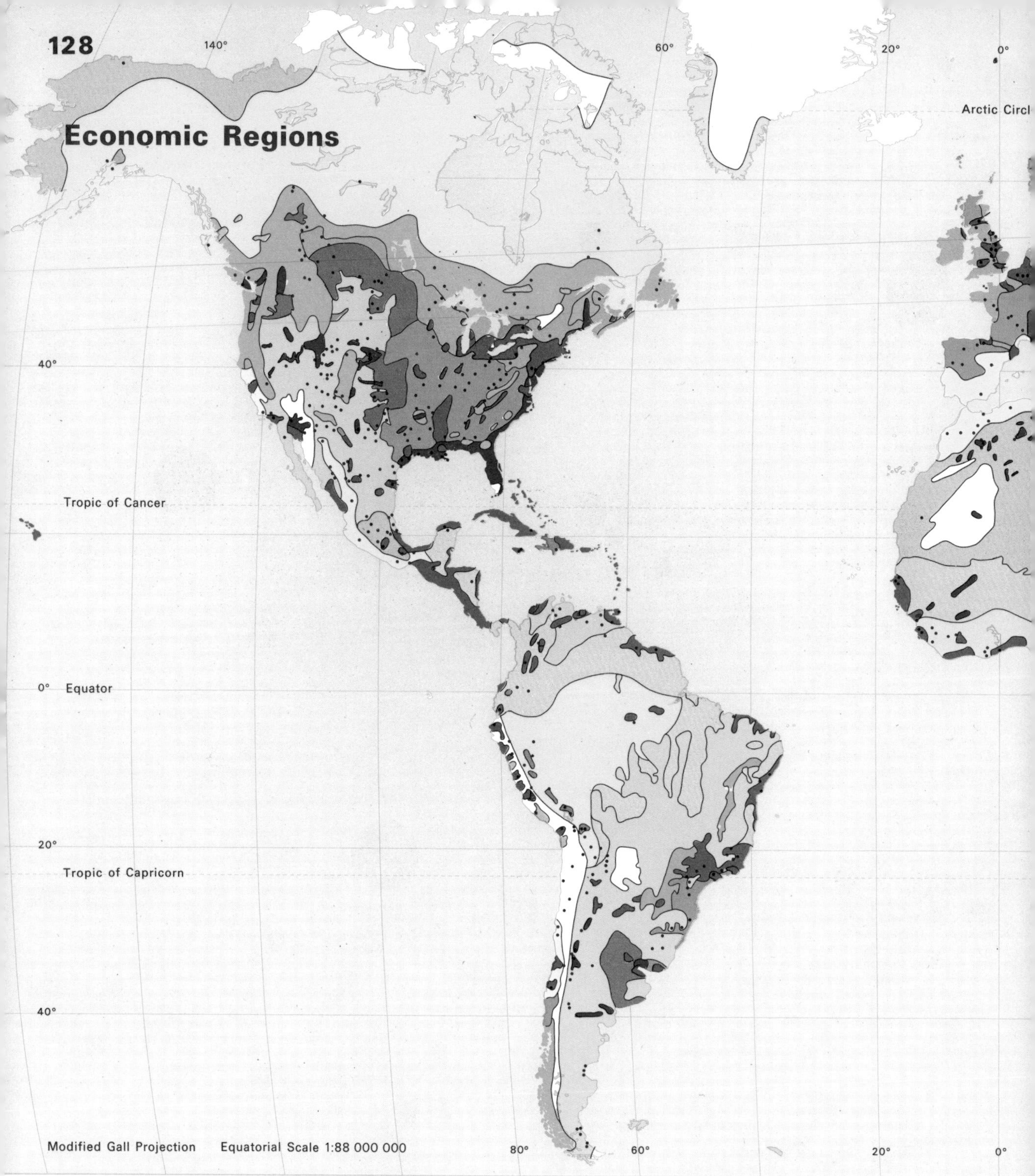

Economic Regions
140°
60°
20°
0°
Arctic Circl
40°
Tropic of Cancer
0° Equator
20°
Tropic of Capricorn
40°
Modified Gall Projection Equatorial Scale 1:88 000 000
80°
60°
20°
0°

Economic regions (by predominant activity)

- Little or no economic activity
- Nomadic herding
- Hunting, gathering, fishing and primitive cultivation
- Shifting and marginal cultivation
- Commercial forestry
- Extensive grazing or stock raising
- Subsistence agriculture: rice dominant
- Subsistence agriculture: rice unimportant
- Subsistence agriculture: mixed crop and livestock
- Mediterranean agriculture
- Plantation crops
- Specialized horticulture
- Other commercial crops: grain dominant
- Commercial agriculture: mixed crop and livestock
- Dairy farming
- Manufacturing and service industries
- Mining and extractive industries

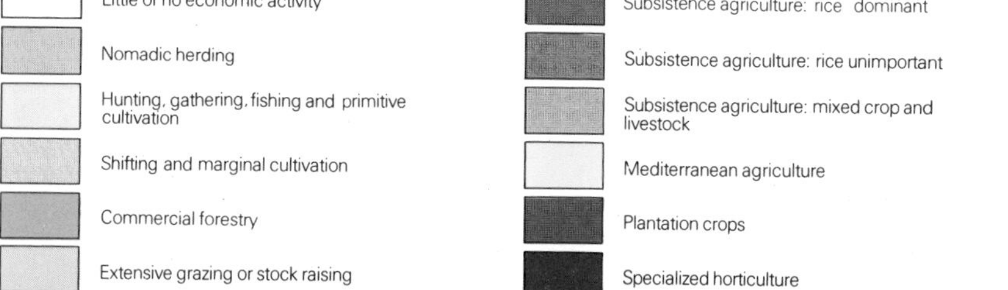

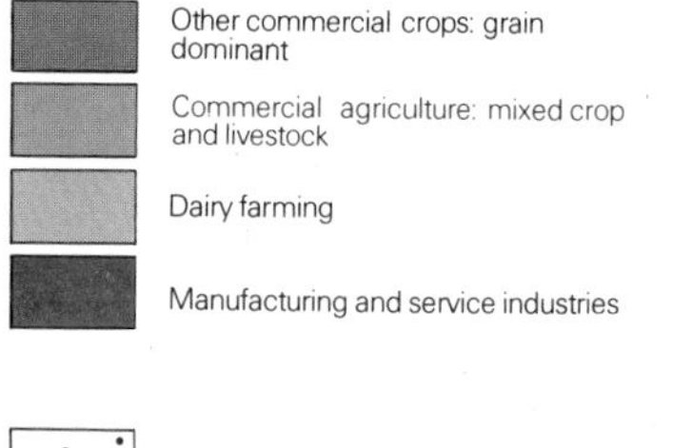

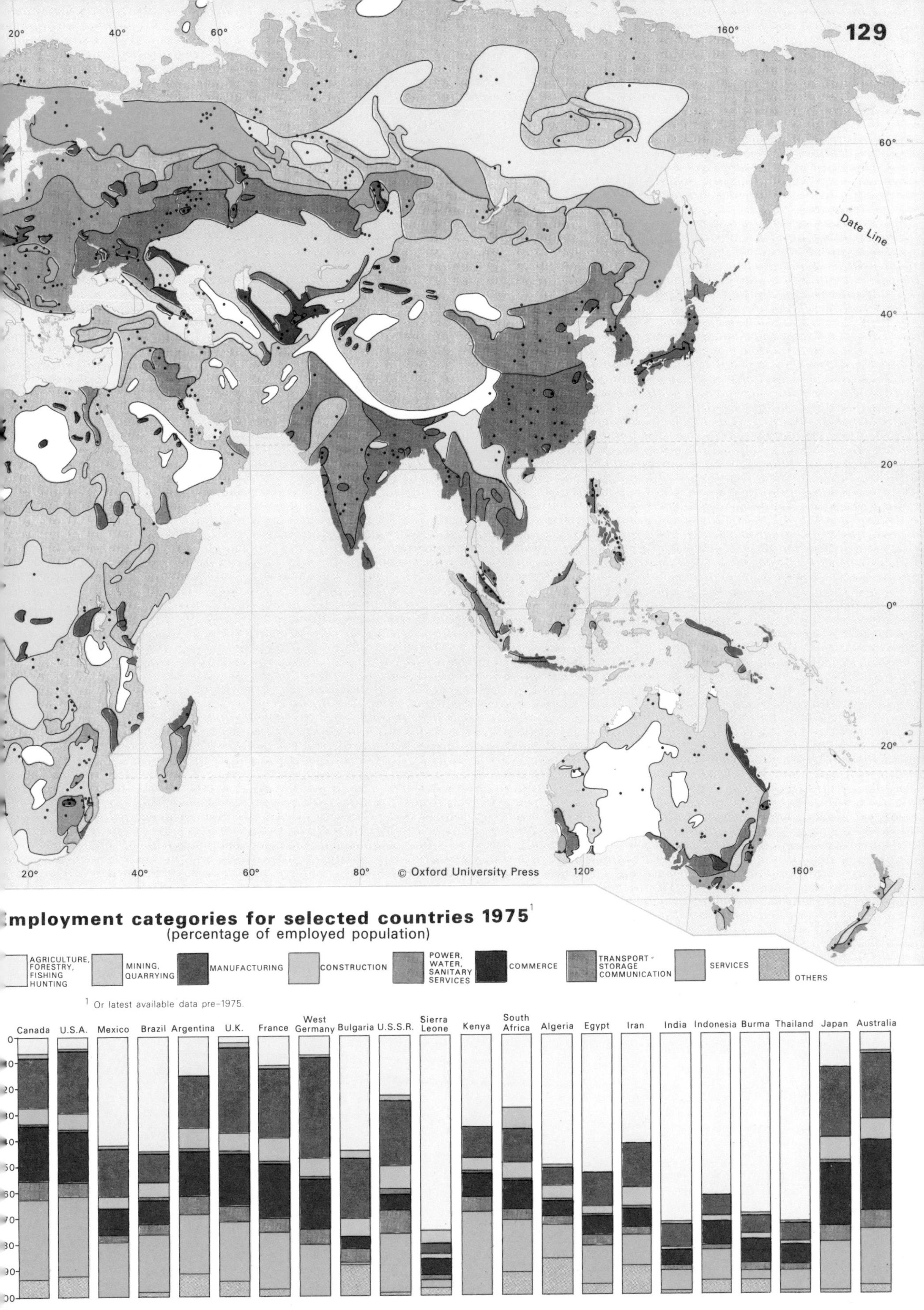

Employment categories for selected countries 1975[1]
(percentage of employed population)

AGRICULTURE, FORESTRY, FISHING HUNTING · MINING, QUARRYING · MANUFACTURING · CONSTRUCTION · POWER, WATER, SANITARY SERVICES · COMMERCE · TRANSPORT - STORAGE COMMUNICATION · SERVICES · OTHERS

[1] Or latest available data pre-1975.

World Political

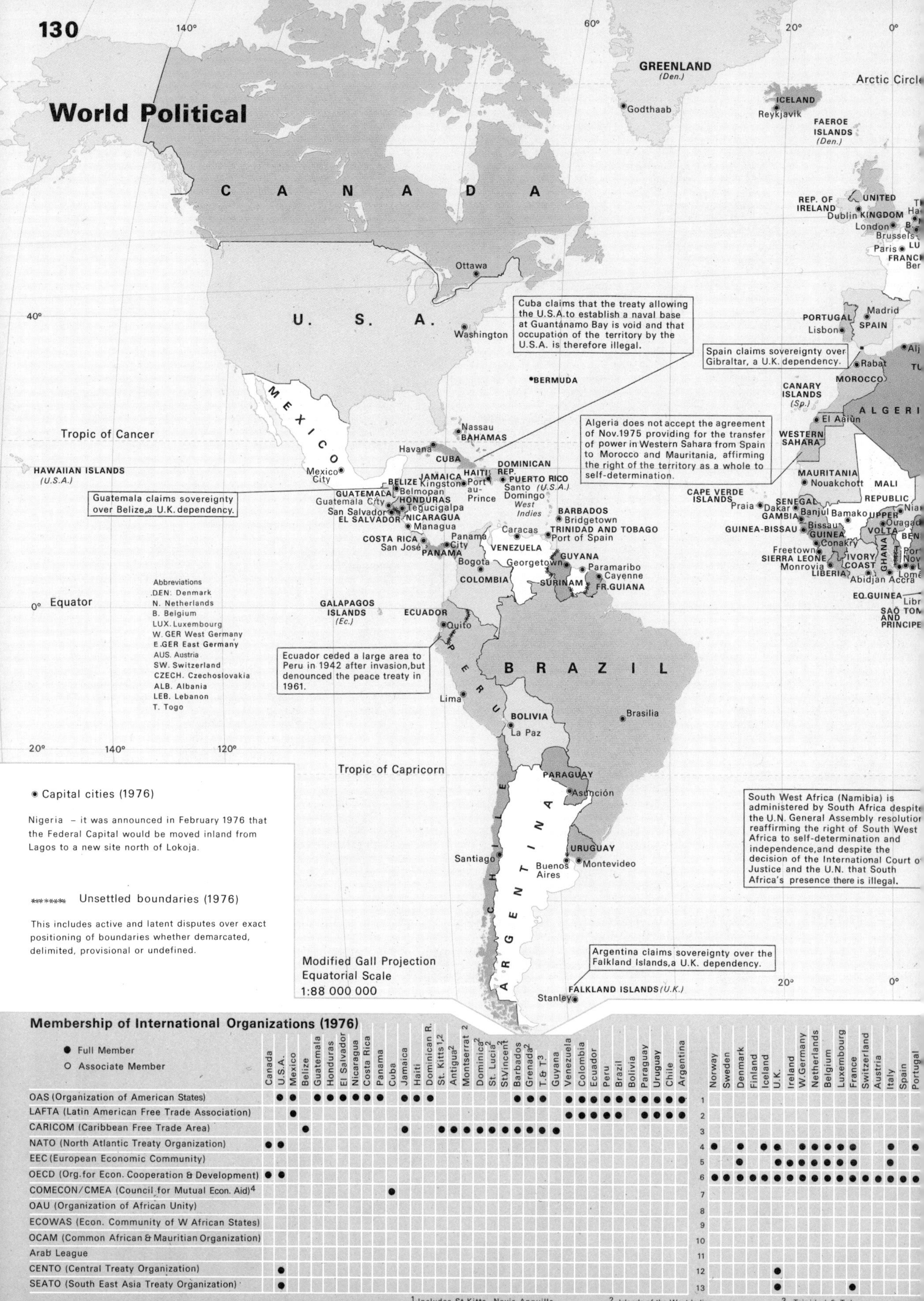

◉ Capital cities (1976)

Nigeria – it was announced in February 1976 that the Federal Capital would be moved inland from Lagos to a new site north of Lokoja.

******* Unsettled boundaries (1976)

This includes active and latent disputes over exact positioning of boundaries whether demarcated, delimited, provisional or undefined.

Membership of International Organizations (1976)

● Full Member
○ Associate Member

Organization	Canada	U.S.A.	Mexico	Belize	Guatemala	Honduras	El Salvador	Nicaragua	Costa Rica	Panama	Cuba	Jamaica	Haiti	Dominican R.	St. Kitts[1,2]	Antigua[2]	Montserrat[2]
OAS (Organization of American States)		●	●		●	●	●	●	●	●		●	●	●			
LAFTA (Latin American Free Trade Association)			●														
CARICOM (Caribbean Free Trade Area)				●								●			●	●	●
NATO (North Atlantic Treaty Organization)	●	●															
EEC (European Economic Community)																	
OECD (Org. for Econ. Cooperation & Development)	●	●															
COMECON/CMEA (Council for Mutual Econ. Aid)[4]											●						
OAU (Organization of African Unity)																	
ECOWAS (Econ. Community of W African States)																	
OCAM (Common African & Mauritian Organization)																	
Arab League																	
CENTO (Central Treaty Organization)		●															
SEATO (South East Asia Treaty Organization)		●															

Organization	Dominica[2]	St. Lucia[2]	St.Vincent[2]	Barbados	Grenada[2]	T.& T[3]	Guyana	Venezuela	Colombia	Ecuador	Peru	Brazil	Bolivia	Paraguay	Uruguay	Chile	Argentina
OAS (Organization of American States)				●	●	●		●	●	●	●	●	●	●	●	●	●
LAFTA (Latin American Free Trade Association)								●	●	●	●	●		●	●	●	●
CARICOM (Caribbean Free Trade Area)	●	●	●	●	●	●	●										
NATO (North Atlantic Treaty Organization)																	
EEC (European Economic Community)																	
OECD (Org. for Econ. Cooperation & Development)																	
COMECON/CMEA (Council for Mutual Econ. Aid)[4]																	
OAU (Organization of African Unity)																	
ECOWAS (Econ. Community of W African States)																	
OCAM (Common African & Mauritian Organization)																	
Arab League																	
CENTO (Central Treaty Organization)																	
SEATO (South East Asia Treaty Organization)																	

	Norway	Sweden	Denmark	Finland	Iceland	U.K.	Ireland	W.Germany	Netherlands	Belgium	Luxembourg	France	Switzerland	Austria	Italy	Spain	Portugal
1																	
2																	
3																	
4	●		●		●	●		●	●	●	●	●			●		●
5			●			●	●	●	●	●	●	●			●		
6	●	●	●	●	●	●	●	●	●	●	●	●	●	●	●	●	●
7																	
8																	
9																	
10																	
11																	
12						●											
13						●						●					

1 Includes St.Kitts-Nevis-Anguilla 2 Islands of the West Indies 3 Trinidad & Tobago

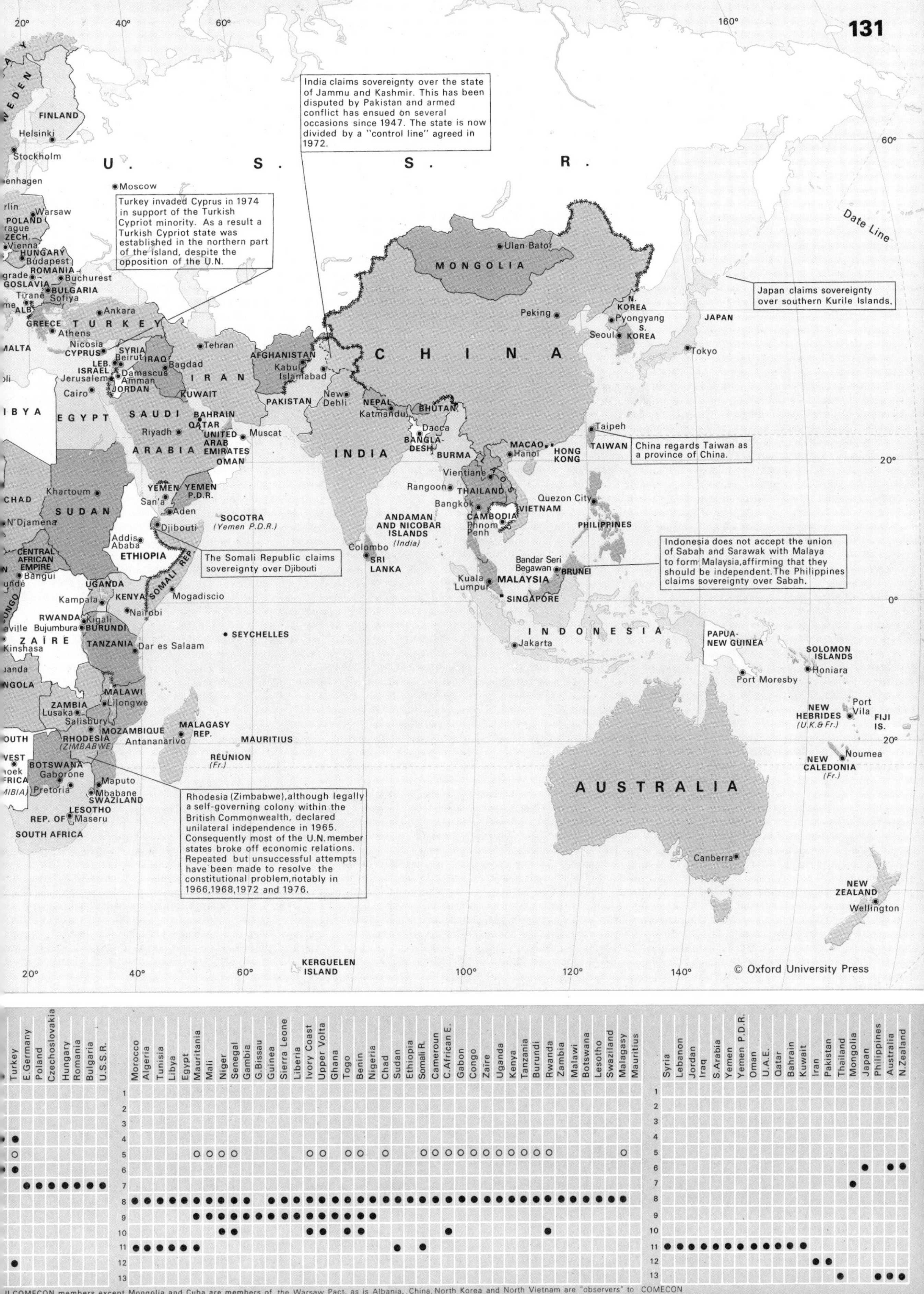

	Turkey	E.Germany	Poland	Czechoslovakia	Hungary	Romania	Bulgaria	U.S.S.R.
1								
2								
3								
4	●							
5	○							
6	●							
7		●	●	●	●	●	●	●
8								
9								
10								
11								
12	●							
13								

	Morocco	Algeria	Tunisia	Libya	Egypt	Mauritania	Mali	Niger	Senegal	Gambia	G.Bissau	Guinea	Sierra Leone	Liberia	Ivory Coast	Upper Volta	Ghana	Togo	Benin	Nigeria
1																				
2																				
3																				
4																				
5						○	○	○	○						○	○		○	○	
6																				
7																				
8	●	●	●	●	●	●	●	●	●	●		●	●	●	●	●	●	●	●	●
9						●	●	●	●	●	●	●	●	●	●	●	●	●	●	●
10								●	●						●	●		●	●	
11	●	●	●	●	●	●														
12																				
13																				

	Chad	Sudan	Ethiopia	Somali R.	Cameroun	C.African E.	Gabon	Congo	Zaïre	Uganda	Kenya	Tanzania	Burundi	Rwanda	Zambia	Malawi	Botswana	Lesotho	Swaziland	Malagasy	Mauritius
1																					
2																					
3																					
4																					
5	○			○	○	○	○	○	○	○	○	○	○	○						○	
6																					
7																					
8	●	●	●	●	●	●	●	●	●	●	●	●	●	●	●	●	●	●	●	●	
9																					
10						●								●							
11		●		●																	
12																					
13																					

	Syria	Lebanon	Jordan	Iraq	S.Arabia	Yemen	Yemen P.D.R.	Oman	U.A.E.	Qatar	Bahrain	Kuwait	Iran	Pakistan	Thailand	Mongolia	Japan	Philippines	Australia	N.Zealand
1																				
2																				
3																				
4																				
5																				
6																	●		●	●
7																●				
8																				
9																				
10																				
11	●	●	●	●	●	●	●	●	●	●	●	●								
12													●	●						
13															●			●	●	●

ll COMECON members except Mongolia and Cuba are members of the Warsaw Pact, as is Albania. China, North Korea and North Vietnam are "observers" to COMECON

Population Distribution and Growth

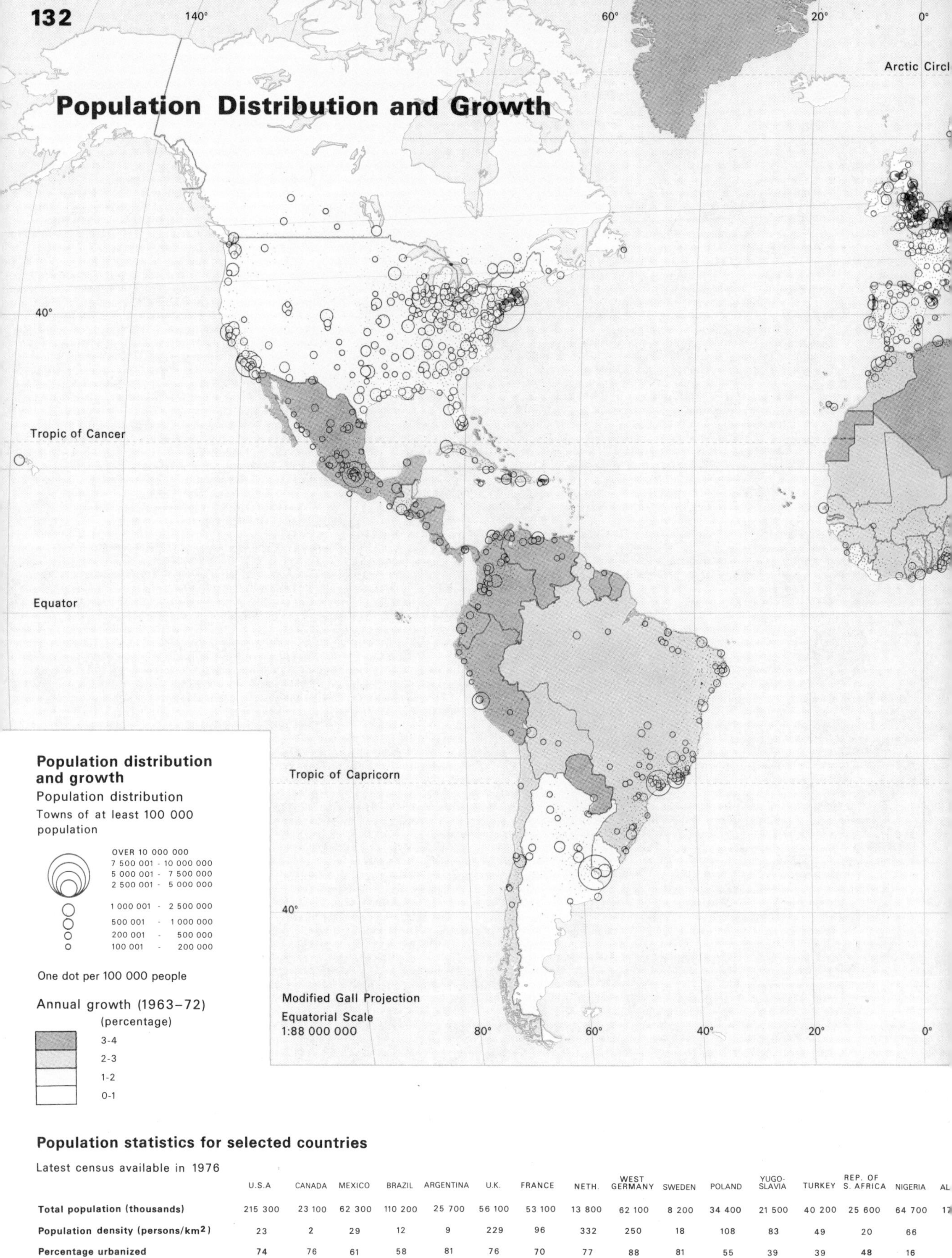

Population statistics for selected countries

Latest census available in 1976

	U.S.A	CANADA	MEXICO	BRAZIL	ARGENTINA	U.K.	FRANCE	NETH.	WEST GERMANY	SWEDEN	POLAND	YUGO-SLAVIA	TURKEY	REP. OF S. AFRICA	NIGERIA	AL
Total population (thousands)	215 300	23 100	62 300	110 200	25 700	56 100	53 100	13 800	62 100	8 200	34 400	21 500	40 200	25 600	64 700	17
Population density (persons/km²)	23	2	29	12	9	229	96	332	250	18	108	83	49	20	66	
Percentage urbanized	74	76	61	58	81	76	70	77	88	81	55	39	39	48	16	
Size of largest urban agglomeration (thousands)	11 571	2 553	7 314	5 186	8 352	7 379	7 369	1 063	2 134	1 344	1 308	565	2 052	1 969	900	9

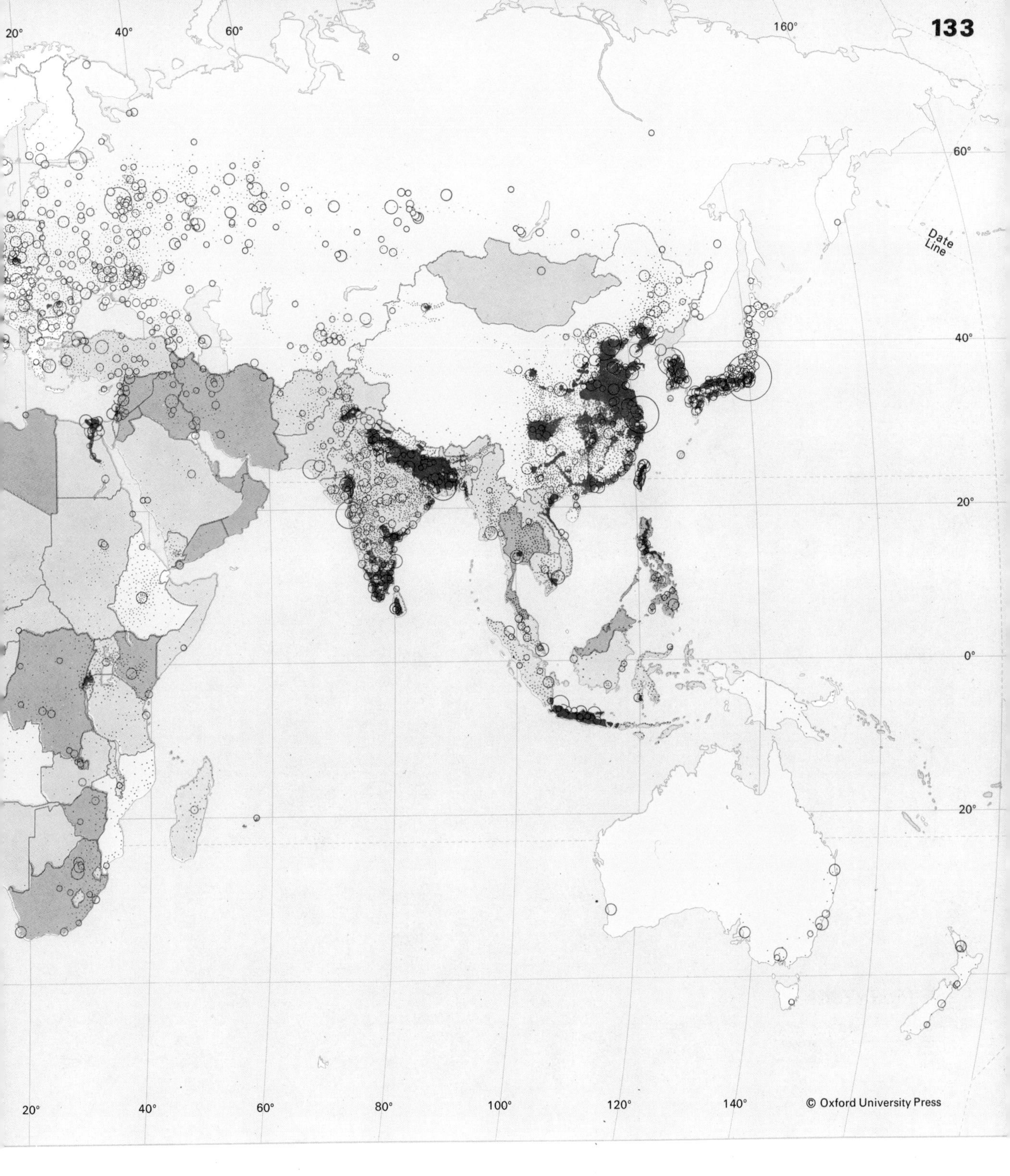

PIA	EGYPT	SAUDI ARABIA	ISRAEL	IRAQ	INDIA	BURMA	THAILAND	CAMBODIA	MALAYSIA	INDO-NESIA	PHILIPPINES	CHINA	TAIWAN	JAPAN	U.S.S.R.	AUSTRALIA
00	38 100	6 400	3 500	11 400	620 700	31 200	43 300	8 300	12 400	134 700	44 000	836 800	16 300	112 300	257 000	13 800
2	36	4	159	25	178	45	80	44	35	86	138	86	433	295	12	2
1	43	18	86	61	20	19	13	19	27	18	32	23	63	72	60	86
96	4 961	225	838	1 657	7 005	1 718	1 867	1 800	452	4 576	1 377	10 820	1 155	11 454	7 172	2 717

Nutrition

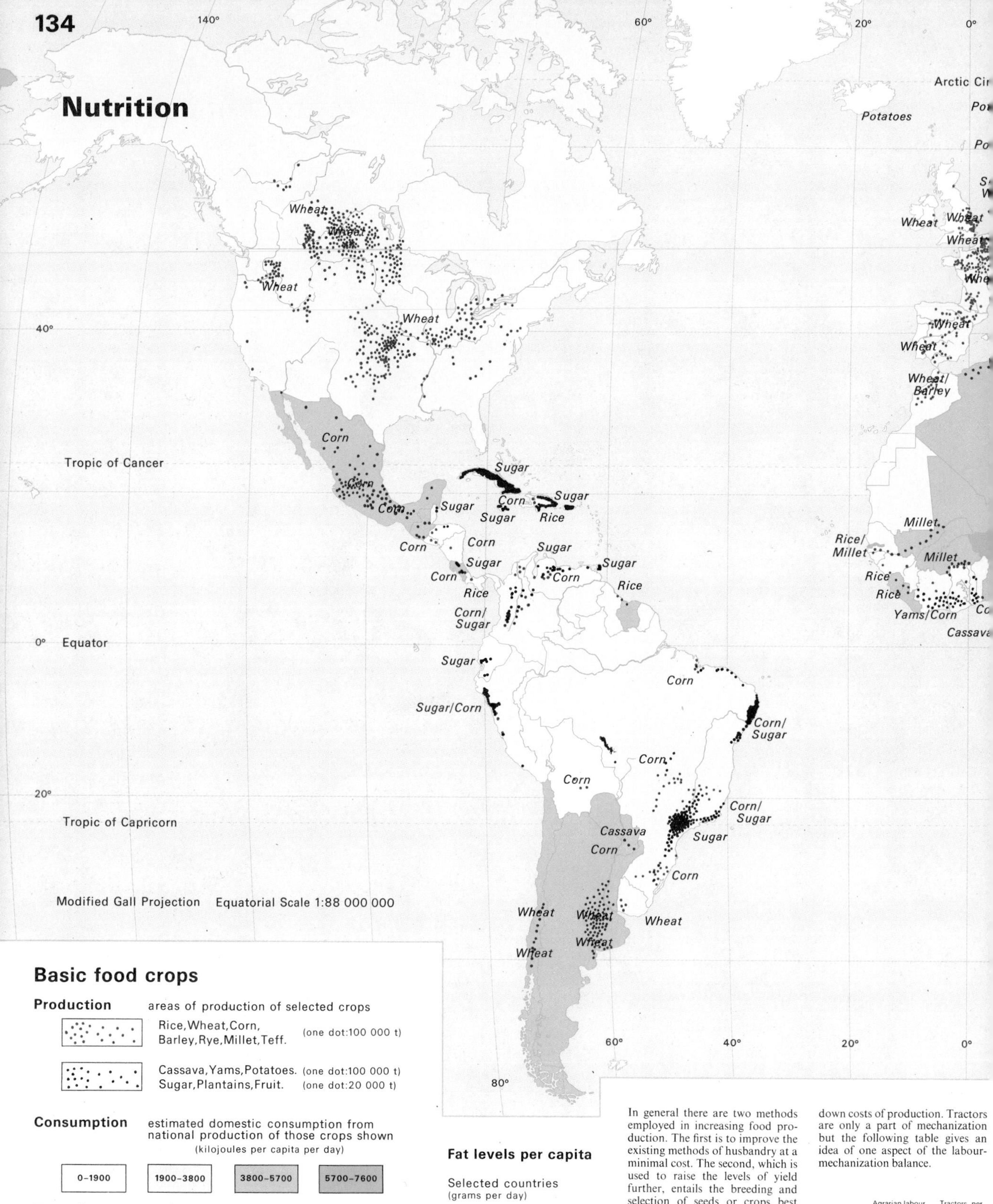

Basic food crops

Production areas of production of selected crops

Rice, Wheat, Corn, Barley, Rye, Millet, Teff. (one dot:100 000 t)

Cassava, Yams, Potatoes. (one dot:100 000 t)
Sugar, Plantains, Fruit. (one dot:20 000 t)

Consumption estimated domestic consumption from national production of those crops shown (kilojoules per capita per day)

0–1900 | 1900–3800 | 3800–5700 | 5700–7600

For each country are shown per capita domestic consumption and areas of production for one or more basic food crop. The crops selected are those carbohydrates which contribute the highest number of kilojoules per capita of any home-grown crop. Selection has been based on national averages, and does not take account of regional or other variations.
Further crops are shown for a country if the contribution to the national average kilojoule intake is at least 75% of that of the first crop selected. When this occurs, the consumption category is based on the aggregate for all crops shown; for example, in Brazil rice provides 2000 kJ/d and sugar 1660 (83% of the rice). Both crops are mapped and kilojoule intake is given as 3650 kJ/d

Fat levels per capita

Selected countries (grams per day)

West Germany	163.6
U.S.A.	159.2
Canada	147.2
U.K.	142.3
Argentina	129.5
U.S.S.R.	74.5
South Africa	66.2
Venezuela	63.3
Japan	51.9
Nigeria	48.7
Iraq	36.7
Bolivia	33.9
Algeria	28.7
India	25.9
Laos	13.6

In general there are two methods employed in increasing food production. The first is to improve the existing methods of husbandry at a minimal cost. The second, which is used to raise the levels of yield further, entails the breeding and selection of seeds or crops best fitted to the environment coupled with the efficient use of fertilizers, pesticides and farm mechanization. Increased productivity of the agrarian labour force is also a requirement. In some areas a high level of mechanization is essential to ensure that the crops are sown and harvested at the right times, as in the Canadian wheat belt. In other regions where, as a consequence of industrialization, farm workers must be paid high wages, mechanization is essential to keep down costs of production. Tractors are only a part of mechanization but the following table gives an idea of one aspect of the labour-mechanization balance.

	Agrarian labour as % of total	Tractors per arable 10 000 ha
India	72.0	11
Thailand	71.8	10
Ghana	58.4	11
Bulgaria	44.4	160
Brazil	44.3	55
Peru	40.6	41
Kenya	34.8	33
Jordan	33.7	24
U.S.S.R.	26.3	94
Japan	12.8	536
New Zealand	11.8	1 177
Netherlands	8.1	2 031
Canada	6.0	143
U.S.A.	4.0	215
U.K.	2.5	634

Estimated megajoules per capita per day

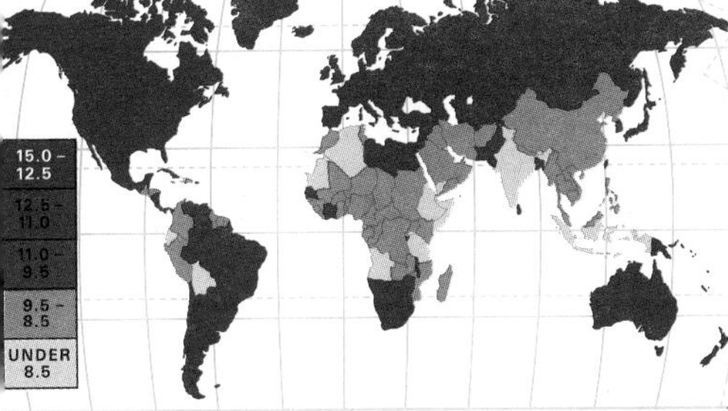

Estimated minimum megajoule requirement to avoid malnutrition, by region

Region	
Europe[1]	10.8
North America	10.8
Latin America	10.1
Middle East	10.0
Africa	9.8
Asia[2]	9.6

Estimated grams per day of protein available, by region

Region	
North America	93
Europe[1]	88
Middle East	76
Latin America	67
Africa	61
Asia[2]	56

[1]Incl. U.S.S.R. [2]Incl. China

Estimated protein per capita (grams per day)

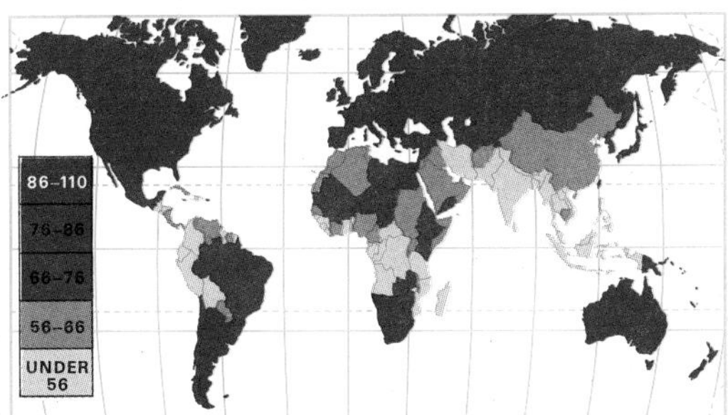

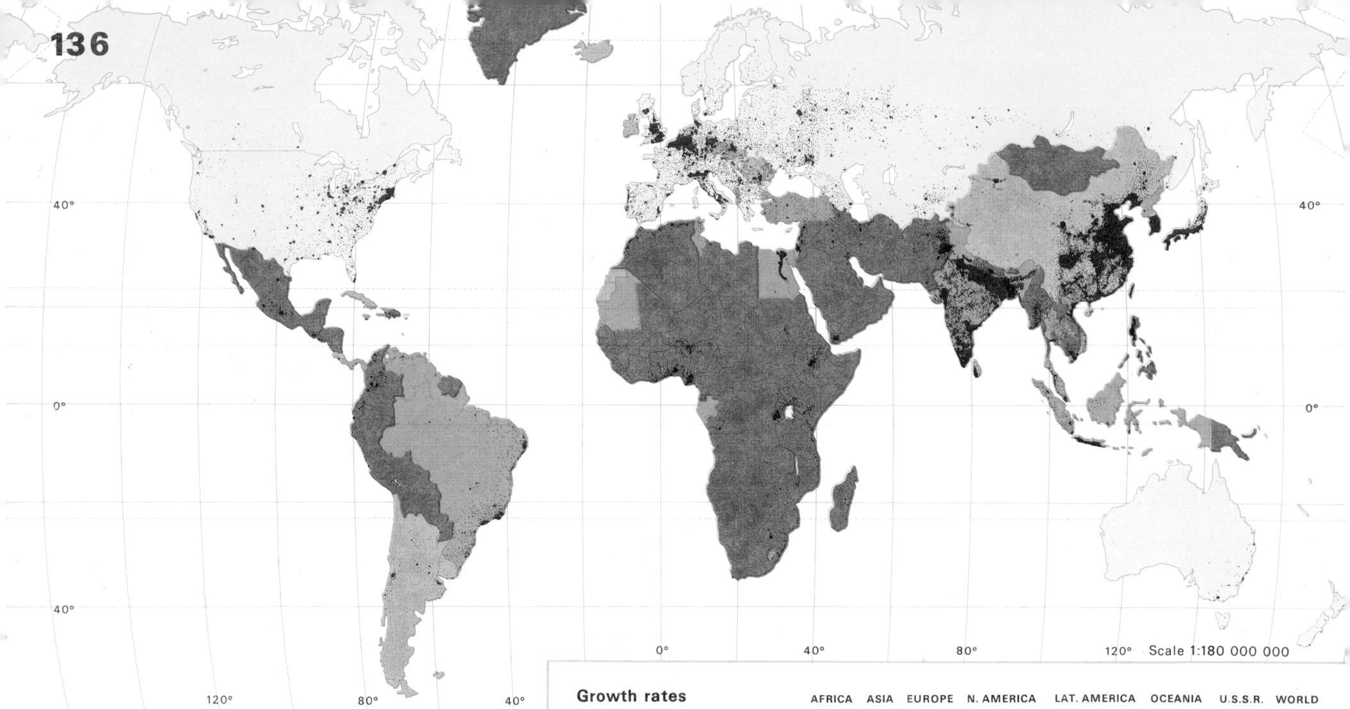

40° 40°
0° 0°
40°
0° 40° 80° 120° Scale 1:180 000 000
120° 80° 40°

Crude birth rate

Annual rate per thousand people (latest available data pre-1975)

	40 & OVER		20 – 30
	30 – 40		10 – 20

One dot to 100 000 population

Data for much of Asia, Africa, Latin America and Oceania are of dubious reliability. Comparison between *any* countries should be treated with care. The extent and type of survey, variation in basis and year of data will all affect the rate.

Growth rates

		AFRICA	ASIA	EUROPE	N. AMERICA	LAT. AMERICA	OCEANIA	U.S.S.R.	WORLD
Population (millions)	1950	*222*	*1 381*	*392*	*166*	*163*	*13*	*180*	*2 517*
	1960	318	1 868	449	217	253	18	233	3 356
	1976	*413*	*2 287*	*476*	*239*	*326*	*22*	*257*	*4 019*
Av. annual birth rate (‰)	1960–66	46	38	18	22	41	26	22	34
	1970–75	*46*	*33*	*15*	*15*	*37*	*22*	*18*	*30*
Av. annual death rate (‰)	1960–66	23	18	10	9	13	11	7	16
	1970–75	*20*	*13*	*10*	*9*	*9*	*10*	*9*	*12*
Av. rate of population increase (%)	1960–66	2.3	2.3	0.9	1.5	2.8	2.1	1.4	1.9
	1970–75	*2.6*	*2.0*	*0.6*	*0.8*	*2.8*	*1.8*	*0.9*	*1.8*

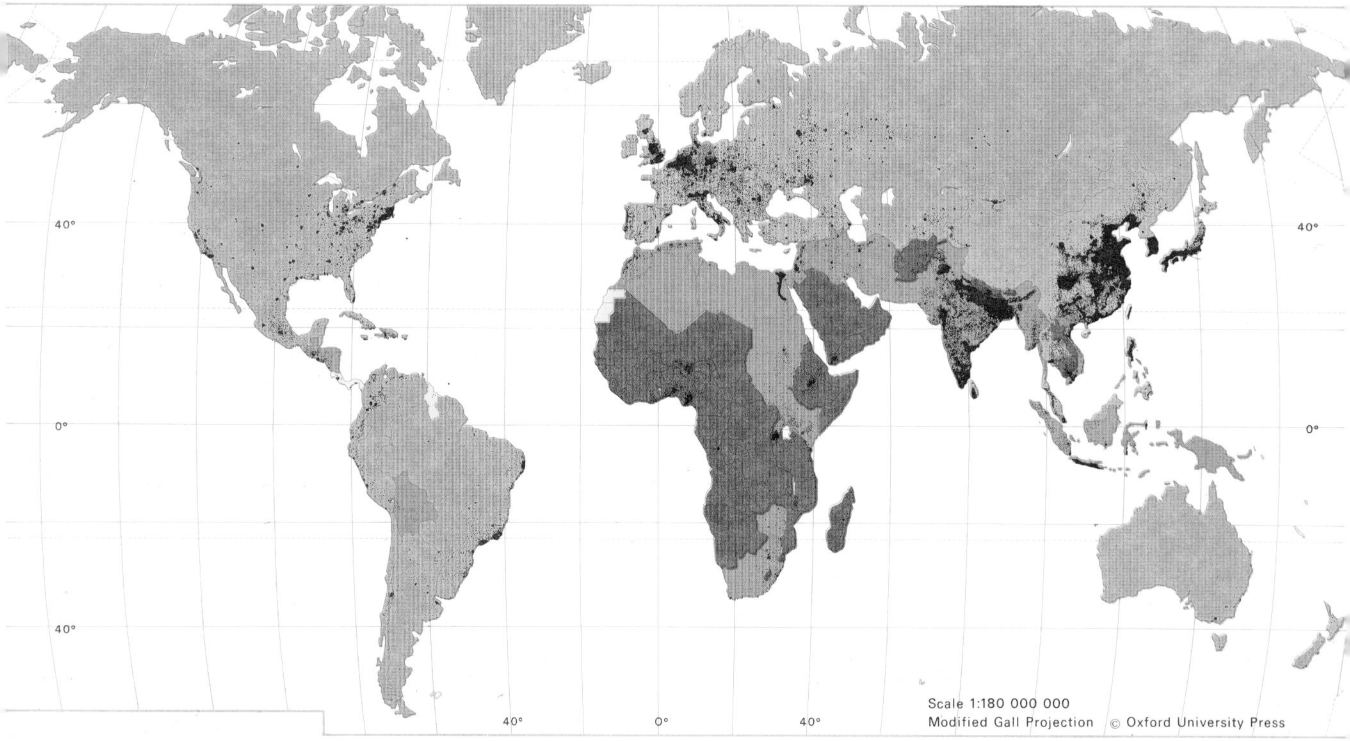

40° 40°
0° 0°
40°
40° 0° 40°

Scale 1:180 000 000
Modified Gall Projection

Crude death rate

Annual rate per thousand people (latest available data pre-1975)

	18 & OVER		6 – 12
	12 – 18		UNDER 6

One dot to 100 000 population

There are many difficulties in obtaining accurate mortality statistics. A major problem is the variation among countries in the basis of tabulation, that is, by date of occurrence or by date of registration. If registration is prompt the difference is slight, but if registration is delayed internationally comparable data will not be produced, especially since the number of events registered may vary due to temporary incentives to encourage registration. There is also a real danger of excluding the deaths of infants who died before registration of their births. Large areas of Latin America, North Africa, the Middle East and Asia are particularly suspect.

Although death rates are still high in many developing nations, great advances are being made with the introduction of advanced medical methods such as in the campaign to fight malaria in Ceylon which started in 1946. The rapidly falling death rates, which are linked with medical technology and socio-political organization, are not matched by equally declining birth rates, which are more responsive to cultural conditions.

Ceylon Death rates

1921–25	27.8
1940–44	19.7
1946	19.8
1948	12.9
1955	10.8
1965	8.1
1975	8.0

Gazetteers

Notes

This atlas has two gazetteers. The Gazetteer of Canada, which covers the topographical maps of Canada (pages 12-31) and the urban plans of Montréal, Ottawa and Toronto (page 32), Winnipeg (page 33) and Vancouver (page 36), is exhaustive and lists all the names shown on the maps. Entries without page numbers are places which do not appear on the maps but their location may be deduced from their latitude and longitude or found by reference to the *Canadian Oxford Atlas*. The World Gazetteer is selective and only lists the more important places and features so the absence of a name in the gazetteer does not necessarily mean that the place or feature is not shown on the map.

All entries are gazetteered to the largest scale map on which the feature appears in its entirety. The geographical co-ordinates are given to the nearest whole degree, thus:

Åland Is.: Finland. Co-ordinates to degrees and minutes: 60°15′N 20°00′E. Gazetteered to 60N 20E.

Port Elizabeth: S.Africa. Co-ordinates to degrees and minutes: 33°58′S 25°36′E. Gazetteered to 34S 26E.

Entries in capital letters denote provincial capitals in Canada (thus: TORONTO) or country capitals in the rest of the world.

Entries in bold face capitals denote countries (thus: **JAPAN**).

Abbreviations

The following abbreviations have been used on the maps and in the gazetteers.

A.C.T. — Australian Capital Territory
admin. — administrative
Afghan. — Afghanistan
Afr. — Africa
Ala. — Alabama
Alg. — Algeria
Alta. — Alberta
Antarc. — Antarctica
A.R. — Autonomous Republic
Arch. — Archipelago
Arab. Sea — Arabian Sea
Arg. — Argentina
Ariz. — Arizona
Ark. — Arkansas
Atl. O. — Atlantic Ocean
Aust. — Austria
Austl. — Australia
B., b. — Baie, Bay
Bangl. — Bangladesh
B.C. — British Columbia
Beds. — Bedfordshire
Belg. — Belgium
Berks. — Berkshire
Bol. — Bolivia
Bots. — Botswana
Br. — British
Braz. — Brazil
Bucks. — Buckinghamshire
Bulg. — Bulgaria
C., c. — Cape, Cabo
Calif. — California
Can. — Canada
cap. — capital
Carib. Sea — Caribbean Sea
Chan. — Channel
Co. — County
Col. — Colombia
Colo. — Colorado
Conn. — Connecticut
C.R. — Costa Rica
Cumb. — Cumbria
Czech. — Czechoslovakia
D.C. — District of Columbia
Del. — Delaware
Den. — Denmark
dep. — depression
Derby. — Derbyshire
dist. — district
Dom. Repub. — Dominican Republic
Dumfr. & Gall. — Dumfries and Galloway
E. — East, Eastern
Ec. — Ecuador
Eng. — England
Eq. — Equatorial
Eth. — Ethiopia
Eur. — Europe
Fd. — Fjord
Fed. — Federal, Federation
Fin. — Finland
Fla. — Florida
Fr. — France, French
Ft. — Fort
G. — Gulf
Ga. — Georgia (U.S.A.)
geog. — geographical
Ger. — German, Germany
Gl. — Glacier
Glos. — Gloucestershire
Gramp. — Grampian
Grnld. — Greenland
Gt. — Great, Greater
Hd. — Head
Herts. — Hertfordshire
Har., Harb. — Harbour
hist. — historical
Hond. — Honduras
Hung. — Hungary
I.(s), i.(s) — island(s)
Ice. — Iceland
Ill. — Illinois
Ind. — Indiana
Ind. O. — Indian Ocean
Indon. — Indonesia
Int. — International
Irel. — Ireland
Jam. — Jamaica
Kans. — Kansas
Ky. — Kentucky
L. — Lago, Lake, Loch
La. — Louisiana
Labr. — Labrador
Lag. — Lagoon
Lancs. — Lancashire
Les. — Lesotho
Lux. — Luxembourg
Mal. — Malaysia
Malag. — Malagasy
Man. — Manitoba
Mass. — Massachusetts
Maur. — Mauritania
Md. — Maryland
Medit. — Mediterranean
Mex. — Mexico
Mich. — Michigan
Minn. — Minnesota
Miss. — Mississippi
Mo. — Missouri
Mong. — Mongolia
Mont. — Montana
Mor. — Morocco
Moz. — Mozambique
Mt.(n) — Mount, Mountain
Mtns. — Mountains
N. — North, Northern
N.B. — New Brunswick
N.C. — North Carolina
N. Dak. — North Dakota
Nebr. — Nebraska
Neth. — Netherlands
Nev. — Nevada
Nfld. — Newfoundland
N.H. — New Hampshire
Nic. — Nicaragua
Nig. — Nigeria
N.J. — New Jersey
N.M. — New Mexico
Nor. — Norway
Northants. — Northhamptonshire
Notts. — Nottinghamshire
N.S. — Nova Scotia
N.W.T. — Northwest Territories
N.Y. — New York
N.Z. — New Zealand
O. — Ocean
Okla. — Oklahoma
Ont. — Ontario
Oreg. — Oregon
P. — Pass
Pa. — Pennsylvania
Pac. O. — Pacific Ocean
Pak. — Pakistan
P.E.I. — Prince Edward Island
Penin. — Peninsula
Phil. — Philippines
Pk. — Peak
Plat. — Plateau
Pol. — Poland
Port. — Portugal, Portuguese
Prov. — Province
Pt.(e) — Point (e)
Pto. — Puerto
Qué. — Québec
R., r. — River, rivière
R., Rep., Repub. — Republic
Reg. — Region
Res. — Reservoir
Rhod. — Rhodesia
R.I. — Rhode Island
Rom. — Romania
R.S.F.S.R. — Russian Soviet Federated Socialist Republic
S. — South, Southern
S. Am. — South America
Sask. — Saskatchewan
Sau. Arab. — Saudi Arabia
S.C. — South Carolina
Scot. — Scotland
Sd. — Sound
S. Dak. — South Dakota
sett. — settlement
Som. Rep. — Somali Republic
Sp. — Spain, Spanish
S.S.R. — Soviet Socialist Republic
St.(e) — Saint (e)
Str. — Strait
Sud. — Sudan
Suff. — Suffolk
Swed. — Sweden
Switz. — Switzerland
Tanzan. — Tanzania
Tenn. — Tennessee
Territ. — Territory
Tex. — Texas
Thai. — Thailand
Tur. — Turkey
U.A.E. — United Arab Emirates
U.S.A. — United States of America
U.S.S.R. — Union of Soviet Socialist Republics
Va. — Virginia
Venez. — Venezuela
volc. — volcano
Vt. — Vermont
W. — West, Western
Wash. — Washington
W. Ind. — West Indies
Wilts. — Wiltshire
Wisc. — Wisconsin
Worcs. — Worcestershire
W. Va. — West Virginia
Wyo. — Wyoming
Yemen A.R. — Yemen Arab Republic
Yemen P.D.R. — Yemen People's Democratic Republic
Yorks. — Yorkshire
Yugo. — Yugoslavia
Zim. — Zimbabwe

Gazetteer of Canada

	Page	N	W
Abbadie, Mt. d': Yukon		62	134
Abbotsford: B.C.	28	49	122
Aberdeen: Sask.	26	52	106
Aberdeen Lake: N.W.T.	31	65	99
Abitibi: *riv.*, Ont.	19	50	81
Abitibi, Lake: Ont./Qué.	19	49	80
Abitibi Game Reserve: Ont.		48	80
Abloviak Fiord: Qué.	14	59	66
Abord-à-Plouffe: Qué.	23	45	74
Acland Bay: N.W.T.	31	72	101
Aconi, Point: N.S.	17	46	60
Actinolite: Ont.	22	45	77
Acton: Ont.	20	44	80
Acton Vale: Qué.	21	45	72
Adams, Lake: B.C.	29	51	119
Adams Sound: N.W.T.	31	73	84
Adelaide Penin.: N.W.T.	31	68	98
Adlavik Is.: Nfld.		55	59
Admiralty Inlet: N.W.T.	31	73	85
Admiralty I.: N.W.T.	31	69	101
Adolphus Reach: Ont.	22	44	77
Agassiz: B.C.	28	49	121
Agawa Bay: Ont.		47	84
Agnew Lake: Ont.	20	46	82
Aguanish: Qué.	16	50	62
Aguanus: *riv.*, Qué.	15	51	62
Agu Bay: N.W.T.	31	70	87
Ahousat: B.C.		49	126
Aigneau: *riv.*, Qué.		57	70
Aigneau, Lac: Qué.		57	70
Aillik: Nfld.		55	59
Ainslie, Lake: N.S.	17	46	61
Airdrie: Alta.	26	51	114
Air Force I.: N.W.T.	14	68	75
Aishihik Lake: Yukon	30	62	138
Aiyansh: B.C.	28	55	129
Ajax: Ont.	22	44	79
Akimiski I.: N.W.T.	18	53	81
Aklavik: N.W.T.	30	68	135
Akpatok I.: Qué.	14	60	68
Alaskan Highway: Canada/U.S.A.	12	—	—
Albanel: Qué.	16	49	72
Albanel, Lac: Qué.	15	51	73
Albany: *riv.*, Ont.	19	51	85
Albert: N.B.	17	46	65
Alberta: *Prov.*, (*cap.* Edmonton)	26	—	—
Albert Edward Bay: N.W.T.	31	69	103
Alberton: P.E.I.	17	47	64
Alert: N.W.T.	13	83	63
Alexandra Falls: N.W.T.		60	116
Alexandria: Ont.	23	45	75
Alexis: *riv.*, Nfld.		53	57
Alexis Creek: *town*, B.C.	29	52	123
Alfred: Ont.	23	46	75
Alfred, Mt.: B.C.	28	50	124
Algonquin Park: *town*, Ont.		46	79
Algonquin Prov. Park: Ont.	20	46	78
Alix: Alta.	26	52	113
Allan: Sask.	27	52	105
Allanwater: Ont.		50	90
Allard, Lac: Qué.	15	51	64
Allenford: Ont.		44	81
Allison Harbour: B.C.	28	51	127
Alliston: Ont.	22	44	80
Allumettes, Île aux: Qué.		46	77
Alma: N.B.	17	45	65
Alma: Qué.	19	47	72
Almonte: Ont.	23	45	76
Alouette Lake: *and riv.*, British Columbia	28	49	122
Alsask: Sask.	26	51	110
Alsek: *riv.*, Yukon		60	138
Alsek Range: Yukon		59	137
Alta Lake: *town*, B.C.	28	50	123
Altona: Man.	27	49	97
Alvin: B.C.	28	50	122
Amadjuak Lake: N.W.T.	14	65	71
Amery: Man.	27	56	94
Amherst: N.S.	17	46	64
Amherstburg: Ont.	20	42	83
Amherst I.: Ont.	22	44	77
Amherst I.: Qué	16	47	62
Amherst View: Ont.	21	44	77
Amisk Lake: Sask.	27	54	102
Amitoke Penin.: N.W.T.	31	68	82
Amos: Qué.	20	48	78
Amqui: Qué.	16	48	68
Amund Ringnes I.: N.W.T.	13	78	97
Amundsen Gulf: N.W.T.	30	71	123
Amyot: Ont.		48	85
Ancaster: Ont.	22	43	80
Anderson: *riv.*, N.W.T.	30	69	128
Anderson Lake: B.C.	28	50	122
Anderson River Bird Sanctuary: N.W.T.	30	70	130
Andrew: Alta.	26	54	112
Andrew Gordon Bay: N.W.T.	14	64	75
Angers: Qué.	23	45	75
Angijak I.: N.W.T.	14	66	62
Angikuni Lake: N.W.T.	31	62	100
Anguille, Cape: Nfld.	17	48	59
Angus: Ont.	22	44	80
Annapolis Royal: N.S.	17	45	66
Annieopsquotch Mts.: Nfld.		48	57
Anstruther Lake: Ont.	22	45	78
Anticosti, Île d': Qué.	16	49	63
Antigonish: N.S.	17	46	62
Anuk, Lac: Qué.		59	75
Anvil Mts.: Yukon	30	62	133
Anyox: B.C.	28	55	130
Apsley: Ont.	22	45	78
Arborfield: Sask.	27	53	103
Arborg: Man.	27	51	97
Arcola: Sask.	27	50	103
Arctic Bay: *town*, N.W.T.	31	73	84
Arctic Red: *riv. & town*, N.W.T.	30	67	134
Arden: Ont.	22	45	77
Argentia: Nfld.	17	47	54
Arichat: N.S.	17	45	61
Aristazabal I.: B.C.	28	53	129
Armstrong: B.C.	29	50	119
Armstrong: Ont.	19	50	89
Arnold's Cove: Nfld.		48	54
Arnot: Man.	27	56	97
Arnprior: Ont.	23	45	76
Arntfield: Qué.	20	48	79
Arrow River: *town*, Man.	27	50	101
Arrowsmith, Mt.: B.C.	28	49	124
Arthabaska: Qué.	21	46	72
Arthur: Ont.	20	44	80
Artillery Lake: N.W.T.	31	63	108
Arvida: Qué.	21	48	71
Asbestos: Qué.	21	46	72
Ascot Corner: Qué.	21	45	72
Ashcroft: B.C.	29	51	121
Ashern: Man.	27	52	99
Asheweig: *riv.*, Ont.	18	54	90
Ashuanipi: Nfld.		53	66
Ashuanipi Lake: Nfld.	15	53	66
Ashuapmuchuan: *riv.*, Qué.	16	49	73
Ashville: Man.	27	51	100
Aspen Grove: B.C.		50	121
Aspy Bay: N.S.	17	47	60
Assiniboia: Sask.	27	49	106
Assiniboine: *riv.*, Sask./Man.	27	50	99
Assiniboine, Mt.: Alta./B.C.	29	51	116
Assinica, Lac: Qué.	15	50	75
Aston Bay: N.W.T.	31	74	95
Aston Junction: Qué.		46	72
Astray Lake: Nfld.		55	67
Athabasca: *& riv.*, Alta.	26	55	113
Athabasca, Lake: Alberta/Saskatchewan	26	59	109
Athelstan: Qué.	23	45	74
Athens: Ont.	23	45	76
Atherley: Ont.	22	45	79
Athol: N.S.	17	46	64
Atikokan: Ont.	19	48	91
Atikonak Lake: Nfld.	15	53	64
Atikwa Lake: Ont.	19	50	93
Atlin: *& lake*, B.C.	24	59	134
Atna Peak: B.C.	28	54	128
Attawapiskat: *& riv.*, Ont.	18	53	82
Attawapiskat Lake: Ont.	19	52	88
Attikamagen Lake: Nfld.	15	55	66
Aubert, Lac.: Qué.		55	71
Aubrey Falls: Ont.	20	47	83
Aubry Lake: N.W.T.	30	67	126
Aulneau Penin.: Ont.	27	49	94
Aurora: Ont.	22	44	79
Austin Channel: N.W.T.	31	75	103
Authier: Qué.		48	79
Aux Outardes: *riv.*, Qué.	15	49	68
Aux Pekans: *riv.*, Qué.		53	67
Aux Sables: *riv. & lake*, Ont.	20	46	82
Avalon, Isthmus of: Nfld.		48	54
Avalon Penin.: Nfld.	17	47	53
Aviron Bay: *town*, Nfld.		47	57
Avola: B.C.	29	52	119
Avon: *riv.*, N.S.	17	45	64
Avonmore: Ont.	22	45	75
Axel Heiberg I.: N.W.T.	13	80	90
Aylen Lake: Ont.		46	78
Aylesford: N.S.	17	45	65
Aylesworth, Mt.: U.S.A./Canada		60	139
Aylmer: Ont.	20	43	81
Aylmer: Qué.	32	45	76
Aylmer, Lake: N.W.T.	31	64	110
Aylmer, Lac: Qué.	21	46	71
Aylmer, Mt.: Alta.	26	51	115
Ayton: Ont.		44	81
Azure Lake: B.C.	29	52	120
Babine Lake: B.C.	29	55	126
Bacalieu I.: Nfld.		48	53
Back: *riv.*, N.W.T.	31	65	105
Backbone Ranges: N.W.T.	30	63	129
Baddeck: N.S.	17	46	61
Baden: Ont.	20	43	81
Badger: Nfld.	17	49	56
Baffin Bay: Canada/Grnld.	13	73	70
Baffin I.: N.W.T.	13	70	75
Bagotville: Qué.	21	48	71
Baie Comeau: Qué.	16	49	68
Baie des Sables: Qué.		48	68
Baie Ste. Catherine: Qué.		48	70
Baie Ste. Claire: Qué.	16	50	64
Baie St. Paul: Qué.	21	47	70
Baie Trinité: Qué.	16	49	67
Baillie: *riv.*, N.W.T.	31	65	106
Baillie Hamilton I.: N.W.T.	31	76	95
Baillie Is.: N.W.T.	30	71	128
Baine Harbour: Nfld.		47	55
Baird Penin.: N.W.T.	14	69	76
Baker Lake: *& settlement*, N.W.T.	31	64	96
Bakers Dozen Is.: N.W.T.	18	57	79
Bala: Ont.	22	45	80
Balcarres: Sask.	27	51	104
Baldock Lake: Man.	27	56	98
Baleine, R. à la: Qué.	15	57	67
Balgonie: Sask.	27	50	104
Ballard, Cape: Nfld.		47	53
Balmertown: Ont.	19	51	98
Balsam Lake: Ont.	22	45	79
Bamfield: B.C.	28	49	125
Bancroft: Ont.	20	45	78
Banff: Alta.	26	51	116
Banff National Park: Alta.	26	51	116
Banks I.: B.C.	28	53	130
Banks I.: N.W.T.	30	73	120
Banks I. Bird Sanctuary: N.W.T.	30	74	125
Bannockburn: Ont.	22	45	78
Baptiste Lake: Ont.		45	78
Baring, Cape: N.W.T.	30	70	117
Barkerville: B.C.	29	53	121
Bark Lake: Ont.		45	78
Bark Lake: Ont.	20	47	82
Barkley Sound: B.C.	28	49	125
Barraute: Qué.	20	48	77
Barrhead: Alta.	26	54	114
Barrie: Ont.	22	44	80
Barrie I.: Ont.	20	46	82
Barriere: B.C.	29	51	120
Barrière, Barrage de: Qué.	21	47	76
Barrington: N.S.	17	43	66
Barrington Lake: Man.	27	57	100
Barrow Head: Nfld.		49	54
Barrow Str.: N.W.T.	31	74	93
Barrys Bay: *town*, Ont.	20	45	78
Barton Lake: Ont.	27	52	94
Bashaw: Alta.	26	53	113
Basin Lake: Sask.	27	52	105
Baskatong, Réservoir: Qué.	21	47	76
Bassano: Alta.	26	51	112
Basseterre Pt.: Nfld.		47	56
Basswood L.: Ont.		48	92
Batchawana: *& riv.*, Ont.	20	47	84
Batchawana, Mt.: Ont.	20	47	84
Bath: N.B.	16	46	67
Bath: Ont.	22	44	77
Bathurst: N.B.	16	47	66
Bathurst, Cape: N.W.T.	30	71	128
Bathurst Inlet: *settlement*, N.W.T.	31	67	108
Bathurst I.: N.W.T.	31	76	100
Batiscan: Qué.		46	72
Batiscan: *riv.*, Qué.	21	47	72
Batteau: Nfld.		53	56
Battle: *riv.*, Alta.	26	53	110
Battleford: Sask.	26	53	108
Bauld, Cape: Nfld.		51	55
Bay Bulls: Nfld.	17	47	53
Bay de Verde: *town*, Nfld.		48	53
Bayfield: *& riv.*, Ont.	20	43	82
Bay Roberts: Nfld.	17	48	53
Bays, Lake of: Ont.	20	45	79
Bazin: *riv.*, Qué.	21	48	75
Beaconsfield: Qué.	32	45	74
Beale, Cape: B.C.	28	49	125
Beamsville: Ont.	20	43	79
Bear: *riv.*, Ont.	32	45	75
Bear, Cape: P.E.I.	17	46	62
Bear Bay: N.W.T.		76	87
Bear Creek: Ont.	20	43	82
Beardmore: Ont.		50	88
Bear Head: Qué.	16	49	62
Bear I.: Nfld.		47	57
Bear I.: N.W.T.	18	54	81
Bear Lake: *town*, B.C.	29	56	127
Bear Lake: Man.	27	55	96
Bear River: *town*, N.S.	17	45	66
Bearskin Lake: Ont.		54	91
Beatton: *riv.*, B.C.	29	57	121
Beauce, Lac à: Qué.	21	47	73
Beauceville: Qué.	21	46	71
Beauchêne: Qué.	20	46	79
Beaufort Sea: Arctic O.	12	73	140
Beauharnois: Qué.	23	45	74
Beauharnois Canal: Qué.	23	45	74
Beaumont: Nfld.		50	56
Beaupré: Qué.	21	47	71
Beauséjour: Man.	27	50	97
Beauval: Sask.	26	55	108
Beaver: *riv.*, Ont.	25	56	88
Beaver: *riv.*, Sask.	26	55	108
Beaverdell: B.C.	28	49	119
Beaverhill Lake: Alta.	26	53	112
Beaverhill Lake: Man.	27	54	95
Beaverlodge: Alta.	26	55	119
Beaverton: Ont.	22	44	79
Bécancour: *& riv.*, Qué.	21	46	72
Bedford: N.S.	17	45	64
Bedford: Qué.	21	45	73
Beechey Head: B.C.	28	48	123
Beeton: Ont.	22	44	80
Beiseker: Alta.	26	51	114
Belcher Is.: N.W.T.	18	56	79
Belcourt: Qué.	20	48	77
Bella Bella: B.C.	28	52	128
Bella Coola: *& riv.*, B.C.	29	52	127
Belle Bay: Nfld.	17	47	55
Belledune: N.B.	17	48	66
Belle Isle: Nfld.	15	52	55
Belle Isle, Str. of: Nfld.	15	51	57
Belle River: Ont.	20	42	83
Belleterre: Qué.	20	47	79
Belleville: Ont.	22	44	77
Bellevue: Alta.	26	50	114
Bellevue: Nfld.		47	54
Bell I.: Nfld.	17	48	53
Bell I.: Nfld.	15	51	55
Bellot Str.: N.W.T.	31	72	95
Bell Penin.: N.W.T.	14	64	82
Bells Corners: Ont.	32	45	76
Belly: *riv.*, Alta.	26	49	113
Belmont: N.S.	17	45	63
Beloeil: Qué.	22	46	73
Belot, Lac: N.W.T.	30	67	127
Bengough: Sask.	27	49	105
Benito: Man.	27	52	101
Bennett: B.C.	24	60	135
Bennett Lake: Yukon/B.C.		60	135
Bentley: Alta.	26	52	114
Berkley, Cape: N.W.T.	31	74	101
Berens River: *town & riv.*, Manitoba	27	52	97
Bereziuk Lac: Qué.		54	76
Berlinguet Inlet: N.W.T.	31	71	86
Bermen, Lac: Qué.	15	53	69
Bernard Lake, Ont.	22	46	79
Bernier Bay: N.W.T.	31	71	88
Bernierville: Qué.	21	46	74
Berrys Mills: N.B.	17	46	65
Berté, Lac: Qué.		51	68
Berwick: N.S.	17	45	65
Berwyn: Alta.	26	56	118
Bethany: Ont.	22	44	79
Betsiamites: *& riv.*, Qué.	19	49	69
Beverly Lake: N.W.T.	31	65	100
Bewdley: Ont.	22	44	78
Bic: Qué.		48	69
Bienfait: Sask.	27	49	103
Bienville, Lac: Qué.	15	55	73
Big: *riv.*, Nfld.		55	59
Big Bay Point: Lake Simcoe	22	44	79
Big Beaver Falls: Ont.		49	82
Big Beaver House: Ont.	18	53	90
Biggar: Sask.	26	52	108
Big Gull Lake: Ont.	22	45	77
Big I.: Nfld.		58	62
Big I.: Great Slave Lake, N.W.T.	30	61	117
Big I.: N.W.T.	30	63	71
Big Muddy Creek: Canada/U.S.A.		48	104
Big Muddy Lake: Sask.	27	49	105
Big River: *town*, Sask.	26	54	107
Big Salmon: *& riv.*, Yukon		62	135
Big Sand Lake: Man.	27	58	99
Big Stick Lake: Sask.	26	50	109
Bigstone Lake: Man.	27	54	96
Big Trout Lake: Ont.		46	79
Big Trout Lake: Ont.	18	54	90
Bigwood: Ont.	20	46	80
Billings, Mt.: Yukon		61	129
Bilodeau: Qué.		48	72
Birch: *riv.*, Alta.	26	58	113
Birch Hills: *town*, Sask.	27	53	105
Birch Island: *town*, Ont.	20	46	82
Birch Lake: Alta.	26	53	112
Birch Lake: Nfld.		54	66
Birch Mtns.: Alta.	26	57	113
Bird Creek: *town*, Ont.		45	78
Bird Rocks: *i.*, Qué.	17	48	61
Birds Hill: Man.	33	50	97
Birken: B.C.	28	50	122
Birtle: Man.	27	50	101
Biscotasing: Ont.		47	82
Bishops Falls: *town*, Nfld.	17	49	55
Biskotasi Lake: Ont.	20	47	82
Bissett: Ont.	20	46	78
Bistcho Lake: Alta.	24	60	119
Bittern Lake: *town*, Alta.		53	113
Bittern Lake: Sask.	27	54	106
Bitumount: Alta.		57	112
Bizard, I.: Qué.	32	45	74
Black: *riv.*, Ont.	20	48	80
Black, Mt.: Yukon		61	134
Black Bay: Ont.		48	88
Black Bear Bay: *town*, Nfld.		53	56
Black Bear Island Lake: Saskatchewan	27	55	105
Black Birch Lake: Sask.	26	57	108
Black Diamond: Alta.	26	51	114
Blackfalds: Alta.	26	52	114
Blackhead Bay: Nfld.		48	53
Black I.: Man.	27	51	96
Black Lake: *town*, Qué.	21	46	71
Black Lake: Sask.	27	59	105
Black Rock Point: Nfld.		60	64
Blacks Harbour: N.B.	17	46	67
Blackville: N.B.	16	47	66
Blackwater Lake: N.W.T.	30	64	123
Blaine Lake: *town*, Sask.	26	53	107
Blairmore: Alta.	26	50	114
Blanc Sablon: Qué.		51	57
Blenheim: Ont.	20	42	82
Blind River: *town*, Ont.	20	46	83
Bloedel: B.C.	28	50	125
Bloodvein: *riv.*, Man.	27	52	96

	Page	N	W
Bloomfield: Ont.	**22**	44	77
Blubber Bay: *town*, B.C.	**28**	50	125
Blue Mt.: Nfld.	**17**	50	57
Blue Mt.: Ont.	**20**	44	80
Bluenose Lake: N.W.T.	**30**	68	119
Blue Ridge: *town*, Alta.	**26**	54	115
Blue River: *town*, B.C.	**29**	52	119
Bluff, Cape: Nfld.		53	56
Blyth: Ont.	**20**	44	81
Boat Basin: *town*, B.C.		49	126
Bobcaygeon: Ont.	**22**	45	79
Bobs Lake: Ont.	**23**	45	77
Boiestown: N.B.	**16**	46	66
Bois, Lac des: N.W.T.	**30**	67	126
Boissevain: Man.	**27**	49	100
Boivin, Lac: Qué.		52	70
Boland: *riv.*, Ont.	**20**	46	82
Bolger: Qué.		48	76
Bolkow: Ont.	**20**	48	84
Bolton: Ont.	**22**	44	80
Bonaventure: Qué.	**16**	48	65
Bonaventure Head: Nfld.		48	53
Bonaventure, Île de: Qué.	**16**	48	64
Bonavista: Nfld.	**17**	49	53
Bonavista Bay: Nfld.	**17**	49	53
Bonfield: Ont.	**20**	46	79
Bonne Bay: Nfld.	**17**	49	58
Bonnechère: *riv.*, Ont.	**21**	45	77
Bonnet, Lac du: Man.	**27**	50	96
Bonnet Plume: *riv.*, Yukon	**30**	65	133
Bonnyville: Alta.	**26**	54	111
Boothia Penin.: N.W.T.	**13**	72	95
Boothia, G. of: N.W.T.	**31**	70	90
Borden: P.E.I.	**17**	46	64
Borden I.: N.W.T.	**12**	78	110
Borden Penin.: N.W.T.	**31**	73	82
Boston Creek: *town*, Ont.	**20**	48	80
Bostonnais: *riv.*, Qué.	**21**	47	72
Botwood: Nfld.	**17**	49	55
Boucherville: *& is.*, Qué.	**32**	46	73
Boundary: B.C.	**28**	57	132
Boundary Ranges: U.S.A./Canada		59	134
Bourget: Ont.	**23**	45	75
Bourkes: Ont.	**20**	48	80
Bourlamaque: Qué.	**15**	48	78
Bourmont: Qué.		48	76
Bow: *riv.*, Alta.	**26**	51	114
Bowden: Alta.	**26**	52	114
Bowdoin Canyon: Nfld.		53	64
Bowen I.: B.C.	**28**	49	123
Bowesville: Ont.	**23**	45	76
Bow Island: *town*, Alta.	**26**	50	111
Bowman Bay: N.W.T.	**14**	66	74
Bowmanville: Ont.	**22**	44	79
Bowness: Alta.	**26**	51	114
Bowron Lake Prov. Park: B.C.	**29**	54	122
Boxey Point: Nfld.		47	56
Boyd Lake: N.W.T.		61	103
Boyd, Lac: Qué.		53	77
Boyle: Alta.	**26**	54	113
Bracebridge: Ont.	**22**	45	79
Brackendale: B.C.	**28**	50	123
Bradford: Ont.	**22**	44	80
Braeburn: Yukon		61	136
Braeside: Ont.	**23**	45	76
Bralorne: B.C.	**28**	51	123
Brampton: Ont.	**22**	44	80
Branch: Nfld.	**17**	47	54
Brandon: Man.	**27**	50	100
Brantford: Ont.	**20**	43	80
Bras d'Or Lake: N.S.	**17**	46	61
Bray I.: N.W.T.	**14**	69	77
Brazeau: *riv.*, Alta.	**26**	53	116
Brazeau, Mt.: Alta.	**26**	53	117
Brazil Pond: Nfld.		48	56
Brechin: Ont.	**22**	45	79
Brent: Ont.		46	78
Breton, Cape: N.S.	**17**	46	60
Brew Mt.: B.C.	**28**	50	122
Briconnet, Lac: Qué.		51	60
Bridge: *riv.*, B.C.	**28**	51	122
Bridgetown: N.S.	**17**	45	65
Bridgewater: N.S.	**17**	44	64
Brier I.: N.S.	**17**	44	66
Brig Bay: *town*, Nfld.		51	57
Brighton: Ont.	**22**	44	78
Brion I.: Qué.	**17**	48	61
Brisay, Lac: Qué.		54	70
Bristol: N.B.	**16**	46	67
Britannia Beach: B.C.	**28**	50	123
British Columbia: *Prov.*, (*cap.* Victoria)	**28/29**	—	—
British Mts.: Can./U.S.A.	**30**	69	140
Britt: Ont.	**20**	46	80
Broadview: Sask.	**27**	50	102
Brochet: Man.	**27**	58	101
Brochet, Lac: Man.	**27**	59	101
Brochet, Lac: Qué.		49	69
Brochu, Lac: Qué.	**21**	48	75
Brockville: Ont.	**23**	45	76
Brodeur Penin.: N.W.T.	**31**	73	87
Bromptonville: Qué.	**21**	45	72
Bronte: Ont.	**22**	43	80
Brookfield: N.S.	**17**	45	63
Brooklin: Ont.	**22**	44	79
Brooklyn: N.S.	**17**	44	64
Brooks: Alta.	**26**	50	112
Brooks Penin.: B.C.	**28**	50	127
Broughton I.: B.C.	**29**	51	127
Broughton I.: N.W.T.		57	77

	Page	N	W
Brower: Ont.		49	81
Browne Bay: N.W.T.		73	98
Brown Lake: N.W.T.	**31**	66	92
Brownsburg: Qué.	**23**	46	74
Bruce Mines: Ont.	**20**	46	84
Bruce Peninsula: Ont.	**20**	45	81
Bruce Point: P.E.I.	**17**	46	62
Bruderheim: Alta.	**26**	54	113
Brûlé Lake: *town*, Ont.		46	79
Brunette I.: Nfld.		47	56
Bruno: Sask.	**27**	52	106
Brunswick Lake: Ont.		49	83
Brussels: Ont.	**20**	43	81
Bryde, Mt.: Yukon		60	133
Brysoné: Qué.	**23**	46	77
Buchans: Nfld.	**17**	49	57
Buchans Junction: Nfld.		49	56
Buckhorn Lake: Ont.	**22**	44	78
Buckingham: Qué.	**23**	46	75
Buctouche: N.B.	**17**	46	65
Buffalo: *riv.*, Alta.	**26**	59	114
Buffalo Head Hills: Alta.	**26**	57	116
Buffalo Lake: Alta.	**26**	52	113
Buffalo Lake: N.W.T.	**30**	60	116
Buffalo Narrows: *town*, Saskatchewan	**26**	57	108
Buffalo River: *town*, N.W.T.	**30**	61	115
Bulkley: *riv.*, B.C.	**28**	55	127
Burden, Mt.: B.C.	**29**	56	123
Bureau, Lac: Qué.	**21**	48	75
Burgeo: Nfld.	**17**	48	58
Burin Penin.: Nfld.	**17**	47	55
Burks Falls: *town*, Ont.	**22**	46	79
Burlington: Ont.	**22**	43	80
Burlington Beach: Ont.	**22**	43	80
Burnaby: B.C.	**36**	49	123
Burnside: Nfld.		49	54
Burnside: *riv.*, N.W.T.	**31**	66	110
Burns Lake: *town*, B.C.	**29**	54	126
Burnt Creek: *town*, Qué.		55	67
Burnt Lake: Qué.	**15**	52	64
Burntroot Lake: Ont.		46	79
Burntwood: *riv.*, Man.	**27**	55	100
Burrard Inlet: B.C.	**36**	49	123
Burstall: Sask.	**26**	51	110
Burton, Lac: Qué.		55	78
Bute Inlet: B.C.	**28**	50	125
Buttle Lake: B.C.	**28**	49	125
Button Bay: Man.	**27**	59	94
Byam Channel: N.W.T.	**31**	75	105
Byam Martin I.: *& Chan.*, N.W.T.	**31**	75	104
Bylot I.: N.W.T.	**31**	73	78
Bylot Island Bird Sanctuary: N.W.T.	**31**	74	80
Byron Bay: Nfld.		55	58
Cabano: Qué.	**16**	48	69
Cabonga, Barrage de: *& res.*, Québec	**21**	47	76
Cabot Head: Ont.	**20**	45	81
Cabot, Lac: Qué.		55	64
Cabot Strait: N.S./Nfld.	**15**	47	60
Cabri: Sask.	**26**	51	108
Cache Bay: *town*, Ont.	**20**	46	80
Cache Creek: *town*, B.C.		51	121
Cadillac: Qué.	**20**	48	79
Cairns Lake: Ont.	**27**	52	94
Calabogie Lake: Ont.	**21**	45	77
Caledonia: N.S.	**17**	44	65
Caledonia: Ont.	**20**	43	80
Calgary: Alta.	**26**	51	114
Callander: Ont.	**20**	46	80
Calling Lake: Alta.	**26**	55	113
Calmar: Alta.	**26**	53	114
Calumet: Qué.		46	77
Calumet I.: Qué.		46	77
Calvert I.: B.C.	**28**	51	128
Camachigama, Lac: Qué.	**21**	48	76
Cambridge Bay: *settlement*, N.W.T.	**31**	69	105
Cambrien, Lac: Qué.		56	69
Cameron Falls: Ont.		49	88
Cameron Hills: N.W.T.	**24**	60	120
Cameron I.: N.W.T.	**31**	76	104
Campbell: Alta.	**26**	54	114
Campbell, Mt.: Yukon	**30**	64	139
Campbellford: Ont.	**22**	44	78
Campbell River: *town*, B.C.	**28**	50	125
Campbells Bay: *town*, Qué.	**22**	46	77
Campbellton: N.B.	**16**	48	67
Campbellton: Nfld.		49	55
Camp Borden: Ont.	**20**	44	80
Camperville: Man.	**27**	52	100
Camp Gagetown: N.B.	**17**	45	66
Campobello I.: N.B.	**17**	45	67
Camrose: Alta.	**26**	53	113
Camsell Range: N.W.T.	**30**	62	124
Canada Bay: Nfld.		51	56
Canairiktok: *riv.*, Nfld.	**15**	55	61
Canal Flats: B.C.	**29**	51	116
Candle Lake: *town*, Sask.	**27**	54	105
Canford: B.C.	**28**	50	121
Caniapiscau, Lac: Qué.	**15**	54	70
Caniapiscau: *riv.*, Qué.	**14**	57	69
Canica: *i.*, Qué.		49	77
Canmore: Alta.	**29**	52	116
Canning: N.S.	**17**	45	64

	Page	N	W
Cannington: Ont.	**22**	44	79
Canoe: *riv.*, B.C.	**29**	52	119
Canoe Lake: Sask.	**26**	55	108
Canora: Sask.	**27**	52	102
Canso: *& cape*, N.S.	**17**	45	61
Canso Causeway: N.S.	**17**	45	61
Canton Bégin: Qué.		48	71
Canyon: Yukon		61	137
Canyon Ranges: N.W.T.	**30**	63	128
Cap à l'Aigle: Qué.	**21**	47	70
Cap Chat: Qué.	**16**	49	67
Cap de la Madeleine: Qué.	**21**	46	72
Cap-Pelé: N.B.	**17**	47	64
Cape Breton Highlands Nat. Park: Nova Scotia	**17**	47	61
Cape Breton I.: N.S.	**17**	46	61
Cape Broyle: Nfld.		47	53
Cape Chidley Is.: Québec/Nfld.		60	65
Cape Dorset: N.W.T.	**14**	64	77
Cape Dyer: *settlement*, N.W.T.	**14**	66	62
Cape North: N.S.	**17**	47	60
Cape St. Charles: Nfld.		52	56
Cape St. George: Nfld.	**17**	48	59
Cape Smoky: N.S.	**17**	47	60
Cape Tormentine: N.B.	**17**	46	64
Capitachouane: *riv.*, Qué.	**21**	48	76
Capitachouane, Lac: Qué.	**21**	48	76
Capreol: Ont.	**20**	47	81
Capstick: N.S.		47	61
Caraquet: N.B.	**16**	48	65
Carberry: Man.	**27**	50	99
Carbonear: Nfld.	**17**	48	53
Carcajou: Alta.		58	117
Carcross: Yukon	**30**	60	135
Cardigan: P.E.I.	**17**	46	63
Cardinal: Ont.	**23**	45	75
Cardston: Alta.	**26**	49	113
Cargill: Ont.		44	81
Cariboo Mtns.: B.C.	**29**	53	121
Caribou: Man.	**27**	59	98
Caribou: *riv.*, Man.	**27**	59	95
Caribou Hide: B.C.	**28**	57	127
Caribou I.: N.S.	**17**	46	63
Caribou I.: Ont.	**19**	47	86
Caribou Lake: Ont.		50	89
Caribou Mtns.: Alta.	**26**	59	115
Carillon: Qué.	**23**	46	74
Carleton: Qué.	**16**	48	66
Carleton, Mt.: N.B.	**16**	47	67
Carleton Place: Ont.	**23**	45	76
Carleton Point: Qué.	**16**	50	62
Carlyle: Sask.	**27**	50	102
Carmacks: Yukon	**30**	62	137
Carman: Man.	**27**	49	98
Carmanville: Nfld.	**17**	49	54
Carmel: Qué.		46	72
Carnduff: Sask.	**27**	49	102
Carnwath: *riv.*, N.W.T.	**30**	67	127
Carp: Ont.	**23**	45	76
Carp Lake: B.C.	**29**	55	123
Carrière, Lac: Qué.	**20**	48	78
Carrot: *riv.*, Man.	**27**	55	96
Carrot River: *& riv.*, Sask.	**27**	53	103
Carstairs: Alta.	**26**	52	114
Cartier: Ont.	**20**	47	81
Cartmel Mt.: B.C.	**28**	58	129
Cartwright: Nfld.	**15**	53	57
Cascade Range: Can./U.S.A.	**28**	49	121
Casse, Lac: Qué.		49	70
Casselman: Ont.	**23**	45	75
Cassiar: B.C.	**24**	59	130
Cassiar Mtns.: B.C.	**24**	59	130
Castel Bay: N.W.T.	**30**	74	120
Castelgar: B.C.	**29**	49	118
Castle I.: N.W.T.		56	77
Castleton: Ont.	**22**	44	78
Castor: Alta.	**26**	52	112
Castor: *riv.*, Ont.	**23**	45	75
Casummit Lake: *town*, Ont.		51	92
Catalina: Nfld.	**17**	48	53
Catchacoma Lake: Ont.	**22**	45	78
Cathedral Prov. Park: B.C.	**29**	49	120
Caughnawaga: Qué.	**32**	45	74
Causapscal: Qué.	**16**	48	67
Cayuga: Ont.	**20**	43	80
Cecil Lake: *town*, B.C.	**29**	56	120
Cedar Lake: Man.	**27**	53	100
Cedar Lake: Ont.	**20**	46	78
Ceepeecee: B.C.		50	127
Central Butte: Sask.	**26**	51	107
Central Patricia: Ont.		51	90
Ceylon: Sask.	**27**	49	105
Chaillon, Cape: Ont.		48	85
Chakonipau Lake: Qué.		56	68
Chaleurs, Baie des: Québec/N.B.	**16**	48	65
Chalk River: *town*, Ont.	**20**	46	77
Chambly: Qué.	**23**	45	73
Chambord: Qué.	**16**	48	72
Chamcook: N.B.		45	67
Chamouchouane: *riv.*, Qué.	**15**	50	73
Champagne: Yukon		60	136
Champcoeur: Qué.		49	78
Champdoré, Lac: Qué.		56	66
Chandler: Qué.	**16**	48	65

	Page	N	W
Chandos Lake: Ont.	**22**	45	78
Change Island: *town*, Nfld.		50	54
Channel: Nfld.		48	59
Channel-Port aux Basques: Newfoundland	**17**	47	59
Chantrey Inlet: N.W.T.	**31**	67	96
Chapais: Ont.	**19**	50	75
Chapeau: Qué.		46	77
Chapel I.: Nfld.		48	55
Chapleau: *& riv.*, Ont.	**20**	48	83
Chapleau Game Preserve: Ontario		48	84
Chaplin Lake: Sask.	**26**	50	107
Chapman, Cape: N.W.T.	**31**	69	89
Chard: Alta.		56	111
Charlemagne: Qué.	**23**	46	73
Charles I.: N.W.T.	**14**	63	74
Charles Lake: Alta.	**26**	60	110
Charleston Lake: Ont.	**23**	45	76
Charlotte Lake: B.C.	**29**	52	125
Charlottetown: Nfld.		48	54
CHARLOTTETOWN: Prince Edward Island	**17**	46	63
Charlton I.: N.W.T.	**19**	52	79
Charny: Qué.	**21**	47	71
Charron Lake: Man.	**27**	53	95
Chase: B.C.	**29**	51	120
Châteauguay: Qué.	**23**	45	74
Châteauguay: *riv.*, Qué.		56	70
Châteauguay, Lac: Qué.		56	70
Château-Richer: Qué.	**16**	47	71
Châteauvert, Lac: Qué.	**21**	48	74
Chateh: Alta.	**26**	59	119
Chatham: N.B.	**16**	47	65
Chatham: Ont.	**20**	42	82
Chatham Sound: B.C.	**28**	54	130
Chats, Lac des: Ont./Qué.	**23**	45	76
Chats Falls Dam: Ont./Qué.	**23**	45	76
Chatsworth: Ont.		44	81
Chaudière: *riv.*, Qué.	**21**	46	71
Chedabucto Bay: N.S.	**17**	45	61
Chelmsford: Ont.	**20**	47	81
Chelsea: Qué.	**23**	45	76
Chemainus: B.C.	**28**	49	124
Cheminis: Ont.		48	79
Chemung Lake: Ont.	**22**	44	78
Chénéville: Qué.	**23**	46	75
Chesley: Ont.	**20**	44	81
Chester: N.S.	**17**	45	64
Chesterfield Inlet: *& town*, N.W.T.	**31**	63	91
Chesterville: Ont.	**23**	45	75
Cheticamp: *& cape*, N.S.	**17**	47	61
Chetwynd: B.C.	**29**	56	121
Chiblow Lake: Ont.	**20**	46	83
Chibougamau: *& lake*, Qué.	**15**	50	75
Chibougamau: *riv.*, Qué.		50	75
Chibougamau, Parc de: Qué.	**15**	49	74
Chicotte: Qué.	**16**	49	63
Chicoutimi: *& riv.*, Qué.	**21**	48	71
Chicoutimi, Parc de: Qué.	**16**	49	71
Chidley, C.: Qué.	**14**	60	65
Chief Lake: *town*, B.C.	**29**	54	123
Chiefs Point: Ont.	**20**	45	81
Chignecto: *cape & bay*, New Brunswick/N.S.	**17**	45	65
Chigoubiche, Lac: Qué.		49	73
Chilanko Forks: B.C.	**29**	42	124
Chilcotin: *riv.*, B.C.	**29**	52	123
Childs Mines: Ont.		45	78
Chilko Lake: B.C.	**29**	51	124
Chilliwack: B.C.	**28**	49	122
Chilliwack Lake: *& riv.*, B.C.	**28**	49	121
Chinchaga: *riv.*, Alta.	**26**	58	119
Chinook Valley: *town*, Alta.		56	118
Chipai Lake: Ont.	**18**	53	88
Chip Lake: Alta.	**26**	54	115
Chipman: N.B.	**17**	46	66
Chippawa: Ont.	**22**	43	79
Chiputneticook Lakes: Canada/U.S.A.	**16**	45	67
Chisel Lake: Man.	**27**	55	100
Chochocauane: *riv.*, Qué.	**21**	47	77
Choiceland: Sask.	**27**	53	104
Chomedey: Qué.	**32**	46	74
Chorkbak Inlet: N.W.T.	**18**	65	74
Chown, Mt.: Alta.	**26**	53	119
Christian I.: Ont.	**20**	45	80
Christie, Mt.: Yukon/N.W.T.	**30**	63	130
Christie Bay: N.W.T.	**31**	62	111
Christina: *riv.*, Alta.	**26**	56	111
Churchbridge: Sask.	**27**	51	102
Churchill: Man.	**27**	59	94
Churchill: *riv.*, Nfld.	**15**	53	64
Churchill: *riv.*, Sask./Man.	**27**	58	95
Churchill, Cape: Man.	**27**	59	93
Churchill Lake: Ont.		51	91
Churchill Lake: Sask.	**26**	56	108
Churchill Peak: B.C.	**24**	58	125
Churchill Reservoir: Nfld.	**15**	55	64
Chute aux Outardes: Qué.	**16**	49	68
Chutine Landing: B.C.	**28**	57	131
Cirque, Mt.: Nfld.	**14**	59	64
City View: Ont.	**32**	45	76
Clair: N.B.		47	69
Clairambault, Lac: Qué.		54	69
Claire, Lake: Alta.	**26**	58	112

	Page	N	W
Clarence, Cape: N.W.T.	31	74	90
Clarence Creek: town, Ont.	23	45	75
Clarenville: Nfld.		48	54
Claresholm: Alta.	26	50	114
Clark Point: Ont.	20	44	82
Clarke City: Qué.	16	50	67
Clarks Harbour: N.S.	17	43	66
Clayoquot Sound: B.C.	29	49	126
Clear, Lake: Ont.	22	45	77
Clear Hills: Alta.	26	57	119
Clearwater: riv., Sask./Alta.	26	57	109
Clearwater Lake: B.C.	29	52	120
Clearwater Lake Prov. Park: Man.	27	54	102
Clearwater Station: B.C.	29	51	120
Clermont: Qué.	21	48	70
Clinton: B.C.	29	51	121
Clinton: Ont.	20	43	82
Clinton-Colden Lake: N.W.T.	31	64	107
Clo-oose: B.C.	28	49	125
Close Lake: Sask.	27	58	105
Clova: Qué.	21	48	75
Clute: Ont.		49	81
Clyde: riv., N.S.	17	44	65
Clyde: riv., Ont.	21	45	76
Coaldale: Alta.	26	50	113
Coalhurst: Alta.	26	50	113
Coalspur: Alta.		53	117
Coast Mtns.: B.C.	28	30	124
Coaticook: Qué.	21	45	72
Coats I.: N.W.T.	14	62	83
Cobalt: Ont.	20	47	80
Cobden: Ont.	21	46	77
Cobequid Bay: N.S.	17	45	64
Cobequid Mtns.: N.S.	17	45	64
Coboconk: Ont.	22	45	79
Cobourg: Ont.	22	44	78
Cochrane: Alta.	26	51	114
Cochrane: Ont.	19	49	81
Cochrane: riv., Man.	27	58	102
Cockburn, Cape: N.W.T.	31	75	100
Cockburn I.: Ont.	20	46	83
Cockram Strait: N.W.T.	14	68	75
Cod I.: Nfld.	14	58	62
Coe Hill: town, Ont.	22	45	78
Coffin I.: Magdalen Is.	17	47	61
Cognac, Lac: Qué.		55	70
Colborne: Ont.	22	44	78
Cold Lake: & town, Alta.	26	54	110
Coldspring Head: N.S.	17	46	64
Cold Spring Pond: Nfld.		48	56
Coldwater: Ont.	22	45	80
Coleman: Alta.	26	50	115
Colinet: Nfld.		47	54
Collingwood: Ont.	20	44	80
Collins Bay: Ont.	22	44	77
Collins Mt.: Ont.	20	48	81
Colombier, Cap: Qué.		49	69
Colonsay: Sask.	27	53	105
Columbia: riv., Can./U.S.A.	29	51	117
Columbia, Cape: N.W.T.	13	83	70
Columbia, Mt.: Alta.	26	52	117
Columbia Mtns.: B.C.	29	52	120
Colville Bay: N.W.T.	31	68	88
Colville Lake: Nfld.		54	66
Colville Lake: N.W.T.	30	67	125
Comber: Ont.	20	42	82
Combermere: Ont.		45	78
Comfort, Cape: N.W.T.	14	65	83
Comfort Bight: Nfld.		53	56
Commissaires, Lac des: Qué.	21	48	72
Committee Bay: N.W.T.	31	68	87
Como, Lake: Ont.	20	48	83
Comox: B.C.	28	50	125
Comox Lake: B.C.	28	50	125
Conception Bay: Nfld.	17	48	53
Conception Harbour: Nfld.		47	53
Conche: Nfld.		51	56
Conestogo: riv., Ont.	20	43	81
Coniston: Ont.	20	46	81
Conklin: Alta.	26	56	111
Connors: N.B.		47	69
Conrad: Yukon		60	134
Consecon: Ont.	22	44	77
Consort: Alta.	26	52	111
Contrecoeur: Qué.	23	46	73
Contwoyto Lake: N.W.T.	31	66	111
Cook, Cape: B.C.		50	128
Cook, Mt.: U.S.A./Can.		60	140
Cook Bay: Lake Simcoe	22	44	79
Cookshire: Qué.	21	45	72
Co-op Point: Sask.	27	57	102
Coppell: Ont.		50	84
Copper Cliff: Ont.	20	46	81
Coppermine: & riv., N.W.T.	30	67	115
Copper Mountain: town, British Columbia	28	49	120
Coquitlam: riv., B.C.	36	49	123
Coral Harbour: town, N.W.T.	18	64	83
Coral Rapids: town, Ont.		50	82
Corbeil Point: Ont.		47	85
Corbett Inlet: N.W.T.	31	62	92
Cormac: Ont.		45	77
Cormack, Mt.: Nfld.	17	48	56
Cormorant: & lake, Man.	27	54	101

	Page	N	W
Cornelius Grinnell Bay: N.W.T.	14	63	65
Corner Brook: Nfld.	17	49	58
Cornwall: Ont.	23	45	75
Cornwall I.: N.W.T.	13	77	95
Cornwallis I.: N.W.T.	31	75	95
Coronation: Alta.	26	52	111
Coronation Gulf: N.W.T.	31	68	110
Cortes I.: B.C.	28	50	125
Corunna: Ont.	20	43	82
Corvette, Lac: & riv., Qué.		53	74
Côteau Station: Qué.	23	45	74
Cottel I.: Nfld.		49	54
Couchiching, Lake: Ont.	22	45	79
Coulonge: riv., Qué.	20	47	77
Coulonge Est: riv., Qué.	21	46	76
Courtenay: B.C.	28	49	125
Coutts: Alta.	26	49	112
Couture, Lac: Qué.		60	75
Cove I.: Ont.	20	45	82
Cowansville: Qué.	21	45	73
Cox's Cove: Nfld.		49	58
Crabtree: Qué.	23	46	73
Cracroft I.: B.C.		50	126
Craik: Sask.	27	52	105
Cramolet, Lac: Qué.		56	68
Cranberry Portage: Man.	27	55	101
Cranbrook: B.C.	29	49	116
Crane Lake: Sask.	26	50	109
Crauford, Cape: N.W.T.	31	74	84
Cree: riv., Sask.	27	58	106
Cree Lake: Sask.	26	57	107
Creighton: Ont.	20	46	81
Creighton: Sask.	27	55	102
Creston: Nfld.		47	55
Creswell Bay: N.W.T.	31	73	94
Croche: riv., Qué.	21	48	73
Crofton: N.S.	28	49	123
Croix, Lac à la: Qué.		51	70
Croker, Cape: Ont.	20	45	81
Croker Bay: N.W.T.	31	75	83
Crooked Lake: Nfld.	17	48	56
Crosby: Ont.		45	76
Crossfield: Alta.	26	51	114
Cross Lake: Ont.	22	45	77
Cross Lake: & town, Man.	27	55	98
Crown Prince Frederick I.: N.W.T.	31	70	87
Crowsnest Pass: B.C./Alta.	29	50	115
Crozier Chan.: N.W.T.	30	76	118
Crystal Falls: town, Ont.	20	46	80
Crysler: Ont.	23	45	75
Cudworth: Sask.	27	52	106
Cumberland: B.C.	28	50	125
Cumberland: penin. & sound, N.W.T.	14	66	65
Cumberland: Ont.	32	46	75
Cumberland Bay: town, N.B.	17	46	66
Cumberland Lake: Sask.	27	54	102
Cupar: Sask.	27	51	104
Cutknife: Sask.	26	53	109
Cuvillier, Lac: Qué.		49	77
Cypress Hills: & park, Sask.	26	50	109
Dalhousie: N.B.	16	48	66
Dalhousie: Qué.	15	48	66
Dalhousie, Cape: N.W.T.	30	70	130
Dalmas, Lac: Qué.		53	72
Dalmeny: Sask.	26	52	107
Dalquier: Qué.		48	78
Dalton: Ont.		48	84
Dalton Mills: Ont.	20	48	84
Daly Bay: N.W.T.	31	64	90
Dana, Lac: Qué.		51	77
Dane: Ont.	20	48	80
Daniels Harbour: Nfld.	17	50	58
Danville: Qué.	21	46	72
Darnley Bay: N.W.T.	30	70	124
Dartmouth: N.S.	17	45	64
Dauphin: Man.	27	51	100
Dauphin: riv., Man.	27	52	99
Dauphin Lake: Man.	27	51	100
Davangus: Qué.		48	79
Davidson: Sask.	27	51	106
Davidson Mtns.: Can./U.S.A.	30	68	142
Davieau I.: N.W.T.		57	77
Davis Inlet: settlement, Newfoundland	15	56	61
Davis Str.: Can./Grnld.	13	67	58
Davy Lake: Sask.	26	59	108
Dawson: Yukon	30	64	139
Dawson, Mt.: B.C.	29	51	117
Dawson Bay: Man.	27	53	101
Dawson Creek: town, B.C.	29	56	120
Dawson Inlet: N.W.T.	31	62	93
Dawson Range: Yukon	30	62	139
Daysland: Alta.	26	53	112
Dayton: Ont.		46	83
Deadman Bay: Nfld.		49	54
Dean: riv., B.C.	29	53	126
Deans Dundas Bay: N.W.T.	30	72	119
Dease: riv., B.C.		59	129
Dease Arm: Great Bear Lake, N.W.T.	30	67	120
Dease Lake: & settlement, British Columbia	24	58	130

	Page	N	W
Dease Plateau: B.C.		60	128
Dease Str.: N.W.T.	31	69	107
Déception: Qué.	18	63	75
Deep River: town, Ont.		46	77
Deer Hill: town, Alta.	26	56	118
Deer I.: N.B.		45	67
Deer Lake: town, Ont.	27	53	94
Deer Lake: town & lake, Newfoundland	17	49	58
Deer Pond, Nfld.		48	55
Defot: B.C.		59	130
Delhi: Ont.	20	43	80
Delisle: Sask.	26	52	107
Deloraine: Man.	27	49	100
Delorme, Lac: Qué.	15	54	70
Deloro: Ont.	22	44	78
Delson: Qué.	23	45	74
Denholm: Sask.		53	108
Denman I.: B.C.	28	50	125
Departure Bay: B.C.	28	53	124
De Pas: riv., Qué.	15	56	65
Depot Harbour: Ont.	20	45	80
De Salis Bay: N.W.T.	30	72	122
Desbarats: Ont.	20	46	84
Desbiens: Qué.	21	48	72
Deschaillons: Qué.	21	47	72
Deschambault Lake: Sask.	27	55	103
Deschênes: lake & town, Québec	32	45	75
Deseronto: Ont.	22	44	77
Desmaraisville: Qué.	15	49	76
Desolation Lake: Nfld.		55	63
Detah: N.W.T.	31	62	114
Detroit: riv., Can./U.S.A.	20	42	83
Deux Montagnes: town, Québec	32	46	74
Deux Montagnes, Lac des: Québec	32	45	74
Deux Rivières: town, Ont.	20	46	78
Devenyns, Lac: Qué.	21	47	74
Devon: Alta.	26	53	114
Devon I.: N.W.T.	31	75	85
Dezadeash Lake: Yukon		60	137
D'Iberville, Lac: Qué.	15	56	73
Dickson Lake: Ont.		46	78
Dickson Peak: B.C.	28	51	123
Didsbury: Alta.	26	52	114
Didyme: Qué.		49	73
Diefenbaker, Lake: Sask.	26	51	107
Digby: N.S.	17	45	66
Digby Neck: penin., N.S.	17	44	66
Digges Is.: Qué.	14	62	68
Dihourse, Lac: Qué.		56	64
Dildo: Nfld.		47	54
Dingwall: N.S.	17	47	60
Disappointment Lake: Newfoundland		54	62
Disaster Rapids: Nfld.		53	64
Dismal Lakes: N.W.T.	30	67	117
Disraeli: Qué.	21	46	71
Dix: Qué.	21	48	76
Dixon Entrance: str., U.S.A./Canada	28	54	132
Doating Cove: Nfld.		49	54
Doda, Lac: Qué.		49	75
Dodge Lake: Sask.	27	60	106
Dodsland: Sask.	26	52	109
Doe Lake: Ont.	22	46	79
Dog Creek: town, B.C.	29	52	122
Dog Lake: Man.	27	51	98
Dog Lake: Ont.		49	89
Dog Lake: Ont.		48	84
Dolbeau: Qué.	21	49	72
Dolphin & Union Str.: N.W.T.	30	69	115
Dome Peak: N.W.T.		61	127
Domes, The: mtn., Nfld.		58	63
Dominion, Cape: N.W.T.	14	66	74
Dominion Lake: Nfld.		53	62
Don: riv., Ont.	32	44	79
Donald Lake: Ont.	27	51	95
Donjek: riv., Yukon	30	62	140
Donkin: N.S.	17	46	60
Donnacona: Qué.	21	47	72
Dorchester: N.B.	17	46	64
Dorchester, Cape: N.W.T.	14	65	78
Doré, Lac: Qué.	21	47	75
Doré Lake: Sask.	26	55	107
Dorion: Qué.	23	45	74
Dorset: Ont.	20	45	79
Dorset, Cape: N.W.T.	14	64	77
Dorval: Qué.	32	45	74
Dosquet: Qué.	21	46	71
Dot: B.C.	28	50	121
Double Mer.: inlet, Nfld.		54	59
Douglas Point: Ont.	20	44	82
Dowling Lake: Alta.	26	52	112
Downton, Mt.: B.C.	29	53	125
Dozois, Réservoir: Qué.	20	47	77
Drayton Valley: town, Alta.	26	54	115
Dresden: Ont.	20	43	82
Driftwood: Ont.		49	81
Drumbo: Ont.	20	43	81
Drumheller: Alta.	26	51	113
Drummondville: Qué.	21	46	72
Dryden: Ont.	19	50	93
Dubawnt: riv., N.W.T.	31	62	103
Dubawnt Lake: N.W.T.	31	63	102
Dubuisson: Qué.	20	48	78
Duck Bay: town, Man.	27	52	100
Duck I.: Ont.	22	44	77

	Page	N	W
Duck Lake: town, Sask.	26	53	106
Duck Mt.: & Prov. Pk., Manitoba	27	51	101
Duffey Lake: B.C.		50	122
Du Gué: riv., Qué.	15	57	72
Duke of York Bay: N.W.T.	14	65	85
Du Lièvre: riv., Qué.	23	46	75
Du Loup: riv., Qué.	21	46	73
Dumoine: riv. & lake, Qué.	20	47	78
Duncan: B.C.	28	49	124
Duncan, Cape: Akimiski I.		53	81
Duncan Dam: B.C.	29	50	117
Duncan Lake: B.C.	29	51	117
Duncan, Lac: Qué.	18	53	78
Dundalk: Ont.	20	44	80
Dundas: Ont.	20	43	80
Dundas I.: B.C.	28	55	131
Dundas Penin.: N.W.T.	31	75	112
Dunkirk: Sask.	27	50	106
Dunnville: Ont.	20	43	80
Dunville: Nfld.		47	54
Duparquet: Qué.	20	49	79
Dupuy: Qué.		49	79
Durham: Ont.	20	44	81
Duvernay: Alta.		54	112
Dyer, Cape: N.W.T.	14	67	61
Dyer Bay: N.W.T.	30	76	122
Dyer Bay: town, Ont.		45	81
Dyke Lake: Nfld.		54	66
Eabamet Lake: Ont.	19	52	88
Eagle: riv., Nfld.		53	58
Eagle Lake: Ont.	19	50	93
Ear Falls: Ont.	19	51	93
Earlton: Ont.	20	48	80
East Angus: Qué.	21	45	71
East Bay: Nfld.		47	55
East Broughton: Qué.	21	46	71
East Chezzetcook: N.S.	17	45	63
East Cub I.: N.W.T.		54	80
Eastend: Sask.	26	49	109
East Jordan: N.S.	17	44	65
Eastmain: & riv., Qué.	15	52	78
Eastman: Qué.	21	45	72
East Point: P.E.I.	17	46	62
Eastport: Nfld.		49	54
East Thurlow I.: B.C.		50	125
Eastview: Ont.	32	45	76
East York: Ont.	32	44	79
Eatonia: Sask.	26	51	110
Ebbegunbaeg Lake: Nfld.		48	56
Echo Bay: town, Ont.	20	46	84
Eclipse: riv & chan., Nfld.		60	64
Eclipse Sound: N.W.T.	31	73	79
E. C. Manning Prov. Park: British Columbia	28	49	121
Ecum Secum: N.S.	17	45	62
Edehon Lake: N.W.T.	31	60	97
Edgell I.: N.W.T.	14	62	65
Edgewood: B.C.	29	50	118
EDMONTON: Alta.	26	54	114
Edmund Lake: Man.	27	55	93
Edmundston: N.B.	16	47	68
Edson: Alta.	26	54	116
Eduni, Mt.: N.W.T.	30	64	128
Edziza Peak: B.C.	28	58	131
Edzo: N.W.T.	30	63	116
Eganville: Ont.	20	45	77
Egmont: B.C.	27	50	124
Egmont Bay: P.E.I.	18	46	64
Eileen Lake: N.W.T.	31	62	107
Eisenhower, Mt.: Alta.	26	51	116
Ekwan Point: Ont.		53	82
Eldorado: Sask.	26	58	109
Eldridge Bay: N.W.T.	31	76	110
Elgin: N.B.	17	46	65
Elgin: Ont.	23	45	76
Eliot, Mt.: Nfld.		59	64
Elkhorn: Man.	27	50	101
Elk Lake: town, Ont.	20	48	80
Elk Point: town, Alta.	26	54	111
Ell Bay: N.W.T.	18	64	87
Ellef Ringnes I.: N.W.T.	12	78	103
Ellesmere I.: N.W.T.	13	80	80
Ellice: riv., N.W.T.	31	67	104
Ellice I.: N.W.T.	30	69	136
Elliot Lake: town, Ont.	19	46	83
Elliston: Nfld.		49	53
Elmira: Ont.	20	43	80
Elmira: P.E.I.	17	46	62
Elmsdale: N.S.	17	45	63
Elmvale: Ont.	22	45	80
Elrose: Sask.	26	51	108
Elsas: Ont.		48	83
Elsie I.: N.W.T.		59	79
Elu Inlet: N.W.T.	31	68	106
Elvira, Cape: N.W.T.	31	74	107
Embarras Portage: Alta.		58	111
Embrun: Ont.	23	45	75
Emerald I.: N.W.T.	31	76	114
Emerson: Man.	27	49	97
Emo: Ont.	27	49	93
Emsdale: Ont.	22	46	79
Enderby: B.C.	29	50	119
Enfield: N.S.	17	45	64
Engineer: B.C.		59	134
Englee: Nfld.	15	51	56
Englehart: Ont.	20	48	80
Englewood: B.C.		51	127
English: riv., Ont.	19	50	95

	Page	N	W
English River: *town*, Ont.		49	91
Ennadai: *& lake*, N.W.T.	**31**	61	101
Enterprise: N.W.T.	**30**	61	116
Enterprise: Ont.		44	77
Entrance: Alta.		53	118
Entry I.: Qué.	**17**	47	61
Erebus Bay: N.W.T.	**31**	69	99
Erie, Lake: Can./U.S.A.	**20**	42	81
Erieau: Ont.	**20**	42	82
Erin: Ont.	**22**	44	80
Erlandson, Lac: Qué.	**15**	57	68
Erskine Inlet: N.W.T.		76	103
Escuminac, Point: N.B.	**16**	47	65
Esker: Nfld.	**15**	54	66
Eskimo Lakes: N.W.T.	**30**	69	131
Eskimo Point: *town*, N.W.T.	**31**	61	94
Eskwahani, Lac: Qué.	**21**	48	76
Esnagi Lake: Ont.		49	84
Espanola: Ont.	**20**	46	82
Espoir, Baie d': Nfld.		48	56
Espoir, Cap d': Qué.	**16**	48	64
Esquimalt: B.C.	**28**	48	123
Essex: Ont.	**20**	42	83
Esterhazy: Sask.	**27**	50	102
Estevan: Sask.	**27**	49	103
Estevan Point: B.C.	**29**	49	126
Eston: Sask.	**26**	51	109
Etawney Lake: Man.	**27**	58	96
Ethelbert: Man.	**26**	51	100
Etobicoke: *& creek*, Ont.	**32**	44	80
Eton Station: Ont.	**20**	47	84
Eureka River: *town*, Alta.	**26**	56	119
Eutsuk Lake: B.C.	**29**	53	126
Evans, Lac: Qué.	**15**	51	77
Evans, Mt.: Alta.	**26**	52	118
Evansburg: Alta.	**26**	54	115
Evans Strait: N.W.T.	**18**	63	82
Evansville: Ont.	**20**	46	83
Everett Mts.: N.W.T.	**14**	63	68
Exeter: Ont.	**20**	43	81
Exeter Bay: N.W.T.	**14**	67	62
Exeter Sound: N.W.T.	**14**	66	62
Exploits: *riv.*, Nfld.	**17**	49	56
Faber Lake: N.W.T.	**30**	63	117
Faillon, Lac: Qué.	**21**	48	76
Fair Ness: N.W.T.	**14**	63	72
Fairview: Alta.	**26**	56	118
Fairweather, Mt.: U.S.A./Canada	**30**	59	138
Falaise Lake: N.W.T.		61	116
Falconbridge: Ont.	**20**	47	81
Falher: Alta.	**26**	56	117
Family Lake: Man.	**27**	52	96
Faribault, Lac: Qué.		59	72
Farmer I.: N.W.T.		58	81
Farnham: Qué.	**21**	45	73
Farnham, Mt.: B.C.	**29**	50	116
Faro: N.W.T.	**30**	63	133
Fassett: Qué.	**23**	46	75
Father, Lac: Qué.		49	75
Fatima: Qué.	**15**	47	62
Fauquier: Ont.		49	82
Favourable Lake: *town*, Ontario	**27**	53	94
Fawcett Lake: Ont.		51	92
Fawn: *riv.*, Ont.	**18**	54	88
Felix, Cape: N.W.T.	**31**	70	98
Fenelon Falls: *town*, Ont.	**22**	45	79
Fergus: Ont.	**20**	44	80
Ferguson Lake: N.W.T.	**31**	70	105
Ferme Neuve: Qué.	**21**	47	75
Fernie: B.C.	**29**	49	115
Ferolle Point: Nfld.		51	57
Ferryland: Nfld.	**17**	47	53
Feuilles, Lac aux: Qué.	**14**	59	70
Feuilles, R. aux: Qué.	**14**	58	73
Field: B.C.	**26**	51	116
Field: Ont.	**20**	47	80
Fife Lake: Sask.	**27**	49	106
Finch: Ont.		45	75
Fingal: Ont.		43	81
Finlay: *riv.*, B.C.	**29**	56	124
Finlay Forks: B.C.	**29**	56	124
Finlay Range: B.C.	**29**	57	126
Finnie Bay: N.W.T.	**14**	65	77
Firebag: *riv.*, Alta.	**26**	57	110
Firebag Hills: Sask.	**26**	58	110
Fire River: *town*, Ont.		49	83
Firth: *riv.*, U.S.A./Can.	**30**	69	140
Fisher: Qué.		49	78
Fisher, Mt.: B.C.	**29**	50	116
Fisher Strait: N.W.T.	**14**	63	84
Fishing Lake: Man.	**27**	52	95
Fishing Ship Harbour: Newfoundland		53	56
Fitzgerald Bay: N.W.T.	**31**	72	90
Fitzhugh Sound: B.C.	**28**	52	128
Fitzpatrick: Qué.		47	73
Fitzwilliam I.: Ont.	**20**	45	82
Fitzwilliam Str.: N.W.T.		76	116
Flaherty I.: N.W.T.		56	80
Flamand, Lac.: Qué.	**21**	48	73
Flatbush: Alta.		55	114
Flat I.: Nfld.		47	55
Fleur de Lys: Nfld.		50	56
Fleur de Mai, Lac: Qué.		52	65
Flin Flon: Man.	**27**	55	102
Flint Lake: N.W.T.	**14**	69	74
Flores I.: B.C.	**29**	49	126

	Page	N	W
Florida: Ont.		49	81
Flower's Cove: *town*, Nfld.	**15**	52	57
Flower Station: Ont.		45	77
Foam Lake: *town*, Sask.	**27**	52	103
Foch: B.C.	**28**	50	124
Fogo: *& i.*, Nfld.	**17**	50	54
Foleyet: Ont.	**20**	48	82
Foley I.: N.W.T.	**14**	68	75
Fond du Lac: Sask.	**26**	59	107
Fond du Lac: *riv.*, Sask.	**27**	59	105
Fontas: *riv.*, B.C.	**24**	58	121
Fonteneau, Lac: Qué.		52	61
Fonthill: Ont.	**22**	43	79
Forbes, Mt.: Alta.	**26**	52	117
Foremost: Alta.	**26**	49	111
Forest: Ont.	**20**	43	82
Forestburg: Alta.	**26**	53	112
Forest Lawn: Alta.	**26**	51	114
Forestville: Qué.	**15**	49	69
Forget: Qué.	**21**	48	77
Fornier, Lac: Qué.		51	65
Forrest Lake: Sask.	**26**	58	109
Forsythe: Qué.	**21**	48	76
Fort Albany: Ont.	**19**	52	82
Fort Babine: B.C.	**29**	55	127
Fort Chimo: Qué.	**14**	58	68
Fort Chipewyan: Alta.	**26**	59	111
Fort Coulonge: Qué.	**21**	46	77
Forteau Bay: *town*, Nfld.		51	57
Fort Erie: Ont.	**22**	43	79
Fort Fitzgerald: Alta.	**26**	60	112
Fort Frances: Ont.	**19**	49	93
Fort Franklin: N.W.T.	**30**	66	124
Fort Fraser: B.C.	**29**	54	125
Fort Garry: Man.	**33**	50	97
Fort George: Qué.	**15**	54	79
Fort Good Hope: N.W.T.	**30**	66	128
Fort Grahame: B.C.	**29**	57	125
Fort Hope: Ont.		51	88
Fortierville: Qué.	**21**	46	72
Fortin, Lac: Qué.		51	68
Fort Langley: B.C.	**28**	49	123
Fort Liard: N.W.T.	**30**	60	124
Fort McKenzie: Qué.	**15**	57	63
Fort Macleod: Alta.	**26**	50	113
Fort McMurray: Alta.	**26**	57	111
Fort McPherson: N.W.T.	**30**	67	135
Fort Nelson: *& riv.*, B.C.	**24**	59	123
Fort Norman: N.W.T.	**30**	65	125
Fort Providence: N.W.T.	**30**	61	118
Fort Qu'Appelle: Sask.	**27**	51	104
Fort Resolution: N.W.T.	**30**	61	114
Fort Rupert: Qué.	**15**	52	79
Fort St. James: B.C.	**29**	54	124
Fort St. John: B.C.	**29**	56	121
Fort Saskatchewan: Alta.	**26**	54	113
Fort Selkirk: Yukon	**30**	63	137
Fort Severn: Ont.	**18**	56	88
Fort Simpson: N.W.T.	**30**	62	122
Fort Smith: N.W.T.	**31**	60	112
Fortune: *& bay*, Nfld.	**17**	47	56
Fortune Harbour: Nfld.		50	55
Fort Vermilion: Alta.	**26**	58	116
Fort William: Ont. *see* Thunder Bay			
Forty Mile: *riv.*, Canada/U.S.A.	**30**	64	141
Fossmill: Ont.		46	79
Foster: *riv.*, Sask.	**27**	56	106
Fourchu: N.S.	**17**	46	60
Fournière, Lac: Qué.	**20**	48	78
Fox Bay: *town*, Qué.	**16**	49	62
Fox Creek: *town*, Alta.	**26**	54	117
Foxe Basin: N.W.T.	**14**	68	79
Foxe Channel: N.W.T.	**14**	65	80
Foxe Penin.: N.W.T.	**14**	64	77
Foxford: Sask.	**27**	53	105
Fox Harbour: Nfld.	**15**	52	56
Fox Harbour: Nfld.		47	54
Fox Valley: *town*, Sask.	**26**	50	109
Frances Lake: Yukon	**30**	61	129
Francois Lake: B.C.	**29**	54	126
Frankford: Ont.	**22**	44	78
Franklin, District of: N.W.T.	**31**	—	—
Franklin Bay: N.W.T.	**30**	70	126
Franklin Bay: N.W.T.	**31**	69	85
Franklin Lake: N.W.T.	**31**	67	96
Franklin Mts.: N.W.T.	**30**	64	125
Franklin Strait: N.W.T.	**31**	71	97
Franz: Ont.		48	84
Fraser: *riv.*, B.C.	**36**	50	121
Fraser: *riv.*, Nfld.	**15**	57	64
Fraserdale: Ont.		50	82
Fraser Plateau: B.C.	**29**	52	124
Frater: Ont.	**20**	47	84
Frederick House: *lake & riv.*, Ontario		49	81
FREDERICTON: New Brunswick	**17**	46	67
Fredericton Junc.: N.B.	**17**	46	67
Frederikshald Bay: N.W.T.	**31**	71	105
Freels, Cape: Nfld.	**17**	49	53
Freeport: N.S.	**17**	44	66
French: *riv.*, Ont.	**20**	46	80
Frenchman: *riv.*, Canada/U.S.A.		49	107
Frenchman Butte: Sask.	**26**	54	110
Freshwater Bay: Nfld.		49	54
Frobisher Bay: *& town*, N.W.T.	**14**	63	68
Frobisher Lake: Sask.	**26**	56	108

	Page	N	W
Frog Lake: Alta.	**26**	54	110
Frozen Strait: N.W.T.	**14**	66	85
Fruitvale: B.C.	**29**	49	118
Fullerton, Cape: N.W.T.	**31**	64	88
Fundy, Bay of: N.B./N.S.	**17**	45	66
Fundy Nat. Park: N.B.	**17**	45	65
Fury & Hecla Strait: N.W.T.	**31**	70	84
Gabarus Bay: N.S.	**17**	46	60
Gabbro Lake: Nfld.		54	65
Gabriel Str.: N.W.T.	**14**	62	65
Gabriola I.: B.C.	**28**	49	124
Gage, Cape: P.E.I.	**17**	47	64
Gagetown: N.B.	**17**	46	66
Gagnon: Qué.	**15**	52	68
Gagnon, Lac: Qué.	**21**	46	75
Galbraith: B.C.		59	132
Galiano I.: B.C.	**28**	49	123
Galiote: Qué.	**16**	49	63
Gambier I.: B.C.	**28**	49	123
Gambo: Nfld.	**17**	49	54
Gananoque: Ont.	**23**	44	76
Gander: *& lake*, Nfld.	**17**	49	55
Gander: *riv.*, Nfld.	**17**	49	55
Gander Bay: *town & bay*, Newfoundland		49	54
Garden River: *& riv.*, Ont.	**20**	46	84
Gardiner: Ont.		49	81
Gardiner Dam: Sask.	**26**	51	107
Gardner Canal: B.C.	**28**	53	128
Gargantua, Cape: Ont.		47	85
Garibaldi: B.C.	**28**	50	123
Garibaldi: *mtn. & lake*, B.C.	**28**	50	123
Garibaldi Prov. Park: B.C.	**28**	50	123
Garnet Bay: N.W.T.	**14**	65	75
Garry Bay: N.W.T.	**31**	69	85
Garry Lake: N.W.T.	**31**	66	100
Garson: Ont.	**20**	46	81
Garthby: Qué.	**21**	46	71
Gaspé: *& cape*, Qué.	**16**	49	64
Gaspé, Péninsule de: Québec	**16**	48	66
Gaspésie, Parc de la: Québec	**16**	49	66
Gataga: *riv.*, B.C.		58	129
Gate, The: *falls*, N.W.T.		61	125
Gateshead I.: N.W.T.	**31**	71	100
Gatineau: *& riv.*, Qué.	**32**	45	75
Gatineau, Parc de la: Qué.	**23**	46	76
Gauer Lake: Man.	**27**	57	98
Gavot, Lac: Qué.		56	71
Geikie: *riv.*, Sask.	**27**	57	105
Gensart, Lac: Qué.		53	68
George, Cape: N.S.	**17**	46	62
George: *riv.*, Qué.	**15**	58	66
George, Lake: Ont.	**20**	46	84
Georges Brook: *town*, Nfld.	**20**	48	54
Georges Cove: Nfld.		53	56
Georgetown: Ont.	**22**	44	80
Georgetown: P.E.I.	**17**	46	62
Georgia, Strait of: B.C.	**28**	49	124
Georgian Bay: Ont.	**20**	45	81
Georgian Bay Prov. Forest: Ontario	**20**	46	80
Georgina I.: Ont.	**22**	44	79
Geraldton: Ont.	**19**	50	87
Germaine, Lac: Qué.		53	68
Germansen Landing: B.C.	**29**	56	125
Gerrard: B.C.	**29**	50	117
Gethsémani: Qué.	**17**	50	60
Ghost River: *town*, Ont.		51	83
Giaque Lake: N.W.T.	**31**	63	114
Gibsons: B.C.	**28**	49	123
Gifford: *Fd. & riv.*, N.W.T.	**22**	70	83
Gilbert, Mt.: B.C.	**28**	51	124
Gilbert Plains: *town*, Man.	**27**	51	100
Gilford I.: B.C.	**29**	51	126
Gil I.: B.C.	**28**	53	129
Gillam: Man.	**27**	56	95
Gillian Lake: N.W.T.	**14**	69	75
Gillies Bay: *town*, B.C.	**28**	50	124
Gimli: Man.	**27**	51	97
Giradrin, Lac: Qué.		58	66
Girardville Centre: Qué.		49	73
Giscome: B.C.	**29**	54	122
Gjoa Haven: N.W.T.	**31**	69	96
Glace Bay: *town*, N.S.	**17**	46	60
Glacier Creek: *town*, Yukon	**30**	64	141
Glacier Nat. Park: B.C.	**29**	51	117
Gladmar: Sask.		49	104
Gladstone: Man.	**27**	50	99
Glenannan: Ont.		44	81
Glenboro: Man.	**27**	50	99
Glencoe: Ont.	**20**	43	82
Glen Robertson: Ont.	**23**	45	75
Glover I.: Nfld.		49	58
Glovertown: Nfld.		49	54
Goat I.: B.C.	**28**	50	124
Godbout: Qué.	**16**	49	67
Goderich: Ont.	**20**	44	82
Gods: *riv.*, Man.	**27**	56	92
Gods Lake: *town & lake*, Manitoba	**27**	55	94
God's Mercy, Bay of: N.W.T.	**31**	64	86
Goëland, Lac au: Qué.		50	77
Gogama: Ont.	**20**	48	82
Gold Bridge: B.C.	**28**	51	123

	Page	N	W
Gold Cove: Nfld.		50	57
Gold River: B.C.	**29**	50	125
Golden: B.C.	**29**	51	117
Golden Hinde: *mtn.*, B.C.	**29**	50	126
Golden Spike: Alta.	**26**	53	114
Gooderham: Ont.	**22**	45	78
Goodeve: Sask.	**27**	51	103
Goodhope, Mt.: B.C.	**29**	51	124
Goodsoil: Sask.	**26**	54	109
Goose: *riv.*, Nfld.		53	61
Goose Bay: *town*, Nfld.	**15**	53	60
Gordonhorne Peak: B.C.	**29**	52	119
Gordon Lake: Alta.	**26**	56	110
Gore Bay: *town*, Ont.	**20**	46	82
Goshen: N.S.	**17**	45	62
Gott Peak: B.C.	**28**	50	122
Goudreau: Ont.	**20**	48	84
Gouin, Barrage: Qué.	**16**	48	74
Gouin, Réservoir: Qué.	**15**	48	75
Goulais: *riv.*, Ont.	**20**	47	84
Goulais Point: Ont.	**20**	47	84
Goulais River Game Preserve: Ontario	**20**	47	84
Gourlay Lake: Ont.		49	85
Gowganda: Ont.	**20**	48	81
Gracefield: Qué.	**22**	46	76
Graham: Ont.		49	91
Graham I.: B.C.	**28**	54	132
Graham Moore, Cape: N.W.T.	**31**	73	76
Granby: Qué.	**21**	45	73
Granby: *riv.*, B.C.	**29**	50	118
Grand: *riv.*, Ont.	**20**	43	80
Grand Bank: *town*, Nfld.	**17**	47	56
Grand Bay: *town*, N.B.	**17**	45	66
Grand Beach: *town*, Nfld.		47	55
Grand Bend: Ont.	**20**	43	82
Grand Cache: Alta.	**29**	54	119
Grande Baie: Qué.	**21**	48	71
Grande Prairie: *town*, Alta.	**26**	55	119
Grande Rivière de la Baleine: Québec	**15**	55	77
Grandes Bergeronnes: Qué.	**16**	48	69
Grand Etang: *town*, N.S.	**17**	47	61
Grande Vallée: *town*, Qué.	**16**	49	65
Grand Falls: Nfld.	**15**	54	64
Grand Falls: *town*, N.B.	**16**	47	67
Grand Falls: *town*, Nfld.	**17**	49	56
Grand Falls: Ont.	**20**	46	83
Grand Forks: B.C.	**29**	49	118
Grand Harbour: N.B.	**17**	44	67
Grandin, Lac: N.W.T.	**30**	64	118
Grand Lac Germain: Qué.		51	67
Grand Lac Jacques Cartier: Québec	**21**	48	71
Grand Lac Témiscamie: Québec		51	73
Grand Lac Victoria: Qué.	**20**	48	77
Grand Lake: N.B.	**17**	46	66
Grand Lake: Nfld.		54	61
Grand Lake: Nfld.	**17**	49	57
Grand Ligne: Qué.	**23**	45	73
Grand Manan I.: *& chan.*, New Brunswick	**17**	45	67
Grand' Mère: Qué.	**21**	47	73
Grand Narrows: *town*, N.S.	**17**	46	61
Grand Rapids: *town*, Man.	**27**	53	99
Grand Valley: *town*, Ont.	**20**	44	80
Grand View: Man.	**27**	51	101
Granet, Lac: Qué.	**20**	48	77
Granisle: B.C.	**29**	55	127
Grant Point: N.W.T.	**31**	68	98
Granville Lake: *& falls*, Manitoba	**27**	56	100
Gras, Lac de: N.W.T.	**31**	64	111
Grass: *riv.*, Man.	**27**	56	97
Grass River Prov. Pk.: Man.	**27**	55	101
Grassy Narrows: *town*, Ontario	**19**	50	94
Grates Point: Nfld.		48	53
Gravelbourg: Sask.	**26**	50	107
Gravell Point: N.W.T.	**14**	67	77
Gravenhurst: Ont.	**22**	45	79
Great Bear Lake: N.W.T.	**30**	66	120
Great Central: B.C.	**28**	49	125
Great Central Lake: B.C.	**28**	49	125
Great Colinet I.: Nfld.		47	54
Great Duck I.: Ont.	**20**	46	83
Great Sand Hills: Sask.	**26**	50	109
Great Slave Lake: N.W.T.	**30**	61	115
Great Village: N.S.	**17**	45	64
Green: *riv.*, N.B.		48	68
Green Bay: *town*, Nfld.		52	56
Green Bay: Nfld.		50	56
Greening: Qué.		48	75
Green Lake: B.C.	**29**	51	121
Greenough Point: Ont.	**20**	45	81
Green Point: Nfld.		50	58
Greenspond: Nfld.		49	54
Greenville: B.C.	**28**	55	130
Greenwater Lake Prov. Pk.: Saskatchewan	**27**	52	104
Greenwood: B.C.	**29**	49	119
Grenfell: Sask.	**27**	50	103
Grenville: Qué.	**23**	46	75
Grenville, Mt.: B.C.	**28**	51	124
Gretna: Man.	**27**	49	97
Grey: *riv.*, Nfld.	**17**	48	57
Grey Is.: Nfld.		51	55

	Page	N	W
Griffith I.: N.W.T.	**31**	75	96
Griffith I.: Ont.	**20**	45	81
Grimsby: Ont.	**22**	43	80
Grimshaw: Alta.	**26**	56	118
Grindstone: *& i.*, Qué.	**16**	47	62
Grindstone Prov. Park: Man.	**27**	52	98
Grinnell Ice Cap: N.W.T.	**14**	62	67
Groais I.: Nfld.	**15**	51	55
Gronlid: Sask.	**27**	53	104
Gros Morne: *mtn.*, Nfld.	**17**	50	58
Gros Morne Nat. Park: Nfld.	**17**	49	58
Groswater Bay: Nfld.	**15**	54	58
Groundhog: *riv.*, Ont.	**19**	49	82
Gueguen, Lac: Qué.	**20**	48	77
Guelph: Ont.	**20**	43	80
Guers, Lac: Qué.		57	66
Guigues: Qué.	**20**	47	77
Gull Lake: Alta.	**26**	52	114
Gull Lake: Nfld.		53	61
Gull Lake: Ont.	**22**	45	79
Gull Lake: *town*, Sask.	**26**	50	108
Gunisao: *riv.*, Man.	**27**	54	97
Gun Lake: B.C.	**28**	51	123
Gunnar: Sask.	**26**	59	109
Gushing, Mt.: B.C.	**28**	58	127
Guysborough: N.S.	**17**	45	62
Gypsum Point: N.W.T.	**30**	62	115
Gyrfalcon, Îles de: Qué.	**14**	59	69
Habay: Alta.	**26**	59	119
Hadley Bay: N.W.T.	**31**	72	109
Hagersville: Ont.	**22**	43	80
Haileybury: Ont.	**20**	47	80
Haines Junction: Yukon		61	137
Hale: Ont.		49	84
Halfway: *riv.*, B.C.	**29**	56	122
Halfway Point: Ont.		52	81
Haliburton: *& lake*, Ont.	**20**	45	78
HALIFAX: Nova Scotia	**17**	45	64
Hall Beach: N.W.T.	**31**	69	81
Hall Harbour: N.S.	**17**	45	65
Hall Lake: N.W.T.	**31**	69	82
Hall Penin.: N.W.T.	**14**	63	66
Halls Bay: Nfld.		50	56
Hamber Prov. Park: B.C.	**29**	52	118
Hamilton: Ont.	**22**	43	80
Hamilton Inlet: Nfld.	**15**	54	58
Hamilton Sound: Nfld.	**17**	49	54
Hamiota: Man.	**27**	50	100
Ham Mt.: Qué.	**21**	46	71
Hampden: Nfld.	**17**	50	57
Hampton: N.B.	**17**	46	66
Haney: B.C.	**28**	49	123
Hanmer: Ont.	**20**	47	81
Hanna: Alta.	**26**	52	112
Hannah Bay: Ont.	**19**	51	80
Hanover: Ont.	**20**	44	81
Hantsport: N.S.	**17**	45	64
Happy Valley: *town*, Nfld.	**15**	53	60
Harbour Breton: Nfld.	**17**	47	56
Harbour Grace: Nfld.	**17**	48	53
Harbour Mille: Nfld.		48	55
Hardisty: Alta.	**26**	53	111
Hardisty Lake: N.W.T.	**30**	65	118
Hardwicke I.: B.C.		50	126
Hare Bay: Nfld.	**15**	51	56
Hare Bay: *town*, Nfld.		49	54
Hare Indian: *riv.*, N.W.T.	**30**	66	127
Hare Lake: Nfld.		55	62
Hares: *riv.*, N.W.T.	**31**	67	93
Harkin Bay: N.W.T.	**14**	65	78
Harricanaw: *riv.*, Qué.	**15**	51	79
Harricanaw Ouest: Qué.		48	78
Harrigan, Cape: Nfld.		56	60
Harrington Harbour: Qué.	**15**	50	59
Harrison, Cape: Nfld.	**15**	55	58
Harrison Hot Springs: B.C.	**28**	49	122
Harrison Lake: B.C.	**28**	49	122
Harriston: Ont.	**20**	44	81
Hart: *riv.*, Yukon	**30**	65	137
Hartland: N.B.	**16**	46	67
Hartney: Man.	**27**	49	100
Harty: Ont.		50	83
Harvey: N.B.		46	67
Harwood: Ont.	**22**	44	78
Hastings: Ont.	**22**	44	78
Hauterive: Qué.	**15**	49	68
Havelock: N.B.	**17**	46	65
Havelock: Ont.	**22**	44	78
Havre Aubert: Qué.	**16**	47	62
Havre St. Pierre: Qué.	**16**	50	64
Hawke Harbour: Nfld.		53	65
Hawke I.: Nfld.		53	56
Hawke Mt.: Nfld.		47	53
Hawkesbury: Ont.	**23**	46	75
Hawk Junction: Ont.	**20**	48	84
Hay: *riv.*, Alta/N.W.T.	**30**	60	116
Hay, Cape: N.W.T.	**31**	74	80
Hay, Cape: N.W.T.	**31**	74	112
Hayes: *riv.*, Man.	**27**	56	93
Hayes: *riv.*, N.W.T.	**31**	67	94
Hay I.: Ont.	**20**	45	81
Hay Lake: Alta.	**26**	59	119
Hay Lake: Ont.		45	78
Hay River: *town*, N.W.T.	**30**	61	116
Hazelton: B.C.	**28**	55	128
Head Lake: Ont.	**22**	45	79
Hearst: Ont.	**19**	50	84
Hearts Content: Nfld.	**17**	48	53
Heaslip: Ont.	**20**	48	80
Heath, Pointe: Qué.	**17**	49	61
Hébert, Lac: Qué.		49	75
Hébertville: Qué.	**16**	48	72
Hebron: Nfld.	**14**	58	63
Hebron: N.S.	**17**	44	66
Hecate: B.C.		50	127
Hecate Strait: B.C.	**28**	53	131
Hecla & Griper Bay: N.W.T.	**31**	76	112
Hecla I.: Man.	**27**	51	97
Hecla Prov. Park: Man.	**27**	52	97
Hedley: B.C.	**28**	49	120
Helena I.: N.W.T.	**31**	76	101
Helen Mine: Ont.		48	85
Hemmingford: Qué.	**23**	45	74
Henley Harbour: Nfld		52	56
Henrietta Maria, C.: Ont.	**18**	55	82
Henry Kater, Cape: N.W.T.	**14**	69	66
Henryville: Qué.	**23**	45	73
Hensall: Ont.	**20**	43	81
Herbert: Sask.	**26**	50	107
Hermitage Bay: Nfld.	**17**	47	56
Hérodier, Lac: Qué.		57	69
Heron Bay: *town*, Ont.		49	86
Herring Cove: *town*, N.S.	**17**	45	64
Herschel: *& i.*, Yukon	**30**	69	139
Hess: *riv.*, Yukon	**30**	63	133
Hess Mts.: Yukon	**30**	63	132
Hickman, Mt.: B.C.	**28**	57	131
Hickman's Harbour: Nfld.		48	54
Hicks Lake: N.W.T.		61	100
High I.: Nfld.		57	61
Highland Creek: Ont.	**32**	44	79
High Level: Alta.	**26**	58	117
High Prairie: *town*, Alta.	**26**	55	116
High River: *town*, Alta.	**26**	50	114
Highrock: *& lake*, Man.	**27**	56	100
Hilda: Ont.		49	84
Hill Island Lake: N.W.T.		60	110
Hillsborough: N.B.	**17**	46	65
Hillsborough Bay: P.E.I.	**17**	46	63
Hillsdale: Ont.	**22**	45	80
Hinds Lake: Nfld.		49	57
Hines Creek: *town*, Alta.	**26**	56	119
Hinton: Alta.	**26**	53	118
Hjalmar Lake: N.W.T.		61	109
Hoare Bay: N.W.T.	**14**	65	66
Hodges Hill: Nfld.		49	56
Hodgeville: Sask.	**26**	50	107
Hogem Range: B.C.	**29**	55	125
Holden: Alta.	**26**	53	112
Holman: N.W.T.	**30**	71	117
Holton: Nfld.		54	57
Holyrood: Nfld.	**17**	47	53
Holyrood Pond: Nfld.		47	54
Homathko: *riv.*, B.C.	**29**	51	125
Home Bay: N.W.T.	**14**	68	67
Home I.: Nfld.		60	64
Honfleur: Qué.		49	72
Honguedo, Détroit d': *chan.*, Qué.	**16**	49	64
Honmer: Ont.	**19**	47	81
Hood: *riv.*, N.W.T.	**31**	67	110
Hootalinqua: Yukon		62	135
Hope: B.C.	**28**	49	121
Hopedale: Nfld.	**15**	55	60
Hope I.: B.C.	**28**	50	128
Hopes Advance, Cap: Qué.	**14**	61	70
Hopes Advance, Baie de: Qué.	**14**	50	70
Hopewell: N.S.	**17**	45	63
Hopewell Is.: N.W.T.		58	78
Hornell Lake: N.W.T.		62	119
Hornepayne: Ont.	**19**	49	85
Horn Mt.: B.C.	**28**	58	129
Horn Mts.: N.W.T.	**30**	62	120
Horsefly, Lake: B.C.	**29**	52	121
Horton: *riv.*, N.W.T.	**30**	69	124
Horwood Lake: Ont.	**20**	48	82
Hotchkiss: Alta.		57	118
Hottah Lake: N.W.T.	**30**	65	118
Houston: B.C.	**29**	54	126
Houston Point: Akimiski I.		53	81
Howe I.: Ont.	**23**	44	76
Howe Point: P.E.I.	**17**	46	62
Howe Sound: B.C.	**28**	49	123
Howick: Qué.		45	74
Howley: Nfld.		49	57
Huard, Pte. au: Qué.		53	79
Hubbard, Mt.: U.S.A./Canada		60	139
Hubbards: N.S.	**17**	45	64
Hubbart Point: Man.	**27**	59	95
Huberdeau: Qué.	**23**	46	75
Hudson: Ont.	**19**	50	92
Hudson: Qué.	**23**	45	74
Hudson Bay	**18**	60	85
Hudson Bay: *town*, Sask.	**27**	53	102
Hudson Hope: B.C.	**29**	56	122
Hudson Strait: N.W.T./Québec	**14**	63	73
Hull: Qué.	**32**	45	75
Humber: *riv.*, Nfld.	**17**	49	57
Humber: *riv.*, Ont.	**32**	44	80
Humber Bay: Ont.	**32**	44	79
Humboldt: Sask.	**27**	52	105
Hundred Mile House: B.C.	**29**	52	121
Hundred Mile Landing: Yukon		61	134
Hunter I.: B.C.	**28**	52	128
Hunter I.: Ont.		48	91
Hunter River: *town*, P.E.I.	**17**	46	63
Huntingdon: Qué.	**23**	45	74
Huntingdon I.: Nfld.	**15**	54	57
Huntsville: Ont.	**22**	45	79
Hurd, Cape: Ont.	**20**	45	82
Huron, Lake: Canada/U.S.A.	**20**	45	82
Hutte Sauvage, Lac de la: Qué.	**15**	56	65
Hyde Lake: N.W.T.		61	95
Hyland: *riv.*, Yukon		61	128
Hyland Post: B.C.	**28**	57	128
Hythe: Alta.	**26**	56	120
Iberville: Qué.	**23**	45	73
Icefield Range: Yukon		61	140
Igloolik: N.W.T.	**31**	69	82
Ignace: Ont.		49	91
Île à la Crosse: *& lake*, Sask.	**26**	55	108
Île aux Coudres: Qué.	**21**	47	70
Île aux Lièvres: Qué.	**21**	48	70
Ilford: Man.	**27**	56	96
Indian Arm: *lake*, B.C.	**36**	49	123
Indian Bay: Nfld.		49	54
Indian Harbour: Nfld.		54	57
Indian Harbour: Nfld.		55	57
Indian Head: Sask.	**27**	50	104
Ingersoll: Ont.	**20**	43	81
Ingleside: Ont.	**23**	45	75
Inglewood: Ont.	**22**	44	80
Ingonish: N.S.	**17**	47	60
Inklin: B.C.		59	133
Innisfail: Alta.	**26**	52	114
Innuksuak: *riv.*, Qué.		58	77
Inoucdjouac: Qué.	**14**	58	78
International Peace Garden: Canada/U.S.A.	**27**	49	100
International Rapids: Canada/U.S.A.	**23**	45	75
Inugsuin Fiord: N.W.T.	**14**	70	69
Inuvik: N.W.T.	**30**	68	133
Invermere: B.C.	**29**	50	116
Inverness: N.S.	**17**	46	61
Ioco: B.C.	**36**	49	123
Irma: Alta.	**26**	53	111
Irondale: *riv.*, Ont.	**22**	45	78
Iroquois: Ont.	**23**	45	75
Iroquois Falls: *town*, Ont.	**19**	48	81
Irvines Landing: B.C.	**28**	50	124
Isabella Bay: N.W.T.	**14**	69	67
Isabella Falls: Nfld.		54	63
Iskut: *riv.*, B.C.	**28**	57	131
Island Cove: *town*, Nfld.		48	53
Island Falls: *town*, Sask.	**27**	56	102
Island Falls Junc.: Ont.		50	81
Island Lake: *& town*, Man.	**27**	54	95
Island Rapids: Qué.		60	71
Islands, Bay of: Nfld.	**17**	49	58
Islands, Bay of: Ont.	**20**	46	82
Isle Madame: N.S.	**17**	45	61
Isle St. Ignace: Ont.	**19**	48	80
Isle Verte: *town*, Qué.	**16**	48	69
Itchen Lake: N.W.T.	**31**	65	113
Ituns: Sask.	**27**	52	104
Ivanhoe: *lake*, Ont.	**20**	48	83
Ivujivik: Qué.	**14**	62	78
Jack Lake: Ont.	**22**	45	78
Jack Lane Bay: Nfld.		56	61
Jacob I.: N.W.T.		52	79
Jacopie Lake: Nfld.		54	64
Jacques Cartier: Qué.	**32**	46	73
Jacques Cartier: *riv.*, Qué.	**21**	47	71
Jacques Cartier, Mt.: Qué.	**16**	49	66
Jacques Cartier, Détroit de: Québec	**16**	50	64
Jacquet River: *town*, N.B.	**16**	48	66
James Bay: Ont./Qué.	**18**	53	80
James Ross, Cape: N.W.T.	**31**	75	114
James Ross Strait: N.W.T.	**31**	70	97
Jamestown: Nfld.		48	54
Jamestown: Ont. *see* Wawa		48	85
Janeville: N.B.	**16**	48	65
Jarvis: Ont.	**20**	43	80
Jasper: Alta.	**26**	53	118
Jasper: Ont.	**23**	45	76
Jasper Nat. Park: Alta.	**26**	53	118
Jasper Place: Alta.	**26**	54	114
Jeannin, Lac: Qué.		56	66
Jellicoe: Ont.		50	88
Jennings: *riv.*, B.C.		59	131
Jenny Lind I.: N.W.T.	**31**	69	102
Jens Munk I.: N.W.T.	**31**	70	80
Jervis Inlet: B.C.	**28**	50	124
Jésus, Île: Qué.	**32**	46	74
Joe Batts Arm: Nfld.		50	54
Joggins: N.S.	**17**	46	64
Johnstone Strait: B.C.	**29**	50	126
Joliette: Qué.	**23**	46	73
Jones Sound: N.W.T.	**13**	76	85
Jonquière: Qué.	**20**	48	71
Joseph, Lac.: Nfld.	**15**	53	65
Joseph Lake: Alta.	**26**	53	113
Joseph, Lake: Ont.	**22**	45	80
Juan de Fuca, Str. of: Canada/U.S.A.	**28**	48	124
Jubilee Lake: Nfld.		48	55
Jude I.: Nfld.		47	55
Judique: N.S.	**17**	46	61
Julian, Lac: Qué.		54	78
Jupiter: *riv.*, Qué.		49	63
Kabinakagami: *lake & riv.*, Ontario		49	84
Kaegudeck Lake: Nfld.		48	55
Kagawong: Ont.		46	82
Kaipokok Bay: Nfld.		55	59
Kakagi Lake: Ont.	**19**	49	94
Kakisa Lake: N.W.T.	**30**	61	118
Kaladar: Ont.	**22**	45	77
Kamaniskeg Lake: Ont.	**20**	45	78
Kamilukuak Lake: N.W.T.	**31**	62	102
Kaminak Lake: N.W.T.	**31**	62	95
Kaministikwia: Ont.		48	89
Kaminuriak Lake: N.W.T.	**31**	63	96
Kamiskotia: *riv.*, Ont.		48	82
Kamloops: *& lake*, B.C.	**29**	51	120
Kamsack: Sask.	**27**	52	102
Kanaaupscow: Qué.	**15**	54	76
Kanaaupscow: *riv.*, Qué.	**15**	55	74
Kane Basin: Can./Grnld.	**13**	79	70
Kapiskau: *riv.*, Ont.	**19**	52	84
Kapuskasing: *& riv.*, Ont.	**19**	49	83
Kapuskasing Lake: Ont.		48	83
Kasba Lake: N.W.T.	**31**	60	102
Kasheshibaw Lake: Nfld.		54	63
Kaskattama: *riv.*, Man.	**25**	56	91
Kaslo: B.C.	**29**	50	117
Kasshabog Lake: Ont.	**22**	45	78
Kates Needle: *mtn.*, Canada/U.S.A.	**28**	57	132
Kawagama Lake: Ont.	**20**	45	79
Kawartha Lakes: Ont.	**22**	45	78
Kazabazua: Qué.	**23**	46	76
Kazan: *riv.*, N.W.T.	**31**	62	100
Kearney: Ont.	**22**	46	79
Kechika: *riv.*, B.C.	**24**	58	127
Kechika Range: B.C.		58	127
Kedgwick: N.B.	**16**	48	67
Kedgwick: *riv.*, N.B.		48	68
Keefers: B.C.	**28**	50	121
Keele: *riv.*, N.W.T.	**30**	64	127
Keele Peak: Yukon/N.W.T.	**30**	63	130
Keels: Nfld.		49	53
Keene: Ont.	**22**	44	78
Keenleyside Dam: B.C.	**27**	49	118
Keewatin: Ont.	**19**	50	95
Keewatin, District of: N.W.T.	**31**	—	—
Kegaska: Qué.	**17**	50	61
Keglo Bay: Qué.		59	66
Keg River: *town*, Alta.	**26**	58	118
Keith Arm: Gt. Bear Lake, N.W.T.	**30**	65	122
Kejimkujik Nat. Pk.: N.S.	**17**	44	65
Kekertaluk I.: N.W.T.	**14**	68	67
Keller Lake: N.W.T.	**30**	64	122
Kellet Str.: N.W.T.	**30**	76	117
Kellett, Cape: N.W.T.	**30**	72	126
Kelligrews: Nfld.	**17**	48	53
Kelliher: Sask.	**27**	51	104
Kelowna: B.C.	**29**	50	119
Kelsey Bay: *town*, B.C.	**29**	50	126
Kelvington: Sask.	**27**	52	103
Kemano: B.C.	**28**	54	128
Kempt, Lac: Qué.	**21**	47	74
Kemptville: Ont.	**23**	45	76
Kenabeek: Ont.	**20**	48	80
Kenamu: *riv.*, Nfld.		53	60
Kendall, Cape: N.W.T.	**18**	63	87
Kennebecasis: *riv.*, N.B.	**17**	46	65
Kennedy: Sask.	**27**	50	102
Kennedy Lake: B.C.	**28**	49	125
Kennetcook: N.S.	**17**	45	64
Kenney Dam: B.C.	**29**	54	125
Kennisis Lake: Ont.		45	79
Kénogami, Lac: Qué.	**21**	48	71
Kénogami: *riv.*, Ont.	**19**	50	85
Kenogamissi: *lake & falls*, Ontario	**20**	48	81
Kenora: Ont.	**19**	50	94
Kensington: P.E.I.	**17**	46	64
Kent Junction: N.B.	**17**	47	65
Kent Penin.: N.W.T.	**31**	68	107
Kentville: N.S.	**17**	45	64
Keremeos: B.C.	**28**	49	120
Kerrobert: Sask.	**26**	52	109
Kesagami Lake: Ont.		50	80
Keswick: N.B.		46	67
Keswick: Ont.	**22**	44	79
Kettle: *riv.*, B.C.	**29**	49	118
Kettle Point: Ont.	**20**	43	82
Kettle Rapids: Man.	**27**	57	95
Kettlestone, Baie: Qué.	**14**	62	78
Key Harbour: Ont.		46	81
Kiamika: Qué.	**21**	46	75
Kicking Horse Pass: B.C./Alberta	**29**	51	116
Kiglapait, Cape: Nfld.	**14**	57	62
Kiglapait Mts.: Nfld.		57	62
Kikerk Lake: N.W.T.	**31**	67	113
Kikkertavak I.: Nfld.		56	61
Kikkertorsoak, I.: Qué.	**14**	59	66
Kildare, Cape: P.E.I.	**17**	47	64
Killaloe Station: Ont.	**20**	46	77
Killam: Alta.	**26**	53	112
Killarney: Man.	**27**	49	100
Killinek I.: Qué.		60	64
Killiniq: Qué.	**14**	60	65

	Page	N	W
Kilmar: Qué.	**23**	46	75
Kimakto Penin.: N.W.T.	**31**	70	88
Kimberley: B.C.	**29**	49	116
Kincardine: Ont.	**20**	44	82
Kindersley: Sask.	**26**	51	109
Kingcome Inlet: *& town,* British Columbia	**29**	51	126
King Cove: Nfld.		49	53
King George, Mt.: B.C.	**29**	51	115
King George IV Lake: Newfoundland		48	58
King George Is.: N.W.T.	**18**	57	79
King I.: B.C.	**28**	52	127
King Kirkland: Ont.	**20**	48	80
Kings Point: *town,* Nfld.	**17**	50	56
Kingston: Ont.	**23**	44	76
Kingsville: Ont.	**20**	42	83
Kingurutik Lake: Nfld.		57	63
King William I.: N.W.T.	**31**	69	97
Kinistino: Sask.	**27**	53	105
Kinnaird: B.C.	**29**	49	118
Kinojevis, Lac: Qué.	**20**	48	79
Kinosis: Alta.		56	111
Kinsella: Alta.		53	112
Kiosk: Ont.	**20**	46	79
Kipahigan Lake: Sask./Man.	**27**	55	102
Kipawa: *town & lake,* Qué.	**20**	47	79
Kipawa, Parc de: Qué.	**20**	47	79
Kipling: Sask.	**27**	50	102
Kirkfield: Ont.	**22**	45	79
Kirkland Lake: *town,* Ont.	**20**	48	80
Kirkpatrick Lake: Alta.	**26**	52	111
Kirkpatrick Lake: Ont.	**20**	47	83
Kirton: B.C.		50	120
Kisgegas: B.C.	**28**	56	128
Kississing Lake: Man.	**27**	55	101
Kistigan Lake: Man.	**27**	55	92
Kitchener: Ont.	**20**	43	80
Kitimat: B.C.	**28**	54	129
Kittigazuit: N.W.T.	**30**	69	134
Klappan: *riv.,* B.C.	**28**	57	129
Kleinburg: Ont.	**32**	44	80
Klinaklini: *riv.,* B.C.	**29**	51	126
Klondike, *riv.,* Yukon	**30**	64	138
Kluane Lake: Yukon	**30**	61	138
Kluane Nat. Park: N.W.T.	**30**	61	140
Klukshu: Yukon		60	137
Knee Lake: Man.	**27**	55	95
Knight Inlet: B.C.	**29**	51	126
Knob Lake, *see* Schefferville			
Knowlton: Qué.	**21**	45	72
Knox, Cape: B.C.	**28**	54	133
Koch I.: N.W.T.	**14**	70	78
Kogaluc: *riv.,* Qué.	**14**	59	77
Kogaluc, Baie: Qué.	**14**	59	78
Kokanee Park: B.C.	**29**	50	117
Koksoak: *riv.,* Qué.	**14**	58	69
Kootenay: *riv.,* Can./U.S.A.	**29**	49	115
Kootenay Lake: B.C.	**29**	49	117
Kootenay Nat. Park: B.C.	**29**	51	116
Koraluk: *riv.,* Nfld.	**15**	56	63
Koruk: *riv.,* Qué.		59	66
Kotcho Lake: B.C.		59	121
Koukdjuak: *riv.,* N.W.T.	**14**	67	72
Kovik, Baie: Qué.	**14**	62	78
Kowkash: Ont.		50	87
Kugmallit Bay: N.W.T.	**30**	70	133
Kunghit I.: B.C.	**28**	52	131
Kusawa Lake: Yukon		60	136
Kwadacha Wilderness Prov. Park: B.C.	**29**	58	125
Kyle: Sask.	**26**	51	108
Kynocks: Yukon		61	136
Labelle: Qué.	**21**	46	75
Laberge, Lake: Yukon	**30**	61	135
Labrador: Nfld.	**15**	—	—
Labrador City: Nfld.	**15**	53	67
Labrador Sea: Atl. O.	**14/15**	—	—
Lac aux Sables: Qué.	**21**	47	72
La Cave: Ont.	**20**	46	79
Lac Baker: N.B.		47	69
Lac Bouchette: Qué.	**21**	48	72
Lac Castagnier: Qué.		49	78
Lac Decelles: Qué.	**20**	48	78
Lac de l'Est: Qué.	**21**	47	70
Lac du Bonnet: Man.	**27**	50	96
Lac Edouard: Qué.	**21**	48	72
Lac Etchemin: Qué.	**16**	46	70
Lac Frontière: Qué.	**16**	47	70
Lachine: *& rapids,* Qué.	**32**	45	74
Lac Humqui: Qué.		48	68
Lachute: Qué.	**23**	46	74
Lac la Biche: Alta.	**26**	55	112
Lac La Marie: N.W.T.	**30**	53	117
Lac La Ronge Prov. Park: Saskatchewan	**27**	55	105
Lac Mégantic: *town,* Qué.	**21**	45	71
Lacolle: Qué.	**23**	45	73
Lacombe: Alta.	**26**	52	114
Lacoste: Qué.		46	75
Lac Rémi: Qué.	**23**	46	75
La Croche: Qué.	**16**	48	73
Lac St. Paul: Qué.		47	75
Ladner: B.C.	**28**	49	123
Lady Evelyn Falls: N.W.T.		61	117
Lady Evelyn Lake: Ont.	**20**	47	80
Ladysmith: B.C.	**28**	49	124
Laflèche: Sask.	**26**	50	107

	Page	N	W
Laforest: Ont.		47	81
La Grande: *riv.,* Qué.	**15**	54	77
Lahave: *riv.,* N.S.	**17**	45	65
La Hune, Cap: Nfld.		48	57
Lake Cowichan: *& lake,* British Columbia	**29**	49	124
Lakefield: Ont.	**22**	44	78
Lake Harbour: N.W.T.	**14**	63	70
Lake Louise: Alta.	**26**	51	116
Lake River: Ont.	**18**	54	82
Lake St. Peter: Ont.	**22**	45	78
Lake Superior Prov. Park: Ontario	**20**	48	85
La Loche: Sask.	**26**	56	109
La Malbaie: Qué.	**21**	48	70
Lamaline: Nfld.		47	56
Lamartine: Qué.		47	70
La Martre, Lac: N.W.T.	**30**	63	118
Lambeth: Ont.	**20**	43	81
Lambton: Qué.	**16**	46	71
Lambton, Cape: N.W.T.	**30**	71	123
La Moinerie, Lac: Qué.		57	67
Lamorandière: Qué.	**20**	49	77
La Motte: *& lake,* Qué.	**20**	48	78
Lampman: Sask.	**27**	49	103
Lanark: Ont.	**23**	45	76
Lancaster: N.B.	**17**	45	66
Lancaster: Ont.	**23**	45	75
Lancaster Sound: N.W.T.	**31**	74	85
Lance Point: Nfld.		47	54
Langenburg: Sask.	**27**	51	101
Langham: Sask.	**26**	52	107
Langlade: Qué.	**21**	48	76
Langley: *town,* B.C.	**28**	49	123
Laniel: Qué.	**20**	47	79
Lanigan: Sask.	**27**	52	105
Lanoraie: Qué.	**23**	46	73
Lansdowne: Ont.	**23**	44	76
Lansdowne House: Ont.		52	88
L'Anse au Loup: Nfld.		51	57
L'Anse-aux-Meadows: Nfld.	**15**	52	55
L'Anse St. Jean: Qué.	**21**	48	70
Lantzville: B.C.	**28**	49	124
Lapêche, Lac: Qué.	**23**	46	76
La Perade: Qué.	**21**	46	72
La Plonge, Lac: Sask.	**26**	55	107
La Pocatière: Qué.	**21**	47	70
La Poile Bay: Nfld.	**17**	48	58
Lapointe, Lac: Qué.		53	69
La Potherie, Lac: Qué.	**14**	59	72
Laprairie: Qué.	**32**	45	73
La Providence: Qué.	**21**	46	73
Larder Lake: *town,* Ont.	**20**	48	80
L'Ardoise: N.S.	**17**	46	61
La Reine: Qué.		49	79
Larive, Lac: Qué.	**20**	47	77
Lark Harbour: Nfld.	**17**	49	58
La Ronge: *& lake,* Sask.	**27**	55	105
Larry's River: *town,* N.S.	**17**	45	61
Larus Lake: Ont.	**27**	51	95
La Salle: Qué.	**32**	45	74
La Sarre: Qué.	**15**	49	79
L'Ascension: Qué.		49	72
La Scie: Nfld.	**17**	50	55
Lashburn: Sask.	**26**	53	110
Lasqueti I.: B.C.	**28**	49	124
L'Assomption: Qué.	**23**	46	73
L'Assomption: *riv.,* Qué.	**21**	46	74
Last Mountain Lake: Sask.	**27**	51	105
Latchford: Ont.	**20**	47	80
La Tuque: Qué.	**21**	47	73
Laurentides, Parc des: Qué.	**20**	47	71
Lauzon: Qué.	**21**	47	71
Laval-des-Rapides: Qué.	**32**	46	74
Lavaltrie: Qué.	**23**	46	73
Lavant Station: Ont.		45	77
La Vérendrye, Parc de: Qué.	**20**	47	77
Lavieille, Lac: Ont.	**20**	46	78
Lawn: Nfld.		47	56
Lawrencetown: N.S.	**17**	45	65
Leader: Sask.	**26**	51	110
Leamington: Ont.	**20**	42	83
L'Eau Claire, Lac à: Qué.	**15**	56	74
L'Ecorce, Lac de: Qué.	**21**	47	76
Leduc: Alta.	**26**	53	114
Lefroy: Ont.	**22**	44	80
Lemieux Is.: N.W.T.	**14**	64	65
Lennoxville: Qué.	**21**	45	72
Lenore Lake: Sask.	**27**	52	105
Leopold I.: N.W.T.	**14**	65	64
Leoville: Sask.	**26**	54	108
L'Epiphanie: Qué.	**23**	46	73
Lepreau, Pointe: N.B.	**17**	45	66
Léry: Qué.	**23**	45	74
L'Escalier, Lac: Qué.	**21**	46	76
Les Escoumains: Qué.	**16**	48	69
Les Etroits: Qué.		47	69
Lesser Slave Lake: Alta.	**26**	55	115
L'Est, Pointe de: Qué.	**17**	49	62
Lethbridge: Alta.	**26**	50	113
Lethbridge: Nfld.		48	54
Levack: Ont.	**20**	47	81
Level Mt.: B.C.		58	131
Lévis: Qué.	**21**	47	71
Lewisporte: Nfld.	**17**	49	55
Leyson Point: N.W.T.	**14**	63	81
Liard: *riv.,* B.C./N.W.T.	**30**	61	123
Liard Plain: Yukon/B.C.		60	126

	Page	N	W
Liard Range: N.W.T.	**30**	61	123
Liddon Gulf: N.W.T.	**31**	75	114
Lillooet: B.C.	**28**	51	122
Lillooet: *riv.,* B.C.	**28**	50	122
Lillooet Lake: B.C.	**28**	50	122
Lime Ridge: *town,* Qué.		46	72
Limoges: Ont.	**23**	45	75
Lindsay: Ont.	**22**	44	79
Lingman Lake: *town,* Ont.	**27**	54	93
Linton: Qué.	**21**	47	72
Linzee, Cape: N.S.	**17**	46	62
Liot Point: N.W.T.	**30**	74	125
Lipton: Sask.	**27**	51	104
Lismore: N.S.	**17**	46	62
Listowel: Ont.	**20**	44	81
Little Bay I.: *& town,* Nfld.		50	56
Little Current: Ont.	**20**	46	82
Little Dover: N.S.	**17**	45	61
Little Grand Lake: Nfld.		49	58
Little Grand Rapids: *town,* Manitoba	**27**	52	95
Little Longlac: Ont.		50	87
Little Missinaibi Lake: Ont.	**20**	48	84
Little Narrows: N.S.	**17**	46	61
Little Pic: *riv.,* Ont.		49	86
Little Smoky: *riv.,* Alta.	**26**	54	117
Little Vermilion Lake: Ont.	**27**	51	94
Lively: Ont.	**20**	46	81
Liverpool: N.S.	**17**	44	65
Liverpool, Cape: N.W.T.	**31**	74	78
Liverpool Bay: N.W.T.	**30**	70	130
Lizotte: Qué.		48	72
Lloyd George, Mt.: B.C.	**29**	58	125
Lloyd Lake: Sask.	**26**	57	109
Lloydminster: Alta./Sask.	**26**	53	110
Lobstick Lake: Nfld.	**15**	54	65
Lochalsh: Ont.		48	84
Lock Barrage: Qué.	**21**	48	75
Lockeport: N.S.	**17**	44	65
Logan, Mt.: Qué.	**16**	49	67
Logan, Mt.: Yukon	**30**	60	140
Logan Mts.: Yukon/N.W.T.	**30**	62	128
Logan Point: N.S.	**17**	46	63
Loks Land: *i.,* N.W.T.	**14**	63	65
London: Ont.	**20**	43	81
Lonely I.: Ont.	**20**	45	81
Lone Star: Alta.		57	118
Long Harbour: B.C.	**26**	49	123
Long I.: Nfld.		48	56
Long I.: Nfld.		50	56
Long I.: Nfld.		47	54
Long I.: N.W.T.	**18**	55	80
Long I.: N.S.	**17**	44	66
Longlac: Ont.	**19**	50	86
Long Lake: N.B.	**16**	47	67
Long Lake: Ont.		50	87
Long Point: Man.	**27**	53	98
Long Point: *& bay,* Ont.	**20**	43	80
Long Pond: Nfld.		48	56
Long Range: Nfld.	**17**	48	59
Long Range: Nfld.	**17**	50	57
Long Sault: Ont.	**23**	45	75
Longueuil: Qué.	**32**	46	73
Lookout, Cape: Ont.		55	84
Lookout Mt.: Nfld.		53	64
Loon Lake: *town,* Sask.	**26**	54	109
Lord Mayor Bay: N.W.T.	**31**	70	92
Lord's Cove: Nfld.		47	56
Loretteville: Qué.	**21**	47	71
L'Orignal: Ont.	**23**	46	75
Lorrainville: Qué.	**20**	47	79
Lotbinière: Qué.	**21**	47	72
Loughborough Inlet: B.C.	**28**	50	125
Louisbourg: N.S.	**17**	46	60
Louise I.: B.C.	**28**	53	132
Louis XIV, Pointe: Qué.	**15**	55	80
Louiseville: Qué.	**21**	46	73
Low: Qué.	**23**	46	76
Low, Cape: N.W.T.	**18**	63	85
Low Bush: Ont.		49	80
Lower Arrow Lake: B.C.	**29**	49	118
Lower Foster Lake: Sask.	**27**	57	105
Lower Post: B.C.	**24**	60	128
Lowther: Ont.		50	83
Lowther I.: N.W.T.	**31**	75	93
Lubicon Lake: Alta.	**26**	56	116
Lucan: Ont.	**20**	43	81
Lucania, Mt.: Yukon		61	140
Lucas Channel: Ont.	**20**	45	82
Luceville: Qué.	**16**	48	68
Ludgate: Ont.		46	80
Lulu I.: B.C.	**36**	49	123
Lumière, Cap: N.B.	**17**	47	65
Lumsden: Nfld.		49	54
Lumsden: Sask.	**27**	51	105
Lund: B.C.	**28**	50	125
Lundar: Man.	**27**	51	98
Lunenburg: N.S.	**17**	44	64
Luseland: Sask.	**26**	52	109
Lyall, Mt.: B.C./Alta.	**29**	50	115
Lynn Lake: Man.	**27**	57	101
Lynx Lake: N.W.T.	**31**	62	106
Lyon, Cape: N.W.T.	**30**	70	123
Lyon Inlet: N.W.T.	**14**	66	84
Lyster Station: Qué.	**21**	46	72
Lytton: B.C.	**28**	50	122
Mabel Lake: B.C.	**29**	50	119
Mabou: N.S.	**17**	46	61

	Page	N	W
McAdam: N.B.	**16**	45	67
MacAlpine Lake: N.W.T.	**31**	67	103
Macamic: *& lake,* Qué.		49	79
Mcbeth Fiord: N.W.T.	**14**	69	69
McBride: B.C.	**29**	53	120
Maccan: N.S.	**17**	46	64
Maccles Pond: Nfld.		49	54
McClintock: Man.	**27**	58	94
McClintock Chan.: N.W.T.	**31**	73	104
McClure, Cape: N.W.T.	**30**	75	121
McClure Str.: N.W.T.	**30**	75	118
McConnell Creek: *town,* British Columbia	**29**	57	126
McConnell Range: N.W.T.	**30**	64	124
McDame: B.C.		59	129
Macdougall Lake: N.W.T.	**31**	66	99
MacDowell Lake: Ont.	**27**	52	92
Macduff: Ont.		49	84
McFarlane: *riv.,* Sask.	**26**	58	108
McGillivray: B.C.	**28**	51	122
McGivney: N.B.	**16**	46	66
MacGregor: Man.	**27**	50	99
McGregor Lake: Alta.	**26**	50	113
McGuire: B.C.	**28**	50	123
McInnes Lake: Ont.	**27**	52	94
MacKay Lake: N.W.T.	**31**	64	112
Mackenzie: B.C.	**29**	56	124
Mackenzie: *riv.,* N.W.T.	**30**	67	133
Mackenzie, District of: N.W.T.	**30/31**	—	—
Mackenzie Bay: Yukon	**30**	69	138
Mackenzie Bison Sanctuary: N.W.T.	**30**	62	117
Mackenzie Highway: Alta.	**26**	57	118
McKenzie Island: *town,* Ontario	**27**	51	94
Mackenzie Mtns.: Yukon/N.W.T.	**30**	64	130
Mackies: Ont.		48	90
Macklin: Sask.	**26**	52	110
McLellan Strait: Nfld.		60	64
McLennan: Alta.	**26**	55	117
Macleod Bay: N.W.T.	**31**	63	110
McLeod Lake: B.C.	**29**	55	125
McLoughlin Bay: N.W.T.	**31**	67	99
McMasterville: Qué.	**23**	46	73
Macmillan: *riv.,* Yukon	**30**	63	133
McNamee: N.B.	**16**	46	66
McNaughton Lake: B.C.	**29**	52	118
McNutt I.: N.S.	**17**	44	65
Macoun Lake: Sask.	**27**	56	104
MacRae: Yukon		61	135
Mactaquac: N.B.	**17**	46	67
McTavish Arm: Great Bear Lake, N.W.T.	**30**	66	118
MacTier: Ont.	**22**	45	80
McVicar Arm: Great Bear Lake, N.W.T.	**30**	65	120
Madawaska: *& riv.,* Ont.	**20**	45	78
Madeleine, Îles de la: Qué.	**15**	47	61
Madoc: Ont.	**22**	45	77
Madsen: Ont.	**19**	51	94
Magaquadavic: *riv.,* N.B.		45	67
Magnet: Man.	**27**	51	99
Magnetawan: Ont.	**22**	46	80
Magog: Qué.	**21**	45	72
Magpie: *riv.,* Ont.	**20**	48	84
Magpie: Qué.	**16**	50	65
Magpie, Lac: Qué.	**15**	51	65
Magrath: Alta.	**26**	49	113
Maguse Lake: N.W.T.	**31**	62	95
Maguse Point: N.W.T.		61	94
Maguse River: *town,* N.W.T.	**31**	61	94
Maher: Ont.		49	81
Mahone Bay: *& town,* N.S.	**17**	44	64
Maidstone: Sask.	**26**	53	109
Main Brook: *town,* Nfld.		51	56
Maitland: *riv.,* Ont.	**20**	44	81
Makkovik: Nfld.	**15**	55	59
Makobe Lake: Ont.	**20**	47	80
Malartic: Qué.	**20**	48	78
Malaspina Strait: B.C.	**28**	50	124
Malbaie: *riv.,* Qué.		48	70
Malcolm I.: B.C.	**28**	51	127
Mallery Lake: N.W.T.	**31**	64	98
Mallorytown: Ont.	**23**	44	76
Malpeque Bay: P.E.I.	**17**	47	64
Mamainse-Hill: Ont.	**20**	47	84
Mamainse Point: Ont.		47	85
Mamette Lake: *town,* B.C.		50	121
Mammamattawa: Ont.		50	84
Manicouagan: Qué.	**15**	51	69
Manicouagan: *riv.,* Qué.	**15**	50	68
Manicouagan: *penin.,* Qué.		49	68
Manicouagan, Réservoir: Qué.	**15**	51	68
Manigotagan Lake: Man.	**27**	51	95
Manitoba: *Prov.* (*cap.* Winnipeg)	**27**	—	—
Manitoba, Lake: Man.	**27**	51	99
Manito Lake: Sask.	**26**	53	110
Manitou: Man.	**27**	49	98
Manitou, Lac: Qué		51	65
Manitou Lake: Ont.	**20**	46	82
Manitou Lakes: Ont.		49	93
Manitoulin I.: Ont.	**20**	46	82
Manitouwadge: Ont.	**19**	49	86
Manitowaning: *& bay,* Ont.	**20**	46	82

	Page	N	W
Manitowik Lake: Ont.	**20**	48	84
Maniwaki: Qué.	**15**	46	76
Manning: Alta.	**26**	57	118
Manning, Cape: N.W.T.	**30**	76	122
Mannville: Alta.	**26**	54	112
Manotick: Ont.	**32**	45	76
Manouane, Lac: Qué.	**15**	51	70
Manseau: Qué.	**21**	46	72
Mansel I.: N.W.T.	**14**	62	80
Manson Creek: *town,* B.C.	**29**	56	124
Maple: Ont.	**32**	44	79
Maple Creek: *town,* Sask.	**26**	50	109
Marathon: Ont.	**19**	49	86
Margaree: N.S.	**17**	46	61
Margaret, Cape: N.W.T.	**31**	70	92
Margaret Bay: *town,* B.C.	**28**	51	127
Margaret Lake: Alta.	**26**	59	115
Marguerite: *riv.,* Qué.	**15**	51	67
Maria: Qué.	**16**	48	66
Marian Lake: N.W.T.	**30**	63	116
Maricourt: Qué.	**14**	62	72
Marieville: Qué.	**21**	45	73
Marilla: B.C.	**29**	54	126
Markdale: Ont.	**20**	44	80
Markham: Ont.	**32**	44	79
Markham Bay: N.W.T.	**14**	63	72
Marmette, Lac: Qué.		49	75
Marmion Lake: Ont.		49	91
Marmora: Ont.	**22**	44	78
Marsh Lake: Yukon		60	134
Marsoui: Qué.		49	66
Marten: *riv.,* Qué.		51	76
Maryfield: Sask.	**27**	50	102
Mary Jones Bay: N.W.T.	**31**	70	92
Marystown: Nfld.	**17**	47	55
Marysville: N.B.	**17**	46	66
Mascouche: Qué.	**23**	46	74
Maskinongé: *& riv.,* Qué.	**21**	46	73
Massawippi, Lac: Qué.	**21**	45	72
Masset: B.C.	**28**	54	132
Masset Inlet: B.C.	**28**	54	132
Massey: Ont.	**20**	46	82
Masson: Qué.	**23**	46	75
Matachewan: Ont.	**20**	48	81
Matagami: Qué.	**15**	50	78
Matane: Qué.	**16**	49	68
Matapédia: Qué.	**16**	48	67
Matapédia, Lac: Qué.		48	68
Matheson: Ont.	**20**	48	80
Matinenda Lake: Ont.	**20**	46	83
Mattagami: *riv.,* Ont.	**19**	50	82
Mattagami Lake: Ont.		48	81
Mattawa: Ont.	**20**	46	79
Mattawin: *riv.,* Qué.	**21**	47	73
Maunoir, Lake: N.W.T.	**30**	67	126
Mauricie, Parc National de la: Qué	**16**	46	73
Maury Channel: N.W.T.	**31**	76	95
Maxville: Ont.	**23**	45	75
Maxwell Bay: N.W.T.	**31**	75	89
May, Point: Nfld.		47	56
Mayerthorpe: Alta.	**26**	54	115
Maynooth: Ont.	**20**	45	78
Mayo: Yukon	**30**	63	136
Mayo Lake: Yukon	**30**	64	135
Mayson Lake: Sask.	**26**	58	107
Mazinaw Lake: Ont.	**22**	45	77
M'Clintock: Yukon		61	134
M'Clintock Chan.: N.W.T.	**13**	72	102
Meadow Lake: *town,* Sask.	**26**	54	108
Meadow Lake Prov. Park: Saskatchewan	**26**	54	109
Meaford: Ont.	**20**	45	81
Meaghers Grant: N.S.	**17**	45	63
Mealy Mtns.: Nfld.	**15**	53	59
Meander River: *town,* Alta.	**26**	59	118
Meddonegonnix Lake: Newfoundland		48	55
Medicine Hat: Alta.	**26**	50	111
Medway: *riv.,* N.S.	**17**	44	65
Meelpaeg Lake: Nfld.	**17**	48	57
Mégantic, Lac: Qué.	**21**	45	71
Mégantic, Mont: Qué.	**21**	45	71
Mégiscane: Qué.	**20**	48	77
Mégiscane: *riv.,* Qué.	**21**	49	76
Mégiscane, Lac: Qué.		48	76
Mékinac, Lac: Qué.	**21**	47	73
Melbourne I.: N.W.T.	**31**	68	104
Meldrum Bay: *town,* Ont.		46	83
Mélèzes, R. aux: Qué.	**14**	57	70
Melfort: Sask.	**27**	53	105
Melita: Man.	**27**	49	101
Melville: Sask.	**27**	51	103
Melville, Lake: Nfld.	**15**	54	59
Melville Hills: N.W.T.	**30**	68	120
Melville I.: N.W.T.	**31**	75	110
Melville Penin.: N.W.T.	**14**	68	84
Melville Sound: N.W.T.	**31**	68	108
Memphrémagog, Lac: Québec.	**21**	45	72
Memramcook: N.B.	**17**	46	65
Menako Lakes: Ont.		52	90
Menihek Lakes: Nfld.	**15**	54	66
Menistouc, Lac: Qué.		53	66
Merasheen I.: Nfld.		47	54
Mercier Barrage: Qué.	**21**	47	76
Mercy Bay: N.W.T.	**30**	74	119
Merigomish: N.S.	**17**	46	62
Merrickville: Ont.	**23**	45	76
Merritt: B.C.	**29**	50	121

	Page	N	W
Merry I.: N.W.T.		56	77
Mesgouez, Lac: Qué.	**15**	51	75
Métabetchouan: Qué.		48	72
Metagama: Ont.	**20**	47	82
Meta Pond: Nfld.		48	55
Metcalfe: Ont.	**32**	45	75
Metchosin: B.C.	**28**	48	124
Meteghan: N.S.	**17**	44	66
Methy Lake: Sask.	**26**	56	110
Métis Beach: *town,* Qué.		48	68
Métis, Lac: Qué.		48	68
Mica Creek: B.C.	**29**	52	118
Mica Dam: B.C.	**29**	52	118
Michael, Lake: Nfld.		55	58
Michael Point: Ont.	**20**	46	82
Michaud Point: N.S.	**17**	46	61
Michel, Pte. à: Qué.	**16**	49	69
Michel Peak: B.C.	**29**	54	126
Michelson, Cape: N.W.T.	**31**	71	103
Michikamau Lake: Nfld.	**15**	54	64
Michipicoten: Ont.	**20**	48	85
Michipicoten I.: Ont.	**19**	48	86
Midale: Sask.	**27**	49	103
Middle I.: Ont.	**20**	42	83
Middle Ridge: Nfld.		48	55
Middleton: N.S.	**17**	45	65
Midland: Ont.	**22**	45	80
Midway Mts.: B.C.	**29**	49	119
Mikkwa: *riv.,* Alta.	**26**	58	115
Milbanke Sound: B.C.	**28**	51	128
Mildmay: Ont.	**20**	44	81
Milestone: Sask.	**27**	50	104
Milk: *riv.,* Alta.	**26**	49	111
Milk River: *town,* Alta.	**26**	49	112
Mill Bay: *town,* B.C.	**28**	55	130
Millbrook: Ont.	**22**	44	78
Mille Îles, R. des: Qué.	**32**	46	74
Mille Lacs, Lac des: Ont.		48	90
Millertown: Nfld.		49	57
Millertown Junction: Nfld.		49	56
Millet: Alta.	**26**	53	113
Mill I.: N.W.T.	**14**	64	78
Mills Lake: N.W.T.	**30**	61	118
Milltown: N.B.	**16**	45	67
Mill Village: N.S.	**17**	44	65
Milne Inlet: N.W.T.	**31**	72	80
Milnet: Ont.	**20**	47	81
Milson: N.S.	**17**	44	65
Milson: P.E.I.	**17**	46	63
Milton: Ont.	**22**	43	80
Milverton: Ont.	**20**	43	81
Minaki: Ont.	**27**	50	95
Minas Basin: *& chan.,* N.S.	**17**	45	64
Minden: Ont.	**22**	45	79
Mingan: *& is.,* Qué.	**16**	50	64
Minipi: *riv. & rapids,* Nfld.		53	62
Minipi Lake: Nfld.		52	61
Minitonas: Man.	**27**	52	101
Minnedosa: Man.	**27**	50	100
Minto: N.B.	**17**	46	66
Minto, Lac: Qué.	**14**	57	75
Minto Head: N.W.T.	**31**	73	103
Minto Inlet: N.W.T.	**30**	71	117
Mira Bay: N.S.	**17**	46	60
Miramichi, N.W.: *riv.,* N.B.	**16**	47	66
Miramichi, S.W.: *riv.,* N.B.	**16**	46	67
Miramichi Bay: N.B.	**16**	47	65
Miscou: *i. & cape,* N.B.	**16**	48	64
Miscouche: P.E.I.	**17**	46	64
Misery Point: Nfld.		52	55
Missanabie: Ont.		48	84
Missinaibi: *riv.,* Ont.	**19**	50	83
Missinaibi Lake: Ont.	**20**	48	84
Mission City: B.C.	**28**	49	122
Missisa Lake: Ont.	**19**	52	83
Mississagi: *riv.,* Ont.	**20**	46	83
Mississagi Strait: Ont.	**20**	46	83
Mississagi Prov. Forest: Ontario	**20**	47	83
Mississauga: Ont.	**22**	44	80
Mississippi: *riv. & lake,* Ont.	**23**	45	76
Missouri Coteau: Sask.	**26**	50	106
Mistassibi: *riv.,* Qué.	**15**	49	72
Mistassini: *& riv.,* Qué.	**16**	49	72
Mistassini, Lac: Qué.	**15**	51	74
Mistassini, Parc de: Qué.	**15**	50	74
Mistastin Lake: Nfld.		56	63
Mistinibi, Lac: Qué.		56	64
Mitchell: Ont.	**20**	43	81
Mitchinamekus: *riv.,* Qué.	**21**	47	75
Moak Lake: Man.	**27**	56	97
Moar Lake: Man./Ont.	**27**	52	95
Moira: *riv.,* Ont.	**22**	44	77
Moisie: *& riv.,* Qué.	**15**	50	66
Mojikit Lake: Ont.		51	88
Molson: Man.	**27**	50	96
Molson Lake: Nfld.		53	66
Molson Lake: Man.	**27**	54	97
Monarch Mt.: B.C.	**29**	52	126
Monashee Mts.: B.C.	**29**	51	118
Moncton: N.B.	**17**	46	65
Monet: Qué.	**21**	48	76
Monkman Pass: B.C.	**29**	55	121
Montague: P.E.I.	**17**	46	63
Mont Alverne: Qué.		48	72
Montauban: Qué.		47	72
Montcerf: Qué.		46	76
Montebello: Qué.	**23**	46	75
Monte Creek: *town,* B.C.		51	120
Monteith: Ont.		49	81

	Page	N	W
Montigny, Lac.: Qué.	**20**	48	78
Mont Joli: Qué.	**16**	48	68
Mont Laurier: Qué.	**21**	47	75
Mont Louis: Qué.	**16**	49	66
Montmagny: Qué.	**16**	47	70
Montmartre: Sask.	**27**	50	103
Montmorency: *& riv.,* Qué.	**21**	47	71
Montor, Lac: Qué.		55	64
Montréal: *City & i.,* Qué.	**32**	46	74
Montreal: *riv.,* Ont.	**20**	47	84
Montreal: *riv.,* Ont.		48	80
Montreal: *riv.,* Sask.	**27**	55	106
Montréal Est: Qué.	**32**	46	74
Montreal Lake: *& town,* Saskatchewan	**27**	54	106
Montréal Nord: Qué.	**32**	46	74
Montreal River: *town,* Ont.	**20**	47	79
Mont Rolland: Qué.	**23**	46	74
Montrose: B.C.	**29**	49	118
Monts, Pte. des: Qué.	**16**	49	67
Mont Tremblant, Parc du: Québec	**21**	46	74
Moonbeam: Ont.		49	82
Moose: *riv.,* Ont.	**19**	51	81
Moose Creek: *town,* Ont.	**23**	45	75
Moose Factory: Ont.		51	81
Moose Jaw: Sask.	**27**	50	106
Moose Lake: Man.	**27**	54	100
Moose Mtn. Park: Sask.	**27**	50	102
Moosonee: Ont.	**19**	51	81
Moosomin: Sask.	**27**	50	102
Morden: Man.	**27**	49	98
Morell: P.E.I.	**17**	46	63
Moresby I.: B.C.	**28**	52	132
Morhiban, Lac de: Qué.		52	63
Moriarty, Mt.: B.C.	**28**	49	124
Morice Lake: B.C.	**28**	54	127
Moricetown: B.C.	**28**	55	127
Morin Heights: Qué.	**23**	46	74
Morinville: Alta.	**26**	54	114
Morris: Man.	**27**	49	97
Morrisburg: Ont.	**23**	45	75
Morse: Sask.	**26**	50	107
Mostoos Hills: Sask.	**26**	55	109
Mouni Rapids: Nfld.		53	62
Mount Albert: Ont.	**22**	44	79
Mount Forest: Ont.	**20**	44	81
Mount Hope: Ont.	**22**	43	80
Mount Robson Prov. Park: British Columbia	**29**	53	119
Mount Stewart: P.E.I.	**17**	46	63
Mount Uniacke: N.S.	**17**	45	64
Mozhabong Lake: Ont.	**20**	47	82
Muddy Bay: *settlement,* Newfoundland		54	57
Mudjatik: *riv.,* Sask.	**26**	57	107
Mugford, Cape: Nfld.		58	62
Mukutawa: *riv.,* Man.	**27**	53	97
Mulgrave: N.S.	**17**	46	61
Mundare: Alta.	**26**	54	112
Munuscong Lake: Canada/U.S.A.	**20**	46	84
Murdochville: Qué.	**16**	49	65
Murray Harbour: P.E.I.	**17**	46	62
Murray Maxwell Bay: N.W.T.	**31**	70	80
Murray River: *town,* P.E.I.	**17**	46	62
Murtie Lake: B.C.	**29**	52	120
Musgrave Town: Nfld.		48	54
Mushalagan: *riv.,* Qué.		52	69
Muskoka, Lake: Ont.	**22**	45	79
Muskrat Falls: Nfld.		53	61
Musquaro, Lac: Qué.		51	61
Musquodoboit: N.S.	**17**	45	63
Musquodoboit Harbour: Nova Scotia	**17**	45	63
Mutton Bay: *town,* Nfld.		51	59
Myrnam: Alta.	**26**	54	111
Myrtle: Ont.	**22**	44	79
Mystery Lake: Man.	**27**	56	98
Nabisipi: *riv.,* Qué.		51	62
Nachicapau, Lac: Qué.		57	68
Nachvak Fiord: Nfld.		59	63
Nackawic: N.B.	**16**	46	67
Nagagami Lake: Ont.		49	85
Nahanni Mt.: N.W.T.		62	123
Nahanni Nat. Park: N.W.T.	**30**	62	125
Nahanni Range: N.W.T.	**30**	61	123
Nahlin: B.C.		59	131
Nahma: Ont.		49	81
Naicam: Sask.	**27**	52	104
Nain: Nfld.	**15**	56	62
Nakina: Ont.	**19**	50	87
Nakusp: B.C.	**29**	50	118
Namur: Qué.	**23**	46	75
Nanaimo: B.C.	**28**	49	124
Nanton: Alta.	**26**	50	114
Naococane, Lac: Qué.	**15**	53	77
Napanee: Ont.	**22**	44	77
Napartokh Bay: Nfld.		58	62
Napierville: Qué.	**23**	45	73
Nappan: N.S.	**17**	46	64
Naskaupi: *riv.,* Nfld.	**15**	54	63
Nass: *riv.,* B.C.	**28**	55	129
Nastapoka: *riv.,* Qué.	**15**	57	76
Nastapoka Is.: N.W.T.		57	77
Nastigouche, Parc: Qué.	**16**	46	74
Natashquan: Qué.	**15**	50	62
Natashquan: *riv.,* Qué.	**15**	51	62

	Page	N	W
Nation: *riv.,* B.C.	**29**	55	124
Native Bay: N.W.T.	**18**	64	83
Naughton: Ont.	**20**	46	81
Nauwigewauk: N.B.	**17**	45	66
Nazko: B.C.	**29**	53	124
Nechako: *riv.,* B.C.	**29**	54	125
Nechako Plateau: B.C.	**29**	54	124
Neddy Harbour: Nfld.		50	58
Nedluk Lake: Qué.		57	73
Neeb: Sask.	**26**	54	108
Neepawa: Man.	**27**	50	99
Neguac: N.B.	**16**	48	66
Nejanilini Lake: Man.	**27**	60	98
Nelson: B.C.	**29**	49	117
Nelson: *riv.,* Man.	**27**	57	93
Nelson Forks: B.C.	**24**	59	124
Nelson House: Man.	**27**	56	99
Nelson I.: B.C.	**28**	50	124
Nelson-Miramichi: N.B.	**16**	48	66
Nemegos: Ont.	**20**	48	83
Nemegosenda: *riv.,* Ont.	**20**	48	83
Nemiskam Nat. Park: Alta.	**26**	49	111
Neoskweskau: Qué.		52	74
Nepewassi Lake: Ont.	**20**	46	81
Nestawkanow: *riv.,* Qué.		50	73
Nettilling Fiord: N.W.T.	**14**	66	68
Nettilling Lake: N.W.T.	**14**	66	70
Neudorf: Sask.	**27**	51	103
Neustadt: Ont.	**20**	44	81
New Bay: Nfld.		49	55
Newboro: Ont.	**23**	45	76
New Brunswick: *Prov.* (*cap.* Fredericton)	**16**	46	66
Newburgh: Ont.	**22**	44	77
New Carlisle: Qué.	**16**	48	65
Newcastle: N.B.	**16**	47	65
Newcastle: Ont.	**22**	44	79
New Denver: B.C.	**29**	50	117
Newell, Lake: Alta.	**26**	50	112
Newfoundland: *Prov.* (*cap.* St. John's)	**14/15**	—	—
Newfoundland: *i.,* Canada	**15**	49	56
New Germany: N.S.	**17**	45	65
New Glasgow: N.S.	**17**	46	63
New Hamburg: Ont.	**20**	43	81
Newington: Ont.	**23**	45	75
New Liskeard: Ont.	**20**	47	80
Newmarket: Ont.	**22**	44	79
Newport: N.S.	**17**	45	64
Newport: Qué.	**16**	48	65
New Richmond: Qué.	**16**	48	66
New Ross: N.S.	**17**	45	64
Newville: N.S.	**17**	46	64
New Waterford: N.S.	**17**	46	60
New Westminster: B.C.	**36**	49	123
New World I.: Nfld.		50	55
Niagara: *riv.,* Can./U.S.A.	**22**	43	79
Niagara Escarpment: Ont.	**22**	43	79
Niagara Falls: *town,* Ont.	**22**	43	79
Niagara-on-the-Lake: Ont.	**22**	43	79
Nichicun, Lac: Qué.		53	71
Nicholson: *& dam,* Ont.	**20**	48	84
Nicobi, Lac: Qué.		49	76
Nicola: *& lake,* B.C.		50	121
Nicola: *riv.,* B.C.	**28**	50	121
Nicolet: *& riv.,* Qué.	**21**	46	73
Nictau: N.B.	**16**	47	67
Nig Creek: *town,* B.C.	**29**	57	121
Nigei I.: B.C.	**28**	50	127
Night Hawk Lake: Ont.	**20**	48	81
Nimpkish Lake: B.C.	**28**	50	127
Nipawin: Sask.	**27**	53	104
Nipawin Prov. Park: Sask.	**27**	54	105
Nipigon: Ont.	**19**	48	88
Nipigon, Lake: Ont.	**19**	50	88
Nipigon Bay: Ont.		49	88
Nipigon-Onaman Game Preserve: Ontario		50	87
Nipigon Prov. Forest: Ont.	**19**	50	88
Nipishish Lake: Nfld.		54	60
Nipisiquit: *riv.,* N.B.	**16**	47	66
Nipissi, Lac: Qué.		50	72
Nipissing, Lake: Ont.	**20**	46	80
Nipissing Game Preserve: Ontario	**20**	47	80
Nisling: *riv. & range,* Yukon	**30**	62	139
Nisutlin: *riv.,* Yukon		61	133
Nitchequon: Qué.	**15**	53	71
Nith: *riv.,* Ont.	**20**	43	81
Nitinat Lake: B.C.	**28**	49	125
Niverville: Man.	**27**	50	97
Nobel: Ont.	**20**	45	80
Nobleton: Ont.	**22**	44	80
Noelville: Ont.	**20**	46	80
Noire: *riv.,* Qué.	**20**	46	77
Nokomis: Sask.	**27**	57	103
Nokomis Lake: Sask.	**27**	57	103
Nomansland Point: Ont.		52	81
Nominingue: Qué.	**21**	46	75
Nonacho Lake: N.W.T.	**31**	62	109
Nootka: B.C.		50	127
Nootka: *i. & sound,* B.C.	**29**	50	127
Noralee: B.C.	**29**	54	126
Noranda: Qué.	**20**	48	79
Nord, R. du: Qué.	**21**	46	74
Norembega: Ont.		49	81
Norman, Cape: Nfld.		52	56
Normandin: Qué.	**16**	49	72
Norman Wells: N.W.T.	**30**	65	126
Normétal: Qué.	**15**	49	79
Norquay: Sask.	**27**	52	102

	Page	N	W
Norris Arm: Nfld.		49	55
North: *riv.*, Nfld.	14	57	63
North, Cape: N.S.	17	47	60
North Aulatsivik I.: Nfld.	14	60	64
North Battleford: Sask.	26	53	108
North Bay: *riv.*, Nfld.		48	55
North Bay: *town*, Ont.	20	46	79
North Cape: P.E.I.	17	47	64
North Caribou Lake: Ont.	18	53	90
North Channel: Ont.	20	46	83
Northern Bay: Nfld.		48	53
Northern Indian Lake: Manitoba	27	57	97
North Gower: Ont.	23	45	76
North Head: Nfld.		49	58
North Head: *town*, Great Manan I.		45	67
North Henik Lake: N.W.T.	31	62	98
North Knife: *riv.*, Man.	27	59	96
North Knife Lake: Man.	27	58	97
North Magnetic Pole: N.W.T.	31	76	101
North Payne: *riv.*, Qué.	14	60	73
North River: *settlement*, Newfoundland		54	57
North River: *town*, Man.	27	59	95
North River Bridge: N.S.	17	46	61
North Saskatchewan: *riv.*, Alberta/Saskatchewan	26	53	107
North Saugeen: *riv.*, Ont.		44	81
North Seal: *riv.*, Man.	27	59	100
North Sydney: N.S.	17	46	60
North Thames: *riv.*, Ont.	20	43	81
North Thompson: *riv.*, British Columbia	29	52	120
Northumberland Strait: Canada	17	46	64
North Vancouver: B.C.	36	49	123
North Wabiskaw Lake: Alberta	26	56	114
North West River: *settlement*, Nfld.	15	53	60
Northwest Territories: (*seat of Govt.* Yellowknife)	30/31	—	—
North York: Ont.	32	44	79
Norton: N.B.	17	46	66
Norway Bay: N.W.T.	31	71	105
Norway House: Man.	27	54	98
Norway I.: N.W.T.	30	74	125
Norwich: Ont.	20	43	81
Norwood: Ont.	22	44	78
Notre Dame: N.B.	17	46	65
Notre Dame Bay: Nfld.	17	50	55
Notre-Dame-de-la-Paix: Québec	23	46	75
Notre-Dame-de-la-Salette: Québec		46	76
Notre Dame du Lac: Qué.		48	69
Notre-Dame-du-Laus: Québec	21	46	76
Notre-Dame-du-Nord: Québec	20	48	80
Notre Dame Junction: Nfld.		49	55
Notre Dame, Monts: Qué.	16	48	67
Notta: *riv.*, Ont.	22	44	80
Nottawasaga Bay: Ont.	20	45	80
Nottaway: *riv.*, Qué.		51	79
Nottingham I.: *& town*, N.W.T.	14	63	78
Nouveau Comptoir: Qué.	18	53	78
Nouvelle France, Cap de: Qué.	14	63	74
Nova Scotia: *Prov.* (*cap.* Halifax)	17	—	—
Novar: Ont.	22	45	79
Noyan: Qué.	23	45	73
Nueltin Lake: N.W.T.	31	60	100
Nungesser Lake: Ont.	27	51	93
Nutak: Nfld.	14	58	62
Nut Mountain: *town & mt.*, Saskatchewan	27	52	103
Nwabasca Lake: B.C.	29	50	122
Oak Bluff: Man.	33	50	97
Oak Lake: Man.	27	50	101
Oakville: Ont.	22	43	80
Obalski, Lac: Qué.		49	78
Oban: Sask.	26	52	108
Obatogameau, Lac: Qué.	16	50	74
Observatory Inlet: B.C.	28	55	130
Ocean Falls: *town*, B.C.	28	52	128
Odessa: Ont.	22	44	77
O'Donnell Point: Ont.	20	45	80
Ogahalla: Ont.		50	86
Ogilvie Mtns.: Yukon	30	65	138
Ogoki: Ont.		52	86
Ogoki: *riv.*, Ont.	19	51	88
Ogoki Reservoir: Ont.		51	88
Oka: Qué.	23	45	74
Okak Is.: Nfld.		58	62
Okanagan Lake: B.C.	29	50	120
Okotoks: Alta.	26	51	114
Old Crow: *& riv.*, Yukon	30	68	140
Oldman: *riv.*, Alta.	26	50	114
Old Perlican: Nfld.		48	53
Olds: Alta.	26	52	114
Old Wives Lake: Sask.	27	50	106
Oliver: B.C.	29	50	120
Olomanc: *riv.*, Qué.		51	61
Omemee: Ont.	22	44	79
Omineca: *riv.*, B.C.	29	56	125
Omineca Mtns.: B.C.	28	57	127
Ommanney Bay: N.W.T.	31	73	101
Onaman Lake: Ont.		50	87
Onaping Lake: *& riv.*, Ont.	20	47	81
Onistagan, Lac: Qué.		51	71
Ontario: *Prov.* (*cap.* Toronto)	18/19	—	—
Ontario, Lake: Can./U.S.A.	20	44	78
Ootsa Lake: *town*, B.C.	29	54	126
Opasatica, Lac: Qué.	20	48	79
Opasatika: Ont.		50	83
Opataca, Lac: Qué.		50	75
Opawica: *lake & riv.*, Qué.		50	76
Opeongo Lake: Ont.	20	46	78
Opinaca: *riv.*, Qué.		53	77
Opinnagau Lake: Ont.		54	84
Opiscotéo, Lac: Qué.	15	53	68
Orange Bay: Nfld.		50	56
Orangeville: Ont.	20	44	80
Ordale: Sask.	26	53	107
Orillia: Ont.	22	45	79
Orleans: Ont.	32	45	76
Orleans, Île d': Qué.	21	47	71
Ormstown: Qué.	23	45	74
Oromocto: N.B.	17	46	66
Orono: Ont.	22	44	79
Osgoode: Ont.	23	45	75
Oshawa: Ont.	22	44	79
Oskélanéo: Qué.	21	48	75
Osnadorgh House: Ont.		51	90
Osoyoos: B.C.	29	49	120
Ospika: *riv.*, B.C.	29	57	124
Osprey Lake: *town*, B.C.		50	120
Ossokmanuan Lake: Nfld.	15	53	65
Otelnuk Lake: Qué.		56	68
Otish Mts.: Qué.	15	52	70
Otoskwin: *riv.*, Ont.	19	51	89
OTTAWA: Ontario	32	45	75
Ottawa: *riv.*, Qué./Ont.	23	46	75
Ottawa Is.: N.W.T.	18	59	80
Otter: Qué.	16	50	64
Otter Head: Ont.		48	86
Otter Lake: Ont.	22	45	80
Otter Lake: Sask.	27	55	104
Ouest, Pointe: Qué.	16	50	65
Ouimet: Ont.		49	89
Oureau: *riv.*, Qué.	21	46	74
Outlook: Sask.	26	51	107
Outremont: Qué.	32	46	74
Owen Sound: *& town*, Ont.	20	45	81
Owl: *riv.*, Man.	27	58	93
Oxbow: Sask.	27	49	102
Oxford: N.S.	17	46	64
Oxford House: Man.	27	55	95
Oxford Junction: N.S.	17	46	64
Oxford Lake: Man.	27	55	95
Oyen: Alta.	26	51	110
Pacific: B.C.	28	55	128
Packenham: Ont.	23	45	76
Pack's Harbour: Nfld.		54	57
Paddle Prairie: *town*, Alta.	26	58	117
Paddockwood: Sask.	27	53	105
Padlei: N.W.T.	31	62	97
Pagwa River: *town*, Ont.	19	50	85
Pakenham: Ont.	23	45	76
Pakowki Lake: Alta.	26	49	111
Pakwash Lake: Ont.	27	51	93
Palling: B.C.	29	54	126
Palmarolle: Qué.		48	79
Palmer Point: N.W.T.	31	75	108
Palmerston: Ont.	20	44	81
Panache, Lake: Ont.	20	46	81
Pancake Point: Ont.		47	85
Pangnirtung: N.W.T.	14	66	66
Papineau, Lac: Qué.	23	46	75
Papineauville: Qué.	23	46	75
Paradis: Qué.	21	48	77
Paradise: *riv.*, Nfld.		53	58
Paradise Sound: Nfld.		47	55
Parc, Lac du: Qué.		57	67
Parent, Lac: Qué.	20	48	77
Parent, Pointe: Qué.	16	50	62
Paris: Ont.	20	43	80
Parisienne, I.: Ont.		46	84
Park Head: *town*, Ont.		45	81
Park Hill: *town*, Ont.	20	43	82
Parksville: B.C.	28	49	124
Parrsboro: N.S.	17	45	64
Parry, Cape: N.W.T.	30	70	125
Parry Bay: N.W.T.	14	68	82
Parry Is.: N.W.T.	31	76	110
Parry Sound: *town*, Ont.	22	45	80
Parsnip: *riv.*, B.C.	29	55	123
Partridgeberry Hills: Nfld.		48	56
Pascalis, Lac: Qué.	20	48	77
Pasfield Lake: Sask.	27	58	105
Pashkokogan Lake: Ont.		51	90
Pasley Bay: N.W.T.	31	71	97
Pasqua: Sask.	27	50	105
Pasquia Hills: Sask.	27	53	103
Passamaquoddy Bay: N.B.	17	45	67
Pattullo, Mt.: B.C.	28	56	130
Paulatuk: N.W.T.	30	69	123
Paul I.: Nfld.	15	56	62
Pavilion: B.C.		51	122
Payne: *riv.*, Qué.	14	60	72
Payne, Baie: Qué.	14	60	70
Payne, Lac: Qué.	14	59	74
Peace: *riv.*, B.C./Alta.	26	58	114
Peace River: *town*, Alta.	26	56	117
Peachland: B.C.		50	120
Pearl I.: Nfld.		49	58
Peary Chan.: N.W.T.	13	79	100
Peel: *plat. & riv.*, Yukon	30	67	134
Peel Point: N.W.T.	31	73	115
Peel Sound: N.W.T.	31	73	97
Peerless Lake: Alta.	26	57	114
Pefferlaw: Ont.	22	44	79
Peggy's Cove: *town*, N.S.	17	44	64
Pelee Island: *town & i.*, Ont.	20	42	83
Pelee Passage: *chan.*, Ont.	20	42	83
Pelee Point, Ont.	20	42	83
Pélican, Lac: Qué.		60	74
Pelican Bay: Man.	27	53	100
Pelican Lake: Man.	27	52	100
Pelican Mtns.: Alta.	26	56	114
Pelican Narrows: *town*, Saskatchewan	27	55	103
Pelly: *riv.*, Yukon	30	62	133
Pelly Bay: *& settlement*, N.W.T.	31	69	90
Pelly Lake: N.W.T.	31	66	102
Pelly Mtns. Yukon	30	62	133
Pemberton: B.C.	28	50	123
Pembina: Alta.	26	53	115
Pembina: *riv.*, Alta.	26	53	116
Pembroke: Ont.	20	46	77
Penetanguishene: Ont.	22	45	80
Penguin Is.: Nfld.		45	57
Penhold: Alta.	26	52	114
Pennant Point: N.S.	17	44	64
Pennask Lake: B.C.		50	120
Pennfield: N.B.	17	45	67
Penny Highland: N.W.T.	14	67	66
Penticton: B.C.	29	49	120
Penzance: Sask.	27	51	105
Percé: Qué.	16	49	64
Perdu, Lac: Qué.		51	70
Perdue: Sask.	26	52	108
Péribonca: Qué.		49	72
Péribonca: *riv.*, Qué.	15	49	71
Péribonca, Lac: Qué.		50	71
Perow: B.C.	29	54	126
Perrault Lake: Ont.	27	50	93
Perron: Qué.	20	48	78
Perrot, Île: Qué.	23	45	74
Perry River: *town*, N.W.T.	31	67	103
Perth: Ont.	23	45	76
Perth-Andover: N.B.	16	47	68
Petawawa: Ont.	20	46	78
Peterbell: Ont.		48	83
Peterborough: Ont.	22	44	78
Peter Pond Lake: Sask.	26	56	109
Peters Arm: Nfld.		49	55
Petitcodiac: N.B.	17	46	65
Petite Rivière de la Baleine: Québec	15	56	76
Petit Etang: *town*, N.S.	17	47	61
Petit Mécatina, R. du: Qué.	15	52	62
Petit Nord Penin.: Nfld.		51	57
Petitot: *riv.*, B.C.	24	60	121
Petitsikapau Lake: Nfld.	15	54	66
Petre, Point: Ont.	22	44	77
Petries: Nfld.		49	58
Petrolia: Ont.	20	43	82
Peyton, Mt.: Nfld.		49	55
Philomena: Alta.		55	112
Piacoudie, Lac: Qué.		51	71
Pickering: Ont.	22	44	79
Pickle Lake: Ont.	19	51	90
Picton: Ont.	22	44	77
Pictou: *& i.*, N.S.	17	46	63
Picture Butte: Alta.	26	50	113
Piedmont: Qué.	23	46	74
Pie I.: Ont.		48	89
Pierrefonds: Qué.	32	45	74
Pierreville: Qué.	21	46	73
Pigeon: *riv.*, Can./U.S.A.		48	90
Pigeon Bay: Man.	27	52	97
Pigeon Bay: Ont.	20	42	83
Pigeon Lake: Alta.	26	53	114
Pigeon Lake: Ont.	22	44	78
Pikangikum Lake: Ont.	19	52	94
Pike: B.C.		59	133
Pikwitonei: Man.	27	56	97
Pilley's I.: Nfld.		50	56
Pilot Mound: Man.	27	49	99
Pinawa: Man.	27	51	96
Pincher Creek: *town*, Alta.	26	49	114
Pinchi Lake: B.C.	29	55	124
Pine, Cape: Nfld.	17	47	54
Pine Falls: *town*, Man.	27	51	96
Pine Pass: B.C.	29	55	122
Pine Point: N.W.T.	30	61	114
Pine River: *town*, Sask.	26	56	107
Pins, Pte. aux: Ont.	20	42	82
Pinto Butte: *mtn.*, Sask.	26	49	107
Pipestone: *riv.*, Ont.		52	90
Pipmuacan, Lac: Qué.	19	49	70
Piscatosin Lac: Qué.	21	47	75
Pistolet Bay: Nfld.		51	56
Pitt: *riv. & lake*, B.C.	28	49	123
Pitt I.: B.C.	28	53	130
Pitt Sound: Nfld.		49	54
Placentia: *& bay*, Nfld.	17	47	54
Plaisance: Qué.	23	46	75
Plantagenet: Ont.	23	45	75
Plaster Rock: N.B.	16	47	67
Plate Cove: Nfld.		49	53
Playgreen Lake: Man.	27	54	98
Pledger Lake: Ont.		50	84
Plessisville: Qué.	21	46	72
Plétipi, Lac: Qué.	15	51	70
Plonge, Lac la: Sask.	26	55	107
Plum Coulee: Man.	27	49	98
Pointe-aux-Trembles: Qué.	32	46	74
Pointe-Claire: Qué.	32	45	74
Pointe Fortune: Ont.	23	46	74
Pointe-Gatineau: Qué.	32	45	76
Pointe Le Bel: Qué.		49	68
Point Lake: N.W.T.	31	65	113
Point Leamington: Nfld.		49	55
Poisson Blanc, Lac: Qué.	23	46	76
Polaris, Lac: Qué.		53	73
Poltimore: Qué.	23	46	76
Pomquet: N.S.	17	46	62
Pond Inlet: *& settlement*, N.W.T.	31	73	78
Ponds, I. of: Nfld.		53	56
Ponoka: Alta.	26	53	114
Pons: *riv.*, Qué.		56	69
Pontax: *riv.*, Qué.		52	77
Ponteix: Sask.	26	50	108
Pont Rouge: Qué.	21	47	72
Pontypool: Ont.	22	44	79
Poplar: *riv.*, Man./Ont.	27	53	97
Poplar Hill: *town*, Ont.	27	52	94
Porcher I.: B.C.	28	54	130
Porcupine: Ont.	20	48	81
Porcupine: *riv.*, U.S.A./Can.	30	67	138
Porcupine, Cape: Nfld.		54	57
Porcupine Hills: Sask./Man.	27	52	101
Porcupine Plain: *town*, Sask.	27	53	103
Porquis Junction: Ont.		48	81
Portage Bay: Man.	27	51	99
Portage-du-Fort: Qué.		46	77
Portage la Prairie: Man.	27	50	98
Port Alberni: B.C.	28	49	125
Port Alfred: Qué.	21	48	71
Port Alice: B.C.	28	50	127
Port Anson: Nfld.		50	56
Port Arthur: Ont. *see* Thunder Bay			
Port-au-Port: *penin. & bay*, Newfoundland	17	49	59
Port Bolster: Ont.	22	44	79
Port Burwell: Ont.	20	42	81
Port Carling: Ont.	22	45	80
Port Cartier: Qué.	15	50	67
Port Cartier, Parc de: Qué.	15	51	67
Port Clements: B.C.	28	53	132
Port Colborne: Ont.	22	43	79
Port Coquitlam: B.C.	36	49	123
Port Credit: Ont.	32	44	80
Port Daniel: Qué.	16	48	65
Port Dover: Ont.	20	43	80
Port Edward: B.C.	28	54	130
Port Edward: Ont.	20	43	82
Port Elgin: N.B.	17	46	64
Port Elgin: Ont.	20	44	81
Porter: B.C.		58	130
Porter Lake: Sask.	26	56	107
Port Essington: B.C.	28	54	130
Port Hardy: B.C.	28	51	128
Port Hawkesbury: N.S.	17	46	61
Port Hood: N.S.	17	46	62
Port Hope: Ont.	22	44	78
Port Hope Simpson: Nfld.		53	56
Portland: Ont.	23	45	76
Portland Canal: B.C.	28	55	130
Portland Inlet: B.C.	28	55	130
Portland Promontory: Qué.		58	78
Port Logan: N.W.T.	31	72	93
Port Loring: Ont.	20	46	80
Port McNeill: B.C.	28	51	128
Port McNicoll: Ont.	22	45	80
Port Maitland: N.S.	17	44	66
Port Mellon: B.C.	28	49	123
Port Menier: Qué.	16	50	64
Port Moody: B.C.	29	49	123
Port Morien: N.S.	17	46	60
Port Mouton: N.S.	17	44	65
Port Nelson: Man.	27	57	93
Portneuf, Parc de: Qué.	16	48	73
Portneuf: *& riv.*, Qué.	21	47	72
Portneuf sur Mer: Qué.		48	69
Port Neville: B.C.		50	126
Port-Nouveau-Québec: Qué.	14	58	66
Port Perry: Ont.	22	44	79
Port Radium: N.W.T.	30	66	118
Port Renfrew: B.C.	28	49	124
Port Rexton: Nfld.		48	53
Port Rowan: Ont.	20	43	80
Port Royal: N.S.	17	44	66
Port Saunders: Nfld.	15	51	57
Port Severn: Ont.		45	80
Port Simpson: B.C.	28	55	130
Port Stanley: Ont.	20	43	81
Port Viau: Qué.	23	46	74
Poste-de-la-Baleine: Qué.	15	55	78
Poste-Mistassini: Qué.	15	50	74
Postville: Nfld.		55	60
Pouce Coupé: B.C.	29	55	120

	Page	N	W
Poularies: Qué.		48	79
Poulin de Courval, Lac: Québec		49	70
Poutrincourt, Lac: Qué.	**16**	49	74
Povungnituk: *&* *riv.*, Qué.	**14**	60	76
Powassan: Ont.	**20**	46	79
Powderview: Man.	**27**	51	97
Powell Lake: B.C.	**28**	50	124
Powell River: *town*, B.C.	**28**	50	125
Prairies, R. des: Qué.	**32**	46	74
Preeceville: Sask.	**27**	52	103
Preissac, Lac: Qué.	**20**	48	78
Prelate: Sask.	**26**	51	109
Prescott: Ont.	**23**	45	76
Prescott I.: N.W.T.	**31**	73	97
Presqu'ile Point: Ont.	**22**	44	78
Press: Qué.	**21**	48	77
Press Lake: Ont.		50	92
Price: Qué.		48	68
Priestly: B.C.	**29**	54	125
Prim Point: P.E.I.	**17**	46	63
Primrose Lake: Sask.	**26**	55	110
Prince Albert: Sask.	**27**	53	106
Prince Albert Hills: N.W.T.	**31**	67	85
Prince Albert Nat. Park: Saskatchewan	**26**	54	106
Prince Albert Penin.: N.W.T.	**30**	72	117
Prince Albert Sound: N.W.T.	**30**	70	115
Prince Alfred, Cape: N.W.T.	**30**	75	121
Prince Charles I.: N.W.T.	**14**	67	76
Prince-de-Galles, Cap: Qué.	**14**	62	72
Prince Edward Bay: Ont.	**22**	44	77
Prince Edward I.: *Prov.* (*cap.* Charlottetown)	**16**	46	63
Prince Edward I. Nat. Park: P.E.I.	**17**	46	63
Prince George: B.C.	**29**	54	123
Prince Leopold I.: N.W.T.	**31**	74	90
Prince of Wales I.: N.W.T.	**31**	72	100
Prince of Wales Str.: N.W.T.	**30**	73	118
Prince Patrick I.: N.W.T.	**30**	77	120
Prince Regent Inlet: N.W.T.	**31**	74	90
Prince Rupert: B.C.	**28**	54	130
Princes Lake (Wallace): *town*, Ontario	**22**	45	78
Princess Royal I.: B.C.	**28**	53	129
Princeton: B.C.	**28**	49	120
Princetown: P.E.I.	**17**	46	64
Profits Cape: P.E.I.	**17**	47	64
Prophet: *riv.*, B.C.	**29**	58	123
Providence Bay: *town*, Ont.		46	82
Provost: Alta.	**26**	52	110
Pubnico: N.S.	**17**	44	66
Pugwash: N.S.	**17**	46	64
Pukatawagan: Man.	**27**	56	101
Pukeashun Mt.: B.C.	**29**	51	119
Purcell Mtns.: B.C.	**29**	50	117
Puskitamika, Lac: Qué.		49	76
Quadra I.: B.C.	**28**	50	125
Qualicum Beach: B.C.	**28**	49	124
Qu'Appelle: Sask.	**27**	51	104
Qu'Appelle: *riv.*, Sask.	**27**	51	104
Qu'Appelle Arm Dam: Saskatchewan	**26**	57	107
Quatsino Sound: B.C.	**28**	50	128
QUÉBEC: Québec	**16**	47	71
Québec: *Prov.* (*cap.* Québec)	**14/15**	—	—
Queen Bess, Mt.: B.C.	**29**	51	124
Queen Charlotte: *&* *is.*, British Columbia	**28**	53	132
Queen Charlotte Sd.: B.C.	**28**	52	129
Queen Charlotte Str.: B.C.	**28**	50	128
Queen Elizabeth Is.: N.W.T.	**13**	78	100
Queen Maud Gulf: N.W.T.	**31**	67	102
Queen Maud Gulf Bird Sanctuary: N.W.T.	**31**	67	105
Queens Channel: N.W.T.	**31**	76	97
Quesnel: *&* *riv.*, B.C.	**29**	53	122
Quesnel Lake: B.C.	**29**	53	121
Quetico Park: Ont.	**19**	48	90
Quévillon, Lac: Qué.		49	77
Quiet Lake: Yukon		61	133
Quilchena: B.C.		50	120
Quill Lake: *town*, Sask.	**27**	52	104
Quill Lakes: Sask.	**27**	52	104
Quinsam: B.C.	**28**	50	125
Quinte, Bay of: Ont.	**22**	44	77
Quinze, Lac des: Qué.	**20**	48	79
Quirke Lake: Ont.	**20**	46	83
Quispamsis: N.B.	**17**	46	67
Quoich: *riv.*, N.W.T.	**31**	65	95
Quorn: Ont.	**19**	49	91
Quyon: Qué.	**23**	46	76
Rabast, C. de: Qué.	**16**	50	64
Race, Cape: Nfld.	**17**	47	53
Racine de Bouleau: *riv.*, Québec		52	69
Radisson: Ont.	**18**	54	78
Radisson: Sask.	**26**	52	107
Radvers: Sask.	**27**	49	102
Radville: Sask.	**27**	49	104
Rae: N.W.T.	**30**	63	116
Rae: *riv.*, N.W.T.	**30**	68	117
Rae Isthmus: N.W.T.	**14**	67	87
Rae Lakes: N.W.T.	**30**	64	116
Rae Strait: N.W.T.	**31**	69	95
Rafael Point: B.C.		49	126
Ragged Lake: Ont.		45	79
Ragueneau: Qué.		49	68
Rainbow Lake: *town*, Alta.	**26**	58	119
Rainy Lake: Ont.	**19**	48	93
Rainy River: *town*, Ont.	**19**	49	95
Ralleau, Lac: Qué.		58	67
Ralston: Alta.	**26**	51	112
Ramah: *&* *bay*, Nfld.		59	63
Rambau, Lac: Qué.		54	70
Ramea Is.: Nfld.	**17**	48	57
Ramore: Ont.	**20**	48	80
Ramusio, Lac: Qué.		55	64
Rancheria: Yukon		60	130
Rancheria: *riv.*, Yukon		60	129
Random I.: Nfld.		48	54
Ranger Lake: Ont.	**20**	47	84
Rankin Inlet: N.W.T.	**31**	63	92
Rapides des Joachims: Qué.	**22**	46	78
Rat: *riv.*, Man.	**27**	56	99
Rathburn: Ont.	**22**	45	79
Rat Rapids: *town*, Ont.		51	90
Ratz, Mt.: B.C.	**28**	57	132
Ravensworth: Ont.		46	79
Rawdon: Qué.	**23**	46	74
Ray, Cape: Nfld.	**17**	48	59
Raymond: Alta.	**26**	49	113
Raymore: Sask.	**27**	52	105
Razorback: *mt.*, B.C.	**29**	51	124
Read I.: B.C.	**28**	50	125
Read Island: *settlement*, N.W.T.	**31**	69	114
Red: *riv.*, Can./U.S.A.	**13**	48	97
Red Bay: *settlement*, Nfld.		52	57
Redberry Lake: Sask.	**26**	53	107
Red Cedar Lake: Ont.	**20**	47	80
Redcliff: Alta.	**26**	50	111
Red Deer: Alta.	**26**	52	114
Red Deer: *riv.*, Alta.	**26**	51	111
Red Deer: *riv.*, Sask.	**27**	53	102
Red Deer Lake: Man.	**27**	53	101
Redditt: Ont.	**27**	50	94
Red Indian Lake: Nfld.	**17**	49	57
Red I.: Nfld.		47	54
Red Lake: *town*, B.C.		51	121
Red Lake: *&* *town*, Ont.	**27**	51	94
Redonda Bay: *town*, B.C.	**28**	50	125
Redonda Is.: B.C.	**28**	50	125
Redstone: *riv.*, N.W.T.	**30**	63	126
Redstone Lake: Ont.		45	78
Red Sucker Lake: Man.	**27**	54	94
Redwater: Alta.	**26**	54	113
Redwater: Ont.		47	80
Red Wine: *riv.*, Nfld.		54	62
Refuge Cove: *town*, B.C.	**28**	50	125
REGINA: Saskatchewan	**27**	50	105
Reindeer: *riv.*, Sask.	**27**	56	103
Reindeer Depot: N.W.T.	**30**	69	134
Reindeer I.: Man.	**27**	52	98
Reindeer Lake: Sask./Man.	**27**	57	102
Reliance: N.W.T.	**31**	63	109
Renews: Nfld.	**17**	47	53
Renfrew: Ont.	**21**	45	77
Renison: Ont.		51	81
Rennie Lake: N.W.T.		61	105
Renouard Point: N.B.	**17**	46	65
Repulse Bay: *settlement*, N.W.T.	**14**	67	86
Resolute: N.W.T.	**31**	75	95
Resolution I.: N.W.T.	**14**	61	65
Resolution, Lac: Qué.		55	65
Restigouche: Qué.	**16**	48	67
Reston: Man.	**27**	50	102
Revelstoke: B.C.	**29**	51	118
Rexton: N.B.	**17**	47	65
Reynaud: Sask.	**27**	53	105
Rice Lake: Ont.	**22**	44	78
Rich, Cape: Ont.	**20**	45	81
Richan: Ont.	**27**	50	93
Richard Collinson Inlet: N.W.T.	**31**	72	114
Richards I.: N.W.T.	**30**	69	135
Richardson: *riv.*, Alta.	**26**	58	110
Richardson Is.: N.W.T.	**31**	68	110
Richardson Mtns.: Yukon	**30**	67	136
Richelieu: *riv.*, Qué.	**23**	46	73
Riche Pt.: Nfld.	**15**	51	57
Richibucto: N.B.	**17**	47	65
Richmond: B.C.	**36**	49	123
Richmond: Ont.	**23**	45	76
Richmond: Qué.	**21**	46	72
Richmond, Golfe de: Qué.	**15**	56	76
Richmond Hill: Ont.	**32**	44	79
Rideau: *riv.*, Ont.	**32**	45	76
Rideau Canal: Ont.	**23**	44	76
Rideau Lakes: Ont.	**23**	45	76
Ridgetown: Ont.	**20**	42	82
Riding Mt.: *&* *Nat. Park*, Manitoba	**27**	51	100
Rigaud: Qué.	**23**	45	74
Rigolet: Nfld.	**15**	54	58
Rimbey: Alta.	**26**	53	114
Rimouski: *&* *riv.*, Qué.	**16**	48	68
Rimouski, Parc de: Qué.	**16**	48	68
Riondel: B.C.	**29**	50	117
Riou Lake: Sask.	**26**	59	106
Ripley: Ont.		44	82
Ripon: Qué.	**23**	46	75
Riverbend: Qué.		49	72
River Hébert: N.S.	**17**	46	64
River John: N.S.	**17**	46	63
River Jordan: B.C.	**28**	48	124
Rivers: Man.	**27**	50	100
Rivers, Lake of the: Sask.	**27**	50	106
Riverside: Ont.	**20**	42	83
Rivers Inlet: *&* *town*, B.C.	**28**	52	127
Riverton: Man.	**27**	51	97
River Valley: *town*, Ont.	**20**	47	80
Rivière à Pierre: Qué.	**21**	47	72
Rivière au Doré: Qué.		49	73
Rivière aux Graines: Qué.		50	65
Rivière au Renard: Qué.	**16**	49	64
Rivière Blanche: Qué.		49	68
Rivière Bleue: Qué.		47	69
Rivière-des-Prairies: Qué.	**23**	46	74
Rivière du Loup: Qué.	**16**	48	70
Rivière du Moulin: Qué.	**21**	49	71
Rivière Pentecôte: Qué.	**16**	50	67
Rivière Pigou: Qué.	**16**	50	66
Robenoire, Lac la: Qué.		51	63
Robert, Cape: Ont.	**20**	46	83
Robert Brown, Cape: N.W.T.	**14**	67	81
Roberts Bank: B.C.	**28**	49	123
Roberts Creek: *town*, B.C.	**28**	49	124
Roberval: Qué.	**16**	48	72
Robillard I.: N.W.T.	**30**	74	124
Robinson: Yukon		60	135
Roblin: Man.	**27**	51	101
Robsart: Sask.		49	109
Robson, Mt.: B.C.	**29**	53	119
Robson Prov. Park: B.C.	**19**	53	119
Rochebaucourt: Qué.		48	77
Rocher River: *town*, N.W.T.		61	113
Rock Bay: *town*, B.C.	**28**	50	125
Rockcliffe Park: Ont.	**32**	45	76
Rockglen: Sask.	**27**	49	106
Rock Lake: *town*, Ont.		45	78
Rockland: Ont.	**23**	46	75
Rockport: Ont.	**23**	44	76
Rocky Bay: *town*, Qué.		51	58
Rocky Harbour: Nfld.	**17**	50	58
Rocky Island Lake: Ont.	**20**	47	83
Rocky Mt. House: Alta.	**26**	52	115
Rocky Mtns.: Can./U.S.A.	**12**	—	—
Rocky Saugeen: *riv.*, Ont.	**20**	44	81
Roddickton: Nfld.		51	56
Roes Welcome Sound: N.W.T.	**18**	65	87
Roger, Lac: Qué.	**20**	48	79
Rogersville: N.B.	**16**	47	65
Roggan River: *town*, Qué.		54	79
Rohault Lake: Man.		49	74
Romaine: *riv.*, Qué.	**15**	51	63
Romanet, Lac: Qué.		56	68
Rorketon: Man.	**27**	51	100
Rose Blanche: Nfld.	**17**	48	59
Rosée Point: Nfld.		47	55
Rosemere: Qué.	**23**	46	74
Rose Point: B.C.	**28**	54	131
Rosetown: Sask.	**26**	51	108
Rose Valley: *town*, Sask.	**27**	52	104
Rosevear: Alta.	**26**	54	116
Roseway: *riv.*, N.S.		44	65
Rosseau: *&* *lake*, Ont.	**22**	45	80
Rosser: Man.	**33**	50	97
Rossignol, Lac: Qué.		53	74
Rossignol, Lake: N.S.	**17**	44	65
Ross I.: Man.	**27**	54	98
Ross Lake: Can./U.S.A.	**28**	49	131
Rossland: B.C.	**29**	49	118
Ross River: *&* *river*, Yukon	**30**	62	132
Rosswood: B.C.	**28**	55	129
Rosthern: Sask.	**26**	53	106
Rothesay: N.B.	**17**	45	66
Rouge River: Ont.	**32**	44	79
Rouleau: Sask.	**27**	50	105
Round Lake: Ont.	**20**	46	78
Round Pond: Nfld.	**17**	48	56
Rouyn: Qué.	**20**	48	79
Rowley I.: N.W.T.	**14**	69	79
Roy: B.C.	**28**	50	125
Ruby Ranges: Yukon	**30**	61	138
Ruel: Ont.		47	81
Rupert: *riv.*, Qué.	**15**	51	77
Rushy Pond: *town*, Nfld.		49	56
Russell: Man.	**27**	51	101
Russell: Ont.	**32**	45	75
Russell, Cape: N.W.T.	**30**	75	117
Russell I.: N.W.T.	**31**	74	99
Russell Point: N.W.T.	**31**	73	116
Rustico: P.E.I.	**17**	46	63
Rutherglen: Ont.		46	79
Sabine, Lac: Qué.		59	73
Sabine Penin.: N.W.T.	**31**	76	109
Sable, Cape: N.S.	**17**	43	66
Sable, Rivière du: Qué.	**15**	55	68
Sable I.: N.S.	**15**	44	60
Sable River: *town*, N.S.	**17**	44	65
Sabourin, Lac: Qué.	**20**	48	78
Sachigo: *riv.*, Ont.		55	91
Sachigo Lake: Ont.	**27**	54	92
Sachs Harbour: N.W.T.	**30**	72	126
Sackville: N.B.	**17**	46	64
Sackville: N.S.	**17**	45	64
Sacré Coeur: Qué.		48	70
Sacré Coeur: Qué.		48	68
Saffray, Lac: Qué.		58	67
Saganaga Lake: Ont.	**19**	48	90
Saglek Bay: Nfld.	**14**	58	63
Saglouc: Qué.	**14**	62	75
Saguenay: *riv.*, Qué.	**21**	48	70
Ste. Adèle: Qué.	**23**	46	74
St. Agapit: Qué.	**21**	46	71
Ste. Agathe: Qué.	**23**	46	74
St. Albans: Nfld.	**17**	48	56
St. Alexandre: Qué.	**21**	48	70
St. Alexis-de-Montcalm: Québec	**23**	46	74
St. Alexis des Monts: Qué.	**21**	46	73
St. Ambroise: Qué.		48	71
St. Anaclet: Qué.		48	68
St. André-Avellin: Qué.	**23**	46	75
St. André-Est: Qué.	**23**	46	74
St. Andrews: N.B.	**16**	45	67
St. Andrew's Channel: N.S.	**17**	46	60
Ste. Angèle: Qué.		48	68
Ste. Angèle de Laval: Qué.	**21**	46	72
Ste. Anne: Man.	**27**	50	97
Ste. Anne: Qué.	**23**	46	74
Ste. Anne, Lac: Qué.	**16**	50	68
Ste. Anne de Beaupré: Qué.	**21**	47	71
Ste. Anne de Bellevue: Qué.	**32**	45	74
Ste. Anne de Chicoutimi: Québec		48	71
Ste. Anne de Portneuf: Québec	**16**	49	69
Ste. Anne des Monts: Qué.	**16**	49	66
St. Anns: N.S.	**17**	46	61
St. Anselme: Qué.	**21**	47	71
St. Anthony: Nfld.	**15**	51	55
St. Antoine: N.B.	**17**	47	64
St. Antoine: Qué.	**23**	46	73
St. Antoine du Lac St. Jean: Québec		49	72
St. Augustin: Qué.	**23**	46	74
St. Augustin: *&* *riv.*, Qué.	**15**	51	59
St. Barbe Is.: Nfld.	**17**	50	56
St. Barthelemi: Qué.		46	73
St. Basile: Qué.	**21**	47	72
Ste. Blandine: Qué.		48	68
St. Boniface: Man.	**33**	50	97
St. Brendans: Nfld.		49	54
St. Bride's: Nfld.		47	54
St. Bruno: Qué.		48	72
St. Calixte-de-Kilkenny: Québec	**23**	46	74
Ste. Camille: Qué.	**21**	46	70
St. Catharines: Ont.	**22**	43	79
St. Césaire: Qué.	**21**	45	73
St. Charles: Qué.	**21**	47	71
St. Chrysostome: Qué.	**23**	45	74
St. Clair: *riv.*, Can./U.S.A.	**20**	43	82
St. Clair, Lake: Can./U.S.A.	**20**	42	83
St. Clément: Qué.		48	69
St. Clet: Qué.	**23**	45	74
St. Coeur de Marie: Qué.	**16**	49	72
St. Côme: Qué.	**21**	46	74
St. Constant: Qué.	**23**	45	74
St. Croix: *riv.*, Can./U.S.A.	**16**	45	67
St. Croix Lake: N.S.	**17**	45	64
St. Cyr: *riv.*, Qué.		49	75
St. Cyr, Mt.: Yukon		61	133
St. Denis: Qué.	**23**	46	73
St. Donat: Qué.	**21**	46	74
St. Edouard: Qué.	**23**	45	74
St. Eleuthère: Can.		47	69
St. Elias, Mt.: Can./U.S.A.	**12**	60	140
St. Elias Mtns.: Yukon/B.C.	**30**	60	140
St. Eloi: Qué.		48	69
Ste. Emélie: Qué.	**21**	46	74
St. Emile-de-Suffolk: Qué.	**23**	46	75
St. Ephrem: Qué.		49	79
St. Esprit: Qué.	**23**	46	74
St. Eugène: Ont.	**23**	45	74
St. Eusebe: Qué.		48	69
St. Eustache: Qué.	**32**	46	74
St. Fabien: Qué.		48	69
Ste. Famille: Qué.	**21**	47	71
St. Faustin: Qué.		46	74
St. Félicien: Qué.	**16**	48	72
St. Félix de Valois: Qué.	**21**	46	73
Ste. Foy: Qué.	**21**	47	71
St. Francis: *riv.*, Canada/U.S.A.		47	69
St. Francis, Cape: Nfld.	**17**	48	53
St. Francis, Lake: Ont./Qué.	**23**	45	74
St. François: *riv.*, Canada/U.S.A.	**19**	47	69
St. François, Lac: Qué.	**16**	46	71
St. Gabriel: Qué.	**21**	46	73
St. Gabriel: Qué.		48	68
St. Gédéon: Qué.	**21**	46	71
St. Gédéon: Qué.		48	72
Ste. Geneviève: Qué.	**23**	45	74
St. George: N.B.	**17**	45	67
St. Georges: Nfld.	**17**	48	58

	Page	N	W
St. George's: Qué.	**20**	46	71
St. George's Bay: Nfld.	**17**	48	59
St. George's Bay: N.S.	**17**	46	62
St. Gerard: Qué.	**21**	46	71
St. Grégoire: Qué.	**23**	45	73
St. Gregory: *mt.*, Nfld.	**17**	49	58
St. Guillaume: Qué.	**21**	46	73
St. Hedwidge: Qué.	**21**	48	72
Ste. Hélène, I.: Qué.	**32**	45	74
St. Henri: Qué.	**21**	47	71
St. Henri de Taillon: Qué.		49	72
St. Hilaire: Qué.	**23**	46	73
St. Honoré: Qué.	**16**	48	71
St. Hubert: Qué.		48	69
St. Hyacinthe: Qué.	**21**	46	73
St. Ignace, Isle: Ont.		49	88
St. Irénée: Qué.		48	70
St. Isidore: Qué.	**23**	45	74
St. Jacques: Nfld.		47	55
St. Jacques: Qué.	**23**	46	74
St. James, Cape: B.C.	**28**	52	131
St. Janvier: Qué.	**23**	46	74
St. Jean: Qué.	**23**	45	73
St. Jean: *riv.*, Qué.		51	64
Saint-Jean, Lac: Qué.	**16**	48	72
St. Jean de Dieu: Qué.		48	69
St. Jean de Matha: Qué.	**21**	46	74
St. Jean Port Joli: Qué.	**21**	47	70
St. Jérôme: Qué.	**21**	47	72
St. Jérôme: Qué.	**23**	46	74
St. Joachim: Qué.	**21**	47	71
Saint John: N.B.	**17**	45	66
Saint John: *riv.*, Canada/U.S.A.	**16**	46	67
St. John, Cape: Nfld.	**17**	50	56
St. John, Lake: Nfld.		48	55
St. John, Mt.: Ont.		50	89
St. John Bay: Nfld.		51	57
ST. JOHN'S: Nfld.	**17**	48	53
St. Joseph: Qué.		46	73
St. Joseph: *i.*, Ont.	**20**	46	84
St. Joseph, Lake: Ont.	**19**	51	91
St. Joseph d'Alma: Qué.	**16**	48	72
St. Joseph-du-Lac: Qué.	**23**	46	74
St. Josephs: Nfld.		47	55
St. Jovite: Qué.	**21**	46	75
Ste. Julienne: Qué.	**23**	46	74
St. Kyrans: Nfld.		47	54
St. Lambert: Qué.	**32**	45	73
St. Laurent: Qué.	**32**	46	74
St. Lawrence: Nfld.	**17**	47	55
St. Lawrence: *riv.*, Canada/U.S.A.	**21**	—	—
St. Lawrence (Upper): *riv. & seaway*, Canada/U.S.A.	**22**	—	—
St. Lawrence, Cape: N.S.		47	61
St. Lawrence, Gulf of: Can.	**16**	48	62
St. Lawrence, Lake: Qué.	**23**	45	75
St. Léon: Qué.		48	71
St. Leonard: N.B.	**16**	47	68
St. Léonard: Qué.	**21**	46	72
St. Lewis: *riv.*, Nfld.		52	57
St. Lin: Qué.	**23**	46	74
St. Louis, Lac: Qué.	**32**	45	74
St. Louis-de-Gonzague: Québec	**23**	45	74
St. Ludger: Qué.		45	71
St. Malachie: Qué.	**21**	46	71
St. Malo: Man.	**27**	50	97
St. Marc: Qué.	**23**	46	73
St. Marc des Carrières: Québec	**21**	47	72
St. Margaret's Bay: N.S.	**17**	45	64
Ste. Marguerite: *riv.*, Qué.	**21**	48	70
Ste. Marie: Qué.	**21**	46	71
Ste. Marie: Qué.	**23**	46	73
St. Martin, Lake: Man.	**27**	52	98
Ste. Martine: Qué.	**23**	45	74
St. Martins: N.B.	**17**	45	66
St. Mary: *riv.*, Alta.	**26**	49	113
St. Mary, Cape: N.S.	**17**	45	62
St. Mary, Cape: *& bay*, N.S.	**17**	44	66
St. Mary's Bay: Nfld.	**17**	47	54
St. Mary's: Ont.	**20**	43	81
St. Mary's: *riv.*, N.S.	**17**	45	62
St. Mary's: *riv.*, Ont.	**20**	46	84
St. Mary's, Cape: Nfld.		47	54
St. Mary's Harbour: Nfld.	**15**	52	56
St. Maurice, Parc du: Qué.	**16**	48	74
St. Maurice: *riv.*, Qué.	**21**	47	73
St. Méthode: Qué.		48	72
St. Michael's Bay: Nfld.		53	56
St. Michel: Qué.	**32**	45	74
St. Michel des Saintes: Qué.	**21**	47	74
St. Moïse: Qué.		48	68
St. Nazaire: Qué.		48	72
St. Norbert: Man.	**33**	50	97
St. Ours: Qué.	**23**	46	73
St. Pacôme: Qué.	**16**	47	70
St. Pamphile: Qué.	**21**	47	70
St. Pascal: Qué.	**21**	48	70
St. Paul: Alta.	**26**	54	111
St. Paul: Qué.		52	58
St. Paul: *riv.*, Qué.	**15**	52	58
St. Paul du Nord: Qué.		48	69
St. Paul l'Ermite: Qué.	**21**	46	74
St. Peter's: N.S.	**17**	46	61
St. Peters: P.E.I.	**17**	46	63
St. Philémon: Qué.		47	70
St. Philippe de Neri: Qué.	**21**	47	70
St. Pie: Qué.	**21**	45	73
St. Pierre: Man.	**27**	50	97
St. Pierre, Lac: Qué.	**21**	46	73
St. Pierre, Pointe: Qué.	**16**	49	64
St. Pierre Bank: Nfld.		46	56
St. Prime: Qué.	**16**	48	72
St. Prosper: Qué.	**21**	46	70
St. Quentin: N.B.	**16**	47	67
St. Raphaël: Qué.	**21**	47	71
St. Raphael Lake: Ont.		51	91
St. Raymond: Qué.	**21**	47	72
St. Rémi: Qué.	**23**	45	74
St. Roch: Qué.	**23**	46	73
St. Roch-de-l'Achigan: Qué.	**23**	46	74
St. Romuald: Qué.	**21**	47	71
Ste. Rose: Qué.	**32**	46	74
Ste. Rose du Dégelé: Qué.		48	69
Ste. Rose du Lac: Man.	**27**	51	99
Ste. Rose du Nord: Qué.	**21**	48	70
Ste. Scholastique: Qué.	**23**	46	74
St. Shotts: Nfld.		47	54
St. Siméon: Qué.	**16**	48	70
St. Simon: Qué.		48	69
St. Stanislas: Qué.	**16**	49	72
St. Stephen: N.B.	**16**	45	67
St. Theresa Point: Man.	**25**	54	95
Ste. Thérèse: Qué.	**32**	46	74
St. Thomas: Ont.	**20**	43	81
St. Timothée: Qué.	**23**	45	74
St. Tite: Qué.	**21**	47	73
St. Urbain: Qué.	**23**	45	74
St. Vallier: Qué.	**21**	47	71
St. Vincent: Nfld.		47	54
St. Vincent-de-Paul: Qué.	**23**	46	74
St. Walburg: Sask.	**26**	54	109
Sakami: *riv.*, Qué.	**15**	53	76
Sakami, Lac: Qué.	**15**	53	77
Sakatawi Lake: Ont.	**20**	48	82
Sakwaso Lake: Ont.		53	92
Sale: *riv.*, Man.	**33**	50	97
Salisbury: N.B.	**17**	46	65
Salisbury I.: N.W.T.	**14**	63	77
Salmo: B.C.	**29**	50	118
Salmon: *riv.*, N.B.	**17**	46	66
Salmon: *riv.*, Ont.	**22**	44	77
Salmon Arm: B.C.	**29**	51	119
Salmon River: *town*, N.S.	**17**	44	66
Saltcoats: Sask.	**27**	51	102
Saltspring I.: B.C.	**28**	49	123
Samaqua: *riv.*, Qué.		49	72
Sandgirt Lake: Nfld.		54	65
Sand Lake: Ont.	**27**	40	94
Sand Lake Station: Ont.	**20**	48	84
Sandspit: B.C.	**28**	53	132
Sandwich Bay: Nfld.	**15**	53	57
Sandy Bay: *town*, Sask.	**27**	56	103
Sandy Lake: Nfld.	**17**	49	57
Sandy Lake: *& town*, Ont.	**27**	53	93
Sardis: B.C.	**28**	49	122
Sarnia: Ont.	**20**	43	82
Sarsfield: Ont.	**32**	45	75
Sasaginnigak Lake: Man.	**27**	52	96
Saskatchewan: *Prov. (cap. Regina)*	**26/27**	—	—
Saskatchewan: *riv.*, Sask./Manitoba	**27**	54	103
Saskatoon: Sask.	**26**	52	107
Saugeen: *riv.*, Ont.	**20**	44	81
Sauker Head: Nfld.		47	55
Saulte Ste. Marie: Ont.	**20**	46	84
Sauvolles, Lac: Qué.		53	73
Savant Lake: *town*, Ont.	**19**	50	91
Sawyer Lake: Nfld.		54	66
Sayabec: Qué.	**16**	49	68
Sayward: B.C.		50	126
Scarborough: Ont.	**32**	44	79
Scatari I.: N.S.	**17**	46	60
Schefferville (Knob Lake): Québec	**15**	55	66
Schomberg: Ont.	**22**	44	80
Schreiber: Ont.	**19**	49	87
Schultz Lake: N.W.T.	**31**	65	97
Schumacher: Ont.	**20**	48	81
Scoresby, Cape: N.W.T.	**31**	72	94
Scotsburn: N.S.	**17**	46	63
Scotstown: Qué.	**21**	45	71
Scott Chan.: B.C.	**28**	51	128
Scott Is.: B.C.	**28**	51	129
Scott Lake: N.W.T./Sask.	**26**	60	106
Scudder: Ont.	**20**	42	83
Scugog, Lake: Ont.	**22**	44	79
Seaforth: Ont.	**20**	43	81
Seahorse Point: N.W.T.	**14**	64	80
Seal: *riv.*, Man.	**27**	59	96
Seal Cove: *town*, N.B.	**17**	45	67
Seal I.: B.C.	**29**	49	123
Seal Lake: Nfld.	**15**	54	62
Searchmont: Ont.	**20**	47	84
Seattle, Mt.: U.S.A./Can.		60	139
Sechelt: B.C.	**28**	49	124
Sechelt Penin.: B.C.	**28**	49	124
Seeleys Bay: *town*, Ont.	**23**	44	76
Seignelay: *riv.*, Qué.		52	69
Seine: *riv.*, Man.	**33**	50	97
Seldom: Nfld.		50	54
Selkirk: Man.	**27**	50	97
Selkirk Mtns.: B.C.	**29**	51	118
Sellwood: Ont.	**20**	47	81
Selwyn Lake: Sask./N.W.T.	**31**	60	104
Selwyn Mtns.: Yukon	**30**	63	130
Senneterre: Qué.	**20**	48	77
Sentinel Peak: B.C.	**29**	55	122
Separation Point: *settlement*, Nfld.		64	58
Sept Îles: *town*, Qué.	**15**	50	66
Sérigny: *riv.*, Qué.	**15**	55	69
Seseganaga Lake: Ont.		50	90
Seton Lake: B.C.	**28**	51	122
Seul, Lac: Ont.	**19**	50	92
Seven Islands Bay: Nfld.	**14**	59	64
Seven Sisters: *mt.*, B.C.	**28**	55	128
Seventy Mile House: B.C.	**29**	51	121
Severn Bridge: Ont.	**22**	45	79
Severn: *riv.*, Ont.	**18**	55	88
Sexsmith: Alta.	**26**	55	119
Seymour Inlet: B.C.	**28**	51	127
Shabogamo, Lac: Qué.		53	67
Shabotik: *riv.*, Ont.		49	85
Shag Harbour: N.S.	**17**	43	66
Shalalth: B.C.	**28**	51	122
Shallop: Qué.	**16**	59	62
Shallow Lake: *town*, Ont.		45	81
Shamattawa: Man.	**27**	56	92
Shapio Lake: Nfld.		55	61
Sharbot Lake: Ont.	**22**	45	77
Shaunavon: Sask.	**26**	50	108
Shawanaga: Ont.		45	80
Shawbridge: Qué.	**23**	46	74
Shawville: Qué.	**23**	46	76
Shawinigan: Qué.	**21**	46	73
Shebandowan Lake: Ont.		48	90
Shediac: *& bay*, N.B.	**17**	46	65
Sheet Harbour: N.S.	**17**	45	63
Sheffield Pond: Nfld.		49	57
Shelburne: N.S.	**17**	44	65
Shelburne: Ont.	**20**	44	80
Sheldrake: Qué.	**16**	50	65
Shellbrook: Sask.	**26**	53	106
Shelter Bay: *town*, Qué.	**16**	50	67
Shenacadie: N.S.	**17**	46	61
Shepherd Bay: N.W.T.	**31**	68	95
Sherard, Cape: N.W.T.	**31**	75	81
Sherbrooke: N.S.	**17**	45	62
Sherbrooke: Qué.	**21**	45	72
Sherbrooke Lake: N.S.	**17**	45	65
Sherman Inlet: N.W.T.	**31**	68	98
Sherridon: Man.	**27**	55	101
Sheslay: B.C.	**28**	58	132
Shibogama Lake: Ont.	**18**	54	88
Shickshock, Monts: Qué.	**16**	49	66
Shikag Lake: Ont.		50	90
Ship Cove: Nfld.		48	56
Shippegan: *& i.*, N.B.	**16**	48	64
Shipshaw: Qué.		48	71
Shirley Lake: Ont.		46	78
Shoal Cove: Nfld.		51	57
Shoal Harbour: Nfld.		48	54
Shoal Lake: *town*, Man.	**27**	50	101
Shoal Lake: Man./Ont.	**27**	49	95
Shoal Lakes: Man.	**27**	50	97
Shoe Point: Nfld.		49	54
Short Point: P.E.I.	**17**	46	62
Shubenacadie: *& riv.*, N.S.	**17**	45	63
Shuswap Lake: B.C.	**29**	51	119
Sicamous: B.C.	**29**	51	119
Sidney: B.C.	**28**	49	123
Sidney Dobson, Mt.: N.W.T.		62	128
Sifton: Man.	**27**	51	100
Sifton Pass: B.C.	**29**	58	126
Signai: Qué.		48	77
Sikanni: B.C.	**29**	58	122
Sikanni Chief: *riv.*, B.C.	**29**	57	123
Silene, Mt.: Nfld.		59	64
Silver Mt.: Nfld.		50	57
Silvertip Mt.: B.C.	**28**	49	121
Simard, Lac: Qué.	**20**	48	79
Simcoe: Ont.	**20**	43	80
Simcoe, Lake: Ont.	**22**	44	79
Similkameen: *riv.*, B.C.	**28**	49	120
Simon, Lac: Qué.	**23**	46	75
Simoom Sound: *town*, B.C.		51	126
Simpson Bay: N.W.T.	**30**	69	114
Simpson I.: Ont.	**19**	48	88
Simpson Lake: N.W.T.	**31**	68	91
Simpson Penin.: N.W.T.	**31**	68	89
Simpson Strait: N.W.T.	**31**	68	98
Sinclair, Mt.: Ont.	**20**	48	81
Sioux Lookout: Ont.	**19**	50	92
Sipiwesk: Man.	**27**	56	97
Sipiwesk Lake: Man.	**27**	55	97
Sir Alexander, Mt.: B.C.	**29**	54	120
Sir Francis Drake, Mt.: British Columbia	**28**	51	125
Sir James McBrien, Mt.: N.W.T.	**30**	62	127
Sir Wilfred, Mt.: Qué.	**21**	47	76
Sir Wilfrid Laurier: *mt.*, British Columbia	**29**	53	120
Sitidgi Lake: N.W.T.	**30**	68	132
Siwhe Mt.: B.C.	**28**	50	122
Skagit: *riv.*, Can./U.S.A.	**29**	48	121
Skeena: *riv.*, B.C.	**28**	54	129
Skeena Mtns.: B.C.	**28**	57	130
Skeleton Lake: Ont.	**22**	45	79
Skihist Mt.: B.C.	**28**	50	122
Skootamatta Lake: Ont.	**22**	45	77
Skownan: Man.	**27**	52	99
Slate Is.: Ont.	**19**	49	87
Slave: *riv.*, Alta./N.W.T.	**26**	60	112
Slave Lake: *town*, Alta.	**26**	55	115
Slave Point: N.W.T.		61	116
Slocan Lake: B.C.	**29**	50	117
Smith: Alta.	**26**	55	114
Smith, Cape: Ont.	**20**	46	82
Smith Arm: Great Bear Lake: N.W.T.	**30**	66	123
Smithers: B.C.	**28**	55	127
Smith Point: N.S.	**17**	46	63
Smiths Falls: Ont.	**23**	45	76
Smith Sound: Nfld.		48	54
Smithville: Ont.	**22**	43	80
Smoky: *riv.*, Alta.	**26**	55	118
Smoky, Cape: N.S.	**17**	47	60
Smoky Falls: Ont.	**19**	50	82
Smoky Lake: *town*, Alta.	**26**	54	112
Smooth Rock Falls: *town*, Ontario	**19**	49	82
Smoothrock Lake: Ont.		51	89
Snag: Yukon	**30**	62	140
Snake: *riv.*, Yukon	**30**	66	133
Snake Lake: Sask.	**26**	55	107
Snare: *riv.*, N.W.T.	**30**	63	115
Snegamook Lake: Nfld.		55	61
Snowbird Lake: N.W.T.	**31**	61	103
Snowdrift: N.W.T.	**31**	63	111
Snow Lake: *town*, Man.	**27**	55	100
Snow Road Station: Ont.	**22**	45	77
Snowy Mt.: B.C.	**28**	49	120
Snug Harbour: Nfld.		53	56
Somerset: Man.	**27**	50	99
Somerset I.: N.W.T.	**31**	73	93
Sooke: B.C.	**28**	48	124
Sops I.: Nfld.	**17**	50	57
Sorel: Qué.	**21**	46	73
Soscumica, Lac: Qué.		50	77
Soulanges: Qué.	**23**	45	74
Sounding Lake: Alta.	**26**	52	110
Souris: Man.	**27**	50	100
Souris: P.E.I.	**17**	46	62
Souris: *riv.*, Man.	**27**	49	101
South: *riv.*, Ont.	**20**	46	79
Southampton: Ont.	**20**	44	81
Southampton Cape: N.W.T.	**14**	62	84
Southampton Island: *town & i.*, N.W.T.	**18**	64	83
South Aulatsivik I.: Nfld.	**15**	57	61
South Bay: N.W.T.	**14**	64	83
South Baymouth: Ont.	**20**	46	82
South Brook: *town*, Nfld.		49	56
South Brookfield: N.S.	**17**	44	65
Southend: Sask.	**27**	56	103
Southern Indian Lake: Manitoba	**27**	57	99
Southey: Sask.	**27**	51	104
South Gloucester: Ont.	**32**	45	76
South Henik Lake: N.W.T.	**31**	61	97
South Indian Lake: *town*, Manitoba	**27**	57	99
South Knife: *riv.*, Man.	**27**	58	96
South Nahanni: N.W.T.		61	123
South Nahanni: *riv.*, N.W.T.	**30**	61	126
South Nation: *riv.*, Ont.	**21**	45	75
South Porcupine: Ont.	**20**	48	81
Southport: Nfld.		48	54
South River: *town*, Ont.	**22**	46	79
South Roxton: Qué.		45	73
South Saskatchewan: *riv.*, Saskatchewan/Alberta	**26**	51	109
South Seal: *riv.*, Man.	**27**	58	99
South Sleeper Is.: N.W.T.		58	80
South Thompson: *riv.*, B.C.		51	120
Spanish: Ont.	**20**	46	82
Spanish: *riv.*, Ont.	**20**	47	82
Sparwood: B.C.	**29**	50	115
Spatsizi Plat. Wilderness Prov. Park: B.C.	**28**	58	130
Spatsum: B.C.		51	121
Spear, Cape: Nfld.	**17**	47	53
Speers: Sask.	**26**	53	107
Spence Bay: *settlement*, N.W.T.	**31**	69	93
Spencer, Cape: N.B.	**17**	45	66
Spencerville: Ont.	**23**	45	76
Spicer Is.: N.W.T.	**14**	68	78
Spirit River: *town*, Alta.	**26**	56	119
Split, Cape: N.S.	**17**	45	64
Split Lake: *& town*, Man.	**27**	56	96
Spotted I.: Nfld.		54	56
Spragge: Ont.	**20**	46	83
Springdale: Nfld.	**17**	49	56
Springer, Mt.: Qué.		50	75
Springfield: N.S.	**17**	45	65
Springhill: N.S.	**17**	46	64
Sproat Lake: B.C.	**28**	49	125
Sproule Point: Qué.	**16**	50	67
Spruce Brook: *town*, Nfld.		49	58
Sprucedale: Ont.	**22**	45	79
Spruce Woods Prov. Park: Man.	**27**	49	99
Squamish: B.C.	**28**	50	123
Squamish: *riv.*, B.C.	**28**	50	123
Square I.: Nfld.		53	56
Squatteck: Qué.		48	69
Squaw Rapids Dam: Sask.	**27**	54	103
Stackpool: Ont.	**20**	48	82
Stallworthy, Cape: N.W.T.	**13**	81	95
Stang, Cape: N.W.T.	**31**	71	105
Stanley: N.B.	**16**	46	67
Star City: Sask.	**27**	53	104

	Page	N	W
Stave Lake: B.C.	**28**	49	122
Stayner: Ont.	**20**	44	80
Steep Rock Lake: Ont.		48	91
Stefansson I.: N.W.T.	**31**	73	107
Steinbach: Man.	**27**	49	97
Stellarton: N.S.	**17**	46	63
Stephenville: Nfld.	**17**	49	69
Stephenville Crossing: Newfoundland		48	58
Stettler: Alta.	**26**	52	113
Steveston: B.C.	**36**	49	123
Stewart: B.C.	**28**	56	130
Stewart: *riv.*, Yukon	**30**	63	138
Stewiacke: *& riv.*, N.S.	**17**	45	63
Stikine: *riv.*, B.C.	**28**	57	131
Stikine Ranges: B.C.		59	130
Stillwater: B.C.	**28**	50	124
Stillwater Creek: Sask.	**26**	50	108
Stimson: Ont.		49	81
Stirling: Alta.	**26**	50	113
Stirling: Ont.	**22**	44	78
Stittsville: Ont.	**32**	45	76
Stonecliffe: Ont.	**20**	46	78
Stonewall: Man.	**27**	50	97
Stoney Creek: *town*, Ont.	**22**	43	80
Stony Lake: Man.	**27**	59	99
Stony Lake: Ont.	**22**	45	78
Stony Mountain: *town*, Manitoba	**27**	50	97
Stony Plain: *town*, Alta.	**26**	54	114
Stony Rapids: *town*, Sask.	**27**	59	106
Storkerson Bay: N.W.T.	**30**	73	125
Stouffville: Ont.	**22**	44	79
Stoughton: Sask.	**27**	50	103
Stout Lake: Ont.	**27**	52	94
Strasbourg: Sask.	**27**	51	105
Stratford: Ont.	**20**	43	81
Strathcona Prov. Park: B.C.	**28**	50	126
Strathcona Sound: N.W.T.	**31**	73	83
Strathmore: Alta.	**26**	51	113
Strathnaver: B.C.	**29**	53	123
Strathroy: Ont.	**20**	43	82
Streetsville: Ont.	**22**	44	80
Strickland: Ont.		49	82
Strzelecki Harbour: N.W.T.		72	97
Stuart Lake: B.C.	**29**	55	124
Sturgeon: *riv.*, Ont.	**20**	47	81
Sturgeon: *riv.*, Sask.	**26**	53	106
Sturgeon Bay: Man.	**27**	52	98
Sturgeon Falls: Ont.	**19**	46	80
Sturgeon Falls: *town*, Ont.	**20**	46	80
Sturgeon Lake: Alta.	**26**	55	117
Sturgeon Lake: Ont.	**22**	44	79
Sturgeon Lake: Ont.		50	91
Sturgeon Landing: Man.	**27**	54	102
Sturgis: Sask.	**27**	52	102
Sudbury: Ont.	**20**	46	81
Sud-Ouest, Pointe: Québec	**16**	49	64
Sullivan Bay: *town*, B.C.		51	127
Sullivan Lake: Alta.	**26**	52	112
Sully: Qué.		47	69
Sultan: Ont.	**20**	48	83
Summerside: P.E.I.	**17**	46	64
Sunderland: Ont.	**22**	44	79
Sundre: Alta.	**26**	52	115
Sundridge: Ont.	**22**	46	79
Superior, Lake: Canada/U.S.A.	**19**	48	88
Surf Inlet: *town*, B.C.	**28**	53	129
Surprise, Lac: Qué.		49	75
Surrey: P.E.I.	**17**	46	63
Sussex: N.B.	**17**	46	66
Sutherland: Sask.	**26**	52	107
Sutton: Ont.	**22**	44	79
Sutton: Qué.	**21**	45	73
Sutton: *riv.*, Ont.		55	84
Sverdrup Is.: N.W.T.	**13**	78	100
Swain Post: Ont.	**27**	51	93
Swan Hills: Alta.	**26**	55	116
Swan Lake: Man.	**27**	52	101
Swannell Range: B.C.	**29**	56	126
Swan River: *town*, Man.	**27**	52	101
Swastika: Ont.	**20**	48	80
Swift Current: Nfld.		48	54
Swift Current: Sask.	**26**	50	108
Swinburne, Cape: N.W.T.	**31**	71	99
Sydenham: Ont.	**22**	44	77
Sydenham: *riv.*, Ont.	**20**	43	82
Sydney: N.S.	**17**	46	60
Sydney Lake: Ont.	**27**	51	95
Sydney Mines: N.S.	**17**	46	60
Sykes, Mt.: Nfld.		49	57
Sylvan Lake: *town*, Alta.	**26**	52	114
Sylvester, Mt.: Nfld.		48	55
Taber: Alta.	**26**	50	112
Table Bay: Nfld.		54	56
Tadoule Lake: Man.	**27**	59	98
Tadoussac: Qué.	**21**	48	70
Tagish: *& lake*, Yukon		60	134
Tahaetkun Mt.: B.C.		50	120
Tahiryuak Lake: N.W.T.	**31**	71	112
Tahoe Lake: N.W.T.	**31**	70	109
Tahsis: B.C.	**29**	50	126
Tahtsa Lake: B.C.	**28**	54	127
Takhini: Yukon		60	135
Takiyuak Lake: N.W.T.	**31**	66	113
Takla Lake: B.C.	**29**	55	126

	Page	N	W
Takla Landing: B.C.	**29**	56	126
Taku: B.C.		60	133
Taku: *riv.*, B.C.	**24**	59	133
Taltson: *riv.*, N.W.T.	**31**	60	111
Tamworth: Ont.	**22**	44	77
Tapani Lac: Qué.	**21**	47	75
Taschereau: Qué.		48	79
Taseko: *riv. & mtn.*, B.C.	**29**	51	123
Tashota: Ont.		50	88
Tasiat, Lac: Qué.		59	75
Tassialouc, Lac: Qué.		59	74
Tatamagouche: *& bay*, N.S.	**17**	46	63
Tathlina Lake: N.W.T.		60	118
Tatla Lake: B.C.	**29**	52	124
Tatlatui Prov. Park: B.C.	**28**	57	129
Tatlayoko Lake: B.C.	**29**	52	124
Tatnam, Cape: Man.	**18**	57	91
Taureau, Rés.: Qué.	**21**	47	74
Tavani: N.W.T.	**31**	62	93
Taverner Bay: N.W.T.	**14**	67	73
Tavistock: Ont.	**20**	43	81
Taylor: B.C.	**29**	56	121
Taylors Head: N.S.	**17**	45	62
Tazin Lake: Sask.	**26**	60	109
Tecumseh: Ont.	**20**	42	83
Teeswater: Ont.	**20**	44	81
Tehek Lake: N.W.T.	**31**	65	95
Tehkummah: Ont.		46	82
Telegraph Creek: *town*, British Columbia	**28**	58	131
Temagami: Ont.	**20**	47	80
Témiscamie: *riv.*, Qué.		52	72
Témiscaming: Qué.	**20**	47	79
Témiscamingue, Lac: Ontario/Québec	**20**	47	79
Témiscamingue Reserve: Québec	**20**	47	79
Témiscouata, Lac: Qué.	**16**	48	69
Templeton: Qué.	**32**	45	76
Terence Bay: *town*, N.S.	**17**	44	64
Terrace: B.C.	**28**	55	129
Terrace Bay: *town*, Ont.		49	87
Terra Nova Nat. Park: Nfld.	**17**	48	54
Terrebonne: Qué.	**23**	46	74
Terrenceville: Nfld.		48	55
Terror Point: N.W.T.	**14**	64	81
Teslin: *& lake*, Yukon	**30**	60	132
Teslin: *riv.*, Yukon	**30**	61	134
Teslin Crossing: Yukon		61	135
Tessik Lake: N.W.T.	**14**	65	75
Tessisoak Lake: Nfld.		57	63
Tetu Lake: Man./Ont.	**27**	50	95
Teulon: Man.	**27**	50	97
Texada I.: B.C.	**28**	49	124
Tha-anne: *riv.*, N.W.T.	**31**	60	96
Thames: *riv.*, Ont.	**20**	43	81
Thamesville: Ont.	**20**	42	82
Theano Point: Ont.		47	85
Thedford: Ont.	**20**	43	82
Thekulthili Lake: N.W.T.		61	110
Thelon: *riv. & Game Sanctuary*, N.W.T.	**31**	64	104
The Pas: Man.	**27**	54	101
Thesiger Bay: N.W.T.	**30**	72	125
Thessalon: Ont.	**20**	46	84
Thetford Mines: Qué.	**21**	46	71
The Two Rivers: *town*, Saskatchewan	**27**	56	103
Thévenet, Lac: Qué.		58	69
Thicket Portage: Man.	**27**	55	98
Thirty Thousand Is.: Ont.	**20**	45	80
Thlewiaza: *riv.*, N.W.T.	**31**	61	97
Thoa: *riv.*, N.W.T.		61	109
Thomaston: N.B.	**16**	46	67
Thom Bay: N.W.T.	**31**	70	92
Thomlinson, Mt.: B.C.	**28**	56	128
Thompson: Man.	**27**	56	98
Thompson: *riv.*, B.C.	**29**	51	121
Thompson Landing: N.W.T.	**31**	63	110
Thomsen: *riv.*, N.W.T.	**30**	74	120
Thorburn Lake: *town*, Newfoundland		48	54
Thorhild: Alta.	**26**	54	113
Thornbury: Ont.	**19**	45	80
Thornhill: Ont.	**32**	44	79
Thorold: Ont.	**22**	43	79
Thorsby: Alta.	**26**	53	114
Thousand Is.: Can./U.S.A.	**23**	44	76
Three Hills: *town*, Alta.	**26**	52	113
Three Mile Plains: N.S.	**17**	44	64
Thunder Bay: Ont.	**19**	48	89
Thurlow: B.C.	**28**	50	125
Thurso: Qué.	**23**	46	75
Thutade Lake: B.C.	**28**	57	127
Thwart I.: Nfld.		49	55
Tiblemont: *lake*, Qué.	**20**	48	77
Tichborne: Ont.		45	77
Tidehead: N.B.	**16**	48	67
Tignish: P.E.I.	**17**	47	64
Tilbury: Ont.	**20**	42	82
Tillsonburg: Ont.	**20**	43	81
Tilt Cove: Nfld.	**17**	50	56
Tilting: Nfld.		50	54
Timagami: *lake*, Ont.	**20**	47	80
Timagami Prov. Forest: Ontario	**20**	47	81
Timberlea: N.S.	**17**	45	64
Timmins: Ont.	**20**	48	81
Tingin Fiord: N.W.T.	**14**	69	68

	Page	N	W
Tinniswood, Mt.: B.C.	**28**	50	124
Tionaga: Ont.	**20**	48	82
Tisdale: Sask.	**27**	53	104
Tiverton: N.S.	**17**	44	66
Tlogotsha Range: N.W.T.		61	125
Toba: *inlet & riv.*, B.C.	**28**	50	124
Tobermory: Ont.	**20**	45	82
Tobin Lake: Sask.	**27**	54	103
Tobique: *riv.*, N.B.	**16**	47	67
Tod, Mt.: B.C.		51	120
Tofield: Alta.	**26**	53	113
Tofino: B.C.	**29**	49	126
Tomiko Lake: Ont.	**20**	47	80
Torbay: Nfld.	**17**	48	53
Torch: *riv.*, Sask.	**27**	54	105
Tornado Mt.: B.C./Alta.	**29**	50	115
Torngat Mtns.: Nfld.		60	64
TORONTO: Ontario	**32**	44	79
Toronto Islands: Ont.	**32**	44	79
Torrance: Ont.	**22**	45	80
Tor's Cove: Nfld.		47	53
Tottenham: Ont.	**22**	44	80
Toulnustouc: *riv.*, Qué.		50	68
Tourville: Qué.	**21**	47	70
Tracadie: N.B.	**16**	47	65
Tracadie: N.S.	**17**	46	62
Tracy: Qué.	**23**	46	73
Traffic Mt.: Yukon		62	130
Trail: B.C.	**29**	49	118
Tramping Lake: Sask.	**26**	52	109
Tranquille: B.C.		51	120
Trans-Canada Highway	**12/13**	—	—
Transcona: Man.	**33**	50	97
Trapp Lake: *town*, B.C.		50	120
Treherne: Man.	**27**	50	99
Trembleur Lake: B.C.	**29**	55	125
Trenche: *riv.*, Qué.		48	73
Trent: *riv.*, Ont.	**22**	44	78
Trent Canal: Ont.	**22**	44	79
Trente et Un Milles, Lac des: Québec	**21**	46	76
Trenton: N.S.	**17**	46	63
Trenton: Ont.	**22**	44	78
Trepassey: Nfld.	**17**	47	53
Trinity: Bonavista Bay, Newfoundland		49	54
Trinity: *& bay*, Nfld.	**17**	48	53
Trochu: Alta.	**26**	52	113
Trodley I.: N.W.T.		52	79
Troilus, Lac: Qué.		51	75
Trois Pistoles: Qué.	**16**	48	69
Trois Rivières: Qué.	**21**	46	73
Trout: *riv.*, N.W.T.		61	120
Trout Creek: *town*, Ont.	**20**	46	79
Trout Lake: N.W.T.	**30**	60	121
Trout Lake: Ont.	**20**	46	79
Trout Lake: Ont.	**18**	51	93
Trout Lake: *town*, Alta.		56	115
Trout Lake: *town*, Ont.		54	90
Trout Mills: Ont.		46	79
Trout River: *town*, Nfld.	**17**	50	58
Troy: N.S.	**17**	46	61
Truite, Lac à la: Qué.	**20**	47	78
Truro: N.S.	**17**	45	63
Tsu Lake: N.W.T.		61	112
Tudhope: Ont.		49	82
Tudor, Lac: Qué.	**15**	56	65
Tukarak I.: N.W.T.		56	79
Tuktoyaktuk: N.W.T.	**30**	69	133
Tulsequah Creek: B.C.	**24**	59	134
Tunulik: *riv.*, Qué.		58	66
Tunungayualuk I.: Nfld.	**15**	56	61
Turgeon, Lac: *& riv.*, Qué.		49	79
Turner's Bight: *settlement*, Newfoundland		54	58
Turner Valley: *town*, Alta.	**26**	51	114
Turnor Lake: Sask.	**26**	57	109
Turriff: Ont.		45	78
Turtle: *riv.*, Ont.		49	92
Turtleford: Sask.	**26**	53	109
Tusket: N.S.	**17**	44	66
Tuxedo: Man.	**33**	50	97
Tuya Lake: B.C.		59	131
Tweed: Ont.	**22**	44	77
Tweedsmuir Prov. Park: British Columbia	**29**	53	126
Twenty Mile Creek: Ont.		43	80
Twillingate: Nfld.	**17**	50	55
Twin Falls: Ont.		49	80
Twin Is.: N.W.T.	**18**	53	80
Twin Ponds: Nfld.		49	56
Two Brothers: *is.*, N.W.T.		59	80
Two Rivers, Lake of: Ont.		46	78
Uchi Lake: *town*, Ont.		51	93
Ucluelet: B.C.	**28**	49	126
Uivuk, Cape: Nfld.		58	63
Ukasiksalik I.: Nfld.		56	61
Umfreville Lake: Ont.	**27**	50	95
Ungava Bay: Qué.	**14**	59	67
Ungava, Péninsule d': Qué.	**14**	61	75
Uniacke: Qué.		48	78
Union Bay: *town*, B.C.	**28**	49	125
Unionville: Ont.	**32**	44	79
United States Range: N.W.T.	**13**	83	80
Unity: Sask.	**26**	52	109
Upper Arrow Lake: B.C.	**29**	50	118
Upper Foster Lake: Sask.	**27**	57	105
Upper Goose Lake: Ont.		52	93

	Page	N	W
Upper Island Cove: Nfld.		48	53
Upper Musquodoboit: N.S.	**17**	45	63
Upsalquitch: N.B.	**16**	48	67
Uranium City: Sask.	**26**	60	109
Utik Lake: Man.	**27**	55	96
Utikuma Lake: Alta.	**26**	56	115
Uxbridge: Ont.	**22**	44	79
Val Barrette: Qué.	**21**	47	75
Val Brillant: Qué.	**16**	48	68
Valcourt: Qué.	**21**	45	72
Valdes I.: B.C.	**28**	49	124
Val d'Or: Qué.	**20**	48	78
Valemount: B.C.	**29**	53	119
Vallée Junction: Qué.	**21**	46	71
Valleyfield: Qué.	**23**	45	74
Valleyview: Alta.	**26**	55	117
Van Bruyssel: Qué.		48	72
Vancouver: B.C.	**36**	49	123
Vancouver, Mt.: U.S.A./Canada		60	140
Vancouver I.: B.C.	**28/29**	—	—
Vanderhoof: B.C.	**36**	54	124
Vankleek Hill: *town*, Ont.	**23**	45	75
Vannes, Lac: Qué.		56	67
Vansittart I.: N.W.T.	**14**	66	84
Varennes: Qué.	**23**	46	73
Vars: Ont.	**23**	45	75
Vauban: Qué.		48	69
Vauxhall: Alta.	**26**	50	112
Vegreville: Alta.	**26**	53	112
Venosta: Qué.	**23**	46	76
Verchères: Qué.	**23**	46	73
Verdun: Qué.	**32**	45	74
Verendrye, Parc de la: Qué.	**16**	50	74
Vermette: Man.	**33**	50	97
Vermeulle, Lac: Qué.		55	69
Vermilion: Alta.	**26**	53	111
Vermilion: *riv.*, Qué.	**21**	47	73
Vermilion Bay: *town*, Ont.	**27**	50	93
Vermilion Pass: Alta./B.C.	**26**	51	116
Verner: Ont.	**20**	46	80
Vernon: B.C.	**29**	50	119
Vernon Lake: Ont.	**22**	45	79
Vernon River: *town*, P.E.I.	**17**	46	63
Verona: Ont.	**22**	44	77
Verte, Baie: N.B./N.S.	**17**	46	64
Verte, Baie: Nfld.	**17**	50	56
Verte I.: Qué.	**21**	48	69
VICTORIA: British Columbia	**28**	48	123
Victoria: *riv.*, Nfld.		48	57
Victoria Harbour: Ont.	**22**	45	80
Victoria I.: N.W.T.	**31**	70	110
Victoria Lake: Nfld.		48	57
Victoria Lake: Ont.		46	78
Victoria Peak: B.C.		50	126
Victoria Road: Ont.	**22**	45	79
Victoria Strait: N.W.T.	**31**	69	100
Victoriaville: Qué.	**21**	46	72
Villebon, Lac: Qué.	**20**	48	77
Ville de Laval: Qué.	**32**	46	74
Ville-Marie: Qué.	**20**	47	79
Villemontel: Qué.		49	78
Villeroy: Qué.		46	72
Vimy Ridge: *town*, Ont.		48	80
Virden: Man.	**27**	50	101
Virginia Falls: N.W.T.		62	126
Virginiatown: Ont.	**20**	48	80
Viscount Melville Sound: N.W.T.	**12**	74	110
Voiseys Bay: Nfld.		56	62
Vulcan: Alta.	**26**	50	113
Waasis: N.B.	**17**	46	67
Wabakimi Lake: Ont.		51	90
Wabana: Nfld.	**17**	48	53
Wabano: *riv.*, Qué.		48	74
Wabasca: *riv.*, Alta.	**26**	57	114
Wabatongushi Lake: Ont.		48	84
Wabigoon Lake: Ont.		50	93
Wabowden: Man.	**27**	55	99
Wabuk Point: Ont.	**18**	55	85
Wabush: Nfld.	**15**	53	67
W.A.C. Bennett Dam: British Columbia	**29**	56	122
Wacouna: Qué.		51	66
Waddington, Mt.: B.C.	**29**	51	125
Wadena: Sask.	**27**	52	104
Wager Bay: *& settlement*, N.W.T.	**31**	66	90
Wainwright: Alta.	**26**	53	111
Wakami Lake: Ont.	**20**	47	83
Wakaw: Sask.	**27**	53	106
Wakefield: Qué.	**23**	46	76
Wakomata Lake: Ont.	**20**	47	83
Wakuach Lake: Qué.		56	68
Wakwekobi Lake: Ont.	**20**	46	83
Waldheim: Sask.	**26**	53	107
Wales I.: N.W.T.	**31**	68	87
Walhachin: B.C.		51	121
Walker Bay: N.W.T.	**30**	71	119
Walkerton: Ont.	**20**	44	81
Wallace: N.S.	**17**	46	63
Wallaceburg: Ont.	**20**	43	82
Walsh, Mt.: Yukon		61	140
Walsingham, Cape: N.W.T.	**14**	66	62
Walter Bathurst, Cape: N.W.T.	**31**	73	76

	Page	N	W
Walton: N.S.	17	45	64
Wanapitei: *lake & riv.*, Ont.	20	47	81
Wanapitei Prov. Forest: Ontario	20	47	81
Wanham: Alta.	24	56	118
Wanless: Man.	27	54	101
Wanup: Ont.		46	81
Wapawekka Hills: *& lake*, Saskatchewan	27	54	105
Wapella: Sask.	27	50	102
Wapesi Lake: Ont.		51	92
Wapiti: *riv.*, B.C./Alta.	26	55	120
Wardlow: Alta.	26	51	112
Ware: B.C.	29	58	126
Warkworth: Ont.	22	44	78
Warman: Sask.	26	52	106
Warner: Alta.	26	49	112
Warren: Ont.	20	46	80
Warren Landing: Man.	27	54	98
Warwick: Qué.	21	46	72
Wascana Creek: Sask.	30	50	105
Wasekamio Lake: Sask.	26	57	109
Washagami: Ont.		47	80
Washago: Ont.	22	45	79
Washburn Lake: N.W.T.	31	70	107
Washow Bay: Man.	27	51	97
Waskesiu: Sask.	26	54	106
Waskigomog Lake: Ont.		46	79
Waswanipi: *& lake*, Qué.		50	76
Watabeag Lake: *& riv.*, Ont.	20	48	80
Watcomb: Ont.		50	91
Waterbury Lake: Sask.	27	58	104
Waterdown: Ont.	22	43	80
Waterford: Ont.	20	43	80
Waterhen: *riv.*, Sask.	26	54	109
Waterhen Lake: Man.	27	52	99
Waterloo: Ont.	20	43	81
Waterloo: Qué.	21	45	73
Waterton Glacier Int. Peace Park: Can./U.S.A.	48	49	114
Waterton Lakes Nat. Park: Alberta	26	49	114
Watford: Ont.	20	43	82
Wathaman: *riv.*, Sask.	27	57	104
Watino: Alta.		56	118
Watrous: Sask.	27	52	105
Watson: Sask.	27	52	104
Watson Lake: *town*, Yukon	30	60	129
Waubaushene: Ont.	22	45	80
Waugh: N.B.	16	47	66
Wawa: Ont.	19	48	85
Wawaitin Falls: Ont.	20	48	81
Wawota: Sask.	27	50	102
Weagamow Lake: Ont.		53	91
Weaver Lake: Man.	27	53	97
Webbwood: Ont.	20	46	82
Wedge Mt.: B.C.	28	50	123
Wedgeport: N.S.	17	44	66
Weedon: Qué.	21	46	71
Wekusko: *& lake*, Man.	27	55	100
Welland: *& canal*, Ont.	22	43	79
Welland: *riv.*, Ont.	22	43	80
Wellington: Nfld.		49	54
Wellington: Ont.	22	44	77
Wellington Chan.: N.W.T.	31	75	93
Wellington Station: N.S.	17	45	64
Wellington Station: P.E.I.	17	46	64
Wells: B.C.	29	53	122
Wells Gray Prov. Park: British Columbia	29	52	120
Welsford: N.B.	17	45	66
Wembley: Alta.	26	55	119
Wenebegon: *lake & riv.*, Ontario	20	47	83
Wernecke Mts.: Yukon	30	65	133
Weslemkoon Lake: Ont.	20	45	77
Wesleyville: Nfld.	17	49	54
West Club I.: N.W.T.		54	81
Westfield: N.B.	17	45	66
West Fiord: N.W.T.		76	90
Westlock: Alta.	26	54	114
West Lorne: Ont.	20	43	82
Westmount: Qué.	32	45	74
West Point: P.E.I.	17	47	64
Westport: N.S.	17	44	66
Westport: Ont.	23	45	76
Westree: Ont.		47	82
West Road: *riv.*, B.C.	29	53	123
West Vancouver: B.C.	36	49	123
Westville: N.S.	17	46	63
Westwold: B.C.		50	120
Wetaskiwin: Alta.	26	53	113
Weyburn: Sask.	27	50	104
Weymouth: N.S.	17	44	66
Whale Cove: Ont.	18	63	92
Wharton Lake: N.W.T.	31	64	100
Wheatley: Ont.	20	42	82
Wheeler: *riv.*, Qué.	15	56	67
Wheeler: *riv.*, Sask.	27	57	105
Whipple Point: N.S.	17	44	66
Whiskey Lake: Ont.	20	46	82
Whitby: Ont.	22	44	79
White: *riv.*, Ont.	19	48	85
White: *riv.*, Yukon	30	63	140
White Bay: Nfld.	17	50	57
White Bear: *riv.*, Nfld.		48	57
Whitecap Mt.: B.C.	28	51	123
Whiteclay Lake: Ont.		51	89
Whitecourt: Alta.	26	54	116
Whitefish Bay: Can./U.S.A.		46	84
Whitefish Lake: N.W.T.	31	63	107
Whitegull, Lac: Qué.	15	55	64
WHITEHORSE: Yukon	30	61	135
White I.: N.W.T.	14	66	85
White Lake: Ont.	21	45	76
White Lake: Ont.		49	86
Whitemouth: Man.	27	50	96
Whitemouth Lake: Man.	27	49	96
White Otter Lake: Ont.		49	92
White Pass: *town*, B.C.		60	135
White Rock: B.C.	28	49	123
Whitesail Lake: B.C.	28	53	127
Whiteshell Prov. Park: Manitoba	27	50	95
Whitewater Lake: Ont.		51	89
Whitewood: Sask.	27	50	102
Whitney: Ont.	20	45	78
Whittle, Cap: Qué.	17	50	60
Whitworth: Qué.		48	69
Wholdaia Lake: N.W.T.	31	60	104
Whycocomagh: N.S.	17	46	61
Wiarton: Ont.	20	45	81
Widdifield: Ont.		46	79
Wignes Lake: N.W.T.		60	106
Wikwemikong: Ont.	20	46	82
Wilberforce Falls: N.W.T.	31	67	109
Wilderness Area: *park*, Newfoundland	17	47	53
Wilderness Area: *park*, Newfoundland	17	48	57
Wildwood: Alta.	26	54	115
Wilkie: Sask.	26	52	109
Will, Mt.: B.C.	28	58	129
Willet: Ont.		50	88
William: *riv.*, Sask.	26	59	109
Williamsburg: Ont.	23	45	75
Williams Lake: *town*, B.C.	29	52	122
Willis I.: Nfld.		49	54
Williston Lake: B.C.	29	56	124
Willmore Wilderness Prov. Park: Alta.	26	53	118
Willowbunch Lake: Sask.	27	49	106
Willow Lake: N.W.T.	31	62	119
Wilson, Cape: N.W.T.	14	67	81
Wilson, Mt.: Qué.		48	74
Winchester: Ont.	23	45	75
Windermere Lake: Ont.	20	48	84
Windigo: *riv.*, Qué.		48	73
Windigo Lake: *& riv.*, Ont.	18	53	92
Windsor: Nfld.	17	49	56
Windsor: N.S.	17	45	64
Windsor: Ont.	20	42	83
Windsor: Qué.	21	46	72
Windy Tickle: *str.*, Nfld.		56	60
Winefred Lake: Alta.	26	55	111
Wingham: Ont.	20	44	81
Winisk: *& riv.*, Ont.	18	55	85
Winisk Lake: Ont.	18	53	87
Winkler: Man.	27	49	98
WINNIPEG: Manitoba	33	50	97
Winnipeg: *riv.*, Man.	27	50	95
Winnipeg, Lake: Man.	27	52	98
Winnipeg Beach: Man.	27	51	98
Winnipegosis: Man.	27	52	100
Winnipegosis, Lake: Man.	27	52	100
Winokapau Lake: Nfld.		53	63
Winter Harbour: N.W.T.	31	75	110
Winter I.: N.W.T.	14	66	83
Winterton: Nfld.		48	53
Witless Bay: *town*, Nfld.		47	53
Wolfe, Cape: P.E.I.	17	47	65
Wolf Island: *& i.*, Ont.	23	44	76
Wolf I.: Magdalen Is., Qué.	16	47	62
Wolfville: N.S.	17	45	64
Wollaston, Cape: N.W.T.	30	71	118
Wollaston Lake: Sask.	27	58	103
Wollaston Penin.: N.W.T.	30	70	115
Wolseley: Sask.	27	50	103
Wood Buffalo Park: N.W.T./Alberta	26	59	113
Woodbridge: Ont.	32	44	80
Woodfibre: B.C.	28	50	123
Wood Is.: P.E.I.	17	46	63
Wood Mt.: Sask.	26	49	106
Woods, Lake of the: Canada/U.S.A.	19	49	94
Woods I.: Nfld.		49	58
Woods Lake: Nfld.		54	65
Woodstock: N.B.	16	46	68
Woodstock: Ont.	20	43	81
Woodville: Ont.	22	44	79
Woody Island: *town*, Nfld.		48	54
Wrigley: N.W.T.	30	63	124
Writing on Stone Park: Alberta	26	49	112
Wrong Lake: Man.	27	53	96
Wrottesley Inlet: N.W.T.		72	96
Wunnummin Lake: Ont.	18	53	89
Wurtele: Ont.		49	81
Wynniatt Bay: N.W.T.		72	111
Wynyard: Sask.	27	52	104
Yale: B.C.	28	50	121
Yamaska: Qué.	21	46	73
Yarker: Ont.	22	44	77
Yarmouth: N.S.	17	44	66
Yathkyed Lake: N.W.T.	31	63	98
Yellow Grass: Sask.	27	50	104
Yellowhead Pass: B.C./Alta.	29	53	119
YELLOWKNIFE: N.W.T.	30	62	114
Yellowknife: *riv.*, N.W.T.	31	63	114
Yoho Nat. Park: B.C.	29	51	117
York: Ont.	32	44	79
York, Cape: N.W.T.	31	74	87
York Factory: Man.	27	57	92
Yorkton: Sask.	27	51	102
Youbou: B.C.	28	49	124
Young: Sask.	27	52	106
Yukon: *riv.*, U.S.A./Can.	30	62	137
Yukon: *Territ.* (*cap.* Whitehorse)	30	—	—

Gazetteer of the World

	Page	Lat.	Long.
Aachen: W. Germany	74	51N	6E
Aalst: Belgium	72	51N	4E
Aare: *r.*, Switzerland	75	47N	7E
Ābādān: Iran	87	30N	48E
Abadla: Algeria	108	31N	2W
Abakan: U.S.S.R.	85	54N	91E
Åbenrå (Aabenraa): Denmark	71	55N	9E
Abbeville: France	72	50N	2E
Abbeville: U.S.A.	46	30N	92W
Abbottabad: Pak.	88	34N	73E
Abd al Kuri: *i.*, Indian O.	87	12N	52E
Abeokuta: Nigeria	108	7N	3E
Aberaeron: Wales	63	52N	4W
Abercorn: see Mbala			
Aberdare: Wales	63	52N	4W
Aberdeen: Scotland	62	57N	2W
Aberdeen: S. Dak., U.S.A.	49	45N	99W
Aberdeen: Wash., U.S.A.	48	47N	124W
Aberfeldy: Scotland	62	57N	4W
Aberystwyth: Wales	63	52N	4W
ABIDJAN: Ivory Coast	108	5N	4W
Abilene: U.S.A.	46	32N	100W
Abingdon: England	63	52N	1W
Abqaiq: Saudi Arabia	87	26N	49E
Absaroka Range: U.S.A.	48	45N	110W
Abu: India	88	25N	73E
ABU DHABI: United Arab Emirates	87	24N	54E
ABYSSINIA: see **ETHIOPIA**			
Acapulco de Juárez: Mexico	52	17N	99W
ACCRA: Ghana	108	5N	0
Achill I.: R. of Ireland	61	54N	10W
Achinsk: U.S.S.R.	85	56N	90E
Acklins I.: The Bahamas	45	22N	74W
Aconcagua: *mtn.*, Argentina	55	33S	70W
Acqui: Italy	75	44N	8E
Acre: *see* Akko			
Ada: U.S.A.	49	35N	97W
Adam's Bridge: India/Sri Lanka	88	9N	80E
Adana: Turkey	86	37N	35E
Adapazarı: Turkey	86	41N	30E
Adda: *r.*, Italy	75	46N	9E
ADDIS ABABA: Ethiopia	109	9N	39E
Adelaide: Australia	101	35S	139E
Adelaide I.: Antarctica	116	*Inset*	
ADEN: Yemen P.D.R.	87	13N	45E
Aden: *gulf*, Arabian Sea	87	13N	47E
Adige: *r.*, Italy	75	46N	11E
Adirondack Mts.: U.S.A.	51	43N	75W
Admiralty Is.: Papua New Guinea	99	2S	147E
Adour: *r.*, France	73	44N	1W
Adrian: U.S.A.	47	42N	84W
Adriatic Sea	69	43N	15E
Aduwa: Ethiopia	109	14N	39E
Aegean Is.: *& sea*	69	38N	26E
AFGHANISTAN: *cap.* Kabul	88	—	—
Afyonkarahisar: Turkey	86	39N	30E
Agadir: Morocco	108	30N	10W
Agartala: India	89	24N	91E
Agde, Cap d': France	73	43N	4E
Agen, France	73	44N	1E
Agenais: *reg.*, France	73	44N	1E
Agincourt: *hist.*, France	72	51N	2E
Agordat: Ethiopia	109	15N	37E
Agra: India	88	27N	78E
Agrigento: Sicily	69	37N	14E
Aguascalientes: Mexico	52	22N	102W
Agulhas Basin: Southern Ocean	89	44S	20E
Ahaggar: *mtns.*, Algeria	108	23N	6E
Ahmedabad: India	88	23N	73E
Ahvāz: Iran	87	31N	49E
Aigues-Mortes: *& gulf*, France	73	44N	4E
Ailsa Craig: *i.*, Scot.	62	55N	5W
Aïn Sefra: Algeria	108	33N	1W
Aïr: *mtns.*, Niger	108	18N	8E
Aire: *r.*, England	62	54N	1W
Aisne: *r.*, France	72	49N	3E
Aitape: Papua New Guinea	99	3S	142E
Aix-en-Provence: Fr.	73	44N	5E
Aix-les-Bains: France	73	46N	6E
Aizuwakamatsu: Japan	93	34N	135E
Ajaccio: Corsica	67	42N	9E
Ajmer: India	88	27N	75E
Ajo: U.S.A.	48	32N	113E
Akaroa: N.Z.	104	44S	173E
Akashi: Japan	93	35N	135E
Akhisar: Turkey	69	39N	28E
Akita: Japan	93	40N	140E
Akko (Acre): Israel	86	32N	35E
Akola: India	88	21N	77E
Akritas, C.: Greece	69	37N	22E
Akron: U.S.A.	47	41N	82W
Aksha: U.S.S.R.	83	50N	113E
Aktyubinsk: U.S.S.R.	85	50N	57E
Akureyri: Iceland	70	66N	18W
Akyab: Burma	92	20N	92E
Alabama: *r.*, U.S.A.	47	32N	88W
Alabama: *State*, U.S.A.	47	33N	87W
Alai Range: U.S.S.R.	85	39N	71E
Ala Kul': *l.*, U.S.S.R.	85	46N	82E
Alameda: U.S.A.	48	43N	112W
Alamogordo: U.S.A.	49	33N	106W
Alamosa: U.S.A.	46	37N	106W
Åland Is.: Finland	71	60N	20E
Alapayevsk: U.S.S.R.	85	58N	62E
Ala Shan: *desert*, China	90	40N	103E
Alaska: *State*, U.S.A.	12	65N	150W
Alaska, Gulf of: U.S.A.	12	58N	145W
Alaska Penin.: U.S.A.	12	56N	160W
Alaska Range: U.S.A.	12	64N	147W
Alaskan Highway: Canada/U.S.A.	12	—	—
Alassio: Italy	75	45N	8E
Alaverdi: U.S.S.R.	84	41N	45E
Alba: Italy	75	45N	8E
Albacete: Spain	67	39N	2W
ALBANIA: *cap.* Tiranë	69	41N	20E
Albany: Australia	100	35S	118E
Albany: Ga., U.S.A.	47	32N	84W
Albany: N.Y., U.S.A.	51	43N	74W
Albany: Oregon, U.S.A.	48	45N	123W
Albemarle Sd.: U.S.A.	47	36N	76W
Albert: France	72	50N	3E
Albert, Lake: Uganda	110	2N	31E
Albert Lea: U.S.A.	49	44N	93W
Albi: France	73	44N	2E
Ålborg (Aalborg): Denmark	71	57N	10E
Alborz Mts.: Iran	87	36N	52E
Albret, Pays d': Fr.	73	44N	1W
Albula Pass: Switz.	75	47N	10E
Albuquerque: U.S.A.	48	35N	107W
Albury: Australia	101	36S	147E
Alcázar de San Juan: Spain	67	39N	3W
Alcoy: Spain	67	39N	0
Aldan: U.S.S.R.	83	58N	125E
Alderney: *i.*, Channel Is.	63	*Inset*	

	Page	Lat.	Long.
Aldershot: England	112	51N	1W
Alegranza: *i.*, Canary Islands	108	29N	13W
Alegrete: Brazil	56	30S	56W
Aleksandrov Gay: U.S.S.R.	84	50N	49E
Aleksandrovsk-Sakhalinskiy: U.S.S.R.	83	51N	142E
Alençon: France	72	48N	0
Aleppo: Syria	86	36N	37E
Alès: France	73	44N	4E
Alessandria: Italy	75	45N	9E
Ålesund: Norway	70	62N	6E
Aleutian Abyssal Plain: Pacific Ocean	102	43N	165W
Aleutian Is.: Bering Sea	102	50N	170W
Aleutian Range: U.S.A.	12	60N	155W
Aleutian Trench: Pacific Ocean	102	45N	165W
Alexander Arch.: U.S.A.	24	57N	135W
Alexander City: U.S.A.	47	33N	86W
Alexander I Island: Antarctica	116	*Inset*	
Alexandra: N.Z.	104	45S	169E
Alexandria: Egypt	86	31N	30E
Alexandria: U.S.A.	46	31N	93W
Alexandrina, L.: Australia	101	35S	139E
Algarve: *Prov.*, Port.	67	37N	8W
Algeciras: Spain	67	36N	5W
ALGIERS: Algeria	108	37N	3E
ALGERIA: *cap.* Algiers	108	—	—
Algoa Bay: S. Africa	111	34S	26E
Alicante: Spain	65	38N	0
Alice: U.S.A.	46	28N	98W
Alice Springs: Australia	98	24S	134E
Aligarh: India	88	28N	78E
Aling Kangri: *mtn.*, China	88	33N	81E
Alingsås: Sweden	71	58N	12E
Alkmaar: Neth.	74	53N	5E
Al Kut: Iraq	87	33N	46E
Allahabad: India	88	25N	82E
Allegheny: *r.*, U.S.A.	47	42N	80W
Allegheny Mts.: U.S.A.	47	40N	79W
Allen Park: U.S.A.	33	42N	83W
Allentown: U.S.A.	50	41N	76W
Alleppey: India	88	9N	76E
Allgäuer Alps: Aust./W. Ger.	75	47N	10E
Alliance: U.S.A.	49	42N	103W
Allier: *r.*, France	73	47N	3E
Alma-Ata: U.S.S.R.	85	43N	77E
Almadén: Spain	67	39N	5W
Almeria: Spain	67	37N	2W
Alnwick: England	62	55N	2W
Alor Setar: Malaysia	92	6N	100E
Alpena: U.S.A.	19	45N	83W
Alps, The: *mtns.*, Europe	64	46N	7E
Alsace: *Old Prov.*, Fr.	72	48N	7E
Alta: Norway	70	70N	23E
Altai Range: Mong.	83	46N	93E
Altamaha: *r.*, U.S.A.	47	32N	82W
Altenburg: E. Germany	74	51N	12E
Altlünen: W. Germany	64	52N	7E
Altona: W. Germany	74	54N	10E
Altoona: U.S.A.	50	40N	78W
Alturas: U.S.A.	48	41N	121W
Altus: U.S.A.	49	35N	99W
Altyn Tagh: *mtns.*, China	83	37N	85E
Alva: U.S.A.	49	37N	99W
Alwar: India	88	27N	77E
Al Wudyan: *desert*, Saudi Arabia	87	32N	40E
Amara: Iraq	87	32N	47E
Amarillo: U.S.A.	49	35N	102W
Amazon: *r.*, Brazil	54	3S	60W
Ambala: India	88	31N	77E
Ambarchik: U.S.S.R.	83	70N	162E
Amberg: W. Germany	74	49N	12E
Amboina: Indonesia	91	4S	128E
Amboise: France	73	47N	1E
Ambon: *i.*, Indon.	91	4S	128E
Americus: U.S.A.	47	32N	84W
Amersfoort: Neth.	74	52N	5E
Ames: U.S.A.	49	42N	94W
Amiens: France	72	50N	2E
Amlwch: Wales	63	53N	4W
'AMMAN: Jordan	86	32N	36E
Amne Machen Shan: *mts.*, China	90	35N	100E
Amoy: China	95	24N	117E
Amritsar: India	88	32N	75E
Amsterdam: Neth.	74	52N	5E
Amsterdam: U.S.A.	51	43N	74W
Amu Dar'ya (oxus): *r.*, U.S.S.R.	85	38N	64E
Amur: *r.*, U.S.S.R./China	83	52N	138E
Anabar: *r.*, U.S.S.R.	83	72N	112E
Anaconda: U.S.A.	48	46N	113W
Anacortes: U.S.A.	48	48N	122W
Anadyr': & *gulf*, U.S.S.R.	83	65N	178W
Anaheim: U.S.A.	37	34N	118W
Anaimudi: *mtn.*, India	88	10N	77E
Anaiza: Sau. Arab.	87	26N	44E
Anambas Is.: Indon.	91	3N	106E
Anan'yev: U.S.S.R.	84	48N	30E
Anápolis: Brazil	54	16S	49W
Ancenis: France	73	47N	1W
Anchorage: U.S.A.	12	61N	150W
Ancona: Italy	75	44N	14E
Andalsnes: Norway	70	62N	8E
Andalusia: U.S.A.	47	31N	86W
Andaman Is.: & *sea*, Indian Ocean	92	12N	93E
Andermatt: Switz.	75	47N	9E
Andernach: W. Ger.	75	50N	7E
Anderson: Indiana, U.S.A.	47	40N	86W
Anderson: S.C., U.S.A.	47	34N	83W
Andes: *range*, S.Am.	54/55	—	—
Andhra Pradesh: *State*, India	88	17N	79E
Andizhan: U.S.S.R.	85	41N	73E
ANDORRA: *cap.* Andorra	73	43N	2E
Andover: England	63	51N	1W
Andover: U.S.A.	51	43N	71W
Andreyevka: U.S.S.R.	85	46N	81E
Andros: *i.*, The Bahamas	45	24N	78W
Andros: *i.*, Greece	69	38N	25E
Anegada: *i.*, W. Indies	45	19N	64W
Aneto: *mtn.*, Spain	65	43N	1E
Angara: *r.*, U.S.S.R.	83	58N	97E
Angel de la Guardia: *i.*, Mexico	44	30N	113W
Angel Falls: Venez.	54	6N	62W
Angers: France	73	47N	1W
Angical: Brazil	54	12S	45W
Angkor: *ruins*, Cambodia	91	13N	104E
Anglesey: *i.*, Wales	63	53N	4W
ANGOLA: *cap.* Luanda	110	—	—
Angola Basin: Atl. O.	57	15S	14E
Angoulême: France	73	46N	0
Angoumois: *reg.* France	73	46N	0
Angren: U.S.S.R.	85	41N	70E
Anguilla: *i.*, W. Indies	45	18N	63W
Anhwei: *Prov.*, China	94	32N	117E
Aniak: U.S.A.	12	62N	160W
Aniva Bay: U.S.S.R.	83	46N	143E
Anjou: *Old Prov.*, Fr.	73	48N	1W
Ankang: China	94	33N	109E
ANKARA: Turkey	86	40N	33E
Ankarata Mts.: Malagasy Rep.	116	20S	47E
Anking (Hwaining): China	95	31N	117E
Annaba: Algeria	67	37N	8E
Annaberg: E. Germany	74	51N	13E
Annam Highlands: S.E. Asia	92	18N	105E
Annapolis: U.S.A.	51	39N	76W
Ann Arbor: U.S.A.	47	42N	84W
Annecy: France	73	46N	6E
Anniston: U.S.A.	47	34N	86W
Annonay: France	73	45N	5E
Ansbach: W. Germany	74	49N	11E
Anshan: China	94	41N	123E
Ansi: China	83	41N	96E
Antakya (Antioch): Turkey	86	37N	36E
Antalya: & *Gulf*, Tur.	86	37N	31E
Antarctic, The	116	*Inset*	
Antequera: Spain	67	37N	4W
Anthony: U.S.A.	46	37N	98W
Anti-Atlas: *mtns.*, Alg./Morocco	108	30N	8W
Antibes, Cap d': Fr.	73	44N	7E
Antifer, Cap d': Fr.	72	50N	0
Antigua: Guatemala	58	15N	91W
ANTIGUA: *cap.* St. John's	45	17N	62W
Antipodes Is.: Pacific Ocean	102	50S	179E
Antofagasta: Chile	54	23S	70W
Antrim: & *Co.*, N. Ireland	62	55N	6W
Antrim Mts.: N. Irel.	62	55N	6W
Antsirane (Diego Suarez): Malag. Rep.	110	12S	49E
Antung: China	90	40N	124E
Antwerp (Anvers): Belgium	72	51N	4E
Anyang: China	94	36N	114E
Anzhero-Sudzhensk: U.S.S.R.	85	56N	86E
Aoiz: Spain	73	43N	1W
Aomori: Japan	93	41N	141E
Aosta: Italy	75	46N	7E
Apalachicola: *r.*, U.S.A.	47	30N	85W
Aparri: Philippines	91	18N	122E
Apeldoorn: Neth.	74	52N	6E
Apennines: *mtns.*, Italy	69	43N	12E
Appalachian Mts.: U.S.A.	45	37N	80W
Appleby: England	62	55N	3W
Appleton: U.S.A.	49	44N	88W
Aqaba: Jordan	86	29N	35E
Aquitaine: *Old Prov.*, France	73	45N	0
Arabian Sea	89	15N	55E
Aracajú: Brazil	54	11S	37W
Arad: Romania	68	46N	21E
Arafura Sea: Indonesia	98	10S	135E
Araguaia: *r.*, Brazil	54	12S	51W
Arakan Yoma: *mtns.*, Burma	92	19N	94E
Araks (Araxes): *r.*, U.S.S.R./Iran	84	39N	47E
Aral Sea: U.S.S.R.	85	45N	60E
Aral'sk: U.S.S.R.	85	47N	62E
Aran Is.: R. of Ireland	61	53N	10W
Ararat, Mt.: Turkey	87	40N	44E
Arauca: Colombia	54	7N	71W
Arbroath: Scotland	62	57N	3W
Arcachon: France	72	45N	1W
Arcata: U.S.A.	48	41N	124W
Arctic Ocean	117	*Inset*	
Ardabil: Iran	87	38N	48E
Ardèche: *r.*, France	73	44N	4E
Ardennes: *mtns.*, Belgium	72	50N	5E
Ardmore: U.S.A.	49	34N	97W
Ardrossan: Scotland	62	56N	5W
Arendal: Norway	71	58N	9E
Arequipa: Peru	54	16S	72W
Arezzo: Italy	69	43N	12E
Argentan: France	72	49N	0
Argenteuil: France	70	49N	2E
ARGENTINA: *cap.* Buenos Aires	54/55	—	—
Argentine Basin: Atl. O.	57	45S	45W
Argonne, Forêt d': France	72	49N	5E
Århus (Aarhus): Denmark	71	56N	10E
Arica: Chile	54	18S	70W
Ariège: *r.*, France	73	43N	2E
Arizona: *State*, U.S.A.	48	34N	112W
Arkansas: *r.* & *State*, U.S.A.	46	36N	93W
Arkansas City: U.S.A.	46	37N	97W
Arkhangel'sk: U.S.S.R.	82	64N	40E
Arlberg Pass: Austr.	75	47N	10E
Arles: France	73	44N	5E
Arlington: U.S.A.	33	42N	71W
Arlington Heights: U.S.A.	34	42N	88W
Arlon: Belgium	72	50N	6E
Armagh: & *Co.*, N. Ireland	62	54N	7W
Armavir: U.S.S.R.	84	45N	41E
Armenian S.S.R.: U.S.S.R.	84	40N	45E
Armentières: Fr.	72	51N	3E
Armidale: Australia	101	31S	152E
Arnhem: Neth.	74	52N	6E
Arnhem Land: Australia	98	14S	133E
Arno: *r.*, Italy	75	44N	11E
Arran: *i.*, Scotland	62	56N	5W
Arras: France	72	50N	3E
Arrée, Mts. d': Fr.	72	48N	4W
Arromanches: France	72	49N	1W
Arrowrock Res.: U.S.A.	48	44N	116W
Arrowsmith, Mt.: New Zealand	104	43S	171E
Arta: Greece	69	39N	21E
Artemovskiy: U.S.S.R.	85	57N	62E
Artesia: U.S.A.	49	33N	104W
Arthur's Pass: N.Z.	104	43S	172E
Artois: *Old Prov.*, Fr.	72	50N	2E
Aruba: *i.*, Carib. Sea	45	13N	70W
Aru Is.: Indonesia	91	6S	134E
Arun: *r.*, England	63	51N	1W
Arunachal Pradesh: *State*, India	89	28N	95E
Arvika: Sweden	71	60N	13E
Arys': U.S.S.R.	85	42N	69E
Arzamas: U.S.S.R.	84	56N	44E
Asahigawa: Japan	93	44N	142E
Asansol: India	88	24N	87E
Ascension I.: Atlantic Ocean	57	8S	15W
Aschaffenburg: W. Ger.	74	50N	9E
Ascoli Piceno: Italy	69	43N	14E
Åsele: Sweden	70	64N	17E
Asenovgrad: Bulg.	69	42N	25E
Ashburnham: U.S.A.	51	43N	72W
Ashburton: N.Z.	104	44S	172E
Ashburton: *r.*, Austl.	98	23S	116E
Asheville: U.S.A.	47	35N	83W
Ashford: England	63	51N	1E
Ashington: England	62	55N	2W
Ashkelon: Israel	86	32N	34E
Ashkhabad: U.S.S.R.	85	38N	58E
Ashland: Ky., U.S.A.	47	38N	83W
Ashland: Oregon, U.S.A.	48	42N	123W
Ashland: Wisconsin, U.S.A.	49	47N	91W
Ashtabula: U.S.A.	47	42N	81W
Ashton: U.S.A.	48	44N	111W
Asino: U.S.S.R.	85	57N	86E
Asir: *reg.*, Saudi Arabia	87	20N	42E
Asmara: Ethiopia	109	15N	39E
Aspiring, Mt.: N.Z.	104	44S	169E
Assab: Ethiopia	109	13N	42E
Assam: *State*, India	89	27N	93E
Assen: Netherlands	74	53N	7E
Assisi: Italy	69	43N	13E
Astara: U.S.S.R.	84	39N	49E
Asti: Italy	75	45N	8E
Astipálaia: *i.*, Greece	69	37N	26E
Astoria: U.S.A.	48	46N	124W
Astrakhan': U.S.S.R.	84	46N	48E
ASUNCIÓN: Paraguay	56	25S	58W
Aswân: & *dam*, Egypt	109	24N	33E
Asyut: Egypt	109	27N	31E
Atacama Desert: Chile	54	22S	69W
Atasuskiy: U.S.S.R.	85	49N	72E
Atbara: & *r.*, Sudan	109	18N	34E
Atbasar: U.S.S.R.	85	52N	68E
Atchafalaya: *r.*, U.S.A.	46	31N	92W
Atchison: U.S.A.	49	40N	95W
ATHENS: Greece	69	38N	24E
Athens: Ga., U.S.A.	47	34N	83W
Athens: Tenn., U.S.A.	47	35N	85W
Athlone: R. of Irel.	61	53N	8W
Athos: *mtn.*, Greece	69	40N	24E
Atlanta: U.S.A.	47	34N	84W
Atlantic City: U.S.A.	51	39N	75W
Atlantic Ocean	57	—	—
Atlixco: Mexico	52	19N	98W
Atoka: U.S.A.	46	34N	96W
Atrak: *r.*, Iran	87	38N	57E
Aubagne: France	73	43N	6E
Aube: *r.*, France	72	48N	4E
Aubrac, Mts. d': France	73	45N	3E
Auburn: Ala., U.S.A.	47	33N	85W
Auburn: Maine, U.S.A.	19	44N	70W
Auburn: N.Y., U.S.A.	50	43N	77W
Aubusson: France	73	46N	2E
Auch: France	73	44N	1E
Auckland: N.Z.	104	37S	175E
Auckland Is.: Pacific Ocean	102	50S	166E
Aude: *r.*, France	73	43N	2E
Audierne: & *bay*, Fr.	72	48N	5W
Augathella: Australia	100	26S	147E
Augsberg: W. Germany	75	48N	11E
Augusta: Australia	100	34S	115E
Augusta: Ga., U.S.A.	47	33N	82W
Augusta: Maine, U.S.A.	21	44N	70W
Aumale: France	72	50N	2E
Aunis: *Old Prov.*, Fr.	73	46N	1W
Aurangabad: India	88	20N	75E
Aurignac: France	73	43N	1E
Aurillac: France	73	45N	2E
Austin: Minnesota, U.S.A.	49	44N	93W
Austin: Nev., U.S.A.	48	40N	117W
Austin: Texas, U.S.A.	46	30N	98W
AUSTRALIA: *cap.* Canberra	98/99	—	—
Australian Alps: Australia	101	37S	148E
AUSTRIA: *cap.* Vienna	68	47N	15E
Autun: France	73	47N	4E
Auvergne: *Old Prov.* & *mtns.*, France	73	45N	3E
Auxerre: France	72	48N	4E
Avallon: France	73	47N	4E
Aveiro: Portugal	67	41N	9W
Avellaneda: Arg.	56	35S	58W
Aveyron: *r.*, France	73	44N	2E
Avignon: France	73	44N	5E
Ávila: Spain	67	41N	5W
Avilés: Spain	67	44N	6W
Avon: *Co.*, England	63	52N	3W
Avon: *r.*, Hants., Eng.	63	51N	2W
Avon: *r.*, War., Eng.	63	52N	2W
Avon: *r.*, Wilts., Eng.	63	51N	2W
Avonmouth: Eng.	63	51N	3W
Avranches: France	72	49N	1W
Awash: Ethiopia	109	9N	40E
Awe, L.: Scotland	62	56N	5W
Ayaguz: U.S.S.R.	85	48N	80E
Aydin: Turkey	69	38N	28E
Aylesbury: England	63	51N	0
Ayon I.: U.S.S.R.	83	70N	168E
Ayr: Australia	100	20S	147E
Ayr: Scotland	62	55N	5W
Ayutthaya: Thailand	92	14N	101E
Azerbaydzhan S.S.R.: U.S.S.R.	84	41N	47E
Azizia: Libya	86	32N	13E
Azores: *is.*, Atlantic Ocean	57	39N	29W
Azov, Sea of: U.S.S.R.	84	46N	37E
Babar Is.: Indonesia	91	8S	130E
Bab el Mandeb: *str.*, Ethiopia/Arabia	109	13N	43E
Babushkin: U.S.S.R.	114	55N	38E
Babylon: *hist.*, Iraq	87	33N	44E
Bacău: Romania	68	47N	27E
Bacolod: Philippines	91	11N	123E
Badajoz: Spain	67	39N	7W
Baden: *Old Prov.*, W. Germany	75	49N	8E
Baden: Switzerland	75	49N	8E
Baden-Baden: W. Ger.	75	49N	8E
Bad Kissingen: W. Ger.	74	50N	10E
Bad Kreuznach: W. Ger.	74	50N	8E
Bad Reichenhall: W. Germany	75	48N	13E
Badulla: Sri Lanka	88	7N	81E
Bagé: Brazil	56	31S	54W
BAGHDĀD: Iraq	87	33N	44E
Bagheria: Sicily	69	38N	14E
BAHAMAS, THE:			

	Page	Lat.	Long.
cap. Nassau	45	25N	75W
Bahawalpur: Pak.	88	29N	72E
Bahia: *see* Salvador			
Bahia Blanca: Arg.	55	39S	62W
Bahraich: India	88	28N	82E
BAHRAIN: *cap.* Manama	87	26N	51E
Bahr el Ghazal: *r.*, Chad	108	14N	17E
Bahr el Ghazal: *Prov.*, Sudan	109	10N	27E
Bahr el Jebel: *see* White Nile			
Baia-Mare: Rom.	68	48N	24E
Bailleul: France	72	53N	1E
Bainbridge: U.S.A.	47	31N	85W
Bairnsdale: Australia	101	38S	148E
Baker: Mont., U.S.A.	49	46N	104W
Baker: Oreg., U.S.A.	48	45N	118W
Bakersfield: U.S.A.	48	35N	119W
Baku: U.S.S.R.	84	40N	50E
Balaghat: India	88	22N	80E
Balaklava: *hist.*, U.S.S.R.	84	45N	34E
Bala Lake: Wales	62	53N	4W
Balashikha: U.S.S.R.	114	55N	38E
Balashov: U.S.S.R.	84	51N	43E
Balasore: India	88	21N	87E
Balatón L.: Hungary	68	47N	18E
Balboa: Panama	45	*Inset*	
Balclutha: N.Z.	104	46S	170E
Bâle: *see* Basel			
Balearic, Islas: Spain	67	39N	3E
Balen: Belgium	72	51N	5E
Bali: *i.*, Indonesia	91	8S	115E
Balikesir: Turkey	86	40N	28E
Balikpapan: Indon.	91	1S	117E
Balkan Mts.: Bulgaria	69	43N	25E
Balkhash: & *l.*, U.S.S.R.	85	46N	75E
Ballarat: Australia	101	38S	144E
Ballater: Scotland	62	57N	3W
Ballina: Australia	101	29S	154E
Ballina: R. of Ireland	61	54N	9W
Ballymena: N. Ireland	61	55N	6W
Balmaceda: Chile	55	46S	72W
Balmoral: Scotland	62	57N	3W
Balovale: Zambia	110	14S	23E
Balranald: Australia	101	35S	144E
Balsas: *r.*, Mexico	52	18N	102W
Balta: U.S.S.R.	68	48N	30E
Baltic Sea	71	—	—
Baltimore: U.S.A.	50	39N	77W
Baltrum: *i.*, W. Ger.	74	54N	7E
Baluchistan: *reg.*, Pakistan	88	27N	65E
BAMAKO: Mali	108	13N	8W
Bamba: Mali	108	17N	2W
Bamberg: W. Germany	74	50N	11E
Banbury: England	63	52N	1W
Banchory: Scotland	62	57N	2W
Banda Aceh: Indon.	92	5N	95E
Bandar: India	88	16N	81E
Bandar Abbās: Iran	87	27N	56E
Bandar-e-Shāh: Iran	87	37N	54E
Bandar-e-Shāhpūr: Iran	87	30N	49E
BANDAR SERI BEGAWAN: Brunei	91	5N	115E
Banda Sea: Indon.	91	6S	127E
Banderas, Bahia de: Mexico	52	21N	106W
Bandırma: Turkey	69	40N	28E
Banja Luka: Yugo.	69	45N	17E
Ban Me Thuot: Vietnam	92	12N	108E
Bandjarmasin: Indon.	91	3S	115E
Bandra: India	88	19N	73E
Bandung: Indonesia	91	7S	107E
Bangalore: India	88	13N	78E
Bangka: *i.*, Indonesia	91	2S	106E
BANGKOK: Thailand	92	14N	100E
Bangor: N. Ireland	62	55N	6W
Bangor: U.S.A.	19	45N	69W
Bangor: Wales	63	53N	4W
BANGUI: Central African Empire	109	4N	18E
Bangweulu, L.: Zambia	110	11S	31E
Ban Houei Sai: Laos	92	20N	100E
Baniâs: Syria	86	35N	36E
Banja Luka: Yugo.	69	45N	17E
BANJUL: The Gambia	108	13N	17W
Banks Penin.: N.Z.	104	44S	173E
Bankstown: Australia	115	34S	151E
Bann: *r.*, N. Ireland	62	55N	7W
Bannu: Pakistan	88	33N	71E
Bantry: & *bay*, R. of Ireland	61	52N	9W
Bapaume: France	72	50N	3E
Bārākpur (Barrackpore): India	115	23N	88E
Baranof I.: U.S.A.	24	57N	135W
Baranovichi: U.S.S.R.	84	53N	26E
Barataria Bay: U.S.A.	47	29N	90W
BARBADOS: *cap.* Bridgetown	45	13N	60W
Barbuda: *i.*, W. Indies	45	18N	62W
Barce: Libya	86	33N	21E
Barcelona: Spain	67	41N	2E
Barcelona: Venezuela	45	10N	65W
Barcelonnette: Fr.	73	44N	7E
Barcoo: *r.*, Australia	99	24S	144E
Bardawīl, Lake: Egypt	86	31N	33E
Bardia: Libya	86	32N	25E
Bareilly: India	88	28N	80E
Barents Sea: U.S.S.R.	82	73N	40E
Bari: Italy	69	41N	17E
Barking: England	112	51N	0
Barkly Tableland: Australia	98	18S	136E
Barkly West: S. Africa	111	28S	25E
Bar-le-Duc: France	72	49N	5E
Barlee, L.: Australia	100	29S	119E
Barletta: Italy	69	41N	16E
Barlin: France	72	50N	3E
Barnaul: U.S.S.R.	85	53N	84E
Barnet: England	112	52N	0
Barnsley: England	62	54N	2W
Barnstaple: England	63	51N	4W
Baroda: India	88	22N	73E
Barquisimeto: Venez.	45	10N	69W
Barra: *i.* & *Hd.*, Scot.	61	57N	7W
Barraba: Australia	101	30S	151E
Barrackpore: *see* Bārākpur			
Barra do Pirai: Brazil	56	22S	44W
Barranquilla: Colombia	45	11N	75W
Barrow-in-Furness: England	62	54N	3W
Barrow, Point: U.S.A.	12	72N	156W
Barry: Wales	63	51N	3W
Barstow: U.S.A.	48	35N	117W
Bar-sur-Seine: France	72	48N	4E
Bartlesville: U.S.A.	49	37N	96W
Basel (Bâle): Switzerland	75	48N	7E
Basildon: England	112	51N	0
Basingstoke: England	63	51N	1W
Basra: Iraq	87	30N	48E
Bassein: Burma	92	17N	95E
Basse-Terre: Guadeloupe	45	16N	62W
Bass Strait: Australia	99	40S	146E
Bastogne: Belgium	72	50N	6E
Bastrop: U.S.A.	46	33N	92W
Bataan Penin.: Phil.	91	15N	120E
Batang: China	90	30N	99E
Batesville: Arkansas, U.S.A.	46	36N	92W
Batesville: Miss., U.S.A.	47	34N	90W
Bath: England	63	51N	2W
Bathurst: Australia	101	33S	150E
Bathurst I.: Australia	98	12S	130E
Baton Rouge: U.S.A.	46	31N	91W
Batticaloa: Sri Lanka	88	8N	82E
Battle Creek: *city*, U.S.A.	47	42N	85W
Battle Mountain: *city*, U.S.A.	48	41N	117W
Batu Is.: Indonesia	91	0	99E
Batumi: U.S.S.R.	84	42N	42E
Batz, I. de: France	72	49N	4W
Bautzen: E. Germany	74	51N	14E
Bavaria: *Prov.*, W. Ger.	74/5	49N	11E
Bavarian Forest: W. Germany	74/5	49N	13E
Bawdwin: Burma	92	23N	97E
Bayamo: Cuba	53	20N	77W
Bayan Kara Shan: *mtns.*, China	90	34N	99E
Bay City: Michigan, U.S.A.	19	44N	84W
Bay City: Texas, U.S.A.	46	29N	96W
Bayeux: France	72	49N	1W
Baykal, L.: U.S.S.R.	83	53N	107E
Baykonur: U.S.S.R.	85	48N	66E
Baymak: U.S.S.R.	85	53N	58E
Bayonne: France	73	43N	1W
Bayonne: U.S.A.	35	41N	74W
Bayreuth: W. Germany	75	50N	12E
Baytown: U.S.A.	46	29N	95W
Baza: Spain	67	37N	3W
Beachy Head: Eng.	61	51N	0
Beaconsfield: England	112	51N	0
Beardmore Glacier: Antarctica	116	*Inset*	
Bear I.: U.S.S.R.	82	74N	20E
Béarn: *Old Prov.*, Fr.	73	43N	1W
Beas: *r.*, India	88	32N	76E
Beatrice: U.S.A.	49	40N	97W
Beauce: *reg.*, France	72	48N	2E
Beaufort: U.S.A.	47	32N	81W
Beaufort Sea	12	73N	140W
Beaufort W.: S. Africa	111	32S	23E
Beaujolais, Mts. du: France	73	46N	4E
Beaumont: U.S.A.	46	30N	94W
Beaune: France	73	47N	5E
Beauvais: France	72	49N	2E
Beaver: *i.*, U.S.A.	19	45N	85W
Beaver Dam: *city*, U.S.A.	49	43N	89W
Béchar: Algeria	108	32N	2W
Beckley: U.S.A.	47	38N	81W
Bedford: & *Co.*, Eng.	63	52N	0
Bedford: Mass., U.S.A.	33	42N	71W
Bedford: Ind., U.S.A.	47	39N	86W
Bedford: Pa., U.S.A.	50	40N	79W
Beersheba: Israel	86	31N	35E
Beeville: U.S.A.	46	29N	97W
Bega: Australia	101	37S	150E
Begovat: U.S.S.R.	85	40N	69E
Beira: Mozambique	110	20S	35E
BEIRUT: Lebanon	86	34N	34E
Beit Bridge: Rhod. (Zimbabwe)	111	22S	30E
Beja: Portugal	67	38N	8W
Bejaia: Algeria	67	36N	5E
Bela: Pakistan	88	26N	66E
Belaya: *r.*, U.S.S.R.	84	54N	56E
Belém: Brazil	54	1S	48W
Belen: U.S.A.	48	35N	107W
BELFAST: N. Ireland	62	55N	6W
Belfast L.: N. Ireland	61	55N	6W
Belfort: France	73	48N	7E
Belgaum: India	88	16N	75E
BELGIUM: *cap.* Brussels	72	51N	4E
Belgorod: U.S.S.R.	84	51N	36E
BELGRADE: Yugo.	69	45N	20E
Belitung: *i.*, Indon.	91	3S	108E
BELIZE: *cap.* Belmopan	53	17N	88W
Belize: Belize	53	17N	88W
Bellac: France	73	46N	1E
Bellary: India	88	15N	77E
Belle Fourche: & *r.*, U.S.A.	49	45N	104W
Bellegarde: France	73	46N	6E
Belle Glade: U.S.A.	47	27N	81W
Belle Île-en-Mer: Fr.	72	47N	3W
Belleville: Kansas, U.S.A.	49	40N	98W
Bellingham: U.S.A.	48	49N	122W
Bellinzona: Switz.	75	46N	9E
Belluno: Italy	75	46N	12E
Belmont: S. Africa	111	30S	24E
BELMOPAN: Belize	53	17N	88W
Belo Horizonte: Brazil	54	20S	44W
Beloit: Kans., U.S.A.	49	39N	98W
Beloit: Wisc., U.S.A.	49	43N	89W
Bel'tsy: U.S.S.R.	69	47N	28E
Belyando: *r.*, Australia	100	22S	146E
Belyy I.: U.S.S.R.	83	73N	70E
Bemidji: U.S.A.	49	47N	95W
Benalla: Australia	101	37S	146E
Bend: U.S.A.	48	44N	121W
Bendery: U.S.S.R.	68	47N	30E
Bendigo: Australia	101	37S	144E
Bengal, Bay of: Bangl./India	89	17N	87E
Benghazi: Libya	109	32N	20E
Benguela: Angola	110	13S	13E
Beni: *r.*, Bolivia	54	13S	67W
BENIN: *cap.* Cotonou	108	10N	3E
Benin, Bight of: Africa	108	4N	3E
Beni Saf: Algeria	67	35N	1W
Ben Macdhui: *mt.*, Scotland	62	57N	4W
Ben Nevis: *mt.*, Scot.	62	57N	5W
Bennington: U.S.A.	19	43N	74W
Bensenville: U.S.A.	34	42N	88W
Benton: U.S.A.	46	35N	93W
Benton Harbor: U.S.A.	47	43N	86W
Benue: *r.*, Africa	108	9N	12E
Berar: *reg.*, India	88	21N	77E
Berber: Sudan	109	18N	34E
Berbera: Somali Republic	109	10N	45E
Berdichev: U.S.S.R.	84	50N	29E
Berezovo: U.S.S.R.	85	64N	65E
Bergama: Turkey	69	39N	27E
Bergamo: & *Alps*, It.	75	46N	10E
Bergen: Norway	70	60N	5E
Bergen-op-Zoom: Netherlands	74	51N	4E
Bergerac: France	73	45N	0
Bergisch Gladbach: W. Germany	74	51N	7E
Berhampore: India	88	24N	88E
Bering Sea	12	61N	170W
Bering Str.: U.S.S.R./U.S.A.	12	65N	170W
Berkeley: U.S.A.	36	38N	122W
Berkley: U.S.A.	33	42N	83W
Berkhamsted: Eng.	112	51N	0
Berkshire: *Co.*, Eng.	63	51N	1W
BERLIN: E. & W. Ger.	113	—	—
Berlin: U.S.A.	19	45N	71W
Bermejo: *r.*, Arg.	56	26S	60W
Bermuda: *i.*, Atlantic Ocean	57	32N	65W
BERN: Switzerland	75	47N	7E
Bernay: France	72	49N	1E
Bernese Alps: Switz.	75	46N	7E
Berre, Étg. de: France	73	43N	5E
Berry: *Old Prov.*, Fr.	73	47N	2E
Berry Is.: The Bahamas	47	26N	78W
Berwick upon Tweed: England	62	56N	2W
Berwyn: U.S.A.	34	41N	88W
Besançon: France	73	47N	6E
Bessèges: France	73	44N	4E
Bessemer: U.S.A.	47	33N	87W
Bessines: France	73	46N	1E
Bethlehem: Jordan	86	31N	35E
Bethlehem: S. Africa	111	28S	28E
Bethlehem: U.S.A.	50	41N	75W
Béthune: France	72	51N	3E
Béticas, Cordillera: *mtns.*, Spain	67	38N	2W
Betwa: *r.*, India	88	26N	80E
Betws-y-Coed: Wales	62	53N	4W
Beuvron: *r.*, France	73	47N	2E
Beverley: England	62	54N	0
Beverly: U.S.A.	51	42N	71W
Beverly Hills: U.S.A.	37	34N	118W
Bexley Heath: England	112	51N	0
Bezhitsa: U.S.S.R.	84	53N	34E
Béziers: France	73	43N	3E
Bhagalpur: India	88	25N	88E
Bhamo: Burma	92	24N	97E
Bhavnagar: India	88	22N	72E
Bhima: *r.*, India	88	17N	76E
Bhopal: India	88	23N	77E
Bhubaneswar: India	88	20N	86E
Bhuj: India	88	23N	70E
BHUTAN: *cap.* Punakha	89	27N	90E
Biak: *i.*, Indon.	91	1S	136E
Białystok: Poland	68	53N	23E
Biarritz: France	73	43N	1W
Bicester: England	63	52N	1W
Biddeford: U.S.A.	19	43N	70W
Bideford: England	63	51N	4W
Biel: Switzerland	75	47N	7E
Bielefeld: W. Germany	74	52N	9E
Biella: Italy	75	46N	8E
Big Black: *r.*, U.S.A.	46	33N	90W
Big Blue: *r.*, U.S.A.	46	41N	97W
Big Falls: *city*, U.S.A.	49	48N	94W
Bighorn Mts.: & *r.*, U.S.A.	48	45N	108W
Big Spring: U.S.A.	49	32N	102W
Big Wood: *r.*, U.S.A.	48	43N	115W
Bihać: Yugoslavia	69	45N	16E
Bihar: *State*, India	88	25N	85E
Bikaner: India	88	28N	73E
Bilaspur: India	88	22N	82E
Bilbao: Spain	67	43N	3W
Billericay: England	112	51N	0
Billings: U.S.A.	48	46N	109W
Biloxi: U.S.A.	47	30N	89W
Bimini Is.: The Bahamas	47	26N	79W
Bingen: W. Germany	74	50N	8E
Binghamton: U.S.A.	50	42N	76W
Binjai: Indonesia	92	3N	98E
Birdum: Australia	98	16S	133E
Birjand: Iran	87	33N	59E
Birkenhead: England	63	53N	3W
Bîrlad: Romania	69	46N	28E
Birmingham: England	63	52N	2W
Birmingham: Ala., U.S.A.	47	33N	87W
Birmingham: Mich., U.S.A.	20	42N	83W
Birobidzhan: U.S.S.R.	83	49N	133E
Bisbee: U.S.A.	48	31N	110W
Biscay, Bay of: Atl. Ocean	64	45N	5W
Bishop's Stortford: England	63	51N	0
Biskra: Algeria	108	35N	6E
Bismarck: U.S.A.	49	47N	101W
Bismarck Arch.: Papua New Guinea	99	5S	150E
BISSAU: Guinea-Bissau	108	12N	16W
Bistrita: *r.*, Romania	68	47N	26E
Bitola: Yugoslavia	69	41N	21E
Bitterfeld: E. Germany	74	52N	12E
Bitterfontein: S. Africa	111	31S	18E
Bitterroot Range: U.S.A.	48	46N	115W
Biwa-ko: *l.*, Japan	93	35N	136E
Biysk: U.S.S.R.	85	53N	85E
Black: *r.*, Ark., U.S.A.	46	36N	91W
Black: *r.*, N.Y., U.S.A.	19	43N	75W
Black: *r.*, Wisc., U.S.A.	49	44N	91W
Blackburn: England	62	54N	2W
Blackfoot: U.S.A.	48	43N	112W
Black Forest: W. Ger.	75	48N	8E
Black Irtysh: *r.*, U.S.S.R./China	85	48N	85E
Black Mtns.: Wales	63	52N	3W
Blackpool: England	62	54N	3W
Black Sea: U.S.S.R.	84	43N	35E
Black Volta: *r.*, West Africa	108	10N	2W
Blackwater: *r.*, R. of Ireland	61	52N	8W
Blackwood: *r.*, Austl.	100	34S	115E
Blagoveshchensk: U.S.S.R.	83	50N	127E
Blanc, C.: W. Sahara	108	20N	17W
Blanc, Mt.: Fr./Italy	73	46N	7E
Blankenberghe: Belg.	72	51N	3E
Blantyre: Malawi	110	16S	35E
Blavet: *r.*, France	72	48N	3W
Blaye: France	71	45N	1W
Blenheim: *hist.*, W. Germany	75	49N	10E
Blenheim: N.Z.	104	42S	174E
Bletchley: England	63	52N	1W
Blida: Algeria	67	36N	3E
Bloemfontein: S. Africa	111	29S	26E
Blois: France	71	48N	1E
Bloody Foreland: R. of Ireland	61	55N	8W
Bloomington: Ill., U.S.A.	49	40N	89W
Bloomington: Ind., U.S.A.	47	39N	86W

	Page	Lat.	Long.
Bluefield: U.S.A.	47	37N	81W
Blue Mts.: Jamaica	53	18N	76W
Blue Mts.: U.S.A.	48	45N	120W
Blue Nile: *r.*, Africa	109	10N	37E
Blue Ridge: *mts.*, U.S.A.	47	36N	81W
Bluff: N.Z.	104	46S	168E
Blumenthal: W. Ger.	74	53N	9E
Blythe: U.S.A.	48	34N	115W
Blytheville: U.S.A.	49	36N	90W
Bo: Sierra Leone	108	8N	12W
Boa Vista: Brazil	54	3N	61W
Bobo Dioulasso: Upper Volta	108	12N	4W
Bocholt: W. Germany	74	52N	7E
Bochum: W. Germany	64	51N	7E
Bodelé Depression: Chad	109	17N	17E
Boden: Sweden	70	66N	22E
Bodensee: *see* Constance, L.			
Bodmin: & *moor*, England	63	50N	5W
Bodø: Norway	70	67N	14E
Bogalusa: U.S.A.	47	31N	90W
BOGOTÁ: Colombia	54	5N	74W
Bohol: *i.*, Phil.	91	10N	124E
Boise: U.S.A.	48	44N	116W
Bojador, C.: W. Sahara	108	26N	15W
Boké: Guinea	108	11N	14W
Boknafjorden: Norway	70	59N	6E
Bolama: Guinea-Bissau	108	12N	15W
Bolan Pass: Pakistan	88	30N	68E
Bolivar: U.S.A.	49	38N	93W
BOLIVIA: *cap.* La Paz (government), Sucre (legal)	54	17S	65W
Bollwiller: France	72	48N	7E
Bologna: Italy	75	44N	11E
Bol'shevik I.: U.S.S.R.	83	78N	102E
Bolton: England	62	53N	2W
Bolzano: Italy	75	47N	11E
Boma: Zaire	110	6S	13E
Bombay: India	88	19N	73E
Bon, C.: Tunisia	69	37N	11E
Bonaire: *i.*, Caribbean Sea	45	12N	98W
Bondo: Zaire	110	4N	24E
Bone, G. of: Indon.	91	4S	121E
Bonin Is.: Pacific O.	102	27N	142E
BONN: W. Germany	74	51N	7E
Bonny, Bight of: Gulf of Guinea	108	3N	8E
Borås: Sweden	71	58N	13E
Bordeaux: France	73	45N	1W
Borders: *Reg.*, Scotland	62	55N	3W
Bordertown: Australia	101	36S	141E
Borehamwood: Eng.	112	52N	0
Borger: U.S.A.	49	36N	101W
Borgholm: Sweden	71	57N	17E
Borislav: U.S.S.R.	68	49N	23E
Borisoglebsk: U.S.S.R.	84	51N	42E
Borkum: *i.*, W. Ger.	74	54N	7E
Borlänge: Sweden	71	60N	15E
Borneo: *i.*, Indonesia	91	0	115E
Bornholm: *i.*, Den.	71	55N	15E
Bosporus: *str.*, Tur.	65	41N	29E
Bossier City: U.S.A.	46	33N	94W
Bosso: Niger	108	14N	13E
Boston: England	63	53N	0
Boston: U.S.A.	51	42N	71W
Botany Bay: Australia	115	34S	151E
Bothnia, Gulf of: Baltic Sea	70	63N	20E
Botosani: Romania	68	47N	26E
BOTSWANA: *cap.* Gaborone	110	22S	24E
Bottrop: W. Germany	64	51N	7E
Bougainville: *i.*, Papua New Guinea	99	6S	155E
Boulder: Australia	100	31S	122E
Boulder: U.S.A.	49	40N	105W
Boulder City: U.S.A.	48	36N	115W
Boulogne: France	72	51N	2E
Boulogne-Billancourt: France	113	49N	2E
Bourbonnais: *reg.*, Fr.	73	46N	3E
Bourg: France	73	46N	5E
Bourges: France	73	47N	2E
Bourget, Lac du: Fr.	73	46N	6E
Bourg Madame: Fr.	73	42N	2E
Bourke: Australia	101	30S	146E
Bournemouth: Eng.	63	51N	2W
Bourtanger Moor: Neth./W. Germany	74	53N	7E
Bou Saâda: Algeria	67	35N	4E
Boussac: France	73	46N	2E
Bowling Green: U.S.A.	47	37N	86W
Bowling Green C.: Australia	100	19S	147E
Bowman: U.S.A.	49	46N	103W
Box Hill: England	112	51N	0
Boyome Falls: Zaire	110	0	25E
Boyne: *r.*, R. of Irel.	61	54N	6W
Bozeman: U.S.A.	48	46N	111W
Brabant: Belgium	72	51N	4E
Brač: *i.*, Yugoslavia	69	43N	16E
Bracknell: England	63	51N	0
Bradenton: U.S.A.	47	28N	83W
Bradford: England	62	54N	1W
Braga: Portugal	67	42N	8W
Brahmani: *r.*, India	88	22N	85E
Brahmaputra: *r.*, Bangl./India	89	26N	93E
Braila: Romania	69	45N	28E
Brainerd: U.S.A.	49	46N	94W
Braintree: England	63	52N	0
Braintree: U.S.A.	33	42N	71W
Branco: *r.*, Brazil	54	1N	62W
Brandenburg: E. Ger.	74	52N	13E
BRASÍLIA: Brazil	54	16S	48W
Braşov: Romania	68	46N	26E
Brasstown Bald: *mtn.*, U.S.A.	47	35N	84W
Bratislava: Czech.	68	48N	17E
Bratsk: U.S.S.R.	83	56N	102E
Braunau: Austria	75	48N	13E
Braunschweig: *see* Brunswick, W. Ger.			
Brawley: U.S.A.	48	33N	115W
Bray: R. of Ireland	63	53N	6W
BRAZIL: *cap.* Brasília	54/5	—	—
Brazil Basin: Atl. O.	57	10S	25W
Brazilian Highlands: Brazil	54	15S	50W
Brazos: *r.*, U.S.A.	46	29N	95W
Brazo Sur del Río Pilcomayo: *r.*, Arg./Paraguay	56	24S	59W
BRAZZAVILLE: Congo	110	4S	15E
Breckenridge: U.S.A.	49	46N	97W
Brecon: Wales	63	52N	3W
Brecon Beacons: *mtns.*, Wales	63	52N	3W
Breda: Netherlands	74	52N	5E
Bregenz: Austria	75	47N	10E
Bréhat, Î.: France	72	49N	3W
Breisach: W. Germany	75	48N	8E
Bremen: W. Germany	74	53N	9E
Bremerhaven: W. Germany	74	54N	9E
Bremerton: U.S.A.	48	47N	123W
Brenner Pass: Austria/Italy	75	47N	12E
Brentwood: England	112	51N	0
Brescia: Italy	75	46N	10E
Bressuire: France	73	47N	0
Brest: France	72	48N	4W
Brest: U.S.S.R.	68	52N	24E
Breton Sound: U.S.A.	47	30N	90W
Briançon: France	73	45N	7E
Bridgend: Wales	63	52N	4W
Bridgeport: Conn. U.S.A.	51	41N	73W
Bridgeport: Texas, U.S.A.	46	33N	99W
Bridgetown: Austl.	100	34S	116E
Bridgnorth: England	63	52N	2W
Bridgwater: England	63	51N	3W
Bridlington: England	62	54N	0
Brie: *reg.*, France	72	49N	3E
Brienz, Lake: Switz.	75	47N	8E
Briey: France	72	49N	6E
Brig: Switzerland	75	46N	8E
Brigham: U.S.A.	48	42N	112W
Brighton: England	63	51N	0
Brindisi: Italy	69	41N	18E
Brisbane: Australia	100	27S	153E
Bristol: England	63	51N	3W
Bristol: U.S.A.	47	37N	82W
Bristol Bay: U.S.A.	12	58N	160W
Bristol Channel: Eng.	63	51N	4W
British Isles: Europe	61	—	—
British Mts.: U.S.A./Canada	30	69N	140W
Brittany: *Old Prov.*, France	72	48N	3W
Brive: France	73	45N	2E
Brno: Czech.	68	49N	17E
Broadview: U.S.A.	34	42N	88W
Brockton: U.S.A.	51	42N	71W
Brockway: U.S.A.	49	47N	106W
Brod: Yugoslavia	69	45N	18E
Broken Bow: U.S.A.	49	41N	100W
Broken Hill: Australia	101	32S	141E
Bromley: England	112	51N	0
Bromsgrove: England	63	52N	2W
Bronx, The: U.S.A.	35	41N	74W
Brookfield: U.S.A.	34	43N	83W
Brookings: U.S.A.	49	44N	97W
Brookline: U.S.A.	33	43N	72W
Brooklyn: U.S.A.	35	41N	74W
Brooks Range: U.S.A.	12	68N	150W
Brooksville: U.S.A.	47	29N	82W
Broome: Australia	98	18S	122E
Brough Head: Scotland	61	59N	3W
Brownsville: U.S.A.	52	26N	97W
Brownwood: U.S.A.	49	32N	99W
Bruchsal: W. Germany	74	49N	9E
Bruges (Brugge): Belgium	72	51N	3E
Brühl: W. Germany	74	51N	7E
BRUNEI: *cap.* Bandar Seri Begawan	91	5N	115E
Brunswick: U.S.A.	47	31N	81W
Brunswick (Braunschweig): W. Ger.	74	52N	10E
BRUSSELS: Belgium	72	51N	4E
Bryan: U.S.A.	46	30N	96W
Bryansk: U.S.S.R.	84	53N	34E
Bucaramanga: Colombia	54	7N	73W
Buchan Ness: Scotland	61	57N	2W
BUCHAREST: Romania	69	44N	26E
Buckhaven: Scotland	62	56N	3W
Buckingham: *Co.*, England	63	52N	0
Buckland Tableland: Australia	100	25S	148E
BUDAPEST: Hungary	68	48N	19E
Bude: England	63	51N	5W
Büderich: W. Germany	64	51N	7E
Buenaventura: Colombia	54	4N	77W
BUENOS AIRES: Arg.	56	35S	58W
Buffalo: N.Y., U.S.A.	50	43N	79W
Buffalo: Wyo., U.S.A.	48	44N	107W
Bug: *r.*, Pol./U.S.S.R.	68	51N	24E
Bug: *r.*, U.S.S.R.	84	48N	31E
BUJUMBURA: Burundi	110	3S	30E
Bukachacha: U.S.S.R.	83	53N	117E
Bukama: Zaire	110	9S	26E
Bukavu: Zaire	110	2S	29E
Bukhara: U.S.S.R.	85	40N	65E
Bukittinggi: Indon.	92	0	100E
Bukoba: Tanzania	110	1S	32E
Bulagan: Mongolia	83	49N	103E
Bulawayo: Rhodesia (Zimbabwe)	111	20S	29E
BULGARIA: *cap.* Sofiya (Sofia)	69	42N	25E
Buller: *mtns.*, N.Z.	104	42S	172E
Bulloo: *r.*, Australia	100	26S	143E
Bulloo, L.: Australia	100	28S	142E
Bull Shoals Res.: U.S.A.	46	37N	93W
Bumthang: Bhutan	89	27N	91E
Bunbury: Australia	100	33S	116E
Bundaberg: Austl.	100	25S	152E
Bunguran Is.: *see* Natuna Is.			
Buraida: Saudi Arabia	87	27N	44E
Buraimi: United Arab Emirates	87	24N	56E
Burbank: U.S.A.	37	34N	118W
Burdekin: *r.*, Austl.	100	20S	147E
Burdur: Turkey	86	38N	30E
Bureya: U.S.S.R.	83	50N	130E
Burgas: Bulgaria	69	42N	27E
Burgdorf: Switzerland	75	47N	8E
Burgersdorp: S. Africa	111	31S	26E
Burgos: Spain	67	42N	4W
Burgundy: *Old Prov.*, France	72/3	47N	5E
Burley: U.S.A.	48	42N	114W
Burlington: Colo., U.S.A.	49	39N	103W
Burlington: Iowa, U.S.A.	49	41N	91W
Burlington: Mass., U.S.A.	51	42N	71W
Burlington: N.C., U.S.A.	47	36N	80W
Burlington: Vt., U.S.A.	19	44N	73W
BURMA: *cap.* Rangoon	92	—	—
Burnie: Tasmania	99	41S	146E
Burnley: England	62	54N	2W
Burns: U.S.A.	48	44N	119W
Burra: Australia	101	34S	139E
Burrinjuck Res.: Australia	101	35S	149E
Bursa: Turkey	86	40N	29E
Burton upon Trent: England	63	53N	2W
BURUNDI: *cap.* Bujumbura	110	3S	30E
Bury: England	62	53N	2W
Bury St. Edmunds: England	63	52N	1E
Būshehr: Iran	87	29N	51E
Busselton: Australia	100	34S	115E
Bute: *i.*, Scotland	62	56N	5W
Butler: U.S.A.	47	41N	80W
Butte: U.S.A.	48	46N	113W
Butterworth: Malaysia	92	5N	100E
Butterworth: S. Africa	111	32S	28E
Butt of Lewis: Scotland	61	58N	6W
Butung: *i.*, Indon.	91	5S	123E
Buxton: England	63	53N	2W
Buyaga: U.S.S.R.	83	60N	127E
Buzău: Romania	69	45N	27E
Buzuluk: U.S.S.R.	84	53N	52E
Bydgoszcz: Poland	68	53N	18E
Byelorussian S.S.R.: U.S.S.R.	68	53N	27E
Byrd Land: Antarctica	116	80S	130W
Bytom: Poland	68	50N	19E
Caballo Res.: U.S.A.	48	33N	107W
Cabimas: Venezuela	45	10N	71W
Cabinda: *prov.*, Angola	110	5S	12E
Čačak: Yugoslavia	69	44N	20E
Cáceres: Spain	67	39N	6W
Cadillac: U.S.A.	19	44N	85W
Cádiz: & Golfo de, Spain	67	37N	6W
Caen: France	72	49N	0
Caernarfon: & *Bay*, Wales	63	53N	4W
Cágliari: Sardinia	67	39N	9E
Cahors: France	73	44N	1E
Caicos Is.: Caribbean Sea	45	22N	72W
Cairngorm Mts.: Scotland	62	57N	4W
Cairns: Australia	99	17S	146E
CAIRO: Egypt	86	30N	31E
Calabozo: Venezuela	45	9N	67W
Calais: France	72	51N	2E
Calais: U.S.A.	15	45N	67W
Calamian Group: Philippines	91	12N	120E
Călăraşi: Romania	69	44N	27E
Calcutta: India	88	22N	88E
Caldera: Chile	54	27S	71W
Caldwell: U.S.A.	48	44N	117W
Calexico: U.S.A.	48	33N	115W
Calf of Man: I. of Man	62	54N	5W
Cali: Colombia	54	3N	77W
Caliente: U.S.A.	48	38N	115W
California: *State*, U.S.A.	48	—	—
California, Gulf of: Mexico	44	27N	112W
Calipatria: U.S.A.	48	33N	115W
Callao: Peru	54	12S	77W
Caltanissetta: Sicily	69	37N	14E
Calumet City: U.S.A.	34	41N	87W
Calvi: Corsica	67	43N	9E
Calvinia: S. Africa	111	32S	20E
Cam: *r.*, England	63	52N	0
Camagüy: Cuba	53	21N	78W
Camargue: *reg.*, France	73	44N	4E
Cambay: & *Gulf*, India	88	22N	73E
Camberley: England	112	51N	0
CAMBODIA: *cap.* Phnom Penh	92	13N	105E
Cambrai: France	72	50N	3E
Cambrian Mts.: Wales	63	52N	4W
Cambridge: & *Co.*, England	63	32N	0
Cambridge: Del., U.S.A.	47	39N	76W
Cambridge: Mass., U.S.A.	33	42N	71W
Camden: U.S.A.	46	34N	93W
Cameron: U.S.A.	46	31N	97W
CAMEROUN: *cap.* Yaoundé	108	5N	12E
Camocim: Brazil	54	3S	41W
Camooweal: Australia	98	20S	138E
Campbeltown: Scot.	62	55N	6W
Campeche, & Bahia de: Mexico	53	20N	93W
Campinas: Brazil	56	23S	47W
Campine: *reg.*, Belg./Neth.	72	51N	5E
Campo Grande: Brazil	54	20S	55W
Cam Ranh: Vietnam	92	11N	109E
Canadian: *r.*, U.S.A.	46	35N	97W
Çanakkale: Turkey	69	40N	26E
Canary Basin: Atl. O.	57	32N	25W
Canary Islands: Atlantic Ocean	57	28N	15W
Canaveral, Cape: U.S.A.	47	29N	81W
CANBERRA: Australia	101	35S	149E
Candia: *see* Iráklion			
Canea: *see* Khania			
Canna: *i.*, Scotland	61	57N	7W
Cannes: France	73	44N	7E
Cannock: England	63	53N	2W
Cannonball: *r.*, U.S.A.	49	46N	102W
Canon City: U.S.A.	49	38N	105W
Cantábrica, Cordillera (Cantabrian Mts.): Spain	67	43N	5W
Canterbury: England	63	51N	1E
Canterbury Bight: New Zealand	104	44S	172E
Canterbury Plains: New Zealand	104	43S	172E
Can Tho: Vietnam	92	10N	105E
Canton: China	95	23N	113E
Canton: Ill., U.S.A.	49	41N	90W
Canton: Mass., U.S.A.	51	42N	71W
Canton: Ohio, U.S.A.	47	41N	81W
Canton: S. Dakota, U.S.A.	49	43N	97W
Canudos: Brazil	54	7S	57W
Canvey Island: England	112	52N	1E
Cape Giradeaux: *city*, U.S.A.	47	37N	90W
Cape Province: South Africa	111	32S	23E
Cape Rise: Atl. O.	57	45S	12E
Cape Town: S. Africa	111	34S	18E
Cape Verde Basin: Atl. Ocean	57	25N	25W
Cape Verde Is.: Atlantic Ocean	57	18N	25W
Cape York Penin.: Australia	99	13S	143E
Cap Haitien: *town*, Haiti	45	20N	72W
Capri: *i.*, Italy	69	40N	14E
Capricorn Channel: Australia	100	23S	152E
Capricorn Group:			

	Page	Lat.	Long.
Australia	100	23S	153E
Caprivi Strip: S. W. Africa (Namibia)	111	18S	23E
CARACAS: Venezuela	45	10N	67W
Caravelas: Brazil	54	18S	39W
Carbondale: U.S.A.	47	38N	89W
Carcassonne: France	73	43N	2E
Cardamon Hills: India	88	10N	77E
Cárdenas: Cuba	15	21N	83W
CARDIFF: Wales	63	51N	3W
Cardigan: Wales	63	52N	5W
Cardigan Bay: Wales	63	52N	4W
Caribbean Sea	45	15N	75W
Carinthia: *Prov.*, Austria	75	47N	14E
Carlisle: England	62	55N	3W
Carlow: R. of Ireland	61	53N	7W
Carlsbad: U.S.A.	49	32N	104W
Carlsberg Ridge: Indian Ocean	89	5N	65E
Carmarthen: Wales	63	52N	4W
Carmaux: France	73	44N	2E
Carnac: France	72	48N	3W
Carnarvon: Australia	98	25S	114E
Carnarvon: S. Africa	111	31S	22E
Carnarvon Range: Australia	100	25S	148E
Carnic Alps: Austria/Italy	75	47N	13E
Carnsore Pt.: R. of Ireland	63	52N	6W
Carolina: Brazil	54	7S	47W
Caroline I.: Pacific O.	103	10S	150W
Caroline Is.: Pac. O.	102	2N	145W
Caroni: *r.*, Venezuela	54	6N	63W
Carpathians: *mtns.*, Europe	67	47N	25E
Carpentaria, Gulf of: Australia	98	15S	138E
Carpentras: France	73	44N	5E
Carrara: Italy	75	44N	10E
Carrauntuohil: *mtn.*, R. of Ireland	61	52N	10W
Carrickfergus: N. Ireland	62	55N	6W
Carrick on Shannon: R. of Ireland	61	54N	8W
Carson City: U.S.A.	48	39N	120W
Carson Sink: *dep.* U.S.A.	48	40N	118W
Cartagena: Col.	45	10N	75W
Cartagena: Spain	67	38N	1W
Carthage: U.S.A.	46	32N	94W
Carvin: France	72	50N	3E
Casablanca: *see* El Dar el Beida			
Casale Monferrato: Italy	75	45N	8E
Cascade Range: Canada/U.S.A.	48	46N	121W
Caserta: Italy	69	41N	14E
Casino: Australia	101	29S	153E
Casiquiare: *r.*, Venezuela	54	2N	66W
Casper: U.S.A.	48	43N	106W
Caspian Lowlands: U.S.S.R.	84	47N	51E
Caspian Sea: U.S.S.R./Iran	84	42N	51E
Cassel: France	72	51N	2E
Cassino: Italy	69	41N	14E
Castellón de la Plana: Spain	67	40N	0
Castelo Branco: Portugal	67	40N	7W
Castlebar: R. of Ireland	61	54N	9W
Castlemaine: Australia	101	37S	144E
Castletown: Isle of Man	62	54N	5W
Castres: France	73	44N	2E
Castrop-Rauxel: W. Germany	64	51N	7E
Catamarca: Arg.	54	28S	66W
Catania: Sicily	69	37N	15E
Catanzaro: Italy	69	39N	17E
Catastrophe, C.: Australia	98	35S	136E
Caterham: England	112	51N	0
Cat I.: The Bahamas	45	24N	76W
Catoche, Cabo: Mex.	53	21N	87W
Catskill Mts.: U.S.A.	51	42N	74W
Cauca: *r.*, Colombia	54	7N	76W
Caucasus Mts.: U.S.S.R.	84	43N	45E
Cauvery: *r.*, India	88	12N	77E
Caux, Pays de: *reg.*, Fr.	72	50N	1E
Cavaillon: France	73	44N	5E
Cavan: R. of Ireland	61	54N	7W
Caxias do Sul: Brazil	56	29S	51W
CAYENNE: Fr. Guiana	54	5N	52W
Cayman Is.: Carib. Sea	53	19N	81W
Cayuga L.: U.S.A.	50	43N	77W
Cebu: & *i.*, Phil.	91	10N	124E
Cedar City: U.S.A.	48	38N	114W
Cedar Rapids: U.S.A.	49	42N	92W
Ceduna: Australia	98	32S	134E
Celebes (Sulawesi): *i. & sea*, Indonesia	91	3S	120E
Celje: Yugoslavia	68	46N	15E
Celle: W. Germany	74	53N	10E
Center Line: U.S.A.	33	42N	83W
Centerville: U.S.A.	49	41N	93W
Central: *Reg.*, Scotland	62	56N	5W
Central, Cordillera: *mtns.*, Spain	69	40N	5W
CENTRAL AFRICAN EMPIRE: *cap.* Bangui	109	7N	20E
Centralia: Ill., U.S.A.	47	39N	89W
Centralia: Wash., U.S.A.	48	47N	123W
Central Pacific Basin: Pacific Ocean	102	10N	180
Central Siberian Plateau: U.S.S.R.	83	65N	110E
Cephalonia: *i.*, Greece	69	38N	21E
Ceram: *i., & sea*, Indonesia	91	3S	130E
Cerro de Pasco: Peru	54	11S	76W
Cesena: Italy	75	44N	12E
České Budejovice: Czechoslovakia	68	49N	14E
Cessnock: Australia	101	33S	151E
Ceuta: Spain	67	36N	5W
Cévennes: *mtns.*, Fr.	73	44N	4E
Chablis: France	72	48N	4E
Chaco Central: *geog. reg.*, Arg.	56	25S	60W
CHAD: *cap.* N'Djamena)	108/9	—	—
Chad, Lake: Africa	108	13N	14E
Chagos-Laccadive Plateau: Indian O.	89	0	73E
Chalon-sur-Saône: France	73	47N	3E
Châlons-sur-Marne: France	72	49N	4E
Chaman: Pakistan	88	31N	66E
Chamba: India	88	32N	76E
Chambal: *r.*, India	88	26N	77E
Chamberlain, L.: U.S.A.	15	46N	69W
Chambersburg: U.S.A.	50	40N	78W
Chambéry: France	73	46N	6E
Chamdo: China	90	31N	97E
Chamonix: France	73	46N	7E
Champagne: *Old Prov.*, France	72	49N	4E
Champagne-Pouilleuse: *reg.*, France	72	49N	4E
Champaign: U.S.A.	47	40N	88W
Champéry: Switz.	75	46N	7E
Champlain, L.: U.S.A.	19	45N	74W
Chañaral: Chile	54	26S	71W
Chandalar: & *r.*, U.S.A.	30	68N	146W
Changchih: China	94	36N	113E
Changchow: China	94	32N	120E
Changchun: China	90	44N	125E
Changkiakow (Kalgan): China	94	41N	115E
Changsha: China	95	28N	113E
Changshu: China	95	32N	121E
Changhsientien: China	114	40N	116E
Changteh: China	95	29N	112E
Changtu: China	90	31N	104E
Channel Is.: U.K.	63	*Inset*	
Chanthaburi: Thai.	92	13N	102E
Chanute: U.S.A.	49	38N	95W
Chany, L.: U.S.S.R.	85	55N	77E
Chapan: China	95	24N	116E
Chaotung: China	92	27N	103E
Chaoyang: China	94	42N	120E
Chaoyangchen: China	90	43N	126E
Chapala, L. de: Mex.	52	20N	103W
Chapayevsk: U.S.S.R.	84	53N	50E
Chapra: India	88	26N	85E
Chardzhou: U.S.S.R.	85	39N	64E
Charente: *r.*, France	73	46N	0
Chari: *r.*, Chad	108	11N	16E
Charleroi: Belgium	72	50N	4E
Charleston: Indiana, U.S.A.	47	39N	88W
Charleston: S.C., U.S.A.	47	33N	80W
Charleston: W. Va., U.S.A.	47	38N	81W
Charleville: Australia	100	26S	146E
Charleville: France	72	50N	5E
Charlotte: U.S.A.	47	35N	81W
Charlotte Harbour: *bay*, U.S.A.	47	27N	82W
Charlottesville: U.S.A.	47	38N	79W
Charollais, Mts. du: France	73	46N	4E
Charolles: France	73	46N	4E
Charters Towers: Australia	99	20S	146E
Chartres: France	72	48N	1E
Château, Pte. du: Fr.	72	49N	3W
Châteaubriant: France	72	48N	1W
Châteaudun: France	72	48N	1E
Châteaulin: France	72	48N	4W
Château Renault: Fr.	73	48N	1E
Châteauroux: France	73	47N	2E
Château-Thierry: Fr.	72	49N	3E
Châtellerault: France	73	47N	1E
Chatham: England	112	51N	0
Chatham Is.: Pac. O.	102	44S	177W
Châtillon-sur-Seine: France	72	48N	5E
Chatrapur: India	88	19N	85E
Chattahoochee: & *r.*, U.S.A.	47	31N	85W
Chattanooga: U.S.A.	47	35N	85W
Chaumont: France	72	48N	5E
Chausey, Iles de: Fr.	72	49N	2W
Cheb: Czech.	74	50N	12E
Chefoo: *see* Yentai			
Cheju: *i.*, S. Korea	90	33N	126E
Chekian: *Prov.*, China	95	29N	120E
Chekunda: U.S.S.R.	83	51N	132E
Cheleken: U.S.S.R.	84	39N	54E
Chéliff: *r.*, Algeria	67	36N	1E
Chelkar-Tengiz, L.: U.S.S.R.	85	48N	63E
Chełm: Poland	67	51N	24E
Chelmsford: England	112	52N	0
Chelsea: U.S.A.	33	42N	71W
Cheltenham: England	63	52N	2W
Chelyabinsk: U.S.S.R.	85	55N	61E
Chelyuskin, Cape: U.S.S.R.	83	77N	105E
Chemyakhovsk: U.S.S.R.	68	55N	22E
Chenab: *r.*, India/Pakistan	88	33N	75E
Chengchow: China	94	35N	113E
Chengkiang: China	90	25N	103E
Chengteh (Jehol): China	94	41N	118E
Chepstow: England	63	52N	3W
Cher: *r.*, France	73	47N	1E
Cheraw: U.S.A.	47	35N	80W
Cherbourg: France	72	50N	2W
Cheremkhovo: U.S.S.R.	83	53N	103E
Cherepovets: U.S.S.R.	84	59N	38E
Chernigov: U.S.S.R.	84	52N	31E
Chernogorsk: U.S.S.R.	85	54N	91E
Chernovtsy: U.S.S.R.	84	48N	26E
Chernyakhovsk: U.S.S.R.	68	55N	22E
Cherokees, Lake of the: U.S.A.	46	37N	95W
Cherrapunji: India	89	25N	92E
Cherskiy Range: U.S.S.R.	83	65N	145E
Cherwell: *r.*, England	63	52N	1W
Chesapeake Bay: U.S.A.	47	38N	76W
Chesham: England	112	52N	0
Cheshire: *Co.*, England	63	53N	3W
Cheshunt: England	112	52N	0
Chesil Beach: England	63	51N	3W
Chester: England	63	53N	3W
Chester: U.S.A.	50	40N	76W
Chesterfield: England	63	53N	1W
Chesuncook L.: U.S.A.	15	46N	70W
Cheviot Hills: England/Scotland	62	55N	2W
Cheyenne: U.S.A.	49	41N	105W
Cheyenne: *r.*, U.S.A.	49	44N	102W
Chhindwara: India	88	22N	79E
Chiai: Taiwan	95	23N	120E
Chiang Mai: Thai	92	19N	99E
Chiang Rai: Thai.	92	20N	100E
Chiba: Japan	93	36N	140E
Chibia: Angola	111	15S	14E
Chicago: U.S.A.	34	—	—
Chicagof I.: U.S.A.	24	58N	136W
Chichén Itzá: *hist.*, Mexico	53	21N	89W
Chichester: England	63	51N	1W
Chickasha: U.S.A.	49	35N	98W
Chicken: U.S.A.	30	64N	141W
Chiclayo: Peru	54	7S	80W
Chico: U.S.A.	48	40N	122W
Chico: *r.*, Arg.	55	45S	67W
Chief Joseph Dam: U.S.A.	29	48N	120W
Chiemsee: *l.*, W. Ger.	75	48N	12E
Chieti: Italy	69	42N	14E
Chihli, G. of: China	94	39N	120E
Chihuahua: Mexico	52	29N	106W
Chihuahua: *Prov.*, Mexico	52	29N	105W
CHILE: *cap.* Santiago	54/5	—	—
Chile Rise: Pacific O.	103	35S	95W
Chillán: Chile	55	36S	72W
Chillicothe: U.S.A.	47	39N	83W
Chiloé I.: Chile	55	43S	64W
Chilpancingo de los Braves: Mexico	52	17N	100W
Chiltern Hills: England	63	52N	0
Chimborazo: *volc.*, Ecuador	54	1S	79W
Chimbote: Peru	54	9S	79W
Chimkent: U.S.S.R.	85	42N	70E
CHINA: *cap.* Peking	94/5	—	—
Chinchilla: Australia	100	27S	151E
Chinchow: China	94	41N	121E
Chindwin: *r.*, Burma	92	25N	95E
Chingtechen: China	95	29N	117E
Chin Hills: Burma	92	22N	93E
Chinhsi: China	94	41N	121E
Chinkiang: China	94	32N	120E
Chinnampo: N. Korea	90	39N	125E
Chinon: France	73	47N	0
Chinwangtao: China	94	40N	119E
Chioggia: Italy	75	45N	12E
Chios: *i. & town*, Greece	69	38N	26E
Chipata: Zambia	110	14S	33E
Chippenham: England	63	51N	2W
Chippewa Falls: *city*, U.S.A.	49	45N	91W
Chiquitos Plat.: Bol.	54	17S	62W
Chita: & *Prov.*, U.S.S.R.	83	52N	113E
Chitral: Pakistan	87	36N	72E
Chittagong: Bangladesh	89	22N	92E
Choctawhatchee: *r.*, U.S.A.	47	31N	86W
Choibalsan: Mong.	83	48N	114E
Cholet: France	73	47N	1W
Cholon: Vietnam	92	10N	107E
Chongjin: N. Korea	90	42N	130E
Chonos Arch.: Chile	55	45S	74W
Chorley: England	62	54N	2W
Chôshi: Japan	93	36N	141E
Christchurch: England	63	51N	2W
Christchurch: N.Z.	104	43S	173E
Christmas I.: Indian Ocean	91	11S	106E
Christmas I.: Pac. O.	103	2N	157W
Christmas Ridge: Pacific Ocean	102	10N	167W
Chu: & *r.*, U.S.S.R.	85	44N	74E
Chuanchow: *see* Tsinkiang			
Chubut: *r.*, Arg.	55	43S	66W
Chuchow: China	95	28N	113E
Chugoku-Sanchi: *mtns.*, Japan	93	35N	133E
Chuguchak: China	85	47N	83E
Chuho: China	83	45N	128E
Chukchi Sea: U.S.S.R.	83	70N	170W
Chulym: *r.*, U.S.S.R.	85	57N	87E
Chumphon: Thai.	92	10N	99E
Chungking: China	95	30N	107E
Chuquicamata: Chile	54	22S	69W
Chur (Coire): Switz.	75	47N	9E
Cicero: U.S.A.	34	42N	88W
Ciego de Avila: Cuba	53	22N	79W
Cienfuegos: Cuba	53	22N	80W
Cilician Gates: Turkey	86	37N	35E
Cimarron: *r.*, U.S.A.	46	37N	99W
Cincinnati: U.S.A.	47	39N	84W
Circle: U.S.A.	30	66N	145W
Circle Springs: U.S.A.	30	66N	145W
Cirencester: England	63	52N	2W
Ciudad Acuña: Mexico	46	29N	101W
Ciudad Bolívar: Venezuela	54	8N	64W
Ciudad Guzmán: Mex.	52	20N	103W
Ciudad Juarez: Mex.	48	32N	107W
Ciudad Madero: Mex.	52	22N	98W
Ciudad Real: Spain	67	39N	4W
Ciudad Victoria: Mex.	52	24N	99W
Civitavecchia: Italy	69	42N	12E
Clacton on Sea: Eng.	63	52N	1E
Clamecy: France	73	47N	3E
Claremont: U.S.A.	19	43N	73W
Clarinda: U.S.A.	49	41N	95W
Clark Hill Res.: U.S.A.	47	34N	82W
Clark Range: Australia	100	21S	148E
Clarksburg: U.S.A.	47	39N	80W
Clarksdale: U.S.A.	46	34N	90W
Clarksville: U.S.A.	47	36N	87W
Clausthal-Zellerfeld: W. Germany	74	52N	10E
Clayton: U.S.A.	49	36N	103W
Clear L.: U.S.A.	48	39N	123W
Clearwater: U.S.A.	47	28N	83W
Cleburne: U.S.A.	46	32N	97W
Clermont: Australia	100	23S	148E
Clermont: France	72	49N	2E
Clermont-Ferrand: France	73	46N	3E
Cleveland: Ark., U.S.A.	46	34N	91W
Cleveland: Ohio U.S.A.	47	42N	82W
Cleveland: Tenn., U.S.A.	47	35N	85W
Cleveland: Texas, U.S.A.	46	30N	95W
Cleveland: *Co.*, Eng.	62	55N	1W
Clew Bay: R. of Irel.	61	54N	9W
Clifton: U.S.A.	35	41N	74W
Clingmans Dome: *mtn.*, U.S.A.	47	36N	84W
Clinton: Iowa, U.S.A.	49	42N	90W
Clinton: Mass., U.S.A.	51	42N	72W
Clinton, C.: Australia	100	22S	151E
Clipperton I.: Pacific O.	103	10N	110W
Clogher Hd.: R. of Ireland	63	54N	6W
Cloncurry: Australia	99	21S	140E
Clonmel: R. of Irel.	61	52N	8W
Cloppenburg: W. Ger.	74	53N	8E
Cluj: Romania	68	47N	24E
Clyde: *r.*, Scotland	62	55N	4W
Clyde, Firth of: Scot.	62	56N	5W
Clywd: *Co.*, Wales	93	53N	4W
Coalville: England	63	53N	1W
Coast Ranges: U.S.A.	48	45N	124W
Coatbridge: Scotland	62	56N	4W

The World

	Page	Lat.	Long.
Coats Land: Antarc.	116	78S	30W
Coatzacoalcos: Mexico	53	18N	94W
Cobar: Australia	101	31S	146E
Cobh: R. of Ireland	61	52N	8W
Coburg: W. Germany	74	50N	11E
Cochabamba: Bolivia	54	17S	66W
Cochin: India	88	10N	76E
Cochrane, L.: Chile/Argentina	55	47S	72W
Cocoa: U.S.A.	47	28N	81W
Cocos Is.: Indian O.	102	11S	97E
Cocos Is.: Pacific O.	103	6N	87W
Cocos Ridge: Pacific O.	103	4N	85W
Cod, Cape: U.S.A.	51	42N	70W
Cody: U.S.A.	48	45N	109W
Coeur d'Alene: U.S.A.	48	48N	117W
Coffeyville: U.S.A.	49	37N	96W
Coff's Harbour: Australia	101	30S	153E
Cognac: France	73	46N	0
Cohasset: U.S.A.	51	42N	71W
Coimbatore: India	88	11N	77E
Coimbra: Portugal	67	40N	8W
Colac: Australia	101	38S	144E
Colatina: Brazil	54	20S	40W
Colby: U.S.A.	49	39N	101W
Colchester: England	63	52N	1E
Coleraine: N. Ireland	61	55N	7W
Colfax: U.S.A.	48	47N	117W
Colima: Mexico	52	19N	104W
Coll: *i.*, Scotland	62	57N	7W
Collie: Australia	100	33S	116E
Colmar: France	72	48N	7E
Cologne (Köln) W. Germany	64	51N	7E
COLOMBIA: *cap.* Bogotá	54	5N	72W
COLOMBO: Sri Lanka	88	7N	80E
Colón: Cuba	53	23N	81W
Colón: Panama	45	*Inset*	
Colonsay: *i.*, Scotland	62	56N	6W
Colorado: *r.*, Arg.	55	39S	65W
Colorado: *r.*, Texas, U.S.A.	46	29N	96W
Colorado: *r.*, U.S.A./Mexico	48	33N	114W
Colorado: *State*, U.S.A.	48/9	39N	106W
Colorado Plateaux: U.S.A.	48	37N	111W
Colorado Springs: U.S.A.	49	39N	105W
Columbia: Mo., U.S.A.	49	39N	92W
Columbia: S.C., U.S.A.	47	34N	81W
Columbia: *r.*, U.S.A.	48	46N	120W
Columbia: Tenn., U.S.A.	47	36N	87W
Columbus: Ga., U.S.A.	47	32N	85W
Columbus: Ind., U.S.A.	47	39N	86W
Columbus: Miss., U.S.A.	47	33N	89W
Columbus: Nebr., U.S.A.	49	41N	97W
Columbus: Ohio, U.S.A.	47	40N	83W
Colville: U.S.A.	48	49N	118W
Comilla: Bangladesh	89	23N	91E
Communism, Mt.: U.S.S.R.	85	39N	72E
Como: & *lake*, Italy	75	46N	9E
Comodoro Rivadavia: Argentina	55	46S	67W
Comorin, C.: India	88	8N	77E
Compiègne: France	72	49N	3E
CONAKRY: Guinea	108	10N	14W
Concarneau: France	72	48N	4W
Concepción: Chile	55	37S	73W
Concepción del Uruguay: Uruguay	56	32S	58W
Conchos: *r.*, Mexico	52	28N	105W
Concord: Mass., U.S.A.	33	42N	71W
Concord: N.C., U.S.A.	47	35N	80W
Concord: N.H., U.S.A.	51	43N	71W
Condamine: Australia	100	27S	150E
Condobolin: Austl.	101	33S	147E
Conecuh: *r.*, U.S.A.	47	31N	87W
Coney Island: U.S.A.	35	41N	74W
Congleton: England	63	53N	2W
CONGO: *cap.* Brazzaville	110	0	15E
Congo: *r.*, *see* Zaïre			
Conn, L.: R. of Ireland	61	54N	9W
Connecticut: *r.*, U.S.A.	51	43N	73W
Connecticut: *State*, U.S.A.	51	41N	72W
Connemara: *reg.*, R. of Ireland	61	54N	10W
Connersville: U.S.A.	47	40N	85W
Conrad: U.S.A.	48	48N	112W
Consett: England	62	55N	2W
Constance, Lake (Bodensee): Switz./W. Germany	75	48N	9E
Constanța: Rom.	69	44N	29E
Constantine: Algeria	108	37N	7E
Conway: U.S.A.	47	33N	79W
Cooch Behar: India	89	26N	90E
Cook Is.: Pacific O.	102	20S	160W
Cook, Mt.: N.Z.	104	44S	170E
Cook Strait: N.Z.	104	41S	174E
Cooktown: Australia	99	15S	145E
Coolangatta: Austl.	100	28S	153E
Coolgardie: Australia	100	31S	121E
Coonamble: Australia	101	31S	148E
Cooper Creek: Austl.	100	27S	140E
Coorong, The: *lag.*, Australia	99	36S	139E
Cootamundra: Austl.	101	35S	148E
COPENHAGEN: Den.	71	56N	13E
Copiapó: Chile	54	27S	70W
Coral Gables: U.S.A.	47	26N	80W
Coral Sea: Pacific O.	99	15S	152E
Corbeil-Essonnes: France	113	49N	3E
Corbières: *mtns.*, Fr.	73	43N	2E
Corby: England	63	52N	1W
Cordele: U.S.A.	47	32N	84W
Cordillera de Mérida: Venezuela	45	9N	71W
Córdoba: Argentina	56	31S	64W
Córdoba: Mexico	53	19N	97W
Córdoba: Spain	67	38N	5W
Cordova: U.S.A.	12	61N	145W
Corinth: & *gulf*, Greece	69	38N	23E
Corinth: U.S.A.	47	35N	89W
Cork: R. of Ireland	61	52N	8W
Çorlu: Turkey	69	41N	28E
Cornwall: *Co.*, Eng.	63	50N	5W
Coromandel Ra.: New Zealand	104	37S	176E
Coromandel Coast: India	88	13N	81E
Corpus Christi: & *bay*, U.S.A.	47	28N	79W
Corrib, L.: R. of Ireland	61	53N	9W
Corrientes: Arg.	56	27S	59W
Corsica: *i.*, Medit. Sea	64	42N	9E
Corsicana: U.S.A.	46	32N	96W
Corumbá: Brazil	54	19S	57W
Corunna: *see* La Coruña			
Corvallis: U.S.A.	48	45N	123W
Coryton: England	112	52N	1E
Cosenza: Italy	69	39N	16E
Cosne: France	73	47N	3E
Costa Brava: *coast*, Spain	67	42N	3E
Costa del Sol: *coast*, Spain	67	36N	4W
COSTA RICA: *cap.* San José	45	10N	84W
Côte d'Azur: France	73	43N	7E
Côte d'Or: *mts.*, France	73	47N	5E
Cotentin: *penin.*, France	72	49N	2W
Côtes de Moselle: *hills*, France	72	49N	6E
COTONOU: Benin	108	6N	2E
Cotopaxi: *volc.*, Ec.	54	1S	78W
Cotswolds: *hills*, Eng.	63	52N	2W
Cottbus: E. Germany	74	52N	14E
Cottian Alps: Fr./It.	73	45N	7E
Coubre, Pte. de la: Fr.	73	46N	1W
Council Bluffs: U.S.A.	49	41N	96W
Coutances: France	72	49N	1W
Coventry: England	63	53N	2W
Covilhã: Portugal	67	40N	7W
Covington: U.S.A.	47	37N	80W
Cowal, Lake: Austl.	101	33S	147E
Cowan, Lake: Austl.	100	32S	122E
Cowes: England	63	51N	1W
Cowra: Australia	101	34S	149E
Cozumel, I. de: Caribbean Sea	53	20N	87W
Cracow (Kraków): Poland	68	50N	20E
Craiova: Romania	69	44N	24E
Crater L. Nat. Park: U.S.A.	48	43N	122W
Crawfordsville: U.S.A.	47	40N	88W
Crawley: England	63	51N	0
Crécy: *hist.*, France	72	50N	2E
Creil: France	72	49N	2E
Cremona: Italy	75	45N	10E
Cres: *i.*, Yugoslavia	69	45N	14E
Crescent City: U.S.A.	48	42N	124W
Crestview: U.S.A.	47	31N	87W
Crete: *i.* & *sea*, Greece	69	35N	25E
Crete: U.S.A.	49	41N	97W
Creuse: *r.*, France	71	46N	2E
Crewe: England	63	53N	2W
Crieff: Scotland	62	56N	4W
Crimea: *penin.*, U.S.S.R.	84	45N	34E
Cromer: England	63	53N	1E
Cromwell: N.Z.	104	45S	169E
Cronulla: Australia	115	34S	151E
Crosby: England	62	54N	3W
Crosby: Minn., U.S.A.	49	46N	94W
Crosby: N. Dakota, U.S.A.	49	49N	103W
Cross Sound: U.S.A.	24	58N	137W
Crotone: Italy	69	39N	17E
Croydon: England	112	51N	0
Crozet Basin: Indian Ocean	89	40S	62E
Cruzeiro do Sul: Brazil	54	8S	73W
CUBA: *cap.* La Habana (Havana)	53	*Inset*	
Cubango: *r.*, Angola	111	17S	18E
Cúcuta: Colombia	54	8N	73W
Cuernavaca: Mexico	52	19N	99W
Cuddalore: India	88	12N	80E
Cuddapah: India	88	15N	79E
Cuenca: Spain	67	40N	2W
Cuiabá: Brazil	54	16S	56W
Cuito: *r.*, Angola	111	17S	19E
Culiacán: Mexico	52	23N	106W
Cullman: U.S.A.	47	34N	87W
Culoz: France	73	46N	6E
Cumana: Venezuela	45	10N	64W
Cumberland: U.S.A.	50	40N	79W
Cumberland Is: Australia	100	21S	149E
Cumberland L.: U.S.A.	47	37N	85W
Cumbria: *Co.*, Eng.	62	55N	3W
Cumnock: Scotland	62	55N	4W
Cuneo: Italy	75	44N	8E
Cunnamulla: Austl.	101	28S	146E
Cupar: Scotland	62	56N	3W
Curaçao: *i.*, Carib. Sea	45	12N	69W
Curicó: Chile	55	35S	71W
Curitiba: Brazil	56	25S	49W
Cuttack: India	88	20N	86E
Cuxhaven: W. Germany	74	54N	9E
Cuzco: Peru	54	14S	72W
Cyclades: *is.*, Greece	69	37N	25E
CYPRUS: *cap.* Nicosia	86	35N	33E
CZECHOSLOVAKIA: *cap.* Prague	68	49N	17E
Czestochowa: Poland	68	51N	19E
Dacca: Bangladesh	89	24N	90E
Dagenham: England	112	52N	0
Dahlak Arch.: Red Sea	87	16N	40W
Dajarra: Australia	99	22S	140E
DAKAR: Senegal	108	15N	17W
Dakhla: W. Sahara	108	24N	16W
Dakhla Oasis: Egypt	109	25N	29E
Dalabandin: Pakistan	88	29N	64E
Dalby: Australia	100	27S	151E
Dalhousie: India	88	33N	76E
Dallas: U.S.A.	46	33N	97W
Dall I.: U.S.A.	24	55N	133W
Dalton: U.S.A.	47	35N	85W
Daltonganj: India	88	24N	84E
Daly: *r.*, Australia	98	14S	132E
Daly Waters: *town*, Australia	98	16S	133E
Daman: *Union Territ.*, India	88	20N	73E
DAMASCUS: Syria	86	34N	36E
Damietta: Egypt	86	31N	32E
Damodar: *r.*, India	88	24N	86E
Dampier Land: Australia	98	17S	123E
Danilovka: U.S.S.R.	85	53N	71E
Dannevirke: N.Z.	104	40S	176E
Danube: *r.*, Europe	68/9	—	—
Danushkodi: India	88	9N	80E
Danville: Ill., U.S.A.	47	40N	88W
Danville: Va., U.S.A.	47	37N	79W
Dardanelles: *str.*, Turkey	86	40N	26E
Dar es Salaam: Tanzania	110	7S	40E
Darfur: *Prov.*, Sudan	109	13N	25E
Dargaville: N.Z.	104	36S	174E
Darien, Gulf of: Colombia	54	9N	77W
Darjeeling: India	88	27N	88E
Darling: *r.*, Australia	101	31S	145E
Darling Downs: Australia	100	27S	150E
Darling Range: Australia	100	32S	116E
Darlington: England	62	55N	2W
Darmstadt: W. Ger.	74	50N	9E
Dart: *r.*, England	63	50N	4W
Dartford: England	112	51N	0
Dartmoor: England	63	51N	4W
Dartmouth: England	63	50N	4W
Darwin: Australia	98	12S	131E
Dasht-e Kavīr: *desert*, Iran	87	34N	55E
Dasht-e Lūt: *desert*, Iran	87	32N	57E
Datteln: W. Germany	64	52N	7E
Daugava: *r.*, *see* West Dvina			
Daugavpils: U.S.S.R.	68	56N	26E
Dauphiné: *Old Prov.*, France	73	45N	6E
Dauphiné Alps: France	73	45N	6E
Davao: Philippines	91	7N	126E
Davenport: U.S.A.	49	41N	90W
Davis: Antarc.	116	64S	92E
Davos: Switzerland	75	47N	10E
Dawna Range: Burma/Thailand	92	13N	99E
Dawson: *r.*, Australia	100	24S	150E
Dax: France	73	44N	1W
Dayton: U.S.A.	47	40N	84W
Daytona Beach: U.S.A.	47	29N	81W
De Aar: S. Africa	111	31S	24E
Dead Sea: Israel/Jordan	86	32N	35E
Deadwood: U.S.A.	49	44N	104W
Dearborn: & *Heights*, U.S.A.	33	42N	83W
Death Valley: & *Nat. Monument*, U.S.A.	48	37N	117W
Deauville: France	72	49N	0
Debrecen: Hungary	68	48N	22E
Decatur: Alabama, U.S.A.	47	35N	87W
Decatur: Ill., U.S.A.	47	40N	89W
Decazeville: France	73	45N	2E
Deccan: *reg.*, India	88	17N	77E
Děčín: Czech.	74	51N	14E
Dee: *r.*, Eng./Wales	63	53N	3W
Dee: *r.*, Gramp., Scot.	62	57N	3W
Dee: *r.*, Dumfr. & Gall. Scotland	62	55N	4W
Deerfield: U.S.A.	34	42N	88W
Deer Lodge: U.S.A.	48	46N	113W
Dehra Dun: India	88	30N	78E
Deir ez Zor: Syria	87	35N	40E
De Kalb: U.S.A.	49	42N	89W
Delagoa Bay: Moz.	111	25S	33E
Delano: U.S.A.	48	36N	119W
Delano Peak: U.S.A.	48	38N	114W
Delaware: *State*, & *bay*, U.S.A.	47	39N	75W
Delft: Netherlands	74	52N	4E
Delmenhorst: W. Ger.	74	53N	9E
Delray Beach: *city*, U.S.A.	47	26N	80W
Del Rio: U.S.A.	46	29N	101W
DELHI: India	88	29N	77E
Demarcation Pt.: U.S.A.	12	70N	141W
Demavand: *mtn.*, Iran	87	36N	52E
Deming: U.S.A.	48	32N	108W
Demmin: E. Germany	74	54N	13E
Denbigh: Wales	63	53N	3W
Dendermonde: Belg.	72	51N	4E
Denham Range: Australia	100	22S	148E
Den Helder: Neth.	74	53N	5E
Deniliquin: Australia	101	36S	145E
Denison: U.S.A.	49	34N	97W
Denizli: Turkey	86	38N	29E
DENMARK: *cap.* Copenhagen	71	56N	10E
Denton: U.S.A.	49	33N	98W
D'Entrecasteaux Is.: Papua New Guinea	99	10S	151E
D'Entrecasteaux, Pt.: Australia	100	35S	116E
Denver: U.S.A.	49	40N	105W
Denville: U.S.A.	51	41N	74W
De Pere: U.S.A.	49	44N	88W
Dera'a: Syria	86	32N	36E
Dera Ghazi Khan: Pakistan	88	30N	70E
Dera Ismail Khan: Pakistan	88	32N	71E
Derbent: U.S.S.R.	84	42N	48E
Derby: Australia	98	17S	123E
Derby: & *Co.*, Eng.	63	53N	1W
Derg, L.: R. of Ireland	61	53N	8W
Derna: Libya	86	33N	22E
Derwent: *r.*, Cumbria, England	62	55N	4W
Derwent: *r.*, Derby., England	63	53N	2W
Derwent: *r.*, N. Yorks., England	63	54N	1W
Des Moines: & *r.*, U.S.A.	46	42N	94W
Des Plaines: U.S.A.	34	42N	88W
Dessau: E. Germany	74	52N	12E
Detroit: U.S.A.	33	—	—
Dettingen: *hist.*, W. Ger.	74	50N	9E
Deva: Romania	68	46N	23E
Deventer: Neth.	74	52N	6E
Dévoluy: *mtns.*, France	73	45N	6E
Devonport: England	63	50N	4W
Devonshire: *Co.*, England	63	51N	4W
Dewsbury: England	63	54N	2W
Dexter: U.S.A.	15	45N	69W
Dhahran: Saudi Arabia	87	26N	50E
Dharwar: India	88	15N	75E
Dhulia: India	88	21N	75E
Diamantina: Brazil	54	18S	44W
Dibrugarh: India	89	28N	95E
Dieciocho de Marzo: Mexico	46	26N	98W
Diego Suarez: *see* Antsirane			
Dieppe: France	72	50N	1E
Digne: France	73	44N	6E
Dijon: France	73	47N	5E
Dili: Indon.	90	8S	126E
Dimitrovgrad: Bulgaria	69	42N	26E
Dinajpur: Bangladesh	88	26N	89E
Dinan: France	72	48N	2W
Dinant: Belgium	72	50N	5E
Dinard: France	72	49N	2W
Dinaric Alps: Yugo.	69	44N	16E
Dingwall: Scotland	61	58N	4W
Dinslaken: W. Germany	64	52N	7E
Diomede Is: Bering Strait	12	66N	169E
Diredawa: Ethiopia	109	10N	42E
Dirk Hartog I.:			

	Page	Lat.	Long.
Australia	**98**	26S	113E
Dirranbandi: Australia	**100**	28S	148E
Disappointment, L.: Australia	**98**	23S	123E
Disko: *i.*, Greenland	**13**	69N	54W
Divriği: Turkey	**87**	40N	38E
Dixmunde: Belgium	**72**	51N	3E
Dixon: U.S.A.	**49**	42N	90W
Dixon Entrance: *chan.*, U.S.A.	**24**	55N	132W
Diyarbakir: Turkey	**87**	38N	40E
DJAKARTA (Jakarta): Indonesia	**91**	6S	107E
Djelfa: Algeria	**108**	35N	3E
Djerba I.: Tunisia	**108**	34N	11E
DJIBOUTI: Djibouti	**109**	13N	43E
Dneprodzerzhinsk: U.S.S.R.	**84**	48N	34E
Dnepropetrovsk: U.S.S.R.	**84**	48N	35E
Dnieper: *r.*, U.S.S.R.	**84**	50N	31E
Dnieper: *r.*, U.S.S.R.	**82**	50N	31E
Doberai Penin.: Indon.	**98**	2S	132E
Dodecanese: *is.*, Greece	**69**	37N	27E
Dodge City: U.S.A.	**46**	38N	100W
DODOMA: Tanzania	**110**	6S	36E
DOHA: Qatar	**87**	26N	51E
Dolak I.: Indonesia	**98**	8S	138E
Dôle: France	**73**	47N	5E
Dolgellau: Wales	**63**	53N	4W
Dolomites: *mtns.*, Italy	**75**	46N	12E
Dolton: U.S.A.	**34**	42N	88W
Dombås: Norway	**70**	62N	9E
DOMINICA: *cap.* Roseau	**45**	15N	61W
DOMINICAN REPUBLIC: *cap.* Santo Domingo	**45**	19N	70W
Don: *r.*, England	**62**	54N	1W
Don: *r.*, Scotland	**61**	57N	2W
Don: *r.*, U.S.S.R.	**84**	50N	40E
Donbass: *reg.*, U.S.S.R.	**84**	48N	38E
Doncaster: England	**62**	54N	1W
Dondra Head: Sri Lanka	**88**	6N	81E
Donegal: R. of Ireland	**61**	55N	8W
Donegal Bay: R. of Ireland	**61**	55N	8W
Donerak, Mt.: U.S.A.	**12**	68N	152W
Donets: *r.*, U.S.S.R.	**84**	49N	37E
Donetsk: U.S.S.R.	**84**	48N	37E
Dongara: Australia	**100**	29S	115E
Donzère: France	**73**	44N	5E
Dorchester: Dorset, England	**63**	51N	2W
Dordogne: *r.*, France	**73**	45N	0
Dordrecht: Neth.	**74**	52N	5E
Dore: *r.*, France	**73**	46N	4E
Dorking: England	**112**	51N	0
Dormagen: W. Ger.	**64**	51N	7E
Dornbirn: Austria	**75**	47N	10E
Dornoch: Scotland	**61**	58N	4W
Dorset: *Co.*, England	**63**	51N	2W
Dorsten: W. Germany	**64**	52N	7E
Dortmund: W. Ger.	**64**	52N	7E
Dortmund-Ems Canal: W. Germany	**74**	52N	7E
Dothan: U.S.A.	**47**	31N	85W
Douai: France	**72**	50N	3E
Douala: Cameroun	**108**	4N	10E
Douarnenez: *& bay*, France	**72**	48N	4W
Doubs: *r.*, France	**73**	47N	6E
Doubtful Sound: New Zealand	**104**	45S	167E
DOUGLAS: I. of Man	**62**	54N	4W
Dounreay: Scotland	**61**	59N	4W
Douro (Duero): *r.*, Spain/Portugal	**67**	41N	8W
Dove: *r.*, England	**63**	53N	2W
Dover: England	**63**	51N	1E
Dover: U.S.A.	**50**	39N	76W
Dover, Strait of: England/France	**63**	51N	1E
Dovey: *r.*, Wales	**63**	53N	4W
Dovrefjell: *mtns.*, Norway	**70**	62N	10E
Down: *Co.*, N. Ireland	**62**	54N	6W
Downpatrick: N. Ireland	**61**	54N	6W
Dra: *r.*, Mor./Alg.	**108**	29N	8W
Draguignan: France	**73**	44N	6E
Drakensberg: *mtns.*, S. Africa	**111**	31S	28E
Drake Passage: S. America	**54**	57S	65W
Dráma: Greece	**69**	41N	24E
Drammen: Norway	**71**	60N	10E
Drava (Drau or Drave): *r.*, Eur.	**68**	46N	16E
Dresden: E. Germany	**74**	51N	14E
Dreux: France	**72**	49N	1E
Drogheda: R. of Irel.	**62**	54N	6W
Drôme: *r.*, France	**73**	45N	5E
Dubai: United Arab Emirates	**87**	25N	55E
Dubbo: Australia	**101**	32S	149E
DUBLIN: R. of Ireland	**63**	53N	6W
Dublin: U.S.A.	**47**	32N	83W
Dubno: U.S.S.R.	**68**	50N	26E
Dubrovnik: Yugo.	**69**	43N	18E
Dubuque: U.S.A.	**49**	42N	91W
Ducie I.: Pacific O.	**103**	25S	124W
Dudelange: Lux.	**72**	50N	6E
Dudinka: U.S.S.R.	**83**	70N	86E
Dudley: England	**63**	53N	2W
Duisburg: W. Germany	**64**	51N	7E
Dulce: *r.*, Arg.	**54**	29S	64W
Duluth: U.S.A.	**49**	47N	92W
Dumbarton: Scotland	**62**	56N	5W
Dum Dum: India	**115**	23N	88E
Dumfries & Galloway: *Reg.*, Scotland	**62**	55N	4W
Dunaújváros: Hungary	**68**	47N	19E
Dunbar: Scotland	**62**	56N	3W
Duncan: U.S.A.	**46**	34N	98W
Duncansby Head: Scotland	**61**	59N	3W
Dundalk: *& bay*, R. of Ireland	**62**	54N	6W
Dundee: Scotland	**62**	56N	3W
Dunedin: N.Z.	**104**	46S	171E
Dunfermline: Scotland	**62**	56N	3W
Dungeness: *hd.*, Eng.	**63**	51N	1E
Dunkirk: France	**72**	51N	2E
Dunkirk: U.S.A.	**47**	42N	79W
Dun Laoghaire: R. of Ireland	**63**	53N	6W
Dunoon: Scotland	**62**	56N	5W
Dunstable: England	**63**	52N	0
Durance: *r.*, France	**73**	44N	6E
Durango: Mexico	**52**	24N	105W
Durango: U.S.A.	**48**	37N	108W
Durant: U.S.A.	**46**	34N	96W
Durban: S. Africa	**111**	30S	31E
Düren: W. Germany	**74**	51N	6E
Durge Nor: *l.*, Mong.	**90**	49N	94E
Durham: *& Co.*, Eng.	**62**	55N	2W
Durham: U.S.A.	**47**	36N	79W
Durrës: Albania	**69**	41N	19E
D'Urville I.: N.Z.	**104**	41S	174E
Düsseldorf: W. Ger.	**64**	51N	7E
Dyersburg: U.S.A.	**47**	36N	89W
Dyushambe: U.S.S.R.	**85**	39N	69E
Dyfed: *Co.*, Wales	**63**	52N	5W
Dzerzhinsk: U.S.S.R.	**84**	56N	43E
Dzhambul: U.S.S.R.	**85**	43N	71E
Dzherba: U.S.S.R.	**83**	60N	116E
Dzhetygara: U.S.S.R.	**85**	52N	61E
Dzhezkazgan: U.S.S.R.	**85**	48N	68E
Dzungarian Gate: *pass*, China/U.S.S.R.	**85**	45N	82E
Eagle: U.S.A.	**30**	65N	141W
Eagle Pass: *city*, U.S.A.	**46**	29N	100W
Ealing: England	**112**	52N	0
Earn: *r.*, Scotland	**62**	56N	4W
East Anglia: *reg.*, Eng.	**63**	52N	1E
Eastbourne: England	**63**	51N	0
East Cape: N.Z.	**104**	38S	178E
East Chicago: U.S.A.	**34**	42N	87W
East China Sea	**90**	30N	123E
Easter I.: Pacific O.	**103**	27S	110W
Eastern Desert: Egypt	**86**	27N	32E
Eastern Ghats: *mtns.*, India	**88**	16N	80E
Eastern Sierra Madre: *see* Sierra Madre Oriental			
East Liverpool: U.S.A.	**47**	41N	81W
East London: S. Africa	**111**	33S	28E
East Pacific Basin: Pacific Ocean	**103**	15N	155W
East Pacific Ridge: Pacific Ocean	**103**	20S	110W
East Retford: England	**63**	53N	1W
East Rift Valley: Kenya/Ethiopia	**110**	5N	37E
East Siberian Sea: U.S.S.R.	**83**	73N	160E
Eau Claire: U.S.A.	**49**	45N	92W
Eauripik Ridge: Pacific Ocean	**102**	5N	142E
Eauze: France	**73**	44N	0
Ebberswalde: E. Ger.	**74**	53N	14E
Ebbw Vale: Wales	**62**	51N	3W
Ebi Nor: *l.*, China	**85**	45N	83E
Ebro: *r.*, Spain	**67**	42N	1W
Echuca: Australia	**101**	36S	145E
Ecorse: U.S.A.	**33**	42N	83W
ECUADOR: *cap.* Quito	**54**	2S	77W
Edam: Netherlands	**74**	53N	5E
Ed Damer: Sudan	**109**	17N	34E
Eddystone Rocks: England	**63**	50N	4W
Ede: Netherlands	**74**	52N	6E
Eden: *r.*, England	**62**	55N	3W
Edhessa: Greece	**69**	41N	22E
EDINBURGH: Scotland	**62**	56N	3W
Edirne (Adrianople): Turkey	**69**	42N	26E
Edjelé: Algeria	**108**	28N	9E
Edremit: Turkey	**69**	40N	27E
Edward, Lake: Africa	**110**	0	30E
Edwards Plateau: U.S.A.	**46**	30N	100W
Eekloo: Belgium	**72**	51N	4E
Egersund: Norway	**71**	58N	6E
Egmont, Mt.: N.Z.	**104**	39S	174E
EGYPT: *cap.* Cairo	**86**	27N	30E
Eifel: *mtns.*, W. Ger.	**74**	50N	7E
Eigg: *i.*, Scotland	**62**	57N	6W
Eighty Mile Beach: Australia	**98**	21S	121E
Eilat: Israel	**86**	30N	35E
Eilenburg: E. Germany	**74**	51N	13E
Eindhoven: Neth.	**74**	51N	5E
Eisenach: E. Germany	**74**	51N	10E
El Aaïun: Western Sahara	**108**	27N	14W
El Alamein: Egypt	**86**	31N	29E
El Asnam: Algeria	**67**	36N	1E
Elâzığ: Turkey	**87**	39N	39E
Elba: *i.*, Italy	**69**	43N	10E
El Ballah: Egypt	**109**	*Inset*	
Elbasan: Albania	**69**	41N	20E
El Bayadh: Algeria	**108**	34N	2E
Elbe: *r.*, E. & W. Ger.	**74**	53N	11E
Elbert, Mt.: U.S.A.	**48**	39N	107W
Elbeuf: France	**72**	49N	1E
Elbląg: Poland	**68**	54N	20E
El'brus: *mtn.*, U.S.S.R.	**84**	43N	42E
El Centro: U.S.A.	**48**	33N	116W
Elche: Spain	**67**	38N	1W
El Dorado: Ark., U.S.A.	**46**	33N	93W
El Dorado: Kansas U.S.A.	**46**	38N	97W
Elephant Butte Res.: U.S.A.	**48**	33N	107W
Eleuthera: *i.*, The Bahamas	**45**	25N	76W
El Faiyum: Egypt	**86**	29N	31E
El Fasher: Sudan	**109**	14N	25E
El Ferrol del Caudillo: Spain	**67**	43N	8W
El Firdân: Egypt	**109**	*Inset*	
Elgin: Scotland	**61**	58N	3W
El'gyay: U.S.S.R.	**83**	62N	117E
Elizabeth: Australia	**101**	35S	139E
Elizabeth: U.S.A.	**35**	41N	74W
Elizabeth City: U.S.A.	**47**	36N	76W
Elizabeth Point: S. W. Africa (Namibia)	**111**	27S	15E
Elizabethton: U.S.A.	**47**	36N	82W
Elizabethtown: U.S.A.	**47**	38N	86W
Elk City: U.S.A.	**46**	35N	99W
El Kharga: Egypt	**86**	25N	30E
Elkhart: U.S.A.	**47**	42N	86W
Elkins: U.S.A.	**47**	39N	80W
Elko: U.S.A.	**48**	41N	116W
Elk River: *city*, U.S.A.	**48**	47N	116W
Ellensburg: U.S.A.	**48**	47N	121W
Ellesmere Port: Eng.	**63**	53N	3W
Ellsworth Land: Antarctica	**116**	77S	90W
El Mansura: Egypt	**86**	31N	32E
El Matarîya: Egypt	**109**	*Inset*	
Elmhurst: U.S.A.	**34**	42N	88W
El Minya: Egypt	**86**	28N	31E
Elmira: U.S.A.	**50**	42N	77W
Elmshorn: W. Germany	**74**	54N	10E
Elmwood Park: U.S.A.	**34**	42N	88W
El Obeid: Sudan	**109**	13N	30E
El Paso: U.S.A.	**48**	32N	106W
El Qantara: Egypt	**109**	*Inset*	
El Reno: U.S.A.	**46**	36N	98W
EL SALVADOR: *cap.* San Salvador	**44**	14N	89W
El Shatt: Egypt	**109**	*Inset*	
Ely: England	**63**	52N	0
Ely: U.S.A.	**48**	39N	115W
Emba: *& r.*, U.S.S.R.	**84/5**	49N	58E
Embrun: France	**73**	45N	6E
Emden: W. Germany	**74**	53N	7E
Emerald: Australia	**100**	23S	148E
Emi Koussi: *mtn.*, Chad	**109**	20N	19E
Emilia Romagna: *Reg.*, Italy	**75**	44N	11E
Emmen: Netherlands	**74**	53N	7E
Emmerich: W. Germany	**74**	52N	6E
Emory Peak: U.S.A.	**46**	29N	104W
Ems: *r.*, W. Germany	**74**	53N	7E
Enderby Land: Antarctica	**116**	71S	50E
Enderlin: U.S.A.	**49**	47N	98W
Enfield: England	**112**	52N	0
Enggano: *i.*, Indon.	**91**	5S	102E
ENGLAND: *cap.* London	**61**	—	—
Englewood: U.S.A.	**35**	41N	74W
English Channel	**61**	50N	2W
Enid: U.S.A.	**49**	36N	98W
Ennepetal: W. Germany	**64**	51N	7E
Enniscorthy: R. of Ireland	**61**	53N	7W
Enniskillen: N. Ireland	**61**	54N	8W
Enns: *r.*, Austria	**75**	48N	14E
Enschede: Netherlands	**74**	52N	7E
Ensenada: Mexico	**48**	32N	117W
Entebbe: Uganda	**110**	0	33E
Enterprise: U.S.A.	**47**	31N	86W
Entre Rios: Moz.	**111**	15S	38E
Enugu: Nigeria	**108**	6N	8E
Épernay: France	**72**	49N	4E
Épinal: France	**72**	48N	6E
Epping: England	**112**	52N	0
Epping Forest: England	**112**	52N	0
Epsom: England	**112**	51N	0
EQUATORIAL GUINEA: *cap.* Malabo	**110**	2N	10E
Erbil: Iraq	**87**	36N	44E
Erentsab: Mongolia	**83**	50N	115E
Erfurt: E. Germany	**75**	51N	11E
Erie: U.S.A.	**47**	42N	80W
Erie, Lake: U.S.A./Canada	**20**	42N	81W
Erigavo: Somali Republic	**109**	11N	47E
Eritrea: *Prov.*, Eth.	**109**	15N	40E
Erkrath: W. Germany	**64**	51N	7E
Erlangen: W. Germany	**74**	50N	11E
Erne, Lough: N. Ireland	**61**	55N	8W
Eromanga: Australia	**100**	27S	143E
Er Rif Mtns.: Mor.	**67**	35N	5W
Erzgebirge: E. Ger./Czech.	**74**	50N	13E
Erzincan: Turkey	**87**	40N	40E
Erzurum: Turkey	**87**	40N	41E
Esbjaerg (Esbjerg): Denmark	**71**	55N	8E
Escanaba: U.S.A.	**49**	46N	87W
Esch: Luxembourg	**72**	50N	6E
Eschwege: W. Germany	**74**	51N	10E
Escondido: U.S.A.	**48**	33N	117W
Eshowe: S. Africa	**111**	29N	32E
Esk: *r.*, England	**62**	54N	1W
Eskilstuna: Sweden	**71**	59N	17E
Eskişehir: Turkey	**86**	40N	30E
Esperance: Australia	**100**	34S	122E
Espinouse, Mts. de l': France	**73**	44N	3E
Espirito Santo: *State*, Brazil	**54**	20S	40W
Essaouira: Morocco	**108**	32N	10W
Essen: W. Germany	**74**	51N	7E
Essequibo: *r.*, Guyana	**54**	5N	58W
Essex: *Co.*, England	**63**	52N	1E
Esslingen: W. Germany	**75**	49N	9E
Estats, Pic d': France	**73**	43N	1E
Estonian S.S.R.: U.S.S.R.	**84**	59N	26E
Esztergom: Hungary	**68**	48N	19E
Étampes: France	**72**	48N	2E
Étaples: France	**72**	51N	2E
Etawah: India	**88**	27N	79E
ETHIOPIA: *cap.* Addis Ababa	**109**	—	—
Ethiopian Plat.: E. Africa	**109**	10N	37E
Etna, Mt.: *volc.*, Sicily	**69**	38N	15E
Étoile, Chaîne de l': France	**73**	43N	6E
Etosha Pan & Game Park: S. W. Africa (Namibia)	**111**	19S	16E
Etruscan Apennines: *mtns.*, Italy	**75**	44N	10E
Euboea: *i.*, Greece	**69**	38N	24E
Eucla: Australia	**98**	32S	129E
Eudora: U.S.A.	**46**	33N	91W
Eugene: U.S.A.	**48**	44N	123W
Eunice: U.S.A.	**46**	30N	91W
Eupen: Belgium	**72**	51N	6E
Euphrates: *r.*, Asia	**87**	35N	40E
Eure: *r.*, France	**72**	49N	1E
Eureka: California U.S.A.	**48**	41N	124W
Eureka: Montana, U.S.A.	**48**	49N	115W
Eureka: Nev., U.S.A.	**48**	40N	116W
Europa: *i.*, Indian O.	**111**	23S	40E
Evanston: U.S.A.	**48**	41N	111W
Evansville: U.S.A.	**47**	38N	88W
Everard, C.: Australia	**101**	38S	149E
Everest: *mtn.*, Himalayas	**88**	28N	87E
Everett: U.S.A.	**48**	48N	122W
Everglades: *swamp*, U.S.A.	**47**	26N	81W
Evesham: England	**63**	52N	2W
Evian: France	**73**	46N	7E
Évora: Portugal	**67**	39N	8W
Évreux: France	**72**	49N	1E
Exe: *r.*, England	**63**	51N	4W
Exeter: England	**63**	51N	4W
Exmoor: England	**63**	51N	4W
Exmouth: England	**63**	51N	3W
Exmouth Gulf: Austl.	**98**	22S	114E
Eyemouth: Scotland	**62**	56N	2W
Eyre, Lake: Australia	**98**	28S	137E
Faenza: Italy	**75**	44N	12E
Faeroe Is.: Atl. O.	**57**	62N	7W
Fagersta: Sweden	**71**	60N	16E
Faguibine, L.: Mali	**108**	16N	4W
Fairbanks: U.S.A.	**12**	65N	148W
Fair Head: N. Ireland	**62**	55N	6W
Fair Isle: Scotland	**61**	59N	2W
Fair Lawn: U.S.A.	**35**	41N	74W
Fairmont: U.S.A.	**47**	40N	80W
Fairweather, Mt.: U.S.A.	**24**	59N	137W
Faith: U.S.A.	**49**	45N	102W
Faizabad: Afghan.	**85**	37N	71E
Fakenham: England	**63**	53N	1E
Falaise: France	**72**	49N	0
Falkirk: Scotland	**62**	56N	4W
Falkland Is.: Atl. O.	**57**	52S	60W
Falköping: Sweden	**71**	58N	13E

	Page	Lat.	Long.
Fall River: *city*, U.S.A.	**51**	42N	71W
Falmouth: England	**63**	50N	5W
False Bay: S. Africa	**111**	34S	19E
Falun: Sweden	**71**	61N	16E
Famagusta: Cyprus	**86**	35N	34E
Fanning I.: Pacific O.	**102**	4N	159W
Fano: Italy	**75**	44N	13E
Farasan Is.: Red Sea	**87**	17N	42E
Fareham: England	**63**	51N	1W
Farewell: U.S.A.	**12**	63N	154W
Farewell, Cape: Greenland	**13**	60N	44W
Farewell, Cape: N.Z.	**104**	40S	173E
Fargo: U.S.A.	**49**	47N	97W
Faribault: U.S.A.	**49**	44N	93W
Farmington: U.S.A.	**48**	37N	108W
Farnborough: England	**112**	51N	1W
Farnham: England	**112**	51N	1W
Faro: Portugal	**67**	37N	8W
Fārs: *reg.*, Iran	**87**	29N	51E
Faxa Bay: Iceland	**70**	64N	23W
Fayette: U.S.A.	**47**	34N	88W
Fayetteville: Ark., U.S.A.	**46**	36N	94W
Fayetteville: N.C., U.S.A.	**47**	35N	79W
Fayîd: Egypt	**109**	*Inset*	
F'Dérik: Mauritania	**108**	23N	13W
Fear, C.: U.S.A.	**47**	34N	78W
Fécamp: France	**72**	50N	0
Feilding: N.Z.	**104**	40S	176E
Feira de Santana: Brazil	**54**	12S	39W
Feldkirch: Austria	**75**	47N	10E
Fen: *r.*, China	**94**	36N	112E
Fengtai: China	**114**	40N	116E
Fenouillèdes: *mtns.*, France	**73**	43N	2E
Fens, The: *reg.*, Eng.	**63**	53N	0
Fenyang: China	**94**	37N	112E
Fergana: U.S.S.R.	**85**	40N	72E
Fergus Falls: *city*, U.S.A.	**49**	46N	96W
Fernando de Noronha: *i.*, Brazil	**54**	4S	32W
Ferndale: U.S.A.	**33**	42N	83W
Ferrara: Italy	**75**	45N	12E
Ferret, Cap: France	**73**	45N	1W
Fès: Morocco	**108**	34N	5W
Fethiye: Turkey	**86**	36N	29E
Fianarantsoa: Malagasy Rep.	**110**	22S	47E
Fife Ness: Scotland	**62**	56N	3W
Figeac: France	**73**	4N	52E
FIJI: *cap.* Suva	**102**	18S	178E
Filchner Ice Shelf: Antarctica	**116**	78S	50W
Findlay: U.S.A.	**47**	41N	84W
Finistère: *Dept.*, France	**72**	48N	4W
Finisterre, Cape: Sp.	**67**	43N	9W
FINLAND: *cap.* Helsinki	**70/1**	—	—
Finschhafen: Papua New Guinea	**99**	7S	148E
Finsteraarhorn: *mtn.*, Switzerland	**75**	47N	8E
Fiordland: *district & Nat. Park*, N.Z.	**104**	46S	167E
Firenze: *see* Florence			
Fishguard: Wales	**63**	52N	5W
Fitchburg: U.S.A.	**51**	43N	72W
Fitzroy: *r.*, Queens., Australia	**100**	23S	150E
Fitzroy: *r.*, W. Austl.	**98**	18S	124E
Flagstaff: U.S.A.	**48**	35N	112W
Flamborough Head: England	**62**	54N	0
Flanders: *reg.*, Belgium	**72**	51N	4E
Flathead L.: U.S.A.	**48**	48N	114W
Flattery, C.: U.S.A.	**48**	48N	125W
Fleetwood: England	**62**	54N	3W
Flensburg: W. Germany	**68**	55N	9E
Flers: France	**72**	49N	1W
Flinders: *r.*, Australia	**99**	20S	141E
Flinders Range: Australia	**101**	31S	139E
Flinders Reefs: Coral Sea	**100**	18S	149E
Flint: U.S.A.	**19**	43N	84W
Flint: *r.*, U.S.A.	**47**	31N	85W
Flora: Norway	**70**	62N	5E
Florence (Firenze): Italy	**75**	44N	11E
Florence: Alabama U.S.A.	**47**	35N	88W
Florence: Arizona U.S.A.	**48**	33N	111W
Florence: S.C., U.S.A.	**47**	34N	80W
Florencia: Colombia	**54**	2N	76W
Flores: *i. & sea*, Indonesia	**91**	9S	121E
Floreshty: U.S.S.R.	**68**	48N	28E
Floriano: Brazil	**54**	7S	43W
Florianópolis: Brazil	**56**	27S	48W
Florida: Cuba	**53**	22N	78W
Florida: *State*, U.S.A.	**47**	28N	82W
Florida, Straits of: U.S.A.	**47**	24N	81W
Florida Keys: *is.*, U.S.A.	**47**	25N	81W
Flórina: Greece	**69**	41N	21E
Flushing (Vlissingen): Netherlands	**74**	51N	4E
Fly: *r.*, Papua New Guinea	**99**	8S	142E
Foggia: Italy	**69**	41N	16E
Foix: & *Old Prov.*, Fr.	**73**	43N	2E
Foligno: Italy	**69**	43N	13E
Folkestone: England	**63**	51N	1E
Fond du Lac: U.S.A.	**49**	44N	88W
Fontainebleau: France	**72**	48N	3E
Fontainebleau, Forêt de: France	**72**	48N	3E
Fontenoy: *hist.*, Belgium	**72**	51N	3E
Foochow: China	**95**	26N	118E
Forbes: Australia	**101**	33S	148E
Forcalquier: France	**73**	44N	6E
Fordlândia: Brazil	**54**	4S	55W
Forel, Mt.: Greenland	**13**	67N	37W
Forez, Monts du: France	**73**	45N	4E
Forfar: Scotland	**62**	57N	3W
Forli: Italy	**75**	44N	12E
Formentera: *i.*, Balearic Is.	**67**	38N	1E
Formosa (Taiwan): *i. & str.*, China	**90**	24N	121E
Forrest: Australia	**98**	31S	128E
Forrest City: U.S.A.	**46**	35N	91W
Forsayth: Australia	**99**	19S	144E
Forsyth: U.S.A.	**48**	46N	107W
Fortaleza: Brazil	**54**	4S	38W
Fort Collins: U.S.A.	**49**	41N	105W
Fort Dauphin: Malagasy Rep.	**110**	25S	47E
FORT-DE-FRANCE: Martinique	**45**	15N	61W
Fort Dodge: U.S.A.	**49**	43N	94W
Fortescue: *r.*, Austl.	**98**	22S	118E
Forth Bridge: Scotland	**62**	56N	3W
Forth, Firth of: Scot.	**62**	56N	3W
Fort Johnston: Malawi	**111**	15S	35E
Fort Lauderdale: U.S.A.	**47**	26N	80W
Fort Madison: U.S.A.	**48**	41N	91W
Fort Morgan: U.S.A.	**49**	40N	104W
Fort Myers: U.S.A.	**47**	27N	82W
Fort Peck Res.: U.S.A.	**48**	47N	107W
Fort Pierce: U.S.A.	**47**	27N	80W
Fort Sandeman: Pakistan	**88**	31N	70E
Fort Shevchenko: U.S.S.R.	**84**	45N	50E
Fort Smith: U.S.A.	**46**	35N	94W
Fort Sumner: U.S.A.	**49**	34N	104W
Fort Wayne: U.S.A.	**47**	41N	85W
Fort William: Scotland	**61**	57N	5W
Fort Worth: U.S.A.	**46**	33N	97W
Forty Mile: *r.*, U.S.A.	**30**	65N	142W
Fort Yukon: U.S.A.	**30**	67N	145W
Foshan: China	**95**	23N	113E
Fougères: France	**72**	48N	1W
Foul Bay: Red Sea	**86**	23N	36E
Foulness I.: England	**63**	52N	1E
Foulwind, C.: N.Z.	**104**	42S	172E
Fourmies: France	**72**	50N	4E
Foveaux Strait: N.Z.	**104**	47S	168E
Foyle, L.: Ireland	**61**	55N	7W
Framingham: U.S.A.	**51**	42N	71W
FRANCE: *cap.* Paris	**72/3**	—	—
Franche Comté: *Old Prov.*, France	**72/3**	47N	6E
Francistown: Bots.	**111**	21S	27E
Franconian Heights: W. Germany	**74**	49N	10E
Franconian Jura: W. Germany	**74**	49N	11E
Frankfort: Indiana, U.S.A.	**47**	40N	86W
Frankfort: Kentucky, U.S.A.	**47**	38N	85W
Frankfurt am Main: W. Germany	**74**	50N	9E
Frankfurt an der Oder: E. Germany	**74**	52N	15E
Franklin D. Roosevelt Lake: U.S.A.	**48**	48N	118W
Franz Josef Land: U.S.S.R.	**82/3**	80N	55E
Fraserburgh: S. Africa	**111**	33S	22E
Fraser I.: Australia	**100**	25S	153E
Fray Bentos: Uruguay	**56**	33S	58W
Fredericia: Denmark	**71**	56N	10E
Frederick: U.S.A.	**46**	34N	99W
Fredericksburg: U.S.A.	**47**	38N	78W
Frederikshavn: Den.	**71**	57N	11E
Frederikstad: Norway	**71**	59N	11E
Freeport: U.S.A.	**46**	29N	97W
FREETOWN: Sierra Leone	**108**	7N	13W
Freiburg im Breisgau: W. Germany	**75**	48N	8E
Freising: W. Germany	**75**	48N	12E
Fréjus: France	**73**	43N	7E
Fremantle: Australia	**100**	32S	116E
Fremont: U.S.A.	**49**	41N	97W
FRENCH GUIANA: *cap.* Cayenne	**54**	4N	53W
Frenchman Creek: U.S.A.	**49**	40N	102W
Fresnillo de Gonzáles Echeverría: Mexico	**52**	23N	103W
Fresno: U.S.A.	**48**	37N	120W
Fribourg: Switzerland	**75**	47N	7E
Friedrichshafen: W. Germany	**75**	48N	9E
Friesland: *Prov.*, Netherlands	**74**	53N	6E
Frisian Is., East: W. Ger.	**74**	54N	7E
Frisian Is., North: W. Germany	**71**	55N	8E
Frisian Is., West: Netherlands	**74**	53N	5E
Frome, Lake: Austl.	**101**	31S	140E
Frunze: U.S.S.R.	**85**	43N	75E
Fuchu: Japan	**114**	36N	139E
Fuerteventura: *i.*, Canary Islands	**108**	29N	14W
Fuji San: *mtn.*, Japan	**93**	35N	139E
Fujisawa: Japan	**114**	35N	139E
Fukien: *Prov.*, China	**95**	26N	118E
Fukui: Japan	**93**	36N	136E
Fukuoka: Japan	**93**	34N	130E
Fukushima: Japan	**93**	38N	140E
Fulda: & *r.*, W. Ger.	**74**	50N	10E
Fulton: U.S.A.	**49**	39N	92W
Funabashi: Japan	**114**	36N	140E
Funchal: Madeira	**108**	33N	17W
Furka Pass: Switzerland	**75**	47N	8E
Furneaux Group: *is.*, Australia	**99**	40S	148E
Fürth: Germany	**74**	49N	11E
Fushun: China	**90**	42N	124E
Fyn: *i.*, Denmark	**71**	55N	10E
Fyne, L.: Scotland	**62**	56N	5W
Gabès: & *gulf*, Tunisia	**108**	34N	11E
GABON: *cap.* Libreville	**110**	2N	12E
GABORONE: Botswana	**111**	24S	26E
Gabrovo: Bulgaria	**69**	43N	25E
Gadames: Libya	**108**	30N	10E
Gadsden: U.S.A.	**47**	34N	86W
Gaffney: U.S.A.	**47**	35N	81W
Gail: *r.*, Austria	**75**	47N	13E
Gaillard Cut: Panama Canal	**45**	*Inset*	
Gainesville: Georgia, U.S.A.	**47**	34N	84W
Gainesville: Texas, U.S.A.	**46**	34N	97W
Gainsborough: Eng.	**63**	53N	1W
Gainsville: Florida, U.S.A.	**47**	30N	82W
Gairdner, L.: Austl.	**98**	32S	136E
Galápagos Is.: Pacific O.	**103**	1S	91W
Galashiels: Scotland	**68**	56N	3W
Galati: Romania	**68**	45N	28E
Galena: U.S.A.	**12**	65N	157W
Galesburg: U.S.A.	**49**	41N	90W
Galilee, Sea of: Israel	**86**	33N	36E
Gallarate: Italy	**75**	46N	9E
Galle: Sri Lanka	**88**	6N	80E
Gallegos: *r.*, Arg.	**55**	52S	71W
Gallinas, Pt.: Colombia	**54**	13N	72W
Gällivare: Sweden	**70**	67N	21E
Gallup: U.S.A.	**48**	36N	109W
Galveston: & *bay*, U.S.A.	**46**	30N	95W
Galway: & *bay*, R. of Ireland	**61**	53N	9W
GAMBIA, THE: *cap.* Banjul	**108**	13N	15W
Gambier Is.: Pac. O.	**103**	22S	135W
Gand: *see* Ghent			
Gandak: *r.*, India	**88**	27N	85E
Ganga (Ganges): *r.*, Bangl./India	**88**	25N	86E
Ganges: France	**73**	44N	4E
Ganges: *r.*, *see* Ganga			
Gap: France	**73**	45N	6E
Gard: *r.*, France	**73**	44N	4E
Garda, L. of: Italy	**75**	46N	11E
Garden City: Mich., U.S.A.	**33**	42N	83W
Garden City: N.Y., U.S.A.	**35**	41N	74W
Garden Grove: U.S.A.	**37**	34N	118W
Gardez: Afghan.	**88**	34N	69E
Gardner I.: Pac. O.	**102**	5S	175W
Garfield: U.S.A.	**35**	41N	74W
Gargano, C.: Italy	**69**	42N	16E
Garnett: U.S.A.	**49**	38N	95W
Garonne: *r.*, France	**73**	45N	0
Garoua: Cameroun	**108**	9N	13E
Garrigues: *mtns.*, Fr.	**73**	44N	4E
Garron Pt.: N. Ireland	**62**	55N	6W
Gartok: China	**88**	32N	80E
Gary: U.S.A.	**34**	42N	86W
Gascony: *Old Prov.*, France	**73**	44N	0
Gastonia: U.S.A.	**47**	35N	81W
Gata, C. de: Spain	**67**	37N	2W
Gateshead: England	**62**	55N	2W
Gâtine, Hauteurs de: *hills*, France	**73**	47N	1W
Gatooma: Rhodesia (Zimbabwe)	**111**	18S	30E
Gatun Lake: & *locks*, Panama Canal	**45**	*Inset*	
Gauhati: India	**89**	26N	92E
Gävle: Sweden	**71**	61N	17E
Gawler: Australia	**101**	35S	139E
Gaya: India	**88**	25N	85E
Gaya: Niger	**108**	12N	4E
Gaza: Egypt	**86**	31N	34E
Gaziantep: Turkey	**87**	37N	37E
Gdansk: & *Gulf*, Poland	**68**	54N	19E
Gdynia: Poland	**68**	55N	18E
Geelong: Australia	**101**	38S	144E
Geerardsbergen: Belgium	**72**	51N	4E
Geissen: W. Germany	**75**	51N	9E
Gelibolu: Turkey	**69**	10N	27E
Gelsenkirchen: W. Ger.	**64**	51N	7E
Geneva: & *l.*, Switz.	**75**	46N	6E
Génissiat Dam: France	**73**	46N	6E
Genoa: & *gulf*, Italy	**75**	44N	9E
Gent: *see* Ghent			
George: S. Africa	**111**	34S	22E
George, L.: Austl.	**101**	35S	149E
GEORGETOWN: Guyana	**54**	7N	58W
George Town: Mal.	**92**	5N	100E
Georgetown: U.S.A.	**47**	33N	79W
Georgia: *State*, U.S.A.	**47**	33N	84W
Georgian S.S.R.: U.S.S.R.	**84**	43N	45E
Gera: E. Germany	**74**	51N	12E
Geraldton: Australia	**100**	29S	115E
GERMANY, EAST *cap.* Berlin	**74**	—	—
GERMANY, WEST: *cap.* Bonn	**74/5**	—	—
Gerona: Spain	**67**	42N	3E
Gers: *r.*, France	**73**	44N	1E
Gettysburg: U.S.A.	**47**	40N	77W
Gevelsberg: W. Ger.	**64**	51N	7E
Ghaghra: *r.*, India	**88**	27N	82E
GHANA: *cap.* Accra	**108**	7N	0
Ghardaïa: Algeria	**108**	33N	4E
Ghazipur: India	**88**	26N	83E
Ghent (Gand, Gent): Belgium	**72**	51N	4E
GIBRALTAR: & *strait*	**67**	36N	5W
Gibson Desert: Austl.	**98**	24S	124E
Gien: France	**73**	47N	3E
Gifu: Japan	**93**	35N	137E
Gijón: Spain	**67**	44N	6W
Gila: *r.*, U.S.A.	**48**	33N	113W
Gila Bend: U.S.A.	**48**	33N	113W
Gilbert: *r.*, Australia	**99**	17S	142E
Gilbert Is.: Pacific O.	**102**	0	175E
Gilgit: India	**88**	36N	74E
Gillingham: England	**112**	51N	0
Gineifa: Egypt	**109**	*Inset*	
Ginir: Ethiopia	**109**	7N	41E
Gippsland: *reg.*, Austl.	**101**	38S	148E
Girga: Egypt	**86**	26N	32E
Gironde: *r.*, France	**73**	45N	1W
Girvan: Scotland	**62**	55N	5W
Gisborne: N.Z.	**104**	39S	178E
Giurgiu: Romania	**69**	44N	26E
Givors: France	**73**	46N	5E
Giza: Egypt	**86**	30N	31E
Gjinokastër: Albania	**69**	40N	20E
Gladbeck: W. Germany	**64**	52N	7E
Gladstone: Australia	**100**	24S	151E
Glåma: *r.*, Norway	**71**	61N	12E
Glamorgan, Mid-: *Co.*, Wales	**63**	52N	4W
Glamorgan, South: *Co.*, Wales	**63**	52N	4W
Glamorgan, West: *Co.*, Wales	**63**	52N	4W
Glasgow: Ky., U.S.A.	**47**	37N	86W
Glasgow: Montana, U.S.A.	**48**	48N	107W
Glasgow: Scotland	**62**	56N	4W
Glastonbury: England	**63**	51N	3W
Glauchau: E. Germany	**74**	51N	13E
Glazov: U.S.S.R.	**84**	58N	53E
Glencoe: U.S.A.	**49**	45N	94W
Glen Cove: U.S.A.	**35**	41N	74W
Glenelg: *r.*, Australia	**101**	37S	141E
Glen Innes: Australia	**101**	30S	152E
Glenmorgan: Australia	**100**	27S	150E
Glenwood: U.S.A.	**49**	46N	95W
Gliwice: Poland	**68**	50N	19E
Globe: U.S.A.	**48**	33N	111W
Gloucester: & *Co.*, England	**63**	52N	2W
Gloucester: U.S.A.	**51**	43N	71W
Gloversville: U.S.A.	**51**	43N	74W
Gniezno: Poland	**68**	53N	18E
Goa: *Union Territ.*, India	**88**	15N	74E
Gobabis: S.W. Africa (Namibia)	**111**	23S	18E
Gobi Desert: Mong.	**83**	43N	105E
Godavari: *r.*, India	**88**	20N	81E
GODTHAAB: Grnld.	**13**	64N	52W
Goiânia: Brazil	**54**	17S	49W

Name	Page	Lat.	Long.
Gojás: Brazil	54	16S	50W
Gojás Massif: Brazil	54	15S	48W
Gol: Norway	71	61N	9E
Golden Bay: N.Z.	104	41S	173E
Gomati: r., India	88	26N	82E
Gomel': U.S.S.R.	84	53N	31E
Gómez Palacio: Mexico	52	26N	103W
Gondar: Ethiopia	109	13N	37E
Good Hope, C. of: S. Africa	111	34S	18E
Goodland: U.S.A.	49	39N	103W
Goodwin Sands: Eng.	63	51N	1E
Goole: England	62	54N	1W
Goondiwindi: Austl.	100	29S	150E
Goose L.: U.S.A.	48	42N	120W
Göppingen: W. Ger.	75	49N	10E
Gorakhpur: India	88	27N	83E
Gordon: U.S.A.	30	70N	141W
Gore: Ethiopia	109	8N	36E
Gore: N.Z.	104	46S	169E
Gorizia: Italy	75	46N	14E
Gor'kiy: U.S.S.R.	84	56N	44E
Gorno-Altaysk: U.S.S.R.	85	52N	86E
Gorzów Wielkopolski: Poland	68	53N	15E
Gosford: Australia	101	33S	151E
Goslar: W. Germany	74	52N	10E
Göta: r., Sweden	71	58N	12E
Göteborg: Sweden	71	58N	12E
Gotha: E. Germany	74	51N	11E
Gotland: i., Sweden	71	57N	19E
Göttingen: W. Germany	74	52N	10E
Gottwaldov: Czech.	68	49N	18E
Gouda: Netherlands	74	52N	5E
Goulburn: Australia	101	35S	150E
Gouverneur: U.S.A.	19	44N	76W
Gower: penin., Wales	63	52N	4W
Gozo: i., Medit. Sea	69	36N	14E
Graaff-Reinet: S. Africa	111	32S	25E
Gracias a Dios, C.: Nicaragua	45	15N	83W
Grafton: Australia	101	30S	153E
Grafton: U.S.A.	49	48N	98W
Graham: U.S.A.	46	33N	99W
Grahamstown: S. Africa	111	33S	26E
Graian Alps: Fr./Italy	75	45N	7E
Grampian: mts. & reg., Scotland	62	57N	4W
Granada: Spain	67	37N	4W
Gran Canaria: i., Canary Is.	108	28N	15W
Gran Chaco: reg., Arg./Paraguay	54	25S	61W
Grand: r., U.S.A.	49	46N	102W
Grand Bahama: i., The Bahamas	45	27N	79W
Grand Canyon: & city, U.S.A.	48	36N	112W
Grand Coulee: U.S.A.	48	48N	119W
Grande Ronde: r., U.S.A.	48	46N	118W
Grand Forks: U.S.A.	49	48N	97W
Grand Island: city, U.S.A.	49	41N	98W
Grand Junction: U.S.A.	48	39N	109W
Grand Rapids: city, Mich., U.S.A.	47	43N	86W
Grand Rapids: city, Minn., U.S.A.	49	47N	94W
Grangemouth: Scot.	62	56N	4W
Grant, Mt.: U.S.A.	48	38N	119W
Grantham: England	63	53N	1W
Grants Pass: city, U.S.A.	48	42N	123W
Granville: France	72	49N	2W
Grasse: France	73	44N	7E
Grave, Pte. de: Fr.	72	46N	1W
Gravelines: France	72	51N	2E
Gravesend: England	112	51N	0
Grays Harbour: bay, U.S.A.	48	47N	124W
Grays Thurrock: England	112	51N	0
Graz: Austria	68	47N	15E
Great Abaco: i., The Bahamas	45	27N	11W
Great Australian Bight	98	33S	130E
Great Barrier I.: New Zealand	104	36S	175E
Great Barrier Reef: Australia	99	17S	147E
Great Bend: U.S.A.	49	38N	99W
Great Bitter Lake: Egypt	109	Inset	
Great Dividing Range: Australia	101	—	—
Great Driffield: Eng.	62	54N	0
Greater Antilles: W. Indies	45	18N	75W
Greater Manchester: Reg., England	62	53N	2W
Great Eastern Erg: desert, Algeria	108	30N	8E
Great Falls: city, U.S.A.	48	47N	111W
Great Himalayan Range	88/9	—	—
Great Inagua: i., Bahamas Is.	45	21N	74W
Great Karroo: plat., S. Africa	111	33S	23E
Great Khingan Mts.: China	90	47N	120E
Great Palm Is.: Australia	100	19S	147E
Great St. Bernard Pass: Switz./Italy	75	46N	7E
Great Salt Lake: & Desert, U.S.A.	48	41N	113W
Great Sandy Desert: Australia	98	21S	124E
Great Victoria Desert: Australia	98	28S	130E
Great Wall: China	94	41N	114E
Great Western Erg: desert, Algeria	108	30N	0
Great Yarmouth: England	63	53N	2E
GREECE: cap. Athens	69	40N	23E
Greeley: U.S.A.	49	40N	105W
Green: r., U.S.A.	48	40N	110W
Greenock: Scotland	62	56N	5W
Greenough: r., Austl.	100	28S	115E
Green Bay: & city, U.S.A.	49	45N	88W
GREENLAND: cap. Godthaab	13	70N	40W
Green Mts.: U.S.A.	51	44N	73W
Green River: city, U.S.A.	48	42N	110W
Greensboro: U.S.A.	47	36N	80W
Greenville: Ala., U.S.A.	47	32N	87W
Greenville: Miss., U.S.A.	46	33N	91W
Greenville: S.C., U.S.A.	47	35N	82W
Greenville: Tenn., U.S.A.	47	36N	83W
Greenville: Texas, U.S.A.	46	33N	96W
Greenwich: England	112	51N	0
Greenwich: U.S.A.	35	41N	74W
Greenwood: Miss., U.S.A.	46	34N	90W
Greenwood: S.C., U.S.A.	47	34N	82W
GRENADA: cap. St. George's	45	12N	62W
Grenadines: is., W. Indies	45	12N	61W
Grenay: France	72	50N	3E
Grenoble: France	73	45N	6E
Gretna Green: Scotland	62	55N	3W
Greymouth: N.Z.	104	42S	171E
Grey Range: Austl.	100	28S	142E
Greystones: R. of Ireland	63	53N	6W
Greytown: S. Africa	111	29S	31E
Griefswald: E. Germany	74	54N	13E
Griffin: U.S.A.	47	33N	84W
Griffith: Australia	101	34S	146E
Grimsby: England	62	54N	0
Grimsel Pass: Switz.	75	47N	8E
Grindelwald: Switz.	75	47N	8E
Griqualand: reg., S. Africa	111	29S	24E
Griquatown: S. Africa	111	29S	25E
Gris Nez: cape, France	72	51N	2E
Grodno: U.S.S.R.	68	54N	24E
Groix, Ile de: France	72	48N	3W
Gronau: W. Germany	74	52N	7E
Grong: Norway	70	64N	12E
Groningen: Neth.	74	53N	7E
Groote Eylandt: i., Australia	98	14S	137E
Grootfontein: S.W. Africa (Namibia)	111	20S	18E
Grosseto: Italy	69	43N	11E
Groznyy: U.S.S.R.	84	43N	46E
Grudziądz: Poland	68	53N	18E
Gruyères: Switzerland	75	47N	7E
Guadalajara: Mexico	52	21N	103W
Guadalajara: Spain	67	41N	3W
Guadalcanal: i., Pacific Ocean	102	10S	160E
Guadalquivir: r., Spain	67	37N	6W
Guadalupe: i., Pac. O.	44	29N	118W
Guadalupe: r., U.S.A.	46	29N	97W
Guadeloupe: i., W. Indies	45	16N	61W
Guadiana: r., Spain/Portugal	67	38N	8W
Guajará-mirim: Brazil	54	11S	65W
Guam: i., Pacific O.	102	14N	145E
Guanabacoa: Cuba	53	23N	82W
Guanajuato: Mexico	52	21N	101W
Guantánamo: Cuba	53	20N	75W
Guarda: Portugal	67	41N	7W
Guardafui, C.: Somali Republic	109	12N	51E
GUATEMALA: cap. Guatemala	45	15N	91W
Guayaquil: & gulf, Ecuador	54	2S	80W
Guaymas: Mexico	44	28N	111W
Gubakha: U.S.S.R.	85	58N	57E
Guebwiller: France	72	48N	7E
Guéret: France	73	46N	2E
Guernsey: i., Channel Islands	63	Inset	
Guiana Highlands: S. America	54	3N	60W
Guildford: England	112	51N	1W
GUINEA: cap. Conakry	108	11N	1W
Guinea, G. of	108	3N	0
GUINEA-BISSAU: cap. Bissau	108	12N	15W
Guingamp: France	72	49N	3W
Güines: Cuba	53	23N	82W
Gujarat: reg., India	88	22N	74E
Gujerat: State, India	88	23N	72E
Gujranwala: Pakistan	88	32N	74E
Gulfport: U.S.A.	47	30N	89W
Gunnedah: Australia	101	31S	150E
Guntersville L.: U.S.A.	47	34N	86W
Guntur: India	88	16N	80E
Gurgan: Iran	87	37N	55E
Gur'yev: U.S.S.R.	84	47N	52E
GUYANA: cap. Georgetown	54	5N	58W
Guymon: U.S.A.	46	37N	101W
Gwaai: Rhodesia (Zimbabwe)	111	19S	27E
Gwadar: Pakistan	88	25N	62E
Gwalior: India	88	26N	78E
Gwelo: Rhodesia (Zimbabwe)	111	20S	30E
Gwent: Co., Wales	63	53N	5W
Gwynedd: Co., Wales	63	53N	5W
Gyangtse: China	88	29N	90E
Gyda Peninsula: U.S.S.R.	83	71N	77E
Gydan Range (Kolyma Ra.) U.S.S.R.	83	62N	160E
Gympie: Australia	100	26S	153E
Györ: Hungary	68	48N	18E
Haarlem: Neth.	74	52N	5E
Haast: & Pass, N.Z.	104	44S	169E
Hab: r., Pakistan	88	25N	67E
Habbānīyah: Iraq	87	34N	43E
Hackensack: U.S.A.	35	41N	74W
Haddington: Scotland	62	56N	3W
Hadhramaut: valley, Yemen P.D.R.	87	16N	48E
Hadibu: Socotra	87	13N	54E
Hadithah: Iraq	87	34N	42E
Hadrian's Wall: Eng.	62	55N	2W
Hageland: reg., Belg.	72	51N	5E
Hagen: W. Germany	74	51N	7E
Hague, Cap de la: Fr.	72	50N	2W
HAGUE, THE (S'GRAVENHAGE) Netherlands	74	52N	4E
Haguenau: France	72	49N	8E
Haifa: Israel	86	33N	35E
Haikow: China	92	20N	110E
Hail: Saudi Arabia	87	27N	42E
Hailar: China	90	49N	120E
Hainan: i. & str., China	92	19N	110E
Hainault: reg., Belgium	72	51N	4E
Haines: U.S.A.	24	59N	135W
Haiphong: Vietnam	92	21N	107E
HAITI: cap. Port-au-Prince	45	19N	73W
Hajara: desert, Sau. Arabia	87	31N	42E
Hakodate: Japan	93	42N	141E
Halaib: Sudan	86	22N	36E
Halberstadt: E. Ger.	74	52N	11E
Haldensleben: E. Ger.	74	52N	11E
Halifax: England	62	54N	2W
Halle: E. Germany	74	51N	12E
Hall's Creek: town, Australia	98	18S	128E
Halmahera: i., Indon.	91	1N	128E
Halmstad: Sweden	71	57N	13E
Hälsingborg: Sweden	71	56N	13E
Hama: Syria	86	35N	37E
Hamadān: Iran	87	35N	48E
Hamamatsu: Japan	93	35N	138E
Hamar: Norway	71	61N	11E
Hambantota: Sri Lanka	88	7N	81E
Hamburg: W. Ger.	74	54N	10E
Hämeenlinna: Finland	71	61N	24E
Hameln: W. Germany	74	52N	9E
Hamersley Range: Australia	98	22S	118E
Hami (Qomul): China	83	43N	93E
Hamilton: Australia	101	38S	142E
Hamilton: N.Z.	104	38S	175E
Hamilton: Scotland	62	56N	4W
Hamilton: U.S.A.	47	39N	85W
Hamlin: U.S.A.	46	33N	100W
Hamm: W. Germany	74	52N	8E
Hammerfest: Norway	70	71N	24E
Hammersmith: England	112	51N	0
Hammond: U.S.A.	34	42N	86W
Hampshire: Co., Eng.	63	51N	1W
Hampton: U.S.A.	47	37N	76W
Hamtramck: U.S.A.	33	42N	83W
Hancock: U.S.A.	49	47N	88W
Hanford: U.S.A.	48	36N	120W
Hangchow: China	95	30N	120E
Hanko: Finland	71	60N	23E
Hankow: China	95	31N	114E
Hannibal: U.S.A.	49	40N	91W
Hanöbukten: bay, Sweden	71	56N	15E
HANOI: Vietnam	92	21N	106E
Hanover (Hannover): W. Germany	74	52N	10E
Hantan: China	94	37N	114E
Hanyang: China	95	31N	114E
Haogoundou, L.: Mali	108	15N	3W
Häora (Howrah): India	115	23N	88E
Haradh: Saudi Arabia	87	24N	49E
Harar: Ethiopia	109	9N	42E
Harbin (Pinkiang): China	90	46N	127E
Hardangerfjorden: fd., Norway	71	60N	6E
Hardangervidda: plat., Norway	71	60N	8E
Hardenberg: Neth.	74	53N	7E
Hargeisa: Somali Republic	109	10N	44E
Harlingen: Neth.	74	53N	5E
Harlingen: U.S.A.	47	26N	98W
Harlow: England	112	52N	0
Harney Basin: U.S.A.	48	43N	120W
Härnösand: Sweden	70	63N	18E
Harris: i., Scotland	61	58N	7W
Harrisburg: U.S.A.	50	40N	77W
Harrismith: S. Africa	111	28S	29E
Harrisonburg: U.S.A.	47	39N	79W
Harrogate: England	62	54N	2W
Harrow: England	112	52N	0
Harstad: Norway	70	69N	16E
Hartford: U.S.A.	51	42N	73W
Hartland Pt.: England	63	51N	5W
Hartlepool: England	63	55N	1W
Harvey: U.S.A.	34	41N	88W
Harwell: England	62	52N	1W
Harwich: England	63	52N	1E
Haryana: India	88	29N	76E
Harz: mtns., E. & W. Germany	74	52N	11E
Hasa: reg., Saudi Arabia	87	27N	48E
Haskovo: Bulgaria	69	42N	26E
Haslemere: England	63	51N	1W
Hassan: India	88	13N	76E
Hasselt: Belgium	72	51N	5E
Hassi Messaoud: Alg.	108	32N	6E
Hässleholm: Sweden	71	56N	14E
Hastings: England	63	51N	1E
Hastings: N.Z.	104	40S	177E
Hastings: U.S.A.	49	41N	98W
Ha Tinh: Vietnam	92	18N	106E
Hatteras, C.: U.S.A.	47	35N	75W
Hattiesburg: U.S.A.	47	31N	89W
Hattingen: Germany	64	51N	7E
Hat Yai: Thailand	92	7N	100E
Haugesund: Norway	71	59N	5E
Hauraki Gulf: N.Z.	104	37S	175E
Hauta: Saudi Arabia	87	23N	47E
HAVANA (La Habana): Cuba	53	23N	82W
Havre: U.S.A.	48	48N	110W
Hawaii: i. & State, Pacific O., U.S.A.	101	20N	155W
Hawaiian Is.: arch., Pacific Ocean	102/3	20N	160W
Hawera: N.Z.	104	40S	174E
Hawick: Scotland	62	55N	3W
Hawke Bay: N.Z.	104	39S	177E
Hawthorne: U.S.A.	48	38N	119W
Hay: Australia	101	34S	145E
Hayama: Japan	114	35N	140E
Hayden: U.S.A.	48	33N	111W
Hays: U.S.A.	49	39N	99W
Hazaribagh: India	88	24N	85E
Hazelbrouck: France	72	51N	3E
Hazel Park: U.S.A.	33	42N	83W
Hazleton: U.S.A.	50	41N	76W
Heanor: England	63	53N	1W
Hebron: Jordan	86	32N	35E
Heidelberg: W. Ger.	74	49N	9E
Heidelberg: S. Africa	111	26S	28E
Heilbronn: W. Germany	74	49N	9E
Heiligenhaus: W. Ger.	64	51N	7E
Hekla: volc., Iceland	70	64N	19W
Helena: Ark., U.S.A.	46	35N	91W
Helena: Montana, U.S.A.	48	47N	112W
Helensville: N.Z.	104	37S	174E
Heligoland (Helgoland): i., W. Germany	71	54N	8E
Heligoland Bight: W. Germany	74	54N	8E
HELSINKI (Helsingfors): Finland	71	60N	25E
Helvellyn: mtn., Eng.	62	55N	3W
Helwan: Egypt	86	29N	31E
Hemel Hempstead: England	63	52N	1W
Hempstead: U.S.A.	35	41N	74W
Henderson: Ky., U.S.A.	47	38N	88W
Henderson: Nev., U.S.A.	48	36N	115W
Henderson: N.C., U.S.A.	47	36N	78W
Hengelo: Netherlands	74	52N	7E
Hengyang: China	95	27N	112E
Henlopen, C.: U.S.A.	47	39N	75W

Name	Page	Lat.	Long.
Henry, C.: U.S.A.	47	37N	76W
Henzada: Burma	92	17N	95E
Herat: Afghanistan	87	34N	62E
Hérault: r., France	73	44N	3E
Herberton: Australia	99	18S	145E
Hereford: & Co., England	63	52N	3W
Hereford: U.S.A.	46	35N	102W
Herford: W. Germany	74	52N	9E
Herisau: Switzerland	75	47N	9E
Hermitage: N.Z.	104	44S	170E
Herne: W. Germany	64	52N	7E
Herning: Denmark	71	56N	9E
Heroica Zitácuaro: Mexico	52	19N	100W
Herstal: Belgium	72	51N	6E
Hertford: & Co., Eng.	63	52N	0
Hervey Bay: Australia	100	25S	153E
Hexham: England	62	55N	2W
Heysham: England	62	54N	3W
Hiawatha: U.S.A.	49	40N	96W
Hibbing: U.S.A.	49	47N	93W
Hicksville: U.S.A.	35	41N	74W
Hidalgo del Parral: Mexico	52	27N	106W
Higashiosaka: Japan	93	35N	136E
High Atlas: mtns., Morocco	108	31N	7W
Highland: Reg., Scot.	62	57N	5W
Highland Park: Ill., U.S.A.	34	42N	87W
Highland Park: Mich., U.S.A.	33	42N	83W
Highlands, The: reg., Scotland	61	57N	5W
High Point: city, U.S.A.	47	36N	80W
High Veld: plat., S. Africa	111	30S	28E
High Wycombe: Eng.	112	52N	1W
Hiiumaa (Khumaa): i., U.S.S.R.	71	59N	23E
Hijaz: reg., Saudi Arabia	87	25N	39E
Hilden: W. Germany	64	51N	7E
Hildesheim: W. Ger.	74	52N	10E
Hillah: Iraq	87	32N	44E
Hillegom: Netherlands	74	52N	4E
Hilversum: Netherlands	74	52N	5E
Himachal Pradesh: State, India	88	32N	77E
Himeji: Japan	93	35N	135E
Hinckley: England	63	53N	1W
Hindu Kush: mtns., Afghanistan	85	36N	70E
Hirakata: Japan	93	35N	136E
Hiroshima: Japan	93	34N	132E
Hirson: France	72	50N	4E
Hispaniola: i., W. Indies	45	20N	70W
Hjørring: Denmark	71	57N	10E
Hobart: Australia	99	43S	147E
Hobbs: U.S.A.	46	32N	103W
Hoboken: Belgium	72	51N	4E
Hoboken: U.S.A.	35	41N	74W
Ho Chi Minh City (Saigon): Vietnam	92	11N	107E
Hodeida: Yemen	87	15N	43E
Hódmezövásárhely: Hungary	68	46N	20E
Hof: W. Germany	74	50N	12E
Hofei: China	94	32N	117E
Hofsjökull: volc., Ice.	70	65N	19W
Hohenlimburg: W. Germany	64	51N	8E
Hohe Rhön: mtns., W. Germany	74	50N	10E
Hohe Tauern: mtns., Austria	74	47N	12E
Hohsien: China	95	24N	112E
Hokang: China	90	47N	130E
Hokianga Harbour: bay, New Zealand	104	36S	173E
Hokitika: N.Z.	104	43S	171E
Hokkaido: i., Japan	93	43N	143E
Holbaek: Denmark	71	56N	12E
Holbrook: Australia	101	36S	147E
Holderness: penin., England	62	54N	0
Holdrege: U.S.A.	49	40N	99W
Holguin: Cuba	53	21N	76W
Holland: district, Eng.	63	53N	0
Holland: U.S.A.	47	43N	86W
Holland: see Netherlands			
Hollick-Kenyon Plat.: Antarctica	116	78S	105W
Hollywood: California, U.S.A.	37	34N	118W
Hollywood: Florida, U.S.A.	47	26N	80W
Holstebro: Denmark	71	56N	9E
Holyhead: Wales	63	53N	5W
Holy I.: England	62	56N	2W
Holy I.: Wales	63	53N	5W
Homberg: W. Germany	64	51N	7W
Home Hill: Australia	100	20S	147E
Homestead: U.S.A.	47	25N	80W
Homs: Libya	86	33N	14E
Homs: Syria	86	35N	37E
Hon: Libya	86	29N	16E
Honan: prov., China	94	34N	113E
HONDURAS: cap. Tegucigalpa	44/5	15N	87W
Honefoss: Norway	71	60N	10E
Honfleur: France	72	49N	0
HONG KONG: cap. Victoria	95	22N	114E
Honiton: England	63	51N	3W
Honshu: i., Japan	93	36N	137E
Hood, Mt.: U.S.A.	48	45N	122W
Hood Point: Australia	100	34S	120E
Hooghly: r., India	88	22N	88E
Hook I.: Australia	100	20S	149E
Hook of Holland: Netherlands	74	52N	4E
Hopeh: prov., China	94	39N	116E
Hopewell: U.S.A.	47	37N	77W
Hopkinsville: U.S.A.	47	37N	87W
Hoppo (Limchow): China	95	22N	109E
Hoquiam: U.S.A.	48	47N	124W
Hormuz, Str. of: Iran/Oman	87	27N	56E
Horn, Cape: Chile	55	56S	67W
Horncastle: England	63	53N	0
Hornell: U.S.A.	50	42N	78W
Horsham: Australia	101	37S	142E
Horsham: England	63	51N	0
Hoshangabad: India	88	23N	78E
Hot Springs: Ark., U.S.A.	46	35N	93W
Hot Springs: S. Dakota, U.S.A.	49	43N	104W
Houma: U.S.A.	46	30N	91W
Hounslow: England	112	51N	0
Hourtin, Étg. d': France	73	45N	1W
Houston: U.S.A.	46	30N	95W
Hovd: Mongolia	83	48N	91E
Howe, Cape: Australia	101	37S	150E
Howrah: see Hāora			
Hoy: i., Scotland	61	59N	3W
Hsichang: China	90	28N	102E
Hsinchu: Taiwan	95	25N	121E
Hsin-hai-lien: China	94	35N	120E
Hsinhsiang: China	94	35N	114E
Hsiyuan: China	114	40N	116E
Hualien: Taiwan	95	24N	121E
Huallaga: r., Peru	54	8S	76W
Huambo (Nova Lisboa): Angola	111	13S	16E
Huancavelica: Peru	54	13S	75W
Huancayo: Peru	54	12S	75W
Hubli: India	88	15N	75E
Huchow: China	95	31N	120E
Huddersfield: England	62	54N	2W
Hudson: r., U.S.A.	51	42N	74W
Hué: Vietnam	92	16N	107E
Huelva: Spain	67	37N	7W
Huesca: Spain	67	42N	0
Hufhuf: Saudi Arabia	87	25N	49E
Hughenden: Australia	99	21S	144E
Huhehot: China	94	41N	112E
Huitse: China	90	26N	103E
Hull: see Kingston upon Hull			
Hüls: W. Germany	64	51N	6E
Hulun Chih: l., China	90	49N	118E
Humber: r., England	62	54N	0
Humboldt: r., U.S.A.	48	40N	119W
Humboldt Glacier: Greenland	13	80N	63W
Hume, Lake: Australia	101	36S	147E
Hunan: Prov., China	95	27N	111E
HUNGARY: cap. Budapest	68	47N	20E
Hunger Steppe: U.S.S.R.	85	47N	70E
Hunsrück: mtns., W. Germany	74	50N	7E
Huntingdon: England	63	52N	0
Huntington: Indiana, U.S.A.	47	41N	86W
Huntington: N.Y., U.S.A.	51	41N	73W
Huntington: W. Va., U.S.A.	47	38N	82W
Huntly: N.Z.	104	37S	175E
Huntsville: Alabama, U.S.A.	47	35N	87W
Huntsville: Texas, U.S.A.	46	31N	96W
Hupeh: Prov., China	95	31N	112E
Huron: U.S.A.	49	44N	98W
Huron, Lake: U.S.A./Canada	20	45N	83W
Hürth: W. Germany	64	51N	7E
Hurunui: r., N.Z.	104	43S	172E
Huskvarna: Sweden	71	58N	14E
Hutchinson: U.S.A.	49	38N	98W
Hutt: N.Z.	104	41S	175E
Hwainan: China	94	33N	117E
Hwaining: see Anking			
Hwaiyang: China	94	34N	115E
Hwangshih: China	95	30N	115E
Hwang (Yellow): r., China	94	41N	110E
Hyderabad: & reg. India	88	17N	78E
Hyderabad: Pakistan	88	25N	68E
Hyères: France	73	43N	6E
Hyères, Îles d': France	73	43N	6E
Iaşi: Romania	68	47N	28E
Ibadan: Nigeria	108	7N	4E
Ibagué: Colombia	54	4N	75W
Ibaraki: Japan	93	35N	136E
Ibiza: i. & town, Balearic Is.	67	39N	2E
Ica: Peru	54	14S	76W
ICELAND: cap. Reykjavik	70	—	—
Ichang: China	95	31N	111E
Ichikawa: Japan	114	36N	140E
Ichinomiya: Japan	93	35N	137E
Idaho: State, U.S.A.	48	44N	115W
Idaho Falls: city, U.S.A.	48	43N	112W
Igarka: U.S.S.R.	83	67N	86E
Iglesias: Sardinia	67	39N	8E
Iguala de la Independencia: Mexico	52	18N	100W
Ijmuiden: Netherlands	74	52N	4E
Ijssel: r., Netherlands	74	52N	6E
Ijsselmeer (Zuider Zee): Netherlands	74	53N	5E
Ikaria: i., Greece	69	38N	26E
Île de France: Old Prov., France	72	49N	2E
Ilford: England	112	51N	0
Ilfracombe: England	63	51N	4W
Ilhéus: Brazil	54	15S	39W
Iliamna Lake: U.S.A.	12	59N	155W
Ilkley: England	62	54N	2W
Illimani: mtn., Bolivia	54	17S	67W
Illinois: State, U.S.A.	49	40N	90W
Il'men', L.: U.S.S.R.	84	58N	32E
Ilmenau: E. Germany	74	51N	11E
Iloilo: Philippines	93	11N	122E
Imabari: Japan	93	34N	133E
Imatra: Finland	70	61N	29E
Imperia: Italy	75	44N	8E
Imphal: India	89	25N	94E
Inari: l., Finland	70	69N	28E
Inchon: S. Korea	90	37N	127E
Indaw: Burma	90	24N	96E
Independence: U.S.A.	49	37N	96W
INDIA (Bharat): cap. Delhi	88/9	—	—
Indiana: State, U.S.A.	47	40N	86W
Indianapolis: U.S.A.	47	40N	86W
Indian Ocean	89	—	—
Indigirka: r., U.S.S.R.	83	68N	146E
INDONESIA: cap. Djakarta	91	5S	115E
Indore: India	88	23N	76E
Indre: r., France	73	47N	1E
Indus: r., S.W. Asia	88	26N	68E
Ingolstadt: W. Germany	75	49N	11E
Inhambane: Moz.	111	24S	35E
Inhaminga: Moz.	111	18S	35E
Inishowen Penin. R. of Ireland	61	55N	7W
Inkerman: hist., U.S.S.R.	84	45N	34E
Inkster: U.S.A.	33	42N	83W
Inn: r., W. Ger./Austria	75	47N	12E
Inner Mongolian A.R.: China	89	42N	112E
Innsbruck: Austria	75	47N	11E
Inowrocław: Poland	68	53N	18E
Interlaken: Switzerland	75	47N	8E
International Falls: city, U.S.A.	49	48N	93W
Inverary: Scotland	62	56N	5W
Invercargill: N.Z.	104	46S	168E
Inverell: Australia	101	30S	151E
Inverness: Scotland	61	57N	4W
Investigator Strait: Australia	101	35S	137E
Ioannina (Yanina): Greece	69	40N	21E
Iona: i., Scotland	62	56N	6W
Ionian Is.: Greece	69	38N	20E
Ionian Sea	69	38N	18E
Ios: i., Greece	69	37N	25E
Iowa: State, U.S.A.	49	42N	93W
Iowa City: U.S.A.	49	42N	92W
Ipin: China	90	29N	105E
Ipoh: Malaysia	92	5N	101E
Ipswich: Australia	100	28S	153E
Ipswich: England	63	52N	1E
Ipswich: U.S.A.	51	43N	71W
Iquique: Chile	54	20S	70W
Iquitos: Peru	54	4S	73W
Iráklion (Candia): Crete	69	35N	25E
IRAN: cap. Tehrān	87	—	—
IRAQ: cap. Baghdād	87	33N	44E
Ira puato: Mexico	52	21N	101W
IRELAND, REPUBLIC OF: cap. Dublin	61	—	—
Irish Sea	61	53N	5W
Irkutsk: U.S.S.R.	83	52N	105E
Iron Gates: gorge, Yugo./Rom.	69	45N	23E
Iron Knob: town, Australia	101	33S	137E
Iron Mt.: U.S.A.	48	43N	117W
Iron Mountain: city, U.S.A.	49	46N	88W
Ironwood: U.S.A.	43	46N	90W
Irawaddy: r., Burma	92	24N	96E
Irtysh: r., U.S.S.R.	85	57N	73E
Irvine: Scotland	62	56N	5W
Isafjördhur: Iceland	70	66N	23W
Isalmi: Finland	70	64N	27E
Isar: r., W. Germany	75	48N	11E
Isarco: r., Italy	75	47N	12E
Ise: Japan	93	34N	137E
Iseo, L.: Italy	75	46N	10E
Isère: r., France	73	45N	5E
Iserlohn: W. Germany	74	51N	8E
Isfahan: Iran	87	33N	52E
Ishim: r., U.S.S.R.	85	54N	67E
Ishimbay: U.S.S.R.	84	53N	56E
Ishpeming: U.S.A.	49	46N	88W
Isiro: Zaire	110	3N	28E
Iskenderun: Turkey	86	37N	36E
ISLAMABAD: Pakistan	88	34N	73E
Islay: i., Scotland	62	55N	6W
Ismailia: Egypt	86	30N	32E
Isna: Egypt	86	25N	33E
Isonzo: r., Yugo./Italy	75	46N	14E
ISRAEL: cap. Jerusalem	86	32N	35E
Issigeac: France	73	45N	1E
Issoudun: France	73	47N	2E
Issyk Kul': l., U.S.S.R.	85	42N	77E
Istanbul: Turkey	86	41N	29E
Istria (Istra): penin., Yugoslavia	75	45N	14E
Itabuna: Brazil	54	15S	39W
ITALY: cap. Rome	68/9	—	—
Itami: Japan	93	35N	135E
Itchen: r., England	63	51N	1W
Ithaca: U.S.A.	50	42N	77W
Ivanhoe: Australia	101	33S	144E
Ivano-Frankovsk: U.S.S.R.	68	49N	25E
Ivanovo: U.S.S.R.	84	57N	41E
Ivdel': U.S.S.R.	85	61N	60E
Iviza: see Ibiza	65	39N	2E
IVORY COAST: cap. Abidjan	108	7N	6W
Izhevsk: U.S.S.R.	84	57N	53E
Izmir: Turkey	86	38N	27E
Izmit: Turkey	86	41N	30E
Izu-Shotō: is., Japan	93	34N	139E
Jabal Akhdhar: mt., Oman	87	24N	57E
Jabalpur: India	88	23N	80E
Jabal Shammar: plat., Saudi Arabia	87	27N	41E
Jabal Tuwaiq: mtns., Saudi Arabia	87	25N	46E
Jaca: Spain	67	43N	1W
Jackson: Mich., U.S.A.	47	42N	84W
Jackson: Miss., U.S.A.	46	32N	90W
Jackson: Tenn., U.S.A.	47	36N	89W
Jackson Bay: N.Z.	104	44S	169E
Jacksonville: Fla., U.S.A.	47	30N	82W
Jacksonville: Ill., U.S.A.	49	40N	90W
Jacobabad: Pakistan	88	28N	69E
Jaén: Spain	67	38N	4W
Jaffa-Tel Aviv: Israel	86	32N	35E
Jaffa, C.: Australia	101	37S	140E
Jaffna: Sri Lanka	88	10N	80E
Jaipur: India	88	27N	76E
Jaisalmer: India	88	27N	71E
Jakarta: see Djakarta			
Jalalabad: Afghanistan	88	34N	71E
Jalapa Enríquez: Mexico	53	20N	97W
JAMAICA: cap. Kingston	53	18N	77W
Jambin: Australia	100	24S	150E
Jambol: Bulgaria	69	12N	27E
James: r., S. Dakota U.S.A.	49	44N	98W
James: r., Va., U.S.A.	47	37N	78W
Jamestown: N.Y., U.S.A.	47	42N	79W
Jamestown: N. Dakota, U.S.A.	49	47N	99W
Jammu: & Kashmir: disputed State: India	88	35N	77E
Jamnagar: India	88	22N	70E
Jamshedpur: India	88	23N	86E
Janesville: U.S.A.	49	43N	89W
JAPAN: cap. Tokyo	93	—	—
Japan, Sea of	90	40N	135E
Japan Trench: Pacific Ocean	102	35N	145E
Japen: i., Indonesia	91	2S	136E
Jasło: Poland	68	50N	22E
Jauf: Saudi Arabia	87	30N	40E
Java: i. & sea, Indon.	91	7S	110E
Jaxartes: r., see Syr Dar'ya			
Jebba: Nigeria	108	9N	4E
Jebel Aulia Dam: Sudan	86	15N	32E
Jebel el Akhdar: hills, Libya	86	32N	21E
Jedburgh: Scotland	62	55N	3W
Jefferson City: U.S.A.	49	39N	92W
Jehol: see Chengteh			
Jena: E. Germany	74	51N	12E
Jerez: Spain	67	37N	6W
Jericho: Jordan	86	31N	35E
Jersey: i., Channel Isles	63	Inset	
Jersey City: U.S.A.	35	41N	74W
JERUSALEM: Israel/Jordan	86	32N	35E
Jervis Bay: Australia	101	35S	151E

	Page	Lat.	Long.
Jessore: Bangladesh	88	23N	89E
Jesup: U.S.A.	47	32N	82W
Jhansi: India	88	25N	79E
Jhelum: *r.*, Pakistan	88	31N	72E
Jibhalanta: *see* Uliastay			
Jidda: Saudi Arabia	87	22N	39E
Jiménez: Mexico	52	27N	105W
João Pessoa: Brazil	54	7S	35W
Jodhpur: India	88	26N	73E
Joensuu: Finland	70	63N	30E
Jofra Oasis: Libya	86	30N	15E
Jogjakarta: Indon.	91	8S	110E
Johannesburg: S. Afr.	111	26S	28E
Johnson City: U.S.A.	47	36N	82W
Johnstown: U.S.A.	50	40N	79W
Johor Bahru: Malaysia	92	1N	104E
Joliet: U.S.A.	34	42N	88W
Jolo: *i.*, Philippines	91	6N	121E
Jonesboro: U.S.A.	[illegible]	[illegible]	91W
Jurua: *r.*, Brazil	[illegible]	[illegible]	[illegible]
Jussey: France	72	48N	6E
Juticalpa: Honduras	53	15N	86W
Jyekundo: *see* Yushu			
Jylland: *penin.*, Den.	71	36N	9E
Jyväskylä: Finland	70	62N	26E
K2: *mtn.*, India	88	36N	77E
Kabaena: *i.*, Indonesia	91	5S	122E
KABUL: Afghanistan	88	35N	69E
Kabwe: Zambia	111	15S	29E
Kadina: Australia	101	34S	138E
Kaduna: Nigeria	108	11N	7E
Kafue: & *r.*, Zambia	111	16S	28E
Kagoshima: Japan	93	32N	131E
Kahsing: China	95	31N	121E
Kaieteur Falls: Guyana	54	5N	59W
Kaifeng: China	94	35N	115E
Kai Is.: Indonesia	91	6S	133E
Kaikohe: N.Z.	104	35S	174E
Kaikoura: & *Range*, N.Z.	104	42S	173E
Kailas Range: China	88	32N	81E
Kaimanawa Mts.: New Zealand	104	39S	176E
Kaipara Harbour: New Zealand	93	36S	174E
Kaiserslautern: W. Ger.	74	49N	8E
Kaitangata: N.Z.	104	46N	170E
Kajaani: Finland	70	64N	28E
Kakinada: India	88	17N	82E
Kakogawa: Japan	93	35N	135E
Kalachinsk: U.S.S.R.	85	55N	75E
Kalahari Desert: Botswana	111	24S	23E
Kalamata: Greece	69	37N	22E
Kalamazoo: U.S.A.	47	42N	86W
Kalat: Pakistan	88	29N	67E
Kalemie: Zaire	110	6S	29E
Kalgan: *see* Changkiakow			
Kalgoorlie: Australia	100	31S	122E
Kalinin: U.S.S.R.	84	57N	36E
Kaliningrad: U.S.S.R.	68	55N	20E
Kalispell: U.S.A.	48	48N	114W
Kalisz: Poland	68	52N	18E
Kalmar: Sweden	71	57N	16E
Kalomo: Zambia	111	17S	26E
Kaluga: U.S.S.R.	84	55N	36E
Kama: *r.*, U.S.S.R.	84	55N	51E
Kamakura: Japan	114	35N	140E
Kamaran Is.: Yemen P.D.R.	87	15N	42E
Kamchatka: *penin.*, U.S.S.R.	83	55N	160E
Kamchatka Bay: U.S.S.R.	83	55N	163E
Kamenskoye: U.S.S.R.	83	63N	165E
Kamensk-Uralskiy: U.S.S.R.	85	57N	62E
Kamet: *mtn.*, India/China	88	31N	79E
Kamina: Zaire	110	9S	25E
KAMPALA: Uganda	110	0	33E
Kampen: Netherlands	74	53N	6E
Kamp-Lintfort: W. Ger.	64	52N	7W
Kamyshlov: U.S.S.R.	85	57N	63E
Kananga: Zaire	110	6S	22E
Kanazawa: Japan	93	37N	137E
Kanchanaburi: Thailand	92	14N	99E
Kanchow: China	95	26N	115E
Kandagach: U.S.S.R.	85	49N	57E
Kandahar: Afghanistan	88	32N	66E
Kandalaksha: U.S.S.R.	70	67N	32E
Kandi: Benin	108	11N	3E
Kandla: India	88	23N	70E
Kandy: Sri Lanka	88	7N	81E
Kangaroo I.: Australia	101	36S	137E
Kangchenjunga: *mtn.*, Nepal/India	89	27N	88E
Kangean Is.: Indonesia	91	7S	116E
Kangting: China	90	30N	102E
Kanin, C.: U.S.S.R.	82	68N	45E
Kankakee: U.S.A.	47	41N	88W
Kankan: Guinea	108	10N	9W
Kannapolis: U.S.A.	47	35N	80W
Kano: Nigeria	108	12N	8E
Kanoya: Japan	93	31N	131E
Kanpur: India	88	26N	80E
Kansas: *State*, U.S.A.	46	39N	98W
Kansas City: Kansas, U.S.A.	46	39N	95W
Kansas City: Mo., U.S.A.	46	39N	95W
Kansk: U.S.S.R.	85	56N	95E
Kansu: *Prov.*, China	94	35N	105E
Kaohsiung: Taiwan	95	23N	120E
Kapellen: W. Germany	64	51N	7E
Kaposvár: Hungary	68	46N	18E
Kapurthala: India	88	31N	75E
Kara: U.S.S.R.	82	69N	65E
Kara-Bogaz-Gol: *l.*, U.S.S.R.	84	42N	54E
Karabük: Turkey	86	41N	32E
Karachi: Pakistan	88	25N	67E
Karaganda: U.S.S.R.	85	50N	73E
Karakoram Pass: China/India	88	35N	76E
Kara-Kum: *desert*, U.S.S.R.	84	39N	60E
Karasberg: S.W. Africa (Namibia)	111	28S	19E
Kara Sea: U.S.S.R.	82	72N	62E
Kara-Tau: *mtns.*, U.S.S.R.	85	44N	68E
Karaul: U.S.S.R.	83	70N	83E
Karbalā: Iraq	87	33N	44E
Kargil: India	88	35N	76E
Kariba: *l., dam & gorge*, Rhod. (Zim.)/Zambia	111	17S	29E
Karibib: S.W. Africa (Namibia)	111	22S	16E
Karl-Marx-Stadt: E. Germany	74	51N	13E
Karlovac: Yugoslavia	69	45N	16E
Karlovy Vary: Czech.	69	50N	13E
Karlshamn: Sweden	71	56N	15E
Karlskoga: Sweden	71	59N	15E
Karlskrona: Sweden	71	56N	16E
Karlsruhe: W. Germany	74	49N	8E
Karlstad: Sweden	71	59N	13E
Karnataka: *State*, India	88	14N	76E
Kárpathos: *i.*, Greece	69	36N	27E
Kartaly: U.S.S.R.	85	53N	60E
Karwar: India	88	15N	74E
Kasai: *r.*, Zaire	110	4S	19E
Kasempa: Zambia	111	13S	26E
Kasese: Uganda	110	0	30E
Kāshān: Iran	87	34N	51E
Kashgar: China	82	39N	76E
Kaskaskia: *r.*, U.S.A.	49	39N	89W
Kasli: U.S.S.R.	85	56N	61E
Kásos: *i. & str.*, Greece	69	35N	27E
Kassala: Sudan	86	15N	36E
Kassala: *Prov.*, Sudan	86	20N	35E
Kassel: W. Germany	74	51N	9E
Katahdin, Mt.: U.S.A.	15	46N	69W
Katanning: Australia	100	34S	118E
Katase: Japan	114	35N	139E
Katherine: Australia	98	14S	133E
Kathiawar: *penin.*, India	88	22N	71E
KATMANDU: Nepal	88	28N	85E
Katoomba: Australia	101	34S	150E
Katowice: Poland	68	50N	19E
Katrineholm: Sweden	71	59N	16E
Kattegat: *str.*, Denmark/Sweden	71	57N	11E
Kauai: *i.*, Pacific O.	103	22N	160W
Kaufman: U.S.A.	46	33N	96W
Kaunas: U.S.S.R.	68	55N	24E
Kaura Namoda: Nigeria	108	13N	7E
Kavacha: U.S.S.R.	83	60N	170E
Kavālla: Greece	69	41N	24E
Kavieng: Papua New Guinea	99	3S	151E
Kawagoe: Japan	93	36N	139E
Kawaguchi: Japan	114	36N	140E
Kawasaki: Japan	114	36N	140E
Kawerau: N.Z.	104	38S	177E
Kayes: Mali	108	14N	11W
Kayseri: Turkey	86	39N	36E
Kazach'ye: U.S.S.R.	83	71N	136E
Kazakh S.S.R.: U.S.S.R.	84/5	—	—
Kazakh Uplands: U.S.S.R.	85	49N	75E
Kazalinsk: U.S.S.R.	85	46N	62E
Kazan': U.S.S.R.	84	56N	49E
Kazanlák: Bulgaria	69	43N	25E
Kéa: *i.*, Greece	69	38N	24E
Kearney: U.S.A.	49	41N	99W
Kebbi: *r.*, Nigeria	108	13N	4E
Kecskemét: Hungary	68	47N	20E
Keene: U.S.A.	51	43N	72W
Keetmanshoop: S.W. Africa (Namibia)	111	26S	18E
Keflavik: Iceland	70	64N	22W
Keighley: England	62	54N	2W
Kelang: Malaysia	92	3N	101E
Kelso: U.S.A.	48	46N	123W
Kemerovo: U.S.S.R.	85	55N	86E
Kemi: & *r.*, Finland	70	66N	25E
Kempsey: Australia	101	31S	153E
Kendal: England	62	54N	3W
Kenitra: Morocco	108	34N	7W
Kenmare: R. of Ireland	61	52N	10W
Kenmore: U.S.A.	49	49N	102W
Kennebec: *r.*, U.S.A.	15	45N	70W
Kennett: U.S.A.	46	36N	90W
Kennewick: U.S.A.	48	46N	119W
Kennicott: U.S.A.	12	62N	143W
Kenosha: U.S.A.	47	43N	88W
Kensington: England	112	51N	0
Kent: *Co.*, England	63	51N	1E
Kentucky: *State*, U.S.A.	47	37N	85W
Kentucky L.: U.S.A.	47	36N	88W
KENYA: *cap.* Nairobi	110	0	37E
Kenya, Mt.: Kenya	110	0	37E
Keokuk: U.S.A.	46	40N	92W
Keppel Bay: Australia	100	23S	151E
Kerala: *State*, India	88	10N	76E
Kerang: Australia	101	36S	144E
Kerch': U.S.S.R.	84	45N	36E
Kerki: U.S.S.R.	85	38N	65E
Kerkira: *i. & town*, Greece	69	40N	20E
Kermadec Islands: & *trench*, Pacific Ocean	102	30S	179W
Kermān: Iran	87	30N	57E
Kermānshāh: Iran	87	34N	47E
Kerulen: *r.*, Mongolia	90	48N	111E
Keswick: England	62	55N	3W
Ketchikan: U.S.A.	24	55N	132W
Kettering: England	63	52N	1W
Kewanee: U.S.A.	49	41N	90W
Keweenaw Penin.: U.S.A.	49	47N	88W
Key West: U.S.A.	47	25N	82W
Khabarovsk: U.S.S.R.	83	48N	135E
Khairpur: Pakistan	88	28N	69E
Khalkís: Greece	69	38N	24E
Khandwa: India	88	22N	76E
Khaniá: (Canea) Crete	69	35N	24E
Khanka, L.: U.S.S.R.	83	45N	133E
Khan Tengri: *mtn.*, China	85	42N	80E
Khanty-Mansiysk: U.S.S.R.	85	61N	69E
Kharagpur: India	88	22N	87E
Kharan Kalat: Pakistan	88	28N	65E
Khārg: *i.*, Persian G.	87	29N	50E
Khar'kov: U.S.S.R.	84	50N	36E
KHARTOUM: Sudan	86	16N	33E
Khasi Hills: India	89	26N	91E
Khatanga: U.S.S.R.	83	72N	102E
Khemmarat: Thailand	92	16N	105E
Kherson: U.S.S.R.	84	47N	33E
Khimki: U.S.S.R.	114	55N	38E
Khiumaa: *i.*, *see* Hiiumaa			
Khiva: U.S.S.R.	85	41N	60E
Khodzheyli: U.S.S.R.	85	42N	60E
Kholmsk: U.S.S.R.	83	47N	142E
Khorāsān: *reg.*, Iran	87	35N	57E
Khorog: U.S.S.R.	85	37N	72E
Khorramshahr: Iran	87	30N	48E
Khrom-Tau: U.S.S.R.	85	50N	58E
Khuzestān: *reg.*, Iran	87	31N	50E
Khyber Pass: Afghan./Pak.	88	34N	71E
Kiamusze: China	90	47N	130E
Kian: China	95	27N	115E
Kiangsi: *Prov.*, China	95	27N	115E
Kiangsu: *Prov.*, China	94	33N	119E
Kiangtu: China	95	32N	119E
Kidderminster: England	63	52N	2W
Kiel: W. Germany	68	54N	10E
Kiel Canal: W. Germany	74	54N	10E
Kielce: Poland	68	51N	21E
Kiev: U.S.S.R.	68	51N	30E
Kigoma: Tanzania	110	5S	30E
Kii-suidō: *chan.*, Japan	93	34N	135E
Kildare: R. of Ireland	61	53N	7W
Kildonan: Rhodesia (Zimbabwe)	111	17S	31E
Kilimanjaro: *mt.*, Tanzania	110	3S	37E
Kilkeel: N. Ireland	62	54N	6W
Kilkenny: R. of Ireland	61	53N	7W
Killarney: R. of Ireland	61	52N	9W
Kilmarnock: Scotland	62	56N	4W
Kilrush: R. of Ireland	61	53N	9W
Kimberley: S. Africa	111	29S	25E
Kindu: Zaire	110	3S	26E
Kingaroy: Australia	100	27S	152E
King I.: Australia	99	40S	144E
Kingman: Arizona, U.S.A.	48	35N	114W
Kingman: Kansas, U.S.A.	49	38N	98W
King's Lynn: England	63	53N	0
Kingsport: U.S.A.	47	37N	84W
Kingston: Australia	101	37S	140E
KINGSTON: Jamaica	53	18N	77W
Kingston: N.Z.	104	45S	169E
Kingston: U.S.A.	51	42N	74W
Kingston upon Hull: England	63	54N	0
Kingston-upon-Thames: England	112	51N	0
Kingsville: U.S.A.	46	28N	98W
King William's Town: S. Africa	111	33S	27E
Kinhwa: China	95	29N	120E
Kinleith: N.Z.	104	38S	176E
Kinsha: *r.*, *see* Yangtze			
KINSHASA: Zaire	110	4S	15E
Kinston: U.S.A.	47	35N	78W
Kintyre: *penin.*, Scot.	62	55N	6W
Kirchheim: W. Germany	75	49N	9E
Kirgiz S.S.R.: U.S.S.R.	85	42N	75E
Kirin: China	90	44N	126E
Kirkcaldy: Scotland	62	56N	3W
Kirkenes: Norway	70	70N	30E
Kirklareli: Turkey	69	42N	27E
Kirksville: U.S.A.	49	40N	93W
Kirkuk: Iraq	87	35N	44E
Kirkwall: Scotland	61	59N	3W
Kirov: U.S.S.R.	84	59N	50E
Kirovabad: U.S.S.R.	84	41N	46E
Kirovograd: U.S.S.R.	84	49N	32E
Kirovsk: U.S.S.R.	85	38N	60E
Kiruna: Sweden	70	68N	20E
Kisangani: Zaire	110	1N	25E
Kisarazu: Japan	93	35N	140E
Kishinev: U.S.S.R.	84	47N	29E
Kishi Wada: Japan	93	34N	135E
Kishm: Afghanistan	85	37N	70E
Kiskunfélegyháza: Hungary	68	47N	20E
Kissimmee: *r.*, U.S.A.	47	27N	81W
Kisumu: Kenya	110	0	35E
Kithira: *i.*, Greece	69	36N	23E
Kithnos: *i.*, Greece	69	37N	24E
Kitwe: Zambia	111	13S	28E
Kitzbühel Alps: Austria	75	47N	12E
Kiuchüan: China	90	40N	99E
Kiukiang: China	95	30N	116E
Kivak: U.S.S.R.	83	65N	174W
Kivu, L.: Zaire	110	2S	29E
Kızılırmak: *r.*, Turkey	86	41N	34E
Kjølen Mts.: Nor./Sweden	75	65N	15E
Kjustendil: Bulgaria	69	42N	23E
Klagenfurt: Austria	75	47N	14E
Klaipeda: U.S.S.R.	71	56N	21E
Klamath Falls: U.S.A.	48	42N	122W
Klerksdorp: S. Africa	111	27S	26E
Klipplaat: S. Africa	111	33S	24E
Knokke: Belgium	72	51N	3E
Knoxville: U.S.A.	47	36N	84W
Kobe: Japan	93	35N	135E
København: *see* Copenhagen			
Koblenz: W. Germany	74	50N	8E
Kobrin: U.S.S.R.	68	52N	24E
Kōchi: Japan	93	34N	134E
Kodiak I.: U.S.A.	12	57N	154W
Kodaira: Japan	114	36N	139E
Kodok: Sudan	109	10N	32E
Kōfu: Japan	93	36N	139E
Kohat: Pakistan	88	34N	71E
Kohima: India	89	26N	94E
Koganei: Japan	114	36N	140E
Kokand: U.S.S.R.	85	40N	71E
Kokchetav: U.S.S.R.	85	54N	70E
Kokkola: Finland	70	64N	23E
Kokomo: U.S.A.	47	41N	86W
Koko Nor: *see* Tsing Hai			
Kola Penin.: U.S.S.R.	82	67N	38E
Kolhapur: India	88	17N	74E
Köln: *see* Cologne			
Kolomna: U.S.S.R.	84	55N	39E
Kolomyya: U.S.S.R.	68	48N	25E
Kolyma Plain: U.S.S.R.	83	68N	155E
Kolyma Range: *see* Gydan Range			
Kolyuchin, Gulf of: U.S.S.R.	83	67N	175W
Kolyvan': U.S.S.R.	85	51N	83E
Komandor Is.: U.S.S.R.	83	55N	166E
Komárno: Czech.	68	48N	18E
Komatipoort: S. Africa	111	25S	32E
Komba: Zaire	110	3N	24E
Kompong Cham: Cambodia	92	11N	105E
Kompong Som			

Place	Page	Lat.	Long.
(Sihanoukville): Cambodia	92	10N	103E
Komsomol'sk-na-Amur: U.S.S.R.	83	51N	137E
Kongmoon: China	95	23N	113E
Kongola: Zaire	110	5S	27E
Kongsvinger: Norway	70	60N	12E
Konosha: U.S.S.R.	84	61N	40E
Konotop: U.S.S.R.	84	51N	33E
Konstanz: W. Germany	75	48N	9E
Konya: Turkey	86	38N	32E
Koppeh Dāgh: *range*, Iran/U.S.S.R.	85	38N	57E
Korçë: Albania	69	41N	21E
Korčula: *i.*, Yugoslavia	69	43N	17E
Kordofan: *Prov.*, Sudan	109	13N	30E
Kortrijk: Belgium	72	51N	3E
Kos: *i.*, Greece	69	37N	27E
Kosciusko, Mt.: Austl.	101	36N	148E
Kosh-Agach: U.S.S.R.	85	50N	89E
Kosi: *r.*, Nepal/India	88	26N	87E
Košice: Czech.	68	49N	21E
Kosovska Mitrovica: Yugoslavia	69	43N	21E
Kostroma: U.S.S.R.	84	57N	41E
Koszalin: Poland	68	54N	17E
Kota: India	88	25N	76E
Kota Bahru: Malaysia	92	6N	102E
Kota Kinabalu: Malaysia	91	6N	116E
Köthen: E. Germany	74	52N	12E
Kotka: Finland	71	60N	27E
Kotlas: U.S.S.R.	84	61N	47E
Kotri: Pakistan	88	25N	68E
Kounradskiy: U.S.S.R.	85	47N	75E
Kovel': U.S.S.R.	68	51N	25E
Kovrov: U.S.S.R.	84	56N	41E
Kowloon: Hong Kong	95	22N	114E
Kozáni: Greece	69	40N	22E
Kra, Isthmus of: Thailand	92	10N	99E
Kragujevac: Yugo.	69	44N	21E
Krakatau: *volc.*, Indonesia	91	6S	105E
Kraków: *see* Cracow			
Kraljevo: Yugoslavia	69	44N	21E
Kramfors: Sweden	70	63N	18E
Krasnodar: U.S.S.R.	84	45N	39E
Krasnovodsk: U.S.S.R.	84	40N	53E
Krasnoyarsk: U.S.S.R.	85	56N	96E
Krasnyy Kut: U.S.S.R.	84	51N	47E
Krasnyy Luch: U.S.S.R.	84	48N	38E
Kratié: Cambodia	92	12N	106E
Krefeld: W. Germany	64	51N	6E
Kremenchug: U.S.S.R.	84	49N	33E
Krishna: *r.*, India	88	17N	75E
Krishnagar: India	88	23N	88E
Kristiansand: Norway	71	58N	8E
Kristianstad: Sweden	71	56N	14E
Kristiansund: Norway	70	63N	8E
Kristinehamn: Sweden	71	59N	14E
Krivoy Rog: U.S.S.R.	84	48N	33E
Krk: *i.*, Yugoslavia	69	45N	15E
Kronotskiy Bay: U.S.S.R.	83	54N	162E
Kronštadt: U.S.S.R.	71	60N	30E
Kroonstad: S. Africa	111	27S	27E
Kruševac: Yugoslavia	69	44N	21E
KUALA LUMPUR: Malaysia	92	3N	102E
Kuala Terengganu: Malaysia	92	5N	103E
Kuantan: Malaysia	92	4N	103E
Kuban: *r.*, U.S.S.R.	84	45N	38E
Kuching: Malaysia	92	2N	110E
Kudat: Malaysia	91	7N	117E
Kufra Oases: Libya	109	25N	22E
Kufstein: Austria	75	48N	12E
Kükong: *see* Shaokuan			
Kulmbach: W. Germany	74	50N	11E
Kulunda Steppe: U.S.S.R.	85	53N	77E
Kulundinskoye, L.: U.S.S.R.	85	53N	80E
Kumagaya: Japan	32	36N	139E
Kumamoto: Japan	93	33N	131E
Kumasi: Ghana	108	7N	2W
Kunene: *r.*, Angola/S.W. Afr. (Namibia)	111	17S	13E
Kungrad: U.S.S.R.	85	43N	59E
Kunming: China	92	25N	103E
Kunshan: China	95	31N	121E
Kuntsevo: U.S.S.R.	114	55N	38E
Kuopio: Finland	70	63N	28E
Kupang: Indonesia	91	10S	124E
Kurdistan: *reg.*, Turkey/Iran	86/7	37N	45E
Kure: Japan	93	34N	133E
Kurgan: U.S.S.R.	85	55N	65E
Kuria Muria Is.: Arabian Sea	87	17N	56E
Kuril: *is.*, *Trench & Ridge*, Pacific O.	102	45N	150E
Kurnool: India	88	16N	78E
Kursk: U.S.S.R.	84	52N	36E
Kushka: U.S.S.R.	85	35N	62E
Kushva: U.S.S.R.	85	58N	60E
Kustanay: U.S.S.R.	85	53N	64E
Kütahya: Turkey	86	39N	30E
Kutaisi: U.S.S.R.	84	42N	42E
Kutno: Poland	68	52N	19E
KUWAIT: *cap.* Kuwait	87	29N	48E
Kuybyshev: U.S.S.R.	85	55N	78E
Kuybyshev: U.S.S.R.	84	53N	50E
Kuzbass: *reg.*, U.S.S.R.	85	55N	85E
Kwangsi Chuang: China	95	24N	108E
Kwanting Penin.: *see* Liaotung Penin.			
Kwantung: *Prov.*, China	95	23N	113E
Kweichow: *Prov.*, China	95	26N	107E
Kweichu: *see* Kweiyang			
Kweilin: China	95	25N	110E
Kweisui: *see* Huhehot			
Kweiyang (Kweichu): China	95	26N	107E
Kyle of Lochalsh: Scotland	61	57N	6W
Kynsna: S. Africa	111	34S	23E
Kyoga, L.: Uganda	110	2N	33E
Kyōga-saki: *pt.*, Japan	93	36N	135E
Kyongsong: *see* Seoul			
Kyōto: Japan	93	35N	136E
Kyūshū: *i.*, Japan	93	33N	131E
Kyūshū-sanchi: *mtns.*, Japan	93	32N	131E
Kyushu-Palau Ridge Pacific Ocean	102	20N	136E
Kyzl: U.S.S.R.	83	52N	95E
Kyzyl-Kum: *desert*, U.S.S.R.	85	43N	64E
Kzyl-Orda: U.S.S.R.	85	45N	65E
la Bastide: France	73	39N	7W
la Baule: France	72	47N	2W
Labe: *r.*, Czech.	74	50N	14E
Labuan: *i.*, Malaysia	91	5N	15E
Lacapelle-Marival: France	73	45N	2E
Lacaune, Mts. de: Fr.	73	44N	3E
Laccadive Sea: Indian Ocean	88	12N	73E
la Chârtre: France	73	47N	2E
la Chaux: France	73	46N	6E
la Chaux-de-Fonds: Switzerland	73	47N	7E
Lachlan: *r.*, Australia	101	33S	148E
la Ciotat: France	73	43N	6E
Laconia: U.S.A.	19	43N	72W
La Coruña (Corunna): Spain	67	43N	8W
Lacq: France	73	43N	1W
La Crosse: U.S.A.	49	44N	91W
Ladakh Ra.: India	88	34N	77E
Ladismith: S. Africa	111	34S	21E
Ladoga, L.: U.S.S.R.	84	61N	31E
Ladysmith: S. Africa	111	28S	30E
Lae: Papua New Guin.	99	7S	147E
La Fayette: U.S.A.	47	40N	87W
Lafayette: U.S.A.	46	30N	92W
la Flèche: France	72	48N	0
Laghouat: Algeria	108	34N	3E
LAGOS: Nigeria	108	6N	3E
La Grande: U.S.A.	48	45N	118W
La Grange: U.S.A.	47	33N	85W
La Guaira: Venez.	45	11N	67W
Laguna Madre: U.S.A.	46	26N	97W
LA HABANA (Havana): Cuba	53	23N	82W
Lahn: *r.*, W. Germany	74	50N	8E
Lahore: Pakistan	88	32N	75E
Lahr: W. Germany	75	48N	8E
Lahti: Finland	71	61N	26E
Lajes: Brazil	56	28S	50W
La Junta: U.S.A.	46	38N	104W
Lake Chad Basin: Chad	108	13N	15E
Lake Charles: *city*, U.S.A.	46	30N	93W
Lake City: U.S.A.	47	30N	83W
Lake District: England	62	54N	3W
Lakeland: U.S.A.	47	28N	82W
Lakhimpur: India	88	28N	81E
Lakshadweep: *is.*, Indian Ocean	89	12N	73E
La Linea: Spain	67	36N	5W
La Louvière: Belgium	72	50N	4E
Lamballe: France	72	48N	3W
Lambeth: England	112	51N	0
Lame Deer: U.S.A.	48	46N	107W
Lamesa: U.S.A.	46	33N	102W
Lamia: Greece	69	39N	22E
La Montaña: *reg.*, Peru	54	11S	72W
Lampedusa: *i.*, Italy	69	36N	13E
Lampeter: Wales	63	52N	4W
Lanak Pass: China/Kashmir	88	34N	80E
Lanark: Scotland	62	56N	4W
Lancashire: *Co.*, Eng.	62	54N	3W
Lancaster: England	62	54N	3W
Lancaster: Ohio, U.S.A.	47	40N	83W
Lancaster: Pa., U.S.A.	50	40N	76W
Lanchow: China	90	36N	104E
Landerneau: France	72	48N	4W
Land's End: England	63	50N	6W
Landshut: W. Germany	75	49N	12E
Langenberg: W. Ger.	64	51N	7E
Langenfeld: W. Ger.	64	51N	7E
Langeoog: *i.*, W. Ger.	74	54N	7E
Langon: France	73	45N	0
Langres: France	72	48N	5E
Langres, Plateau de: France	72/3	48N	5E
Langsa: Indonesia	92	4N	98E
Languedoc: *Old Prov.*, France	73	44N	4E
Lannion: France	72	49N	4W
Lans, Mts. de: France	73	45N	6E
Lansing: U.S.A.	47	43N	85W
Lanús: Argentina	56	35S	58W
Lanzarote: *i.*, Canary Islands	108	29N	13W
Lao Cai: Vietnam	92	23N	104E
Laon: France	72	50N	4E
LAOS: *cap.* Vientiane	92	18N	104E
Lapalisse: France	73	46N	4E
LA PAZ: Bolivia	54	16S	68E
La Plata: Argentina	56	35S	58W
Lappeenranta: Finland	71	61N	28E
Laptev Sea: U.S.S.R.	83	75N	125E
Laptev Str.: U.S.S.R.	83	73N	142E
L'Aquila: Italy	69	42N	13E
Larache: Morocco	67	35N	6W
Laramie: U.S.A.	49	41N	106W
Larche: France	73	44N	7E
Laredo: U.S.A.	46	28N	99W
Lārestān: *reg.*, Iran	87	28N	54E
Largs: Scotland	62	56N	5W
Lárisa: Greece	69	40N	22E
Larne: N. Ireland	61	55N	6W
la Rochelle: France	73	46N	1W
la Roche sur Yon: Fr.	73	47N	1W
La Romana: Dominican Rep.	45	19N	69W
Larsen Ice Shelf: Antarctica	116	68S	64W
Larzac, Causse du: Fr.	73	44N	3E
Las Cruces: U.S.A.	48	32N	107W
La Serena: Chile	55	30S	71W
La Seyne-sur-mer: France	73	43N	6E
Lashio: Burma	92	23N	98E
Las Palmas: Canary Islands	108	28N	15W
La Spezia: Italy	75	44N	10E
Lassalle: France	73	44N	4E
Lassen Peak: U.S.A.	48	41N	121W
Lastoursville: Gabon	110	1S	13E
Las Vegas: Nevada, U.S.A.	48	36N	115W
Las Vegas: N. Mexico, U.S.A.	49	36N	105W
Latakia: Syria	86	36N	36E
la Tour-du-Pin: France	73	46N	5E
Latvian S.S.R.: U.S.S.R.	84	57N	35E
Lauder: Scotland	62	56N	3W
Launceston: Australia	99	41S	147E
Laurel: Miss., U.S.A.	47	32N	89W
Laurel: Mont., U.S.A.	48	46N	109W
Lausanne: Switzerland	75	46N	7E
Laut: *i.*, Indonesia	91	4S	116E
Laval: France	72	48N	1W
Laverton: Australia	100	29S	123E
Lawgi: Australia	100	25S	151E
Lawrence: U.S.A.	51	43N	71W
Lawton: U.S.A.	46	35N	98W
Lead: U.S.A.	49	44N	104W
Leatherhead: England	112	51N	0
LEBANON: *cap.* Beirut	86	34N	36E
Lebanon: U.S.A.	47	36N	86W
le Blanc: France	73	47N	1E
le Cateau: France	72	50N	4E
Lecce: Italy	69	40N	18E
Lecco: Italy	75	46N	9E
Lech: *r.*, Austria/W. Germany	75	48N	11E
le Chambon-Feugerolles: France	73	45N	4E
le Conquet: France	72	48N	5W
le Creusot: France	73	47N	4E
le Croisic: France	72	47N	2W
Lectoure: France	73	44N	1E
Lee: *r.*, R. of Ireland	61	52N	9W
Leeds: England	62	54N	2W
Leeds: U.S.A.	49	48N	100W
Leek: England	63	53N	2W
Leer: W. Germany	74	53N	7E
Leeton: Australia	101	35S	146E
Leeuwarden: Neth.	74	53N	6E
Leeuwin, C.: Australia	100	34S	115E
Leeward Is.: W. Indies	45	17N	63W
Legaspi: Philippines	91	13N	124E
Leghorn (Livorno): Italy	75	44N	10E
Legnano: Italy	73	46N	9E
Leh: India	88	34N	78E
le Havre: France	72	50N	0
Lehrte: W. Germany	74	52N	10E
Leicester: & *Co.*, England	63	53N	1W
Leichhardt Ra.: Austl.	100	21S	148E
Leichlingen: W. Ger.	64	51N	7E
Leiden: Netherlands	74	52N	4E
Leigh Creek: *town*, Australia	101	31S	138E
Leipzig: W. Germany	74	51N	12E
Leith: Scotland	62	56N	3W
Lek: *r.*, Netherlands	74	52N	5E
Léman, L.: *see* Geneva, L. of			
le Mans: France	72	48N	0
le Monastier: France	73	45N	4E
Lena: *r.*, U.S.S.R.	83	64N	126E
Leninabad: U.S.S.R.	85	40N	70E
Leninakan: U.S.S.R.	84	41N	44E
Leningrad: U.S.S.R.	84	60N	30E
Leninogorsk: U.S.S.R.	85	50N	84E
Lenin Pk.: U.S.S.R.	85	39N	73E
Leninsk-Kuznetskiy: U.S.S.R.	85	55N	86E
Lens: France	72	50N	3E
Leoben: Austria	68	47N	15E
Leominster: England	63	52N	3W
Leominster: U.S.A.	51	43N	72W
León: Mexico	52	21N	102W
León: Spain	67	43N	6W
Leonora: Australia	100	29S	121E
Lepontine Alps: Switzerland/Italy	75	46N	8E
le Puy: France	73	45N	4E
Lérida: Spain	67	42N	1E
les Bains du Mont Dore: France	73	46N	3E
les Baux: France	73	44N	5E
Lesbos: *i.*, Greece	69	39N	26E
Les Ecréhou: *is.*, Channel Islands	63	*Inset*	
Les Landes: *reg.*, France	73	44N	1W
Les Monts Faucilles: France	72	48N	6E
LESOTHO: *cap.* Maseru	111	29S	27E
Les Sables d'Olonne: France	72	47N	2W
les Saintes Maries: France	73	43N	4E
Les Sept Îles: France	72	49N	3W
Lesser Antilles: *arch.*, West Indies	45	15N	62W
Letchworth: England	63	52N	0
Leticia: Colombia	54	4S	70W
le Touquet: France	72	51N	2E
le Tréport: France	72	50N	1E
Leuven: Belgium	72	51N	5E
Leveque, C.: Australia	98	17S	123E
le Verdon: France	73	46N	1W
Leverkusen: W. Ger.	64	51N	7E
le Vigan: France	73	44N	4E
Levittown: U.S.A.	35	41N	74W
Lewes: England	63	51N	0
Lewis: *i.*, Scotland	61	58N	7W
Lewisham: England	112	51N	0
Lewiston: Maine, U.S.A.	19	44N	70W
Lewiston: Wash., U.S.A.	48	46N	117W
Lewistown: U.S.A.	48	47N	109W
Lexington: Ken., U.S.A.	47	38N	84W
Lexington: Mass., U.S.A.	33	42N	71W
Leydsdorp: S. Africa	111	24S	31E
Leyre: *r.*, France	73	45N	1W
Leyte: *i.*, Philippines	91	11N	125E
Lhasa: China	89	30N	91E
l'Hospitalet: France	73	43N	2E
Liaoning: *Prov.*, China	94	41N	121E
Liaotung Bay: China	94	41N	121E
Liaotung Penin. (Kwantung Penin.): China	94	40N	123E
Liaoyang: China	94	42N	124E
Libby: U.S.A.	48	48N	116W
Liberal: U.S.A.	49	37N	101W
Liberec: Czech.	68	51N	15E
LIBERIA: *cap.* Monrovia	108	7N	10W
Libourne: France	73	45N	0
LIBREVILLE: Gabon	110	0	10E
LIBYA: *cap.* Tarabulus	108/9	—	—
Libyan Desert: Libya/Egypt	109	25N	25E
Libyan Plat.: Egypt	109	30N	27E
Lichfield: England	63	53N	2W
Lichtenburg: S. Africa	111	26S	26E
Licking: *r.*, U.S.A.	47	38N	84W
Lida: U.S.S.R.	68	54N	25E
Lidköping: Sweden	71	58N	13E
LIECHTENSTEIN: *cap.* Vaduz	75	47N	10E
Liège: Belgium	72	51N	6E
Lienz: Austria	75	47N	13E
Liepāja: U.S.S.R.	71	57N	21E
Lier: Belgium	72	51N	5E
Liestal: Switzerland	75	47N	8E
Liévin: France	72	50N	3E
Liffey: *r.*, R. of Ireland	61	53N	6W
Ligny: Belgium	72	50N	5E
Liguria: *Reg.*, Italy	75	44N	9E
Ligurian Apennines: Italy	75	44N	9E
Ligurian Sea: Italy	64	43N	9E
Likasi: Zaire	110	11S	27E
Lilla Baelt: *str.*, Den.	71	55N	10E
Lille: France	72	51N	3E
Lillehammer: Norway	71	61N	11E
LILONGWE: Malawi	111	14S	34E
LIMA: Peru	54	12S	77W
Lima: U.S.A.	47	41N	84W
Limagne: *reg.*, France	73	46N	3E
Limassol: Cyprus	86	40N	33E
Limburg: W. Germany	74	50N	8E
Limburg: *Prov.*,			

	Page	Lat.	Long.
Netherlands	74	51N	6E
Limerick: R. of Ireland	61	53N	9W
Limnos: i., Greece	69	40N	25E
Limoges: France	73	46N	1E
Limousin: Old Prov., France	73	46N	1E
Limpopo: r., Moz.	111	23S	33E
Linares: Mexico	52	25N	100W
Linares: Spain	67	38N	4W
Lincoln: & Co., Eng.	63	53N	1W
Lincoln: U.S.A.	49	41N	97W
Lincoln Park: U.S.A.	33	42N	83W
Lincolnwood: U.S.A.	34	42N	87W
Line Is.: Pacific O.	102/3	0	158W
Lingen: W. Germany	74	52N	7E
Lingga: i., Indonesia	91	0	105E
Linguère: Senegal	108	15N	15W
Linköping: Sweden	71	58N	16E
Linnhe, L.: Scotland	62	57N	5W
Linton: U.S.A.	49	46N	100W
Linz: Austria	75	48N	14E
Lions, G. of (Golfe du Lion): France	73	43N	4E
Lipari Is.: Italy	69	38N	15E
Lipetsk: U.S.S.R.	84	53N	40E
Lippstadt: W. Germany	74	52N	8E
LISBON: Portugal	67	39N	9W
Lisburn: N. Ireland	62	55N	6W
Lisburne, C.: U.S.A.	12	69N	166W
Lisianski: i., Pacific O.	102	27N	175W
Lisieux: France	72	49N	0
Lismore: Australia	101	29S	153E
Lithgow: Australia	101	33S	150E
Lithuanian S.S.R.: U.S.S.R.	84	55N	24E
Little Bitter Lake: Egypt	109	Inset	
Little Black: r., U.S.A.	30	67N	144W
Littlefield: U.S.A.	46	34N	102W
Little Karroo: plat., S. Africa	111	34S	22E
Little Minch: chan., Scotland	61	58N	7W
Little Rock: U.S.A.	46	35N	92W
Little St. Bernard Pass: France/Italy	75	46N	7E
Liuchow: China	95	24N	109E
Livermore, Mt.: U.S.A.	46	30N	105W
Liverpool: Australia	115	34S	151E
Liverpool: England	62	53N	3W
Liverpool Range: Australia	101	32N	150E
Livingstone: see Maramba			
Livingstone Falls: Zaire	110	5S	14E
Livorno: see Leghorn			
Livradois, Massif du: mtns., France	73	45N	3E
Lizard Point: England	63	50N	5W
Ljubljana: Yugoslavia	68	46N	14E
Ljungan: r., Sweden	70	62N	17E
Llandrindod Wells: Wales	63	52N	3W
Llandudno: Wales	63	53N	4W
Llanelli: Wales	63	52N	4W
Llangollen: Wales	63	53N	3W
Llanidloes: Wales	63	52N	4W
Llano Estacado: plat., U.S.A.	46	33N	103W
Llanos de Guarayos: plains, Bolivia	54	15S	63W
Lleyn: penin., Wales	63	53N	5W
Lo: r., China	94	36N	109E
Lobito: Angola	111	12S	14E
Lockerbie: Scotland	62	55N	3W
Lod (Lydda): Israel	86	32N	35E
Lodi: Italy	75	45N	9E
Łodź: Poland	68	52N	19E
Lofoten Is.: Norway	70	69N	15E
Logan: Utah, U.S.A.	48	42N	112W
Logan W. Va., U.S.A.	47	38N	82W
Logansport: U.S.A.	47	41N	86W
Logroño: Spain	67	42N	2W
Loir: r., France	72	48N	0
Loire: r., France	73	47N	1W
Lója: Ecuador	54	4S	79W
Lokchang: China	95	25N	113E
Lolland: i., Denmark	71	55N	11E
Lombard: U.S.A.	34	42N	88W
Lombardy: & Plain, Italy	75	45N	9E
Lomblen: i., Indonesia	91	8S	123E
Lombok: i. & str., Indonesia	91	8S	116E
LOMÉ: Togo	108	6N	1E
Lommel: Belgium	72	51N	5E
Lomond, L.: Scotland	62	56N	5W
LONDON: England	112	—	—
Londonderry: N. Ireland	61	55N	7W
Londrina: Brazil	56	23S	51W
Long Bay: U.S.A.	47	34N	79W
Long Beach: city, Calif. U.S.A.	37	34N	118W
Long Beach: city, N.Y. U.S.A.	35	41N	73W
Longford: R. of Ireland	61	54N	8W
Long I.: Australia	100	22S	150E
Long I.: The Bahamas	45	23N	75W
Long I.: U.S.A.	47	41N	73W
Longmont: U.S.A.	49	40N	105W

	Page	Lat.	Long.
Longreach: Australia	99	23S	144E
Longuyon: France	72	49N	6E
Longview: Oregon, U.S.A.	48	46N	123W
Longview: Texas, U.S.A.	46	33N	95W
Longwy: France	72	49N	6E
Lons-le-Saunier: Fr.	73	47N	6E
Lookout, C.: U.S.A.	47	35N	77W
Lopei: China	90	48N	131E
Lorain: U.S.A.	47	41N	83W
Lorca: Spain	67	38N	2W
Lord Howe Rise: Pacific Ocean	102	30S	163E
Lorestān: reg., Iran	87	33N	48E
Lorient: France	72	48N	3W
Lorne, Firth of: Scot.	62	56N	6W
Lörrach: W. Germany	75	48N	8E
Lorraine: Old Prov., France	72	49N	6E
Los Alamos: U.S.A.	48	36N	106W
Los Andes: Chile	55	33S	71W
Los Angeles: U.S.A.	37	—	—
Lossiemouth: Scotland	61	58N	3W
Lot: r., France	73	44N	1E
Lothian: Reg., Scotland	62	56N	4W
Loue: r., France	73	47N	6E
Loughborough: Eng.	63	53N	1W
Loughton: England	112	52N	0
Louislade Archipelago: Coral Sea	99	11S	153E
Louisiana: State, U.S.A.	46	33N	93W
Louis Trichardt: S. Africa	111	23S	30E
Louisville: U.S.A.	47	38N	86W
Loup City: U.S.A.	46	41N	99W
Lourdes: France	73	43N	0
Louth: England	63	53N	0
Louvain: see Leuven			
Lowell: U.S.A.	51	43N	71W
Lower California: Territ., Mexico	44	27N	113W
Lower Tunguska: r., U.S.S.R.	83	64N	95E
Lowestoft: England	63	52N	2E
Lowville: U.S.A.	19	44N	75W
Loyalty Is.: Pac. O.	102	20S	165E
Loyang: China	94	35N	112E
Lu (Salween): r., China	90	30N	97E
Lualaba: r., Zaïre	110	6S	26E
LUANDA: Angola	110	9S	13E
Luang Prabang: Laos	92	20N	102E
Luanshya: Zambia	111	13S	28E
Lubango (Sá da Bandiera): Angola	111	15S	14E
Lubbock: U.S.A.	46	34N	102W
Lübeck: & bay, W. Germany	74	54N	11E
Lubéron, Montagne du: France	73	44N	5E
Lublin: Poland	68	51N	23E
Lubumbashi: Zaïre	110	12S	27E
Lucca: Italy	75	44N	10E
Luce Bay: Scotland	62	55N	5W
Lucerne, L.: Switz.	75	47N	8E
Lucin: U.S.A.	48	41N	114W
Luckenwalde: E. Ger.	74	52N	13E
Lucknow: India	88	27N	81E
Lüdenscheid: W. Ger.	74	51N	8E
Lüderitz: S.W. Africa (Namibia)	111	27S	15E
Ludhiana: India	88	31N	76E
Ludlow: England	63	52N	3W
Ludlow: U.S.A.	48	35N	116W
Ludvika: Sweden	71	60N	15E
Ludwigsburg: W. Ger.	74	49N	9E
Ludwigshafen: W. Ger.	74	49N	8E
Ludwigslust: E. Ger.	74	53N	12E
Lufkin: U.S.A.	46	31N	95W
Luga: U.S.S.R.	71	59N	30E
Lugano: Switzerland	75	46N	9E
Lugo: Spain	67	43N	8W
Lugoj: Romania	68	46N	22E
Luichow Penin.: China	90	21N	110E
Luleå: Sweden	70	66N	22E
Lüleburgaz: Turkey	69	41N	27E
Lumberton: U.S.A.	47	34N	79W
Lumsden: N.Z.	104	46S	168E
Lund: Sweden	71	56N	13E
Lundy I.: England	63	51N	5W
Lune: r., England	62	54N	3W
Lüneburg: & Heath, Germany	74	53N	10E
Lunéville: France	72	49N	6E
Lungkiang: see Tsitsihar			
Lure: France	72	48N	6E
Lurgan: N. Ireland	62	54N	6W
LUSAKA: Zambia	111	15S	28E
Lusambo: Zaïre	110	5S	23E
Lushai Hills: India	89	23N	93E
Lushun: China	94	39N	121E
Lussac-les-Châteaux: France	73	46N	1E
Lüta: China	94	39N	121E
Luton: England	63	52N	0
Lutsk: U.S.S.R.	68	51N	25E
LUXEMBOURG: cap. Luxembourg	72	50N	6E
Luxor: Egypt	86	26N	33E

	Page	Lat.	Long.
Luzern (Lucerne): Switzerland	75	47N	8E
Luzon: i., Phil.	91	15N	121E
Luzy: France	73	47N	4E
L'vov: U.S.S.R.	68	50N	24E
Lyakhov Is.: U.S.S.R.	83	73N	142E
Lyallpur: Pakistan	88	31N	73E
Lydda: see Lod			
Lydenburg: S. Africa	111	25S	30E
Lyme Bay: England	63	51N	3W
Lynchburg: U.S.A.	47	37N	79W
Lynn: U.S.A.	33	42N	71W
Lyonnais: Old Prov., France	73	46N	4E
Lyons (Lyon): France	73	46N	5E
Lys: r., France/Belgium	72	51N	3E
Lys'va: U.S.S.R.	85	58N	58E
Lyttleton: N.Z.	104	44S	173E
Lyubertsy: U.S.S.R.	114	55N	38E
Lyublino: U.S.S.R.	114	55N	38E
Ma'ān: Jordan	86	30N	36E
Maanshan: China	94	32N	119E
Maarianhamina: Fin.	71	60N	20E
Maas: r., Netherlands	74	52N	5E
Maastricht: Neth.	74	51N	6E
McAlester: U.S.A.	46	35N	96W
McAllen: U.S.A.	46	26N	98W
Macao: China	95	22N	113E
Macclesfield: England	63	53N	2W
McComb: U.S.A.	46	31N	90W
McCook: U.S.A.	46	40N	101W
Macdonnell Ranges: Australia	98	24S	132E
Maceió: Brazil	54	10S	36W
Macequece: Moz.	111	19S	33E
Macerata: Italy	69	43N	13E
McGehee: U.S.A.	46	34N	91W
Macgillycuddy's Reeks: mtns., R. of Ireland	61	52N	10W
Machida: Japan	114	36N	139E
Machrihanish: Scotland	62	55N	6W
McIntosh: U.S.A.	49	46N	101W
Mackay: Australia	100	21S	149E
Mackay, L.: Australia	98	23S	128E
Mackenzie: Guyana	54	6N	58W
Mackenzie: r., Australia	100	23S	149E
Mackinac, Str. of: U.S.A./Canada	19	46N	85W
McKinley, Mt.: U.S.A.	12	63N	151W
McKinney: U.S.A.	46	33N	97W
McMurdo: Antarctica	116	78S	168E
Macias Nguema Biyogo: i., Eq. Guinea	108	4N	9E
Mâcon: France	73	46N	5E
Macon: U.S.A.	47	33N	84W
Macquarie I.: Pac. O.	102	55S	159E
McRae: U.S.A.	47	32N	83W
Madagascar: see **MALAGASY REP.**			
Madagascar Basin: Indian Ocean	89	25S	55E
Madagascar Ridge: Indian Ocean	89	30S	45E
Madang: Papua New Guinea	99	5S	146E
Maddalena Pass: France/Italy	75	44N	7E
Madeira: i., Atlantic Ocean	57	33N	17W
Madeira: r., Brazil	54	5S	61W
Madera: U.S.A.	48	37N	120W
Madhya Pradesh: State, India	88	23N	78E
Madison: Florida, U.S.A.	47	30N	84W
Madison: Ind., U.S.A.	47	39N	85W
Madison: S. Dakota, U.S.A.	49	44N	97W
Madison: Wisc., U.S.A.	49	43N	89W
Madison Heights: U.S.A.	33	43N	83W
Madisonville: U.S.A.	47	37N	88W
Madiun: Indonesia	91	8S	112E
Madras: India	88	13N	80E
MADRID: Spain	67	40N	4W
Madura: i., Indon.	91	7S	113E
Madurai: India	88	10N	78E
Maebashi: Japan	93	36N	139E
Mafeking: S. Africa	111	26S	25E
Magadan: U.S.S.R.	83	60N	150E
Magallenes: see Punta Arenas			
Magdalena: r., Colombia	54	7N	74W
Magdeburg: E. Ger.	74	52N	12E
Magellan, Str. of: Chile/Argentina	55	53S	70W
Maggiore, Lake: Italy/Switzerland	75	46N	9E
Magnitogorsk: U.S.S.R.	85	53N	59E
Magnolia: U.S.A.	46	33N	93W
Magude: Moz.	111	25S	33E
Magwe: Burma	92	20N	95E
Mahanadi: r., India	88	22N	83E
Maharashtra: State, India	88	24N	76E
Mahia Penin.: N.Z.	104	39S	178E
Mahón: Minorca	67	40N	4E
Maidenhead: England	112	52N	1W

	Page	Lat.	Long.
Maidstone: England	112	51N	1E
Maiduguri: Nigeria	108	12N	13E
Maimana: Afghan.	85	36N	65E
Main: r., W. Germany	74	50N	10E
Main: Old Prov., France	72	48N	1W
Main Barrier Range: Australia	101	32S	141E
Mai Ndombe, L.: Zaire	110	2S	17E
Maine: State, U.S.A.	19	45N	70W
Mainland: i., Orkney Is.	61	59N	3W
Mainz: W. Germany	74	50N	8E
Maiskhal: Bangladesh	89	21N	92E
Maitland: Australia	101	33S	152E
Majorca (Mallorca): i., Balearic Is.	67	39N	3E
Majunga: Malagasy Republic	110	16S	46E
Makeni: Sierra Leone	108	9N	12W
Makarikari Salt Pan: Botswana	111	21S	26E
Makassar: str., Indonesia	91	5S	120E
Makeyevka: U.S.S.R.	84	48N	38E
Makhachkala: U.S.S.R.	84	43N	48E
Makran: reg., Iran/Pakistan	87	26N	62E
Makushino: U.S.S.R.	85	55N	67E
Malabar Coast: India	88	12N	75E
Malacca: str., Malaysia	92	2N	102E
Maladetta Massif: France/Spain	73	43N	1E
Málaga: Spain	67	37N	4W
MALAGASY REP.: cap. Tananarive	110	Inset	
Malahide: R. of Ireland	62	53N	6W
Malaita: i., Solomon Is.	99	9S	161E
Malakal: Sudan	109	10N	32E
Malang: Indonesia	91	8S	112E
Malanje: Angola	110	9S	16E
Mälar, L.: Sweden	71	59N	17E
Malatya: Turkey	87	38N	38E
MALAWI: cap. Lilongwe	110	13S	34E
Malawi (Nyasa), Lake: Africa	110	13S	34E
Malaya: State, Malaysia	91	4N	102E
MALAYSIA: Fed. cap. Kuala Lumpur	91	5N	110E
Malbork: Poland	68	54N	19E
Malden: U.S.A.	33	42N	71W
Malden I.: Pacific O.	103	5S	155W
MALDIVES: cap. Mahé	89	7N	73E
Malebo, Pool: l., Zaire	110	4S	15E
Malesherbes: France	72	48N	2E
Malheur L.: U.S.A.	48	43N	119W
MALI: cap. Bamako	108	15N	5W
Malines: see Mechelen			
Malin Head: R. of Ireland	61	55N	7W
Malinmore Head: R. of Ireland	61	55N	9W
Mallaig: Scotland	62	57N	6W
Mallorca (Majorca): i., Spain	67	39N	3E
Mallow: R. of Ireland	61	52N	9W
Malmberget: Sweden	70	67N	21E
Malmédy: Belgium	72	50N	6E
Malmesbury: S. Africa	111	33S	19E
Malmö: Sweden	71	56N	13E
Maloja Pass: Switz.	75	46N	10E
Malonga: Zaire	110	10S	23E
Malpelo I.: Pacific O.	54	4N	82W
Malplaquet: hist., France	72	50N	4E
MALTA: cap. Valletta	69	36N	14E
Malta: U.S.A.	48	48N	108W
Malvan: India	88	16N	73E
Malvern: England	63	52N	2W
Man, I. of: cap. Douglas	62	54N	5W
Manaar: & gulf, Sri Lanka	88	9N	80E
Manado: Indonesia	91	2N	125E
MANAGUA: Nic.	45	12N	86W
MANAMA: Bahrain	87	26N	51E
Mana Pass: China	88	31N	79E
Manaus: Brazil	54	3S	60W
Manchester: England	62	54N	2W
Manchester: U.S.A.	51	43N	71W
Mandalay: Burma	92	22N	96E
Mandan: U.S.A.	49	47N	101W
Mandasor: India	88	24N	75E
Mangalore: India	88	13N	75E
Mangyshlak Penin.: U.S.S.R.	84	44N	51E
Manhattan: Kansas, U.S.A.	49	39N	97W
Manhattan: N.Y., U.S.A.	35	41N	74W
Manifold, C.: Australia	100	23S	151E
Manila: Philippine Is.	91	15N	121E
Manipur: State, India	89	25N	94E
Manistee: r., U.S.A.	19	44N	85W
Manitou Is.: U.S.A.	49	47N	87W
Manitowoc: U.S.A.	19	44N	88W
Manizales: Colombia	54	5N	76W

Place	Page	Lat.	Long.
Manjra: r., India	88	18N	76E
Mankato: U.S.A.	49	44N	94W
Mankoya: Zambia	111	15S	25E
Manly: Australia	115	34S	151E
Mannheim: W. Ger.	74	49N	8E
Manokwari: Indonesia	98	1S	134E
Manresa: Spain	67	42N	2E
Mansfield: Australia	101	37S	146E
Mansfield: England	63	53N	1W
Mansfield: U.S.A.	47	41N	83W
Manta: Ecuador	54	1S	81W
Mantes-Gassicourt: France	72	49N	2E
Mantua (Mantova): Italy	75	45N	11E
Manus: i., Papua New Guinea	99	3S	147E
Manzala, L.: Egypt	109	Inset	
Manzanillo: Cuba	53	20N	77W
Manzanillo: Mexico	52	19N	104W
MAPUTO: Mozambique	111	26S	33E
Maracaibo: & lake, Venezuela	45	11N	72W
Maracay: Venezuela	45	10N	68W
Marajó, I. of: Brazil	54	1S	50W
Maramba (Livingstone): Zambia	111	18S	26E
Marampa: Sierra Leone	108	8N	12W
Marañon: r., Peru	54	5S	77W
Marble Bar: Australia	98	21S	120E
Marburg: W. Germany	74	51N	9E
Marche: Old Prov., France	73	46N	2E
Mar Chiquita, Laguna: Arg.	56	31S	62W
Marchienne: Belgium	72	50N	4E
Marcos Paz: Argentina	56	35S	59W
Marcus I.: Pacific O.	102	25N	154E
Marcus Necker Rise: Pacific Ocean	102	20N	170E
Marcy, Mt.: U.S.A.	19	44N	74W
Mar del Plata: Arg.	55	38S	58W
Mardin: Turkey	87	37N	41E
Marfa: U.S.A.	46	30N	104W
Marganets: U.S.S.R.	85	48N	67E
Margarita I.: Venezuela	45	11N	64W
Margate: England	63	51N	1E
Margate: S. Africa	111	31S	30E
Margeride, Monts de la: France	73	45N	4E
Marianas: Is. & Trench, Pacific Ocean	102	18N	145E
Maria van Diemen, C.: New Zealand	104	34S	173E
Maribor: Yugoslavia	68	47N	16E
Marie Galante: i., West Indies	45	16N	61W
Mariental: S.W. Africa (Namibia)	111	25S	18E
Mariinsk: U.S.S.R.	85	56N	88E
Marinett: U.S.A.	49	45N	88W
Marion: Ind., U.S.A.	47	41N	86W
Marion: Ohio, U.S.A.	47	41N	83W
Maritime Alps: France	73	44N	7E
Market Harborough: England	63	52N	1W
Markovo: U.S.S.R.	83	65N	170E
Marlborough: England	63	51N	2W
Marles: France	72	51N	2E
Marlow: England	112	51N	1W
Marmande: France	73	44N	0
Marmara, Sea of: Turkey	69	41N	28E
Marne: r., France	72	49N	4E
Marquesas Is.: Pac. O.	103	10S	140W
Marquette: U.S.A.	49	46N	87W
Marrakesh: Mor.	108	32N	8W
Marra Mts.: Sudan	109	13N	24E
Marree: Australia	101	30S	138E
Marsala: Sicily	69	38N	12E
Marseilles (Marseille):	73	43N	5E
Marshall: U.S.A.	46	33N	94W
Marshall Is.: Pac. O.	102	10N	166E
Marshalltown: U.S.A.	46	42N	93W
Marshfield: U.S.A.	49	45N	90W
Martaban, G. of: Burma	91	16N	97E
Martha's Vineyard: i., U.S.A.	51	41N	71W
Martigny: Switzerland	75	46N	7E
Martigues: France	73	43N	5E
Martinique: i., West Indies	45	15N	61W
Martinsville: U.S.A.	47	37N	80W
Marton: N.Z.	104	40S	175E
Mary (Merv): U.S.S.R.	85	38N	62E
Maryborough: Queens., Australia	100	25S	153E
Maryborough: Victoria, Australia	101	37S	144E
Maryland: State, U.S.A.	47	38N	75W
Maryport: England	62	55N	4W
Maryville: U.S.A.	47	36N	84W
Mascara: Algeria	67	35N	0
MASERU: Lesotho	111	29S	27E
Mashhad: Iran	87	36N	60E
Mashkel: r., Pakistan	88	27N	63E
Masira: i., Oman	87	20N	59E
Mask, L.: R. of Ireland	61	54N	9W
Mason City: U.S.A.	49	43N	93W
Massachusetts: State, U.S.A.	51	42N	73W
Massawa: Ethiopia	109	16N	39E
Massena: U.S.A.	19	45N	75W
Massif Central: France	73	46N	3E
Masterton: N.Z.	104	41S	176E
Mastung: Pakistan	88	30N	67E
Matadi: Zaire	110	6S	14E
Matagorda I.: U.S.A.	46	28N	97W
Matamoros: Mexico	52	26N	97W
Matanzas: Cuba	53	23N	82W
Matapan, C.: Greece	69	36N	22E
Matatiele: S. Africa	111	30S	28E
Mateka Falls: Zaire	110	5S	15E
Matera: Italy	69	41N	17E
Mathura: India	88	27N	78E
Matlock: England	63	53N	2W
Mato Grosso, Plat. of: Brazil	54	15S	54W
Matopo Hills: Rhodesia (Zimbabwe)	111	21S	30E
Matrah: Oman	87	24N	58E
Matrûh: Egypt	86	32N	27E
Matsudo: Japan	114	36N	140E
Matsue: Japan	93	35N	133E
Matsumoto: Japan	93	36N	138E
Matsusaka: Japan	93	35N	137E
Matsuyama: Japan	93	34N	133E
Matterhorn: mtn., Switzerland	75	46N	8E
Mattoon: U.S.A.	47	39N	88W
Maturín: Venezuela	45	10N	63W
Maubeuge: France	72	50N	4E
Maui: i., Pacific O.	103	20N	155W
Maumee: r., U.S.A.	47	41N	84W
Maumere: Indonesia	91	8S	122E
Maun: Botswana	111	20S	23E
MAURITANIA: cap. Nouakchott	108	20N	10W
MAURITIUS: cap. Port Louis	89	20S	57E
Mawlaik: Burma	92	24N	94E
May, C.: U.S.A.	47	39N	75W
Mayapán: hist., Mexico	53	20N	89W
Mayenne: & r., Fr.	72	48N	1W
Mayfield: U.S.A.	47	36N	89W
Maykop: U.S.S.R.	84	45N	40E
Maymyo: Burma	92	22N	96E
Mayoumba: Gabon	110	4S	11E
Maywood: U.S.A.	34	42N	88W
Mazamet: France	73	43N	2E
Mazar-i-Sharif: Afghanistan	85	37N	67E
Mazatlán: Mexico	52	23N	107W
Mazoe: Rhodesia (Zimbabwe)	111	17S	31E
Mbala: Zambia	110	9S	32E
Mbandaka: Zaïre	110	0	18E
Mead, Lake: U.S.A.	48	36N	114W
Meaux: France	72	49N	3E
Mecca: Saudi Arabia	87	21N	40E
Mechelen: Belgium	72	51N	4E
Medan: Indonesia	92	4N	99E
Medéa: Algeria	67	36N	3E
Medellín: Colombia	54	6N	76W
Medford: U.S.A.	33	42N	71W
Medias: Romania	68	46N	25E
Medina: Saudi Arabia	87	25N	40E
Medinat-ash-Sha'b: Aden	87	13N	45E
Mediterranean Sea	64/5	—	—
Mednogorsk: U.S.S.R.	85	51N	58E
Médoc: reg., France	73	45N	1W
Medway: r., England	63	51N	0
Meerut: India	88	29N	77E
Mega: Ethiopia	109	4N	38E
Mégara: Greece	69	38N	23E
Meghalaya: State, India	89	26N	91E
Meiningen: E. Ger.	74	51N	10E
Meissen: E. Germany	74	51N	13E
Meiktila: Burma	92	21N	96E
Mekong: r., S.E. Asia	91	33N	96E
Melaka: Malaysia	92	2N	102E
Melanesia: reg., Pacific O.	102	—	—
Melbourne: Austl.	101	38S	145E
Melbourne: U.S.A.	47	28N	81W
Melilla: Spain	67	35N	3W
Melo: Uruguay	56	32S	54W
Melrose: U.S.A.	33	42N	71W
Melrose Park: U.S.A.	34	42N	88W
Melton Mowbray: England	63	53N	1W
Melun: France	72	49N	3E
Melville Bay: Grnld.	13	76N	62W
Melville I.: Austl.	98	11S	131E
Memmingen: W. Ger.	75	48N	10E
Memphis: hist., Egypt	86	30N	31E
Memphis: U.S.A.	47	35N	90W
Menai Strait: Wales	63	53N	4W
Menderes: r., Turkey	86	37N	27E
Mendip Hills: Eng.	63	51N	3W
Mendocino, Cape: U.S.A.	44	40N	125W
Mendoza: Argentina	55	33S	69W
Mène: Congo	108	2N	16E
Mengtsz: China	92	23N	103E
Menindee: & lake, Australia	101	32S	142E
Menommee: U.S.A.	49	45N	88W
Menorca (Minorca): i., Spain	67	40N	4E
Mentawai Is.: Indon.	91	3S	100E
Menton: France	73	44N	7E
Meppel: Neth.	74	53N	6E
Meramec: r., U.S.A.	46	38N	91W
Merano: Italy	75	47N	11E
Merauke: Indon.	98	9S	140E
Mercara: India	88	12N	76E
Merced: U.S.A.	48	37N	120W
Mergui: Burma	92	12N	98E
Mergui Arch.: Burma	92	10N	97E
Mérida: Mexico	53	21N	90W
Mérida: Spain	67	39N	6W
Meridian: U.S.A.	47	32N	89W
Meridional, Meseta: plat., Spain	67	39N	5W
Merowe: Sudan	86	18N	32E
Merredin: Australia	100	31S	118E
Merrick: mtn., Scot.	62	55N	5W
Merseburg: W. Ger.	74	51N	12E
Mersey: r., England	63	53N	3W
Merseyside: Co., England	63	53N	3W
Mersin: Turkey	86	37N	34E
Merthyr Tydfil: Wales	63	52N	3W
Merv: see Mary			
Mesa: U.S.A.	48	33N	112W
Mesabi Ra.: U.S.A.	49	48N	93W
Messina: & str., Sicily	69	38N	16E
Messina: S. Africa	111	23S	30E
Mestre: Italy	75	45N	12E
Methuen: U.S.A.	51	43N	71W
Mettman: W. Ger.	64	51N	7E
Mettur: India	88	12N	78E
Metz: France	72	49N	6E
Meuse: r., Fr./Belg.	72	50N	5E
Mexicali: Mexico	48	33N	115W
Mexican Plat.: Mex.	44	24N	103W
MEXICO: cap. Ciudad de México	52/3	—	—
Mexico, Gulf of	44/5	25N	90W
MÉXICO, CIUDAD DE (Mexico City): Mexico	52	19N	99W
Mézières: France	72	50N	5E
Mezquital: r., Mexico	52	23N	105W
Miami: Ariz., U.S.A.	48	33N	111W
Miami: Fla., U.S.A.	47	26N	80W
Miami: Okla., U.S.A.	46	37N	95W
Miami: r., U.S.A.	47	39N	85W
Miami Beach: U.S.A.	47	26N	80W
Mianeh: Iran	87	37N	47E
Michelson, Mt.: U.S.A.	30	69N	144W
Michigan: State, U.S.A.	19	45N	85W
Michigan, Lake: U.S.A./Canada	19	44N	87W
Michigan City: U.S.A.	47	42N	86W
Micronesia: reg., Pacific Ocean	102	—	—
Mid-Atlantic Ridge: Atlantic Ocean	57	—	—
Middelburg: Neth.	74	51N	3E
Middelburg: S. Africa	111	26S	30E
Middle Atlas: mtns., Morocco	108	33N	5W
Middlesboro: U.S.A.	47	37N	84W
Middlesbrough: Eng.	62	55N	1W
Middletown: N.Y., U.S.A.	51	41N	74W
Middletown: Ohio, U.S.A.	47	40N	84W
Mid-Indian Basin: Indian O.	89	7S	80E
Midland: Michigan, U.S.A.	19	43N	85W
Midland: Texas, U.S.A.	46	32N	102W
Midnapore: India	88	22N	87E
Midway I.: Pacific O.	102	29N	179W
Midwest: U.S.A.	48	43N	106W
Mijares: r., Spain	67	40N	0
Mikkeli: Finland	70	62N	27E
Milan (Milano): Italy	75	45N	9E
Milbank: U.S.A.	49	45N	97W
Mildura: Australia	101	34S	142E
Miles City: U.S.A.	49	46N	106W
Milford: U.S.A.	33	42N	72W
Milford Haven: Wales	63	52N	5W
Milford Sound: N.Z.	104	44S	168E
Milk: r., U.S.A.	48	48N	109W
Millau: France	73	44N	3E
Milledgeville: U.S.A.	47	33N	83W
Mille Lacs: U.S.A.	49	46N	94W
Millicent: Australia	101	38S	140E
Millinocket: U.S.A.	15	46N	69W
Milos: i., Greece	69	37N	24E
Milparinka: Austl.	101	30S	142E
Milton: U.S.A.	33	42N	71W
Milwaukee: U.S.A.	49	43N	88W
Min: r., China	95	27N	117E
Minatitlán: Mexico	53	17N	95W
Mindanao: i., Phil.	91	8N	125E
Minden: U.S.A.	46	33N	93W
Mindoro: i., Phil.	91	13N	121E
Minehead: England	63	51N	3W
Mine Hd.: R. of Irel.	61	52N	8W
Mineral Wells: U.S.A.	46	33N	98W
Minneapolis: U.S.A.	49	45N	93W
Minnesota: State, U.S.A.	49	47N	95W
Minorca (Menorca): i., Balearic Is.	67	40N	4E
Minot: U.S.A.	49	48N	101W
Minquiers, Plat. des: is., Channel Is.	72	49N	2W
Minsk: U.S.S.R.	71	54N	28E
Minusinsk: U.S.S.R.	85	54N	92E
Miraflores Locks: Panama Canal	45	Inset	
Miram Shah: Pak.	88	33N	70E
Mirande: France	73	44N	0
Mirecourt: France	72	48N	6E
Mirim, Lagoa dos: Brazil	56	31S	51W
Mirtoon Sea: Greece	69	37N	24E
Mirzapur: India	88	25N	82E
Miskolc: Hungary	68	48N	21E
Misoöl: i., Indon.	98	2S	130E
Mississippi: r., U.S.A.	46	31N	92W
Mississippi: State, U.S.A.	46/7	33N	90W
Missoula: U.S.A.	48	47N	114W
Missouri: r., U.S.A.	49	39N	94W
Missouri: State, U.S.A.	49	39N	93W
Misurata: Libya	108	32N	15E
Mitaka: Japan	114	36N	140E
Mitchell: Australia	100	26S	148E
Mitchell: U.S.A.	49	44N	98W
Mitchell: r., Queens., Australia	99	16S	142E
Mitilini: Greece	69	39N	26E
Mito: Japan	93	36N	141E
Mittelland Canal: W. Germany	74	52N	8E
Mitu: Colombia	54	1N	70W
Mizoram: State, India	89	23N	93E
Mizunami: Japan	93	35N	137E
Mjøsa: l., Norway	71	61N	11E
Mława: Poland	68	53N	20E
Moascar: Egypt	109	Inset	
Mobara: Japan	93	35N	140E
Mobaye: Central Afr. Empire	109	4N	22E
Moberly: U.S.A.	46	39N	92W
Mobile: U.S.A.	47	31N	88W
Moçâmedes: Angola	110	15S	12E
Mocuba: Moz.	111	17S	37E
Modane: France	73	45N	7E
Modder River: sett., South Africa	111	29S	25E
Modena: Italy	75	45N	11E
Modeste: U.S.A.	48	38N	121W
Moengo: Surinam	54	6N	54E
Moers: W. Germany	64	6N	7E
Moffat: Scotland	62	55N	3W
MOGADISCIO: Somali Republic	109	2N	45E
Mogilev Podol'skiy: U.S.S.R.	68	48N	28E
Mogocha: U.S.S.R.	83	53N	120E
Mogollon Plateau: U.S.A.	48	35N	111W
Mointy: U.S.S.R.	85	47N	74E
Mojave Desert: U.S.A.	48	35N	117W
Mold: Wales	63	53N	3W
Moldavian S.S.R.: U.S.S.R.	84	47N	28E
Mole: r., England	112	51N	0
Molières: France	73	44N	1E
Mollendo: Peru	54	17S	72W
Molndal: Sweden	71	58N	12E
Molodechno: U.S.S.R.	68	54N	27E
Molopo: r., S. Afr.	111	26S	23E
Moluccas: is., Indon.	91	0	127E
Molucca Sea: Indon.	91	0	125E
Mombasa: Kenya	110	4S	39E
MONACO: cap. Monte Carlo	73	44N	7E
Monadhliath Mts.: Scotland	62	57N	4W
Monaghan: R. of Ireland	61	54N	7W
Mona Passage: W. Indies	45	18N	68W
Monchegorsk: U.S.S.R.	70	68N	33E
Monchen-Gladbach: W. Germany	64	51N	6E
Monclova: Mexico	52	27N	101W
Mondovi: Italy	75	44N	8E
Monfalcone: Italy	75	46N	13E
Mong Cai: Vietnam	92	22N	108E
MONGOLIA: cap. Ulan Bator	83	47N	105E
Mongu: Zambia	111	15S	23E
Monheim: W. Ger.	64	51N	7E
Monmouth: Wales	63	52N	3W
Monmouth: U.S.A.	49	41N	91W
Monroe: La., U.S.A.	46	33N	92W
Monroe: Michigan,			

	Page	Lat.	Long.
U.S.A.	47	42N	83W
Monroeville: U.S.A.	47	31N	87W
MONROVIA: Liberia	108	6N	11W
Mons: Belgium	72	50N	4E
Montague I.: U.S.A.	12	60N	147W
Montana: *State*, U.S.A.	48	47N	110W
Montargis: France	72	48N	3E
Montauban: France	73	44N	1E
Montauk Pt.: U.S.A.	51	41N	72W
Montbéliard: France	73	47N	7E
Montceau-les-Mines: France	73	47N	4E
Mont Cenis Pass: France/Italy	75	45N	7E
Montclair: U.S.A.	35	41N	74W
Mont de Marsan: Fr.	73	44N	1W
Montdidier: France	72	50N	3E
Monte Bello Is.: Australia	98	20S	115E
MONTE CARLO: Monaco	73	44N	7E
Montego Bay: *town*, Jamaica	53	18N	78W
Montélimar: France	73	45N	5E
Monterey: & *Bay*, U.S.A.	48	37N	122W
Monterrey: Mexico	52	26N	100W
MONTEVIDEO: Uruguay	56	35S	56W
Montgomery: U.S.A.	47	32N	86W
Montluçon: France	73	46N	3E
Montmédy: France	72	50N	5E
Montmirail: France	72	49N	4E
Montpelier: U.S.A.	19	44N	73W
Montpellier: France	73	44N	4E
Montreuil: France	72	50N	2E
Montreuil Bellay: Fr.	73	47N	0
Montreux: Switz.	75	46N	7E
Montrose: Scotland	62	57N	2W
Montrose: U.S.A.	48	38N	108W
Mont St. Michel: Fr.	72	49N	2W
Montserrat: *i.*, West Indies	45	17N	62W
Montvalier, Pic de: Spain/France	73	43N	1E
Monza: Italy	75	46N	9E
Moorhead: U.S.A.	49	47N	97W
Moorreesburg: South Africa	111	33S	18E
Moosehead, L.: U.S.A.	15	46N	69W
Moradabad: India	88	29N	79E
Morava: *r.*, Czech.	68	49N	17E
Moray Firth: Scot.	61	58N	4W
Morbihan: *Dept.*, Fr.	72	48N	3W
Moreau: *r.*, U.S.A.	49	45N	102W
Morecambe: England	62	54N	3W
Moree: Australia	101	29S	150E
Morelia: Mexico	52	20N	101W
Moreton in Marsh: England	63	52N	2W
Morgan City: U.S.A.	46	30N	91W
Morgantown: U.S.A.	47	40N	80W
Morkalla: Australia	101	34S	141E
Morlaix: France	72	49N	4W
MOROCCO: *cap.* Rabat	108	32N	5W
Morón: Cuba	53	22N	78W
Morotai: *i.*, Indon.	91	3N	128E
Morpeth: England	62	55N	2W
Morristown: U.S.A.	35	41N	75W
Morton Grove: U.S.A.	34	42N	87W
Morvan: *reg.*, France	73	47N	4E
Moscow: U.S.A.	48	47N	117W
MOSCOW: U.S.S.R.	84	56N	37E
Mosel (Moselle): *r.*, Fr./W. Ger.	74	50N	7E
Moses Lake: *city*, U.S.A.	48	47N	119W
Moshi: Tanzania	110	3S	37E
Moss: Norway	70	59N	11E
Mosselbaai: *town*, South Africa	111	34S	22E
Most: Czech.	74	50N	14E
Mostaganem: Algeria	67	36N	0
Mostar: Yugoslavia	69	43N	18E
Mosul: Iraq	87	36N	43E
Motala: Sweden	71	59N	15E
Motherwell: Scot.	62	56N	3W
Motueka: N.Z.	104	41S	173E
Moulins: France	73	47N	3E
Moulmein: Burma	92	17N	97E
Moultrie: U.S.A.	47	31N	84W
Moundsville: U.S.A.	47	40N	81W
Mountain Home: U.S.A.	48	43N	116W
Mount Eba: *town*, Australia	98	30S	136E
Mount Gambier: *town*, Australia	101	38S	141E
Mount Isa: *town*, Australia	98	21S	140E
Mount Lofty Range: Australia	101	35S	138E
Mount Lyell: *town*, Australia	99	42S	146E
Mount Magnet: *town*, Australia	100	28S	118E
Mount Morgan: *town*, Australia	100	24S	150E
Mount Pleasant: *city*, U.S.A.	19	44N	85W
Mount Prospect: *city*, U.S.A.	34	42N	88W
Mount Vernon: *city*, Ill., U.S.A.	47	38N	89W
Mount Vernon: *city*, N.Y., U.S.A.	35	41N	74W
Mount Vernon: *city*, Wash., U.S.A.	48	48N	122W
Mourne Mts.: N. Irel.	61	54N	6W
Moyale: Kenya	110	4N	39E
MOZAMBIQUE: *cap.* Maputo	110	—	—
Mozambique: Moz.	111	15S	40E
Mozambique Chan.	110	15S	41E
Mpanda: Tanzania	110	6S	31E
Mtwara: Tanzania	110	10S	40E
Muang Khon Kaen: Thailand	92	16N	103E
Muang Lamsang: Thailand	92	18N	99E
Muang Nan: Thailand	92	19N	101E
Muang Phrae: Thailand	92	18N	100E
Muang Phitsanulok: Thailand	92	17N	100E
Muchinga Mts.: Zambia	111	13S	32E
Mudgee: Australia	101	32S	150E
Muğla: Turkey	86	37N	28E
Muhammad Qol: Sudan	86	21N	37E
Mühlhausen: E. Ger.	74	51N	10E
Mukachevo: U.S.S.R.	68	48N	23E
Mukallā: Yemen P.D.R.	87	15N	49E
Mukden (Shenyang): China	94	42N	124E
Mülheim: W. Ger.	74	51N	7E
Mülheim an der Ruhr: W. Germany	64	51N	7E
Mulhouse: France	72	48N	7E
Mull: *i.*, Scotland	62	56N	6W
Müller Mts.: Indon.	91	1N	114E
Mullewa: Australia	100	28S	116E
Mull Hd.: Scotland	61	59N	3W
Mullinger: R. of Irel.	61	54N	7W
Mull of Oa.: Scotland	62	56N	6W
Mulobezi: Zambia	111	17S	25E
Multan: Pak.	88	30N	71E
Muna: *i.*, Indonesia	91	5S	122E
Muncie: U.S.A.	47	40N	85W
Mungbere: Zaire	110	3N	28E
Munich(München): W. Germany	75	48N	12E
Münster: W. Ger.	74	52N	8E
Muonio: *r.*, Finland	70	68N	24E
Mur: France	72	48N	3W
Mur: *r.*, Austria	75	47N	14E
Murat: France	73	45N	3E
Murchison: *r.*, Austl.	98	27S	116E
Murcia: Spain	67	38N	1W
Muret: France	73	43N	1E
Murfreesboro: U.S.A.	47	36N	86W
Murmansk: U.S.S.R.	70	69N	33E
Murom: U.S.S.R.	84	56N	42E
Muroran: Japan	93	42N	141E
Murray: *r.*, Austl.	101	35S	139E
Murray Bridge: Australia	101	35S	139E
Murrumbidgee: *r.*, Australia	101	35S	146E
Murupara: N.Z.	104	38S	177E
Murwillumbah: Australia	100	28S	153E
Musashino: Japan	114	36N	140E
MUSCAT: Oman	85	24N	59E
Muscatine: U.S.A.	49	41N	91W
Muskegon: *r.*, U.S.A.	19	43N	86W
Muskogee: U.S.A.	46	36N	95W
Mussoorie: India	88	30N	78E
Mustafakemalpaşa: Turkey	69	40N	28E
Mustang I.: U.S.A.	46	27N	97W
Muswellbrook: Austl.	101	32S	151E
Mutankiang: China	90	45N	130E
Mutano: Angola	111	17S	15E
Muyun-Kum: *desert*, U.S.S.R.	85	44N	71E
Muzaffarpur: India	88	26N	85E
Mwanza: Tanzania	110	3S	33E
Mweru, L.: Zambia/Zaire	110	9S	29E
Myingyan: Burma	92	21N	95E
Myitkyina: Burma	92	26N	97E
Mymensingh: Bangl.	88	25N	90E
Mysore: India	88	12N	77E
My Tho: Vietnam	92	10N	106E
Naas: R. of Ireland	61	53N	7W
Nacala: Mozambique	111	15S	40E
Nacogdoches: U.S.A.	46	32N	95W
Naestved: Denmark	71	55N	12E
Nafud: *desert*, Saudi Arabia	87	28N	41E
Naga Hills: India/Burma	89	26N	95E
Nagaland: *State*, India	89	26N	95E
Nagaoka: Japan	93	37N	139E
Nagapattinam: India	88	11N	80E
Nagasaki: Japan	93	33N	130E
Nagoya: Japan	93	35N	137E
Nagpur: India	88	21N	79E
Nagykanizsa: Hung.	68	46N	16E
Naha: Okinawa I.	92	26N	127E
Naini Tal: India	88	29N	80E
Nairn: Scotland	61	58N	4W
NAIROBI: Kenya	110	2S	37E
Najaf: Iraq	87	32N	44E
Najd: *reg.*, Saudi Arabia	87	26N	42E
Najran: Saudi Arabia	87	17N	44E
Nakhon Phanom: Thailand	92	17N	105E
Nakhon Ratchasima: Thailand	92	15N	102E
Nakhon Sawan: Thailand	92	16N	100E
Nakhon Si Thammarat: Thailand	92	8N	100E
Namangan: U.S.S.R.	85	41N	72E
Nam Dinh: Vietnam	92	20N	106E
Namib Desert: S.W. Afr. (Namibia)	111	23S	15E
NAMIBIA: *see* South West Africa			
Nampa: U.S.A.	48	44N	117W
Nampula: Moz.	111	15S	40E
Namsos: Norway	70	64N	11E
Namur: Belgium	72	50N	5E
Nanchang: China	95	28N	116E
Nancy: France	72	49N	6E
Nanda Devi: *mtn.*, India	88	30N	80E
Nangchen Japo: *mtn.*, China	90	33N	94E
Nanking: China	94	32N	119E
Nanling: *mts.*, China	95	25N	112E
Nanning: China	95	23N	108E
Nanping: China	95	27N	118E
Nansei Is.: *see* Ryukyu Is.			
Nan Shan: *mts.*, China	90	38N	100E
Nantes: France	72	47N	2W
Nantung: China	94	32N	121E
Nanumea: *i.*, Pac. O.	102	5S	176E
Nanyang: China	94	33N	112E
Nanyüan: China	114	40N	116E
Nanyuki: Kenya	110	0	37E
Nao, C. de la: Spain	67	39N	0
Napa: U.S.A.	46	38N	122W
Napier: N.Z.	104	39S	177E
Naples: Italy	69	41N	14E
Naracoorte: Austl.	101	37S	141E
Narbada: *r.*, India	88	22N	75E
Narbonne: France	73	43N	3E
Narrabri: Australia	101	30S	150E
Narrandera: Austl.	101	35S	147E
Narrogin: Australia	100	33S	117E
Narva: U.S.S.R.	84	59N	28E
Narvik: Norway	70	68N	17E
Nar'yan-Mar: U.S.S.R.	82	67N	53E
Nashua: U.S.A.	51	43N	72W
Nashville: U.S.A.	47	36N	87W
Nasik: India	88	20N	74E
Nasiriya: Iraq	87	31N	46E
NASSAU: The Bahamas	45	25N	77W
Nassau Mts.: Indonesia	98	4S	136E
Nasser, L.: Egypt	86	23N	33E
Nässjö: Sweden	71	58N	15E
Natal: Brazil	54	6S	35W
Natal: *Prov.*, S. Afr.	111	28S	31E
Natchez: U.S.A.	46	32N	91W
Natchitoches: U.S.A.	46	33N	93W
Natick: U.S.A.	33	41N	71W
Natuna Is. (Bunguran Is.): Indon.	91	4N	108E
Naturaliste, Cape: Australia	100	34S	115E
Nauru: *i.*, Pac. O.	102	1S	167E
Navan: R. of Irel.	61	54N	7W
Navarin, C.: U.S.S.R.	83	62N	179E
Navasota: *r.*, U.S.A.	46	31N	96W
Návpaktos: Greece	69	38N	21E
Návplion: Greece	69	38N	23E
Náxos: *i.*, Greece	69	37N	26E
Nazareth: Israel	86	33N	35E
Naze, The: *marshes*, England	63	52N	1E
N'DJAMENA: Chad	108	12N	15E
Ndola: Zambia	111	13S	29E
Neagh, L.: N. Irel.	61	55N	6W
Nebit-Dag: U.S.S.R.	84	40N	55E
Nebraska: *State*, U.S.A.	49	42N	100W
Nebraska City: U.S.A.	49	41N	96W
Neches: *r.*, U.S.A.	46	31N	95W
Neckar: *r.*, W. Germany	74	49N	9E
Needham: U.S.A.	33	42N	71W
Needles, The: *cliffs*, England	63	51N	2W
Negeb: *desert*, Israel	86	30N	35E
Negro: *r.*, Argentina	55	40S	64W
Negro: *r.*, Brazil	54	1S	64W
Negros: *i.*, Phil.	91	10N	123E
Nehbandān: Iran	87	32N	60E
Neisse (Nysa): *r.*, Pol./E. Ger.	74	52N	15E
Neiva: Colombia	54	3N	75W
Nellore: India	88	14N	80E
Nelson: N.Z.	104	41S	173E
Neman: *r.*, U.S.S.R.	71	53N	25E
Nemours: France	72	48N	3E
Nemuro: Japan	90	43N	145E
Nenagh: R. of Irel.	61	53N	8W
Nenana: U.S.A.	12	64N	149W
Nene: *r.*, England	63	53N	0
Neosho: *r.*, U.S.A.	46	38N	96W
NEPAL: *cap.* Katmandu	88	28N	85E
Nerchinsk: U.S.S.R.	83	52N	116E
Neskaupstadhur: Ice.	70	65N	14W
Ness, L.: Scotland	61	57N	4W
NETHERLANDS: *cap.* The Hague	74	52N	5E
Neubrandenburg: E. Germany	74	53N	13E
Neuchâtel: & *lake*, Switzerland	75	47N	7E
Neufchâteau: Belg.	72	50N	5E
Neufchâteau: France	72	48N	6E
Neukirchen-Vluyn: W. Germany	64	51N	7E
Neumünster: W. Ger.	72	54N	10E
Neunkirchen: W. Ger.	74	49N	7E
Neuquén: Argentina	55	39S	68W
Neuse: *r.*, U.S.A.	47	35N	78W
Neuss: W. Germany	64	51N	7E
Neustrelitz: E. Ger.	74	53N	13E
Nevada: *State*, U.S.A.	48	39N	117W
Nevada City: U.S.A.	48	39N	121W
Never: U.S.S.R.	83	54N	124E
Nevers: France	73	47N	3E
Nevis: *i.*, W. Indies	45	17N	63W
New Amsterdam: *i.*, Indian Ocean	89	38S	78E
Newark: N.J., U.S.A.	35	41N	74W
Newark: Ohio, U.S.A.	47	40N	82W
Newark upon Trent: England	63	53N	1W
New Bedford: U.S.A.	51	42N	71W
New Bern: U.S.A.	47	35N	77W
Newberry: U.S.A.	19	46N	85W
New Braunfels: U.S.A.	46	30N	98W
New Britain: *i.*, Papua, New Guinea	99	6S	150E
New Brunswick: U.S.A.	35	40N	74W
Newbury: England	63	51N	1W
New Caledonia: *i.*, Pacific Ocean	102	21S	165E
Newcastle: Australia	101	33S	152E
Newcastle: N. Ireland	62	54N	6W
New Castle: Pa., U.S.A.	47	41N	80W
Newcastle: S. Africa	111	28S	30E
Newcastle: Wyo., U.S.A.	49	44N	104W
Newcastle under Lyme: England	63	53N	2W
Newcastle upon Tyne: England	62	55N	2W
Newdegate: Austl.	100	33S	119E
New Delhi: India	115	28N	77E
Newenham, Cape: U.S.A.	12	59N	162W
New Forest: *reg.*, England	63	51N	2W
New Guinea: *i.*, East Indies	98/9	5S	140E
New Hampshire: *State*, U.S.A.	19	44N	72W
Newhaven: England	63	51N	0
New Haven: U.S.A.	51	41N	73W
New Hebrides: *is.*, Pacific Ocean	102	15S	168E
New Hyde Park: U.S.A.	35	41N	74W
New Iberia: U.S.A.	46	30N	92W
New Ireland: *i.*, Papua New Guinea	99	3S	152E
New Jersey: *State*, U.S.A.	50/1	40N	75W
Newmarket: Eng.	63	52N	0
New Mexico: *State*, U.S.A.	48/9	34N	107W
Newnan: U.S.A.	47	33N	85W
New Orleans: U.S.A.	46	30N	90W
New Plymouth: N.Z.	104	39S	174E
Newport: Wales	63	52N	3W
Newport: England	63	51N	1W
Newport: Rhode Island, U.S.A.	51	41N	71W
Newport: Vt., U.S.A.	19	45N	72W
Newport News: U.S.A.	47	37N	76W
New Providence: *i.*, The Bahamas	47	25N	77W
Newquay: England	63	50N	5W
New Rochelle: U.S.A.	35	41N	74W
Newry: N. Ireland	62	54N	6W
New South Wales: *State*, Australia	101	32S	146E
Newton: Iowa, U.S.A.	49	42N	93W

Place	Page	Lat.	Long.
Newton: Kansas, U.S.A.	49	38N	97W
Newton Abbot: England	63	51N	4W
Newton Stewart: Scotland	62	55N	5W
Newtownabbey: N. Ireland	62	55N	6W
Newtownards: N. Ireland	62	55N	6W
New Ulm: U.S.A.	49	44N	95W
New York: U.S.A.	35	—	—
New York: *State*, U.S.A.	50/1	—	—
NEW ZEALAND: *cap.* Wellington	104	—	—
Neyagawa: Japan	93	35N	136E
Ngami, Lake: Bots.	111	21S	23E
Ngauruhoe: *mtn.*, N.Z.	104	39S	175E
Nguru: Nigeria	108	13N	10E
Nha Trang: Vietnam	92	12N	109E
NIAMEY: Niger	108	14N	2E
Nias: *i.*, Indonesia	91	1N	98E
NICARAGUA: *cap.* Managua	45	13N	85W
Nicaragua, Lake: Nic.	45	11N	85W
Nice: France	71	44N	7E
Nicobar Is.: Ind. O.	92	7N	93E
NICOSIA: Cyprus	86	35N	33E
Niedere Tauern: *mtns.*, Austria	75	47N	14E
Nienburg: W. Ger.	74	53N	9E
Nieuwpoort: Belg.	72	51N	3E
Nieuwveld Range: S. Africa	111	32S	21E
NIGER: *cap.* Niamey	108	17N	10E
Niger: *r.*, W. Afr.	108	8N	6E
NIGERIA: *cap.* Lagos	108	—	—
Nihau: *i.*, Pacific O.	102	22N	162W
Nihoa: *i.*, Pacific O.	102	22N	162W
Niigata: Japan	93	38N	139E
Niihama: Japan	93	34N	133E
Nijmegen: Neth.	74	52N	6E
Nikolayev: U.S.S.R.	84	47N	32E
Nikolayevsk: U.S.S.R.	84	53N	142E
Nikopol': U.S.S.R.	84	48N	34E
Nile: *r.*, N. Africa	109	21N	31E
Niles: U.S.A.	34	42N	88W
Nilgiri Hills: India	88	11N	77E
Nîmes: France	73	44N	4E
Nimule: Sudan	109	4N	32E
Ninety Mile Beach: Australia	101	38S	147E
Nineveh: *hist.*, Iraq	87	37N	43E
Ninghsia: *see* Yinchwan			
Ninghsia Hui: China	94	37N	106E
Ningpo: China	95	30N	122E
Niobrara: *r.*, U.S.A.	49	43N	99W
Niort: France	73	46N	0
Niš: Yugoslavia	69	43N	22E
Niterói: Brazil	56	23S	43W
Nith: *r.*, Scotland	62	55N	4W
Nivelles: Belgium	72	51N	4E
Nivernais: *Old Prov.*, France	73	47N	3E
Nizhniy-Tagil: U.S.S.R.	85	58N	60E
Nobeoka: Japan	93	33N	132E
Nogent-sur-Seine: France	72	48N	3E
Noirmoutier, Île de: France	72	47N	2W
Nome: U.S.A.	12	65N	165W
Norden: W. Germany	74	54N	7E
Nordenham: W. Ger.	74	53N	8E
Norderney: *i.*, W. Ger.	74	54N	7E
Nordhausen: E. Ger.	74	52N	11E
Nordhorn: W. Ger.	74	52N	7E
Nördlingen: W. Ger.	75	49N	10E
Nordvik: U.S.S.R.	83	74N	110E
Norfolk: *Co.*, Eng.	63	53N	1E
Norfolk: Nebraska, U.S.A.	49	42N	97W
Norfolk: Va., U.S.A.	47	37N	76W
Norfolk Broads: *reg.*, England	63	53N	1E
Norfolk I.: Pac. O.	102	29S	168E
Norfork, L.: U.S.A.	46	36N	92W
Noril'sk: U.S.S.R.	83	69N	90E
Norman: *r.*, Austl.	99	19S	142E
Normandy: *Old Prov.*, France	72	49N	0
Normanton: Austl.	99	18S	141E
Norrköping: Sweden	71	59N	16E
Norseman: Austl.	100	32S	122E
Northallerton: Eng.	62	54N	1W
Northam: Australia	100	32S	117E
North America Basin: Atlantic Ocean	57	32N	55W
Northampton: Austl.	100	28S	115E
Northampton: & *Co.*, England	63	52N	1W
Northampton: U.S.A.	51	42N	73W
North Bend: U.S.A.	48	43N	124W
North Bergen: U.S.A.	35	41N	74W
North Cape: N.Z.	104	34S	173E
North Canadian: *r.*, U.S.A.	46	37N	103W
North Cape: Nor.	70	71N	26E
North Carolina: *State*, U.S.A.	47	35N	80W
North Channel: Scot./N. Irel.	62	55N	6W
North Chelmsford: U.S.A.	51	43N	71W
North Chicago: U.S.A.	34	42N	88W
Northcliffe: Austl.	100	35S	116E
North Dakota: *State*, U.S.A.	49	47N	100W
North Downs: *hills*, England	63	51N	1E
North Dvina: *r.*, U.S.S.R.	82	63N	43E
NORTHERN IRELAND: *cap.* Belfast	61	—	—
Northern Sporades: *is.*, Greece	69	39N	24E
Northern Territory: *State*, Austl.	98	20S	135E
North Foreland: *c.*, England	63	51N	1E
North Island: N.Z.	104	—	—
NORTH KOREA: *cap.* Pyongyang	90	40N	127E
Northland: *district*, N.Z.	104	36S	174E
North Minch: *chan.*, Scotland	61	58N	6W
North Platte: & *r.*, U.S.A.	49	41N	100W
North Sea	64	—	—
North Uist: *i.*, Scot.	61	58N	7W
Northumberland: *Co.*, England	62	55N	2W
Northumberland Is.: Australia	100	22S	150E
Northway: U.S.A.	30	63N	142W
North West Highlands: Scotland	61	57N	5W
Northwest Pacific Basin: Pacific Ocean	102	35N	155E
Northwich: England	62	53N	3W
North York Moors: England	62	54N	1W
Norton Sound: *bay*, U.S.A.	12	64N	163W
Norwalk: U.S.A.	51	41N	73W
NORWAY: *cap.* Oslo	70/1	—	—
Norwich: England	63	53N	1E
Norwood: U.S.A.	51	42N	71W
Nossob: *r.*, S. Africa	111	26S	21E
Nosy Bé: *i.*, Malagasy Republic	110	13S	48E
Noto-Hanto: *penin.*, Japan	93	37N	137E
Nottingham: & *Co.*, England	63	53N	1W
Nouadhibou: Mauritania	108	21N	17W
NOUAKCHOTT: Mauritania	108	18N	17W
Nova Iguaçu: Brazil	56	23S	43W
Nova Lisboa (Huambo): Angola	111	13S	16E
Novara: Italy	75	45N	9E
Novaya Zemlya: *is.*, U.S.S.R.	82	75N	60E
Novgorod: U.S.S.R.	84	58N	31E
Novi Ligure: Italy	75	45N	9E
Novi Pazar: Yugo.	69	43N	20E
Novi Sad: Yugo.	69	45N	20E
Novocherkassk: U.S.S.R.	84	47N	40E
Novograd Volynskiy: U.S.S.R.	68	51N	28E
Novokuznetsk: U.S.S.R.	85	54N	87E
Novomoskovsk: U.S.S.R.	84	54N	38E
Novonazyvayevka: U.S.S.R.	85	56N	72E
Novorossiysk: U.S.S.R.	84	45N	38E
Novosibirsk: U.S.S.R.	85	55N	83E
Novosibirskiye Ostrova: *is.*, U.S.S.R.	83	76N	140E
Novouzensk: U.S.S.R.	84	50N	48E
Novyy Port: U.S.S.R.	83	67N	74E
Nowy Sącz: Poland	68	50N	21E
Nubian Desert: Sud.	109	21N	33E
Nueces: *r.*, U.S.A.	46	28N	98W
Nueva Rosita: Mexico	52	28N	101W
Nuevitas: Cuba	53	22N	77W
Nuevo Laredo: Mex.	52	27N	100W
Nuits St. Georges: France	73	47N	5E
Nullarbor Plain: Australia	98	30S	128E
Numazu: Japan	93	35N	139E
Nuneaton: England	63	53N	1W
Nunivak: *i.*, U.S.A.	12	60N	166W
Nunkiang: China	90	49N	125E
Nuremberg (Nürnberg): W. Germany	74	49N	11E
Nuseybin: Turkey	87	37N	41E
Nushki: Pakistan	88	29N	66E
Nuwara Eliya: Sri Lanka	88	7N	81E
Nyahururu: Kenya	110	0	36E
Nyala: Sudan	109	12N	25E
Nyasa (Malawi), L.: Africa	110	13S	34E
Nyenchen Tanglha Range: China	88/9	30N	90E
Nyíregyháza: Hung.	68	48N	22E
Nykøbing: Denmark	71	55N	12E
Nykøping: Sweden	71	59N	17E
Nyngan: Australia	101	32S	147E
Nysa: Poland	68	51N	18E
Nysa (Neisse): *r.*, Pol./E. Ger.	74	50N	15E
Oahu: *i.*, Pacific O.	103	21N	158W
Oakdale: U.S.A.	48	38N	121W
Oakland: U.S.A.	36	38N	122W
Oak Lawn: U.S.A.	34	42N	88W
Oak Park: Illinois, U.S.A.	34	42N	88W
Oak Park: Michigan, U.S.A.	33	42N	83W
Oak Ridge: U.S.A.	47	36N	84W
Oamaru: N.Z.	104	45N	171E
Oaxaca de Juárez: Mexico	53	17N	97W
Ob': *r.*, U.S.S.R.	82	63N	65E
Ob', Gulf of: U.S.S.R.	82/3	67N	76E
Oban: Scotland	62	56N	5W
Obbia: Somali Rep.	109	5N	48E
Oberammergau: W. Germany	75	48N	11E
Oberhausen: W. Ger.	64	51N	7E
Obidos: Brazil	54	2S	56W
Obi Is.: Indonesia	91	2S	128E
Ocala: U.S.A.	47	29N	82W
Ocean I.: Pacific O.	102	1S	170E
Odawara: Japan	93	35N	139E
Odda: Norway	71	60N	7E
Odemiş: Turkey	69	38N	28E
Odense: Denmark	71	55N	10E
Odenwald: *mts.*, W. Germany	74	50N	9E
Oder (Odra): *r.*, E. Ger./Pol.	74	53N	14E
Odessa: U.S.A.	46	32N	102W
Odessa: U.S.S.R.	84	46N	31E
Oeno I.: Pacific O.	103	24S	130W
Oer-Erkenschwick: W. Germany	64	52N	7E
Offenburg: W. Ger.	75	48N	8E
Ogaden: *reg.*, Ethiopia	109	7N	43E
Ogaki: Japan	93	35N	137E
Ogden: U.S.A.	48	41N	112W
Oglio: *r.*, Italy	75	45N	10E
Ohai: N.Z.	104	46S	168E
Ohakune: N.Z.	104	39S	175E
Ohio: *r.*, U.S.A.	47	37N	89W
Ohio: *State*, U.S.A.	47	40N	83W
Ohře: *r.*, Czech.	74	50N	14E
Oise: *r.*, France	72	49N	2E
Oita: Japan	93	33N	132E
Oka: *r.*, U.S.S.R.	84	55N	40E
Okanogan: *r.*, U.S.A.	48	49N	120W
Okayama: Japan	93	35N	134E
Okazaki: Japan	93	35N	137E
Okeechobee, L.: U.S.A.	47	27N	81W
Okehampton: Eng.	63	51N	4W
Okhotsk: U.S.S.R.	83	59N	143E
Okhotsk, Sea of	83	55N	150E
Oki-gunto: *i.*, Japan	93	36N	133E
Okinawa: *i.*, Japan	90	27N	128E
Oklahoma: *State*, U.S.A.	46	35N	97W
Oklahoma City: U.S.A.	46	35N	98W
Oklawaha: *r.*, U.S.A.	47	29N	82W
Okmulgee: U.S.A.	46	36N	96W
Okovango: *r.*, Angola/S.W. Afr. (Namibia)	111	18S	21E
Okovango Basin: Botswana	111	19S	23E
Öland: *i.*, Sweden	71	57N	17E
Oldenburg: W. Ger.	74	53N	8E
Oldenzaal: Neth.	74	52N	7E
Oldham: England	62	54N	2W
Olean: U.S.A.	50	42N	78W
Olekminsk: U.S.S.R.	83	60N	120E
Olenek: *r.*, U.S.S.R.	83	71N	120E
Oléron, Île d': Fr.	73	46N	1W
Olomouc: Czech.	68	50N	17E
Olonzac: France	73	43N	3E
Oloron-Ste.-Marie: France	73	43N	1W
Olsztyn: Poland	68	54N	20E
Olten: Switzerland	74	47N	8E
Olympia: U.S.A.	48	47N	123W
Olympic Nat. Park: U.S.A.	48	48N	124W
Olympus: *mtn.*, Greece	69	40N	22E
Omagh: N. Ireland	61	55N	7W
Omaha: U.S.A.	49	41N	96W
OMAN: *cap.* Muscat, & *Gulf*	87	25N	57E
Omaruru: S.W. Afr. (Namibia)	111	21S	16E
Omdurman: Sudan	84	16N	32E
Ommaney, C.: U.S.A.	24	56N	135W
Omsk: U.S.S.R.	85	55N	73E
Omuta: Japan	93	33N	131E
Omutinskoye: U.S.S.R.	85	56N	68E
Onega, L.: U.S.S.R.	84	63N	35E
O'Neill: U.S.A.	49	42N	99W
Onekotan: *i.*, U.S.S.R.	83	50N	155E
Oneonta: U.S.A.	50	42N	75W
Onslow Bay: U.S.A.	47	34N	77W
Onstwedde: Neth.	74	53N	7E
Ontario, Lake: Canada/U.S.A.	20/1	44N	78W
Oodnadatta: Austl.	98	27S	135E
O'Okiep: S. Africa	111	30S	18E
Ooldea: Australia	98	30S	132E
Oosterhesselen: Netherlands	74	53N	7E
Oosterhout: Neth.	74	52N	5E
Ootacamund: India	88	11N	77E
Opava: Czech.	68	50N	18E
Opelika: U.S.A.	47	33N	85W
Opelousas: U.S.A.	46	31N	92W
Opladen: W. Ger.	64	51N	7E
Opole: Poland	68	51N	18E
Oporto: Portugal	67	41N	9W
Opotiki: N.Z.	104	38S	177E
Opunake: N.Z.	104	39S	174E
Oradea: Romania	68	47N	22E
Oraison: France	73	44N	6E
Oran: Algeria	108	36N	1W
Orange: Australia	101	33S	149E
Orange: France	73	44N	5E
Orange: N.J., U.S.A.	35	41N	74W
Orange: Texas, U.S.A.	46	30N	94W
Orange: *r.*, S. Africa	111	28S	18E
Orangeburg: U.S.A.	47	33N	81W
Orange Free State: *Prov.*, S. Africa	111	29S	27E
Oranienburg: E. Ger.	113	53N	13E
Orbost: Australia	101	39S	149E
Ord: *r.*, Australia	98	16S	128E
Ordos Plat.: China	94	39N	108E
Ordzhonikidze: U.S.S.R.	84	43N	45E
Orebro: Sweden	71	59N	15E
Oregon: *State*, U.S.A.	48	44N	120W
Oregon City: U.S.A.	48	45N	123W
Orekhovo-Zuyevo: U.S.S.R.	84	55N	39E
Orel: U.S.S.R.	84	53N	36E
Orem: U.S.A.	48	40N	112W
Orenburg: U.S.S.R.	84	52N	55E
Orense: Spain	67	42N	8W
Orford Ness: *spit*, England	63	52N	1E
Orgeyev: U.S.S.R.	68	48N	29E
Orihuela: Spain	67	38N	1W
Orinoco: *r.*, Venez.	45	8N	64W
Orissa: *State*, India	88	20N	84E
Oristano: Sardinia	67	40N	9E
Orizaba: & *mt.*, Mex.	52	19N	97W
Orkney Is.: Scotland	61	59N	3W
Orlando: U.S.A.	47	29N	81W
Orléanais: *Old Prov.*, France	72	48N	2E
Orléans: France	72	48N	2E
Ornain: *r.*, France	72	49N	5E
Orne: *r.*, France	72	49N	0
Orsk: U.S.S.R.	85	51N	59E
Orthez: France	73	43N	1W
Ortler: *mt.*, Italy	75	47N	10E
Oruro: Bolivia	54	18S	67W
Osage: *r.*, U.S.A.	46	38N	94W
Osaka: Japan	93	35N	135E
Osh: U.S.S.R.	85	41N	73E
Oshkosh: U.S.A.	49	44N	88W
Osijek: Yugoslavia	69	46N	19E
Oskaloosa: U.S.A.	49	41N	93W
Oskarshamm: Sweden	71	57N	16E
OSLO: Norway	71	60N	11E
Oslofjorden: *fd.*, Norway	71	59N	11E
Osmanabad: India	88	18N	76E
Osnabruck: W. Ger.	74	52N	8E
Ostend: Belgium	72	51N	3E
Osterath: W. Ger.	64	51N	7W
Östersund: Sweden	70	63N	15E
Ostrava: Czech.	68	50N	18E
Ostrovnoye: U.S.S.R.	83	68N	164E
Ostrów Wielkopolski: Poland	68	52N	18E
Osumi Is.: Japan	90	31N	131E
Oswego: U.S.A.	19	43N	76W
Otago: *district*, N.Z.	104	46S	169E
Otago Penin.: N.Z.	104	46S	171E
Otaru: Japan	93	43N	141E
Othe, Forêt d': Fr.	72	48N	4E
Otranto, Strait of: Italy	69	40N	18E
Otsu: Japan	93	35N	136E

	Page	Lat.	Long.
Ottawa: Ill., U.S.A.	**49**	41N	89W
Ottawa: Kansas, U.S.A.	**49**	39N	95W
Otway Cape: Austl.	**101**	39S	144E
Ötztal Alps: Austria	**75**	47N	11E
Ouachita: *r.*, U.S.A.	**46**	33N	92W
OUAGADOUGOU: Upper Volta	**108**	12N	2W
Ouargla: Algeria	**108**	32N	5E
Oubangui: *r.*, Africa	**109**	4N	21E
Oudenaarde: Belg.	**72**	51N	4E
Oudtshoorn: S. Afr.	**111**	34S	22E
Ouessant, Î. d': Fr.	**72**	48N	5W
Oulu: & *lake*, Fin.	**70**	65N	25E
Ou-sammyaku: *mtns.*, Japan	**93**	39N	141E
Ourthe: *r.*, Belgium	**72**	50N	6E
Ouse: *r.*, East Anglia, England	**63**	53N	0
Ouse: *r.*, Sussex, England	**63**	51N	0
Oust: *r.*, France	**72**	48N	2W
Outer Hebrides: *is.*, Scotland	**61**	58N	7W
Outjo: S.W. Africa (Namibia)	**111**	20S	17E
Ouyen: Australia	**101**	35S	142E
Oviedo: Spain	**67**	43N	6W
Owen, Mt.: N.Z.	**104**	42S	172E
Owen Falls: Uganda	**110**	0	33E
Owens: *l.*, U.S.A.	**48**	36N	118W
Owensboro: U.S.A.	**47**	38N	87W
Owen Stanley Range: Papua New Guinea	**99**	9S	147E
Owyhee Res.: & *r.*, U.S.A.	**48**	43N	118W
Oxford: & *Co.*, Eng.	**63**	52N	1W
Oxnard: U.S.A.	**48**	34N	119W
Oxus: *r. see* Amu Dar'ya			
Oyonnax: France	**73**	46N	6E
Ozark Plat.: U.S.A.	**46**	37N	93W
Ozarks, L. of the: U.S.A.	**46**	38N	93W
Ózd: Hungary	**68**	48N	20E
Paarl: S. Africa	**111**	34S	19E
Pachuca de Soto: Mexico	**52**	27N	99W
Pacific Grove: U.S.A.	**48**	37N	122W
Pacific Ocean	**102/3**	—	—
Padang: Indonesia	**91**	1S	100E
Padangsidempuan: Indonesia	**92**	1N	99E
Paderborn: W. Ger.	**74**	52N	9E
Padre I.: U.S.A.	**46**	27N	97W
Padua (Padova): It.	**75**	45N	12E
Paducah: U.S.A.	**47**	37N	89W
Pafuri: Moz.	**111**	22S	33E
Paignton: England	**63**	50N	4W
Paimboeuf: France	**73**	47N	2W
Paimpol: France	**72**	49N	3W
Paisley: Scotland	**62**	56N	4W
Pakanbaru: Indonesia	**92**	1N	102E
PAKISTAN: *cap.* Islamabad	**88**	—	—
Pak Lay: Laos	**92**	18N	101E
Pakokku: Burma	**92**	21N	95E
Pakse: Laos	**92**	15N	105E
Palapye Road: Botswana	**111**	22S	26E
Palatka: U.S.A.	**47**	30N	82W
Palau Is.: Caroline Is.	**91**	7N	135E
Palawan: *i.*, Phil.	**91**	10N	119E
Palembang: Indonesia	**91**	3S	105E
Palencia: Spain	**67**	42N	5W
Palermo: Sicily	**69**	38N	13E
Palestine: U.S.A.	**46**	32N	96W
Palghat: India	**88**	11N	76E
Palisade: U.S.A.	**48**	41N	116W
Palk Strait: India/Sri Lanka	**88**	10N	80E
Palliser, C.: N.Z.	**104**	42S	175E
Palma de Mallorca: Spain	**67**	40N	3E
Palma Sorlano: Cuba	**53**	20N	76W
Palmas, C.: Liberia	**108**	4N	8W
Palm Beach: U.S.A.	**45**	27N	80W
Palmer Land: Antarctica	**116**	64S	63W
Palmerston North: New Zealand	**104**	40S	176E
Palmyra I.: Pac. O.	**102**	6N	162W
Palo Alto: U.S.A.	**36**	36N	122W
Palos, C. de: Spain	**67**	38N	1W
Pamiers: France	**73**	43N	2E
Pamirs: *mts.*, U.S.S.R./Afghanistan	**85**	37N	73E
Pamlico Sd.: U.S.A.	**47**	35N	76W
Pampa: *reg.*, Argentina	**49**	33S	64W
Pampa: U.S.A.	**46**	35N	101W
Pamplona: Spain	**67**	43N	2W
PANAMA: *cap.* Panama	**45**	8N	80W
Panama Canal	**45**	*Inset*	
Panama City: U.S.A.	**47**	30N	86W
Panay: *i.*, Phil.	**91**	11N	122E
Pangong Ra.: China	**88**	34N	80E
Panjim: India	**88**	15N	74E
Pantar: *i.*, Indonesia	**91**	8S	124E
Pantellaria: *i.*, Italy	**69**	37N	12E

	Page	Lat.	Long.
Paoki: China	**94**	34N	107E
Paoshan: China	**92**	25N	99E
Paoting: China	**94**	39N	115E
Paotow: China	**94**	41N	110E
Papua: & *gulf*, Papua New Guinea	**99**	7S	145E
PAPUA NEW GUINEA: *cap.* Port Moresby	**99**	5S	145E
Pará: *r.*, Brazil	**54**	1S	48W
Paracel Is.: S. China S.	**91**	16N	112E
PARAGUAY: *cap.* Asuncion	**56**	23S	58W
Paraguay: *r.*, S. Am.	**49**	26S	58W
Parakou: Benin	**108**	9N	3E
PARAMARIBO: Surinam	**54**	6N	55W
Paramus: U.S.A.	**35**	41N	74W
Paramushir: *i.*, U.S.S.R.	**83**	51N	155E
Paraná: Argentina	**56**	32S	60W
Paraná: *r.*, S. Am.	**56**	25S	53W
Parbati: *r.*, India	**88**	23N	77E
Parbhani: India	**88**	19N	77E
Parchim: E. Germany	**74**	53N	12E
Pardubice: Czech.	**68**	50N	16E
PARIS: France	**113**	—	—
Paris: U.S.A.	**46**	34N	96W
Parkersburg: U.S.A.	**47**	39N	82W
Parkes: Australia	**101**	33S	148E
Park Range: U.S.A.	**48**	40N	107W
Park Rapids: *town*, U.S.A.	**49**	47N	95W
Parma: Italy	**75**	45N	10E
Parma: U.S.A.	**47**	41N	82W
Parnaiba: Brazil	**54**	3S	42W
Parnassós: *mtn.*, Greece	**69**	38N	22E
Páros: *i.*, Greece	**69**	37N	25E
Parramatta: Austl.	**115**	34S	151E
Parsons: U.S.A.	**49**	37N	95W
Parthenay: France	**73**	47N	0
Partizansk: U.S.S.R.	**83**	43N	133E
Pasadena: U.S.A.	**37**	34N	118W
Pascagoula: & *r.*, U.S.A.	**47**	30N	89W
Pasco: U.S.A.	**48**	46N	119W
Passaic: U.S.A.	**35**	41N	74W
Passau: W. Germany	**75**	49N	13E
Passchendaele: Belg.	**72**	51N	3E
Passero, C.: Sicily	**69**	37N	15E
Pasto: Colombia	**54**	1N	77W
Patagonia: *reg.*, Arg.	**55**	45S	70W
Patay: France	**72**	48N	2E
Paterson: U.S.A.	**35**	41N	74W
Pathankot: India	**88**	32N	76E
Pathfinder Res.: U.S.A.	**48**	42N	107W
Patiala: India	**88**	30N	76E
Patna: India	**88**	26N	85E
Patos, Lagoa dos: Brazil	**56**	31S	51W
Pátrai (Patras): Greece	**69**	38N	22E
Pattani: Thailand	**92**	6N	101E
Pau: France	**73**	43N	0
Paulistana: Brazil	**54**	8S	41W
Paulo Afonso Falls: Brazil	**54**	9S	38W
Pavia: Italy	**75**	45N	9E
Pavlodar: U.S.S.R.	**85**	52N	77E
Payette: & *r.*, U.S.A.	**48**	44N	117W
Paysandu: Uruguay	**56**	32S	58W
Pearl: *r.*, U.S.A.	**46**	32N	90W
Pease: *r.*, U.S.A.	**46**	34N	100W
Pechenga: U.S.S.R.	**70**	70N	31E
Pechora: *r.*, U.S.S.R.	**84**	63N	56E
Pecos: & *r.*, U.S.A.	**46**	31N	104W
Pécs: Hungary	**68**	46N	18E
Pedro, Pt.: Sri Lanka	**88**	10N	80E
Pedro Miguel Locks: Panama Canal	**45**	*Inset*	
Peebinga: Australia	**101**	35S	141E
Peebles: Scotland	**62**	56N	3W
Pee Dee: *r.*, U.S.A.	**47**	34N	79W
Peel: I. of Man	**62**	54N	5W
Pegasus Bay: N.Z.	**104**	43S	173E
Pegu: Burma	**92**	17N	96E
Peh: *r.*, China	**95**	24N	113E
Peian: China	**90**	48N	127E
Peine: W. Germany	**74**	52N	10E
Peipus, L.: U.S.S.R.	**71**	58N	27E
PEKING (Peiping): China	**114**	—	—
Pelee: *i.*, U.S.A.	**47**	42N	83W
Pelican Point: S.W. Afr. (Namibia)	**111**	23S	14E
Peloponnese: *penin.*, Greece	**69**	38N	22E
Pelotas: Brazil	**56**	32S	52W
Pelusium, Bay of: Egypt	**109**	*Inset*	
Pelvoux, Mont: Fr.	**73**	45N	6E
Pematangsiantar: Indonesia	**92**	2N	99E
Pemba: Zambia	**111**	17S	27E
Pemba: *i.*, Tanzan.	**110**	5S	40E
Pembroke: Wales	**63**	52N	5W
Pendembu: Sierra Leone	**108**	8N	11W
Pendleton: U.S.A.	**48**	46N	119W
Pend Oreille L.: U.S.A.	**48**	48N	116W

	Page	Lat.	Long.
Penganga: *r.*, India	**88**	20N	77E
Pengpu: China	**94**	33N	117E
Penmarch, Pte. de: France	**72**	48N	4W
Pennar: *r.*, India	**88**	14N	77E
Pennine Alps: Switzerland/Italy	**75**	46N	7E
Pennines: *mtns.*, Eng.	**62**	54N	2W
Pennsylvania: *State*, U.S.A.	**47**	41N	77W
Penobscot: *r.*, U.S.A.	**15**	45N	68W
Penrith: Australia	**101**	34S	151E
Penrith: England	**62**	55N	3W
Pensacola: U.S.A.	**47**	30N	87W
Pentland Firth: Scot.	**61**	59N	3W
Penza: U.S.S.R.	**84**	53N	45E
Penzance: England	**63**	50N	6W
Peoria: U.S.A.	**49**	41N	90W
Perche, Collines du: *hills*, France	**72**	49N	1E
Percy Is.: Australia	**100**	22S	150E
Perdu, Mont: Fr./Sp.	**73**	43N	0
Pergamino: Arg.	**56**	34S	61W
Périgord: *reg.*, France	**73**	45N	1E
Périgueux: France	**73**	45N	1E
Perim I.: Yemen P.D.R.	**87**	13N	43E
Perm: U.S.S.R.	**84**	57N	55E
Pernik: Bulgaria	**69**	43N	23E
Péronne: France	**72**	50N	3E
Perpignan: France	**73**	43N	3E
PERSIA: *see* **IRAN**			
Persian Gulf	**87**	27N	52E
Perth: Australia	**100**	32S	116E
Perth: Scotland	**62**	56N	3W
Perth Amboy: U.S.A.	**35**	41N	74W
PERU: *cap.* Lima	**54**	10S	75W
Peru Basin: Pacific O.	**103**	15S	85W
Peru-Chile Trench: Pacific Ocean	**103**	20S	75W
Perugia: Italy	**69**	43N	12E
Pesaro: Italy	**75**	44N	13E
Pescadores: *is.*, Taiwan	**95**	24N	120E
Pescara: Italy	**69**	42N	14E
Peshawar: Pakistan	**88**	34N	71E
Pessac: France	**73**	45N	1W
Petange: Lux.	**72**	50N	6E
Peterborough: Austl.	**101**	33S	139E
Peterborough: Eng.	**63**	53N	0
Peterhead: Scotland	**61**	57N	2W
Petersburg: Alaska, U.S.A.	**24**	57N	133W
Petersburg: Va., U.S.A.	**47**	37N	78W
Petone: N.Z.	**104**	41S	175E
Petoskey: U.S.A.	**19**	45N	85W
Petropavlovsk: U.S.S.R.	**85**	55N	69E
Petropavlovsk-Kamchatskiy: U.S.S.R.	**83**	53N	159E
Petrópolis: Brazil	**56**	23S	43W
Petroşeni: Romania	**69**	45N	23E
Petrozavodsk: U.S.S.R.	**84**	62N	35E
Petukhovo: U.S.S.R.	**85**	55N	68E
Pfälzer Bergland: *plat.*, W. Germany	**74**	49N	8E
Pforzheim: W. Ger.	**74**	49N	9E
Phanom Dongrak: *mtns.*, Thailand	**92**	14N	103E
Phan Rang: Vietnam	**92**	12N	109E
Phan Thiet: Vietnam	**92**	10N	108E
Phenix City: U.S.A.	**47**	32N	85W
Phet Buri: Thailand	**92**	13N	99E
Philadelphia: U.S.A.	**50**	40N	75W
PHILIPPINES, THE: *cap.* Manila	**91**	10N	123E
Philippine Sea	**91**	18N	130E
Philip Smith Mts.: U.S.A.	**30**	68N	147W
PHNOM PENH: Cambodia	**93**	11N	105E
Phoenix: U.S.A.	**48**	34N	112W
Phoenix Is.: Pac. O.	**102**	3S	175W
Phong Saly: Laos	**92**	21N	102E
Phu Cuong: Vietnam	**92**	10N	106E
Phuket: Thailand	**93**	8N	98E
Piacenza: Italy	**75**	45N	10E
Piatra-Neamţ: Rom.	**68**	47N	26E
Piave: *r.*, Italy	**75**	46N	12E
Picardy: *Old Prov.*, France	**72**	50N	2E
Picton: N.Z.	**104**	41S	174E
Piedmont: *Reg.*, It.	**75**	45N	8E
Piedras Negras: Mex.	**52**	29N	101W
Pierre: U.S.A.	**49**	44N	100W
Pietarsaari: Finland	**70**	64N	23E
Pietermaritzburg: South Africa	**111**	30S	30E
Piet Retief: S. Africa	**111**	27S	31E
Pigeon: *r.*, U.S.A./Canada	**49**	48N	90W
Pikeville: U.S.A.	**47**	37N	83W
Pilcomayo: *r.*, S. Am.	**54**	23S	62W
Pilsen: *see* Plzen			
Pinang: *i.*, Malaysia	**92**	5N	100E
Pinar del Rio: Cuba	**53**	22N	84W
Pindus Mts.: Greece	**69**	40N	21E
Pine Bluff: U.S.A.	**46**	34N	92W

	Page	Lat.	Long.
Pine Island Sound: U.S.A.	**47**	27N	82W
Pinerolo: Italy	**75**	45N	7E
Pinkiang: *see* Harbin			
Pinnaroo: Australia	**101**	35S	141E
Pinos, I. de: Cuba	**53**	22N	83W
Pinsk: U.S.S.R.	**71**	52N	26E
Piraieus: Greece	**69**	38N	24E
Pirgos: Greece	**69**	38N	22E
Pirmasens: W. Ger.	**74**	49N	8E
Pisa: Italy	**75**	44N	10E
Pistoia: Italy	**75**	44N	11E
Pit: *r.*, U.S.A.	**48**	41N	121W
Pitcairn I.: Pac. O.	**103**	25S	130W
Piteşti: Romania	**69**	45N	25E
Pittsburg: Kansas, U.S.A.	**49**	37N	95W
Pittsburg: Texas, U.S.A.	**46**	33N	95W
Pittsburgh: U.S.A.	**47**	40N	80W
Piura: Peru	**54**	5S	81W
Placetas: Cuba	**53**	22N	80W
Plainfield: U.S.A.	**35**	41N	74W
Plantaurel, Mts. du: France	**73**	43N	1E
Plata, Rio de la: *r.*, S. America	**56**	35S	57W
Platte: *r.*, U.S.A.	**49**	41N	100W
Plattsburg: U.S.A.	**19**	45N	74W
Plauen: E. Germany	**74**	50N	12E
Plenty, Bay of: N.Z.	**104**	38S	177E
Plentywood: U.S.A.	**49**	49N	105W
Pleven: Bulgaria	**69**	43N	25E
Ploeşti: Romania	**69**	45N	26E
Plomb du Cantal: *mtn.*, France	**73**	45N	3E
Plombières: France	**72**	48N	6E
Plovdiv: Bulgaria	**69**	42N	25E
Plumtree: Rhodesia (Zimbabwe)	**111**	20S	28E
Plymouth: England	**63**	50N	4W
Plzen (Pilsen): Czech.	**68**	50N	13E
Po: *r.*, Italy	**75**	45N	10E
Pocatello: U.S.A.	**48**	43N	112W
Poçoes: Brazil	**54**	15S	40W
Pointe Noire: Congo	**110**	5S	12E
Poissy: France	**72**	49N	2E
Poitiers: France	**73**	47N	0
Poitou: *Old Prov.*, Fr.	**73**	47N	1W
Poix: France	**72**	50N	2E
POLAND: *cap.* Warsaw	**68**	52N	20E
Polotsk: U.S.S.R.	**68**	55N	29E
Poltava: U.S.S.R.	**84**	50N	35E
Polunochnoye: U.S.S.R.	**85**	62N	60E
Pomeranian Bay: E. Ger./Pol.	**71**	54N	14E
Pomona: S.W. Africa (Namibia)	**111**	27S	15E
Ponape: *i.*, Pacific O.	**102**	8N	159E
Ponca City: U.S.A.	**49**	37N	97W
Ponce: Puerto Rico	**45**	18N	67W
Pondicherry: India	**88**	12N	80E
Ponta Grossa: Brazil	**56**	24S	47W
Pont-à-Mousson: Fr.	**72**	49N	6E
Ponta Porã: Brazil	**54**	22S	56W
Pontarlier: France	**73**	47N	6E
Pontchartrain, L.: U.S.A.	**47**	30N	90W
Pontevedra: Spain	**67**	42N	9W
Pontiac: U.S.A.	**47**	43N	83W
Pontianak: Indonesia	**91**	0	109E
Pontic Mts.: Turkey	**86/7**	42N	35E
Pontivy: France	**72**	48N	3W
Pontoise: France	**113**	49N	2E
Pontresina: Switz.	**75**	46N	10E
Pontypool: Wales	**63**	52N	3W
Pontypridd: Wales	**63**	52N	3W
Poole: England	**63**	51N	2W
Poona: India	**88**	18N	74E
Poopo, L.: Bolivia	**54**	18S	67W
Poperinghe: Belg.	**72**	51N	3E
Poplar Bluff: U.S.A.	**46**	37N	90W
Popocatepetl: *volc.*, Mexico	**52**	19N	99W
Porbandar: India	**88**	22N	70E
Porcupine: *r.*, Canada/U.S.A.	**30**	67N	142W
Pori: Finland	**70**	61N	22E
Port Adelaide: Austl.	**101**	35S	139E
Portadown: N. Irel.	**62**	54N	6W
Portaferry: N. Irel.	**62**	54N	6W
Portalegre: Portugal	**67**	39N	7W
Port Alfred: S. Afr.	**111**	34S	27E
Port Angeles: U.S.A.	**48**	48N	123W
Port Antonio: Jam.	**53**	18N	76W
Port Arthur: U.S.A.	**46**	30N	94W
Port Augusta: Austl.	**101**	32S	138E
PORT-AU-PRINCE: Haiti	**45**	19N	72W
Port Chalmers: N.Z.	**104**	46S	171E
Port Elizabeth: South Africa	**111**	34S	26E
Port Ellen: Scotland	**62**	56N	6W
Port Fuad: Egypt	**109**	*Inset*	
Port Harcourt: Nig.	**108**	5N	7E
Port Hedland: Austl.	**98**	20S	119E
Port Huron: U.S.A.	**19**	43N	82W
Port Jackson: *sd.*, Austl.	**115**	34S	151E

	Page	Lat.	Long.
Portland: Australia	101	38S	142E
Portland: Maine, U.S.A.	19	44N	70W
Portland: Oregon, U.S.A.	48	46N	123W
Portland, Bill of: *hd.*, England	63	51N	2W
Portlaoighise, R. of: Ireland	61	53N	7W
Port Lincoln: Austl.	98	35S	136E
Port Macquarie: Australia	101	31S	153E
Portmadoc: Wales	63	53N	4W
PORT MORESBY: Papua New Guinea	99	9S	147E
Port Nolloth: S. Afr.	111	29S	17E
Pôrto Alegre: Brazil	56	30S	51W
Pôrto Alexandre: Angola	111	16S	12E
Portobello: *hist.*, Panama	47	10N	80W
PORT OF SPAIN: Trinidad & Tobago	45	11N	61W
Porto Novo: Benin	108	6N	3E
Pôrto Velho: Brazil	54	9S	64W
Port Phillip Bay: Australia	101	38S	145E
Port Pirie: Australia	101	33S	138E
Portree: Scotland	61	57N	6W
Portrush: N. Ireland	62	55N	7W
Port Safaga: Egypt	86	27N	34E
Port St. Joe: U.S.A.	47	30N	85W
Port Said: Egypt	86	31N	32E
Port Shepstone: South Africa	111	31S	31E
Portsmouth: England	63	51N	1W
Portsmouth: N.H., U.S.A.	51	43N	71W
Portsmouth: Ohio, U.S.A.	47	39N	83W
Portsmouth: Va., U.S.A.	47	37N	76W
Port Sudan: Sudan	86	20N	37E
Port Sulphur: U.S.A.	47	29N	90W
Port Talbot: Wales	63	52N	4W
Port Taufiq: Egypt	109	*Inset*	
PORTUGAL: *cap.* Lisbon	67	—	—
Port Vendres: Fr.	73	43N	3E
Porz: W. Germany	64	51N	7E
Posadas: Argentina	56	27S	56W
Postmasburg: S. Afr.	111	28S	23E
Poteet: U.S.A.	46	29N	99W
Potenza: Italy	69	41N	16E
Potgietersrus: S. Afr.	111	24S	29E
Poti: U.S.S.R.	84	42N	42E
Potomac: *r.*, U.S.A.	47	38N	77W
Potosi: Bolivia	54	20S	66W
Potrerillos: Chile	54	26S	69W
Potsdam: E. Germany	113	52N	13E
Potsdam: U.S.A.	19	45N	75W
Potters Bar: England	112	52N	0
Pottstown: U.S.A.	50	40N	76W
Poughkeepsie: U.S.A.	51	42N	74W
Poverty Bay: N.Z.	104	39S	178E
Powder: *r.*, U.S.A.	49	45N	106W
Powys: *Co.*, Wales	63	52N	4W
Poyang: & *l.*, China	95	29N	116E
Poznań: Poland	68	52N	17E
Prades: France	73	43N	2E
PRAGUE (Praha): Czechoslovakia	75	50N	14E
Prato: Italy	75	44N	11E
Prescott: U.S.A.	48	35N	112W
Presque Isle: *city*, U.S.A.	15	47N	68W
Preston: England	62	54N	3W
Prestwick: Scotland	62	55N	5W
PRETORIA: Republic of South Africa	111	26S	28E
Préveza: Greece	69	39N	21E
Prichard: U.S.A.	47	31N	88W
Prieska: S. Africa	111	30S	22E
Prilep: Yugoslavia	69	41N	22E
Prince of Wales I.: U.S.A.	24	56N	133W
Princeton: U.S.A.	50	40N	75W
Pripet (Pripyet'): *r.* & *marshes*, U.S.S.R.	84	52N	29E
Priština: Yugoslavia	69	43N	21E
Privas: France	73	45N	5E
Prizren: Yugoslavia	69	42N	21E
Progreso: Mexico	53	21N	90W
Prokop'yevsk: U.S.S.R.	85	54N	86E
Prome: Burma	92	19N	95E
Proserpine: Austl.	100	20S	149E
Prosser: U.S.A.	48	39N	119W
Provence: *Old Prov.*, France	73	44N	6E
Provence Alps: France	73	44N	6E
Providence: U.S.A.	51	42N	71W
Providence, C.: N.Z.	104	46S	166E
Provo: U.S.A.	48	40N	112W
Prut: *r.*, U.S.S.R./Romania	68	48N	27E
Przemyśl: Poland	68	50N	23E
Pskov: U.S.S.R.	82	58N	28E
Puebla: Mexico	52	19N	98W
Pueblo: U.S.A.	49	38N	105W
Puerto Ayacucho: Venezuela	54	6N	66W
Puerto Cabello: Venezuela	54	10N	68W
Puerto Deseado: Arg.	55	48S	66W
Puerto Limón: Costa Rica	45	10N	83W
Puerto Montt: Chile	55	41S	71W
Puerto Peñasco: Mex.	48	31N	114W
PUERTO RICO: *cap.* San Juan	45	18N	66W
Pukekohe: N.Z.	104	37S	175E
Pula: Yugoslavia	69	45N	14E
Pulaski: U.S.A.	47	37N	81W
Pullman: U.S.A.	48	47N	117W
PUNAKHA: Bhutan	89	28N	90E
Punjab: *State*, India	88	30N	75E
Puno: Peru	54	16S	70W
Punta Arenas: Chile	55	53S	71W
Purbeck, I. of: *reg.*, England	63	51N	2W
Puri: India	88	20N	86E
Purnea: India	88	26N	88E
Purús: *r.*, Brazil	54	5S	64W
Pusan: S. Korea	90	35N	129E
Pushkin: U.S.S.R.	84	59N	30E
Putoran Mts.: U.S.S.R.	83	69N	95E
Putumayo: *r.*, S. Am.	54	2S	72W
Puy de Sancy: *mtn.*, France	73	45N	3E
Pwllheli: Wales	63	53N	4W
Pyatigorsk: U.S.S.R.	84	44N	43E
PYONGYANG: N. Korea	90	39N	126E
Pyramid Lake: U.S.A.	48	40N	120W
Pyramids: *hist.*, Egypt	86	30N	31E
Pyrenees: *mtns.*, Spain/France	73	43N	0
Qasr Farafra: Egypt	109	27N	28E
QATAR: *cap.* Doha	87	25N	51E
Qattara Depression: Egypt	86	29N	28E
Qazvīn: Iran	87	36N	50E
Qena: Egypt	86	26N	33E
Qila Saifullah: Pakistan	88	31N	69E
Qomul: *see* Hami			
Queanbeyan: Austl.	101	35S	149E
Quedlinburg: E. Ger.	74	52N	11E
Queen Adelaide Arch.: Chile	55	52S	75W
Queen Maud Land: Antarctica	116	75S	10E
Queens: U.S.A.	35	41N	74W
Queensland: *State*, Australia	99	23S	145E
Queenstown: N.Z.	104	45S	169E
Quelimane: Moz.	111	18S	37E
Quelpart I.: *see* Cheju I.			
Quemoy: China	95	24N	118E
Que Que: Rhodesia (Zimbabwe)	111	19S	30E
Querétaro: Mexico	52	21N	100W
Quetta: Pakistan	88	30N	67E
Quiberon: & *bay*, Fr.	72	47N	3W
Quilpie: Australia	100	27S	144E
Quimper: France	72	48N	4W
Quimperlé: France	72	48N	4W
Quincy: U.S.A.	33	42N	71W
Qui Nhon: Vietnam	92	13N	109E
QUITO: Ecuador	54	0	78W
Qum: Iran	87	35N	50E
Qunfidha: Sau. Arab.	87	19N	41E
Quorn: Australia	101	32S	138E
Quwaiiya: Sau. Arab.	87	24N	45E
RABAT: Morocco	108	34N	7W
Rabaul: Papua New Guinea	99	4S	152E
Rach Gia: Vietnam	92	10N	105E
Racine: U.S.A.	47	43N	88W
Radom: Poland	68	51N	21E
Ragusa: Sicily	69	37N	15E
Raichur: India	88	16N	77E
Rainier, Mt.: U.S.A.	48	47N	122W
Raipur: India	88	21N	82E
Rajahmundry: India	88	17N	82E
Rajasthan: *State*, India	88	27N	74E
Rajkot: India	88	22N	71E
Rajshahi: Bangladesh	88	24N	88E
Rakaia: *r.*, N.Z.	104	44S	172E
Raleigh: U.S.A.	47	36N	79W
Rambouillet: France	72	49N	2E
Ramillies: *hist.*, Belgium	72	51N	5E
Rampur: India	88	29N	79E
Ramsey: I. of Man	62	54N	4W
Ramsey, I.: Wales	63	52N	5W
Ramsgate: England	63	51N	1E
Rancagua: Chile	55	34S	71W
Ranchi: India	88	23N	85E
Randers: Denmark	71	56N	10E
Rangitaiki: *r.*, N.Z.	104	38S	177E
RANGOON: Burma	92	17N	96E
Rangpur: Bangladesh	88	26N	89E
Raniganj: India	88	24N	87E
Rann of Kutch: *marsh*, India/Pak.	88	24N	69E
Rapallo: Italy	75	44N	9E
Rapid City: U.S.A.	49	44N	103W
Ras al Hadd: *c.*, Oman	87	23N	60E
Rasht: Iran	87	37N	50E
Rastatt: W. Germany	74	49N	8E
Rathenow: E. Germany	74	53N	13E
Rathlin I.: N. Irel.	62	55N	6W
Ratingen: W. Germany	64	51N	7E
Ratlam: India	88	23N	75E
Ratnagiri: India	88	17N	73E
Raton: U.S.A.	49	37N	105W
Raukumara Ra.: N.Z.	104	38S	178E
Ravenna: Italy	75	44N	12E
Ravi: *r.*, Pakistan	88	31N	72E
Rawalpindi: Pakistan	88	34N	73E
Rawson: Argentina	55	43S	65W
Rayleigh Bay: U.S.A.	47	35N	76W
Raymond: U.S.A.	48	47N	124W
Ré, Île de: France	72	46N	1W
Reading: England	63	51N	1W
Reading: U.S.A.	50	40N	76W
Recherche, Arch. of the: Australia	100	34S	122E
Recife: Brazil	54	8S	35W
Recklinghausen: W. Germany	64	52N	7E
Red: *r.*, Can./U.S.A.	49	48N	97W
Red: *r.*, U.S.A.	46	31N	92W
Red Basin of Szechwan: China	95	30N	105E
Red Bluff: U.S.A.	48	40N	122W
Red Cedar: *r.*, U.S.A.	49	45N	92W
Redcliffe: Australia	100	27S	153E
Red Cliffs: Australia	101	34S	142E
Redding: U.S.A.	48	41N	122W
Redditch: England	63	52N	2W
Redfield: U.S.A.	49	45N	99W
Redhill: England	112	51N	0
Red L.: U.S.A.	49	48N	95W
Redon: France	72	48N	2W
Red Sea	86/7	—	—
Red Sea Hills: Egypt	86	27N	33E
Red Wing: U.S.A.	49	45N	93W
Regensburg: W. Ger.	74	49N	12E
Reggio di Calabria: Italy	69	38N	16E
Reggio nell'Emilia: Italy	75	45N	11E
Reidsville: U.S.A.	47	36N	80W
Reigate: England	112	51N	0
Reims: *see* Rheims			
Reinosa: Mexico	52	26N	98W
Remoulins: France	73	44N	5E
Remscheid: W. Germany	64	51N	7E
Renkum: Neth.	74	52N	6E
Renmark: Australia	101	34S	141E
Rennes: France	72	48N	2W
Reno: U.S.A.	48	39N	120W
Republican: *r.*, U.S.A.	49	40N	97W
REPUBLIC OF SOUTH AFRICA: *cap.* Pretoria	111	—	—
Repulse Bay: Austl.	100	21S	149E
Resistencia: Arg.	56	27S	59W
Reşiţa: Romania	69	45N	22E
Rethimnon: Crete	69	35N	25E
Reus: Spain	67	41N	1E
Reuss: *r.*, Switz.	75	47N	8E
Reutlingen: W. Ger.	75	48N	9E
Revere: U.S.A.	33	42N	71W
Revermont: *hills*, France	73	46N	5E
Revilla Gigedo Is.: Pacific Ocean	103	19N	112W
Rewari: India	88	28N	76E
Rexburg: U.S.A.	48	44N	112W
Reykjanis Ridge: Atlantic Ocean	57	60N	34W
REYKJAVIK: Iceland	70	64N	22W
Rezā'īyeh: Iran	87	38N	45E
Rēzekne: U.S.S.R.	71	56N	28E
Rhaetian Alps: Switzerland	75	47N	10E
Rhayader: Wales	62	52N	4W
Rheden: Neth.	74	52N	6E
Rheims (Reims): France	72	49N	4E
Rheinberg: W. Ger.	64	52N	7E
Rheine: W. Germany	74	52N	7E
Rheinhausen: W. Germany	64	51N	7E
Rheinkamp: W. Germany	64	51N	7E
Rheydt: W. Germany	64	51N	6E
Rhine: *r.*, Europe	74	52N	6E
Rhode Island: *State*, U.S.A.	51	42N	72W
Rhodes (Ródhos): *i.* & *town*, Greece	69	36N	28E
RHODESIA (ZIMBABWE): *cap.* Salisbury	111	20S	30E
Rhodope Mts.: Bulg.	69	42N	24E
Rhône: *r.*, Europe	73	45N	5E
Rhum: *i.*, Scotland	62	57N	6W
Rhyl: Wales	63	53N	4W
Riau Arch.: Indon.	91	0	105E
Ribble: *r.*, England	62	53½N	2½W
Ribeirão Prêto: Brazil	54	21S	48W
Riberalta: Bolivia	54	11S	66W
Riccarton: N.Z.	104	44S	173E
Richfield: U.S.A.	48	39N	112W
Richland: U.S.A.	48	46N	119W
Richmond: England	112	51N	0
Richmond: Indiana, U.S.A.	47	40N	85W
Richmond: Ky., U.S.A.	47	38N	84W
Richmond: Virginia, U.S.A.	47	38N	77W
Richwood: U.S.A.	47	38N	81W
Rickmansworth: Eng.	112	52N	0
Ridgewood: U.S.A.	35	41N	74W
Riga: & *gulf*, U.S.S.R.	71	57N	24E
Rijeka: Yugoslavia	69	45N	15E
Rijswijk: Neth.	74	52N	4E
Rimini: Italy	75	44N	13E
Riobamba: Ecuador	54	2S	79W
Rio Branco: Brazil	54	10S	68W
Rio Cuarto: *sett.*, Arg.	56	33S	64W
Rio de Janeiro: Brazil	56	23S	43W
Rio Gallegos: Arg.	55	52S	69W
Rio Grande: Brazil	56	32S	52W
Rio Grande: *r.*, U.S.A./Mexico	44	29N	102W
Rio Grande de Santiago: *r.*, Mexico	52	21N	104W
Rio Grande do Sul: *State*, Brazil	56	30S	53W
Riom: France	73	46N	3E
Ripon: England	62	54N	2W
Ritter, Mt.: U.S.A.	48	38N	120W
Rive-de-Gier: France	73	46N	5E
Rivera: Uruguay	56	31S	56W
Riverina: *reg.*, Australia	101	36S	145E
Riverside: U.S.A.	48	34N	117W
RIYADH: Saudi Arabia	87	25N	47E
Roanne: France	73	46N	4E
Roanoke: U.S.A.	47	37N	80W
Roanoke Rapids: *city*, U.S.A.	47	37N	78W
Robstown: U.S.A.	46	28N	97W
Rochdale: England	62	54N	2W
Rochechouart: Fr.	73	46N	1E
Rochefort-sur-Mer: France	73	46N	1W
Rochester: England	112	51N	1E
Rochester: Minn., U.S.A.	49	44N	92W
Rochester: N.H., U.S.A.	51	43N	71W
Rochester: N.Y., U.S.A.	50	43N	78W
Rock: *r.*, U.S.A.	47	42N	89W
Rockall Plateau: Atlantic Ocean	57	58N	14W
Rockford: U.S.A.	49	42N	89W
Rockhampton: Australia	100	23S	151E
Rock Hill: *city*, U.S.A.	47	35N	81W
Rock Island: *city*, U.S.A.	49	41N	91W
Rock Springs: *city*, U.S.A.	48	42N	109W
Rockville Centre: U.S.A.	35	41N	74W
Rockwood: U.S.A.	15	46N	70W
Rocky Ford: *city*, U.S.A.	46	38N	104W
Rocky Mount: *city*, U.S.A.	47	36N	78W
Rocky Mts.: Canada/U.S.A.	12	55N	117W
Rocroi: France	72	50N	5E
Rodenkirchen: W. Ger.	64	51N	7E
Rodez: France	73	44N	3E
Ródhos (Rhodes): *i.* & *town*, Greece	69	36N	28E
Roermond: Neth.	74	51N	6E
Roeselare: Belgium	72	51N	3E
Rogers, Mt.: U.S.A.	47	37N	82W
Rogers City: U.S.A.	19	45N	84W
Rolla: U.S.A.	46	38N	92W
Roma: Australia	100	27S	149E
Roman: Romania	68	47N	26E
ROMANIA: *cap.* Bucharest	68/9	—	—
Romans: France	73	45N	5E
ROME: Italy	69	42N	12E
Rome: U.S.A.	47	34N	85W
Romford: England	112	52N	0
Romilly-sur-Seine: France	72	49N	4E
Romulus: U.S.A.	33	42N	83W
Rona: *i.*, Scotland	61	59N	6W
Roncesvalles: Spain	73	43N	1W
Ronda: Spain	67	37N	5W
Roosendaal: Neth.	74	52N	4E
Roosevelt I.: Antarc.	116	80S	161W
Roquefort: France	73	44N	0
Roraima: *mtn.*, S. America	54	5N	61W
Rorschach: Switz.	75	48N	9E
Rorvik: Norway	70	65N	11E
Rosa, Monte: Switz./Italy	75	46N	8E

Name	Page	Lat.	Long.
Rosario: Argentina	56	33S	61W
Roscoff: France	72	49N	4W
Roseburg: U.S.A.	48	43N	123W
Roseires: Sudan	109	12N	34E
Rosendaël: France	72	51N	2E
Rosenheim: W. Ger.	75	48N	12E
Rosetta: Egypt	86	32N	30E
Ross Ice Shelf: Antarctica	116	80S	180
Rosslare Harbour: R. of Ireland	62	52N	6W
Ross-on-Wye: Eng.	62	52N	3W
Ross Sea: Antarctica	116	76S	175W
Rostock: E. Germany	74	54N	12E
Rostov: U.S.S.R.	84	47N	40E
Roswell: U.S.A.	49	33N	105W
Rothbury: England	62	55N	2W
Rothenburg: W. Ger.	74	49N	10E
Rotherham: England	63	53N	1W
Rothesay: Scotland	62	56N	5W
Roti: i., Indonesia	91	10S	124E
Roto: Australia	101	33S	146E
Rotorua: N.Z.	104	38S	176E
Rotterdam: Neth.	74	52N	4E
Rottweil: W. Ger.	74	48N	9E
Roubaix: France	72	51N	3E
Rouen: France	72	49N	1E
Roundup: U.S.A.	48	46N	109W
Roussillon: Old Prov., France	73	43N	3E
Rovaniemi: Finland	70	66N	26E
Rovereto: Italy	75	46N	11E
Rovigo: Italy	75	45N	12E
Rovno: U.S.S.R.	84	51N	26E
Roxburgh: N.Z.	104	46S	169E
Royale, Isle: U.S.A.	49	48N	89W
Royal Tunbridge Wells: England	63	51N	0
Royan: France	72	46N	1W
Royston: England	63	52N	0
Ruahine Range: N.Z.	104	40S	176E
Ruapehu: mtn., N.Z.	104	39S	176E
Rub' al Khali: desert, Saudi Arabia	87	20N	50E
Rubtsovsk: U.S.S.R.	85	52N	81E
Rudok: China	88	34N	80E
Ruffec: France	73	46N	0
Rugby: England	63	52N	1W
Rugen: i., E. Germany	68	54N	13E
Ruhr: district, W. Ger.	64	Inset	
Rukwa, L.: Tanzania	110	8S	32E
Rum Jungle: Austl.	98	13S	131E
Ruse: Bulgaria	69	44N	26E
Rush: R. of Ireland	62	54N	6W
Russian Soviet Fed. Socialist Rep.: U.S.S.R.	82/3	—	—
Rutland: U.S.A.	19	44N	73W
Ruvuma: r., Africa	110	11S	37E
Ruwenzori, Mt.: Uganda	110	1N	30E
RWANDA: cap. Kigali	110	2S	30E
Ryazn': U.S.S.R.	84	55N	40E
Rybach'ye: U.S.S.R.	85	43N	76E
Rybinsk: & res., U.S.S.R.	84	58N	38E
Ryukyu Is. (Nansei Is.): Japan	90	27N	127E
Ryukyu Trench: Pacific Ocean	102	27N	130E
Rzeszów: Poland	68	50N	22E
Rzhev: U.S.S.R.	84	56N	35E
Saale: r., E. Germany	74	50N	12E
Saalfeld: E. Germany	74	51N	11E
Saar: Land, W. Ger.	74	49N	7E
Saar: r., W. Germany	74	50N	7E
Saarbrücken: W. Ger.	74	49N	7E
Saaremaa: i., U.S.S.R.	71	58N	23E
Sabadell: Spain	67	42N	2E
Sabah: State, Malaysia	91	5N	118E
Sabinas: Mexico	52	28N	101W
Sabine: r., U.S.A.	46	31N	94W
Sabkhat Minjora: salt flat, Saudi Arabia	87	20N	53E
Sable, Cape: U.S.A.	47	25N	81W
Saco: U.S.A.	19	43N	70W
Sacramento: & r., U.S.A.	48	39N	121W
Sacramento Mts.: U.S.A.	46	34N	105W
Sá da Bandeira (Lubango): Angola	111	15S	14E
Sado: i., Japan	93	38N	138E
Safford: U.S.A.	48	32N	110W
Safi: Morocco	108	32N	9W
Sagaing: Burma	92	21N	95E
Saginaw: U.S.A.	19	44N	84W
Sagua la Grande: Cuba	53	23N	80W
Sahara Desert: North Africa	108/9	—	—
Saharan Atlas: mts., Algeria	108	33N	3E
Saharanpur: India	88	30N	78E
Sai: r., India	88	26N	82E
Saigon: see Ho Chi Minh City			
St. Affrique: France	73	44N	3E
St. Albans: England	62	52N	0
St. Amand: France	72	50N	3E
St. Amand-Mont-Rond: France	73	47N	2E
St. André, Plaine de: France	72	49N	1E
St. Andrews: Scot.	62	56N	3W
St. Anne's: England	62	54N	3W
St. Augustine: U.S.A.	47	30N	81W
St. Bride's Bay: Wales	63	52N	5W
St. Brieuc: France	72	49N	3W
St. Catherine's Pt.: England	63	51N	1W
St. Chamond: France	73	45N	5E
St. Christopher (St. Kitts): i., W. Indies	45	17N	63W
St. Clair, L.: U.S.A.	19	43N	83W
Saint Clair Shores: U.S.A.	33	42N	83W
St. Claude: France	73	46N	6E
St. Cloud: U.S.A.	49	46N	94W
St. Croix: i., W. Ind.	45	18N	65E
St. David's Head: Wales	63	52N	5W
St. Denis: France	113	49N	2E
St. Dié: France	72	48N	7E
St. Dizier: France	72	49N	5E
St. Elias, Mt.: & mtns., U.S.A./Canada	12	60N	140W
Saintes: France	73	46N	1W
Saintes, Les: is., West Indies	45	16N	62W
St. Étienne: France	73	45N	4E
St. Flour: France	73	45N	3E
St. Francis: r., U.S.A.	46	35N	90W
St. Francis, C.: South Africa	111	34S	25E
St. Gallen: Switz.	75	47N	9E
St. George: U.S.A.	48	37N	114W
St. George, C.: U.S.A.	47	30N	85W
St. George's Chan.: Wales/R. of Irel.	63	52N	6W
St. Germain-en-Laye: France	113	49N	2E
St. Gothard Pass: Switzerland	75	47N	9E
St. Govan's Head: Wales	63	52N	5W
St. Helena: i., Atl. O.	57	16S	8W
St. Helena Bay: South Africa	111	32S	18E
St. Helens: England	62	53N	3W
Saint Helens: U.S.A.	48	46N	123W
St. Helier: Chan. Is.	63	Inset	
St. Ingbert: Germany	74	49N	7E
St. Ives: England	63	50N	5W
St. Jean-de-Luz: Fr.	73	43N	2W
St. Jean de Maurienne: Fr.	73	45N	6E
St. Jean Pied-de-Port: France	73	43N	1W
St. John: r., U.S.A.	15	47N	69W
St. Johns: r., U.S.A.	47	30N	82W
St. Joseph: Mo., U.S.A.	46	40N	95W
St. Joseph: & r., Mich., U.S.A.	47	42N	87W
St. Julien: France	73	46N	6E
St. Junien: France	73	46N	1E
St. Kitts: see St. Christopher			
St. Lawrence: i., Bering Sea	12	63N	170W
St. Lô: France	72	49N	1W
St. Louis: U.S.A.	46	39N	90W
St. Louis: Senegal	108	16N	16W
St. Lucia: i., W. Ind.	45	14N	61W
St. Malo: & gulf, Fr.	72	49N	2W
St. Martin: i., West Indies	45	18N	63W
St. Mary's: England	63	50N	6W
St. Mary's: Australia	99	42S	148E
St. Marys: U.S.A.	50	41N	79W
St. Matthew: i., Bering Sea	12	60N	172W
St. Maurice: Switz.	75	46N	7E
Ste. Menehould: Fr.	72	49N	5E
St. Moritz: Switz.	75	46N	10E
St. Nazaire: France	72	47N	2W
St. Omer: France	72	51N	2E
Saintonge: Old Prov., France	75	45N	1W
St. Paul: i., Indian O.	89	39S	78E
St. Paul: U.S.A.	49	45N	93W
St. Paul, C.: Ghana	108	6N	1E
St. Paul Rocks: Atlantic Ocean	57	0	30W
St. Peter Port: Channel Islands	63	Inset	
St. Petersburg: U.S.A.	47	28N	83W
St. Pierre-Quilbignon: France	72	48N	5W
St. Pol: France	72	50N	2E
St. Pons: France	73	43N	3E
St. Quentin: France	72	50N	3E
St. Raphaël: France	73	43N	7E
Ste. Savine: France	72	48N	4E
St. Servan: France	72	49N	2W
St. Thomas: i., West Indies	45	18N	65W
St. Tropez: France	73	43N	7E
St. Valéry en Caux: France	72	50N	1E
St. Vincent, C. (Cabo de São Vincent): Portugal	67	37N	9W
St. Vincent: i., West Indies	45	13N	61W
Saipan: i., Pac. O.	102	15N	145E
Saiwūn: Yemen P.D.R.	87	16N	49E
Sakai: Japan	93	35N	135E
Sakaka: Sau. Arab.	87	30N	40E
Sakakawea, L.: U.S.A.	49	48N	102W
Sakata: Japan	93	39N	140E
Sakhalin: i., U.S.S.R.	83	50N	143E
Sakhalin Bay: U.S.S.R.	83	54N	141E
Sakishima Group: Japan	90	24N	124E
Salado: r., Argentina	56	30S	61W
Salala: Oman	87	17N	54E
Salamanca: Mexico	52	21N	101W
Salamanca: Spain	67	41N	6W
Sala-y-Gomez: i., Pacific Ocean	103	26S	105W
Salekhard: U.S.S.R.	82	66N	66E
Salem: India	88	12N	78E
Salem: Mass., U.S.A.	51	42N	71W
Salem: Oregon, U.S.A.	48	45N	123W
Salem: Va., U.S.A.	47	37N	80W
Salerno: Italy	69	41N	15E
Salida: U.S.A.	49	38N	106W
Salima: Malawi	110	14S	35E
Salina: U.S.A.	49	39N	98W
Salinas: U.S.A.	48	37N	122W
Saline: r., U.S.A.	46	34N	92W
Salisbury: Australia	101	35S	139E
Salisbury: & Plain, England	63	51N	2W
SALISBURY: Rhodesia (Zimbabwe)	111	18S	31E
Salmon: r., U.S.A.	48	45N	116W
Salmon River Mts.: U.S.A.	48	45N	115W
Salon de Provence: France	73	44N	5E
Salonica: see Thessalonica			
Salop: Co., England	63	53N	3W
Salpausselka: moraine, Finland	71	61N	25E
Salt: r., U.S.A.	46	40N	92W
Salta: Argentina	56	25S	65W
Saltillo: Mexico	52	25N	101W
Salt Lake City: U.S.A.	48	41N	112W
Salt Range: Pakistan	88	33N	73E
Salto: Uruguay	56	31S	58W
Saluzzo: Italy	75	45N	7E
Salvador (Bahia): Brazil	54	13S	38W
Salween: r., Burma	90	20N	98E
Salzach: r., Austria	75	47N	12E
Salzburg: & Prov., Austria	75	48N	13E
Salzgitter: W. Ger.	74	52N	10E
Samah de Langreo: Spain	67	43N	7W
Samah: China	93	18N	110E
Samar: i., Phil.	91	12N	125E
Samarinda: Indon.	91	0	117E
Samarkand: U.S.S.R.	85	40N	67E
Samarra: Iraq	87	34N	44E
Sambalpur: India	88	22N	84E
Sambor: U.S.S.R.	68	50N	23E
Sambre: r., France/Belgium	72	50N	4E
Samoa Is.: Pac. O.	102	12S	172W
Sámos: i., Greece	69	38N	27E
Samothrace: i., Greece	69	40N	26E
Samsun: Turkey	86	41N	36E
SAN'A: Yemen	87	15N	44E
Sanandaj: Iran	87	35N	47E
San Angelo: U.S.A.	46	31N	100W
San Antonio: U.S.A.	46	29N	99W
San Antonio: r., U.S.A.	46	29N	97W
San Benito Is.: Mex.	44	28N	115W
San Bernardino: U.S.A.	48	34N	117W
San Blas, C.: U.S.A.	47	30N	85W
Sancerre: France	73	47N	3E
San Clemente: i., U.S.A.	48	33N	118W
San Cristóbal: Venez.	54	8N	72W
Sancti Spiritus: Cuba	53	22N	79W
Sandakan: Malaysia	91	6N	118E
Sandgate: Australia	100	27S	153E
San Diego: U.S.A.	48	33N	117W
Sandpoint: U.S.A.	48	48N	117W
Sandringham: Eng.	63	53N	1E
Sandusky: U.S.A.	47	41N	83W
San Félix I.: Pac. O.	103	26S	80W
San Fernando: Chile	54	34S	71W
San Fernando: r., Mexico	52	25N	98W
San Fernando: Phil.	91	17N	120E
Sanford: Fla., U.S.A.	47	29N	80W
Sanford: Maine, U.S.A.	19	43N	71W
Sanford: N.C., U.S.A.	47	35N	79W
San Francisco: r., U.S.A.	48	33N	109W
San Francisco: U.S.A.	36	—	—
Sangar: U.S.S.R.	83	64N	127E
Sangre de Cristo Range: U.S.A.	49	37N	105W
San Joaquin: r., U.S.A.	48	37N	120W
SAN JOSÉ: Costa Rica	45	10N	84W
San Jose: U.S.A.	48	37N	122W
San Jose: r., U.S.A.	48	35N	108W
San Juan: Argentina	55	32S	69W
SAN JUAN: Puerto Rico	45	18N	66W
San Juan Mts.: U.S.A.	48	37N	107W
San Justo: Argentina	56	31S	61W
San Luis: Argentina	55	33S	66W
San Luis Obispo: U.S.A.	48	35N	121W
San Luis Potosi: Mex.	52	22N	101W
San Marcos: U.S.A.	46	30N	98W
SAN MARINO: cap. San Marino	75	44N	12E
San Mateo: U.S.A.	36	38N	122W
San Pedro: r., U.S.A.	48	33N	111W
Sanquhar: Scotland	62	55N	4W
San Rafael: Arg.	54	35S	68W
San Rafael: U.S.A.	36	38N	123W
San Remo: Italy	75	44N	8E
SAN SALVADOR: El Salvador	44	14N	89W
San Sebastián: Spain	67	43N	2W
San Severo: Italy	69	42N	15E
Santa Ana: U.S.A.	37	34N	118W
Santa Barbara: & chan., U.S.A.	48	34N	120W
Santa Barbara Is.: U.S.A.	48	34N	120W
Santa Catalina: i. & gulf, U.S.A.	48	33N	118W
Santa Clara: Cuba	53	22N	80W
Santa Clara: U.S.A.	48	37N	122W
Santa Cruz: Bolivia	54	18S	63W
Santa Cruz: U.S.A.	48	37N	122W
Santa Cruz: i., U.S.A.	48	34N	120W
Santa Cruz de Tenerife: Canary Islands	108	28N	16W
Santa Fé: Argentina	56	32S	61W
Santa Fe: U.S.A.	49	36N	106W
Santa Maria: Brazil	56	30S	54W
Santa Maria: U.S.A.	48	35N	120W
Santa Marta: Col.	45	11N	74W
Santa Monica: U.S.A.	37	34N	118W
Santana do Livramento: Brazil	56	31S	55W
Santander: Spain	67	43N	4W
Santa Paula: U.S.A.	48	34N	119W
Santarém: Portugal	67	39N	9W
Santa Rosa: Arg.	55	37S	64W
Santa Rosa: Calif., U.S.A.	48	38N	123W
Santa Rosa: N. Mex., U.S.A.	49	35N	105W
Santa Rosa: i., U.S.A.	48	34N	120W
SANTIAGO: Chile	55	33S	71W
Santiago: Dom. Rep.	45	20N	71W
Santiago, Rio Grande de: r., Mexico	52	21N	104W
Santiago de Compostelo: Spain	67	43N	9W
Santiago de Cuba: Cuba	53	20N	76W
Santiago del Estero: Argentina	54	28S	64W
Santo André: Brazil	56	24S	47W
Santo Antônio: Brazil	54	9S	64W
SANTO DOMINGO: Dom. Repub.	45	19N	70W
Santos: Brazil	56	24S	46W
Sanvic: France	72	49N	0
Sanyate: r., Rhodesia (Zimbabwe)	111	17S	29E
São Bernardo do Campo: Brazil	56	24S	47W
São Francisco: r., Brazil	54	12S	43W
São Leopoldo: Brazil	56	30S	51W
São Luis: Brazil	54	3S	44W
Saône: r., France	73	46N	5E
São Paulo: Brazil	56	24S	46W
São Roque, C. de: Brazil	54	5S	35W
São Vicente: Brazil	56	24S	46W
São Vicente, Cabo de (C. St. Vincent): Portugal	67	37N	9W
Sapporo: Japan	93	43N	141E
Saragossa: see Zaragoza			
Sarajevo: Yugo.	69	44N	18E
Saranac Lake: city, U.S.A.	19	44N	74W

	Page	Lat.	Long.
Saransk: U.S.S.R.	**84**	54N	45E
Sarasota: U.S.A.	**47**	27N	83W
Saratov: U.S.S.R.	**84**	52N	46E
Saravane: Laos	**92**	15N	106E
Sarawak: *State,* Malaysia	**91**	3N	113E
Sardina: *i.,* Medit. Sea	**64**	40N	9E
Sargasso Sea	**57**	30N	60W
Sark: *i.,* Chan. Is.	**63**	*Inset*	
Sarny: U.S.S.R.	**84**	51N	27E
Sarpsborg: Norway	**71**	59N	11E
Sarrebourg: France	**72**	49N	7E
Sarreguemines: Fr.	**72**	49N	7E
Sarthe: *r.,* France	**72**	48N	0
Sasebo: Japan	**93**	33N	130E
Sassari: Sardinia	**67**	41N	9E
Satara: India	**88**	17N	74E
Satpura Range: India	**88**	22N	77E
Satu-Mare: Romania	**68**	48N	23E
SAUDI ARABIA: *cap.* Riyadh	**87**	—	—
Sauerland: *upland,* W. Germany	**74**	51N	8E
Saugor: India	**88**	24N	79E
Sauk Center: U.S.A.	**49**	46N	95W
Sault Ste. Marie: U.S.A.	**19**	46N	84W
Saumur: France	**73**	47N	0
Sauternes: France	**73**	45N	0
Sava: *r.,* Yugoslavia	**69**	45N	17E
Savannah: *& r.,* Ga., U.S.A.	**47**	32N	81W
Savannah: Tenn., U.S.A.	**47**	35N	88W
Savannakhet: Laos	**93**	17N	105E
Saverne: France	**72**	49N	7E
Savigliano: Italy	**75**	45N	8E
Savona: Italy	**75**	44N	8E
Savonlinna: Finland	**70**	62N	29E
Savoy: *Old Prov.,* Fr.	**73**	46N	6E
Savoy Alps: France	**73**	46N	7E
Sawu: *i. & sea,* Indon.	**91**	10S	122E
Saxmundham: Eng.	**63**	52N	1E
Sayn Shanda: Mong.	**83**	45N	110E
Sca Fell: *mtn.,* Eng.	**62**	54N	3W
Scapa Flow: *inlet,* Scotland	**61**	59N	3W
Scarborough: Eng.	**62**	54N	0
Schaerbeek: Belgium	**72**	51N	4E
Schaffhausen: Switz.	**75**	48N	8E
Scheldt: *r.,* Belgium/Netherlands	**72**	51N	4E
Schenectady: U.S.A.	**51**	43N	74W
Schiedam: Neth.	**74**	52N	4E
Schio: Italy	**75**	46N	11E
Schleswig: W. Ger.	**68**	54N	10E
Schmalkalden: E. Ger.	**74**	51N	10E
Schoonebeek: Neth.	**74**	53N	7E
Schouwen-Duiveland: *i.,* Netherlands	**72**	52N	4E
Schwäbisch-Gmünd: W. Germany	**75**	49N	10E
Schwandorf: W. Ger.	**74**	49N	12E
Schweinfurt: W. Ger.	**74**	50N	10E
Schwelm: W. Ger.	**64**	51N	7E
Schwerin: E. Ger.	**74**	54N	11E
Schwerte: W. Ger.	**64**	51N	8E
Schwyz: Switz.	**75**	47N	9E
Scilly, Is. of: Eng.	**63**	50N	6W
Scoresby Sound: Greenland	**13**	71N	23W
Scotia Sea: S. Atlantic Ocean	**55**	57S	50W
SCOTLAND: *cap.* Edinburgh	**61**	—	—
Scottsbluff: U.S.A.	**49**	42N	104W
Scranton: U.S.A.	**50**	41N	76W
Scunthorpe: England	**62**	54N	1W
Seal, C.: S. Africa	**111**	34S	24E
Seattle: U.S.A.	**36**	—	—
Sebakwe: *r.,* Rhodesia (Zimbabwe)	**111**	18S	30E
Sebcha di Tauorga: *bay,* Libya	**86**	32N	15E
Sebha Oasis: Libya	**108**	27N	15E
Sechura Desert: Peru	**54**	6S	80W
Sedalia: U.S.A.	**46**	39N	93W
Sedan: France	**72**	50N	5E
Sedbergh: England	**62**	54N	3W
Seeheim: S.W. Afr. (Namibia)	**111**	27S	18E
Segovia: Spain	**67**	42N	4W
Segovia: *r.,* Hond./Nicaragua	**45**	15N	84W
Ségre: *r.,* Spain	**67**	42N	1E
Segura: *r.,* Spain	**67**	38N	2W
Seine: *r.,* France	**72**	49N	1E
Seine, Baie de la: Fr.	**72**	49N	1W
Sekondi-Takoradi: Ghana	**108**	5N	2W
Selby: England	**62**	54N	1W
Selenga: *r.,* Mongolia	**83**	49N	101E
Sélestat: France	**72**	48N	7E
Selety-Tengiz, L.: U.S.S.R.	**85**	53N	73E
Selkirk: Scotland	**62**	56N	3W
Selma: U.S.A.	**47**	32N	87W
Selsey Bill: *hd.,* Eng.	**63**	51N	1W
Selukwe: Rhodesia (Zimbabwe)	**111**	20S	30E
Selvas: *geog. reg.,* Brazil	**54**	6S	65W
Semarang: Indonesia	**91**	7S	110E
Seminoe Res.: U.S.A.	**48**	42N	107W
Semiozernoye: U.S.S.R.	**85**	52N	64E
Semipalatinsk: U.S.S.R.	**85**	50N	80E
Semnān: Iran	**87**	35N	53E
Senanga: Zambia	**111**	16S	23E
Sendai: Japan	**93**	38N	141E
Seneca L.: U.S.A.	**50**	43N	77W
SENEGAL: *& r., cap.* Dakar	**108**	15N	15W
Senja: *i.,* Norway	**70**	69N	18E
Senlis: France	**72**	49N	3E
Sennar: *& dam,* Sudan	**86**	13N	34E
Sens: France	**72**	48N	3E
SEOUL (KYONGSONG): S. Korea	**90**	38N	127E
Septentrional, Meseta: *plat.,* Spain	**67**	42N	5W
Seremban: Malaysia	**92**	3N	102E
Seria: Brunei	**91**	4N	114E
Serian: Malaysia	**92**	1N	111E
Serio: *r.,* Italy	**75**	45N	10E
Serov: U.S.S.R.	**85**	60N	60E
Serowe: Botswana	**111**	23S	27E
Serra dos Parecis: Brazil	**54**	12S	60W
Serra Geral: *mtns.,* Brazil	**56**	25S	51W
Sérrai: Greece	**69**	41N	23E
Sète: France	**73**	43N	4E
Sétif: Algeria	**67**	36N	5E
Setúbal: Portugal	**67**	38N	9W
Sevan, L.: U.S.S.R.	**84**	41N	46E
Sevastopol': U.S.S.R.	**84**	45N	34E
Sevenoaks: England	**112**	51N	0
Severn: *r.,* England	**63**	52N	2W
Severnaya Zemlya: *is.,* U.S.S.R.	**83**	79N	95E
Severn Tunnel: Eng.	**63**	52N	3W
Severoural'sk: U.S.S.R.	**85**	60N	60E
Seville: Spain	**67**	37N	6W
Sèvre Nantaise: *r.,* France	**73**	47N	1W
Sèvre Niortaise: *r.,* France	**73**	46N	1W
Sèvres: France	**113**	49N	2E
Seward: U.S.A.	**12**	60N	150W
Seward Peninsula: U.S.A.	**12**	66N	165W
Seychelles-Mauritius Plateau: Indian O.	**89**	10S	57E
Seydhisfjördhur: Ice.	**70**	65N	14W
Seymour: U.S.A.	**46**	33N	99W
Sézanne: France	**72**	49N	4E
Sfax: Tunisia	**108**	35N	11E
'S-GRAVENHAGE: *see* HAGUE, THE			
Shabwah: Yemen P.D.R.	**87**	16N	47E
Shackleton Range: Antarctica	**116**	82S	160E
Shaftesbury: England	**63**	51N	2W
Shahjahanpur: India	**88**	28N	80E
Shahrezā: Iran	**87**	32N	52E
Shahrūd: Iran	**87**	36N	55E
Shakhty: U.S.S.R.	**84**	48N	40E
Shalym: U.S.S.R.	**85**	53N	88E
Shamrock: U.S.A.	**46**	35N	100W
Shamva: Rhodesia (Zimbabwe)	**111**	17S	32E
Shangani: *r.,* Rhod. (Zimbabwe)	**111**	19S	28E
Shanghai: China	**95**	31N	121E
Shangkiu: China	**94**	34N	116E
Shanklin: England	**63**	51N	1W
Shannon: *r.,* R. of Ireland	**61**	53N	9W
Shansi: *Prov.,* China	**94**	37N	112E
Shan States: Burma	**93**	22N	98E
Shantung: *Prov.,* China	**94**	36N	117E
Shantung Peninsula: China	**94**	37N	120E
Shaohing: China	**95**	30N	121E
Shaokuan (Kükong): China	**95**	25N	113E
Shaoyang: China	**95**	27N	111E
Sharjah: U.A.E.	**87**	25N	55E
Sharon: U.S.A.	**47**	41N	81W
Shasta, Lake: U.S.A.	**48**	41N	122W
Shasta, Mt.: U.S.A.	**48**	41N	122W
Shawnee: U.S.A.	**46**	35N	97W
Sheboygan: U.S.A.	**49**	44N	88W
Sheenjek: *r.,* U.S.A.	**30**	68N	144W
Sheffield: England	**63**	53N	1W
Sheffield: U.S.A.	**47**	35N	88W
Shelby: U.S.A.	**48**	48N	112W
Shelbyville: U.S.A.	**47**	35N	86W
Shelekhov Bay: U.S.S.R.	**83**	60N	157E
Shenandoah: *r.,* U.S.A.	**47**	38N	79W
Shensi: *Prov.,* China	**94**	35N	109E
Shenyang (Mukden): China	**94**	42N	123E
Shepparton: Austl.	**101**	36S	145E
Sheppey, I. of: Eng.	**63**	51N	1E
Sherborne: England	**63**	51N	3W
Sheridan: U.S.A.	**48**	45N	107W
Sherlovaya Gora: U.S.S.R.	**83**	51N	116E
Sherman: U.S.A.	**46**	34N	97W
's-Hertogenbosch: Netherlands	**74**	52N	5E
Shetland Is.: Scot.	**61**	60N	2W
Sheyenne: *r.,* U.S.A.	**49**	48N	99W
Shibeli: *r.,* Ethiopia/Somali Republic	**109**	6N	43E
Shigatse: China	**89**	29N	89E
Shihchan: China	**83**	51N	126E
Shihkiachwang: China	**94**	38N	115E
Shikoku: *i.,* Japan	**93**	34N	134E
Shillong: India	**89**	26N	92E
Shimoga: India	**88**	14N	76E
Shimonoseki: Japan	**93**	34N	131E
Shipki Pass: India/China	**88**	32N	79E
Shiraz: Iran	**87**	30N	53E
Shire: *r.,* Malawi	**111**	16S	35E
Shizuoka: Japan	**93**	35N	139E
Shkodër: Albania	**69**	42N	19E
Shoalwater Bay: Australia	**100**	22S	150E
Sholapur: India	**88**	18N	76E
Shortland Is.: Solomon Is.	**99**	7S	156E
Shreveport: U.S.A.	**46**	32N	94W
Shrewsbury: England	**63**	53N	3W
Shrewsbury: U.S.A.	**51**	42N	72W
Shuntak: China	**95**	23N	113E
Shwangliao: China	**90**	44N	123E
Shwebo: Burma	**92**	23N	96E
Si: *r.,* China	**95**	23N	112E
Sialkot: Pakistan	**88**	32N	75E
SIAM: *see* **THAILAND**			
Siam, Gulf of	**92**	10N	102E
Sian: China	**94**	34N	109E
Siang: *r.,* China	**95**	27N	112E
Siangfan: China	**94**	32N	112E
Siangtan: China	**95**	28N	112E
Siauliai: U.S.S.R.	**68**	56N	23E
Sibenik: Yugoslavia	**69**	44N	16E
Sibi: Pakistan	**88**	30N	68E
Sibiu: Romania	**68**	46N	25E
Sibu: Malaysia	**92**	2N	112E
Sicilian Channel: Medit. Sea	**69**	37N	12E
Sicily: *i. & Reg.,* Italy	**69**	—	—
Sidi-bel-Abbès: Alg.	**67**	35N	1W
Sidmouth: England	**63**	51N	3W
Sidney: U.S.A.	**49**	48N	104W
Sidra, Gulf of: Libya	**109**	32N	17E
Sieg: *r.,* W. Germany	**74**	51N	8E
Siegburg: W. Germany	**74**	51N	7E
Siegen: W. Germany	**74**	51N	8E
Siem Reap: Cambodia	**92**	13N	103E
Siena: Italy	**69**	43N	11E
Sierra de Juárez: *mtns.,* Mexico	**48**	32N	116W
SIERRA LEONE: *cap.* Freetown	**108**	8N	12W
Sierra Madre Occidental (W. Sierra Madre): *mtns.,* Mexico	**52**	25N	105W
Sierra Madre Oriental (E. Sierra Madre): *mtns.,* Mexico	**52**	25N	100W
Sierra Madre del Sur (S. Sierra Madre): *mtns.,* Mexico	**52**	17N	100W
Sierra Morena: *mtns.,* Spain	**67**	38N	5W
Sierra Névada: *mtns.,* Spain	**67**	37N	3W
Sierra Nevada: *mtns.,* U.S.A.	**48**	38N	120W
Siglufjördhur: Ice.	**70**	66N	19W
Sihanoukville: *see* Kompong Som			
Siirt: Turkey	**87**	38N	42E
Sikeston: U.S.A.	**47**	37N	89W
Sikhote Alin' Range: U.S.S.R.	**83**	47N	137E
Sikkim: *State,* India	**88**	27N	88E
Silchar: India	**89**	25N	93E
Silistra: Bulgaria	**69**	44N	27E
Silverton: Colorado, U.S.A.	**48**	38N	108W
Silverton: Oregon, U.S.A.	**48**	45N	123W
Simanggang: Malaysia	**92**	1N	111E
Simferopol': U.S.S.R.	**84**	45N	34E
Simla: India	**88**	31N	77E
Simonstown: S. Afr.	**111**	34S	18E
Simplon Pass: Switz.	**75**	46N	8E
Simpson Desert: Australia	**98**	25S	137E
Sinai: *penin. & mtn.,* Egypt	**86**	28N	34E
Sind: *Prov.,* Pakistan	**88**	26N	69E
SINGAPORE: *cap.* Singapore	**92**	1N	104E
Singaradja: Indon.	**91**	8S	115E
Singkep: *i.,* Indon.	**91**	1S	104E
Singleton: Australia	**101**	33S	151E
Singtai: China	**94**	37N	114E
Sining: China	**90**	36N	102E
Sinkiang Uighur A.R.: China	**82/3**	40N	85E
Sinuiju: N. Korea	**90**	40N	124E
Sinyang: China	**94**	32N	113E
Sion: Switzerland	**75**	46N	7E
Sioux City: U.S.A.	**49**	42N	96W
Sioux Falls: *city,* U.S.A.	**49**	44N	97W
Siretul: *r.,* Romania	**68**	47N	26E
Sirte: Libya	**84**	31N	17E
Sisak: Yugoslavia	**69**	45N	16E
Sisseton: U.S.A.	**49**	46N	97W
Sīstān: *geog. reg.,* Iran/Afghan.	**87**	31N	61E
Sisteron: France	**73**	44N	6E
Sitapur: India	**88**	27N	81E
Sittang: *r.,* Burma	**92**	18N	97E
Sivas: Turkey	**86**	40N	37E
Siwa: Egypt	**86**	29N	25E
Skagerrak: *str.,* Denmark/Nor.	**71**	57N	8E
Skagway: U.S.A.	**24**	60N	135W
Skåne: *reg.,* Sweden	**71**	56N	14E
Skegness: England	**63**	53N	0
Skellefte: *r.,* Sweden	**70**	65N	20E
Skellefteå: Sweden	**70**	65N	21E
Skerries: R. of Irel.	**62**	54N	6W
Skien: Norway	**71**	59N	10E
Skikda: Algeria	**67**	37N	7E
Skipton: England	**62**	54N	2W
Skiros: *i.,* Greece	**69**	39N	25E
Skive: Denmark	**71**	57N	9E
Skokie: U.S.A.	**34**	42N	88W
Skomer I.: Wales	**63**	52N	5W
Skopje: Yugoslavia	**69**	42N	21E
Skövde: Sweden	**71**	58N	14E
Skye: *i.,* Scotland	**61**	57N	6W
Slavonski Brod: Yugoslavia	**69**	49N	18E
Slieve Donard: *mtn.,* N. Ireland	**62**	54N	6W
Sligo: R. of Ireland	**61**	54N	8W
Sliven: Bulgaria	**69**	43N	26E
Slonim: U.S.S.R.	**68**	53N	25E
Slough: England	**112**	52N	1W
Smoky Hill: *r.,* U.S.A.	**49**	39N	100W
Smolensk: U.S.S.R.	**84**	55N	32E
Snaefell: *mtn.,* I. of Man	**62**	54N	4W
Snake: *r.,* U.S.A.	**48**	46N	118W
Snowdon: *mtn.,* Wales	**63**	53N	4W
Snowy: *mtns. & r.,* Australia	**101**	37S	148E
Snyder: U.S.A.	**46**	33N	101W
Sochi: U.S.S.R.	**84**	44N	40E
Society Is.: Pac. O.	**103**	17S	150W
Socotra: *i.,* Arab. Sea	**87**	13N	54E
Soda Mts.: Libya	**84**	29N	15E
Söderhamn: Sweden	**71**	61N	17E
Soest: W. Germany	**74**	52N	8E
Soest: Netherlands	**74**	52N	5E
Sofala: Moz.	**111**	20S	35E
SOFIYA: Bulgaria	**69**	43N	23E
Sognafjorden: *fd.,* Norway	**71**	61N	6E
Soissons: France	**72**	49N	3E
Sokoto: Nigeria	**108**	13N	5E
Solent, The: *chan.,* England	**63**	51N	1W
Solihull: England	**63**	52N	2W
Solikamsk: U.S.S.R.	**84**	60N	57E
Solimões: *r., see* Amazon			
Solingen: W. Germany	**64**	51N	7E
Sologne: *reg.,* France	**72**	48N	2E
Solomon Is.: Pacific O.	**99**	10S	155E
Solothurn: Switz.	**75**	47N	8E
Solway Firth: Eng./Scotland	**62**	55N	4W
SOMALI REPUBLIC: *cap.* Mogadiscio	**109**	—	—
Sombor: Yugoslavia	**68**	46N	19E
Sombrero: *i.,* West Indies	**45**	18N	63W
Somerset: *Co.,* Eng.	**63**	51N	3W
Somerset: U.S.A.	**47**	37N	85W
Somerville: Mass., U.S.A.	**33**	42N	71W
Somerville: N.J., U.S.A.	**50**	41N	75W
Somme: *r.,* France	**72**	50N	2E
Sommières: France	**73**	44N	4E
Son: *r.,* India	**88**	24N	81E
Sondre Stromfjörd: Greenland	**13**	67N	52W
Songea: Tanzania	**110**	11S	36E
Songkhla: Thailand	**92**	7N	101E
Sonoyta: Mexico	**48**	32N	113W
Soonwald: *mtns.,* W. Germany	**74**	50N	8E
Sopron: Hungary	**68**	48N	16E
Soria: Spain	**67**	42N	2W
Sorocaba: Brazil	**56**	23S	48W
Souk Ahras: Algeria	**67**	36N	8E
Souris: *r.,* U.S.A./Canada	**49**	49N	101W
Sousse: Tunisia	**108**	36N	11E
Southampton: Eng.	**63**	51N	1W
South Australia:			

	Page	Lat.	Long.
State, Australia	**98**	30S	135E
South Bend: U.S.A.	**47**	42N	86W
South Carolina: *State*, U.S.A.	**47**	34N	81W
South China Sea	**91**	15N	115E
South Dakota: *State*, U.S.A.	**49**	45N	100W
South Downs: Eng.	**63**	51N	0
Southeast Indian Ridge: Indian Ocean	**89**	45S	95E
Southeast Pacific Basin: Pacific Ocean	**103**	45S	100W
Southend-on-Sea: England	**63**	52N	1E
Southern Alps: N.Z.	**104**	43S	170E
Southern Cross: Australia	**100**	31S	119E
Southern Ocean	**102/3**	—	—
Southern Sierra: *see* Sierra Madre del Sur			
Southern Uplands: Scotland	**62**	55N	4W
Southfield: U.S.A.	**33**	42N	83W
South Foreland: Eng.	**63**	51N	1E
Southgate: U.S.A.	**33**	42N	83W
South Georgia: *i.*, Atlantic Ocean	**55**	54S	37W
South Island: N.Z.	**104**	—	—
SOUTH KOREA: *cap.* Seoul	**90**	37N	127E
Southland: *district*, N.Z.	**104**	46S	168E
South Orkney Is.: Southern Ocean	**57**	61S	45W
Southport: England	**62**	54N	3W
South Sandwich Is.: Southern Ocean	**55**	57S	27W
South Sandwich Trench: Southern O.	**57**	57S	25W
South Shetland Is.: Antarctica	**55**	62S	60W
South Shields: Eng.	**62**	55N	1W
South Sioux City: U.S.A.	**49**	42N	96W
South Uist: *i.*, Scot.	**53**	57N	7W
South West Africa (Namibia): S. Africa	**111**	24S	17E
Southwest Indian Ridge: Indian Ocean	**89**	35S	55E
Southwest Pacific Basin: Pacific Ocean	**103**	35S	150W
Southwark: England	**112**	52N	0
Southwest Cape: New Zealand	**104**	47S	168E
Sovetsk: U.S.S.R.	**68**	55N	22E
Soviet Harbour: U.S.S.R.	**83**	49N	140E
SPAIN: *cap.* Madrid	**67**	—	—
Spalding: England	**63**	53N	0
Spandau: W. Germany	**113**	53N	13E
Spanish Town: Jam.	**53**	18N	77W
Sparks: U.S.A.	**48**	40N	120W
Spartanburg: U.S.A.	**47**	35N	82W
Spárti: Greece	**69**	37N	22E
Spartivento, C.: Italy	**69**	38N	16E
Spasskoye: U.S.S.R.	**85**	52N	69E
Speedwell, C.: U.S.S.R.	**82**	75N	55E
Spencer Gulf: Austl.	**101**	34S	137E
Spennymoor: Eng.	**62**	55N	2W
Spenser Mts.: N.Z.	**104**	42S	173E
Spessart: *mts.*, W. Ger.	**74**	50N	9E
Spey: *r.*, Scotland	**61**	57N	3W
Speyer: W. Germany	**74**	49N	8E
Spiekeroog: *i.*, W. Ger.	**74**	54N	8E
Spitsbergen (Svalbard): *i.*, Arctic Ocean	**82**	78N	20E
Split: Yugoslavia	**69**	44N	16E
Spokane: U.S.A.	**48**	48N	117W
Spree: *r.*, E. & W. Ger.	**113**	52N	14E
Springbok: S. Africa	**111**	30S	18E
Springdale: U.S.A.	**46**	36N	94W
Springfield: Colo., U.S.A.	**49**	37N	103W
Springfield: Illinois, U.S.A.	**49**	40N	90W
Springfield: Mass., U.S.A.	**51**	42N	73W
Springfield: Mo., U.S.A.	**49**	37N	93W
Springfield: Ohio, U.S.A.	**47**	40N	84W
Springfield: Oregon, U.S.A.	**48**	44N	123W
Springsure: Austl.	**100**	24S	148E
Spungabera: Moz.	**111**	20S	33E
Spurn Hd.: England	**62**	54N	0
Sretensk: U.S.S.R.	**83**	52N	118E
SRI LANKA: *cap.* Colombo	**88**	7N	81E
Srinagar: India	**88**	34N	75E
Stafford: & *Co.*, Eng.	**62**	53N	2W
Staines: England	**112**	51N	1W
Stamford: England	**63**	53N	0
Stamford: U.S.A.	**51**	41N	74W
STANLEY: Falkland Is.	**55**	52S	58W
Stanthorpe: Austl.	**101**	29S	152E
Stara Zagora: Bulg.	**69**	42N	26E
Start Pt.: England	**63**	50N	4W
Stassfurt: E. Germany	**74**	52N	12E
State College: *city*, U.S.A.	**50**	41N	78W
Staten I.: U.S.A.	**35**	41N	74W
Statesville: U.S.A.	**47**	36N	81W
Staunton: U.S.A.	**47**	38N	79W
Stavanger: Norway	**71**	59N	6E
Stavelot: Belgium	**72**	50N	6E
Stavropol': U.S.S.R.	**84**	45N	42E
Steigerwald: *mts.*, W. Germany	**74**	50N	10E
Steinkjer: Norway	**70**	64N	11E
Stellenbosch: S. Afr.	**111**	34S	19E
Stelvio Pass: Switz./Italy	**75**	47N	10E
Stendal: E. Germany	**74**	53N	12E
Steppes: *geog. reg.*, U.S.S.R.	**82**	50N	70E
Sterling: Colorado, U.S.A.	**49**	41N	103W
Sterling: Ill., U.S.A.	**49**	42N	90W
Sterlitamak: U.S.S.R.	**84**	54N	56E
Steubenville: U.S.A.	**47**	40N	81W
Stevens Point: *City*, U.S.A.	**49**	45N	89W
Stewart I.: N.Z.	**104**	47S	168E
Steyr: Austria	**75**	48N	14E
Stillwater: U.S.A.	**46**	36N	97W
Štip: Yugoslavia	**69**	42N	22E
Stirling: Scotland	**62**	56N	4W
Stirling Range: Austl.	**100**	34S	118E
STOCKHOLM: Sweden	**71**	59N	18E
Stockport: England	**63**	53N	2W
Stockton: U.S.A.	**48**	38N	121W
Stockton on Tees: England	**62**	55N	1W
Stockton Plateau: U.S.A.	**46**	30N	102W
Stoke on Trent: Eng.	**63**	53N	2W
Stonehaven: Scot.	**62**	57N	2W
Stonehenge: *hist.*, England	**63**	51N	2W
Stonington I.: Antarctica	**116**	67S	67W
Stony Tunguska: *r.*, U.S.S.R.	**83**	61N	95E
Store Bælt: *str.*, Den.	**71**	55N	11E
Stor L.: Sweden	**61**	63N	14E
Stornoway: Scot.	**70**	58N	6W
Storuman: Sweden	**70**	65N	17E
Stour: *r.*, Dorset, England	**63**	51N	2W
Stour: *r.*, Kent, Eng.	**63**	51N	1E
Stour: *r.*, Suff., Eng.	**63**	52N	1E
Stowmarket: Eng.	**63**	52N	1E
Stralsund: E. Germany	**68**	54N	13E
Strangford L.: N. Ireland	**62**	54N	6W
Stranraer: Scotland	**62**	55N	5W
Strasbourg: France	**72**	49N	8E
Stratford on Avon: England	**63**	52N	2W
Stratford: N.Z.	**104**	39S	174E
Strathclyde: *Reg.*, Scot.	**62**	56N	4W
Strathmore: *valley*, Scotland	**62**	57N	3W
Straubing: W. Ger.	**74**	49N	12E
Strawberry Mt.: U.S.A.	**48**	44N	119W
Stromboli: *volc.*, Italy	**69**	39N	15E
Stroud: England	**63**	52N	2W
Strumble Head: Wales	**63**	52N	5W
Stuart Highway: Australia	**98**	20S	134E
Sturt Desert: Austl.	**101**	28S	141E
Stuttgart: W. Germany	**75**	49N	9E
Stuttgart: U.S.A.	**46**	35N	91W
Suakin: Sudan	**109**	19N	37E
Suanhwa: China	**94**	41N	115E
Subotica: Yugoslavia	**68**	46N	20E
Suceava: Romania	**68**	48N	26E
Suchiate: Mexico	**44**	15N	92W
Suchow (Tungshan): China	**94**	34N	117E
Suchow: China	**95**	32N	121E
Sucre: Bolivia	**54**	19S	65W
SUDAN: *cap.* Khartoum	**109**	—	—
Sudbury: England	**63**	52N	1E
Sudeten Mts.: Czech./Poland	**68**	51N	16E
Sue Peaks: *mtn.*, U.S.A.	**46**	30N	103W
Suez: & *gulf*, Egypt	**86**	30N	32E
Suez Canal: Egypt	**109**	*Inset*	
Suffolk: *Co.*, Eng.	**63**	52N	1E
Suffolk: U.S.A.	**47**	37N	77W
Sugarloaf Pt.: Austl.	**101**	32S	153E
Suir: *r.*, R. of Ireland	**61**	52N	7W
Suita: Japan	**93**	35N	135E
Sukhona: *r.*, U.S.S.R.	**84**	60N	42E
Sukhumi: U.S.S.R.	**84**	43N	41E
Sukkur: Pakistan	**88**	28N	69E
Sula: *is.*, Indonesia	**91**	2S	125E
Sulaiman Range: Pakistan	**88**	30N	70E
Sulawesi: *see* Celebes			
Sulphur Springs: U.S.A.	**46**	33N	96W
Sulu Sea: Phil.	**91**	8N	120E
Sumatra: *i.*, Indon.	**91**	0	100E
Sumba: *i.*, Indonesia	**91**	10S	120E
Sumbawa: *i.*, Indon.	**91**	8S	117E
Sumen: Bulgaria	**69**	43N	27E
Sumgait: U.S.S.R.	**84**	40N	50E
Summan Dahna: *desert*, Saudi Arabia	**87**	26N	47E
Summit: Alaska, U.S.A.	**12**	63N	149W
Summit: N.J., U.S.A.	**35**	41N	74W
Sumter: U.S.A.	**47**	34N	80W
Sumy: U.S.S.R.	**84**	51N	35E
Sunbury: U.S.A.	**50**	41N	77W
Sundarbans: *district*, India/Bangladesh	**88**	22N	90E
Sunda Str.: Indon.	**91**	6S	106E
Sunderland: England	**62**	55N	1W
Sundsvall: *l.*, Sweden	**70**	62N	17E
Sungari Res.: China	**90**	43N	127E
Sungkiang: China	**95**	31N	121E
Suo-nada: *gulf*, Japan	**93**	34N	132E
Superior: U.S.A.	**49**	47N	92W
Superior, L.: U.S.A./Canada	**19**	47N	90W
Suphan Buri: Thailand	**92**	14N	100E
Sur (Tyre): Lebanon	**86**	33N	35E
Surabaja: Indonesia	**91**	7S	113E
Surakarta: Indonesia	**91**	7S	111E
Surat: India	**88**	21N	73E
SURINAM: *cap.* Paramaribo	**54**	4N	56W
Surrey: *Co.*, Eng.	**63**	51N	0
Susa: Italy	**75**	45N	7E
Susquehanna: *r.*, U.S.A.	**50**	40N	76W
Sussex, E.: *Co.*, England	**63**	51N	0
Sussex, W.: *Co.*, England	**63**	51N	1W
Susuman: U.S.S.R.	**83**	63N	148E
Sutlej: *r.*, Pakistan/India	**88**	30N	73E
Sutherland: Australia	**115**	34S	151E
Sutton: England	**112**	51N	0
Suttor: *r.*, Australia	**100**	21S	147E
SUVA: Fiji	**99**	18S	178E
Suwannee: *r.*, U.S.A.	**47**	30N	83W
Suzuka: Japan	**93**	35N	137E
Svalbard *see* Spitsbergen			
Svendborg: Den.	**71**	55N	11E
Sverdlovsk: U.S.S.R.	**85**	57N	61E
Svir': *r.*, U.S.S.R.	**84**	61N	34E
Swabian Jura: *mts.*, W. Germany	**75**	48N	9E
Swaffham: England	**63**	53N	1E
Swain Reefs: Austl.	**100**	22S	152E
Swakopmund: S.W. Africa (Namibia)	**111**	23S	14E
Swale: *r.*, England	**62**	54N	2W
Swan: *r.*, Australia	**100**	32S	116E
Swanage: England	**63**	51N	2W
Swan Hill: *town*, Australia	**101**	35S	144E
Swansea: Wales	**63**	52N	4W
Swatow: China	**95**	23N	117E
SWAZILAND: *cap.* Mbabane	**111**	27S	32E
SWEDEN: *cap.* Stockholm	**70/1**	—	—
Sweetwater: U.S.A.	**46**	32N	100W
Sweetwater Canal: Egypt	**109**	*Inset*	
Swellendam: S. Afr.	**111**	34S	20E
Swilly, L.: R. of Irel.	**61**	55N	8W
Swindon: England	**63**	52N	2W
Swinoujście: Poland	**68**	54N	14E
SWITZERLAND: *cap.* Bern	**75**	47N	8E
Sydney: Australia	**115**	34S	151E
Syktyvkar: U.S.S.R.	**84**	62N	51E
Sylacauga: U.S.A.	**47**	33N	86W
Sylhet: Bangladesh	**89**	25N	92E
Syracuse: Sicily	**69**	37N	15E
Syracuse: U.S.A.	**50**	43N	76W
Syr Darya (Jaxartes): *r.*, U.S.S.R.	**85**	43N	67E
SYRIA: *cap.* Damascus	**86/7**	—	—
Syrian Desert: Arabia	**87**	32N	40E
Syzran': U.S.S.R.	**84**	53N	48E
Szczecin: Poland	**68**	53N	15E
Szczecinek: Poland	**68**	54N	17E
Szechwan: *Prov.*, China	**95**	30N	105E
Szeged: Hungary	**68**	46N	20E
Szolnok: Hungary	**68**	47N	20E
Szombathely: Hung.	**68**	47N	17E
Tabora: Tanzania	**110**	5S	33E
Tabriz: Iran	**87**	38N	46E
Tacna: Peru	**54**	18S	70W
Tacoma: U.S.A.	**48**	47N	122W
Tacuarembó: Uruguay	**56**	32S	56W
Tadzhik S.S.R.: U.S.S.R.	**85**	38N	72E
Taegu: S. Korea	**90**	36N	128E
Taejon: S. Korea	**90**	37N	127E
Taff: *r.*, Wales	**63**	52N	3W
Tafilalet Oasis: Mor.	**108**	31N	4W
Taganrog: U.S.S.R.	**84**	47N	39E
Tagliamento: *r.*, Italy	**75**	46N	13E
Tagus: *r.*, Sp./Port.	**67**	40N	8W
Tahiti: *i.*, Pacific O.	**103**	18S	150W
Tahoe, Lake: U.S.A.	**48**	39N	120W
Tai, Lake: China	**95**	31N	121E
Taichow: China	**94**	32N	120E
Taichung: Taiwan	**95**	24N	121E
Taif: Saudi Arabia	**87**	21N	40E
Taihape: N.Z.	**104**	40S	176E
Tainan: Taiwan	**95**	23N	120E
TAIPEI: Taiwan	**95**	25N	122E
Taipeh Shan: *ra.*, China	**95**	31N	116E
Taiping: Malaysia	**92**	5N	101E
Taitao Penin.: Chile	**55**	47S	75W
T'aitung: Taiwan	**93**	23N	121E
TAIWAN *cap.* Taipei	**95**	24N	121E
Taiyuan: China	**94**	38N	112E
Ta'iz: Yemen	**87**	14N	44E
Tak: Thailand	**92**	17N	99E
Takamatsu: Japan	**93**	34N	134E
Takaoka: Japan	**93**	37N	137E
Takla Makan: *desert*, China	**82/3**	39N	83E
Talara: Peru	**54**	5S	81W
Talaud Is.: Indon.	**91**	4N	127E
Talavera de la Reina: Spain	**67**	40N	5W
Talbot, C.: Austl.	**98**	14S	127E
Tali: China	**92**	35N	110E
Talladega: U.S.A.	**47**	33N	86W
Tallahassee: U.S.A.	**47**	30N	84W
Tallinn: U.S.S.R.	**71**	59N	25E
Tamale: Ghana	**108**	9N	1W
Tamana: *r.*, U.S.A.	**30**	63N	143W
Tamar: *r.*, England	**63**	51N	4W
Tamatave: Malagasy Republic	**110**	18S	49E
Tambov: U.S.S.R.	**84**	53N	41E
Tamil Nadu: *State*, India	**88**	10N	78E
Tampa: & *bay*, U.S.A.	**47**	28N	82W
Tampere: Finland	**70**	61N	24E
Tampico: Mexico	**52**	23N	98W
Tamsag Bulag: Mongolia	**83**	47N	117E
Tamworth: Australia	**101**	31S	151E
Tana: *fd.*, Norway	**70**	70N	28E
Tana, L.: Ethiopia	**109**	12N	37E
Tanana: U.S.A.	**12**	65N	152W
TANANARIVE: Malagasy Rep.	**110**	18S	47E
Tandil: Argentina	**55**	37S	59W
Tandou, L.: Austl.	**101**	33S	142E
Tanezrouft: *geog. reg.*, Algeria	**108**	23N	0
Tanga: Tanzania	**110**	5S	39E
Tanganyika, L.: Afr.	**110**	8S	30E
Tangier: Morocco	**67**	36N	6W
Tangshan: China	**94**	39N	118E
Tanimbar Is.: Indon.	**91**	7S	131E
Tanta: Egypt	**86**	31N	31E
TANZANIA: *cap.* Dodoma	**110**	—	—
Tapajos: *r.*, Brazil	**54**	6S	57W
Tapa Shan: *mts.*, China	**94**	32N	108E
Tapti: *r.*, India	**88**	21N	75E
TARABULUS: Tripoli	**86**	33N	13E
Tarakan: Indonesia	**91**	3N	118E
Taranaki: *dist.*, N.Z.	**104**	39S	174E
Taranto: & *gulf*, Italy	**69**	40N	17E
Tarare: France	**73**	46N	4E
Tararua Ra.: N.Z.	**104**	41S	175E
Tarascon: France	**73**	44N	5E
Tarawa: *i.*, Pac. O.	**102**	1N	173E
Tarbes: France	**73**	43N	0
Tardenois: *hills*, Fr.	**72**	49N	4E
Taree: Australia	**101**	32S	152E
Tarim: *r.*, China	**85**	41N	83E
Tarko-Sale: U.S.S.R.	**83**	65N	78E
Tarn: *r.*, France	**73**	44N	2E
Târnovo: Bulgaria	**69**	43N	26E
Tarragona: Spain	**67**	41N	1E
Tarsus: Turkey	**86**	37N	35E
Tartary, Gulf of: U.S.S.R.	**83**	50N	140E
Tartu: U.S.S.R.	**71**	58N	27E
Tashkent: U.S.S.R.	**85**	41N	69E
Tasman, Mt.: N.Z.	**104**	44S	170E
Tasman Bay: & *mts.*, New Zealand	**104**	41S	173E
Tasmania: *i.* & *State*, Australia	**99**	42S	146E
Tasman Sea: Pac. O.	**99**	35S	165E
Tassili-n-Ajjer: *plat.*, Algeria	**108**	26N	8E
Tatarsk: U.S.S.R.	**85**	55N	76E
Tateyama: Japan	**93**	35N	140E
Tatry: *mtns.*, Czech.	**68**	49N	20E
Tatung: China	**94**	40N	113E
Taumarunui: N.Z.	**104**	39S	175E
Taunton: England	**63**	51N	3W
Taunton: U.S.A.	**51**	42N	71W
Taunus: *mts.*, W. Ger.	**74**	50N	8E
Taupo: & *lake*, N.Z.	**104**	39S	176E
Tauranga: N.Z.	**104**	38S	176E
Taurus Mts.: Turkey	**86**	37N	35E
Tavda: & *r.*, U.S.S.R.	**85**	58N	65E
Tavistock: England	**63**	51N	4W
Tavoy: Burma	**92**	14N	98E
Taw: *r.*, England	**63**	51N	4W
Tawas Pt.: U.S.A.	**19**	44N	83W
Tawitawi: *i.*, Phil.	**91**	5N	120E
Tay: *r.*, Scotland	**62**	56N	3W

Name	Page	Lat.	Long.
Tay, L.: Scotland	62	56N	4W
Tayside: *Reg.*, Scotland	62	57N	3W
Taymyr, L.: U.S.S.R.	83	75N	102E
Taymyr Peninsula: U.S.S.R.	83	75N	105E
Tayshet: U.S.S.R.	85	56N	97E
Tbilisi: U.S.S.R.	84	42N	45E
Teague: U.S.A.	46	32N	96W
Te Anau, L.: N.Z.	104	45S	168E
Te Awamatu: N.Z.	104	38S	175E
Tecuci: Romania	68	46N	27E
Tees: *r.*, England	62	55N	1W
Teesside: England	62	55N	1W
TEGUCIGALPA: Honduras	45	14N	87W
TEHRĀN: Iran	87	35N	51E
Tehuacán: Mexico	52	18N	97W
Tehuantepec: *gulf & isthmus*, Mexico	53	17N	94W
Teifi: *r.*, Wales	63	52N	4W
Tekely: U.S.S.R.	85	45N	79E
Tekirdağ: Turkey	69	41N	27E
Tell Atlas: *mtns.*, Algeria	67	37N	7E
Tell el Kebir: Egypt	109	*Inset*	
Telok Anson: Malaysia	92	4N	101E
Telukbetung: Indon.	91	5S	105E
Temir-Tau: U.S.S.R.	85	50N	73E
Temora: Australia	101	34S	148E
Temple: U.S.A.	46	31N	97W
Temuco: Chile	55	39S	73W
Tenda Pass: Fr./Italy	75	44N	7E
Tende: France	73	44N	8E
Tenerife: *i.*, Canary Is.	108	28N	16W
Tengchung: China	92	25N	98E
Tengiz, L.: U.S.S.R.	85	50N	69E
Tenkiller Ferry Res.: U.S.A.	46	36N	95W
Tennant Creek: *town*, Australia	98	20S	134E
Tennessee: *r.*, & *State*, U.S.A.	47	36N	88W
Tenterfield: Austl.	101	29S	152E
Ten Thousand Is.: U.S.A.	47	26N	82W
Tepic: Mexico	52	21N	105W
Teramo: Italy	69	43N	14E
Teresina: Brazil	54	5S	43W
Terme di Valdieri: Italy	75	44N	7E
Termez: U.S.S.R.	85	37N	67E
Ternate: *i.*, Indon.	91	1N	127E
Terneuzen: Neth.	74	51N	4E
Terni: Italy	69	43N	13E
Ternopol': U.S.S.R.	68	50N	26E
Terre Haute: U.S.A.	47	39N	87W
Terschelling: *i.*, Netherlands	74	53N	5E
Teruel: Spain	67	40N	1W
Tessenei: Ethiopia	109	15N	37E
Test: *r.*, England	63	51N	1W
Tete: Mozambique	111	16S	34E
Tetlin Junction: U.S.A.	30	63N	142W
Tetuan: Morocco	67	36N	5W
Teutoburger Wald: W. Germany	74	52N	8E
Tewkesbury: Eng.	63	52N	2W
Texarkana: U.S.A.	46	33N	94W
Texas: *State*, U.S.A.	46	32N	100W
Texas City: U.S.A.	46	29N	95W
Texel: *i.*, Neth.	74	53N	5E
Texoma, L.: U.S.A.	46	34N	97W
Tezpur: India	89	27N	93E
Thabazimbi: S. Afr.	111	25S	27E
THAILAND: *cap.* Bangkok	92	15N	102E
Thal: *desert*, Pakistan	88	32N	72E
Thames: N.Z.	104	37S	176E
Thames: *r.*, England	63	52N	0
Thanet, Isle of: *dist.*, England	63	51N	1E
Thanh Hoa: Vietnam	92	19N	105E
Thanjavur: India	88	11N	79E
Thar Desert: India/Pakistan	88	27N	72E
Thásos: *i.*, Greece	69	41N	25E
Thaton: Burma	92	16N	97E
Thayetmyo: Burma	92	19N	95E
Thebes: *hist.*, Egypt	86	26N	33E
The Dalles: U.S.A.	48	46N	121W
The Hague: *see* Hague			
Thermopolis: U.S.A.	48	44N	108W
Thessalonica (Salonica): Greece	69	41N	23E
Thetford: England	63	52N	1E
Thief River Falls: *city*, U.S.A.	49	48N	96W
Thiérache: *hills*, France	72	50N	4E
Thiers: France	73	46N	4E
Thionville: France	72	49N	6E
Thira: *i.*, Greece	69	36N	25E
Thirsk: England	62	54N	1W
Thomasville: Ala., U.S.A.	47	32N	88W
Thomasville: Ga., U.S.A.	47	31N	84W
Thonon: France	73	46N	7E
Thore: *r.*, France	73	44N	2E
Thouars: France	73	47N	0
Three Kings Is.: N.Z.	104	34S	172E
Three Points, C.: Ghana	108	5N	2W
Three Springs: Austl.	100	30S	116E
Thule: Greenland	13	76N	68W
Thun: & *l.*, Switz.	75	47N	8E
Thur: *r.*, Switz.	75	48N	9E
Thuringer Wald: *mts.*, E. Germany	74	50N	11E
Thursday I.: Austl.	99	11S	142E
Thurso: Scotland	61	59N	3W
Tiaret: Algeria	67	35N	1E
Tiber: *r.*, Italy	69	43N	12E
Tibesti: *highlands*, Chad	108/9	—	—
Tibet: *Aut. Reg.*, China	88/9	33N	85E
Ticino: *r.*, Italy	75	45N	9E
Tien Shan: *range*, China/U.S.S.R.	85	42N	80E
Tientsin: China	94	39N	117E
Tierra del Fuego: *i.*, Argentina	55	54S	67W
Tiffin: U.S.A.	47	41N	83W
Tignes Res.: France	72	45N	7E
Tigris: *r.*, Turkey/Iraq	87	35N	44E
Tihama: *plain*, Sau. Arab.	87	20N	41E
Tijuana: Mexico	48	32N	117W
Tiksi: U.S.S.R.	83	72N	129E
Tilburg: Neth.	74	52N	5E
Tilbury: England	112	51N	0
Tillabéry: Niger	108	14N	1E
Timaru: N.Z.	104	44S	171E
Timbuktu: *see* Tombouctou			
Timişoara: Romania	68	46N	21E
Timor: *i. & sea*, Indonesia	91	10S	125E
Timsah, L.: Egypt	109	*Inset*	
Tipperary: R. of Ireland	61	52N	8W
TIRANË: Albania	69	41N	20E
Tiraspol': U.S.S.R.	68	47N	30E
Tire: Turkey	69	38N	28E
Tiree: *i.*, Scotland	61	56N	7W
Tirgu-Jiu: Romania	69	45N	23E
Tirgu Mureş: Romania	68	46N	25E
Tiruchirappalli: India	88	11N	79E
Tirunelveli: India	88	9N	78E
Tista: *r.*, Bangl./India	88	27N	89E
Titicaca, Lake: Peru/Bolivia	54	16S	69W
Titograd: Yugoslavia	69	42N	19E
Titovo Užice: Yugo.	69	44N	20E
Titov Veles: Yugo.	69	42N	22E
Tiverton: England	63	51N	4W
Tivoli: Italy	69	42N	13E
Tlálpan: Mexico	52	19N	99W
Tlemcen: Algeria	67	35N	1W
Tobago: *i.*, Trinidad & Tobago	45	11N	61W
Tobermory: Scot.	62	57N	6W
Tobol': *r.*, U.S.S.R.	85	56N	66E
Tobol'sk: U.S.S.R.	85	58N	68E
Tobruk: Libya	86	32N	24E
Tocantins: *r.*, Brazil	54	4S	50W
Toccoa: U.S.A.	47	35N	84W
Tocumwal: Austl.	101	36S	146E
TOGO: *cap.* Lomé	108	8N	1E
Tokelau: *is.*, Pac. O.	102	9S	171W
Tokorozawa: Japan	114	36N	139E
Tokushima: Japan	93	34N	134E
TOKYO: Japan	93	36N	140E
Tolbuhin: Bulgaria	69	44N	28E
Toledo: & *mtns.*, Spain	67	40N	4W
Toledo: Ohio, U.S.A.	47	42N	84W
Toledo: Oregon, U.S.A.	48	45N	124W
Tolo, G. of: Indon.	91	2S	122E
Tolstoy, C.: U.S.S.R.	83	59N	155E
Toluca de Lerdo: Mexico	52	19N	100W
Tomatlan: Mexico	44	20N	105W
Tombigbee: *r.*, U.S.A.	47	32N	88W
Tombouctou (Timbuktu): Mali	108	17N	3W
Tomini, Gulf of: Indonesia	91	0	121E
Tomsk: U.S.S.R.	85	56N	85E
Tonbridge: England	112	51N	0
TONGA: & *Trench*, Pacific Ocean	102	20S	175W
Tonkin, Gulf of: S.E. Asia	92	21N	108E
Tonle, Sap: *L.*, Cambodia	92	13N	104E
Tønsberg: Norway	71	59N	11E
Tooele: U.S.A.	48	41N	112W
Toowoomba: Austl.	100	28S	152E
Topeka: U.S.A.	49	39N	96W
Topozero: *L.*, U.S.S.R.	70	66N	32E
Torbay: England	63	60N	4W
Torgau: E. Germany	74	52N	13E
Torne: *r.*, Sweden/Finland	70	68N	19E
Tornio: Finland	70	66N	24E
Tororo: Uganda	110	1N	34E
Torquay: England	63	50N	4W
Torrance: U.S.A.	37	34N	118W
Torrens, L.: Austl.	101	31S	137E
Torreón: Mexico	52	26N	103W
Torres Strait: Austl.	99	10S	142E
Torridge: *r.*, England	61	51N	4W
Tortona: Italy	75	45N	9E
Tortosa: Spain	67	41N	1E
Toruń: Poland	68	53N	19E
Tosa-wan: *bay*, Japan	93	33N	134E
Touba: Senegal	108	15N	16W
Touggourt: Algeria	108	33N	6E
Toul: France	72	49N	6E
Toulon: France	73	43N	6E
Toulouse: France	73	44N	1E
Toungoo: Burma	92	19N	96E
Touraine: *Old Prov.*, France	73	47N	1E
Tourcoing: France	72	51N	3E
Tournai: Belgium	72	51N	3E
Tours: France	73	47N	1E
Towcester: England	63	52N	1W
Townshend I.: Austl.	100	22S	151E
Townsville: Austl.	100	19S	147E
Toyama: Japan	93	37N	137E
Toyohashi: Japan	93	35N	137E
Toyonaka: Japan	93	35N	135E
Toyota: Japan	93	35N	137E
Trabzon: Turkey	87	41N	40E
Trafalgar, C.: Spain	64	36N	6W
Tralee: R. of Ireland	61	52N	10W
Tranås: Sweden	70	58N	15E
Transkei: *self-governing State*, South Africa	111	31S	29E
Transvaal: *Prov.*, Rep. of South Africa	111	25S	29E
Transylvanian Alps: Romania	69	45N	24E
Trapani: Sicily	69	38N	12E
Traunstein: W. Ger.	75	48N	13E
Traveller's L.: Austl.	101	33S	142E
Traverse City: U.S.A.	19	45N	85W
Trelleborg: Sweden	71	55N	13E
Tremadoc Bay: Wales	63	53N	4W
Trent: *r.*, England	63	53N	1W
Trentino: *Reg.*, Italy	75	46N	11E
Trento: Italy	75	46N	11E
Trenton: Missouri, U.S.A.	49	40N	94W
Trenton: N.J., U.S.A.	51	40N	75W
Treviso: Italy	75	46N	12E
Trier: W. Germany	74	50N	7E
Trieste: Italy	75	46N	14E
Trikkala: Greece	69	40N	22E
Trincomalee: Sri Lanka	88	8N	81E
Trinidad: U.S.A.	49	37N	105W
TRINIDAD & TOBAGO: *cap.* Port of Spain	45	10N	61W
Trinity: *r.*, U.S.A.	46	31N	96W
Tripoli: Lebanon	86	34N	36E
Tripolis: Greece	69	38N	22E
Tripura: *State*, India	89	24N	92E
Tristan da Cunha: *i.*, Atlantic Ocean	57	38S	12W
Trivandrum: India	88	8N	77E
Troitsk: U.S.S.R.	85	54N	62E
Trollhattan: Sweden	71	58N	12E
Tromsø: Norway	70	70N	19E
Trona: U.S.A.	48	36N	117W
Trondheim: Norway	70	63N	11E
Trondheimsfjorden: *fd.*, Norway	70	64N	11E
Trowbridge: England	63	51N	2W
Troy: Ala., U.S.A.	47	32N	86W
Troy: N.Y., U.S.A.	51	42N	74W
Troy: *hist.*, Turkey	86	40N	26E
Troyes: France	72	48N	4E
Trujillo: Honduras	45	16N	86W
Trujillo: Peru	54	8S	79W
Truro: England	63	50N	5W
Truth or Consequences: U.S.A.	48	33N	107W
Tsaidam Swamps: China	90	37N	95E
Tsangpo: *r.*, China	89	29N	86E
Tselinograd: U.S.S.R.	85	51N	71E
Tsetserlig: Mong.	90	47N	102E
Tsimlyansk Res.: U.S.S.R.	84	48N	43E
Tsinan: China	94	37N	117E
Tsing Hai (Koko Nor): *l.*, China	90	37N	100E
Tsingtao: China	94	36N	120E
Tsining: Inner Mongolia, China	94	41N	113E
Tsining: Shantung, China	94	35N	117E
Tsinkiang (Chuanchow): China	95	25N	119E
Tsinling Shan: China	94	34N	108E
Tsitsihar: China	90	47N	124E
Tsu: Japan	93	35N	137E
Tsushima: *is.*, Japan	93	34N	129E
Tsumeb: S.W. Africa (Namibia)	111	19S	18E
Tsuni: China	92	27N	106E
Tsuyung: China	92	25N	101E
Tuam: R. of Ireland	61	54N	9W
Tuamotu Arch.: Pacific Ocean	103	15S	140W
Tuapse: U.S.S.R.	84	44N	39E
Tuatapere: N.Z.	104	46S	168E
Tubai Is.: Pac. O.	103	25S	150W
Tubarão: Brazil	56	28S	49W
Tübingen: W. Ger.	75	49N	9E
Tucson: U.S.A.	48	32N	111W
Tucumcari: U.S.A.	49	35N	104W
Tucupita: Venez.	54	9N	62W
Tudela: Spain	67	42N	2W
Tufts Abyssal Plain: Pacific Ocean	103	45N	140W
Tugssâq: Greenland	13	73N	55W
Tula: U.S.S.R.	84	54N	37E
Tulare: U.S.A.	48	36N	119W
Tulear: Malagasy Rep.	110	23S	44E
Tulia: U.S.A.	46	35N	102W
Tullahoma: U.S.A.	47	35N	86W
Tullamore: R. of Ireland	61	53N	7W
Tulle: France	73	45N	2E
Tulsa: U.S.A.	46	36N	96W
Tulufan: China	90	43N	89E
Tumaco: Colombia	54	2N	79W
Tumkur: India	88	13N	77E
Tungabhadra: *r.*, India	88	16N	76E
Tungchuan: China	94	35N	119E
Tunghsien (Tungchow): China	114	40N	117E
Tunghwa: China	90	42N	126E
Tungkwan: China	94	34N	110E
Tungshan: *see* Suchow			
Tungting, L.: China	95	29N	112E
TUNIS: Tunisia	108	37N	10E
TUNISIA: *cap.* Tunis	108	35N	10E
Tunja: Colombia	54	6N	73W
Tupelo: U.S.A.	46	34N	89W
Turanian Plain: U.S.S.R.	85	43N	60E
Turbat: Pakistan	88	26N	63E
Turbo: Colombia	54	8N	77W
Turda: Romania	68	47N	24E
Turfan Depression: China	83	43N	89E
Turgay: & *r.*, U.S.S.R.	85	50N	64E
Turgutlu: Turkey	69	39N	28E
Turin: Italy	75	45N	8E
Turkana (Rudolf), L.: Kenya	110	4N	36E
Turkestan: U.S.S.R.	85	43N	68E
TURKEY: *cap.* Ankara	86/7	—	—
Turkmen S.S.R.: U.S.S.R.	82/3	39N	57E
Turks Is.: W. Indies	45	22N	71W
Turku (Åbo): Finland	71	60N	22E
Turlock: U.S.A.	48	37N	121W
Turnagain, C.: N.Z.	104	40S	177E
Turnhout: Belgium	72	51N	5E
Turnu Măgurele: Romania	69	44N	25E
Turnu Severin: Romania	69	45N	23E
Tuscaloosa: U.S.A.	47	33N	88W
Tuscany: *Reg.*, Italy	75	44N	11E
Tushino: U.S.S.R.	114	55N	38E
Tuttlingen: W. Ger.	75	48N	9E
Tuvalu: *is.*, Pacific O.	102	8S	180
Tuxpan: Mexico	52	21N	97W
Tuxtla Gutiérrez: Mexico	53	17N	93W
Tuy Hoa: Vietnam	92	13N	109E
Tuyun: China	95	26N	107E
Tuz, L.: Turkey	86	38N	33E
Tweed: *r.*, England/Scotland	62	56N	2W
Twenty Mile House: U.S.A.	30	66N	144W
Twin Bridges: U.S.A.	48	45N	112W
Twin Falls: *city*, U.S.A.	48	43N	115W
Tygda: U.S.S.R.	83	53N	126E
Tyler: U.S.A.	46	32N	95W
Tyne, N. & S.: *rivs.*, England	62	32N	2W
Tyne and Wear: *Co.*, England	62	55N	1W
Tynemouth: England	62	55N	1W
Tyre: *see* Sur			
Tyrol: *Prov.*, Austria	75	47N	11E
Tyrrhenian Sea	69	40N	12E
Tywi: *r.*, Wales	63	52N	4W
Tyumen': U.S.S.R.	85	57N	65E
Tzepo: China	94	37N	118E
Ube: Japan	93	34N	131E
Uberaba: Brazil	54	20S	48W
Ubon Ratchathani: Thailand	92	15N	105E
Ubsa Nor.: *L.*, Mong.	90	50N	93E
Ubundi: Zaïre	110	0	25E
Ucayali: *r.*, Peru	54	7S	74W
Udaipur: India	88	25N	74E
Uddevalla: Sweden	71	58N	12E
Udd L.: Sweden	70	66N	18E
Udine: Italy	75	46N	13E
Udon Thani: Thailand	92	17N	103E

	Page	Lat.	Long.
Ufa: & *r.*, U.S.S.R.	84/5	55N	56E
UGANDA: *cap.* Kampala	110	1N	32E
Uinta Mts.: U.S.A.	48	41N	111W
Uitenhage: S. Africa	111	33S	25E
Ujjain: India	88	23N	76E
Ujung Pandang: Indonesia	91	5S	119E
Ukhta: U.S.S.R.	84	63N	54E
Ukiah: U.S.A.	48	39N	123W
Ukrainian S.S.R.: U.S.S.R.	84	50N	30E
ULAN BATOR: Mongolia	83	47N	107E
Ulan Gom: Mongolia	83	50N	92E
Ulan Ude: U.S.S.R.	83	52N	107E
Uldza: Mongolia	83	49N	112E
Uliastay (Jibhalanta): Mongolia	83	47N	97E
Ullapool: Scotland	61	58N	5W
Ullswater: *l.*, Eng.	62	55N	3W
Ulm: W. Germany	75	48N	10E
Ulundi: S. Africa	111	28S	32E
Ulu-Tau: *range*, U.S.S.R.	85	49N	67E
Ul'yanovsk: U.S.S.R.	84	54N	48E
Ulyungur Nor: *l.*, China	85	47N	87E
Ulzen: W. Germany	74	53N	10E
Umarkot: Pakistan	88	25N	70E
Umeå: Sweden	70	64N	20E
Umm Samin: *salt flats*, Oman	87	22N	56E
Umtali: Rhodesia (Zimbabwe)	111	19S	33E
Umtata: S. Africa	111	31S	29E
Union: U.S.A.	35	41N	74W
Uniondale: S. Africa	111	34S	23E
UNION OF SOVIET SOCIALIST REPUBLICS: *cap.* Moscow	82/3	—	—
Uniontown: U.S.A.	47	40N	80W
UNITED ARAB EMIRATES: *cap.* Abu Dhabi	87	24N	55E
UNITED KINGDOM OF GREAT BRITAIN & N. IRELAND *cap.* London	61	—	—
UNITED STATES OF AMERICA: *cap.* Washington	44/5	—	—
UPPER VOLTA: *cap.* Ouagadougou	108	12N	1W
Uppsala: Sweden	71	60N	18E
Ur: *hist.*, Iraq	87	31N	46E
Uraga: Japan	114	35N	140E
Ural: *r.*, U.S.S.R.	84	52N	53E
Ural Mts.: U.S.S.R.	85	55N	59E
Ural'sk: U.S.S.R.	84	51N	51E
Urawa: Japan	93	36N	140E
Urdos: France	73	43N	1W
Ure: *r.*, England	62	54N	2W
Urfa: Turkey	87	37N	39E
Uruapan del Progreso: Mexico	52	19N	102W
Uruguaiana: Brazil	56	30S	57W
URUGUAY: *cap.* Montevideo	56	32S	56W
Uruguay: *r.*, S. Am.	56	29S	56W
Urumchi: *see* Wulumuchi			
Usakos: S.W. Africa (Namibia)	111	22S	15E
Ushant: *see* Ouessant, Île d'			
Uskudar: Turkey	86	41N	29E
Usol'ye: U.S.S.R.	83	53N	103E
Uspallata Pass: Chile/Arg.	55	33S	70W
Uspenskiy: U.S.S.R.	85	49N	73E
Ussurilsk: U.S.S.R.	83	44N	132E
Usti nad Labem: Czechoslovakia	74	51N	14E
Ust'-Kamenogorsk: U.S.S.R.	85	50N	83E
Ust'-Kut: U.S.S.R.	83	57N	105E
Ust'-Urt Plateau: U.S.S.R.	84/5	44N	57E
Ust' Uyskoye: U.S.S.R.	85	54N	65E
Utah: *State*, U.S.A.	48	39N	112W
Utah Lake: U.S.A.	48	40N	112W
Utica: U.S.A.	50	43N	75W
Utrecht: Neth.	74	52N	5E
Uttaradit: Thailand	92	17N	100E
Uttar Pradesh: *State*, India	88	27N	80E
Uvalde: U.S.A.	46	29N	100W
Uxmal: Mexico	53	20N	90W
Uyuni: Bolivia	54	20S	67W
Uzbek S.S.R.: U.S.S.R.	85	41N	62E
Uzhgorod: U.S.S.R.	68	49N	22E
Vaal: *r.*, S. Africa	111	27S	28E
Vaasa: Finland	70	63N	22E
Vaccarès: Étang de: France	73	44N	5E
VADUZ: Liechtenstein	75	47N	10E
Valdai Hills: U.S.S.R.	84	57N	34E
Valdepeñas: Spain	67	39N	3W
Valdés Penin.: Arg.	55	43S	64W
Valdez: U.S.A.	12	61N	146W
Valdivia: Chile	55	40S	74W
Valdosta: U.S.A.	47	31N	83W
Valence: France	73	45N	5E
Valencia: & *gulf*, Spain	67	39N	0
Valencia: Venez.	45	10N	68W
Valenciennes: Fr.	72	50N	4E
Valentia I.: R. of Irel.	61	52N	10W
Valga: U.S.S.R.	71	57N	25E
Valladolid: Spain	67	42N	5W
Vallejo: U.S.A.	42	38N	122W
VALLETTA: Malta	69	36N	14E
Valmiera: U.S.S.R.	71	57N	25E
Valparaiso: Chile	55	33S	72W
Valsch, Cape: Indon.	98	8S	137E
Van: & *lake*, Turkey	87	39N	43E
Vancouver: U.S.A.	48	46N	123W
Vancouver, Mt.: U.S.A./Canada	12	60N	140W
Vaner, L.: Sweden	71	59N	13E
Vanersborg: Sweden	71	58N	12E
Vannes: France	72	48N	3W
Vannøy: *i.*, Norway	70	70N	20E
Vanua Levu: *i.*, Pacific Ocean	102	16S	179E
Varanasi: India	88	25N	83E
Varanger Penin.: Norway	70	71N	29E
Varangerfjorden: *fd.*, Norway	70	71N	30E
Varaždin: Yugoslavia	68	46N	16E
Vardar: *r.*, Yugo./Greece	69	41N	22E
Vardø: Norway	70	70N	31E
Varese: Italy	75	46N	9E
Varna: Bulgaria	69	43N	28E
Varnamo: Sweden	71	57N	14E
Vasterås: Sweden	71	60N	17E
Vaster Dal: *r.*, Sweden	71	61N	13E
Vastervik: Sweden	71	58N	17E
Vatnajökull: *ice cap*, Iceland	70	64N	17W
Vatter, L.: Sweden	71	58N	14E
Vaupés: *r.*, Col.	54	1N	71W
Vaxjö: Sweden	71	57N	15E
Vaygach I.: U.S.S.R.	82	70N	59E
Vega: *i.*, Norway	70	66N	12E
Velbert: W. Germany	64	51N	7E
Velikiye Luki: U.S.S.R.	84	56N	31E
Vellore: India	88	13N	79E
Velmandois: France	72	50N	3E
Velp: Netherlands	74	52N	6E
Venado Tuerto: Argentina	56	34S	62W
Vendée: *reg.*, France	73	47N	1W
Vendôme: France	72	48N	1E
Venetian Alps: Italy	75	46N	13E
Venetie: U.S.A.	30	67N	146W
Venezia: *reg.*, It.	75	46N	12E
VENEZUELA: *cap.* Caracas	54	7N	65W
Venezuela, Gulf of: Venezuela	45	11N	71W
Venice: & *gulf*, Italy	75	45N	12E
Venlo: Netherlands	74	51N	6E
Ventimiglia: Italy	75	44N	8E
Ventspils: U.S.S.R.	71	57N	22E
Veracruz Llave: Mexico	53	19N	96W
Verde: *r.*, U.S.A.	48	34N	112W
Verdigris: *r.*, U.S.A.	46	38N	96W
Verdon: *r.*, France	73	44N	6E
Verdun: France	72	49N	5E
Vereeniging: S. Afr.	111	26S	28E
Verkhoyansk: U.S.S.R.	83	68N	134E
Verkhoyansk Range: U.S.S.R.	83	65N	130E
Vermilion L.: U.S.A.	49	48N	93W
Vermillion: *r.*, U.S.A.	49	44N	97W
Vermont: *State*, U.S.A.	19	44N	73W
Vernal: U.S.A.	48	40N	110W
Vernon: U.S.A.	46	34N	99W
Verona: Italy	75	45N	11E
Versailles: France	113	49N	2E
Verviers: Belgium	72	51N	6E
Vesle: *r.*, France	72	49N	4E
Vesoul: France	73	48N	6E
Vestfjorden: *fd.*, Norway	70	68N	15E
Vesuvius: *volc.*, Italy	69	41N	15E
Vevey: Switzerland	75	46N	7E
Viareggio: Italy	75	44N	10E
Viborg: Denmark	71	56N	9E
Vicenza: Italy	75	46N	11E
Vichy: France	73	46N	3E
Vicksburg: U.S.A.	46	32N	91W
VICTORIA: Hong Kong	95	22N	114E
Victoria: *r.*, Austl.	98	16S	130E
Victoria: *State*, Austl.	101	37S	145E
Victoria: U.S.A.	46	29N	97W
Victoria de los Tunas: Cuba	53	21N	77W
Victoria Falls: Rhodesia (Zimbabwe)	111	18S	26E
Victoria Land: Antarctica	116	78S	169E
Victoria, L.: Africa	110	1S	33E
Victoria West: South Africa	111	31S	23E
Vidin: Bulgaria	69	44N	23E
Viella: Spain	73	43N	1E
VIENNA: Austria	68	48N	16E
Vienne: France	73	46N	5E
Vienne: *r.*, France	73	47N	1E
VIENTIANE: Laos	92	18N	103E
VIETNAM: *cap.* Hanoi	92	15N	105E
Vierzon-Ville: Fr.	73	47N	2E
Vigevano: Italy	75	45N	9E
Vigo: Spain	69	42N	9W
Vijayawada: India	88	16N	81E
Vikna: *i.*, Norway	70	65N	11E
Vila Cabral: Mozambique	111	13S	35E
Vila de João Bela: Mozambique	111	25S	34E
Vilaine: *r.*, France	72	48N	2W
Villach: Austria	75	47N	14E
Villahermosa: Mexico	53	18N	93W
Villefranche-sur-Saône: France	73	46N	5E
Villeneuve-sur-Lot: France	73	44N	1E
Villeurbanne: France	73	46N	5E
Vilnius: U.S.S.R.	71	55N	25E
Viña del Mar: Chile	54	33S	72W
Vincennes: U.S.A.	47	39N	88W
Vindel: *r.*, Sweden	70	65N	18E
Vindhya Ra.: India	88	23N	77E
Vineland: U.S.A.	51	39N	75W
Vinh: Vietnam	92	19N	106E
Vinh Loi: Vietnam	92	9N	105E
Vinnitsa: U.S.S.R.	68	49N	28E
Vire: France	72	49N	1W
Virgin: *r.*, U.S.A.	48	37N	114W
Virginia: *State*, U.S.A.	47	37N	78W
Virginia: U.S.A.	49	48N	93W
Virgin Is.: W. Indies	45	18N	65W
Vishakhapatnam: India	88	18N	83E
Visalia: U.S.A.	48	36N	119W
Visby: Sweden	71	58N	18E
Viseu: Portugal	66	41N	8W
Vistula: *r.*, Poland	68	53N	19E
Vitebsk: U.S.S.R.	68	55N	30E
Viti Levu: *i.*, Pac. O.	102	18S	178E
Vitim: & *r.*, U.S.S.R.	83	60N	113E
Vitória: Brazil	54	20S	40W
Vitoria: Spain	67	43N	3W
Vitry-en-Artois: Fr.	72	50N	3E
Vitry-le-François: Fr.	72	49N	5E
Vittoria Veneto: It.	75	46N	12E
Vizianagaram: India	88	18N	83E
Vladimir: U.S.S.R.	84	56N	40E
Vladivostok: U.S.S.R.	83	43N	132E
Vlissingen: *see* Flushing			
Vlorë: Albania	69	40N	20E
Vltava: *r.*, Czech.	74	50N	14E
Voerde: W. Germany	64	52N	7E
Voiron: France	73	45N	6E
Volga: *r.*, U.S.S.R.	84	50N	45E
Volga Hills: U.S.S.R.	84	51N	45E
Volgograd: U.S.S.R.	84	49N	45E
Volmarstein: W. Ger.	64	51N	7E
Vologda: U.S.S.R.	84	59N	40E
Vólos: Greece	69	39N	23E
Vol'sk: U.S.S.R.	84	52N	47E
Volta Redonda: Braz.	56	23S	44W
Vorarlberg: *Prov.*, Austria	75	47N	10E
Vorkuta: U.S.S.R.	82	67N	64E
Voronezh: U.S.S.R.	84	52N	39E
Voroshilovgrad: U.S.S.R.	84	48N	40E
Vosges: *mtns.*, Fr.	72	48N	7E
Voss: Norway	71	61N	6E
Vraca: Bulgaria	69	43N	24E
Vryburg: S. Africa	111	27S	25E
Vyaz'ma: U.S.S.R.	84	55N	34E
Vyborg: U.S.S.R.	71	61N	29E
Vyshniy-Volochek: U.S.S.R.	84	58N	35E
Waal: *r.*, Neth.	74	52N	5E
Wabash: *r.*, U.S.A.	47	38N	88W
Waccasassa Bay: U.S.A.	47	29N	83W
Waco: U.S.A.	46	32N	97W
Wadden Zee: Neth.	74	53N	5E
Wadena: U.S.A.	49	46N	95W
Wadi el Milk: *r.*, Sudan	86	17N	30E
Wadi Halfa: Sudan	86	22N	31E
Wad Medani: Sudan	86	14N	34E
Wagga Wagga: Austl.	101	35S	147E
Wagin: Australia	100	33S	117E
Wahpeton: U.S.A.	49	46N	97W
Waiau: & *r.*, N.Z.	104	43S	173E
Waigeo: *i.*, Indonesia	91	0	131E
Waikaremoana, L.: N.Z.	104	39S	177E
Waikato: *r.* & *district*, N.Z.	104	38S	176E
Waikerie: Australia	101	34S	140E
Waingapu: Indon.	91	10S	120E
Waipara: N.Z.	104	43S	173E
Waipawa: N.Z.	104	40S	177E
Wairau: *r.*, N.Z.	104	41S	174E
Wairoa: N.Z.	104	39S	177E
Waitaki: *r.*, N.Z.	104	45S	171E
Waitangi: N.Z.	104	35S	174E
Waitara: N.Z.	104	39S	174E
Wakatipu, L.: N.Z.	104	45S	168E
Wakayama: Japan	93	34N	135E
WaKeeney: U.S.A.	49	39N	100W
Wakefield: England	62	54N	1W
Wakefield: U.S.A.	33	42N	71W
Wake I.: Pac. O.	102	20N	167E
Wakkanai: Japan	90	45N	142E
Walcheren: *i.*, Neth.	74	51N	4E
WALES: *cap.* Cardiff	61	—	—
Walgett: Australia	101	30S	148E
Wallachia: *Old Reg.*, Romania	69	44N	25E
Wallaroo: Australia	101	34S	137E
Walla Walla: U.S.A.	48	46N	118W
Walsenburg: U.S.A.	49	38N	105W
Waltham: U.S.A.	33	42N	71W
Walton-on-Thames: England	112	51N	0
Waltrop: W. Germany	64	52N	7E
Walvis Bay: S. Afr.	111	23S	14E
Wanaka, L.: N.Z.	104	44S	169E
Wandsworth: Eng.	112	51N	0
Wanganui: & *r.*, New Zealand	104	40S	175E
Wangaratta: Austl.	101	36S	146E
Wangeroog: *i.*, W. Ger.	74	54N	8E
Wanhsien: China	95	31N	109E
Wankie: Rhodesia (Zimbabwe)	111	18S	26E
Wanne-Eickel: W. Ger.	64	52N	7E
Wantagh: U.S.A.	35	41N	73W
Warangal: India	88	18N	80E
Ware: England	112	52N	0
Warmbad: S.W. Afr. (Namibia)	111	28S	19E
Warminster: Eng.	63	51N	2W
Warracknabeal: Australia	101	36S	142E
Warragul: Australia	101	38S	146E
Warrego: *r.*, Austl.	100	28S	146E
Warrego Ra.: Australia	100	25S	146E
Warren: Idaho, U.S.A.	48	45N	116W
Warren: Michigan, U.S.A.	33	43N	83W
Warren: Minn., U.S.A.	49	48N	97W
Warren: Ohio, U.S.A.	47	41N	81W
Warren: Pa., U.S.A.	47	42N	79W
Warrnambool: Australia	101	38S	143E
Warroad: U.S.A.	49	49N	95W
WARSAW: Poland	68	52N	21E
Warwick: Australia	101	28S	152E
Warwick: & *Co.*, England	63	52N	2W
Warwick: U.S.A.	51	42N	72W
Wash, The: *bay*, England	63	53N	0
WASHINGTON: D.C., U.S.A.	33	—	—
Washington: Ind., U.S.A.	47	39N	87W
Washington: N.C., U.S.A.	47	36N	77W
Washington: *State*, U.S.A.	48	47N	120W
Washington, Mt.: U.S.A.	19	44N	71W
Waterbury: U.S.A.	51	42N	73W
Waterford: R. of Irel.	61	52N	7W
Waterloo: Belgium	72	51N	4E
Waterloo: U.S.A.	49	42N	92W
Waterton Glacier Int. Peace Park: Canada/U.S.A.	48	49N	114W
Watertown: N.Y., U.S.A.	19	44N	76W
Watertown: S. Dak., U.S.A.	49	45N	97W
Waterville: U.S.A.	15	45N	70W
Watford: England	112	51N	0
Watsonville: U.S.A.	48	37N	122W
Wattenscheid: W. Ger.	64	51N	7E
Wau: Sudan	109	7N	27E
Waukegan: U.S.A.	33	42N	87W
Wausau: U.S.A.	49	45N	90W
Waxahachie: U.S.A.	46	32N	97W
Waycross: U.S.A.	47	31N	83W
Wayne: U.S.A.	35	41N	74W
Waynesboro: U.S.A.	47	38N	79W
Weald, The: *geog. reg.*, England	63	51N	0
Weaverville: U.S.A.	48	41N	123W
Webster: U.S.A.	51	42N	72W
Weddell Sea: Antarctica	116	72S	40W
Weed: U.S.A.	48	41N	122W
Weiden: W. Germany	74	50N	12E

	Page	Lat.	Long.
Weifang: China	**94**	37N	118E
Weihai: China	**94**	38N	122E
Weimar: E. Germany	**74**	51N	11E
Weirton: U.S.A.	**47**	41N	81W
Weiser: U.S.A.	**48**	44N	117W
Weisshorn: *mtn.*, Switzerland	**75**	46N	8E
Welkon: S. Africa	**111**	27S	27E
Welland: *r.*, Eng.	**63**	52N	0
Wellesley Is.: Austl.	**98**	17S	139E
Wellesley: U.S.A.	**33**	42N	71W
Wellingborough: England	**63**	52N	1W
Wellington: Austl.	**101**	32S	149E
Wellington: England	**63**	53N	3W
WELLINGTON: N.Z.	**104**	41S	175E
Wells: U.S.A.	**48**	41N	115W
Welper: W. Germany	**64**	51N	7E
Welshpool: Wales	**63**	53N	3W
Welwyn Garden City: England	**112**	52N	0
Wem: England	**63**	53N	3W
Wembley: England	**112**	52N	0
Wenatchee: U.S.A.	**48**	47N	121W
Wenchow: China	**95**	28N	121E
Wendover: U.S.A.	**48**	41N	114W
Wenshan: China	**92**	23N	104E
Wensum: *r.*, Eng.	**63**	53N	1E
Wentworth: Austl.	**101**	34S	141E
Wernigerode: E. Ger.	**74**	52N	11E
Wesel: W. Germany	**64**	52N	6E
Weser: *r.*, W. Germany	**74**	53N	9E
Wesergebirge: *mts.*, W. Germany	**74**	52N	9E
West Australian Basin: Indian Ocean	**89**	20S	100E
West Bengal: *State*, India	**88**	23N	87E
West Dvina (Daugava): *r.*, U.S.S.R.	**84**	56N	28E
Westerholt: W. Ger.	**64**	52N	7E
Western Australia: *State*, Australia	**98**	25S	120E
Western Ghats: *range*, India	**88**	15N	75E
Western Sahara: *disputed territory* W. Africa	**108**	25N	14W
Western Sayan Mts.: U.S.S.R.	**85**	52N	91E
Western Sierra Madre: *see* Sierra Madre Occidental			
Westerwald: *mts.*, W. Germany	**74**	51N	8E
West Indies	**45**	—	—
West Irian: *State*, Indonesia	**98**	5S	137E
Westland: *district*, N.Z.	**104**	43S	171E
Westland: U.S.A.	**33**	42N	83W
West Midland: *Co.*, England	**63**	52N	2W
Westminster: Eng.	**112**	51N	0
Weston: Malaysia	**91**	5S	116E
Weston-super-Mare: England	**63**	51N	3W
West Palm Beach: U.S.A.	**47**	27N	80W
Westphalia: *Land*, W. Germany	**74**	52N	7E
Westport: N.Z.	**104**	42S	172E
Westport: R. of Ireland	**61**	54N	10W
Westport: U.S.A.	**51**	41N	73W
West Siberian Plain: U.S.S.R.	**82/3**	60N	73E
West Virginia: *State*, U.S.A.	**47**	38N	80W
Westwood: U.S.A.	**48**	40N	121W
Wetar: *i.*, Indonesia	**91**	7S	126E
Wetzlar: W. Germany	**74**	51N	9E
Wexford: R. of Irel.	**61**	52N	6W
Wexford: *Co.*, R. of Ireland	**63**	52N	6W
Wey: *r.*, England	**63**	51N	1W
Weymouth: England	**63**	51N	2W
Weymouth: U.S.A.	**51**	42N	71W
Whakatane: N.Z.	**104**	38S	177E
Whangarei: N.Z.	**104**	36S	174E
Wharfe: *r.*, England	**62**	54N	1W
Wharton Basin: Indian Ocean	**89**	16S	107E
Wheaton: U.S.A.	**34**	42N	88W
Wheeler L.: U.S.A.	**47**	35N	87W
Wheeling: U.S.A.	**47**	40N	81W
Whitby: England	**62**	54N	1W
Whitchurch: Eng.	**63**	53N	3W
White: *r.*, Arkansas, U.S.A.	**46**	35N	91W
White: *r.*, Indiana, U.S.A.	**47**	39N	87W
White: *r.*, S. Dak., U.S.A.	**49**	44N	100W
Whitefish: U.S.A.	**48**	48N	115W
Whitehead: N. Irel.	**62**	55N	6W
White Nile (Bahr el Jebel): *r.*, Sudan	**109**	7N	31E
White Plains: U.S.A.	**51**	41N	74W
White Sea: U.S.S.R.	**82**	65N	37E
White Volta: *r.*, West Africa	**108**	12N	2W
Whitney, Mt.: U.S.A.	**48**	37N	118W
Whitsunday I.: Australia	**100**	20S	149E
Whyalla: Australia	**101**	33S	138E
Wichita: U.S.A.	**46**	38N	97W
Wichita: *r.*, U.S.A.	**46**	34N	100W
Wichita Falls: *city*, U.S.A.	**46**	34N	98W
Wick: Scotland	**61**	58N	3W
Wicklow: R. of Irel.	**61**	53N	6W
Wicklow Mts.: R. of Ireland	**61**	53N	6W
Widnes: England	**63**	53N	3W
Wiener-Neustadt: Austria	**68**	48N	16E
Wiesbaden: W. Ger.	**74**	50N	8E
Wigan: England	**62**	53N	3W
Wight, I. of: Eng.	**63**	51N	1W
Wigtown: Scotland	**62**	55N	4W
Wigtown Bay: Scot.	**62**	54N	4W
Wilcannia: Australia	**101**	32S	143E
Wilhelmshaven: W. Germany	**74**	54N	8E
Wilkes-Barre: U.S.A.	**50**	41N	76W
Wilkes Land: Antarctica	**116**	71S	120E
Willamette: *r.*, U.S.A.	**48**	45N	123W
Williamson: U.S.A.	**47**	37N	82W
Williamsport: U.S.A.	**50**	41N	77W
Willich: W. Germany	**64**	51N	7E
Williston: U.S.A.	**49**	48N	104W
Willmar: U.S.A.	**43**	45N	95W
Willoughby, Cape: Australia	**101**	36S	138E
Willow South: U.S.A.	**12**	62N	150W
Wilmette: U.S.A.	**34**	42N	88W
Wilmington: Del., U.S.A.	**50**	40N	75W
Wilmington: N.C., U.S.A.	**47**	34N	78W
Wilson: U.S.A.	**47**	36N	78W
Wiltshire: *Co.*, Eng.	**63**	51N	2W
Wiluna: Australia	**98**	27S	120E
Winchester: England	**63**	51N	1W
Winchester: Ky., U.S.A.	**47**	38N	84W
Winchester: Va., U.S.A.	**50**	39N	78W
Windermere: *l.*, England	**62**	54N	3W
Windhoek: S.W. Africa (Namibia)	**111**	22S	17E
Wind River Range: U.S.A.	**48**	43N	110W
Windsor: England	**112**	51N	1W
Windward Is.: W. Indies	**45**	13N	62W
Windward Passage: Cuba/Haiti	**45**	20N	73W
Winfield: U.S.A.	**46**	37N	97W
Winnemucca: & *l.*, U.S.A.	**48**	41N	118W
Winner: U.S.A.	**49**	43N	100W
Winnibago, L.: U.S.A.	**49**	44N	88W
Winona: U.S.A.	**47**	33N	90W
Winslow: U.S.A.	**48**	35N	111W
Winston-Salem: U.S.A.	**47**	36N	80W
Winter Haven: U.S.A.	**47**	28N	82W
Winterthur: Switz.	**75**	48N	9E
Winton: Australia	**99**	22S	143E
Wisbech: England	**63**	53N	0
Wisconsin: *State*, U.S.A.	**49**	45N	90W
Wisconsin Rapids: *city*, U.S.A.	**49**	44N	90W
Wismar: E. Germany	**74**	54N	11E
Witbank: S. Africa	**111**	26S	29E
Witdraai: S. Africa	**111**	27S	21E
Witney: England	**63**	52N	2W
Witten: W. Germany	**64**	51N	7E
Wittenberge: E. Ger.	**74**	53N	12E
Wittlaer: W. Germany	**64**	51N	7E
Włocławek: Poland	**68**	52N	19E
Woburn: U.S.A.	**33**	42N	71W
Woking: England	**112**	51N	1W
Wolf: *r.*, U.S.A.	**49**	45N	89W
Wolfenbuttel: W. Ger.	**74**	52N	10E
Wolf Rock: England	**63**	50N	6W
Wolfsburg: W. Ger.	**74**	52N	11E
Wollongong: Austl.	**101**	34S	151E
Wolverhampton: England	**63**	53N	2W
Wolverton: England	**63**	52N	1W
Wonsan: N. Korea	**90**	39N	127E
Wonthaggi: Austl.	**101**	38S	146E
Woodland: U.S.A.	**48**	39N	122W
Woodville: N.Z.	**104**	40S	176E
Woodville: U.S.A.	**46**	31N	94W
Woodward: U.S.A.	**46**	36N	99W
Woomera: Australia	**98**	31S	137E
Woonsocket: U.S.A.	**51**	42N	72W
Woosung: China	**95**	31N	121E
Worcester: & *Co.*, England	**63**	52N	2W
Worcester: S. Africa	**111**	34S	20E
Worcester: U.S.A.	**51**	42N	73W
Workington: Eng.	**62**	55N	3W
Worksop: England	**63**	53N	1W
Worms: W. Germany	**74**	50N	8E
Worms Hd.: Wales	**63**	52N	4W
Worth: U.S.A.	**34**	42N	88W
Worthing: England	**63**	51N	0
Wrangell: U.S.A.	**24**	56N	132W
Wrath, C.: Scotland	**61**	59N	5W
Wrexham: Wales	**63**	53N	3W
Wrocław: Poland	**68**	51N	17E
Wuchang: China	**95**	30N	114E
Wuchow: China	**95**	23N	111E
Wuhan: China	**95**	30N	115E
Wuhsi: China	**95**	32N	120E
Wuhu: China	**95**	31N	118E
Wulanhaote: China	**90**	46N	112E
Wülfrath: W. Germany	**64**	51N	7E
Wulumuchi (Urumchi): China	**83**	44N	87E
Wuppertal: W. Ger.	**64**	51N	7E
Würzburg: W. Ger.	**74**	50N	10E
Wuyi Shan: *mtns.*, China	**95**	27N	117E
Wyandotte: U.S.A.	**33**	42N	83W
Wyangala Res.: Australia	**101**	34S	149E
Wye: *r.*, England	**63**	52N	3W
Wyndham: Austl.	**98**	15S	128E
Wyoming: *State*, U.S.A.	**42/3**	43N	107W
Xánthi: Greece	**69**	41N	25E
Xingu: *r.*, Brazil	**54**	7S	53W
Xochimilco: Mexico	**52**	19N	99W
Yaan: China	**90**	30N	103E
Yakima: & *r.*, U.S.A.	**48**	47N	120W
Yakuta: & *bay*, U.S.A.	**30**	60N	140W
Yakutsk: U.S.S.R.	**83**	62N	130E
Yallourn: Australia	**101**	38S	146E
Yalta: U.S.S.R.	**84**	45N	34E
Yamagata: Japan	**93**	38N	140E
Yamal Peninsula: U.S.S.R.	**82/3**	70N	70E
Yamatu: China	**85**	46N	84E
Yamma Yamma, L.: Australia	**100**	26S	141E
Yampa: *r.*, U.S.A.	**48**	40N	108W
Yampi Sound: Austl.	**98**	16S	123E
Yamuna: *r.*, India	**88**	25N	81E
Yanbu: Saudi Arabia	**87**	24N	38E
Yangchow: China	**94**	38N	113E
Yangtze: *r.*, China	**95**	31N	118E
Yao: Japan	**93**	35N	136E
YAOUNDÉ: Cameroun	**108**	4N	11E
Yaraka: Australia	**99**	25S	144E
Yarkand: China	**82**	38N	77E
Yaroslavl': U.S.S.R.	**84**	58N	40E
Yazd: Iran	**87**	32N	54E
Yazoo City: & *r.*, U.S.A.	**46**	33N	90W
Yellow Sea: China	**90**	35N	122E
Yellowstone: *L.* & *Nat. Park*, U.S.A.	**48**	45N	111W
Yellowstone: *r.*, U.S.A.	**48**	46N	108W
YEMEN: *cap.* San'a	**87**	15N	44E
YEMEN P.D.R.: *cap.* Aden	**87**	15N	50E
Yenakiyevo: U.S.S.R.	**84**	48N	38E
Yenangyaung: Burma	**90**	20N	95E
Yencheng: China	**94**	34N	120E
Yenisey: *r.*, U.S.S.R.	**83**	58N	88E
Yenisey, Gulf of: U.S.S.R.	**83**	72N	83E
Yeniseysk: U.S.S.R.	**85**	58N	92E
Yentai (Chefoo): China	**94**	38N	121E
Yeovil: England	**63**	51N	3W
Yerevan: U.S.S.R.	**84**	40N	44E
Yeungkong: China	**95**	22N	112E
Yeysk: U.S.S.R.	**84**	46N	38E
Yinchwan (Yin-chuan, ~~Ninghsia): China~~	~~**94**~~	~~38N~~	~~106E~~
Yingkow: China	**94**	40N	122E
Yin Shan: *desert*, China	**90**	42N	108E
Yokkaichi: Japan	**93**	35N	137E
Yokohama: Japan	**114**	35N	140E
Yokosuka: Japan	**114**	35N	140E
Yonkers: U.S.A.	**35**	41N	74W
Yonne: *r.*, France	**72**	48N	3E
York: England	**62**	54N	1W
York, Cape: Austl.	**98**	11S	143E
York: Nebr., U.S.A.	**49**	41N	98W
York: Pa., U.S.A.	**50**	40N	77W
Yorke Penin.: Austl.	**99**	35S	138E
Yorkshire, N.: *Co.*, England	**62**	54N	1W
Yorkshire, S.: *Co.*, England	**62**	54N	1W
Yorkshire, W.: *Co.*, England	**62**	54N	2W
Yoshkar-Ola: U.S.S.R.	**84**	57N	48E
Youghal: R. of Irel.	**61**	52N	8W
Young: Australia	**101**	34S	148E
Youngstown: U.S.A.	**47**	41N	81W
Ypres: Belgium	**72**	51N	3E
Yreka: U.S.A.	**48**	42N	123W
Yuan: *r.*, China	**95**	29N	110E
Yuba City: U.S.A.	**48**	39N	122W
Yucatan Channel: Mexico/Cuba	**45**	22N	86W
Yucatán Penin.: Mexico	**53**	20N	88W
YUGOSLAVIA: *cap.* Belgrade	**69**	44N	20E
Yukagir Plateau: U.S.S.R.	**83**	66N	157E
Yukon: *r.*, Canada/U.S.A.	**12**	63N	159W
Yulin: China	**94**	38N	109E
Yuma: U.S.A.	**48**	33N	115W
Yunkwei Plat.: China	**90**	27N	106E
Yunnan: *Prov.*, China	**92**	25N	103E
Yushu (Jyekundo): China	**90**	33N	97E
Yuzhno Sakhalinsk: U.S.S.R.	**83**	47N	143E
Yverdon: Switz.	**75**	47N	7E
Zabul: Iran	**87**	31N	62E
Zacatecas: Mexico	**52**	23N	103W
Zadar: Yugoslavia	**69**	44N	15E
Zagreb: Yugoslavia	**68**	46N	16E
Zagros Mts.: Iran	**87**	32N	50E
Zāhedan: Iran	**87**	29N	61E
ZAÏRE: *cap.* Kinshasa	**110**	—	—
Zaire (Congo): *r.*, Zaire	**110**	2N	21E
Zambezi: *r.*, S. Afr.	**111**	16S	31E
ZAMBIA: *cap.* Lusaka	**110**	—	—
Zamboanga: Phil.	**91**	7N	122E
Zamora: Spain	**67**	41N	6W
Zamora de Hidalgo: Mexico	**52**	20N	102W
Zamość: Poland	**68**	51N	23E
Zanesville: U.S.A.	**47**	40N	82W
Zante: *i.*, Greece	**69**	38N	21E
Zanthus: Australia	**98**	31S	123E
Zanzibar: *State & town*, Tanzania	**110**	6S	39E
Zaporozh'ye: U.S.S.R.	**84**	48N	35E
Zaragoza (Saragossa): Spain	**67**	42N	1W
Zárate: Argentina	**56**	34S	59W
Zaria: Nigeria	**108**	11N	8E
Zaysan, L.: U.S.S.R.	**85**	48N	84E
Zeebrugge: Belgium	**72**	51N	3E
Zeerust: S. Africa	**111**	26S	26E
Zeila: Somali Rep.	**109**	11N	43E
Zeitz: E. Germany	**74**	51N	12E
Zella Mehlis: E. Ger.	**74**	51N	11E
Zemz: *r.*, Libya	**84**	31N	14E
Zermatt: Switz.	**75**	46N	8E
Zeya: U.S.S.R.	**83**	54N	127E
Zhdanov: U.S.S.R.	**84**	47N	37E
Zhigalovo: U.S.S.R.	**83**	55N	105E
Zhitomir: U.S.S.R.	**84**	50N	29E
Zielona Góra: Pol.	**68**	52N	16E
ZIMBABWE: *see* **RHODESIA**			
Zittau: E. Germany	**74**	51N	15E
Ziatoust: U.S.S.R.	**85**	55N	60E
Zliten: Libya	**86**	32N	14E
Znojmo: Czech.	**68**	49N	16E
Zomba: Malawi	**111**	15S	35E
Zongo: Zaire	**109**	4N	18E
Zonguldak: Turkey	**86**	41N	32E
Zrenjanin: Yugo.	**69**	45N	20E
Zuara: Libya	**86**	33N	13E
Zug: Switzerland	**75**	47N	8E
Zuider Zee: *see* Ijsselmeer			
Zuni: *r.*, U.S.A.	**48**	35N	109W
Zurich: & *L.*, Switz.	**75**	47N	8E
Zushi: Japan	**114**	35N	140E
Zwickau: E. Germany	**74**	51N	12E
Zwolle: Neth.	**74**	53N	6E